Whither Opportunity?

Whither Opportunity?

Rising Inequality, Schools, and Children's Life Chances

Greg J. Duncan and Richard J. Murnane
editors

Russell Sage Foundation • New York
Spencer Foundation • Chicago

Library of Congress Cataloging-in-Publication Data

Whither opportunity? : rising inequality, schools, and children's life chances / Greg J. Duncan and Richard J. Murnane, editors.

    p. cm.
  Includes bibliographical references and index.
  ISBN 978-0-87154-372-1 (pbk. : alk. paper)
  1. Poor children—Education—United States. 2. Children with social disabilities—Education—United States. I. Duncan, Greg J. II. Murnane, Richard J.
  LC4091.W495 2011
  379.73—dc23

2011016969

The paper used in this publication meets the minimum requirements of American National Standard for Information Sciences—Permanence of Paper for Printed Library Materials. ANSI Z39.48-1992.

Text design by Genna Patacsil.

RUSSELL SAGE FOUNDATION
112 East 64th Street, New York, New York 10065
10 9 8 7 6 5 4 3 2

CONTENTS

CONTRIBUTORS

Greg J. Duncan is Distinguished Professor in the Department of Education at the University of California, Irvine and adjunct professor in the School of Education and Social Policy at Northwestern University.

Richard J. Murnane is Thompson Professor of Education and Society at the Harvard Graduate School of Education and research associate at the National Bureau of Economic Research.

Joseph G. Altonji is Thomas DeWitt Cuyler Professor of Economics, faculty affiliate at the Economic Growth Center, and member of the executive committee at the Cowles Foundation, all at Yale University, and research associate at the National Bureau of Economic Research.

Elizabeth O. Ananat is assistant professor of public policy and economics in the Sanford School of Public Policy at Duke University.

Emily Art is doctoral student at the University of Chicago.

Martha J. Bailey is assistant professor in the Department of Economics at the University of Michigan, faculty affiliate of the National Poverty Center, research associate of the Population Studies Center, and faculty research fellow at the National Bureau of Economic Research.

Don Boyd is senior fellow at the Nelson A. Rockefeller Institute of Government at the State University of New York at Albany.

Harry Brighouse is professor of philosophy and affiliate professor of educational policy studies at the University of Wisconsin–Madison.

Julia Burdick-Will is Ph.D. candidate in the University of Chicago Department of Sociology and predoctoral fellow at the Institute for Educational Sciences.

Vilsa E. Curto is research associate at the Education Innovation Laboratory at Harvard University.

Susan M. Dynarski is associate professor of public policy in the Gerald R. Ford School of Public Policy, associate professor of education in the School of Education at the University of Michigan, and faculty research associate at the National Bureau of Economic Research.

George Farkas is professor in the Department of Education at the University of California, Irvine.

Roland G. Fryer Jr. is professor in the Department of Economics at Harvard University.

Frank F. Furstenberg is professor of sociology and research associate in the Population Studies Center at the University of Pennsylvania.

Anna Gassman-Pines is assistant professor of public policy and psychology and neuroscience in the Sanford School of Public Policy at Duke University.

Lisa Gennetian is senior research director of economic studies at the Brookings Institution and managing director of economic mobility at ideas42, a social impact organization applying the tools of behavioral economics to social problems.

Christina M. Gibson-Davis is assistant professor of public policy, sociology, and psychology and neuroscience in the Sanford School of Public Policy at Duke University.

David Harding is associate professor in the Department of Sociology and the Ford School of Public Policy, research associate professor in the Population Studies Center and Survey Research Center, and faculty affiliate at the National Poverty Center at the University of Michigan.

Michael Hout is Natalie Cohen Sociology Chair at the University of California, Berkeley.

Meghan L. Howard is project manager at the Education Innovation Laboratory at Harvard University.

Brian A. Jacob is Walter H. Annenberg Professor of Education Policy, professor of economics, and director of the Center on Local, State, and Urban Policy in the Gerald R. Ford School of Public Policy at the University of Michigan, faculty research fellow at the National Bureau of Economic Research, and executive committee member of the National Poverty Center.

Alexander Janus is graduate student in the sociology department at the University of California, Berkeley.

Marshall Jean is doctoral student at the University of Chicago.

Neeraj Kaushal is associate professor at the Columbia University School of Social Work, research associate at the National Bureau of Economic Research, and research fellow at the Institute for the Study of Labor, Bonn, Germany.

David S. Kirk is assistant professor in the Department of Sociology and faculty research associate of the Population Research Center at the University of Texas at Austin.

Jeffrey Kling is associate director for economic analysis at the Congressional Budget Office and faculty research fellow at the National Bureau of Economic Research. He was formerly deputy director of economic studies at the Brookings Institution and faculty member at Princeton University.

Hamp Lankford is professor in the Department of Educational Administration and Policy Studies at the State University of New York at Albany.

Phillip B. Levine is Katharine Coman and A. Barton Hepburn Professor in Economics at Wellesley College, research associate at the National Bureau of Economic Research, research affiliate of the National Poverty Center, and member of the National Academy of Social Insurance.

Tamara Wilder Linkow is postdoctoral fellow at the Center on Local, State, and Urban Policy in the Gerald R. Ford School of Public Policy at the University of Michigan.

Susanna Loeb is professor of education at Stanford University, director of the Institute for Research on Education Policy and Practice, and codirector of Policy Analysis for California Education.

Jens Ludwig is McCormick Foundation Professor of Social Service Administration, Law, and Public Policy in the School of Social Service Administration, the Harris School, and the University of Chicago Law School, director of the University of Chicago Crime Lab, nonresident senior fellow in economic studies at the Brookings Institution, and research associate of the National Bureau of Economic Research.

Katherine Magnuson is associate professor in the School of Social Work at the University of Wisconsin–Madison.

Richard K. Mansfield is Ph.D. candidate in economics at Yale University.

Charles A. Nelson III is professor of pediatrics at Harvard Medical School and Richard David Scott Chair in Pediatric Developmental Medicine Research at Children's Hospital Boston.

Meredith Phillips is associate professor of public policy and sociology at the University of California–Los Angeles.

Stephen W. Raudenbush is Lewis-Sebring Distinguished Service Professor in the Department of Sociology at the University of Chicago and chairman of the Committee on Education.

Sean F. Reardon is associate professor in the School of Education at Stanford University.

Matthew Ronfeldt is assistant professor in the School of Education at the University of Michigan.

Brian Rowan is Burke A. Hinsdale Collegiate Professor in the School of Education at the University of Michigan and research professor at the Institute for Social Research.

Robert J. Sampson is Henry Ford II Professor of the Social Sciences at Harvard University and senior advisor of the social science program at the Radcliffe Institute for Advanced Study.

Lisa Sanbonmatsu is senior researcher at the National Bureau of Economic Research.

Gina Schouten is graduate student in the Department of Philosophy at the University of Wisconsin–Madison.

Amy Ellen Schwartz is professor of public policy, education, and economics at the Robert F. Wagner Graduate School of Public Service and the Steinhardt School of Culture, Education, and Human Development at New York University and director of the NYU Institute for Education and Social Policy.

Patrick Sharkey is assistant professor in the Department of Sociology at New York University.

Margaret A. Sheridan is postdoctoral researcher in the Laboratory of Cognitive Neuroscience at Children's Hospital Boston.

Leanna Stiefel is professor of economics and education policy at the Robert F. Wagner Graduate School of Public Service and the Steinhardt School of Culture, Education, and Human Development at New York University and associate director of the NYU Institute for Education and Social Policy.

Megan M. Sweeney is associate professor of sociology at the University of California, Los Angeles.

Jacob L. Vigdor is professor of public policy and economics at the Sanford School of Public Policy at Duke University, faculty research fellow at the National Bureau of Economic Research, and adjunct fellow at the Manhattan Institute for Policy Research.

Jane Waldfogel is professor of social work and public affairs at the Columbia University School of Social Work and visiting professor at the Centre for Analysis of Social Exclusion at the London School of Economics and Political Science.

Christopher Winship is Diker-Tishman Professor of Sociology at Harvard University and member of the senior faculty at the Harvard Kennedy School of Government.

Jim Wyckoff is professor in the Curry School of Education at the University of Virginia and director of the Center on Education Policy and Workforce Competitiveness.

ACKNOWLEDGMENTS

This book is the brainchild of Rebecca Blank. In 2007 Becky convened two meetings with a group of scholars working on issues related to trends in income inequality, changing labor markets, and the challenges of providing equal access to good education. From these brainstorming sessions, Becky shaped the ideas that led to this project. As the magnitude of the project became more evident, Becky asked Richard Murnane to share the leadership role. With financial support from the Russell Sage Foundation and the Spencer Foundation and intellectual support from their presidents, Eric Wanner and Michael McPherson, they recruited distinguished scholars to write the chapters contained in this volume. When Becky assumed the position of undersecretary of commerce for economic affairs at the Department of Commerce in May 2009, she and Murnane asked Greg Duncan to replace Becky in helping to organize the production of this volume.

The papers written for the project were presented at two conferences hosted by the Brookings Institution in the fall of 2009. We thank the many scholars who provided comments on the conference papers and who contributed to lively and fruitful conversations over four days. We are especially grateful to the project's advisory committee—Deborah Ball, Tom Cook, John Easton, Larry Hedges, Christopher Jencks, Larry Katz, and Sara McLanahan—many of whom attended both conferences and provided valuable feedback, as well as Harry Brighouse, advisor to the Spencer Foundation. We also thank Ron Haskins and his Brookings team for making the arrangements for the conferences and for first-rate logistical support throughout the project. Ron also provided valuable comments on the introductory chapter. Barbara Ray and her team of editors at Hired Pen provided invaluable editorial support. We also thank the reviewers for the Russell Sage Foundation who provided detailed comments on earlier versions of the chapters in the volume.

FOREWORD

The large, multipronged research project reported in this volume represents the most comprehensive effort to date to examine the toll that rising economic inequality is taking on education in the United States. The Spencer Foundation and the Russell Sage Foundation have joined forces, at the intersection of their common interests, to sponsor a definitive assessment of this growing national problem and to bring it squarely to the country's attention. The two foundations come at the issue from different angles, but with a unified purpose.

The Spencer Foundation, long a leader in research on American education, is committed to broadening our understanding of the challenges facing U.S. schools. While contentious debates revolve around various diagnoses of "failing" schools, less attention has been paid to the changing nature of the problems emanating from the surrounding society that schools are confronted with and to the vast differences in the social challenges faced by schools in well-off communities compared to schools in disadvantaged areas. As economic inequality has risen slowly but steadily over the past thirty years, those differences have only become greater.

The Russell Sage Foundation has for many decades supported research on the nature of poverty in the United States and the reasons for its vexing persistence in our wealthy country. Most recently the Foundation has turned its attention to research on the social consequences of the long drift upward in economic inequality that has taken place in the United States over the last three decades. Much of this recent work has sought to delineate the impact of rising inequality on American institutions, particularly institutions, such as education, which we depend upon as a counterweight to rising inequality. Public education is our country's preeminent commitment to equipping the children of rich and poor alike with the capabilities they will need to compete in an increasingly knowledge-driven economy. But if the children of the well-off now systematically receive superior education to that of the children of the disadvantaged, then rising inequality may perpetuate itself, and even accelerate in coming generations.

This project was initially conceived in a series of intense conversations early in 2007 between the presidents of the two sponsoring foundations and economist Rebecca Blank, who was then the dean of the Ford School of Public Policy at the University of Michigan. The three of us agreed that social science badly needs to develop a new strand of research on education, one that examines the ways in which general social and economic conditions in the country affect the educational achievements of our students and the functioning of our schools. Under Becky Blank's leadership this conversation broadened to include a group of relevant experts in education and the social sciences who helped us shape the project and recruit participants. We also teamed with Becky to invite the economist Richard Murnane, Thompson Professor of Education and Society at the Harvard Graduate School of Education, to share the leadership of the project with her. Dick's involvement was of great value in shaping the project and proved providential when Becky joined the Obama administration as the undersecretary of commerce for economic affairs in 2009. At that point, economist Greg Duncan, Distinguished Professor in the School of Education at the University of California, Irvine, graciously agreed to step in for Becky as co-leader of the project with Dick Murnane. We are enormously grateful to all three of them, without whom this large and complicated endeavor could never have been brought to such a successful conclusion.

As it evolved, the conceptual framework for the project parsed the general question about how rising inequality might be having an impact on education into a number of more precise questions about how changes in families, neighborhoods, and local labor markets may affect the educational capabilities of students and the functioning of schools: Does inequality weaken families at the bottom of the income distribution in ways that make it difficult for them to prepare their children for school and support their regular participation? Does inequality tend to concentrate poverty and disadvantage in unstable, high-crime neighborhoods that make it hard for schools to operate effectively? Do local labor markets with high rates of unemployment and a prevalence of low-wage, low-quality jobs create stressful, insecure conditions for families that hinder student performance and discourage student engagement in education?

This volume examines these questions, and many others like them, in twenty-five chapters that summarize existing research and offer a rich variety of new findings about how social and economic inequality influence education. The question looming over all this analytic research, of course, is what to do about these problems. If we assume that economic inequality is likely to persist at high levels in the United States for some time to come, how should we support families and children, and strengthen and redesign the educational system to provide better educational opportunities and outcomes for those who come from increasingly disadvantaged backgrounds? Given limited resources, should we focus primarily on ameliorating the social and economic conditions that make effective education so difficult to achieve, or should we concentrate on developing schools that can operate effectively even in the most difficult circumstances? Many of the key findings reported in this volume should help us understand and address this tradeoff. Greg Duncan and Dick Murnane are now at work on a short, nontechnical book intended for the broader public that will summarize these results and spell out their policy implications.

Americans have long been willing to accept a certain measure of material inequality as inevitable and even as fair in a political and economic system that sustains and encourages free enterprise. But Americans also believe in the democratic ideal of equal opportunity—that everyone should have an equal chance to get ahead in life, and that ability and hard work should be rewarded without regard to the accidents of birth. Education has long been seen as an essential foundation for those opportunities. Educating disadvantaged students not only adds to their opportunities but to the development of a prosperous and healthy democratic society from which all benefit. Over much of our nation's history, expanding educational opportunity has been, in fact and in perception, a key element in the "rising tide that lifts all boats." At the deepest level, the disturbing question this volume raises is whether, after thirty years of steadily rising economic inequality in the United States, that tide is now running out, and our educational system may be doing more to perpetuate and even to increase inequality than to expand educational opportunity. It bears remembering that test score differences between the children of the rich and poor are now much greater than they were thirty years ago and so are the differences in college attendance and graduation. We believe these stark facts signal a real danger that needs to be addressed in many ways, but not least by seriously rethinking and reinvesting in our educational system to make the conception of a democratic society to which all contribute and from which all benefit more a reality and less an empty ideal.

Michael S. McPherson
President
Spencer Foundation

Eric Wanner
President
Russell Sage Foundation

Part I

Overview

Chapter 1

Introduction: The American Dream, Then and Now

Greg J. Duncan and Richard J. Murnane

America has always taken pride in being the land of opportunity, a country in which hard work and sacrifice result in a better life for one's children. Economic growth made that dream a reality for generations of Americans, including many people who started out poor. Between 1947 and 1977, a period in which the gross national product (GDP) per capita doubled, the incomes of the poorest families nearly doubled as well (see figure 1.1).[1] In fact, for the first three-quarters of the twentieth century, economic growth was a rising tide that lifted the boats of the rich and poor alike.

Crucial to this economic growth and the consequent boost to living standards was a rapid increase in educational attainment. In 1900, only 6 percent of teenagers graduated from high school, and only 3 percent of young people graduated from college. The comparable figures in 1975 were 75 and 23 percent, respectively.[2] The skills of the increasing numbers of high school and college graduates constituted the human capital that fueled productivity gains and wage growth (Goldin and Katz 2008).

Of course some families had far greater financial resources than others to invest in their children. In 1947, the income of families at the 80th percentile of the income distribution was 3.1 times that of families at the 20th percentile. However, most Americans were willing to accept this degree of income inequality, for three reasons: First, incomes of families at the bottom of the distribution were growing quite rapidly. Second, inequality remained relatively stable for the first three decades after World War II.[3] The third and perhaps most important factor was a relatively high rate of intergenerational economic mobility. Growing up in a poor family did not have to mean that one's children would repeat that experience.[4]

For many generations of Americans, education was the springboard to upward mobility. Figure 1.2 shows that by the middle of the twentieth century, more than half of young adult men and women had completed more years of formal education than their parents had, a percentage that would continue to climb for the next twenty-five years (see chapter 8 in this volume for more details about trends in intergenerational mobility in educational attainments in the United States). In fact, as Claudia D. Goldin and Lawrence F. Katz (2008) have documented, U.S. educational institutions served the country well for the first three-quarters of the twentieth century. Although the nation never completely fulfilled the promise of equality of educational opportunity, the openness of the American educational system made it possible for hardworking children from low-income families to graduate not only from high school but also from college. The college graduation

FIGURE 1.1   *High and Low Family Incomes, 1947 to 2008*

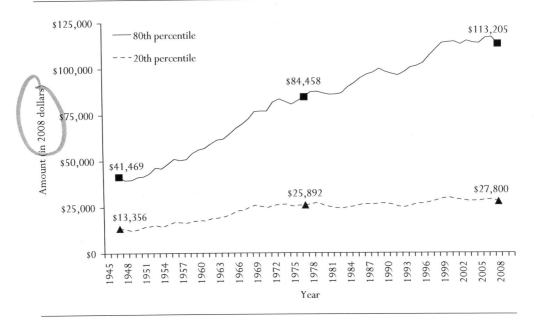

Source: Authors' calculations based on U.S. Bureau of the Census (n.d.).

FIGURE 1.2   *Upward and Downward Intergenerational Mobility, 1933 to 2005*

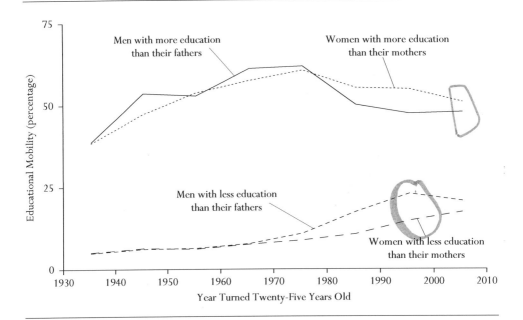

Source: Hout and Janus (this volume, figure 8.3); their calculations of General Social Surveys (Smith et al. 1972–2008).

rates of children whose parents had never attended college exceeded 20 percent between 1950 and 1970. The skills and credentials resulting from these educational investments allowed many Americans who had grown up poor to join the middle class.

Fast-forward three decades, to 2007. Between 1977 and 2007, America's GDP per capita nearly doubled again.[5] This time, however, the fruits of economic growth were confined to a smaller proportion of the population. In 2007, family income at the 20th percentile was a scant 7 percent higher than the comparable figure for 1977, after adjusting for inflation (figure 1.1). On the other hand, the incomes of families at the 80th percentile had grown by 34 percent—nearly five times as much. Yet even these striking differences fail to capture the extent to which economic growth over the three decades after 1977 disproportionately benefited a very small percentage of American families. Between 1977 and 2007, the income of families at the 99th percentile increased by 90 percent, while families at the 99.9th percentile saw their income more than triple.[6]

Many factors contributed to the stagnation of incomes in the bottom tiers and the increase in inequality, including growing numbers of single-parent families and changing norms about appropriate executive compensation (Levy and Temin 2010). Particularly important, however, have been changes in the U.S. economy, including advancing technology and the outsourcing of jobs to lower-wage countries, both of which reduced the demand for U.S. workers with relatively little formal education. During a time (1977 to 2007) when the inflation-adjusted wages of college graduates grew by 25 percent, the wages of high school graduates increased by only 1 percent, and those of high school dropouts fell by 13 percent (for a discussion of these changes, see Levy and Murnane 2004).

Although technological changes and outsourcing are important reasons for the increases in education-related earnings differentials, they play only a little role in explaining the extraordinary increase in the earnings at the top of the distribution. Indeed, the dramatic increase in inequality at the top of the U.S. earnings distribution is not found in other high-income countries in Europe and Asia that experienced the same technological changes.

Taken together, then, two powerful crosscurrents have pushed and pulled at children growing up in low-income families. On the one hand, the rewards for buckling down and graduating from college have never been higher. On the other, the resources available to low-income families to pay for their children's preschool, for access to good public schools or to private education, and for college investments have fallen farther behind those of affluent families. Remarkably, we know very little about how these forces have affected the achievement, educational attainments, and labor-market success of low- and high-income children. One key goal of this book is to provide the evidence we need to answer these questions.

With few exceptions, this volume provides depressing evidence on the relative skills of low- and high-income children. In chapter 5, Sean F. Reardon documents startling growth in the income-based gap in the test scores of children born since the 1950s (figure 1.3). Among children born around 1950, test scores of low-income children lagged behind those of their better-off peers by a little over half a standard deviation, about 60 points on an SAT-type test. Fifty years later, this gap was twice as large.[7] We were surprised to discover how much the income-based gap grew during this period, in view of the fact that racial gaps in test scores have diminished considerably in the fifty years since *Brown v. Board of Education* (figure 1.3) (Jencks and Phillips 1998).[8] We need to know why the trends in income gaps moved in the opposite direction.

Given the importance of cognitive skills in determining educational success, it should come as no surprise that growth in the income-based gap in children's reading and mathematics achievement has translated into a larger gap between children growing up in poor families and their more affluent peers with respect to the amount of schooling they have received. Figure 1.4

FIGURE 1.3   *Estimated Gaps in Reading Achievement Between High- and Low-Income and Black and White Students, by Birth Year*

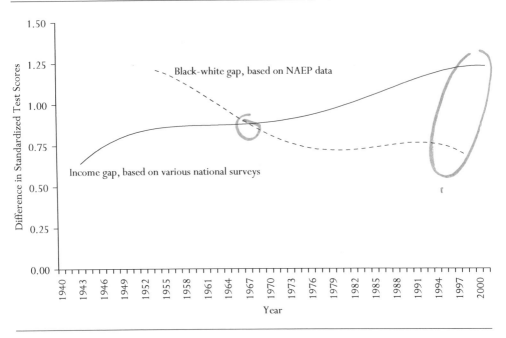

Source: Authors' adaptation of Reardon (this volume, figures 5.4 and 5.7).

plots the trend in years of completed schooling for children from top- and bottom-quintile-income families. The increase in this gap—roughly one year—is comparable to the increase in the test score gap Reardon found.[9] Using different data, in chapter 6 Martha J. Bailey and Susan M. Dynarski document a growing income-based gap in college completion.

Moreover, these growing gaps in educational attainment have translated into less educational mobility, particularly for men. Until about 1970, fewer than one in ten men and women entering adulthood had completed less schooling than their parents (figure 1.2). By the 1990s, more than 20 percent of men and almost as large a fraction of women had less education than their parents. As Michael Hout and Alexander Janus explain in chapter 8, this disturbing trend stems to a large extent from stagnation in educational attainment. High school graduation rates have not budged in the last thirty-five years, and the slow growth we have seen in college graduation rates has been due almost entirely to children from middle-class and affluent families.[10]

Despite these pessimistic trends, one might still hope that America's second-chance educational system and entrepreneurial culture would promote more intergenerational mobility in both educational attainment and income than is found in other developed countries. Yet a great deal of international evidence indicates that this is not the case. Measures of immobility (for example, the simple correlation between the educational attainments of parents and children) are higher in the United States than in most continental European countries (Hertz et al. 2007).[11] The same pattern holds for the correlations between the earnings of fathers and sons (Bjorklund and Jantti 2009).

FIGURE 1.4　　*Gap in Years of Completed Schooling Between Students with Family Income in the Top and Bottom Quintiles, by Year Turned Fourteen*

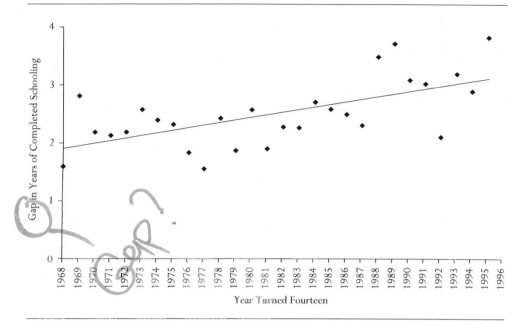

Source: Authors' calculations based on Panel Study of Income Dynamics (1968–2006).

Just how increased income inequality influences the skill acquisition and educational attainment of children born into different circumstances is, of course, a much more complicated question, and one that consumes the bulk of our volume. In the next section we describe our conceptual model of how increasing family income inequality may affect access to high-quality child care, schools, neighborhoods, and other settings that help build children's skills and educational attainments.

HOW RISING INEQUALITY INFLUENCES CHILDREN'S SKILLS AND ATTAINMENT

American society relies on its schools to level the playing field for children born into different circumstances. More than any other institution, schools are charged with making equality of opportunity a reality. During a period of rising inequality, can schools play this critical role effectively? Or has growing income inequality affected families, neighborhoods, and local labor markets in a manner that undercuts the effectiveness of schools serving disadvantaged populations? This is the question at the heart of this project.

To understand the impact of growing inequality, we adopted the ecological perspective illustrated in figure 1.5. According to this framework, income inequality affects families, neighborhoods, and local labor markets. Changes in these social contexts may in turn affect children's skill acquisition and educational attainments directly, as well as indirectly by influencing how schools operate. For example, growing income inequality increases the gap separating the resources of rich and poor families that they can invest in their children. Growing disparities in parental investments may also indirectly widen skill gaps by contributing to residential segregation, as the wealthy

FIGURE 1.5   *Inequality and Children's Attainments*

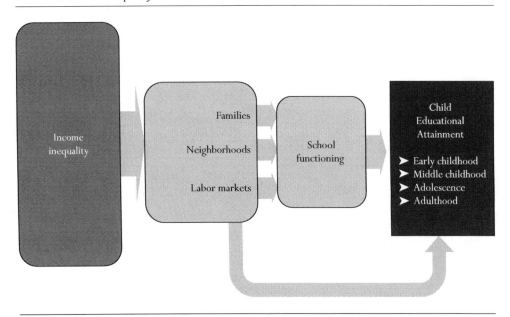

Source: Authors' figure.

purchase housing in neighborhoods where less affluent families cannot afford to live. Indeed, residential segregation by income has increased in recent decades.[12] This can reduce interactions between rich and poor in settings ranging from schools and child-care centers to libraries and grocery stores. Without the financial and human resources and political clout of the wealthy, institutions in poorer neighborhoods, perhaps most importantly schools, may decline in quality, which in turn has detrimental effects on the education and life chances of children born into poor families.

Low family income makes it more difficult for parents to gain access to the high-quality child care that prepares children for kindergarten. It can also lead to classrooms filled with low-achieving, inattentive classmates. Crime in low-income neighborhoods may provide tempting alternatives to working hard at school and at the same time make it more difficult for neighborhood schools to recruit high-quality teachers. Plant closings can disrupt family life for children whose parents lose jobs, as well as deplete community resources that might have been channeled into school improvements.

Rising inequality can have political repercussions as well. As the rich become increasingly isolated in certain neighborhoods and schools, the extent of inequality becomes less visible to them and to society as a whole, which in turn can lead to increased social conflict and a reduced sense of common purpose. This can make it harder to mobilize the public concern necessary to deal with problems of disadvantage among those most at risk. Indeed, growing inequality can create a vicious circle: increasing returns to education create growing social and economic inequalities; these in turn exacerbate educational inequality and limit educational achievement among more disadvantaged populations. Social and economic inequalities become more entrenched and limit social mobility, as more disadvantaged groups fall further behind. Only by understanding the effects of the various contexts depicted in figure 1.5 on educational attainment can we begin to make sense of three decades of rising income inequality.

THE DEVELOPING CHILD AND ADOLESCENT

In order to understand the long-term consequences for children of macro-environmental changes such as increasing income inequality, it is crucial to look at the nature of child development. Since nearly all developmental processes work through the brain, we offer in chapter 2 an accessible overview of brain development by two neuroscientists, Charles A. Nelson III and Margaret A. Sheridan.

Brain Development

Essential properties of most of the brain's architecture are established very early in life by genes and, importantly, early experience. A child's everyday interactions with sights, sounds, and supportive caregivers are important for allowing the brain's wiring to progress appropriately. The brains of children in deprived or traumatic environments often develop differently. Traumatic stress that arises from child maltreatment, for example, produces measurable effects on brain structures and increases the odds of long-lasting disadvantages for adult mental health and labor-market functioning.

Although it is sometimes possible to remedy problematic early brain development, success in doing so is limited by the shrinking plasticity of the brain as time goes by and the inefficiency with which remediated brain circuitry often operates. For example, when children are exposed to the severe psychosocial deprivation that characterizes some orphanages, remediation in the form of foster care that begins before age two can compensates for some, but not all, negative consequences.

It is difficult to generalize from situations of severe deprivation and maltreatment to the more common situations associated with an economically deprived environment. The empirical literature on socioeconomic status and the brain—admittedly based largely on simple correlations—suggests that the stress associated with socioeconomic deprivation may affect important aspects of children's cognitive control which, in turn, may influence their behavior, learning, and educational attainments.

Early Skill Development

Chapters 3, 4, and 5, by Greg J. Duncan and Katherine Magnuson, George Farkas, and Sean F. Reardon, examine the nature of socioeconomic gaps in skills and behaviors in childhood and adolescence. They find large income-related skills gaps that, in the case of children in the top and bottom income quintiles, are often larger than gaps defined by race or ethnicity. Moreover, income-based gaps persist across the school years.

Duncan and Magnuson argue that the domains of achievement, attention, and behavior are useful for organizing the most important children's skills and behaviors. Upon entering kindergarten, children from low-income families have weaker academic and attention skills, on average, and a higher probability of demonstrating antisocial behavior than children from higher-income families. None of these gaps shrinks over the course of elementary school. In fact, the income-based gap in antisocial behavior nearly doubles by fifth grade and, as Farkas shows, persists into high school. This pattern suggests that differences in early skills and behaviors related to family income may be important mechanisms through which socioeconomic status is transmitted from one generation to the next.

Another transfer mechanism is the segregation of children from low-income families into schools not attended by children from more affluent families. As Joseph G. Altonji and Richard Mansfield document in chapter 16, this sorting increased during the 1980s. The result is that a child from a poor family is two to four times as likely as a child from an affluent family to have classmates in both elementary and high school with low skills and with behavior problems (for relevant data see chapters 3 and 4). This sorting matters, because the weaker cognitive skills and worse behavior of low-income children have a negative effect on the learning of their classmates. Once again, economic disadvantage is passed on from one generation to the next.

In chapter 5, Sean F. Reardon assembles information from virtually all the reading and mathematics tests that have been administered to nationally representative samples of American students over the last forty years—something that has never been done before. As we have seen in figure 1.3, he finds that the trends in the test scores of low- and high-income children parallel those of income itself, with income-based gaps in test scores now twice as large as test score gaps between African Americans and whites. Reardon finds mixed evidence as to whether income itself is the cause of these trends or whether they are driven by other, correlated factors such as parental education. Although gaps are much more apparent when family socioeconomic status is measured by income rather than by the educational attainment of parents, it is also the case that test score gaps between poor and middle-income students grew about as fast when income inequality was flat or falling (in the 1950s and 1960s) as when it was rising most rapidly (in the 1980s).[13]

Educational Attainment

In chapter 6, Martha J. Bailey and Susan M. Dynarski detail the growing gaps in college graduation rates between children from low- and high-income families. Graduation rates for children born into high-income families jumped twenty-one percentage points (from 33 to 54 percent) between the early 1960s and the early 1980s. The corresponding increase for children born into low-income families was only four percentage points (from 5 to 9 percent). A little less than half of the gap between rich and poor in college graduation rates can be explained by differences in college enrollment rates, with the rest explained by differences in students' persistence in completing their degrees.

Bailey and Dynarski also document significant differences in the educational trajectories of boys and girls. Particularly striking is the extraordinary growth over a twenty-year period in the college graduation rate for girls from high-income families: from 33 percent for those born in the early 1960s to 60 percent among those born in the early 1980s. In contrast, the college graduation rate among girls from low-income families grew by only five percentage points, from 5 to 10 percent, over this time period. Disturbingly, the rate of college completion among boys—black, Hispanic and white—from low-income families fell in recent decades. Evidence in several of the book's chapters suggests that educational attainment problems are particularly acute among males growing up in low-income families.

Expectations

It is tempting to assume that the growing gap between the college graduation rates of children from differing economic backgrounds is due to the fact that poor children quickly abandon any hope that college might be part of their future. However, Brian A. Jacob and Tamara Wilder Linkow show in chapter 7 that this is not the case. They find that the percentage of children who expect to obtain a four-year college degree has grown rapidly over the last twenty years. Moreover, the increase was greater for children of parents who were not college graduates, suggesting that children from low-income families still expect to graduate from college.[14] In one sense this is encouraging; relatively few students who do not expect to go to college actually do so. However, it is troubling that so many children from low-income families have college expectations that are either

FIGURE 1.6   *Enrichment Expenditures on Children, 1972 to 2006*

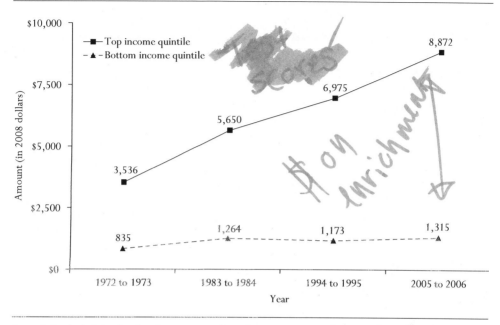

Source: Authors' calculations based on Consumer Expenditure Surveys (U.S. Bureau of Labor Statistics, various years).

thwarted or unrealistic, especially since the gap in average earnings between college graduates and high school graduates is so much higher today than it was in the 1970s.

Families

Very young children tend to be completely dependent on their families to provide what they need for healthy development. As Duncan and Magnuson show in chapter 3, children growing up in families with greater financial resources score higher on many dimensions of school readiness upon entering kindergarten. It is a challenge to identify the extent to which these differences are caused by income itself as opposed to differences in innate capabilities or other family character-istics (such as two-parent family structure or parental education levels).

An obvious advantage of a higher family income is that it provides more resources to buy books, computers, high-quality child care, summer camps, private schooling, and other enrich-ments. Figure 1.6 shows how spending on child-enrichment goods and services jumped for fam-ilies in the top quintiles to a far greater extent than for those in the bottom income quintiles, as reflected in four large consumer expenditure surveys conducted between the early 1970s and 2005 to 2006.[15] In the period from 1972 to 1973, high-income families spent about $2,700 more per year on child enrichment than did low-income families. By 2005 to 2006, this gap had nearly tripled, to $7,500. As detailed in chapter 9 by Neeraj Kaushal, Katherine Magnuson, and Jane Waldfogel, spending differences are largest for enrichment activities such as music lessons, travel, and summer camps. Differential access to such activities may explain the gaps in background knowledge between children from high-income families and those from low-income families that are so predictive of reading skills in the middle and high school years (Snow 2002).

Parents also spend different amounts and quality of time interacting with their children and exposing them to novel environments, and these factors can make a difference in their development (Risley and Hart 1995). In chapter 10, Meredith Phillips reports some striking differences in time-use patterns between low- and high-income families, especially time spent in "novel" places. She estimates that between birth and age six, children from high-income families will have spent 1,300 more hours in novel contexts (that is, other than at home, school, or in the care of another parent or a day-care provider) than children from low-income families. These experiences contribute to the background knowledge that is so critical to comprehending science and social studies texts in the middle-school grades. In addition, the amount of time parents spent in literacy activities was lower for low-income than for high-income families, although not all of the components of that index (for example, time spent conversing or reading with adults) passed tests of statistical significance. Phillips was unable to measure differences in the *quality* of time spent in these interactions.

The money and time expended on behalf of children also differ markedly between single- and two-parent families. As Megan M. Sweeney shows in chapter 11, increases in both marital disruption and births to unmarried women have fueled a large rise in the proportion of children living with only one biological parent. These trends are particularly pronounced among African American children. Numerous studies have established that children who grow up with two biological parents attain more schooling than children who do not. Income differences are a leading explanation for these effects, although characteristics of couples who divorce or separate also matter. Sweeney's analysis suggests that youths who experience family disruption have poorer educational outcomes than those who live in stable families with two parents (original or stepfamily). However, for most outcomes considered, these differences are explained by the characteristics of children and their parents prior to the disruption. Moreover, and contrary to some prior research, educational outcomes for youths living in a stable married stepfamily, or transitioning from a family headed by a single mother to a stepfamily, are similar to those for youth living with two biological parents.

Neighborhoods

Given the differences in school quality, safety, amenities, peer behavior, and social cohesiveness between low-income and affluent neighborhoods, most people believe that neighborhood conditions matter a great deal for children's attainments (Brooks-Gunn, Duncan, and Aber 1997). However, as David Harding and his coauthors explain in chapter 13, separating the effects of neighborhoods from the conditions that lead families to reside in particular kinds of neighborhoods is a very difficult task indeed.

Skepticism regarding the importance of neighborhood, as opposed to family, conditions for poor children has been fueled by recent evidence from the Moving to Opportunity (MTO) experiment. That program offered families living in public housing in high-poverty neighborhoods counseling and financial assistance to enable them to move to less poor neighborhoods. Because a lottery determined which families moved, the results are not overly influenced by the fact that more motivated families—whose motivation might also positively influence children's outcomes—were more likely to apply for the program. As a result, MTO provides a powerful test of the assumption that children's school attainments will improve if they and their families move away from a very poor neighborhood.

Five years later, the average test scores and years of completed schooling of children whose families won the lottery were nearly identical to the results for those who lost (Sanbonmatsu et al. 2006). In chapter 12, Julia Burdick-Will and her coauthors reconcile these results with those emerging in other studies of neighborhood effects on children. They find noteworthy but very selective effects of neighborhood conditions on children's academic achievement. In particular, African American families living in public housing in extremely high-poverty neighborhoods in two of the five MTO cities (Chicago and Baltimore) experienced much higher levels of crime and other dimensions of concentrated neighborhood disadvantage than did families living in other MTO cities. Accordingly, they hypothesize that the relatively small number of African American children living in extremely disadvantaged neighborhoods might benefit much more from improvements in neighborhood conditions than children living in other high-poverty neighborhoods.

Labor Markets

Labor markets affect children's development in at least two ways. First, they affect the financial resources available to parents to care for their children. Second, stresses associated with jobs, the work-family balance, and, especially, the loss of a job can affect parents' mental health and the quality of the emotional environment in the home. As Charles A. Nelson III and Margaret A. Sheridan explain in chapter 2, severe emotional stress can have lasting impacts on children's development. Of course, since parents have some control over where and how much they work, it is difficult to separate the effects of labor-market conditions on children from the effects of difficult-to-measure characteristics of parents that affect both their work choices and how they care for their children.

Elizabeth O. Ananat, Anna Gassman-Pines, and Christina M. Gibson-Davis take an innovative look in chapter 14 at the impacts of adverse local labor-market conditions on children's achievement. They find that spikes in job losses in North Carolina counties are associated with lower test scores for children attending public schools in the same counties, and the effects emerge more rapidly for children from low socioeconomic status (SES) families than for their more affluent peers. It is important to note that these effects are not limited to children from families in which an adult has lost a job. Moreover, in relatively disadvantaged counties, community-level job losses appeared to increase the incidence of students' serious disciplinary offenses reported to the police. Reductions in school spending and increases in teacher mobility do not appear to be the mechanisms through which the negative effects of community job losses occur. Instead, the authors hypothesize that increased stress in families is the primary mechanism through which community job losses influence children's reading and mathematics achievements.

In another wrinkle, however, in chapter 15 Phillip B. Levine finds no evidence of a causal link between parents' employment and children's academic achievement. To reconcile Levine's findings with those of Ananat and her colleagues, it may be helpful to consider the reasons for unemployment. As Levine points out, the unexpected involuntary job losses studied by Ananat and her colleagues are only part of the picture. Levine's approach necessarily assumes that voluntary unemployment (for example, quitting a job to search for a better one) has the same impact on family dynamics and children's well-being as an involuntary job loss. This assumption is likely to be incorrect; in fact, involuntary job losses probably affect children more profoundly and negatively than voluntary unemployment does.

Schools

Researchers have long known that children attending schools with mostly poor classmates have lower academic achievement and graduation rates than those attending schools with more affluent student populations. Less well understood are the ways environmental influences shape school functioning and the particular ways in which schools affect children's developmental trajectories and long-run outcomes. The chapters on schools provide some insight into these issues.

In chapter 16, Joseph G. Altonji and Richard Mansfield highlight the role of schools in linking growing family income inequality and the educational attainments of the nation's teenagers. From 1972 to 1988, schools became more economically segregated, and teenagers from affluent families were less and less likely to have classmates from low-income families.[16] Despite this segregation, differences among schools account for a relatively modest, although growing, part of the variation in high school graduation rates, college enrollment rates, and labor-market earnings. But modest does not imply unimportant. Altonji and Mansfield estimate that moving a high school student in 1972 from a school in the 10th percentile to a school in the 90th percentile of school quality would increase the student's probability of enrollment in a four-year college by about twenty percentage points, a very big change.[17] The corresponding change for a high school student in 1992 or 2002 is even larger.

We have already noted that the chapters contributed by both Duncan and Magnuson and Farkas show that children attending schools with large concentrations of low-income students have several times as many low-achieving and badly behaved classmates as children attending schools with more affluent student bodies. Another threat to achievement is student mobility. In chapter 17, Stephen W. Raudenbush, Marshall Jean, and Emily Art find that urban families living in poverty move frequently, and as a result of school sorting by socioeconomic status, children from poor families are especially likely to attend schools with relatively high rates of new students arriving during the school year. Furthermore, children attending elementary schools with considerable student mobility make less progress in mathematics than do children attending schools with a low level of student mobility.[18] Moreover, the negative effects apply to students who themselves are residentially stable as well as to those who are not, and are likely to be associated with the disruption of instruction caused by the entry of new students into a class.

Teacher quality is another factor contributing to the weak performance of students in high-poverty schools. A substantial body of research has shown that schools serving high concentrations of poor, nonwhite, and low-achieving students find it difficult to attract and retain skilled teachers. Don Boyd and his colleagues examine in chapter 18 the extent to which neighborhood characteristics affect teachers' decisions about where to teach. In addition to preferring schools with relatively low proportions of nonwhite and low-achieving students, teachers also favor schools in neighborhoods with higher-income residents and less violent crime.[19] This is consistent with the evidence David S. Kirk and Robert J. Sampson present in chapter 19, showing that schools with a large percentage of students who have been arrested do not function as well as other schools. Teacher commitment, parental involvement, and student achievement in these schools all tend to be low. Such schools are also likely to be in high-crime neighborhoods, although it is important to note that student arrest rates are not high in all schools located in high-crime neighborhoods.

These patterns highlight the difficult challenges facing schools in high-crime neighborhoods. On the one hand, schools need to deal firmly with students who have been arrested, especially for violent crimes, because these students may disrupt the learning climate of their school. On the other hand, expelling students who have been arrested reduces the probability that these students will graduate from high school. This is one of many issues that occupy the time and resources of teachers and administrators in high-poverty schools and detract attention from teaching and learning.

In chapter 20, Amy Ellen Schwartz and Leanna Stiefel examine yet another challenge facing many of the nation's schools: new immigrants, many of whom speak little English. Today's immigrants are more likely than immigrants in the early 1970s to come from high-poverty countries. The authors also find that black and Hispanic immigrants to New York City are much more likely to be poor than are white immigrants from Eastern Europe, and they are more likely to attend elementary and middle schools with native-born black and Hispanic students who are poor. Thus, although immigrants are not segregated from the native-born in New York City schools, the fact that they tend to move into certain neighborhoods contributes to segregation of schools by socio-economic status and race.

In New York City, as in many other American cities, schools serving large numbers of the city's black and Hispanic students, most of whom are poor, have lower percentages of licensed teachers and higher percentages of novice teachers than other schools. The difficulty these schools experience in attracting and retaining a talented and stable teaching force tends to make them less effective.

In seeking to formulate policies that might address the economic segregation of schools, we can profit from several lessons learned in the nation's most significant school-based social intervention: court-ordered desegregation by race. As Jacob L. Vigdor explains in chapter 21, court-ordered desegregation reduced high school dropout rates for black students; with the end of court-ordered busing, those rates rose again. This pattern supports a theme of this project—namely, that forces external to schools that affect their student body composition influence their effectiveness in creating equal opportunities for children.

However, Vigdor cautions that the evidence concerning younger black children is much less clear-cut. After the end of court-ordered desegregation in Charlotte-Mecklenburg, North Carolina, in 2002, the gap between the achievement of black and white elementary school students did not increase. Vigdor hypothesizes that high schools may be more affected than elementary schools by the racial composition of the student body. He also suggests that measures taken by the school district may have counteracted, at least to some extent, potentially negative effects on black children stemming from the end of court-ordered desegregation. These measures included programs to make disadvantaged schools more attractive workplaces for teachers and a lottery program that enabled some students living in neighborhoods served by relatively low-quality middle schools and high schools to enroll in better schools.[20] Evaluations of the effects of the lottery program show that the opportunity to attend a better middle school or high school imparted long-term benefits for disadvantaged students in Charlotte-Mecklenburg (Deming forthcoming; Deming et al. 2011)

IMPROVING THE LIFE CHANCES OF LOW-INCOME CHILDREN

As the incomes of affluent and poor American families have diverged over the past three decades, so too has the educational performance of the children in these families. Test score differences between rich and poor children are much larger now than thirty years ago, as are differences in rates of college attendance and college graduation. Underachievement problems are particularly acute for low-income males, more and more of whom are lagging behind their own fathers' attainments in school and in the labor market.

What can be done? We identify several possible areas for policy interventions. Foremost among them is K–12 education, which has been battered by adverse changes in families, neighborhoods, and labor markets that have accompanied the last three decades' rising income inequality. Here we need policies that will help to restore public education's historical role as the key social institution for boosting the lifelong opportunities of poor children.

But can investments in improving schools overcome the myriad problems disadvantaged children face, which have been exacerbated by increased income inequality? There is some disagreement among this volume's contributors on this question. They agree that individual schools can make a big difference in the lives of disadvantaged children. However, as Harry Brighouse and Gina Schouten point out in chapter 24, many schools that have experienced success in educating disadvantaged children impose stringent disciplinary codes and require parents to agree to monitor their children's attendance, homework, and behavior, and as a result these schools do not serve children from the most troubled families. To date there is little systematic evidence regarding the extent to which the admission practices of "high commitment" schools are critical to their effectiveness. Even more important, there is little evidence regarding the extent to which the growing number of "high commitment" charter schools spur conventional public schools to improve their performance or, conversely, reduce their quality by leaving them with a disproportionate share of troubled students.

In the interest of drawing policy conclusions, we organize our discussion by childhood stage and context. We first focus on early childhood and opportunities to bolster both early education programs and family functioning. We next review policy ideas for K–12 public education. We conclude with thoughts about neighborhood and labor-market policies.

Early Childhood Interventions

Drawing on neuroscience evidence regarding the plasticity of brain development in early childhood and the importance of ensuring that children's brains are wired correctly from the outset, Nelson and Sheridan conclude in chapter 2 that early childhood represents a particularly promising period for human-capital investments. In the case of profoundly damaging conditions such as maltreatment or institutionalization, they point out that early remediation can help prevent dysfunctional developmental trajectories. Unfortunately, early impairments of brain architecture can give rise to "sleeper effects" that become evident only later. And there may also be spillover costs in schools, as disruptions caused by children with emotional problems reduce the quality of education for their classmates (Carrell and Hoekstra 2010; Neidell and Waldfogel forthcoming).

It can be hazardous to make a direct leap from neuroscience to policy recommendations. Just because early childhood provides opportunities for more efficient interventions does not mean that the early-childhood policies actually implemented by communities, states, or the federal government are worthy investments. In the first place, it may be difficult to design programs that improve children's cognitive or behavioral development. Second, the costs of even effective programs might outweigh the benefits they generate for children, their families, and taxpayers. And third, programs in early childhood require upfront investments that may take decades to pay off. Since society discounts dollars in the future relative to today's dollars, it should prefer an equally effective and costly investment program for adolescents rather than toddlers.

That said, there is considerable evidence of the efficacy of some early-childhood intervention programs, and in particular high-quality, center-based, early-childhood education. Model programs such as Perry Preschool in Ypsilanti, Michigan, and Abecedarian in Chapel Hill, North Carolina, boosted school attainment and earnings; in the case of the Perry program, crime and the risk of adult poverty were reduced as well (Duncan, Ludwig, and Magnuson 2010). These were both expensive model programs designed and run by researchers and they may be hard to replicate, or afford, in a real-life setting.

Fortunately, recent evidence suggests that the larger-scale and less expensive federal Head Start program may also produce long-term improvements in the life chances of participants. Although the estimated effect sizes are smaller than those of the model programs, the benefit-cost ratios are favorable (Deming 2009).[21] Rigorous evaluations of state pre-kindergarten programs are also encouraging, although research has identified only very short-term program impacts (Wong et al. 2008).

Turning from child- to parent-focused programs, Frank F. Furstenberg's review of parenting intervention research in chapter 22 is much more pessimistic. Programs that attempt to enhance parental skills and resources in hopes that parents will do a better job of teaching, nurturing, or in other ways providing for their children generally have a disappointing record. There are two possible exceptions, however. First is the nurse home-visitation program developed by David Olds, in which nurses pay repeated home visits to high-risk, first-time mothers (Duncan, Ludwig, and Magnuson 2010). Second, evidence from a number of experimental and quasi-experimental studies suggests that boosting the incomes of the poor has positive, albeit modest, impacts on the achievement of younger children (Morris, Duncan, and Clark-Kauffman 2005; Dahl and Lochner 2008).

It appears likely that selective investments aimed at improving the school readiness of disadvantaged children are more efficient than attempting to remediate problems among older children or attempting to support schools that serve high percentages of troubled, low-skilled children. In other words, preventing problems is more efficient than ameliorating their effects, although both are necessary.

K-12 Schooling

Several chapters document that consistently high-quality schooling improves the life chances of children from low-income families. Key characteristics of effective schools include an orderly, safe environment in which both teachers and children treat each other with respect and teachers have high expectations for students' success; an intense focus on improving the quality and coherence of instruction; frequent assessment of students' skills and rapid intervention as needed; and an increase in instructional time, typically through a longer school day and often through a longer school year as well. The crucial question, of course, is which policies are best able to create and sustain schools that embody these characteristics.

Vilsa E. Curto, Roland G. Fryer, Jr., and Meghan L. Howard argue in chapter 23 that a growing number of charter schools exhibit these common characteristics and are effective in enhancing the skills of disadvantaged children. They point to the dramatic success of the Promise Academy Middle School in the Harlem Children's Zone in enhancing students' mathematics and reading skills, and to promising evaluations of "high commitment" charter schools that are part of the Knowledge is Power Program (KIPP) (Angrist et al. 2010a; Angrist et al. 2010b). Although the authors are optimistic that more charter schools will result in better education for many disadvantaged children, they also note that we know too little about critical factors that influence the number of truly effective charter schools and the types of disadvantaged children they will serve. Moreover, we need to know more about whether improved test scores will translate into better long-term outcomes and the degree to which the success of many charter schools depends on their strict entry requirements.

Is there hope for better education for disadvantaged children in conventional (noncharter) schools? In chapter 25, Brian Rowan points out that many public elementary schools serving large numbers of poor children have improved their performance by adopting whole-school improvement plans that focus on increasing the coherence and quality of instruction in English language arts and mathematics. He expresses cautious optimism that these reform efforts can improve the education of disadvantaged children. Rowan also suggests a focus on children's behavior problems that interfere with their own learning and that of their classmates, in the form of classroom-based structured modular curricula to develop students' socioemotional skills.

Don Boyd and his colleagues in chapter 18 highlight another significant obstacle to improving the effectiveness of high-poverty schools: the inability to attract and retain skilled teachers. Urban school districts are undertaking promising initiatives to recruit teams of skilled teachers who agree to work together in high-poverty schools, often under the leadership of a strong principal. The teachers receive extra pay in return for working a longer school day and school year.

To date there have been no strong evaluations of the effectiveness of this strategy. However, recent studies show that financial incentives make a difference in recruiting academically talented teachers to high-poverty schools and encouraging them to continue teaching in those schools (Clotfelter et al. 2008; Steele, Murnane, and Willett 2010).

Improving high-poverty middle and high schools has proved to be much more difficult than improving high-poverty elementary schools. As Rowan explains in chapter 25, contributing factors include greater problems in maintaining order, a low level of engagement on the part of many students, and greater resistance from teachers to a focus on improving the coherence and quality of instruction. Partly for these reasons, efforts to improve secondary schools have concentrated on changing their structure, often by breaking up large schools into several smaller ones. Reducing school size has helped ameliorate the order and safety problems that plague many large high schools. However, this strategy, by itself, has not consistently resulted in better teaching and enhanced student learning, in part because it has proved difficult to engage many veteran teachers in sustained efforts to improve instruction (City 2008).

At the same time, breaking up large high schools creates an opportunity for innovative approaches to improving educational performance. For example, starting in 2002, New York City closed more than twenty low-performing high schools and opened more than two hundred smaller schools. Particular emphasis was placed on encouraging innovative approaches to educating low-income urban students and providing widespread access to the 123 new schools that were non-selective. The district invited stakeholders, including educational entrepreneurs and school reform organizations, to submit proposals for new small schools. It introduced a competitive process to select the most promising ideas, and provided the winners with startup funds and support for leadership development and the recruitment of strong teachers. In addition, each school was paired with an intermediary organization that was skilled in launching new schools.

The New York City initiative demonstrates that new approaches to secondary schooling are indeed possible, even in a large urban district widely viewed as excessively bureaucratic and resistant to change. Even more important, the results of a high-quality evaluation show that enrollment in small schools of choice dramatically increased the high school graduation rate of students from low-income families, two-thirds of whom were below grade level when they entered ninth grade. This included males of color, a group that has fared especially poorly in the nation's urban high schools (Bloom, Thompson, and Unterman 2010). The importance of increasing the high school graduation rate cannot be overstated. As Bailey and Dynarski explain in chapter 6, the gap between the high school graduation rates of children from low- and high-income families explains about half of the gap in college entry.

Neighborhoods

Neighborhood conditions loom large in the lives of older children and adolescents. However, we see relatively few opportunities to improve children's life chances by altering neighborhood settings. As Burdick-Will and her coauthors point out in chapter 12, the evidence that dramatic changes in residential location can improve children's academic performance appears to apply only to children living in public housing in the very worst neighborhoods in the country—the kinds of neighborhoods that can be found in Chicago and Baltimore, but perhaps not in cities like Boston, New York, and Los Angeles. They show that the positive academic impacts of the Moving to Opportunity residential mobility program were limited to these kinds of neighborhoods, as were the academic impacts of a more conventional set of housing vouchers offered to Chicago residents.

As for improving the neighborhood conditions of families in situ, none of the countless attempts to do so has led to well-documented improvements in children's educational outcomes.[22]

Indeed, in the case of the successful Harlem Children's Zone (HCZ) Promise Academy charter school, Vilsa E. Curto, Roland G. Fryer, Jr., and Meghan L. Howard show in chapter 23 that whether children lived within the HCZ made no difference in the academic gains for middle-schoolers attending the charter school. This calls into question the benefits to children of the many services available to families living inside the HCZ neighborhood boundaries.

The Promise Academy charter school illustrates another lesson: schools can play a larger role in children's lives than they generally do, and this can reduce the amount of time children spend on troubled neighborhood streets. The Promise Academy and many other schools that are effective in educating poor children living in troubled neighborhoods start early in the morning, often with breakfast. They serve children until late in the afternoon, providing additional time for instruction, remediation of lagging skills, and exposure to enrichment activities. Many offer instruction on Saturdays and well into the summer months. Unlike typical after-school and summer programs that do not improve student outcomes because they are disconnected to the core instructional program, the extended-day and extended-year programs in effective schools in poor neighborhoods are well-integrated parts of a coherent strategy to continually build children's skills (Levy and Murnane 2004). Of course, another benefit of such a comprehensive approach to schooling is that the school becomes the center of children's daily experiences, which reduces their exposure to the lures and dangers of the neighborhood.

Labor Markets

Macroeconomic policies that promote economic growth and strengthen labor markets are vital to the upward mobility of America's children and youth. Higher earnings enable families to enrich the learning environments in which their children develop, while high employment rates help to keep communities healthy. Unfortunately, however, the overall economic growth in the American economy over the past three decades did not translate into the kind of upward mobility that characterized the first three-quarters of the twentieth century. Strong growth, then, is a necessary but insufficient condition for solving the educational attainment problems documented in this volume.

A number of programs providing earnings supplements, child-care subsidies, and other work-related supports for low-income families appear to be effective at boosting children's school achievement. As part of the "make work pay" focus of welfare reform in the 1990s, the federal government increased the generosity of the Earned Income Tax Credit, which provides income supplements to low-income working families that can amount to as much as $5,600 per year—a big boost to the income of a family supported by minimum-wage jobs. One careful study showed that the increased generosity of this program was associated with test score gains among younger children (Dahl and Lochner 2008). A rigorous evaluation of New Hope, a work support program in Milwaukee, also documented gains in achievement and also reductions in antisocial behavior that were particularly strong for boys (Duncan, Huston, and Weisner 2007).

SUMMARY

Although the authors in this volume differ in their views of the most promising strategies for improving the life chances of children growing up in low-income families, all would agree on the importance of increasing these children's academic achievement and educational attainments. How to do this, especially during a time of large government deficits, is a difficult question. We see no prospects for initiatives like the Great Society programs of the mid-1960s, made possible by the federal budget surpluses of that era. But prudent investments in improving the life chances of children born into low-income families will both strengthen the country's frayed social fabric and create the conditions for economic growth.

We draw three conclusions: First, mindful of the biology of human development and the track record of proven programs, we must channel more policy dollars to enrich the early years of children born into poverty. Second, we must improve the educational opportunities of children from low-income families at every stage of their development. Third, we need a national policy debate about the consequences of economic policies that have permitted the growth in family income inequality that the nation has experienced in recent decades. Only if our country faces the consequences of growing income inequality will it be able to maintain its rich heritage of upward social mobility through educational opportunity.

NOTES

Online appendix available at: http://www.russellsage.org/duncan_murnane_online_appendix.pdf.

1. The Census Bureau started its annual tracking of family income in 1947.
2. For the figures on high school graduation rates see U.S. Department of Education, Digest of Education Statistics 2009, table 103 (available at: http://nces.ed.gov/programs/digest/d09; accessed June 25, 2010). The figures on the college graduation rate in 1900 and 1975 are from Goldin and Katz (2008), figure 7.1. We thank Claudia Goldin for providing the data on which the figure is based. We based estimates of the college graduation rates for teenagers in 1900 and 1975 on the figures for cohorts born twenty years before these dates.
3. In 1977, the income of families at the 80th percentile of the income distribution was just slightly higher than it was thirty years before, at 3.3 times that of families at the 20th percentile. Of course, equal relative growth in low and high incomes leads to larger and larger absolute dollar differences. As can be seen in figure 1.1, between 1947 and 1977 the dollar gap between the top and bottom family income quintile threshold more than doubled, from about $28,000 to $58,500.
4. Daniel Aaronson and Bhashkar Mazumder (2007) present evidence indicating that intergenerational economic mobility in the United States increased from 1950 to 1980, but has declined sharply since 1980.
5. Between 1947 and 1977, GDP per capita increased by 98 percent. Between 1977 and 2007, it increased by 80 percent.
6. These earnings figures are available at Emmanuel Saez's website: http://elsa.berkeley.edu?/~saez/. They are updates of the data presented in Thomas Piketty and Saez (2003).
7. Figure 1.3 is based on the trend line fit to reading test scores provided in chapter 5 in this volume. The gap in math test scores increased from about 1.0 standard deviations for cohorts born around 1950 to 1.3 standard deviations for cohorts born around 2000.
8. The white/black gap time series shown in figure 1.3 is from chapter 5 in this volume and is based on the smoothed data from the National Assessment of Educational Progress.
9. Both gaps grew by roughly one-half standard deviations. Figure 1.4 is based on data from the Panel Study of Income Dynamics on children turning 14 between 1969 and 1997 and does not count GEDs as added years of schooling. A linear trend line is statistically significant at the .01 level ($t = 3.17$) and implies a growing gap over the observation period of just under half a standard deviation. A closer look at trends in the components of completed schooling shows no statistically significant trend in failure to complete high school, a significant ($t = 2.04$) adverse trend for completing no more than a high school degree, and a borderline insignificant ($t = 1.85$) adverse trend in completing college.
10. In 2008, the high school graduation rate of young Americans enrolled in public schools was 75 percent, exactly the same as in 1975 (Snyder and Dillow 2010, table 103). Following James J. Heckman and Paul A. LaFontaine (2010), GED recipients are counted as high school graduates in these estimates. The chapter by Martha Bailey and Susan Dynarski document trends in college graduation.
11. The same pattern holds for the correlations between the earnings of fathers and sons, as documented in Bjorklund and Jantti (2009).
12. For evidence on trends in residential segregation by income, see Jargowsky (1997); Reardon and Bischoff (forthcoming); and Watson (2009). Reardon and Kendra Bischoff (forthcoming) show that income segregation for whites and blacks increased between 1970 and 1990 and for whites in large cities between 1990 and 2000.

13.   It is difficult to predict the timing of when changes in family income inequality should affect inequality in cognitive skills. Reardon implicitly assumes that income effects are immediate with, for example, adolescents' test scores determined by their family incomes during adolescence. If, as evidence reviewed in Duncan, Ziol-Guest, and Kalil (2010) suggests, income early in childhood matters more for a child than income in adolescence, then the links between aggregate changes in income inequality and income-based test score gaps are harder to pin down.

14.   These authors use data from surveys that measure parent education but not family income.

15.   As with figure 1.1, all dollar amounts are inflated to 2008 price levels. We are very grateful to Sabino Kornich of the Center for the Advanced Studies in the Social Sciences at the Juan March Institute in Madrid for providing these data. The definition of "enrichment expenditures" in this graph is identical to that given in chapter 9 in this volume.

16.   Altonji and Mansfield find little additional change during the 1990s.

17.   Altonji and Mansfield's definition of school quality includes the influence of peer effects on outcomes, which include the high school graduation rate, college enrollment rate, and the subsequent wages of students attending particular high schools.

18.   Raudenbush, Jean, and Art control for a comprehensive list of school-level compositional factors, including two social class composites, in their models estimating the influence of the school-specific student mobility rate on the mathematics achievement of students (see chapter 17, n. 1).

19.   The influence of neighborhood residents' incomes on teacher transfer decisions is net of the influence of the socioeconomic status of students in the relevant school, as measured by eligibility for a free or reduced price lunch.

20.   C. Kirabo Jackson (2009) shows that the end of court-ordered desegregation led to a decline in teacher quality in schools that experienced an increase in the number of black students. However, the decline in school quality might have been greater in the absence of the district programs that were designed to improve the attractiveness of teaching positions in disadvantaged schools.

21.   David Deming (2009) reports that the internal rate of return to Head Start is 7.9 percent. Since the cost to the federal government of borrowing to pay for social investments such as Head Start is considerably lower than 7.9 percent, the evidence is that this program is a worthwhile social investment.

22.   Policing experiments have shown that it is possible to reduce the crime rate in high-crime neighborhoods (Skogan and Frydl 2004), but the evaluations of these interventions have yet to test for improvements in children's schooling outcomes.

REFERENCES

Aaronson, Daniel, and Bhashkar Mazumder. 2007. "Intergenerational Economic Mobility in the U.S., 1940–2000." Working paper. Chicago: Federal Reserve Bank of Chicago.

Angrist, Joshua D., Susan M. Dynarski, Thomas J. Kane, Parag A. Pathak, and Christopher R. Walters. 2010a. "Inputs and Impacts in Charter Schools: KIPP Lynn." *American Economic Review* 100(2): 239–43.

———. 2010b. "Who Benefits from KIPP?" NBER Working paper No. 15740. Washington, D.C.: National Bureau of Economic Research.

Bjorklund, Anders, and Markus Jantti. 2009. "Intergenerational Income Mobility and the Role of Family Background." In *The Oxford Handbook of Income Inequality,* edited by Wiemer Salvedra, Brian Nolan and Timothy M. Smeeding. New York: Oxford University Press.

Bloom, Howard S., Saskia Levy Thompson, and Rebecca Unterman. 2010. *Transforming the High School Experience: How New York City's New Small Schools Are Boosting Student Achievement and Graduation Rates.* New York: MDRC.

Brooks-Gunn, Jeanne, Greg J. Duncan, and J. Lawrence Aber. 1997. *Neighborhood Poverty.* New York: Russell Sage Foundation.

Carrell, Scott E., and Mark L. Hoekstra. 2010. "Externalities in the Classroom: How Children Exposed to Domestic Violence Affect Everyone's Kids." *American Economic Journal: Applied Economics* 2(1): 211–28.

City, Elizabeth A. 2008. *Resourceful Leadership: Tradeoffs and Tough Decisions on the Road to School Improvement.* Cambridge, Mass.: Harvard Education Press.

Clotfelter, Charles, Elizabeth Glennie, Helen Ladd, and Jacob Vigdor. 2008. "Would Higher Salaries Keep Teachers in High-Poverty Schools? Evidence from a Policy Intervention in North Carolina." *Journal of Public Economics* 92(5–6): 1352–70.

Dahl, Gordon, and Lance Lochner. 2008. "The Impact of Family Income on Child Achievement: Evidence from the Earned Income Tax Credit." NBER Working Paper No. 14599. Washington, D.C.: National Bureau of Economic Research, Inc.

Deming, David. Forthcoming. "Better Schools, Less Crime?" *Quarterly Journal of Economics.*

————. 2009. "Early Childhood Intervention and Life-Cycle Skill Development: Evidence from Head Start." *American Economic Journal: Applied Economics* 1(3): 111–34.

Deming, David, Justine S. Hastings, Thomas J. Kane, and Douglas O. Staiger. 2011. "School Choice, School Quality, and Academic Achievement." Unpublished working paper, Harvard University.

Duncan, Greg J., Aletha Huston, and Thomas Weisner. 2007. *Higher Ground: New Hope for the Working Poor and Their Children.* New York: Russell Sage Foundation.

Duncan, Greg, Jens Ludwig, and Katherine Magnuson. 2010. "Child Development." In *Targeting Investments in Children: Fighting Poverty When Resources Are Limited,* edited by Phillip Levine and David Zimmerman. Chicago: University of Chicago Press.

Duncan, Greg J., Kathleen M. Ziol-Guest, and Ariel Kalil. 2010. "Early-Childhood Poverty and Adult Attainment, Behavior, and Health." *Child Development* 81(1): 306–25.

Goldin, Claudia D., and Lawrence F. Katz. 2008. *The Race Between Education and Technology.* Cambridge, Mass.: Harvard University Press/Belknap Press.

Heckman, James J., and Paul A. LaFontaine. 2010. "The American High School Graduation Rate: Trends and Levels." *Review of Economics and Statistics* 92(2): 244–62.

Hertz, Tom, Tamara Jayasundera, Patrizio Piraino, Sibel Selcuk, Nicole Smith, and Alina Verashchagina. 2007. "The Inheritance of Educational Inequality: International Comparisons and Fifty-Year Trends." *B.E. Journal of Economic Analysis and Policy* 7(2): 1–46.

Jackson, C. Kirabo. 2009. "Student Demographics, Teacher Sorting, and Teacher Quality: Evidence from the End of School Desegregation." *Journal of Labor Economics* 27(2): 213–56.

Jargowsky, Paul A. 1997. *Poverty and Place: Ghettos, Barrios, and the American City.* New York: Russell Sage Foundation.

Jencks, Christopher, and Meredith Phillips. 1998. *The Black-White Test Score Gap.* Washington, D.C.: Brookings Institution Press.

Levy, Frank, and Richard J. Murnane. 2004. *The New Division of Labor: How Computers Are Creating the Next Labor Market.* Princeton, N.J.: Princeton University Press.

Levy, Frank, and Peter Temin. 2010. "Institutions and Wages in Post–World War II America." In *Labor in the Era of Globalization,* edited by Clair Brown, Barry J. Eichengreen, and Michael Reich. New York: Cambridge University Press.

Morris, Pamela, Greg J. Duncan, and Elizabeth Clark-Kauffman. 2005. "Child Well-Being in an Era of Welfare Reform: The Sensitivity of Transitions in Development to Policy Change." *Developmental Psychology* 41(6): 919–32.

Neidell, Matthew, and Jane Waldfogel. Forthcoming. "Cognitive and Non-Cognitive Peer Effects in Early Education." *Review of Economics and Statistics.*

Panel Study of Income Dynamics. 1968–2006. [Public-use dataset]. Institute for Social Research Survey Research Center, University of Michigan, Ann Arbor [producer and distributor].

Piketty, Thomas, and Emmanuel Saez. 2003. "Income Inequality in the United States, 1913–1998." *Quarterly Journal of Economics* 118(1): 1–39.

Reardon, Sean F., and Kendra Bischoff. Forthcoming. "Income Inequality and Income Segregation." *American Journal of Sociology.*

Risley, Todd R., and Betty Hart. 1995. *Differences in the Everyday Experience of Young American Children.* Baltimore: Brookes.

Sanbonmatsu, Lisa, Jeffrey R. Kling, Greg J. Duncan, and Jeanne Brooks-Gunn. 2006. "Neighborhoods and Academic Achievement." *Journal of Human Resources* 41(4): 649–91.

Skogan, Wesley, and Kathleen Frydl, eds. 2004. *Fairness and Effectiveness in Policing: The Evidence.* Washington, D.C.: National Academy Press.

Smith, Tom W., Peter Marsden, Michael Hout, and Jibum Kim. 1972–2008. *General Social Surveys, 1972–2010* [machine-readable data file]. Principal Investigator, Tom W. Smith; Co-Principal Investigator, Peter V. Marsden; Co-Principal Investigator, Michael Hout; Sponsored by National Science Foundation—NORC ed.—Chicago, Ill.: National Opinion Research Center [producer]; Storrs, Conn.: The Roper Center for Public Opinion Research, University of Connecticut [distributor].

Snow, Catherine. 2002. *Reading for Understanding: Toward a Research and Development Program in Reading Comprehension.* Santa Monica: Rand Corporation.

Snyder, T. D., and S. A. Dillow. 2010. *Digest of Education Statistics 2009* (NCES 2010-013). Washington, D.C.: National Center for Education Statistics, Institute of Education Sciences, U.S. Department of Education. Available at: http://nces.ed.gov/pubsearch/pubsinfo.asp?pubid=2010013 (accessed June 25, 2011).

Steele, Jennifer L., Richard J. Murnane, and John B. Willett. 2010. "Do Financial Incentives Help Low-Performing Schools Attract and Keep Academically Talented Teachers? Evidence from California." *Journal of Policy Analysis and Management* 29(3): 451–78.

U.S. Bureau of the Census. (n.d.). *Current Population Survey, 1948–2009* [dataset]. Available at: http://www.census.gov/hhes/www/income/data/historical/families/index.html (accessed May 2, 2011).

U.S. Bureau of Labor Statistics. Various years. *Consumer Expenditure Survey, Public Use Microdata.* Available at: http://www.bls.gov/cex (accessed April 30, 2011).

Watson, Tara. 2009. "Inequality and the Measurement of Residential Segregation by Income in American Neighborhoods." *Review of Income and Wealth* 55(3): 820–44.

Wong, Vivian C., Thomas D. Cook, W. S. Barnett, and Kwanghee Jung. 2008. "An Effectiveness-Based Evaluation of Five State Pre-Kindergarten Programs." *Journal of Policy Analysis and Management* 27(1): 122–54.

Part II

The Developing Child and Adolescent

Chapter 2

Lessons from Neuroscience Research for Understanding Causal Links Between Family and Neighborhood Characteristics and Educational Outcomes

Charles A. Nelson III and Margaret A. Sheridan

What can neuroscience tell us about educational inequality and about the links between families and neighborhoods and between educational and labor-market outcomes? In this chapter we review literature relevant to this question. We posit that families, schools, and neighborhoods play a critical role in influencing the course of child development and, collectively, influence long-term educational success. In addition, we posit that we cannot fully understand child development without also understanding brain development, since all changes in behavior are predicated on changes in the brain.

In this chapter we do the following:

- Briefly review developmental neurobiology, highlighting aspects of development that are most likely to be shaped by families, schools, and neighborhoods. Specifically, in the first section we review the critical difference between developmental and adult plasticity.

- Report on a randomized clinical trial of foster care as an intervention for severe psychosocial deprivation that documents dramatic changes in neural function, IQ, mental health, and language learning for children removed from institutions. We emphasize in particular benefits for children removed before the second year of life.

- Review literature demonstrating the impact of stress exposure on specific neural structures, the hippocampus and amygdala, and describe how different developmental patterns in these structures could influence adult mental health and labor-market outcomes.

- Review how exposures associated with socioeconomic status (for example, school environments and parental language use) may affect neural development, particularly in areas of the "association cortex" that are known to mediate our ability to perform tasks of cognitive control.

- Discuss the implications of neuroscience research for the cost-effectiveness of intervening early versus late in life.

- Provide views about future research directions that would better inform the questions we begin the chapter with, thus more effectively informing the fields of both economics and neuroscience.

The question we seek to answer in this chapter is, what can neuroscience tell us about educational inequality, links between families and neighborhoods, and links between educational and labor-market outcomes? We posit that families, schools, and neighborhoods all play a critical role in influencing the course of child development and, collectively, influence long-term educational success. Moreover, how successful a child is in negotiating the educational challenges that he or she faces during the first two decades of life will ultimately determine how successful that child is in the labor market, which in turn will influence the quality of the society in which we live.

Accordingly, the course of child development influences in whole or in part the success the child has in the labor market. Critically, we cannot fully understand child development without understanding the brain, the engine that drives development. If we hope to understand what regulates behavior, we must dig beneath the surface, to the organ that drives behavior, which is the brain. Overall, then, we cannot understand how families, schools, and neighborhoods affect life outcomes until we first explain how they affect the developing brain.

Families, schools, and neighborhoods can be conceptualized, in different ways and at different levels, as composed of a collection of experiences that the child must incorporate into his or her brain. These experiences range from the discrete and specific (for instance, the quality of caregiving the child experiences as an infant) to the broad and nonspecific (how safe the child feels walking through his or her neighborhood each day to school). (See chapter 12 in this volume for further discussion.)

Not surprisingly, we know most about the effect of discrete and specific experiences on brain development, as those are easiest to control, measure, and study. There is a small and growing literature that directly assesses macro-experiences, such as schools and neighborhoods, on brain and cognitive development; and these studies, while incomplete, generate testable hypotheses about the impact of these forces on brain development. When possible, we review the literature concerning neural development and these macro-experiences. Finally, if we can model the effects of families, schools, and neighborhoods on brain development, we should be able to model how educational attainment and, ultimately, success in the labor market will similarly be derived from how the brain is built over the first two decades of life.

The main thesis we put forth in this chapter is that both micro-experiences (such as the caregiving environment) and macro-experiences (neighborhoods and schools) weave their way into the developing brain and, depending on their timing, exert different effects. Such experiences ultimately influence the course of human development. For example, a child who is reared in a safe, nurturing environment and who is exposed to mild stressors early in life may grow up to be well equipped to handle increasing levels of stress, including those faced in neighborhoods and schools (for example, bullies) and, eventually, in the workplace. In contrast, a child who grows up in a chaotic family environment, in a neighborhood where the specter of violence is commonplace and where the schools are unsafe, may well grow up to be ill equipped to handle even the mildest of stressors, may do poorly in school, and may eventually fail to make a successful transition to the labor market. To support our thesis, we draw heavily on the literature on the effects of maltreatment and neglect, stress and trauma, and poverty on brain development. It follows from this review that exposure to early life adversity can powerfully shape the life course.

BRAIN DEVELOPMENT

Shortly after conception, the embryo begins to develop a neural tube, which when completely formed (three to four weeks postconception) ushers in the next phase of brain development—a process referred to as neurogenesis (birth of neurons—a glossary of scientific terms is found in the online appendix, available at: http://www.russellsage.org/duncan_murnane_online_appendix.pdf). Neurogenesis will continue through the entire gestation period and early postnatal life, and it is responsible for every brain cell that exists. As humans, we massively overproduce brain cells such that the newborn brain has many more cells than the adult brain; gradually, however, over the first months and years of life, the number of brain cells (particularly neurons) is reduced, a process referred to as apoptosis.

Around the sixth prenatal week, a subset of the neurons that have been forming begins to migrate out from the neural tube. Cell migration continues through about the twenty-fifth prenatal week. During this time the cortex, the convoluted outer layer of the brain, is formed. The cortex itself is composed of six layers, each of which possesses some functional significance owing to the composition of cells that make up each layer and to the connections among cells within and across layers. Once a cell has found its correct location, the cell body forms, and branches from the cell body, axons and dendrites, extend from it. In most cases one neuron communicates with another via one axon's connecting with the dendrite of another neuron, which forms a synapse. The synapse is the sine qua non of neural function, as it permits neurons to communicate with one another. Individual synapses eventually begin to connect with other like-minded synapses, forming a neural circuit. Ultimately, it is the neural circuit that underlies all of human behavior, thought, and function.

As is the case with neurons, we massively overproduce synapses, such that the newborn brain has many more synapses than the adult brain. This process of overproducing synapses is largely under genetic control, but the process of synapse elimination is greatly influenced by experience. The rate at which the brain constructs and then eliminates synapses varies by area; thus, the peak of overproduction of synapses in the visual cortex, the locus of our ability to see, occurs at around four months, and adult numbers of synapses are eventually reached by the time a child is four to six years old. In contrast, the peak of overproduction of synapses in the prefrontal cortex—the area of the brain that sits behind the forehead and is involved in higher cognitive functions and regulating emotion—occurs at about one year of age, and adult numbers of synapses are not obtained till mid- to late adolescence.

Myelination occurs in parallel with synaptogenesis. Myelin is a fatty substance that coats some axons and serves the purpose of speeding up the transmission of information. Myelination occurs in waves, beginning with sensory and motor areas in the last trimester of pregnancy and ending with areas involved in higher cognitive function and emotion regulation, such as the frontal lobe, in an individual's early to mid-twenties. (For recent and accessible reviews of brain development, see Nelson and Jeste 2008.)

In summary, brain development begins just a few weeks after conception, and although the bulk of it is completed by mid- to late adolescence, recent research suggests that the process of myelination is likely incomplete until the early to mid-twenties. Accordingly, most neuroscientists now agree that a child's brain does not reach adult status until the mid-twenties. It is also important to emphasize that although genetics supplies the basic blueprint for brain development, experience adjusts the genetic plan for the brain and shapes the architecture of its neural circuits, according to the needs and distinctive environment of the individual. It is not just the postnatal environment that is important; for example, prenatal exposure to teratogens, such as alcohol and other drugs of abuse, illustrates how the fetus's experiences before birth can influence development (Langlois and Mayes 2008; Mattson et al. 2008). For the purposes of this chapter, we confine ourselves to how experiences that occur postnatally influence the course of human development.

NEURAL PLASTICITY

Neural plasticity refers to the process whereby the structure of experience weaves its way into the structure of the brain. There are generally two types of neural plasticity: developmental plasticity, which refers to processes that occur during the time the brain is being built, and adult plasticity, which refers to the remolding or modification of the mature brain. In developmental plasticity, we are using experience to wire an incompletely formed brain, whereas in adult plasticity, we are using experience to rewire a mature, fully formed brain. Thus, acquiring one's first language would be an example of developmental plasticity, but acquiring a second language later in life might be an example of adult plasticity (for a recent review of plasticity, see Fox, Levitt, and Nelson 2010).

Adult Plasticity

Once a circuit is fully formed and functional, in many respects it is difficult if not impossible to change. In addition, the earlier in life a circuit is formed, the harder it is to change later. Thus, most of our sensory systems (for instance, vision and hearing) are fully adultlike in the first few years of life—which is why we do not learn to see or hear better as we get older. In contrast, our learning and memory functions have a very long developmental trajectory, in part because the areas of the brain involved in learning and memory remain plastic for many years; as a result, barring pathology or injury, we are capable of new learning and memory for much of the life span. Motor functions likely fall somewhere in between sensory and learning and memory functions; thus, although we can certainly acquire new motor functions in adulthood, the likelihood is remote of attaining the same level of proficiency as someone who acquired that motor function much earlier in life. (This conclusion likely resonates for readers who learned to play golf or tennis as an adult.)

Developmental Plasticity

As a rule, developmental plasticity typically occurs during the time the brain is still undergoing rapid growth. However, there are constraints on developmental plasticity. First, because different regions of the brain mature at different rates, once a region or circuit is mature, it will prove much more difficult to modify with experience. Thus, timing matters. Second, some regions and circuits require more experience than others to develop normally, and if sufficient experience does not occur during the time that particular region or circuit is forming, the functionality of that region and circuit may be limited. For example, for normal language acquisition to occur, children must be exposed to the sounds of language very early in life. Such experience essentially sculpts and eventually narrows the perceptual window through which language is processed, leading to expertise with one's native language. By six months of age, infants throughout the world can discriminate the sounds of most of the world's languages (for example, an infant being brought up in an English-speaking home can discriminate the phonemes of not only English but also of Thai, Swedish, and Czech). But by twelve months of age, infants are only able to discriminate the sounds from their native language.

Experience has its maximal effect during a particular span of time, which is referred to as a sensitive period. As a rule, sensitive periods vary by domain. For example, for the visual system to develop normally, visual input must be available and be normal during the first year or so of life. Similarly, for a child to develop normal language or a normal relationship with his or her caregiver, access to normal language and caregiving must occur during the first two or so years of life. As a rule, although different functional domains (including vision, hearing, language, and attachment) vary in the precise time when their sensitive periods begin and end, most sensitive periods run their course in the first few years of life. Our point, then, is that brains are built over time, that they depend on access to a normal, expectable environment, and that what happens in the first few years has a profound impact on the course of child development.

Because sensitive periods differ by brain region or circuit, and because it is during a sensitive period that experience can maximally exert its effects, some neuroscientists have adopted the expression "plasticity cuts both ways." If a brain is exposed to good experiences during a sensitive period, then the long-term outcome is biased to be positive. However, if the brain is exposed to bad experiences, then the long-term outcome is biased to be negative. Once a particular region or circuit of the brain has passed through a sensitive period, the principles of developmental plasticity cease to play a role, and the mechanisms of adult plasticity must come into play. And, as mentioned earlier, no amount of experience will improve our eyesight or hearing, suggesting that once sensory systems pass through their sensitive period, no modification is possible. In contrast, because the areas of the brain that subserve many high-level cognitive and emotional functions—the prefrontal cortex, in particular—have such a long developmental trajectory, remaining not fully formed till mid- to late adolescence, these areas maintain considerable plasticity through adolescence. This means that even if the initial construction of the brain gets off to a good start as a result of exposure to good environments and experiences, later development can be compromised if the child is exposed to negative experiences later in his or her life.

THE ROLE OF EXPERIENCE IN BRAIN DEVELOPMENT

Neuroscientists have historically studied the role of experience in brain development in two ways. First, they conduct experiments in which they manipulate the dose, timing, and duration of specific experiences and observe the outcome on behavior and the brain. Not surprisingly, much of this work is done with animals, as the key variables are easier to manipulate. Second, they take advantage of naturally occurring conditions in which the organism is deprived of certain experiences at certain points in time. The reason studies of deprivation or adversity have taken precedence over studies of enrichment is simply because the variables are easier to isolate and control and so these studies are easier to conduct.

It is understandable that there is very little research examining families, neighborhoods, or schools on brain development per se. Rather, what investigators have done is attempt to isolate key components of each of these domains and examine how these components influence the child's behavior and, in some cases, the child's brain. For example, within the context of the family, a great deal of work has focused on caregiving. In contrast, virtually no research has examined the role of schools and neighborhoods in brain development (with the possible exception of the effects of poverty, which we discuss later in this chapter) because these are macro-environments. Because of the paucity of research in this area, we are forced to speculate about the effects of family, neighborhood, and school on brain development.

We have selected four areas to focus on as examples of the impact of environment on neural development: severe psychosocial deprivation, trauma, stress, and poverty. We have done so for two reasons. First, these topics have been examined in the context of brain development. Second, these topics are examples of the importance of families, neighborhoods, and schools. Thus, even though it is currently impossible to examine how families, neighborhoods, and schools directly influence the course of brain development, we can infer their indirect effects by examining key components of families, neighborhoods, and schools. Once we have reviewed this literature, we attempt to integrate across these domains and then speculate as to how labor markets might be affected by alterations in brain development. We conclude by briefly offering some suggestions for future research.

ENVIRONMENTAL DEPRIVATION

It has been known for at least three-quarters of a century that development can be profoundly derailed among children who grow up in institutions (Kreppner et al. 2007; MacLean 2003; Rutter, O'Connor, and the English and Romanian Adoptees [ERA] Study Team 2004). Obviously, the deficits and developmental delays that result from institutional rearing have their origins in compromised brain development. The question is, what is the mechanism that underlies such deficits? In the view of most neuroscientists, the brain requires normative input in order to wire correctly, and if such input is lacking, or is impoverished, errors in brain development can occur. Among children experiencing neglect, normative input is lacking, and errors in brain development are likely to result.

Some domains of function are more experience-dependent than others. For those that are experience-dependent, the timing of experience varies by functional domain; for instance, timing in cognition, attachment, and language vary. As a result, if children are deprived of a normal language environment at a particular point in development, there is a high likelihood of a delay in the acquisition of language or of a language disorder.

The literature on children who have experienced profound and prolonged neglect is substantial (for reviews, see Gunnar, Bruce, and Grotevant 2000; Gunnar and Nelson 1994; Gunnar and van Dulmen 2007), and so we confine our discussion to the Bucharest Early Intervention Project (BEIP), a study that the first author of this chapter has been involved with for nearly ten years (see Zeanah et al. 2003 for a description). The BEIP is a randomized controlled trial of foster care as an intervention for early institutionalization. Specific details about the scope of the project and experimental design are available in the online appendix. We focused our attention on cognitive, social, emotional, and brain development (for a summary see Nelson et al. 2009). Following the baseline assessment, half the children in the institutional group were randomly assigned to care as usual—to remain in the institution—and half to high-quality foster care, which the BEIP team itself designed and built, since there was very little government foster care at the outset of the study. All three groups were then followed at regular intervals until the children were eight years of age.

IQ

We observed that children reared in institutions showed greatly diminished IQ scores compared with children reared with their biological families. For example, prior to randomization (mean age was twenty-two months old) the mean Bayley Mental Developmental Index (MDI) scores were 66 for children in the institutionalized group and 103 for children in the community group (Smyke et al. 2007).[1] Like IQ, the MDI is a test with a normal distribution and a mean of 100 and standard deviation of 15.

Having established that early institutionalization has a very detrimental effect on IQ, we next turned our attention to intervention effects (Nelson et al. 2007). Here we asked whether our intervention was effective and whether there was an effect of age at placement. To answer the first question, we observed that children in the foster-care group (FCG) experienced significant gains in IQ compared with children in the institutional group (IG). For example, at fifty-four months the mean IQ was 81 for children in the FCG, 73 for children in the IG, and 109 for children in the never-institutionalized group (NIG). Regarding the effects of age of placement, we found that at fifty-four months, the IQ of children placed in foster care before eighteen months of age was 85; those placed in care when eighteen to twenty-four months old, 87; those placed when twenty-four to thirty months old, 78; and those placed when after thirty months of age, 72 (for discussion, see Nelson et al. 2007).

Overall, children placed in institutions suffer significant delays in their intellectual functioning. Those placed in foster care, by contrast, show substantial gains, although their IQs never reach the level of the never-institutionalized group. Finally, the earlier the child was placed in foster care (as in, before reaching twenty-four-months old), the greater his or her intellectual recovery.

Mental Health

Throughout the world, psychiatric illness exerts an enormous burden on individuals, families, and societies. In the context of labor markets and the economy, psychiatric illness results in inefficiency at work, lost wages, and a burden on health-care costs. In the BEIP study, to examine the link between early profound deprivation and later mental health outcomes, the researchers assessed psychiatric symptoms, disorders, and impairments when all children were fifty-four months of age (Zeanah et al. 2009). The majority (55 percent) of children who had lived in institutions had diagnosable psychiatric disorders at fifty-four months of age. By contrast, only 22 percent of children in the community met criteria for suffering from a disorder. Children in both the institutional and foster-care groups had higher levels of both emotional and behavioral disorders—for example, they showed evidence of anxiety, were depressive, oppositional, defiant, had attention deficit and hyperactivity disorder (ADHD), and conduct disorders. Approximately 45 percent of children assigned to care as usual—those in the institutional group—suffered from an anxiety disorder and nearly 4 percent from depression; another 18 to 20 percent were diagnosed with ADHD.

The intervention was effective, but not for all types of disorders. Children in the foster-care group exhibited significantly fewer emotional disorders, such as anxiety, than children in the institutionalized group, although, as with IQ, the prevalence of emotional disorders was still higher among children in foster care than among the community children. However, there was no evidence that the intervention reduced behavioral disorders such as ADHD.

Sensitive Periods and Timing Effects

A pronounced theme in BEIP was the importance of timing of placement in foster care. For IQ, attachment, language, and brain function, children placed in foster care before twenty-two to twenty-four months of age had much better outcomes than those placed after this age—although it is important to note that in virtually no domain did children assigned to foster care look indistinguishable from those who were never institutionalized. However, we did not observe sensitive periods in all domains. For example, there was no hint of a sensitive period in our mental health data. Collectively, this speaks to the point we raised earlier: functional domains differ in their dependence on the timing of experience.

Having discussed the effects of early, profound deprivation on the course of child and brain development, we next turn our attention to two other areas that we believe have enormous implications for labor markets: individuals who have experienced unremitting or chronic stress, trauma, or abuse, and those living in poverty.

STRESS AND TRAUMA

Several studies have examined the association between violence or trauma and mental health or achievement. Many of these studies have focused on the mediation of violence exposure by stress and its impact on neurodevelopment. This focus in part reflects the relationship of stress to trauma. For instance, there is evidence that children who are exposed to early adverse experiences, such as abuse, have increased stress hormone exposure (Tarullo, Bruce, and Gunnar 2007). In online appendix 2.A1, we describe the hormonal cascade that follows a stressful or traumatic experience. The neural consequences of mild stressors, such as a child's response to the first day of school or day care, can be neutral or even positive. However, when a child is chronically exposed to more negative stressors (for example, fear for one's safety in a neighborhood or school) or exposed to toxic stress resulting from a traumatic experience (abuse or neglect), the consequences are quite negative and enduring.

Traumatic or Chronic Stress and the Brain

There are several areas of the brain involved in the limbic-hypothalamic-pituitary-adrenal (LHPA)-axis stress response (see online appendix 2.A1). Some of these areas have prolonged developmental trajectories, through at least middle childhood. Others show little change across childhood and, given the principles of developmental plasticity, may subsequently not be as influenced by environmental variables or experiences. This difference in developmental plasticity by area may be important in predicting the effect of environment on neural structure and function.

Two neural structures, the hippocampus and the amygdala, are necessary to initiate and modulate the stress response. In addition, both are affected by chronic stress exposure. The hippocampus plays an important role in learning and memory in adults and children, and it becomes functional early in the first year of life (Richmond and Nelson 2009). The hippocampus has another important role: it provides a negative-feedback mechanism, which modifies the LHPA-axis response (Kim and Yoon 1998). During a typical LHPA-axis stress response, glucocorticoids are released and travel via blood flow to the hippocampus and bind to glucocorticoid receptors, activating a negative-feedback loop and decreasing the LHPA-axis response. Chronic stress disrupts hippocampal function, which may in turn disrupt this negative feedback, resulting in extended LHPA-axis activation following stressful events and initiating a cycle of damage as excessive glucocorticoid exposure occurs. Importantly, damage to the hippocampus via exposure to stress disrupts both the moderation of the LHPA-axis response and memory formation. In disorders associated with increased glucocorticoid exposure, such as post-traumatic stress disorder (PTSD), memory encoding and recall are disrupted (Jelinek et al. 2009).

The amygdala plays an important role in emotion learning and recognition in adults and children, particularly in fear learning and interpretation of visual emotional information such as facial expressions. In bilateral amygdala lesions in humans or nonhuman primates, indiscriminate friendliness and overly trusting behavior are commonly observed (Bechara et al. 1995; Emery and Amaral 1999), and the ability to identify correctly emotional facial expressions, particularly fear, is compromised (Adolphs et al. 1994).

For children as for adults, the amygdala plays a role in fear conditioning (Monk et al. 2003) and in processing facial emotion (Baird et al. 1999; Beesdo et al. 2009). When learning that certain objects or places are to be feared, people do not need to be able to report consciously about the association. In fact, the amygdala prepares the body for negative stimuli by activating the stress response, even when the individual is not aware that he or she "knows" a negative event will occur.

Not all aspects of amygdala function are identical in children and adults. Children tend to activate the amygdala to a broader set of socially relevant stimuli (for example, facial expressions; Thomas et al. 2001). There is ample evidence that the amygdala, unlike the hippocampus, changes in structure and function across childhood, making it a more developmentally "plastic" structure and therefore potentially more susceptible to the impact of stress during childhood.

Effects of Traumatic Stress

It has been widely hypothesized that a variety of adverse experiences can impact the brain's ability to respond to stress. These range from exposure to poverty (Lupien et al. 2000) to exposure to severe neglect (Nelson et al. in press). Observing the effect of exposure to traumatic experiences such as neighborhood violence, war, physical, or sexual abuse is one way to study the role that chronic or traumatic LHPA-axis activation can have on the developing brain. These experiences are associated with severe psychological distress at the time of the event and also when they are remembered later, in late childhood and adulthood.

In human adults, trauma-related mental illness, such as PTSD, correlates with decreased hippocampal volume and increased LHPA-axis activity (Campbell and MacQueen 2004; Geuze, Vermetten, and Bremner 2005; Kitayama et al. 2005; Sheline, Gado, and Kraemer 2003; Smith 2005). In otherwise healthy middle-aged adults, self-reported stress reported over twelve years was associated with decreases in hippocampal volume at year thirteen (Gianaros et al. 2007).

Similarly, in the rodent literature, there is clear evidence that in adult animals stress exposure results in decreased hippocampal volume (see Liu et al. 1997; for review, see Sánchez, Ladd, and Plotsky 2001). However, there is little evidence that these differences in hippocampal volume are present in juvenile animals. Human individuals exposed to abuse during childhood do not differ in hippocampal volume from their nonabused peers (De Bellis et al. 2001; Woon and Hedges 2008), despite evidence that children who experience trauma have increased glucocorticoid exposure (De Bellis et al. 1999). Yet in both mature rodents and human adults, exposure to a highly stressful environment during the juvenile phase of development results in decreased hippocampal volume in adulthood (Bremner et al. 1997). It thus appears that stress-related reductions in hippocampal volume and changes in LHPA-axis activation incurred as a result of childhood trauma exposure are permanent in the sense that they become obvious years later, in adulthood (Seckl and Meaney 2004), even though these effects of stress are not obvious as reduced hippocampal volume at the time of stress in childhood.

Changes in hippocampal function modify the LHPA-axis response, potentially increasing risk for mental health disorders, such as PTSD and depression, both associated with hippocampal reductions. In addition, deficits in the hippocampus result in deficits in long-term memory, potentially making learning difficult. Finally, increases in stress exposure and smaller hippocampal volume may increase the risk for the development of Alzheimer's disease (Fotenos et al. 2008).

Let us now turn our attention to the amygdala, another structure that is key to our understanding of trauma or stress exposure. In adult rodents, stress modulates the amygdala by enhancing reactivity to fear conditioning (Roozendaal, McEwen, and Chattarji 2009) and by increasing corticotropin-releasing hormone (CRH) production (Makino, Gold, and Schulkin 1994). Chronic stress, in addition to changing regulation, also changes amygdala structure. Unlike the hippocampus, where chronic stress exposure decreases hippocampal volume, chronic stress increases amygdala volume and increases fear behavior in rodents (Mitra et al. 2005; Vyas, Bernal, and Chattarji 2003). Again in contrast to the findings relating to the hippocampus, this increased growth in the amygdala does not return to normal after a prolonged time period with no stress (Vyas, Pillai, and Chattarji 2004).

In nonhuman primates, severely impoverished rearing environments are associated with changes in the amygdala even during the juvenile stage of development (Sabatini et al. 2007). Consistent with the animal studies, when children are examined during development, there is evidence that anxiety disorders are associated with increased amygdala volume and increased fear reactivity in childhood as in adulthood (De Bellis et al. 2000; MacMillan et al. 2003; however, see Woon and Hedges 2008 for a counterargument).

Traumatic Stress Exposure: Conclusions

Traumatic and chronic stress during childhood has a lasting effect on amygdala and hippocampal volume and function, leading to decreased emotion regulation and increased risk for mental illness, particularly anxiety and depression. The effect of toxic stress on hippocampal function appears to be evident only years later, in adulthood. Early impacts on amygdala function may potentiate the stress response, which eventually leads to differences in hippocampal volume. Children exposed to traumatic stress are likely to have an increased risk for mental illness during childhood. Childhood mental illness is associated with decreased school attendance and increased difficulties with attention and concentration, which impair one's ability to excel academically. In addition, these children are likely to grow into adults who have impaired long-term memory, relative to that of their non-trauma-exposed peers. In addition to these differences in memory, which are likely to affect post–high school education, childhood mental illness that persists into adulthood often signals a more severe and chronic course. Mental illness in adulthood is associated with increased days off from work, decreased concentration, and increased distress. Each of these is likely to affect job performance.

The findings discussed here also point to two more subtle deficits likely to be experienced by individuals with childhood stress exposure. These individuals may have more difficulty with emotion identification and regulation resulting from differences in amygdala structure and function. In addition, the stable impacts that early stress exposure has on the hippocampus point to long-term differences in memory formation. These two deficits may constitute "noncognitive" contributions to labor-market performance.

Low Socioeconomic Status

Exposure to low socioeconomic status (SES) environments appears to have a profound effect on health and achievement throughout childhood and adulthood (Cohen et al. 2004; Commission on Social Determinants of Health 2008; Marmot et al. 1991; Melchior et al. 2007; Miller and Chen 2007). An association between health and socioeconomic status was reported as early as 1967 (Marmot et al. 1991), where lower SES was associated with increased morbidity and mortality at every age. This association has not decreased in the intervening years, and it is hypothesized that social inequalities become "biologically embedded" (Hertzman 1999), modifying risk for later negative achievement and health outcomes. How this happens is unclear. In longitudinal studies, childhood SES appears to account for variance in adult health outcomes over and above that attributable to adult SES, consistent with the hypothesis that there are long-term effects of early exposures to materially or psychosocially impoverished environments (Goodman, Daniels, and Dolan 2007; Parsons et al. 1999; Poulton et al. 2002). In addition to its relation to health, the social partitioning of childhood experience is strongly associated with a host of other variables such as language development and school achievement (Stipek and Ryan 1997). Using the principles we already discussed, we here propose three major mechanisms by which experiences associated with early childhood SES could come to affect long-term health and achievement: (1) differences in rates of childhood traumatic stress exposure, (2) differences in degree of language-complexity exposure, and (3) differences in degree of structure in educational settings.

Chronic and traumatic stress exposure has been one explanation of the economic gradient in health and achievement (Adler et al. 2000). The association between low SES and undesirable health outcomes is particularly strong for health outcomes such as complications of type II diabetes, heart disease, and hypertension—diseases for which the stress response could easily exacerbate disease outcomes (Marmot et al. 1991; McEwen and Mirsky 2002; Poulton and Caspi 2005). Many material explanations (access to monetary resources and healthy food) and structural explanations (access to health care, proximity to grocery stores) have been put forward to account for this sociodemographic variation in health. However, even when these variables are statistically accounted for, disparities in SES continue to be associated with variation in health outcomes (McGinnis and Foege 1993). Researchers have posited that exposure to stress associated with low SES may lead to increased morbidity and mortality. Individuals living in low-SES neighborhoods are more likely than those who live in more affluent neighborhoods to be exposed to more stressful environments resulting from higher crime rates and crowding (Evans and Kantrowitz 2002). In addition, children from low-SES families are more likely than their high-SES peers to experience instances of abuse and neglect, or to have at least one parent who meets criteria for major depressive disorder (Evans 2006; Lupien et al. 2000). As previously mentioned, these circumstances, in isolation, are known to be associated with changes in amygdala and hippocampal structure and function. Given the description of the impact of stress on brain development already reviewed, we can reasonably propose that early exposure to stress associated with low SES should alter stress reactivity and amygdala function in childhood and in adulthood should alter long-term memory and hippocampal structure.

In childhood, there are consistent findings of increased stress reactivity associated with low parental SES (Boyce et al. 1995). Consistent with the potential effect of SES-associated stress on hippocampal function in adulthood, adults who are exposed to low-SES environments are more likely to experience Alzheimer's disease (Fotenos et al. 2008), a disease associated with decreased hippocampal volume. In one study, Peter Gianaros and colleagues demonstrated an association between amygdala function, self-reported parental SES, and stress reactivity in college students (Gianaros et al. 2008). This study demonstrates the vulnerability of these systems to typical variation in environment associated with SES in the United States.

Prefrontal Cortex

The prefrontal cortex has a long developmental trajectory (Gogtay et al. 2006). Gross changes in volume and connectivity (increased white matter) begin at birth in the prefrontal cortex and continue through early adulthood. This protracted development is reflected in behavioral studies with young children which find that children become competent in performing different tests of executive function across this same time period (Davidson et al. 2006). In addition, changes in activation of the prefrontal cortex are observed as children develop across middle childhood (Bunge et al. 2002; Bunge and Wright 2007; Klingberg, Forssberg, and Westerberg 2002; Rubia et al. 2006; Scherf, Sweeny, and Luna 2006). Like adults, when children experience damage to the prefrontal cortex, they have immediate deficits in executive function and fail to develop typical executive function as adults (Anderson et al. 2002). These findings indicate that, like the amygdala, the prefrontal cortex plays a role in cognition from early on, but this role changes and develops across childhood.

SES and the Prefrontal Cortex

A number of cognitive functions and neural areas are potentially associated with SES. Some researchers have attempted to survey separable cognitive functions to determine whether all aspects of functioning are affected similarly by exposure to low SES. These studies, which used behavioral tests to examine aspects of cognitive function, consistently associated decreased ability to perform tests of executive function, a type of cognition that requires the prefrontal cortex, with decreased parental SES (Farah et al. 2006; Noble, Norman, and Farah 2005). In these studies this association between parental SES and executive function was more robust and consistent than associations between parental SES and other cognitive domains (Hackman and Farah 2009). The association between executive function and SES is not unique to the United States, with studies in Mexico, for example (Ardila et al. 2005), demonstrating comparable associations. In one study the association between childhood poverty exposure and later performance on a test of executive function was statistically mediated by stress exposure measured in childhood (Evans and Schamberg 2009). A few studies have used neuroimaging to examine the link between prefrontal function and socioeconomic status in childhood. These studies have demonstrated that children in low-SES families have a reduced ability to suppress distractors at the neural level (Kishiyama et al. 2009; Stevens, Lauinger, and Neville 2009) and have more general reductions in prefrontal cortex activity even during rest (Otero 1997).

Differences in prefrontal function like those described here could influence a wide variety of experiences in childhood and adulthood. For example, executive function is broadly associated with academic achievement, as learning in the classroom environment requires self-regulatory abilities (Blair and Razza 2007). In adolescents, poor executive function is associated with risky health behaviors (Patrick, Blair, and Maggs 2008); and in adulthood, poor inhibition and is associated with nicotine dependence, smoking, and alcohol abuse (Crews and Boettiger 2009; Giancola and Moss 1998; Jester et al. 2009; Sweitzer, Allen, and Kaut 2008).

The Classroom Environment

Macro-level variables, such as attributes of the school environment, may contribute to helping children learn executive function and modify prefrontal development. In one study of a preschool classroom primarily composed of children from low-SES families, random assignment to a classroom where the management style emphasized learning self-regulation dramatically improved performance on an unrelated test of executive function (Diamond and Amso 2008). In Tools of the Mind classrooms, and in most well-functioning classrooms for young children, the practicing of inhibition and working memory is made explicit and emphasized as part of the classroom experience. The creation of predictable classroom environments that emphasize the child's ability to learn self-regulation may be one way in which executive function develops. To the extent to which well-structured and monitored classroom environments are less common in neighborhoods that are marked by poverty, owing to a lack of school funding and leading to increased risk of violence in schools, this may be another way low SES compromises academic achievement.

Summary

The course of brain development begins in utero and continues through early adulthood. During childhood, brain development is characterized by increased cortical efficiency as irrelevant pathways are pruned, by increased circuit use as connections between areas of the brain strengthen, and by a more differentiated role for some subcortical structures as they grow in volume. The changes that occur during childhood constitute developmental plasticity, an increased responsiveness to environmental inputs the brain has during periods of rapid development. This increased responsiveness mediates the neural effects of a variety of environments, ranging from the kind of language you hear to whether you are exposed to violence. These in turn ultimately influence the course of development and may result in permanent and stable neural differences in adulthood. Given brain plasticity, it is easy to understand how differences in environments early in childhood could go on to affect adult behavior and experiences.

Numerous studies have measured the association between a large variety of environments with cognitive and neural outcomes. These studies allow the variable "environment" to be more specifically defined. Here we described the literature considering the role of stress related to abuse or neglect. Studies that associate abuse exposure to brain outcomes document that the volume, function, and connectivity of the amygdala—a subcortical structure involved in fear learning and stress reactivity—are related to exposure to abuse beginning in childhood and continuing through adulthood. Other environments associated with stress exposure, such as environments associated with low SES, are also associated with changes in amygdala function.

In contrast to the amygdala, the effect of stressful experience on the volume and function of the hippocampus, a subcortical structure involved in long-term memory and stress reactivity, is not obvious until adulthood. We propose that differences such as these in the timing of the effect of stress on structures within the brain may be related to differences in the developmental trajectories of these structures. Future research should consider the timing of environmental inputs in shaping aspects of cognition.

Finally, we reviewed a small but emerging literature examining the association between SES and prefrontal cortex structure and function. The prefrontal cortex has an extended developmental trajectory with large changes in structural development of this area occurring throughout childhood and extending into adolescence. As such, it is likely that there is a co-occurring extension in developmental plasticity in this area, and environmental inputs across childhood are likely to shape the development of the prefrontal cortex. It has been observed that the function and volume of the prefrontal cortex is associated with parental SES beginning in middle childhood. Given the role that the prefrontal cortex plays in health behaviors and achievement, two areas highly correlated with SES, this seems like an important direction for future research to explore.

EARLY VERSUS LATE INTERVENTION: RETURN ON THE DOLLAR?

In this chapter we have argued that in many key respects the brain is more plastic early in life than later in life; accordingly, early experience has the potential for greater impact on adult outcomes than later experience. By this principal it might be argued that early interventions are always more effective overall, and therefore more cost-effective, than later interventions. Examples of this principle include work with social and language interventions in autism. Interventions that remediate language processing and social skills are effective if administered around the age of two, with some children no longer meeting criteria for autism diagnosis at follow-up (Dawson et al. 2010; Lovaas 1987). Children who do not receive these interventions do not exhibit improvement, and across time they show greater disparities in function from typically developing children, resulting in greater costs to society and to themselves (Ganz 2007).

Similarly, interventions designed to treat dyslexia are more effective if administered to children at risk (age five or six) before they have demonstrably failed to learn to read at age seven (Torgesen et al. 2010; Vadasy, Jenkins, and Pool 2000). Further examples of the relative effectiveness of early intervention have already been reviewed in this chapter. For example, in the BEIP study, children who were removed from institutions before the age of two fared far better than those removed later. In certain areas, children removed after the age of two never caught up to their earlier-intervention peers.

Effective interventions for particular deficits such as dyslexia or autism have two effects. First, they treat the presenting disorder, increasing the likelihood that a child will maximize his or her earnings potential in adulthood. Second, they decrease the secondary negative outcomes associated with these disorders, including expensive accommodations required for these children to participate in school (Bodden, Dirksen, and Bogels 2008), loss of wages on the part of parents to accommodate their child's needs (Nyden, Myren, and Gillberg 2008), increased health burden experienced by parents and caretakers of children with special needs (Epel et al. 2004), and disruptions to the learning environment experienced by other children who share their classroom. The exact cost to society of each of these aspects of rearing a child who is not developing typically should be considered when deciding the best time at which to attempt intervention or prevention programs.

In economic models of the relative effectiveness of early intervention, it is clear that social disparities in educational achievement and health emerge early and increase across childhood. Estimations of the effect of early interventions in these models are high (Heckman 2007). Long-term outcomes of some interventions, notably the HighScope Perry Preschool Study, have demonstrated positive effects of early intervention, where random assignment to a particular preschool classroom environment is associated with differences in adult income and health behaviors (Muennig et al. 2009).

However, there are numerous counterexamples where positive outcomes associated with an intervention or prevention project are clear shortly after the intervention but quickly fade and are unobservable even one year post-intervention (Otaiba et al. 2009). These examples may lead researchers to conclude that intervening early is ineffective so that any cost incurred in intervention projects should be delayed until late adolescence or adulthood. There are several reasons that this conclusion may be misleading. First, some studies have observed "sleeper effects," where differences between children who did and did not experience the intervention are minor directly following an intervention but by the time they reach adolescence or adulthood, large differences in outcome can be observed (Weikart 1998). This is consistent with the notion of early interventions modifying developmental trajectories. Early differences in outcome may seem small, but larger effects emerge as the child progresses along a different trajectory. Second, even short-term change may be cost-saving. As described, disrupted development has both short- and long-term associated costs: the future labor-market performance of a child may not be influenced by the intervention, but the current performance of her parents and teachers may be relatively better if these people do not have to exert extra effort caring for a child with untreated special needs. Finally, the principles of neural plasticity dictate that some interventions may only be possible during specific periods of brain development. The most effective programs are those that use developmentally appropriate interventions at a time when the relevant neural architecture is still developing.

It may seem counterintuitive, but this impact period usually occurs before a particular problem behavior emerges, when the neural circuits that support this behavior are still being formed. In addition, the most effective prevention programs may not even directly address the future problem behavior but may promote aspects of neural and cognitive development that can be employed effectively later. Take, for example, different approaches to dealing with teen drug abuse. Prevention and intervention programs to reduce drug abuse among teens who have developed substance dependence or a substance-use disorder have low success rates (Botvin and Griffin 2007). In contrast, programs or clinical interventions implemented during early childhood can decrease the likelihood of adolescent substance use, effectively conferring two benefits (short-term gains during childhood and decreased risk of substance abuse during adolescence) for the price of one. It may be that interventions such as these are effective because they affect neural development during a time of maximal plasticity, allowing modifications to the developmental trajectory.

CONCLUSIONS

Several themes emerged from our review of the research. First, different parts of the brain do not develop at the same rate, and it is likely that environmental exposures interact with developmental plasticity, leading to the same exposure's affecting the brain differently depending on when it occurs. Second, developmental plasticity is important. As we described at length, the timing of environmental exposures must be considered. The entire course of brain development could only be altered if environmental input is experienced at the right—or wrong—time. Alternatively, only an incremental effect may be felt regionally in the brain.

The way the environment shapes brain development continues to be poorly understood. Still, the brain can be an important tool in understanding how neighborhoods, schools, and families affect adult behavior. All behavior is governed by the brain, and so it is the most likely site for the embodiment of social conditions related to all behaviors. Parental SES subjects the child to probabilities of exposure to a variety of different environmental influences, from neighborhood safety to school organization. These exposures are likely to shape brain development in the ways we described: decreased neighborhood safety and increased stress may increase sensitivity of the amygdala to future fear stimuli and change subsequent stress responses, making children more vulnerable to mental illness and stress-related diseases; less structure in school may lead to fewer opportunities to learn and practice executive function and may cause differences to come about in prefrontal cortex structure and function. Difficulties in executive function may manifest as differences in academic and job success, permanently altering the likelihood of successful labor-market competition.

During childhood, the plastic brain receives inputs and quickly adapts to the environment it is in. These adaptations become permanent differences in neural structure and function, altering the opportunities of children as they grow into adulthood. By ensuring that early environments are more positive and more equitably distributed, we increase the chance of success that all children have. By ignoring early inequality, we risk permanently altering the chances that some children have to succeed. These early differences in environment are etched into the structure of our brains; the way we think, react, and feel in adulthood is necessarily related to the environmental exposures we did and did not experience in our childhood.

Charles A. Nelson acknowledges the support of the NIH (MH078829-10), the Richard David Scott endowment, and the John D. and Catherine T. MacArthur Foundation. Margaret A. Sheridan acknowledges the support of the Robert Wood Johnson Health and Society Scholars Program. Information about this chapter should be directed to Charles A. Nelson, Laboratories of Cognitive Neuroscience, Children's Hospital Boston/Harvard Medical School, 1 Autumn Street, 6th floor, Boston, MA 02215; charles.nelson@childrens.harvard.edu.

NOTE

Online appendix available at: http://www.russellsage.org/duncan_murnane_online_appendix.pdf.

1.   The Bayley Mental Developmental Index is a standardized test used to evaluate a child's cognitive developmental status. From the Bayley one derives a "developmental quotient" (DQ), which many view as a proxy for the intelligence quotient (IQ).

REFERENCES

Online appendix available at: http://www.russellsage.org/duncan_murnane_online_appendix.pdf.

Adler, N. E., E. S. Epel, G. Castellazzo, and J. R. Ickovics. 2000. "Relationship of Subjective and Objective Social Status with Psychological and Physiological Functioning: Preliminary Data in Healthy White Women." *Health Psychology* 19(6): 586–92.

Adolphs, R., D. Tranel, H. Damasio, and A. Damasio. 1994. "Impaired Recognition of Emotion in Facial Expressions Following Bilateral Damage to the Human Amygdala." *Nature* 372(6507): 669–72.

Anderson, V. A., P. Anderson, E. Northam, R. Jacobs, and O. Mikiewicz. 2002. "Relationships Between Cognitive and Behavioral Measures of Executive Function in Children with Brain Disease." *Child Neuropsychology* 8(4): 231–40.

Ardila, A., M. Rosselli, E. Matute, and S. Guajardo. 2005. "The Influence of the Parents' Educational Level on the Development of Executive Functions." *Developmental Neuropsychology* 28(1): 539–60.

Baird, A. A., S. A. Gruber, D. A. Fein, L. C. Maas, R. J. Steingard, P. F. Renshaw, B. M. Cohen, and D. A. Yurgelun-Todd. 1999. "Functional Magnetic Resonance Imaging of Facial Affect Recognition in Children and Adolescents." *Journal of the American Academy of Child and Adolescent Psychiatry* 38(2): 195–99.

Bechara, A., D. Tranel, H. Damasio, R. Adolphs, C. Rockland, and A. R. Damasio. 1995. "Double Dissociation of Conditioning and Declarative Knowledge Relative to the Amygdala and Hippocampus in Humans." *Science* 269(5227): 1115–18.

Beesdo, K., J. Lau, A. E. Guyer, E. B. McClure-Tone, C. S. Monk, E. E. Nelson, S. J. Fromm, M. A. Goldwin, H. U. Wittchen, E. Leibenluft, M. Ernst, and D. S. Pine. 2009. "Common and Distinct Amygdala-Function Perturbations in Depressed vs. Anxious Adolescents." *Archives of General Psychiatry* 66(3): 275–85.

Blair, C., and R. P. Razza. 2007. "Relating Effortful Control, Executive Function, and False Belief Understanding to Emerging Math and Literacy Ability in Kindergarten." *Child Development* 78(2): 647–63.

Bodden, D. H. M., C. D. Dirksen, and S. M. Bogels. 2008. "Societal Burden of Clinically Anxious Youth Referred for Treatment: A Cost-of-Illness Study." *Journal of Abnormal Child Psychology* 36(4): 487–97.

Botvin, G., and K. Griffin. 2007. "School-Based Programmes to Prevent Alcohol, Tobacco and Other Drug Use." *International Review of Psychiatry* 19(6): 607–15.

Boyce, W., M. Chesney, A. Alkon, J. Tschaan, S. Adams, B. Chesterman, F. Cohen, P. Kaiser, S. Folkman, and D. Wara. 1995. "Psychobiologic Reactivity to Stress and Childhood Respiratory Illnesses: Results of Two Prospective Studies." *Psychosomatic Medicine* 57(5): 411–22.

Bremner, J. D., P. Randall, E. Vermetten, L. Staib, R. A. Bronen, C. Mazure, S. Capelli, G. McCarthy, R. B. Innus, and D. S. Charney. 1997. "Magnetic Resonance Imaging–Based Measurement of Hippocampal Volume in Post-Traumatic Stress Disorder Related to Childhood Physical and Sexual Abuse: A Preliminary Report." *Biological Psychiatry* 41(1): 23–32.

Bunge, S. A., N. M. Dudukovic, M. E. Thomason, C. J. Vaidya, and J. D. Gabrieli. 2002. "Immature Frontal Lobe Contributions to Cognitive Control in Children: Evidence from fMRI." *Neuron* 33(2): 301–11.

Bunge, S. A., and S. B. Wright. 2007. "Neurodevelopmental Changes in Working Memory and Cognitive Control." *Current Opinion in Neurobiology* 17(2): 243–50.

Campbell, S., and G. MacQueen. 2004. "The Role of the Hippocampus in the Pathophysiology of Major Depression." *Journal of Psychiatry and Neuroscience* 29(6): 417–26.

Cohen, S., W. Doyle, R. Turner, A. Cuneyt, and D. Skoner. 2004. "Childhood Socioeconomic Status and Host Resistance to Infectious Illness in Adulthood." *Psychosomatic Medicine* 66(4): 553–58.

Commission on Social Determinants of Health. 2008. *Closing the Gap in a Generation: Health Equity Through Action on the Social Determinants of Health.* Geneva: World Health Organization.

Crews, F. T., and C. A. Boettiger. 2009. "Impulsivity, Frontal Lobes and Risk for Addiction." *Pharmacology Biochemistry and Behavior* 93(3): 237–47.

Davidson, M. C., D. Amso, L. C. Anderson, and A. Diamond. 2006. "Development of Cognitive Control and Executive Functions from 4 to 13 Years: Evidence from Manipulations of Memory, Inhibition, and Task Switching." *Neuropsychologia* 44(11): 2037–78.

Dawson, G., S. Rogers, J. Munson, M. Smith, J. Winter, A. Donaldson, and J. Varley. 2010. "Randomized, Controlled Trial of an Intervention for Toddlers with Autism: The Early Start Denver Model." *Pediatrics* 125(1): e17–e23.

De Bellis, M. D., A. Baum, B. Birmaher, M. S. Keshavan, C. H. Eccard, A. M. Boring, F. J. Jenkins, and N. D. Ryan. 1999. "Developmental Traumatology. Part I: Biological Stress Systems." *Biological Psychiatry* 45(10): 1259–70.

De Bellis, M. D., B. J. Casey, R. E. Dahl, B. Birmaher, D. E. Williamson, K. M. Thomas, D. A. Axelson, K. Frustaci, A. M. Boring, J. Hall, and N. D. Ryan. 2000. "A Pilot Study of Amygdala Volumes in Pediatric Generalized Anxiety Disorder." *Biological Psychiatry* 48(1): 51–57.

De Bellis, M. D., J. Hall, A. M. Boring, K. Frustaci, and G. Moritz. 2001. "A Pilot Longitudinal Study of Hippocampal Volumes in Pediatric Maltreatment–Related Post-Traumatic Stress Disorder." *Biological Psychiatry* 50(4): 305–9.

Diamond, A., and D. Amso. 2008. "Contributions of Neuroscience to Our Understanding of Cognitive Development." *Current Directions in Psychological Science* 17(2): 136–41.

Emery, N. J., and D. G. Amaral. 1999. "The Role of the Amygdala in Primate Social Cognition." In *Cognitive Neuroscience of Emotion*, edited by R. D. Lane and L. Nadel. Oxford: Oxford University Press.

Epel, E. S., E. H. Blackburn, J. Lin, F. S. Dhabhar, N. E. Adler, J. S. Morrow, and R. M. Cawthon. 2004. "Accelerated Telomere Shortening in Response to Life Stress." *Proceedings of the National Academy of Sciences of the United States of America* 101(49): 17312–15.

Evans, G. W. 2006. "Child Development and the Physical Environment." *Annual Review of Psychology* 57: 423–51.

Evans, G. W., and E. Kantrowitz. 2002. "Socioeconomic Status and Health: The Potential Role of Environmental Risk Exposure." *Annual Review of Public Health* 23: 303–31.

Evans, G. W., and M. A. Schamberg. 2009. "Childhood Poverty, Chronic Stress, and Adult Working Memory." *Proceedings of the National Academy of Sciences of the United States of America* 106(16): 6545–49.

Farah, M. J., D. M. Shera, J. H. Savage, L. Betancourt, J. M. Giannetta, N. L. Brodsky, E. K. Malmud, and H. Hurt. 2006. "Childhood Poverty: Specific Associations with Neurocognitive Development." *Brain Research* 1110(1): 166–74.

Fotenos, A. F., M. A. Mintun, A. Z. Snyder, J. C. Morris, and R. L. Buckner. 2008. "Brain Volume Decline in Aging: Evidence for a Relation Between Socioeconomic Status, Preclinical Alzheimer Disease, and Reserve." *Archives of Neurology* 65(1): 113–20.

Fox, S. E., P. Levitt, and C. A. Nelson. 2010. "How the Timing and Quality of Early Experiences Influence the Development of Brain Architecture." *Child Development* 81(1): 28–40.

Ganz, M. L. 2007. "The Lifetime Distribution of the Incremental Societal Costs of Autism." *Archives of Pediatrics and Adolescent Medicine* 161(4): 343–49.

Geuze, E., E. Vermetten, and J. D. Bremner. 2005. "MR-Based in Vivo Hippocampal Volumetrics: 1. Review of Methodologies Currently Employed." *Molecular Psychiatry* 10(2): 147–59.

Gianaros, P. J., J. A. Horenstein, A. R. Hariri, L. K. Sheu, S. B. Manuck, K. A. Matthews, and S. Cohen. 2008. "Potential Neural Embedding of Parental Social Standing." *Social Cognitive and Affective Neuroscience* 3(2): 91–96. doi:10.1093/scan/nsn003.

Gianaros, P. J., J. R. Jennings, L. K. Sheu, P. J. Greer, L. H. Kuller, and K. A. Matthews. 2007. "Prospective Reports of Chronic Life Stress Predict Decreased Grey Matter Volume in the Hippocampus." *Neuroimage* 35(2): 795–803.

Giancola, P. R., and H. B. Moss. 1998. "Executive Cognitive Functioning in Alcohol Use Disorders." *Recent Developments in Alcoholism* 14: 227–51.

Gogtay, N., T. F. Nugent III, D. H. Herman, A. Ordonez, D. Greenstein, K. M. Hayashi, L. Clasen, A. W. Toga, J. N. Giedd, J. L. Rapoport, and P. M. Thompson. 2006. "Dynamic Mapping of Normal Human Hippocampal Development." *Hippocampus* 16(8): 664–72.

Goodman, E., S. R. Daniels, and L. M. Dolan. 2007. "Socioeconomic Disparities in Insulin Resistance: Results from the Princeton School District Study." *Psychosomatic Medicine* 69(1): 61–68.

Gunnar, M. R., J. Bruce, and H. D. Grotevant. 2000. "International Adoption of Institutionally Reared Children: Research and Policy." *Development and Psychopathology* 12(4): 677–93.

Gunnar, M. R., and C. A. Nelson. 1994. "Event-Related Potentials in Year-Old Infants Predict Negative Emotionality and Hormonal Responses to Separation." *Child Development* 65: 80–94.

Gunnar, M. R., and M. H. van Dulmen. 2007. "Behavior Problems in Postinstitutionalized Internationally Adopted Children." *Development and Psychopathology* 19(1): 129–48.

Hackman, D. A., and M. J. Farah. 2009. "Socioeconomic Status and the Developing Brain." *Trends in Cognitive Science* 13(2): 65–73.

Heckman, J. J. 2007. "The Economics, Technology, and Neuroscience of Human Capability Formation." *Proceedings of the National Academy of Sciences of the United States of America* 104(33): 13250–55.

Hertzman, C. 1999. "The Biological Embedding of Early Experience and Its Effects on Health in Adulthood." *Annals of the New York Academy of Sciences* 896: 85–95.

Jelinek, L., S. Randjbar, D. Seifert, M. Kellner, and S. Moritz. 2009. "The Organization of Autobiographical and Non-autobiographical Memory in Post-Traumatic Stress Disorder (PTSD)." *Journal of Abnormal Psychology* 118(2): 288–98.

Jester, J. M., J. T. Nigg, L. I. Puttler, J. C. Long, H. E. Fitzgerald, and R. A. Zucker. 2009. "Intergenerational Transmission of Neuropsychological Executive Functioning." *Brain and Cognition* 70(1): 145–53.

Kim, J. J., and K. S. Yoon. 1998. "Stress: Metaplastic Effects in the Hippocampus." *Trends in Neuroscience* 21(12): 505–9.

Kishiyama, M. M., W. T. Boyce, A. M. Jimenez, L. M. Perry, and R. T. Knight. 2009. "Socioeconomic Disparities Affect Prefrontal Function in Children." *Journal of Cognitive Neuroscience* 21(6): 1106–15.

Kitayama, N., V. Vaccarino, M. Kutner, P. Weiss, and J. D. Bremner. 2005. "Magnetic Resonance Imaging (MRI) Measurement of Hippocampal Volume in Posttraumatic Stress Disorder: A Meta-Analysis." *Journal of Affective Disorders* 88(1): 79–86.

Klingberg, T., H. Forssberg, and H. Westerberg. 2002. "Increased Brain Activity in Frontal and Parietal Cortex Underlies the Development of Visuospatial Working Memory Capacity During Childhood." *Journal of Cognitive Neuroscience* 14(1): 1–10.

Kreppner, J. M., M. Rutter, C. Beckett, J. Castle, E. Colvert, C. Groothues, A. Hawkins, T. G. O'Connor, S. Stevens, and E. J. Sonuga-Barke. 2007. "Normality and Impairment Following Profound Early Institutional Deprivation: A Longitudinal Follow-up into Early Adolescence." *Developmental Psychology* 43(4): 931–46.

Langlois, E. M., and L. C. Mayes. 2008. "Impact of Prenatal Cocaine Exposure on the Developing Nervous System." In *Handbook of Developmental Cognitive Neuroscience,* 2nd ed., edited by C. A. Nelson and M. Luciana. Cambridge, Mass.: MIT Press.

Liu, D., J. Diorio, B. Tannenbaum, C. Caldji, D. Francis, A. Freedman, S. Sharma, D. Pearson, P. M. Plotsky, and M. J. Meaney. 1997. "Maternal Care, Hippocampal Glucocorticoid Receptors, and Hypothalamic-Pituitary-Adrenal Responses to Stress." *Science* 277(5332): 1659–62.

Lovaas, O. 1987. "Behavioral Treatment and Normal Educational and Intellectual Functioning in Young Autistic Children." *Journal of Consulting and Clinical Psychology* 55(1): 3–9.

Lupien, S. J., S. King, M. J. Meaney, and B. S. McEwen. 2000. "Child's Stress Hormone Levels Correlate with Mother's Socioeconomic Status and Depressive State." *Biological Psychiatry* 48(10): 976–80.

MacLean, K. 2003. "The Impact of Institutionalization on Child Development. *Development and Psychopathology* 15(4): 853–84.

MacMillan, S., P. R. Szeszko, G. J. Moore, R. Madden, E. Lorch, J. Ivey, S. P. Banerjee, and D. R. Rosenberg. 2003. "Increased Amygdala: Hippocampal Volume Ratios Associated with Severity of Anxiety in Pediatric Major Depression." *Journal of Child and Adolescent Psychopharmacology* 13(1): 65–73.

Makino, S., P. W. Gold, and J. Schulkin. 1994. "Corticosterone Effects on Corticotropin-Releasing Hormone mRNA in the Central Nucleus of the Amygdala and the Parvocellular Region of the Paraventricular Nucleus of the Hypothalamus." *Brain Research* 640(1–2): 105–12.

Marmot, M., G. D. Smith, S. A. Stansfeld, C. Patel, F. North, J. Head, I. White, E. Brunner, and A. Feeney. 1991. "Health Inequalities Among British Civil Servants: The Whitehall II Study." *Lancet* 337(8754): 1387–93.

Mattson, S. N., S. L. Fryer, C. I. McGee, and E. P. Riley. 2008. "Fetal Alcohol Syndrome." In *Handbook of Developmental Cognitive Neuroscience,* 2nd ed., edited by C. A. Nelson and M. Luciana. Cambridge, Mass.: MIT Press.

McEwen, B. S., and A. E. Mirsky. 2002. "How Socioeconomic Status May 'Get Under the Skin' and Affect the Heart." *European Heart Journal* 23(22): 1727–28.

McGinnis, J. M., and W. H. Foege. 1993. "Actual Causes of Death in the United States." *Journal of the American Medical Association.* 270(18): 2207–12.

Melchior, M., T. E. Moffitt, B. J. Milne, R. Poulton, and A. Caspi. 2007. "Why Do Children from Socio-economically Disadvantaged Families Suffer from Poor Health When They Reach Adulthood?: A Life-Course Study." *American Journal of Epidemiology* 166(8): 966–74.

Miller, G., and E. Chen. 2007. "Unfavorable Socioeconomic Conditions in Early Life Presage Expression of Proinflammatory Phenotype in Adolescence." *Psychosomatic Medicine* 69(5): 402–9.

Mitra, R., A. Vyas, G. Chatterjee, and S. Chattarji. 2005. "Chronic-Stress Induced Modulation of Different States of Anxiety-like Behavior in Female Rats." *Neuroscience Letters* 383(3): 278–83.

Monk, C. S., C. Grillon, J. M. Bass, E. B. McClure, E. E. Nelson, E. Zarahn, D. S. Charney, M. Ernst, and D. S. Pine. 2003. "A Neuroimaging Method for the Study of Threats in Adolescents." *Developmental Psychobiology* 43(4): 359–66.

Muennig, P., L. Schweinhart, J. Montie, and M. Neidell. 2009. "Effects of a Prekindergarten Educational Intervention on Adult Health: 37-Year Follow-up Results of a Randomized Controlled Trial." *American Journal of Public Health* 99(8): 1431–37.

Nelson, C. A., K. Bos, M. R. Gunnar, and E. Sonuga-Barke. In press. "The Neurobiological Toll of Early Human Deprivation." In *Children Without Permanent Parental Care: Research, Practice, and Policy,* edited by R. B. McCall, M. H. van IJzendoorn, F. Juffer, C. J. Groark, and V. K. Groza. Hoboken, N.J.: Wiley-Blackwell. Monographs of the Society for Research in Child Development.

Nelson, C. A., E. A. Furtado, N. A. Fox, and C. H. Zeanah. 2009. "The Deprived Human Brain." *American Scientist* 97(3): 222–29.

Nelson, C. A., and S. Jeste. 2008. "Neurobiological Perspectives on Developmental Psychopathology." In *Textbook on Child and Adolescent Psychiatry,* 5th ed., edited by M. Rutter, P. Bishop, D. Pine, S. Scott, J. Stevenson, E. Taylor, and A. E. Thapar. London: Blackwell.

Nelson, C. A., C. H. Zeanah, N. A. Fox, P. J. Marshall, A. T. Smyke, and D. Guthrie. 2007. "Cognitive Recovery in Socially Deprived Young Children: The Bucharest Early Intervention Project." *Science* 318(5858): 1937–40.

Noble, K. G., M. F. Norman, and M. J. Farah. 2005. "Neurocognitive Correlates of Socioeconomic Status in Kindergarten Children." *Developmental Science* 8(1): 74–87.

Nyden, A., K. J. Myren, and C. Gillberg. 2008. "Long-Term Psychosocial and Health Economy Consequences of ADHD, Autism, and Reading-Writing Disorder: A Prospective Service Evaluation Project." *Journal of Attention Disorders* 12(2): 141–48.

Otaiba, S. A., C. S. Puranik, R. A. Ziolkowski, and T. M. Montgomery. 2009. "Effectiveness of Early Phonological Awareness Interventions for Students with Speech or Language Impairments." *Journal of Special Education* 43(2): 107–28.

Otero, G. A. 1997. "Poverty, Cultural Disadvantage and Brain Development: A Study Of Pre-School Children in Mexico." *Electroencephalography and Clinical Neurophysiology* 102(6): 512–16.

Parsons, T. J., C. Power, S. Logan, and C. D. Summerbell. 1999. "Childhood Predictors of Adult Obesity: A Systematic Review." *International Journal of Obesity and Related Metabolic Disorders* 23(8): 1–107.

Patrick, M. E., C. Blair, and J. L. Maggs. 2008. "Executive Function, Approach Sensitivity, and Emotional Decision Making as Influences on Risk Behaviors in Young Adults." *Journal of Clinical and Experimental Neuropsychology* 30(4): 449–62.

Poulton, R., and A. Caspi. 2005. "Commentary: How Does Socioeconomic Disadvantage During Childhood Damage Health in Adulthood? Testing Psychosocial Pathways." *International Journal of Epidemiology* 34(2): 344–45.

Poulton, R., A. Caspi, B. J. Milne, W. M. Thomson, A. Taylor, M. R. Sears, and T. E. Moffitt. 2002. "Association Between Children's Experience of Socioeconomic Disadvantage and Adult Health: A Life-Course Study." *Lancet* 360(9364): 1640–45.

Richmond, J., and C. A. Nelson. 2009. "Relational Memory During Infancy: Evidence from Eye Tracking." *Developmental Science* 12(4): 549–56.

Roozendaal, B., B. S. McEwen, and S. Chattarji. 2009. "Stress, Memory, and the Amygdala." *Nature Reviews Neuroscience* 10(6): 423–33.

Rubia, K., A. B. Smith, J. Woolley, C. Nosarti, I. Heyman, E. Taylor, and M. Brammer. 2006. "Progressive Increase of Frontostriatal Brain Activation from Childhood to Adulthood During Event-Related Tasks of Cognitive Control." *Human Brain Mapping* 27(12): 973–93.

Rutter, M., T. G. O'Connor, and the English and Romanian Adoptees (ERA) Study Team. 2004. "Are There Biological Programming Effects for Psychological Development?: Findings from a Study of Romanian Adoptees." *Developmental Psychology* 40(1): 81–94.

Sabatini, M. J., P. Ebert, D. A. Lewis, P. Levitt, J. L. Cameron, and K. Mirnics. 2007. "Amygdala Gene Expression Correlates of Social Behavior in Monkeys Experiencing Maternal Separation." *Journal of Neuroscience* 27(12): 3295–304.

Sánchez, M. M., C. O. Ladd, P. M. Plotsky 2001. "Early Adverse Experience as a Developmental Risk Factor for Later Psychopathology: Evidence for Rodent and Primate Models." *Development and Psychopathology* 13(3): 419–49.

Scherf, K. S., J. A. Sweeny, and B. Luna. 2006. "Brain Basis of Developmental Change in Visuospatial Working Memory." *Journal of Cognitive Neuroscience* 18(7): 1045–58.

Seckl, J. R., and M. J. Meaney. 2004. "Glucocorticoid Programming." *Annals of the New York Academy of Sciences* 1032: 63–84.

Sheline, Y. I., M. H. Gado, and H. C. Kraemer. 2003. "Untreated Depression and Hippocampal Volume Loss." *American Journal of Psychiatry* 160(8): 1516–18.

Smith, M. E. 2005. "Bilateral Hippocampal Volume Reduction in Adults with Post-Traumatic Stress Disorder: A Meta-Analysis of Structural MRI Studies." *Hippocampus* 15(6): 798–807.

Smyke, A. T., S. Koga, D. E. Johnson, N. Fox, P. Marshall, C. A. Nelson, C. H. Zeanah, and the BEIP Core Group. 2007. "The Caregiving Context in Institution-Reared and Family-Reared Infants and Toddlers in Romania." *Journal of Child Psychology and Psychiatry* 48(2): 210–18.

Stevens, C., B. Lauinger, and H. Neville. 2009. "Differences in the Neural Mechanisms of Selective Attention in Children from Different Socioeconomic Backgrounds: An Event-Related Brain Potential Study." *Developmental Science* 12(4): 634–46.

Stipek, D. J., and R. H. Ryan. 1997. "Economically Disadvantaged Preschoolers: Ready to Learn but Further to Go." *Developmental Psychology* 33(4): 711–23.

Sweitzer, M. M., P. A. Allen, and K. P. Kaut. 2008. "Relation of Individual Differences in Impulsivity to Nonclinical Emotional Decision Making." *Journal of the International Neuropsychological Society* 14(5): 878–82.

Tarullo, A. R., J. Bruce, and M. R. Gunnar. 2007. "False Belief and Emotion Understanding in Post-Institutionalized Children." *Social Development* 16(1): 57–78.

Thomas, K. M., W. C. Drevets, R. E. Dahl, N. D. Ryan, B. Birmaher, C. H. Eccard, D. Axelson, P. J. Whalen, and B. J. Casey. 2001. "Amygdala Response to Fearful Faces in Anxious and Depressed Children." *Archives of General Psychiatry* 58(11):1057–63.

Torgesen, J., R. Wagner, C. Rashotte, J. Herron, and P. Lindamood. 2010. "Computer-Assisted Instruction to Prevent Early Reading Difficulties in Students at Risk for Dyslexia: Outcomes from Two Instructional Approaches." *Annals of Dyslexia* 60(1): 40–56.

Vadasy, P. F., J. Jenkins, and K. Pool. 2000. "Effects of Tutoring in Phonological and Early Reading Skills on Students at Risk for Reading Disabilities." *Journal of Learning Disabilities* 33(6): 579–90.

Vyas, A., S. Bernal, and S. Chattarji. 2003. "Effects of Chronic Stress on Dendritic Arborization in the Central and Extended Amygdala. *Brain Research* 965(1–2): 290–94.

Vyas, A., A. G. Pillai, and S. Chattarji. 2004. "Recovery After Chronic Stress Fails to Reverse Amygdaloid Neuronal Hypertrophy and Enhanced Anxiety-like Behavior." *Neuroscience* 128(4): 667–73.

Weikart, D. P. 1998. "Changing Early Childhood Development Through Educational Intervention." *Preventive Medicine* 27(2): 233–37.

Woon, F. L., and D. W. Hedges. 2008. "Hippocampal and Amygdala Volumes in Children and Adults with Childhood Maltreatment-Related Post-Traumatic Stress Disorder: A Meta-Analysis." *Hippocampus* 18(8): 729–36.

Zeanah, C. H., H. Egger, A. T. Smyke, C. A. Nelson, N. Fox, P. Marshall, and D. Guthrie. 2009. "Institutional Rearing and Psychiatric Disorders in Romanian Preschool Children." *American Journal of Psychiatry* 166(7): 777–85.

Zeanah, C. H., C. A. Nelson, N. A. Fox, A. T. Smyke, P. Marshall, S. W. Parker, and S. Koga. 2003. "Designing Research to Study the Effects of Institutionalization on Brain and Behavioral Development: The Bucharest Early Intervention Project." *Development and Psychopathology* 15(4): 885–907.

Chapter 3

The Nature and Impact of Early Achievement Skills, Attention Skills, and Behavior Problems

Greg J. Duncan and Katherine Magnuson

Our chapter investigates links between young children's skills and behaviors and their later attainments. We begin with a conceptual framework for understanding early skills. We argue that the skill categories "cognitive" and "noncognitive" used by many economists are too simplistic and are also inaccurate. "Cognitive" skills mix mental acuity (IQ) with concrete achievements, such as knowing letters, beginning word sounds, and numbers. "Noncognitive" skills encompass diverse capacities such as paying attention (an inherently cognitive task), getting along with classmates and teachers, and maintaining good mental health. We propose and defend the early-skill classification of achievement, attention, behavior problems, and mental health while at the same time acknowledging that these broad categories are related and can be broken down further into more narrowly defined component parts.

Children from different social groups enter school with very different skills and behaviors. Comparing children in the bottom and top quintiles of socioeconomic status (SES), we show that low-SES children are 1.3 standard deviations lower than high-SES children in their kindergarten-entry math skills, nearly two-thirds of a standard deviation below in teacher ratings of attention skills, and one-fourth of a standard deviation worse in terms of teacher-reported antisocial behavior. None of these gaps shrinks over the course of elementary school, and in the case of antisocial behavior, the SES-based gap nearly doubles. More than half of the SES gaps occurred within schools, which suggests that the very different kinds of schools attended by poor and affluent children do not begin to account for all of the gaps.

Next, we summarize what is known about the developmental course of these capacities. Cross-time achievement correlations tend to be higher than correlations for either attention or behavior, but this may be due in part to the fact that achievement is measured more reliably than attention or behavior. Interesting work on behavior problems identified upon school entry shows that they persist for a small but significant number of children. Behavior problems that arise in adolescence also generally fail to persist much beyond the adolescent period.

The heart of our chapter is a review of associations between early achievement, attention, and behavior and later school achievement and such late-adolescent schooling outcomes as dropping out and college attendance. We also consider early-adult criminal behavior as measured by the likelihood of having been arrested.

We find that although school-entry achievement skills prove quite predictive of later school achievement, the *persistence* dimension of early skills and behavior problems matters most for later attainment and crime. Point-in-time assessments of primary school children are, at best, weakly predictive of where children will end up in late adolescence or early adulthood. Associations between skills and outcomes were generally stronger after age ten than before. Using measures based on persistent problems across elementary school boosts the explanatory power of early measures considerably. Children with either persistent math problems or behavior problems were much less likely to graduate from high school or attend college. In the case of early-adult crime, early antisocial behaviors were most predictive. But even when we judged persistent early skill and behavior problems to have strong effects on our outcomes, there were still many exceptions to the rule.

During the 1960s, the HighScope Perry preschool intervention program provided one or two years of high-quality, part-day educational services and home visits to three- and four-year-old low-income, low-IQ African American children in Ypsilanti, Michigan. At program entry, the Perry children averaged 80 on an IQ test normed to a population mean of 100.[1] Shortly after these children completed the program, and around the time they entered kindergarten, their scores had jumped to 95. For the children randomly assigned to a control group, scores increased very little, from 79 to 84. The differential Perry advantage amounted to nearly one standard deviation—a huge advantage. Perry children went on to get better grades, complete more schooling, commit fewer crimes, and, through middle age, enjoy higher earnings and rely less on social services than children in the control group.[2]

It is tempting to draw two conclusions from the Perry evidence. The first is that the skills children develop prior to school entry can have important impacts on lifelong success. Abundant theory and evidence from neuroscience and developmental psychology, as well as evaluations of a number of intensive early-childhood interventions, support the contention that early skills and behavior can indeed matter a great deal for later academic achievement and attainment.

A second possible conclusion is that boosting childhood IQ was the key reason for the Perry program's long-run successes. This is likely false: by third grade, the average IQs of Perry children had fallen to 88—a statistically insignificant single IQ point higher than the third-grade IQs of control-group children. If not IQ, then what other skill or behavior, consequential alone or in combination with early cognitive skills, conveyed the benefits from the Perry "treatment"?

One possibility is that the Perry program improved key literacy and numeracy skills that, independent of pure cognitive ability, can lay the foundation for future success in school and beyond. In fact, measures of school achievement continued to show significant advantages for the Perry children well beyond third grade, although later achievement impacts were certainly smaller than early impacts. Early cognitive and achievement gains might have helped children to avoid early school failure; indeed, children who attended the Perry program were also less likely to receive special education services or to have been held back. Progressing through the early school years without being held back or placed in special education increased the likelihood that they would later go on to complete high school (Deming 2009).

Perhaps it was something about the Perry children's ability to pay attention and become more engaged with their school tasks. A few years after the Perry study ran its preschools, Walter Mischel, Yuichi Shoda, and Monica Rodriguez (1989) measured impulse control by observing whether four-year-olds from affluent California families, when left alone with a marshmallow,

FIGURE 3.1   *Skills, Behaviors, and Attainment Across Childhood*

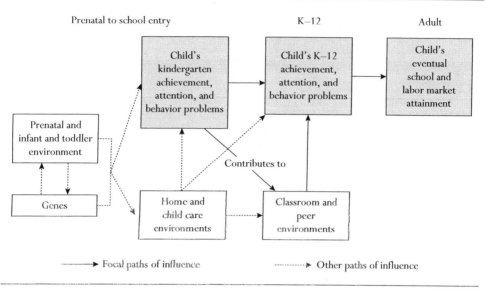

Source: Authors' figure.

could wait long enough before eating it to earn a second marshmallow. He found that children who were better able to control their impulses went on to get higher SAT scores, graduate from better colleges, and have better adult outcomes. Regrettably, the Perry evaluation did not measure children's self-regulation skills, so it cannot answer this question.

Or perhaps Perry taught children inclined toward aggressive behavior how to get along better with their peers and teachers. A number of longitudinal studies have found that adults who commit crimes repeatedly were much more likely to have been aggressive as young children than adults with no criminal records (Leschied et al. 2008). Analyses of the Perry evaluation by Flavio Cunha and James J. Heckman (2009) consider whether children's misbehavior during elementary school as measured in the Perry evaluation accounted for reductions in later crime and achievement. They find that improvement in participants' behavior does explain some of the program's effects on crime and income. However, most of the effects remain unexplained.

This chapter sheds light on the Perry effect and other school-entry puzzles by drawing on theory as well as other empirical studies investigating links between young children's skills and behaviors and their later attainments.

THE NATURE OF EARLY ACHIEVEMENT, ATTENTION, AND BEHAVIOR

We focus on three skill domains: achievement, attention, and behavior. Figure 3.1 presents our theoretical model of how biology and environments interact to produce later school outcomes. It draws on a Bronfenbrennerian perspective which sees children as embedded in multiple contexts and their development as shaped by their interactions within and across these contexts (Bronfenbrenner and Morris 1998). As depicted in the figure, children enter school with a set of skills determined by interactions between their own endowments (genetic and otherwise) and the quality of their early experiences, including interactions in home and child-care settings. How school-entry skills develop is a vital question that has been studied extensively (Shonkoff and Phillips 2000), and is not the focus of our chapter.

Children's skills at school entry facilitate the acquisition of more sophisticated skills later. But they also shape children's environments, particularly interactions with teachers and classmates, school experiences such as placement into ability groups, and interactions with family members. These environments can in turn affect children's learning and skill development throughout the school years.

For example, strong letter identification skills at school entry may enhance a child's ability to map letters onto corresponding sounds, and thus provide a strong foundation for developing reading skills. The presence of highly skilled children clustered in the same classroom may also enable a teacher to target and pace instruction to meet the needs of more children with advanced skills. This instruction may lead the child to enjoy reading and to read more during free-play time in the classroom and with family members. This in turn further builds a child's vocabulary, thus improving language and reading learning. Thus, by influencing both the child and his or her social environment, early academic skills can be linked to subsequent academic achievement because they provide the foundation for positive classroom adaptation (Cunha et al. 2005; Entwisle, Alexander, and Olson 2007).

Negative feedback loops are also possible. A student's early difficulties paying attention or getting along with teachers and classmates can lead to fewer learning-related interactions with teachers and social ostracism by classmates. Classroom disruptions can also interfere with classmates' opportunity to learn. In later grades, antisocial behaviors may lead to suspensions or expulsions, with obvious detrimental consequences for student achievement. Such transactional and recursive models of development are a staple of developmental theory (Sameroff and Fiese 2000).

A broader conception of the classroom environment box in figure 3.1 would include the institutional practices of schools—specifically the ways in which children are sorted across schools and also "tracked" within schools. For example, placement into more or less academically challenging curricular tracks has been linked to students' later outcomes. (The sorting of students within schools is more central to later schooling experiences, and is discussed in chapter 4 of this volume.)

Achievement, Attention, and Behavior Problems and Mental Health

We find "achievement," "attention," and "behavior problems and mental health" to be a productive way of categorizing the general domains of children's school-related functioning (table 3.1), instead of "cognitive" and "noncognitive." By achievement we mean concrete academic skills. Attention refers to the ability to control impulses and focus on tasks. Behavior problems and mental health consists of two important dimensions—the ability to get along with others and sound mental health.

Notably absent from this schema are students' own aspirations, goals, and attitudes, an appropriate omission in light of our focus on younger children. Self-constructs, goals, and aspirations develop during the early school years, and as they become more differentiated and complex, they also become more closely associated with children's behavior and performance (Davis-Kean et al. 2008). For this reason, a discussion of these constructs appears in chapter 4 in this volume.

Achievement Skills

Achievement in the preschool and middle-childhood years refers mainly to a set of reading- and math-related skills. For preschoolers, reading-related skills encompass identification of upper- and lowercase letters as well as decoding skills such as beginning to associate sounds with letters

TABLE 3.1   *Taxonomy of Skill and Behavior Domains*

	Achievement	Attention	Behavior Problems	Mental Health
Description	Concrete academic skills	Ability to control impulses and focus on tasks	Ability to get along with others	Sound mental health
Example test areas or question wording	Knowing letters and numbers; beginning word sounds, word problems	Can't sit still; can't concentrate; score from a computer test of impulse control	Cheats or tells lies, bullies, is disobedient at school	Is sad, depressed, moody
Commonly used index names	IRT (in ECLS-K) or PIAT (in NLSY) composite reading and math scores	"Approaches to learning" index (in ECLS-K) and attention problems (NLSY)	Externalizing behavior problems (in ECLS-K and NLSY)	Internalizing behavior problems (in ECLS-K and NLSY)

Source: Authors' table.

at the beginnings and ends of words. Most early reading problems reflect poor decoding skills and low levels of phonological and phonemic awareness, such as a poor ability to break down words into component sounds. As children progress through childhood, reading skills include recognizing words by sight, understanding words in context, and making literal inferences from passages. By the end of elementary school, students are developing reading comprehension and evaluation skills, which include identifying the main points in a passage as well as understanding an author's intentions and evaluating the adequacy and logical consistency of supporting evidence. Writing skills, specifically a child's ability to express ideas in written form, develop in concert with reading skills.

Rudimentary math skills can be detected in children as young as six months (Posner and Rothbart 2007). Concrete math skills begin with the ability to recognize numbers and shapes and to compare relative sizes. Counting and sequencing skills are followed by the ability to perform addition and subtraction tasks, as well as multiplication and division tasks. Understanding numerical properties such as proportions, fractions, integers, and decimals also develops, as do measurement skills and an understanding of geometry.

These pre-academic and academic skills develop as a result of learning opportunities embedded in everyday activities and specific instruction, which is especially important for code-related reading skills and computational mathematical skills. Achievement trajectories are steepest in the early years of school, as children rapidly learn many new skills and improve existing ones. Although learning continues into later school years, the rate of gaining new skills declines over time as more focus is placed on elaborating and improving existing skills.

More general cognitive skills also play a role in skill development. For example, oral language skills facilitate the acquisition of reading skills such as identifying letter sounds, and they are increasingly important as children make the transition from "learning to read" to "reading to learn." Likewise, a strong foundation of basic number concepts such as one, two, and three dimensions becomes increasingly important as children advance from basic computational tasks to more complex mathematical problems that require flexible problem-solving techniques (Baroody 2003; Hiebert and Wearne 1996).

Although many prior studies have focused on IQ as an important determinant of scholastic skills, we do not discuss IQ per se for several reasons. Many IQ measures include items that are related to the acquisition of basic early reading and math skills and thus overlap with our "achievement" domain. Measures of IQ free of such "content" reflect the speed of cognitive processing, or the ability to recognize patterns. But these types of assessments are rarely included in large studies, and although they may be influenced by instruction, most intervention programs target achievement and behavior rather than IQ.

Attention Skills and Cognitive Self-Regulation

Self-regulation has been defined as the "processes by which the human psyche exercises control over its functions, states, and inner processes" (Baumeister and Vohs 2004, 1). It involves the ability to evaluate the steps and actions required to meet a desired goal and to control behavior deliberately in order to reach that goal. Current theory and research on young children's self-regulation subdivides the construct in a variety of ways, but almost all works in this area separate cognitive (cool) and emotional components (hot) (Eisenberg, Sadovsky, and Spinrad 2005; Raver 2004; Raver et al. 2005). We, too, distinguish between hot and cold self-regulation, placing cognitive self-regulation into our "attention" category and emotional self-regulation into our "behavior problems and mental health" category.

Cognitive self-regulation is a broad construct including such overlapping subcomponents as executive function, planning, sustaining attention, task persistence, and inhibition of impulsive responses. We classify this collection of skills as "attention" but emphasize their diverse nature. Research has shown that attention and impulsivity can be detected as early as age two and a half but continue to develop until reaching relative stability between ages six and eight (Posner and Rothbart 2000). It is widely accepted that some dimensions of executive functioning undergo rapid development during adolescence.

Cognitive self-control can be measured by both direct assessments of particular components and more general descriptions of children's behaviors (especially in structured classroom contexts).[3] Parent and teacher reports of children's cognitive self-regulation assess the behavioral consequences of children's self-regulatory skills, for example, the extent to which children are able to sit still, concentrate on tasks, persist at a task despite minor setbacks or frustrations, listen and follow directions, and work independently or, conversely, are easily distracted, overactive, or forgetful.

Attention skills and cognitive self-regulation are thought to be consequential to children's learning because they increase the time children are engaged and participating in academic endeavors and increase children's ability to solve problems. Studies have consistently found positive associations between measures of children's ability to control and sustain attention with academic gains in the preschool and early elementary school years (Raver et al. 2005; McClelland, Morrison, and Holmes 2000; Yen, Konold, and McDermott 2004; Brock et al. 2009).

Behavior Problems and Mental Health

Perhaps because these are easily identified by the frequently used Child Behavior Checklist (Achenbach 1991, 1992), developmentalists often distinguish between two broad dimensions of behavior problems, externalizing and internalizing. Externalizing behavior refers to a cluster of related behaviors including antisocial behavior, conduct disorders, and more general aggression. Attention problems are also included in most externalizing behavior scales, although we suggest that they should be separated from other forms of behavior problems. Internalizing behavior refers to a similarly broad set of constructs including anxiety and depression as well as somatic complaints and withdrawn behavior. In terms of understanding how behavior shapes children's schooling, greater attention has been devoted to externalizing behavior than to internalizing behavior, likely because of its obvious disruptive consequences in the classroom.

Although both children's behavior problems and their mental health are predicted by their capacity to regulate emotions, these constructs are not the same. Emotional regulation refers to the ability to "modulate the experience and expression of positive and negative emotions" (Bridges, Denham, and Ganiban 2004, 340). It includes the ability to control anger, sadness, joy, and other emotional reactions, which predict behavior such as aggression and internalizing problems (for example, social withdrawal, anxiety) (Eisenberg, Sadovsky, and Spinrad 2005).[4] Poor emotional regulation is not the only reason for poor mental health or behavior problems. Indeed, children differ in the strength of their emotional reactivity to experiences, including the underlying physiological reactions. Children also differ along dimensions of emotional positivity and negativity (Posner and Rothbart 2007). Furthermore, a large body of evidence points to the importance of deviant social information processing, including hostile attribution and other cognitive biases, as an important contributory factor to antisocial behavior (Crozier et al. 2008).

Young children's externalizing behavior problems are assessed by asking parents and teachers how often a child argues, fights, or throws tantrums; gets angry; acts impulsively; and disturbs ongoing activities. Aggression refers to behaviors such as bragging, teasing, fighting, and attacking and is closely related to antisocial behavior, which means behavior that harms another person, whether by imposing physical or mental harm or by creating property loss. Antisocial behaviors also encompass nonaggressive but harmful behaviors such as lying and cheating. In this chapter we focus on antisocial behavior as a particularly important dimension of externalizing behavior.

Externalizing behavior is quite common in young children. Reports of aggression and other forms of externalizing behavior typically peak in the preschool and early school years, as children use aggression as a way to assert control over their environment to compensate for their own nascent but inadequate communication skills. As children's abilities to communicate, self-regulate, and solve problems effectively increase, their aggressive and antisocial behavior typically decreases. However, research suggests that for a small proportion of children, hostile, aggressive, and antisocial behavior remains high throughout childhood and adolescence (Campbell, Shaw, and Gilliom 2000; Moffitt 1993). Boys are more likely to display these "life-course-persistent" patterns of behavior than girls.

Depressive behavior is measured by questions as to how frequently children appear to be in a sad or irritable mood and whether they demonstrate low self-esteem or low energy. Anxiety refers to a set of factors including children's fears related to separation from caregivers, obsessive-compulsive behavior, and social reticence. Socially withdrawn behavior refers specifically to a child's social anxiety and avoidance of social interactions.

Internalizing behavior problems increase over the course of childhood. Research suggests that anxiety may be relatively constant over time, although it takes different forms at different ages. Depressive behaviors, however, increase over time, and do so more for girls than boys (Bongers et al. 2003).

Children's behavior problems are expected to affect both individual learning and classroom dynamics. Externalizing behaviors lead to child-teacher conflict and social exclusion (Newcomb, Bukowski, and Pattee 1993; Parker and Asher 1987), and these stressors may reduce children's participation in collaborative learning activities and adversely affect their achievement (Ladd, Birch, and Buhs 1999; Pianta and Stuhlman 2004). Depressive symptoms and anxiety may also reduce children's engagement in classroom group learning activities (Fantuzzo et al. 2003; Fantuzzo et al.

forthcoming), but evidence of the negative effect of behavior problems on achievement is mixed: correlational evidence points to a detrimental effect, but more controlled models yield no or much smaller associations. One possible explanation for this difference is that teachers do not expect young children to manage their emotional responses well and thus use instructional approaches that minimize children's need to manage their responses independently (Brock et al. 2009).

SKILLS AND BEHAVIORS AT SCHOOL ENTRY AND BEYOND

The Early Childhood Longitudinal Study, Kindergarten Class of 1998–99 (ECLS-K) is a good choice for illustrating basic empirical properties of achievement, attention, and behavioral measures owing to its large and representative national sample of kindergartners, its longitudinal nature, and the quality of its measures. As detailed in the online appendix, the ECLS-K's school-entry reading measures assess skills such as identifying upper- and lowercase letters by name, associating letters with sounds at the beginnings and ends of words, and recognizing common words by sight. Its math measures reflect the ability to identify one- and two-digit numerals, recognize geometric shapes, count up to ten objects, and recognize the next number in a sequence.

Attention and behavior problem measures are based on teacher reports. The attention and cognitive self-regulation scale in the ECLS-K is called "approaches to learning" and includes items that assess the child's attentiveness, task persistence, eagerness to learn, learning independence, flexibility, and organization. The externalizing behavior problem index rates the frequency with which a child argues, fights, gets angry, acts impulsively, and disturbs ongoing activities, and the internalizing behavior problem index covers anxiety, loneliness, low self-esteem, and sadness.

Kindergarten and Cross-Time Correlations

Kindergarten correlations among the ECLS-K measures are shown in table 3.A1 in the online appendix (available at: http://www.russellsage.org/duncan_murnane_online_appendix.pdf). Reading and math achievement have the highest correlation, 0.69. Both reading and math scores correlate substantially with attention; the correlation between achievement and behavior problems is much lower. Attention is moderately correlated with both achievement and behavior problems—all four correlations are in or near the 0.3 to 0.5 range.

By fifth grade, virtually all the correlations have grown, some substantially (see table 3.A1 in online appendix). Most notably, correlations between the two achievement and the two behavior measures are all above 0.2 in absolute value. Although part of the increased correlations may come from better measurement, the early school years may be a time in which children become somewhat more differentiated into groups with higher achievement and good behavior versus lower achievement and poor behavior.

Skill and Behavior Stability Across Primary School

Although stability is the norm, some children do demonstrate both transitory fluctuations and fundamental shifts in their achievement trajectories (Kowaleski-Jones and Duncan 1999; Pungello et al. 1996). A look at the temporal persistence of the ECLS-K's five achievement, attention, and behavior measures shows a clear ranking of these correlations, with both time-dependent math and reading test score correlations always above 0.6, externalizing behavior problem and attention correlations falling to about 0.50 by first grade but then falling only modestly after that, and internalizing behavior problem correlations dropping the most (tables 3.A2, 3.A3, and 3.A4 in

FIGURE 3.2   *Math Gaps in Kindergarten and Fifth Grade*

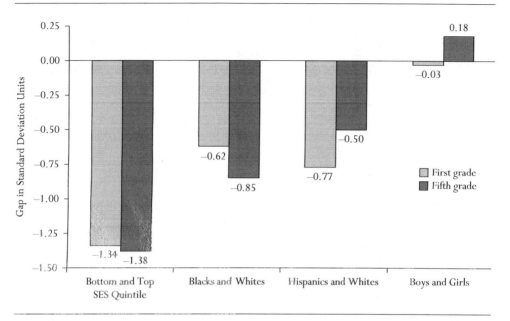

Source: Authors' calculations based on Early Childhood Longitudinal Study, Kindergarten Cohort (National Center for Education Statistics n.d.).

online appendix). The pattern in the attention and behavior problem measures may reflect, in part, the lower reliability of the internalizing behavior problem index ($\alpha = 0.80$ in kindergarten) compared with externalizing behavior problems ($\alpha = 0.90$) and attention ($\alpha = 0.89$ for the ECLS-K's "approaches to learning" scale).

Skill and Behavior Differences Across Groups

Figures 3.2, 3.3, and 3.4, which are based on the detailed data provided in tables 3.A5 and 3.A6 (online appendix), plot differences in math scores, attention, and externalizing behavior problems across socioeconomic, racial and ethnic, and gender groups in both kindergarten and fifth grade.[5] These figures show simple differences across groups; tables 3.A5 and 3.A6 also show counterpart differences within a classroom (that is, adjusting for classroom fixed effects), which account for the way students are clustered within schools and classrooms and, in the case of the attention and behavior measures, in the way individual teachers respond to the scales.

Overall, SES differences in skills and behaviors are larger than racial and ethnic differences. In the case of math achievement, income gaps far exceed racial-ethnic and gender gaps. Students in the bottom SES quintile (with average family income of about $15,500) on average, scored well over one standard deviation below children in the top SES quintile (average family income of $100,000). This result mirrors those found in chapter 5 of this volume (by Sean F. Reardon), which also uses data from the ECLS-K. As shown in table 3.A5 in the online appendix, SES gaps are roughly half as large for children in the same schools as for children overall, suggesting that SES-based family selection into schools accounts for some but by no means all of the achievement gaps.

FIGURE 3.3   *Attention and Engagement Gaps in Kindergarten and Fifth Grade*

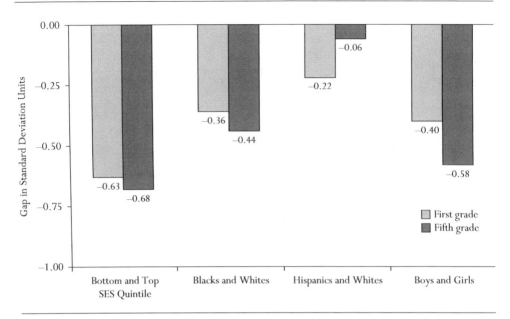

Source: Authors' calculations based on Early Childhood Longitudinal Study, Kindergarten Cohort (National Center for Education Statistics n.d.).

FIGURE 3.4   *Antisocial Behavior Differences in Kindergarten and Fifth Grade*

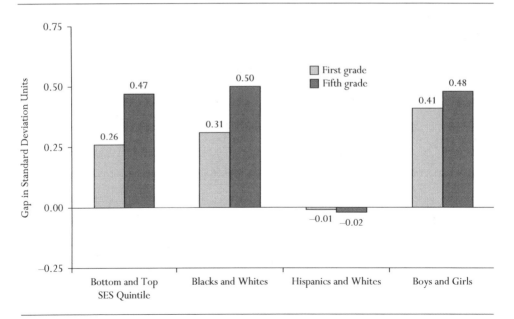

Source: Authors' calculations based on Early Childhood Longitudinal Study, Kindergarten Cohort (National Center for Education Statistics n.d.).

FIGURE 3.5   *Accounting for the Association Between Bottom and Top SES Quintiles in Early-Adult Outcomes*

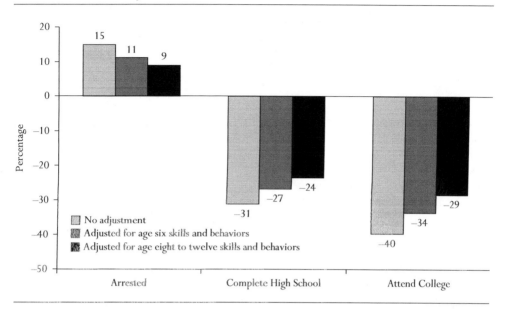

Source: Authors' calculations based on National Longitudinal Survey of Youth, Child and Young Adult (U.S. Bureau of Labor Statistics n.d.).

The picture for attention and behavior problems is relatively favorable for Hispanics; attention gaps between Hispanics and whites virtually disappear by the end of primary school, and behavior problem differences between these two groups are very small through middle childhood. But while achievement gaps do not increase, Hispanic fifth graders still lag far (half a standard deviation) behind their white counterparts.

Most worrisome are the growing skill and behavior gaps between the SES groups and by race. By fifth grade, non-Hispanic black children and children from low-SES families have closed none of their achievement gap with children from white and more advantaged families and have fallen further behind in terms of attention and behavior problems.

SES and Young Adult Outcomes

SES differences in early skills and behavior are worrisome because they may be an important way in which SES is transmitted from parent to child. We turned to data from the children of the National Longitudinal Survey of Youth (details about the data are provided in the online appendix) to examine the mediation role of early skills and behavior. Mother's SES is measured by her highest grade of completed schooling when the child was five or six. Outcomes are measured around age twenty and include the probability of being arrested, completing high school, and attending college.

Bivariate models suggest that children in the bottom SES quintile have arrest rates 15 percentage points higher than children in the top SES quintile, high school completion rates 31 percentage points lower, and college attendance rates 40 percentage points lower (figure 3.5; online appendix table 3.A7). Adding measures of children's achievement and behavior at age six explains about one-fourth of the arrest differences and one-eighth of the two sets of schooling differences.[6] Next we added the children's average level of achievement and behavior at ages eight, ten, and twelve. These more persistent skill and behavior measures accounted for more of the SES differences, but in no case did they account for as much as half of them. This suggests that mechanisms and pathways not involving early skills play an important role in the intergenerational transmission of SES.

School-Level Measures of Skill Distribution

As the description of achievement, attention, and behavior problem gaps suggests, low skill levels are disproportionately concentrated among disadvantaged populations. Given the geographic concentration of disadvantage, low-skilled children are more concentrated in schools that serve disadvantaged children. This imparts a double disadvantage to many low-skilled children—not only do they have low skills but also they encounter classroom environments where concentrations of achievement and behavior problems pose difficult classroom management challenges for teachers.

Using ECLS-K data we examined the possible scope of problem-laden classrooms. We defined math and attention problems as being in the most problematic 25 percent of the national distribution on each of these measures. We tried to do the same for externalizing behavior, but the discrete nature of the measure led us to draw the line at the 18th percentile of its distribution. Taken as a whole, some 5 percent of kindergarteners exhibit problems in all three dimensions (table 3.A8 in the online appendix).

We then characterized schools by the percentage of children qualifying for the federal free school lunch program, the percentage of racial or ethnic minority children, and population density (urban versus suburban). Income-based contrasts are striking, with four times as many triple-problem children in poor (8 percent) as in affluent (2 percent) schools. More generally, the data suggest that schools with higher proportions of low-income or minority children have a greater concentration of children with low math skills and significant behavior and attention problems. Differences between urban and suburban schools are considerably smaller but still apparent. With most peer-effect studies concentrating on the consequences of low- or high-achieving classmates (for example, Betts and Zau 2004; Hanushek et al. 2003; Hoxby and Weingarth 2007), we know relatively little about possible tipping points surrounding the number of multiple-problem classmates it takes for individual problems to become collective problems.

Nor do we know how the concentration of these problems affects the other half of the sorting process, of teachers across schools. Schools serving more affluent children typically have more economic resources and, it would appear from table 3.A8 in the online appendix, more easily managed classrooms. Little wonder they are able to attract and retain more highly qualified teachers than poor schools (Phillips and Chin 2004). Even within a large urban school district, principals of lower-achieving schools assign classroom management skills a much higher priority in looking for new teachers than do principals of higher-achieving schools (Engel 2007).

CONSEQUENCES OF SKILLS AND BEHAVIORS FOR SCHOOL ACHIEVEMENT

We turn now to the "so what?" question for early skills and behaviors: What difference do they really make for later success in school and beyond? Here we review existing evidence linking school-entry skills and behaviors to later school achievement and then generate new evidence on links to early-adult school attainment and crime.

TABLE 3.2   *Effect Sizes of School-Entry Skills and Behaviors on Later Achievement, Meta-Analysis of 236 Coefficients*

	Grades One to Eight	
At School Entry	Math Achievement	Reading Achievement
Reading	0.09*	0.24*
Math	0.41*	0.26*
Attention	0.10*	0.08*
Externalizing behavior (−expected)	0.01 ns	0.01 ns
Internalizing behavior (−expected)	0.01 ns	−0.01 ns

Source: Authors' adaptation of Duncan et al. (2007, table 3).

Note: n = 236 estimated coefficients. Meta-analytic estimates control for time to test, test and teacher outcome, and study fixed effects; coefficients are weighted by inverse of their variances.

*$p < 0.05$; ns $p > 0.05$

School-Entry Skills and Later Achievement

A number of experiments provide encouraging evidence that specially designed intervention programs that target preschool children "at-risk" for school failure produce cognitive and academic achievement gains; long-term reductions in referral for special education services, grade retention, and dropping out; and increases in adult educational attainment (for a review, see Blau and Currie 2006). But most of these programs had a broad curriculum designed to enhance academic and social skills, so it is not possible to disentangle impacts of the self-regulation, behavior, and academic components of the programs.

Another shortcoming of the experimental literature is that interventions that focus more narrowly on just one aspect of skills or behaviors do not consider cross-domain effects. Relatively few studies of behavioral interventions also estimate impacts on later academic outcomes. Joseph Durlak et al.'s (forthcoming) review suggests that at least some of those do find positive impacts on achievement.

Greg Duncan et al. (2007) provide the most comprehensive nonexperimental assessment of the associations between school-entry achievement, attention, and behavior and later school achievement. Using six longitudinal data sets,[7] they regressed reading and mathematics achievement (from tests and, where available, teacher ratings) on kindergarten-entry measures of reading and math achievement, attention, antisocial behavior, and internalizing behavior problems. Importantly, controls for child IQ, behavior, and temperament and parent education and income, all of which were measured prior to kindergarten entry, were included in the regressions. To establish comparability across studies, dependent-variable measures of achievement as well as school-entry skills and behaviors were standardized in all studies using full-sample standard deviations. All post-kindergarten reading and math achievement outcome measures available in the six data sets were treated as dependent variables in separate regressions.

To summarize their results, they conducted a formal meta-analysis of the 236 standardized regression coefficients emerging from the individual study regressions. Average coefficients from the regressions involving math and reading outcomes are presented in table 3.2. A clear conclusion is that only three of the five school-entry skill categories predict subsequent reading and math achievement: reading, math, and attention.[8] Neither behavior problems nor mental health problems were associated with later achievement, holding constant achievement as well as child and family characteristics. Indeed, none had a standardized coefficient that averaged more than 0.01 in absolute value.

Not surprisingly, early reading skills were stronger predictors of later reading achievement than later math achievement. Less expected was that early math skills (adjusting for prior IQ in five of the six studies) were as predictive of later reading achievement as were early reading skills. Children's attention appeared equally important (and several dimensions of socioemotional behaviors appeared uniformly unimportant) for reading and math achievement.[9] These findings did not differ systematically by gender or family SES.

All in all, the Duncan et al. (2007) analysis provides a clear answer to one question involving the relative role of school-entry skills and behavior: early academic skills correlate most strongly for later school achievement, even after adjusting for differences in the fact that early achievers score higher on tests of cognitive ability and come from more advantaged families. A student's school-entry ability to pay attention is modestly predictive of later achievement, and early behavior problems and other dimensions of social skills and mental health problems are not predictive, once the student's initial levels of achievement are taken into account.[10]

Middle-Childhood Skills and High School Completion

It is far from clear whether early academic skills matter as much and early behaviors as little for adolescent and early-adult school attainment as they do for middle-childhood reading and math proficiency. Finishing high school likely requires a combination of achievement, engagement, and perseverance. Antisocial behaviors in primary school may lead to inconsequential trips to the principal's office, whereas such behaviors in middle or high school may lead to suspension, expulsion, or even criminal prosecution. The far-from-perfect temporal correlations in achievement and behaviors shown in online appendix tables 3.A2 to 3.A4 mean that many children perform and behave better and worse over time.

Katherine Magnuson et al. (2009) used the NLSY and Baltimore Beginning School Study (BSS) to study links between middle-childhood skills and behavior problems and high school completion. Here we reproduce and expand upon their NLSY-based results and note that the BSS data produced very similar patterns of effects.

As detailed in the online appendix, the NLSY measures reading and math achievement in its biennial child survey. Attention and self-regulation in the NLSY is drawn from the hyperactivity subscale of the parent-reported Behavior Problems Index (BPI). Antisocial behavior and anxiety scales are drawn from the BPI as well.

Although the NLSY surveys children every other year, it provides concurrent measurements on math, reading, and attention skills as well as internalizing and externalizing behavior problems for school-age children of every age between five and fourteen. To investigate when skills and behaviors begin to predict high school completion, we ran a series of probit regressions that related high school completion to preschool measures of child cognitive skills, temperament, and family background (see the online appendix for a complete list) and middle-childhood skills and behaviors. The first regression measured these skills and behaviors at age five, the second at age six, and so on, up to age fourteen. Regression results are presented in online appendix table 3.A9.

In seeking to understand the role of early skills in determining later outcomes, we adopt a regression method that includes our measures of concurrent skills as well as measures of child and family characteristics from birth through age five. For comparative purposes we also provide bivariate models that provide a sense of the magnitude of associations between each domain and later outcomes. Such simple associations show uniformly significant prediction from all the

FIGURE 3.6   *Effect of an Increase of One Standard Deviation in Composite Achievement at Various Ages on the Probability of High School Graduation, Full Controls*

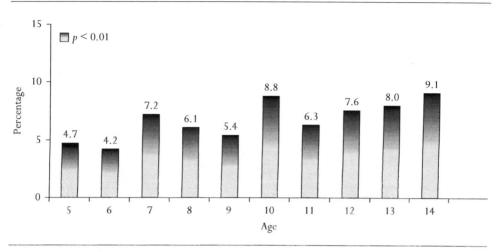

Source: Authors' calculations based on National Longitudinal Survey of Youth, Child and Young Adult (U.S. Bureau of Labor Statistics n.d.).

measures to later educational (and crime) outcomes, albeit larger associations in the later years than in the earlier years (columns 1 and 11 of online appendix tables 3.A9 and 3.A11). This finding is not surprising, and it confirms the common observation that early skill deficits s across range of domains are linked to later outcomes. Such bivariate associations may, however, be simply proxying for other skills or family circumstances that are the true cause of later outcomes. For this reason we focus on results from regression models that hold constant not only other important domains but also family and child characteristics.

In models with a full set of controls, math and reading skills have uniformly positive but often statistically insignificant effects on high school completion, with neither being consistently more predictive than the other (top panel of online appendix table 3.A9). When combined into a single standardized composite, however, achievement effects became uniformly significant (figure 3.6 and bottom panel of online appendix table 3.A9).[11] Standard deviation increases in the achievement composite are generally associated with smaller increases in the probability of high school completion before age ten than after.

For the attention and behavior problem measures, only the measure of antisocial behavior is consistently predictive of high school completion (figure 3.7 and online appendix table 3.A10). Once antisocial behavior is taken into account, attention skills and anxiety and depression do not predict high school completion. As with the achievement composite, behavior problems become more predictive around age ten. Increases of one standard deviation in externalizing behavior problems for ages ten to fourteen are associated with reductions of five to ten percentage points in high school completion rates.

Persistent Problems and High School Completion

Prior research has suggested that a student's trajectory of behavior problems may be more important than the level of behavior problems at any single age in predicting later educational attainment

FIGURE 3.7   *Effect of an Increase of One Standard Deviation in Antisocial Behavior at Various Ages on the Probability of High School Graduation, Full Controls*

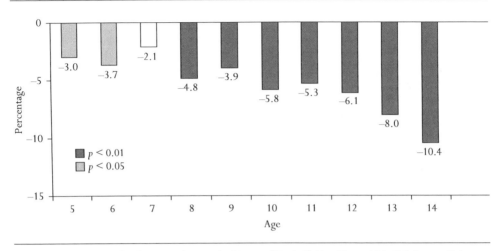

Source: Authors' calculations based on National Longitudinal Survey of Youth, Child and Young Adult (U.S. Bureau of Labor Statistics n.d.).

(Kokko et al. 2006). This might also be true for achievement trajectories. To test whether the persistence of academic, attention, and behavior problems is a stronger predictor of later attainment than early behavior, we categorized children according to their pattern of scores during the early school years (ages six, eight, and ten in the NLSY). In light of prior empirical work, we chose the 75th percentile to demarcate a "high" level of behavior problems and the 25th percentile as the threshold for "low" achievement.

We then sorted children in the NLSY data into three groups—"never," "intermittent," and "persistent"—depending on whether the child fell into the worst quarter of a given measure's distribution on zero, one or two, or all three measurement occasions. Bivariate associations between high school completion and all five of the skill and behavior measures are very strong (first column of online appendix table 3.A10), with the contrasts between the "persistent" and "never" groups associated with drops of 20 to 30 percentage points in high school completion rates. As with the single-year measures, regression adjustments left only the achievement and antisocial behavior problem measures to be predictive of high school completion (table 3.3). Persistent early math achievement and antisocial behavior problems are associated with drops of 13 to 16 percentage points in high school completion rates. Surprisingly, persistent early reading problems are not predictive of high school completion, nor are persistent attention or anxiety problems. Extending the outcomes to college attendance produces similar patterns, with persistent math problems associated with a drop of thirty-four percentage points in the probability of college attendance.

We considered whether the association between both levels and patterns of achievement, attention, and behavior problems differed across several relevant subgroups defined by SES, race, and gender. We found some variation but little systematic differences by SES and race. Associations did, however, differ by gender. In particular, antisocial behavior was more predictive of schooling attainment for boys than for girls.

TABLE 3.3   *Effect of Persistent and Intermittent Problems at Ages Six, Eight, and Ten on the Probabilities of High School Graduation and College Attendance*

Problem Area	Problem Frequency	High School Completion	College Attendance
Reading	Intermittent	−0.08* (0.04)	−0.12* (0.05)
	Persistent	−0.08 (0.07)	−0.09 (0.10)
Math	Intermittent	−0.06† (0.03)	−0.10* (0.05)
	Persistent	−0.13* (0.07)	−0.34** (0.08)
Antisocial behavior	Intermittent	−0.07 (0.04)	−0.05 (0.05)
	Persistent	−0.16* (0.07)	−0.17† (0.10)
Inattention	Intermittent	−0.02 (0.03)	−0.05 (0.05)
	Persistent	0.03 (0.05)	−0.01 (0.09)
Anxiety	Intermittent	−0.02 (0.03)	−0.05 (0.05)
	Persistent	−0.08 (0.07)	−0.11 (0.09)

Source: Authors' calculations based on National Longitudinal Survey of Youth, Child and Young Adult (U.S. Bureau of Labor Statistics n.d.).

Note: A "problem" is defined as being in the worst quartile of distribution at a given age; N = 1,437 for high school completion and N = 1,081 for college attendance.

**$p < 0.01$; *$p < 0.05$; †$p < 0.10$

Crime

Although educational attainment is an important measure of young adults' successful transition into adulthood, it is not the only one. To broaden the scope of our study of adolescent and early-adult outcomes, we repeated the NLSY-based analyses using reports of whether a child had ever been arrested by age twenty. Duncan et al. (2009) show that results from NLSY parallel those for the Beginning School Study sample and its measure of incarceration by age twenty or twenty-one and the Infant Health and Development sample and its measure of arrest by age eighteen.

As with high school completion, we ran a series of probit regressions, all of which related high school completion to preschool measures of child IQ, temperament, and family background as well as middle-childhood skills and behaviors. Regression results are presented in online appendix table 3.A10. Again, results from the bivariate models uniformly indicated that the achievement, attention, and behavior problem domain measures all predicted later arrests. Turning to the fully controlled models, only the antisocial behavior reports were predictive of later crime. Year-by-year patterns are shown in figure 3.8. Coefficient sizes are generally modest (although statistically significant) until age ten, at which point they roughly double. The sample mean is about 22 percent, so a three-percentage-point coefficient amounts to about a 15 percent increase relative to the base rate, and a six-percentage-point coefficient increases the base rate by about 30 percent.

Although the individual-year effects of behavior problems from age five to ten are only modestly predictive of later crime, persistent early antisocial behavior is very predictive. As in the high school completion analysis, we sorted the NLSY data into "never," "intermittent," and "persistent" groups, depending on whether the child fell into the worst quarter of a given measure's distribution on zero, one, or two, or all three measurement occasions (online appendix table 3.A12). Children exhibiting persistent early antisocial behavior had nearly double the chance of being arrested. As shown in online table 3.A12, this effect is somewhat larger for males than for females.[12]

FIGURE 3.8   *Effect of an Increase of One Standard Deviation in Antisocial Behavior at Various Ages on the Probability of Ever Having Been Arrested, Full Controls*

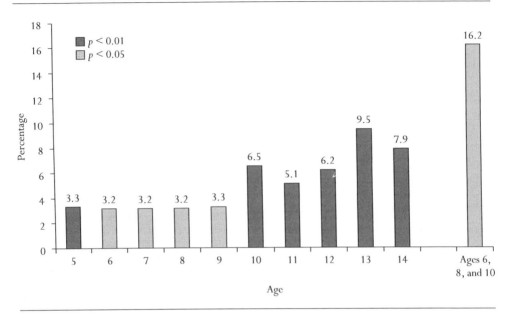

Source: Authors' calculations based on National Longitudinal Survey of Youth, Child and Young Adult (U.S. Bureau of Labor Statistics n.d.).

In sum, most of the action in predicting early adult crime is within the domain of antisocial behavior. Persistent antisocial behavior problems in primary school are quite predictive; persistent achievement, attention, or anxiety problems are not.

SUMMARY

We opened our chapter with a question we called the Perry puzzle: If it was not cognitive skills that kept Perry children on track in school, in good jobs, and out of jail, what other skills or positive behaviors might the Perry preschool intervention have promoted that had these effects? Our bivariate NLSY-based analyses do little to narrow the field of important skills; virtually all of our skill and behavior problem measures have significant correlations with the later outcomes. Holding constant family background and concurrent skills produces a much more selective picture.

In the case of early-adult crime, our guess is that Perry reduced antisocial behavior problems in the intervention group. Our longitudinal analyses consistently point to early antisocial behavior problems, but not early achievement, attention, or internalizing behavior problems, as strong predictors of arrests and incarceration, especially among boys. Children who persistently display such problems between the ages of six and ten had double the chance (roughly 40 percent rather than 20 percent) of ever having been arrested or incarcerated—a result replicated in three data sets in Magnuson et al. (2009). The impressive explanatory power of early antisocial behavior problems for later crime stood in marked contrast to the inability of even persistent early reading, math, attention, or mental health problems to predict later criminal arrest, once such behavior and family background are taken into account.[13]

Speculating about the early-skills antecedents behind Perry's success in promoting school attainment is more tenuous. Here our longitudinal analyses suggest that both early achievement and positive behaviors help children negotiate their way through successful completion of high school and that both may be even more important in distinguishing those who enroll in postsecondary education.

We close with a number of observations. First, although school-entry skills proved quite predictive of later school achievement, the persistence of early achievement and behavior problems was what mattered most for later attainment and crime. Single assessments of primary school children are at best relatively weakly predictive of where children will end up in late adolescence or early adulthood. Repeating these assessments over a number of years boosts the explanatory power of at least some of them considerably.

Second, we were somewhat surprised that early attention did not matter more than it did for long-run outcomes. Much has been written recently about the importance of a child's ability to regulate attention, plan tasks, and engage in the demands of a school curriculum (Baumeister and Vohs 2004). Although our measures of attention leave much to be desired, they appear about as reliably measured as antisocial behaviors, which proved to be predictors of later outcomes. One possibility is that our attainment measures (high school completion and on-time college attendance) focus on the lower end of the attainment distribution and attention skills may be more consequential for persistence and attainment at the higher end. It may also be that attention skills developed by the early grades matter much less than higher-level attention skills that emerge during the transition to adolescence.

Third, we noted, but were unable to test for, how one child's achievement or behavior problems might prove detrimental to his or her classmates. We found that high-poverty classrooms have four times the concentrations of academic, attention, and behavior problems as low-poverty classrooms. Although prior research has produced mixed evidence on spillover effects for low achievers, we know much less about the classroom implications of substantial numbers of children with behavior problems.

Finally, none of the links between middle childhood skills and adult success appeared to be all-determining. Associations between skills and outcomes were generally stronger after age ten than before. And even when we judged persistent early skill problems to have strong effects on our outcomes, there were still many exceptions to the rule.

An optimistic interpretation is that teachers and parents are somehow able to prevent most early skill and behavior problems from translating into long-run attainment problems. Alternatively, perhaps the course of children's development is sufficiently variable, and subjected to so many positive and negative shocks, that cross-time skill-attainment correlations fall quickly to modest levels.

But low correlations do not necessarily mean that early interventions designed to boost skills, attention, or behavior are ill considered. The appropriate policy test involves costs and benefits rather than correlation size. High-quality, intensive interventions like the Perry preschool program have proved their worth. Whether larger-scale early interventions can do so remains a vital policy question.

The authors are grateful to the Spencer Foundation, the Russell Sage Foundation, the Foundation for Child Development, and the NSF–supported Center for the Analysis of Pathways from Childhood to Adulthood (grant no. 0322356) for research support.

NOTES

Online appendix available at: http://www.russellsage.org/duncan_murnane_online_appendix.pdf.

1. These data regarding the Perry program are taken from Lawrence Schweinhart et al. (2005).

2. To be sure, not all outcomes differed significantly between Perry and control children, but the long-run impacts are impressive, as reflected both in the evaluation reports written by the organization that ran the Perry study and in an independent reanalysis of the Perry data (Heckman et al. 2009).

3. Direct assessments of young children's inhibition require children to suppress a dominant or congruent response, yet measures differ in the extent to which the tasks also include an emotional component. A measure of cognitive self-regulation involves suppressions but little emotional work.

4. Emotional self-regulation is measured by tasks that require children to control (typically deescalate) their emotions, usually their excitement. Most often these tasks for young children involve delaying the gratification of a desired reward—candy or a gift. For example, in one task a child is told not to peek as the assessor noisily wraps a present in front of the child.

5. We chose math over reading owing to second-language complications with early reading scores; the online appendix tables show broadly similar patterns for math and reading.

6. For example, the unadjusted 13.8 percent difference between low and high SES and arrest rates falls to 10.2 percent, or by about one quarter.

7. The data sets included the Children of the National Longitudinal Survey of Youth (NLSY), the National Institute of Child Health and Human Development Study of Early Child Care and Youth Development (NICHD SECCYD), the 1970 British Cohort Study (BCS), the Early Childhood Longitudinal Study Kindergarten Cohort (ECLS-K), the Infant Health and Development Program (IHDP), and the Montreal Longitudinal-Experimental Preschool Study (MLEPS).

8. This conclusion held both across studies and within each of the six data sets they examined. Their analysis included a sixth category, school-entry social skills, which also proved to be completely unpredictive of later school achievement.

9. Key results from the meta-analysis appeared robust to a host of potential problems related to measurement and modeling, including the inclusion of controls (see Duncan et al. 2007).

10. The Duncan et al. (2007) analysis was of population-based data sets that provided little to no ability to identify children with diagnosed conduct disorder, attention deficit disorder, or other behavioral conditions. It is best to think of their analyses as focusing on children with relatively high but not clinical levels of learning, attention, and behavior problems.

11. The shading on the bars in figure 3.6 indicates levels of statistical significance, with light shading indicating $p < .05$ and darker shading indicating $p < .01$.

12. No consistently significant differences by family SES were found in either the attainment or crime analyses.

13. Two words of caution to this conclusion. First, arrest is an imperfect and incomplete way to measure criminal behavior, and it does not distinguish between types of criminal behavior (violent versus nonviolent). Second, although Head Start programs rarely match the intensity of model programs such as the Perry one, Deming's (2009) sibling-based analysis of Head Start showed long-run impacts on arrests but not shorter-run impacts on behavior problems.

REFERENCES

Achenbach, Thomas. 1991. *Manual for the Child Behavior Checklist/4–18 and 1991 Profile.* Burlington: University of Vermont Department of Psychiatry.

————. 1992. *Manual for the Child Behavior Checklist/2–3 and 1992 Profile.* Burlington, Vt.: University of Vermont Department of Psychiatry.

Baroody, Arthur J. 2003. "The Development of Adaptive Expertise and Flexibility: The Integration of Conceptual and Procedural Knowledge." In *The Development of Arithmetic Concepts and Skills: Constructing Adaptive Expertise Studies,* edited by Arthur J. Baroody and Ann Dowker. Mahwah, N.J.: Lawrence Erlbaum.

Baumeister, Roy, and Kathleen Vohs. 2004. *Handbook of Self-Regulation: Research, Theory, and Applications.* New York: Guilford Press.

Betts, Julian R., and Andrew Zau. 2004. "Peer Groups and Academic Achievement: Panel Evidence from Administrative Data." Working paper. La Jolla: University of California, San Diego.

Blau, David, and Janet Currie. 2006. "Pre-school, Day Care, and After-School Care: Who's Minding the Kids?" *Handbook of the Economics of Education.* Amsterdam: North-Holland.

Bongers, Ilja L., Hans M. Koot, Jan van der Ende, and Frank C. Verhulst. 2003. "The Normative Development of Child and Adolescent Problem Behavior." *Journal of Abnormal Psychology* 112(5): 179–92.

Bridges, Lisa J., Susanne A. Denham, and Jody M. Ganiban. 2004. "Definitional Issues in Emotion Regulation Research." *Child Development* 75(2): 340–45.

Brock, Laura, Sara E. Rimm-Kaufman, Lori Nathanson, and Kevin J. Grimm. 2009. "The Contributions of Hot and Cool Executive Function to Children's Academic Achievement, Learning-Related Behaviors, and Engagement in Kindergarten." *Early Childhood Research Quarterly* 24(3): 337–49.

Bronfenbrenner, Urie, and Pamela A. Morris. 1998. "The Ecology of Developmental Processes." In *Handbook of Child Psychology: Theoretical Models of Human Development*, edited by Richard M. Lerner. 5th ed. Vol. 1. New York: Wiley.

Campbell, Susan B., Daniel S. Shaw, and Miles Gilliom. 2000. "Early Externalizing Behavior Problems: Toddlers and Preschoolers at Risk for Later Adjustment." *Development and Psychopathology* 12(3): 467–88.

Crozier, Joseph C., Kenneth A. Dodge, Reid Griffith Fontaine, Jennifer E. Lansford, John E. Bates, Gregory S. Pettit, and Robert W. Levenson. 2008. "Social Information Processing and Cardiac Predictors of Adolescent Antisocial Behavior." *Journal of Abnormal Psychology* 117(2): 253–67.

Cunha, Flavio, and James J. Heckman. 2009. "The Economics and Psychology of Inequality and Human Development." *Journal of the European Economic Association* 7(2–3): 320–64.

Cunha, Flavio, James Heckman, Lance Lochner, and Dimitri Masterov. 2005. "Interpreting the Evidence on Life Cycle Skill Formation." In *Handbook of the Economics of Education,* edited by Eric A. Hanushek and Finis Welch. Amsterdam: North-Holland.

Davis-Kean, Pamela E., L. Rowell Huesmann, Justin Jager, W. Andrew Collins, John E. Bates, and Jennifer Lansford. 2008. "Changes in the Relation of Beliefs and Behaviors During Middle Childhood." *Child Development* 79(5): 1257–69.

Deming, David. 2009. "Early Childhood Intervention and Life-Cycle Skill Development: Evidence from Head Start." *American Economic Journal: Applied Economics* 1(3): 111–34.

Duncan, Greg, Chantelle Dowsett, Amy Classens, Katherine Magnuson, Aletha Huston, Pamela Klebanov, Linda Pagani, Leon Feinstein, Mimi Engel, Jeanne Brooks-Gunn, Holly Sexton, Kathryn Duckworth, and Crista Japel. 2007. "School Readiness and Later Achievement." *Developmental Psychology* 43(6): 1428–46.

Duncan, Greg, You-geon Lee, Katherine Magnuson, and Molly Metzger. 2009. "Early School Skills and Behaviors: Precursors to Young Adult Crime?" Paper presented at the biennial meeting of the Society for Research in Child Development. Denver (April 2, 2009).

Durlak, Joseph, Roger Weissberg, Allison Dymnicki, Rebecca Taylor, and Kriston Schellinger. Forthcoming. "The Impact of Enhancing Students' Social and Emotional Learning: A Meta-Analysis of School-Based Universal Interventions." *Child Development.*

Eisenberg, Nancy, Adrian Sadovsky, and Tracy L. Spinrad. 2005. "Associations of Emotion-Related Regulation with Language Skills, Emotion Knowledge, and Academic Outcomes." *New Directions for Child and Adolescent Development* 2005(109): 109–18.

Engel, Miriam 2007. "What Characteristics Do Principals in the Chicago Public Schools Look For in Teachers? A Mixed Methods Study." Paper presented at the annual meeting of the Association for Public Policy Analysis and Management. Washington, D.C. (November 9, 2007).

Entwisle, Doris R., Karl L. Alexander, and Linda S. Olson. 2007. "Early Schooling: The Handicap of Being Poor and Male." *Sociology of Education* 80(2): 114–38.

Fantuzzo, John, Rebecca Bulotsky, Paul McDermott, Samuel Mosca, and Megan N. Lutz. 2003. "A Multivariate Analysis of Emotional and Behavioral Adjustment and Preschool Educational Outcomes." *School Psychology Review* 32(2): 185–203.

Fantuzzo, John, Rebecca Shearer, Douglas Frye, Paul McDermott, Christine McWayne, and Stacy Perlman. Forthcoming. "Investigation of Dimensions of Social-Emotional Classroom Behavior and School Readiness for Low-Income Urban Preschool Children." *School Psychology Review.*

Hanushek, Eric A., John F. Kain, Jacob M. Markman, and Steven G. Rivkin. 2003. "Does Peer Ability Affect Student Achievement?" *Journal of Applied Econometrics* 18(5): 527–44.

Heckman, James, Seong H. Moon, Rodrogo Pinto, Peter A. Savleyev, and Adam Yavitz. 2009. "The Rate of Return to the HighScope Perry Preschool Program." NBER Working Paper No. 15471. Cambridge, Mass.: National Bureau of Economic Research.

Hiebert, James, and Diana Wearne. 1996. "Instruction, Understanding, and Skill in Multidigit Addition and Subtraction." *Cognition and Instruction* 14(3): 251–83.

Hoxby, Caroline M., and Gretchen Weingarth. 2007. "Taking Race Out of the Equation: School Reassignment and the Structure of Peer Effects." Working paper. Cambridge, Mass.: Harvard University.

Kokko, Katja, Richard E. Tremblay, Eric LaCourse, Daniel Nagin, and Frank Vitaro. 2006. "Trajectories of Prosocial Behavior and Physical Aggression in Middle Childhood: Links to Adolescent School Dropout and Physical Violence." *Journal of Research on Adolescence* 16(3): 404–28.

Kowaleski-Jones, Lori, and Greg J. Duncan. 1999. "The Structure of Achievement and Behavior Across Middle Childhood." *Child Development* 70(4): 930–43.

Ladd, Gary W., Sondra H. Birch, and Eric Buhs. 1999. "Children's Social and Scholastic Lives in Kindergarten: Related Spheres of Influence?" *Child Development* 70(6): 1373–1400.

Leschied, Alan, Debbie Chiodo, Elizabeth Nowicki, and Susan Rodger. 2008. "Childhood Predictors of Adult Criminality: A Meta-Analysis Drawn from the Prospective Longitudinal Literature." *Canadian Journal of Criminology and Criminal Justice* 50(4): 435–67.

Magnuson, Katherine, Greg Duncan, Molly Metzger, and You-geon Lee. 2009. "Early School Adjustment and High School Dropout." Paper presented at the biennial meeting of the Society for Research in Child Development. Denver (April 2, 2009).

McClelland, Megan, Frederick J. Morrison, and Deborah L. Holmes. 2000. "Children at Risk for Early Academic Problems: The Role of Learning-Related Social Skills." *Early Childhood Research Quarterly* 15(3): 307–29.

Mischel, Walter, Yuichi Shoda, and Monica Rodriguez. 1989. "Delay of Gratification in Children." *Science* 244(4907): 933–38.

Moffitt, Terrie E. 1993. "Adolescence-Limited and Life-Course-Persistent Antisocial Behavior: A Developmental Taxonomy." *Psychological Review* 100(4): 674–701.

National Center for Education Statistics. n.d. *Early Childhood Longitudinal Study, Kindergarten Cohort.* Available at: http://nces.ed.gov/ecls/kindergarten.asp (accessed May 2, 2011).

Newcomb, Andrew F., William M. Bukowski, and Linda Pattee. 1993. "Children's Peer Relations: A Meta-Analytic Review of Popular, Rejected, Neglected, Controversial, and Average Sociometric Status." *Psychological Bulletin* 113(1): 99–128.

Parker, Jeffrey G., and Steven R. Asher. 1987. "Peer Relations and Later Personal Adjustment: Are Low-Accepted Children at Risk?" *Psychological Bulletin* 86(3): 357–89.

Phillips, Meredith, and Tiffany Chin. 2004. "School Inequality: What Do We Know?" In *Social Inequality,* edited by Kathryn Neckerman. New York: Russell Sage Foundation.

Pianta, Robert, and Megan Stuhlman. 2004. "Teacher-Child Relationships and Children's Success in the First Years of School." *School Psychology Review* 33(3): 444–58.

Posner, Michael, and Mary K. Rothbart. 2000. "Developing Mechanisms of Self-Regulation." *Development and Psychopathology* 12(3): 427–41.

———. 2007. *Educating the Human Mind.* Washington, D.C.: American Psychological Association.

Pungello, Elizabeth P., Janis B. Kupersmidt, Margaret R. Burchinal, and Charlotte Patterson. 1996. "Environmental Risk Factors and Children's Achievement from Middle Childhood to Adolescence." *Developmental Psychology* 32(4): 755–67.

Raver, C. Cybele. 2004. "Placing Emotional Self-Regulation in Sociocultural and Socioeconomic Contexts." *Child Development* 75(2): 346–53.

Raver, C. Cybele, Radiah Smith-Donald, Tiffany Hayes, and Stephanie M. Jones. 2005. "Self-Regulation Across Differing Risk and Sociocultural Contexts: Preliminary Findings from the Chicago School Readiness Project." Paper presented at the biennial meeting of the Society for Research in Child Development. Atlanta, Ga. (April 8, 2005).

Sameroff, Arnold J., and Barbara H. Fiese. 2000. "Transactional Regulation: The Developmental Ecology of Early Intervention." In *Handbook of Early Childhood Intervention,* edited by Jack P. Shonkoff and Samuel J. Meisels. 2nd ed. New York: Cambridge University Press.

Schweinhart, Lawrence, Jeanne Monte, Zongping Xiang, W. Steven Barnett, Clive R. Belfield, and Milagros Nores. 2005. *Lifetime Effects: The HighScope Perry Preschool Study through Age 40.* Ypsilanti, Mich.: High/Scope Press.

Shonkoff, Jack, and Deborah Phillips, eds. 2000. *From Neurons to Neighborhoods: The Science of Early Childhood Development.* Washington, D.C.: National Academy Press.

U.S. Bureau of Labor Statistics. n.d. *National Longitudinal Survey of Youth, Child and Young Adult.* Available at: http://www.bls.gov/nls/nlsy79ch.htm (accessed May 2, 2011).

Yen, Cherng-Jyh, Timothy R. Konold, and Paul A. McDermott. 2004. "Does Learning Behavior Augment Cognitive Ability as an Indicator of Academic Achievement?" *Journal of School Psychology* 42(2): 157–69.

Chapter 4

Middle and High School Skills, Behaviors, Attitudes, and Curriculum Enrollment, and Their Consequences

George Farkas

This chapter complements chapter 3, by Greg Duncan and Katherine Magnuson, by focusing on links between student skills and behaviors in grades eight to twelve and later outcomes (high school and postsecondary degree attainment, arrest, and earnings) for these students. I also examine variables that are particularly appropriate to students in the middle and high school years and thus are not considered by Duncan and Magnuson. These include social psychological and attitudinal variables—self-esteem, sense of personal control, and educational expectations. In addition, I measure the association between enrollment in an academic or nonacademic curriculum track and later outcomes. Prior research by sociologists and psychologists has suggested that these variables play a significant role in determining schooling outcomes.

The findings show that in both eighth and twelfth grade, the gaps between the average reading and math skills of children from families in the top socioeconomic status (SES) quintile and those from families in the bottom SES quintile are more than one standard deviation (with the math gaps somewhat larger than the reading gaps). Consistent with the theme of this volume, these gaps are particularly large, almost twice the size of the achievement gaps between African Americans and whites. The black-white reading and math skill gaps in turn are a little larger than the comparable gaps between Hispanic and non-Hispanic white children. SES- and race-based gaps in learning behaviors are much smaller than comparable test score gaps. SES-based gaps in learning behaviors among eighth-graders are about twice as large as gaps attributable to race or ethnicity. These gaps decline slightly between eighth and twelfth grade.

Test scores, behaviors, and attitudes measured at grade eight explain more than half of the SES-based gaps in the high school graduation rate. They also play a role in explaining SES-based gaps in postsecondary degree attainment and subsequent labor-market earnings. There are substantial SES-related gaps in the probability of obtaining a postsecondary degree and labor-market earnings, even after controlling for skills and behaviors at grade eight. This suggests that parental SES affects children's outcomes not only through the relationship between family social class and children's skills and behaviors, but also via additional mechanisms. Candidates for these include professional contacts and financial support. In general, persistent test score and behavior problems are much more important than intermittent problems for later outcomes. The strongest effects on later outcomes are due to persistently low math test scores in eighth and tenth grade. Among behavior problems, the strongest effects are associated with persistent learning behavior problems, with externalizing and internalizing behavior problems exerting much smaller effects on later outcomes.

Students in a nonacademic track in tenth grade have a high school graduation rate, a postsecondary degree attainment rate, and earnings at age twenty-six that are all fourteen to fifteen percentage points lower than those of students in academic tracks. Much, but not all, of these gaps is explained by differences in eighth-grade test scores and behaviors. A similar pattern is observed for the effects of the student's educational expectations in tenth grade. These psychological and enrollment variables also mediate the effects of social class and race-ethnicity and eighth-grade test scores and behaviors on later outcomes. In sum, the test scores, behaviors, attitudes, and curriculum enrollment of middle and high school students are very consequential for later schooling and earnings outcomes. Equations to predict arrest generally show smaller magnitudes of effect than for the other outcomes, but the patterns are similar to those found by other researchers. Males have higher arrest rates than females. Lower test scores, externalizing behavior problems, and learning behavior problems are associated with a higher probability of arrest. It is interesting that a greater sense of personal control and higher educational expectations are associated with lower probabilities of arrest.

The path to a level of educational attainment adequate for middle-class employment and earnings has never been as long as it is in the United States today. Successful completion of kindergarten followed by five years of elementary school, three years of middle school, and four years of high school are essential, as is completion of at least some postsecondary schooling, preferably a four-year college degree. Further, many college-educated adults now attain postbaccalaureate training and degrees that qualify them for positions in our increasingly differentiated and professionalized occupational structure. Within this stratification system, failure at K–12 schooling tends to predict occupational and earnings attainment below a middle-class level. This is often accompanied by higher rates of unemployment and involvement with the criminal justice system, lower marriage rates, greater health problems, and decreased longevity over the life course.

Thus, at least some success at K–12 is needed for later life success. But what are the determinants of K–12 success? In particular, what processes and mechanisms determine the evolution of schooling careers as students develop from elementary school through middle and high school and in many cases go on to postsecondary education?

Chapter 3 of this volume, by Greg J. Duncan and Katherine Magnuson, examines this question by focusing on elementary school achievement, attention, and behavior problems and how they affect later outcomes—high school graduation, arrest, and college attendance. They find substantial gaps in achievement, attention and engagement, and antisocial behavior across socioeconomic status (SES), racial-ethnic, and gender groups in first and fifth grade. They also find substantial relationships between early achievement and antisocial behavior, and the probabilities of high school graduation, college attendance, and arrest, particularly when the early achievement and antisocial behavior outcomes are persistent rather than intermittent. In this chapter I extend the story to student skills and behaviors in grades eight through twelve and their consequences for later outcomes.

I use data from the National Education Longitudinal Study (NELS), which began with a representative national sample of eighth-graders in 1988 and incorporated successive waves of data collection in 1990 (when the original pupils were in tenth grade) and 1992 (twelfth grade), with further follow-ups in 1994 and 2000. Many of the variables are similar to those analyzed by Duncan and Magnuson. These include standardized, grade-appropriate assessments of math and reading performance, and also teacher-judged measures of the student's attention and engagement and other learning-related behaviors, externalizing behavior problems, and internalizing behavior problems. Ultimate outcome measures include high school and postsecondary degree attainment, whether the individual has ever been arrested, and earnings.

In addition, I also examine variables that are particularly appropriate to the middle and high school years and thus are not considered by Duncan and Magnuson. These include the following sociopsychological and attitudinal variables: self-esteem (measured in eighth grade), locus of control (sense of personal control over life outcomes, also measured in eighth grade), educational expectations (how far the student expects to go in school, measured in tenth grade), and the student's curriculum track enrollment (academic or nonacademic), also measured in tenth grade. Prior research by sociologists and psychologists has suggested that these variables play a significant role in determining schooling outcomes.

Much research has been undertaken on these topics, but this research tends to be fragmented across disciplinary lines. Economists have emphasized cognitive skills, measured by test scores, as both determinants and consequences of schooling success. In this model of human capital formation, skill begets skill as teachers assist students to "invest in their human capital." Economists have also followed psychologists in adding learning-related skills and behaviors, including attention, organization, and effort, to the variables they focus on. Sociologists and psychologists also study test score data and learning-related skills and behaviors, but they tend to further expand the list of variables to include sociopsychological attitudes and student enrollment into school structures, such as curriculum tracks, as determinants of success. In particular, sociologists and some psychologists have a long history of including attitude scales measuring students' self-esteem, sense of personal control over life outcomes, and educational expectations as determinants of educational and occupational attainment. In addition, sociologists have given much attention to students' enrollment into ability groupings and academic and nonacademic curriculum tracks as determinants of schooling outcomes. These variables are likely to be particularly important for understanding educational outcomes in middle and high school, since teenagers formulate and act to attain goals within a world of intense social interaction involving peers, parents, and teachers.

Yet it is rare for these disparate research traditions to be combined in a single study, where the relative magnitudes of the effects of different sets of variables can be assessed. Doing so is a goal of this chapter. I examine disparities in school success that already exist in middle school (eighth grade) and study how these evolve during high school and lead to disparate attainment of postsecondary education and disparate earnings by age twenty-six. The child's background is measured by gender, race-ethnicity, and socioeconomic status. Cognitive performance in eighth grade is measured by standardized test scores in reading and math. Learning-related behaviors in eighth grade are measured by the average of reports from two teachers on the student's absenteeism, tardiness, inattentiveness, and disruptive behaviors. Attitudes in eighth grade are measured by standardized scales of self-esteem and locus of control.

The student's enrollment in the academic or nonacademic curriculum track is measured in tenth grade. A standardized scale of the student's expectations for how many years of schooling he or she will attain is also measured in tenth grade. Ultimate outcomes are whether or not by age twenty-six the student had graduated from high school (this does not include receiving a GED), had ever been arrested, or had obtained a postsecondary degree, and weekly earnings at age twenty-six.

THEORETICAL ORIENTATION

With their focus on standardized test scores as measures of the skills embodied in human capital, and the notion that "skills beget skills" as a model of human capital development over time (Cunha et al. 2006), it is not surprising that economists have long estimated models in which school success in high school, college, and beyond, as well as labor-market success, are driven by students' prior cognitive skills as measured by test scores in kindergarten, elementary school, and middle school. Economists have also added measures of student behaviors—those that are learning-related and attentional as well as social, including both internalizing and externalizing behavior problems—to their models (Duncan and Dunifon 1997; Duncan et al. 2007; Heckman and Rubinstein 2001; Heckman, Stixrud, and Urzua 2006). Doing so builds on an earlier research tradition (Bowles and Gintis 1976; Jencks, Crouse, and Mueser 1979) that enriched the model of educational and labor-market attainment by including measures of socialization, personality, and behavior, as well as variation in these across different levels of family social-class background. In a review of this literature for sociologists, George Farkas (2003, 556–57) characterized it as "a new paradigm for understanding the microprocesses underlying stratification outcomes. Patterns of habitual behavior, particularly the extent of conscientiousness or good work habits, developed from birth through adolescence, in conjunction with the cognitive skills developed alongside these behaviors, determine school success and schooling and occupational attainment. These skills and habits then combine with skills and habits developed on the job to determine employment and earnings success."

An attractive feature of this emerging paradigm is that by adding learning-related behaviors to prior test scores as predictors of later test scores and behaviors, the theoretical framework is expanded to begin to describe the mechanisms by which some students perform better at school and work because they bring strong effort and focused attention to these tasks. Yet despite the increased richness of the resulting models, they still give little or no attention to two important aspects of student life in schools. The first of these is attitudes relating to self-concept (self-esteem and locus of control) and educational expectations. The second is school structures, particularly ability groups and curriculum tracks. The following section begins with a discussion of prior research on the role of learning-related behaviors in the school achievement process. Discussions of self-concept, educational expectations, and curriculum track enrollment follow.

Learning-Related Behaviors

Samuel Bowles and Herbert Gintis (1976) and Christopher Jencks, James Crouse, and Peter Mueser (1979) were the first researchers to prominently contrast the effects of "noncognitive traits" with those of test scores as determinants of educational, occupational, and earnings success.[1] Bowles and Gintis reported that measures of rule orientation, dependability, and internalization predicted high school students' grade-point averages after controlling for test scores. Jencks, Crouse, and Mueser measured the effects of personality self-assessments, self-reported "indirect measures of personality," and teacher-reported student character traits on achievement. The personality self-assessments included sociability, social sensitivity, impulsiveness, vigor, calmness, tidiness, culture, leadership, self-confidence, and mature personality. The indirect measures of personality included study habits, working so quickly that a student fails to do his or her best work, group affiliations, leadership roles, dating activities, reading habits, culture and hobbies, and orientation to the world of work. The teacher-rated personality traits included cooperativeness, dependability, executive ability, emotional control, industriousness, initiative, integrity, perseverance, and appearance. The authors found that a number of these variables had significant effects on achievement.

In an important theoretical article, Anne Swidler (1986) argued that group cultural differences may be relevant to understanding group achievement differences. But rather than thinking of culture as determining action through its effect on values, the ends toward which action is directed, she argued for viewing culture as a tool kit of skills, habits, and styles, the means by which strategies of action are constructed. She goes on to note that "if one asked a slum youth why he did not take steps to pursue a middle-class path to success . . . the answer might well be not 'I don't want that life,' but instead, 'Who, me?' One can hardly pursue success in a world where the accepted skills, styles, and informal know-how are unfamiliar. One does better to look for a line of action for which one already has the cultural equipment" (275).

Farkas et al. (1990; see also Farkas 1996) followed up on this observation by testing the extent to which teacher-judged student work habits (homework, class participation, effort, and organization), disruptiveness, and appearance and dress, combined with basic cognitive skills measured by test scores and coursework mastery measured by a curriculum-referenced test, determine the teacher-assigned course grade in seventh and eighth grade. The authors found that basic cognitive skills and good work habits increase coursework mastery, which increases course grades. Then, after controlling for basic skills and coursework mastery test scores, better student work habits are found to further increase course grades. Thus, learning-related behaviors strongly increase course grades, both indirectly via their positive effect on coursework mastery and directly, since teachers grade on these behaviors over and above the student's coursework mastery.

James Rosenbaum (2001, chapter 8) went further in this research direction, estimating models in which learning-related behaviors, along with test scores, help determine course grades, and then these variables determine educational attainment and earnings. He too found that learning-related behaviors affect grades and that both these behaviors and grades affect later outcomes.

The economists Greg J. Duncan and colleagues (Duncan and Dunifon 1997, 1998; Dunifon, Duncan, and Brooks-Gunn 2001) and James J. Heckman and colleagues (Heckman and Lochner 2000; Heckman and Rubinstein 2001; Cunha et al. 2006; Cunha and Heckman 2008) also examined the relationship between family background and learning-related behaviors and skills, and the consequences of these behaviors and skills for education and employment outcomes across the life cycle. They too found that, even after controlling for test scores, these behaviors and skills play a significant role in explaining achievement differences between individuals.

Self-Concept and Educational Expectations

Behaviors and skills do not develop in a vacuum. Rather, their development is driven by the student's school-related attitudes and expectations. Human agency involves goal setting and goal seeking, and sociologists and psychologists have long hypothesized that these processes are strongly affected by the individual's self-concept—feelings of self-esteem (perception of oneself as a person of worth) and sense of personal control (perception of oneself as an effective person). Among adolescents, self-esteem results from positive interactions with, and support from, parents, peers, teachers, and others (Rosenberg 1979, 1989; Rosenberg, Schooler, and Schoenbach 1989). It is associated with low rates of depression, but its effects on educational success are uncertain (Rosenberg, Schooler, and Schoenbach 1989; Ross and Broh 2000). Sense of control involves feeling able to affect outcomes by one's own actions (internal locus of control) or, by contrast, feeling relatively helpless in the face of outside forces (external locus of control). A sense of personal control is hypothesized to result from past successes and to improve academic performance via increased effort, motivation, and persistence (Rotter 1966; Seeman 1983; Bandura 1986). This has been shown to partially explain the positive relationship between parental social class and children's school success via a mechanism in which well-educated parents help children develop the skills and habits needed for academic success, which not only directly improves achievement but also increases the children's sense of control, thereby further improving achievement (Mirowsky and Ross 1998; Ross and Broh 2000).

Yet empirically separating the effects of self-esteem and locus of control (the individual's ability to affect what happens to her or him) on school achievement can be difficult. One problem is that each may have reciprocal effects with school achievement—each variable may itself be caused by achievement, increasing the difficulty in isolating its effect *upon* achievement. A second problem is that self-esteem and locus of control are likely to be correlated, so that each must be controlled for when estimating the effects of the other. Thus, reviewing findings in this area, Catherine E. Ross and Beckett A. Broh (2000) suggested that although Xiaoru Liu, Howard B. Kaplan, and Will Risser (1992) found reciprocal effects between self-esteem and academic achievement among students in grades seven to twelve, their failure to simultaneously control for locus of control may have led to spurious effect estimates. Ross and Broh observe that this conclusion is consistent with the finding by Mark A. Mone, Douglas D. Baker, and Frank Jeffries (1995) that when both self-efficacy and self-esteem are used as predictors of academic performance, only self-efficacy is found to have an effect. It is also consistent with the finding by Morris Rosenberg, Carmi Schooler, and Carrie Schoenbach (1989) that the correlation between self-esteem and school achievement is due to an effect of achievement on self-esteem, not one in the opposite direction. Finally, Ross and Broh's (2000) own study finds that locus of control, but not self-esteem, affects school achievement.

In the present study, I follow Ross and Broh's admonition to simultaneously include both self-esteem and locus of control in the model when estimating the effects of these variables on school achievement. I also extend Ross and Broh's logic to the inclusion of other relevant variables in the model. In particular, I include a measure of the student's expectations for his or her ultimate level of educational attainment. This variable played an important role in the "Wisconsin model" of socioeconomic attainment.

The Wisconsin model (Sewell, Haller, and Portes 1969; Sewell, Haller, and Ohlendorf 1970; Sewell and Hauser 1976) aimed to add a sociopsychological mechanism to the dominant model of intergenerational socioeconomic attainment (Blau and Duncan 1967). This mechanism involves the process of socialization, in which parents and peers affect the educational aspirations and expectations of students, which in turn affect student motivation and effort, and thus achievement. Indeed, studies have repeatedly found that student aspirations and expectations do indeed affect student achievement, even after controls for many other variables are included. However, these studies almost never include controls for a full set of correlated variables—test scores, self-esteem, locus of control, learning-related behaviors, and curricular track enrollment.[2] Such studies are unable to assess the relative importance of these variables in affecting the process of school achievement as students make the transition from middle childhood to adolescence, high school, and beyond.

Curriculum Track Enrollment

Sociologists of education have a long-standing interest in school structures. Particularly important among these are student enrollment into ability groups and curriculum tracks. Such enrollment has been shown to significantly affect student effort and achievement, even after controlling for prior test scores (Gamoran and Mare 1989; Rosenbaum 2001; Hallinan 2003; Carbonaro 2005; Tach and Farkas 2006). This is not surprising, since students in lower-ability groups and less academically oriented curriculum tracks often experience diminished self-esteem, sense of personal control, educational expectations, and learning-related behaviors. Yet no prior empirical research has included these variables alongside curriculum track enrollment in a comprehensive model of educational achievement. By including all these variables in the estimated models, we assess their relative magnitudes of effect on educational outcomes. Although school and neighborhood differences no doubt affect student test scores, behaviors, and their outcomes, these school and neighborhood effects have generally been found to be weaker in magnitude than family- and student-level variables (Brooks-Gunn, Duncan, and Aber 1997; Rumberger and Palardy 2004), and they are not the focus of this chapter. Instead, some of our models include school fixed effects, thereby eliminating the effects of differences between schools and revealing how student-level variables affect one another within each school. In general, these fixed-effects calculations find similar results to those without fixed effects.

Curriculum-track enrollment and educational expectations are measured in tenth grade. This is appropriate for track enrollment since a student's high school curriculum track often is not firmly established until at least the tenth grade. It is also appropriate for the student's expectations for his or her ultimate educational attainment: educational expectations become increasingly meaningful in tenth grade, when the student's curriculum-track enrollment and school-performance level are becoming established and high school graduation is only about two years in the future.

SKILLS AND BEHAVIORS IN MIDDLE AND HIGH SCHOOL

We use data from the National Education Longitudinal Study to estimate the strength of the relationships discussed above. The NELS began by interviewing a large, nationally representative sample of eighth graders in 1988. These students were then resurveyed in 1990 (tenth grade), 1992 (twelfth grade), 1994 (post–high school), and 2000 (when they were in their mid-twenties). As detailed in the online appendix (available at http://www.russellsage.org/duncan_murnane_online_appendix.pdf) reading, math, and other tests were administered uniformly to the students in 1988, 1990, and 1992. The students responded to questionnaires, providing measures of their self-esteem, sense of personal control, educational expectations, curriculum-track enrollment, arrest record, high school and postsecondary degree completion, and earnings at age twenty-six. Their teachers reported on the students' learning behaviors, externalizing behavior problems, and internalizing behavior problems.

Eighth Grade and Cross-Time Correlations

As Duncan and Magnuson did for kindergarten, I correlated the eighth-grade measures of skills and behaviors—reading and math test scores, teacher-judged learning-related behaviors (measures of attention and engagement), and externalizing and internalizing behavior problems. These eighth-grade correlations are patterned similarly to those for kindergarten. Thus, in both kindergarten and eighth grade, reading and math test scores correlate at about 0.70. Also, at both grade levels, test scores correlate with student attention and engagement at about 0.3 to 0.4, and attention and engagement correlates with externalizing behavior problems at about −0.5. Other correlations are smaller, with patterns generally similar to those for kindergarten. I also calculated cross-time (eighth- and twelfth-grade) correlations. Patterns are similar to those calculated by Duncan and Magnuson for kindergarten and fifth grade: the highest correlations are for test scores with themselves over time, with other variables showing lower correlations over time.

Skill and Behavior Differences Across Groups

On the basis of the detailed calculations in online appendix tables 4.A1 and 4.A2, in-text figures 4.1 to 4.4 plot differences in reading, math, learning behaviors, and externalizing behavior problems across socioeconomic, racial-ethnic, and gender groups in both eighth and twelfth grade.

FIGURE 4.1   *Reading Gaps in Eighth and Twelfth Grades*

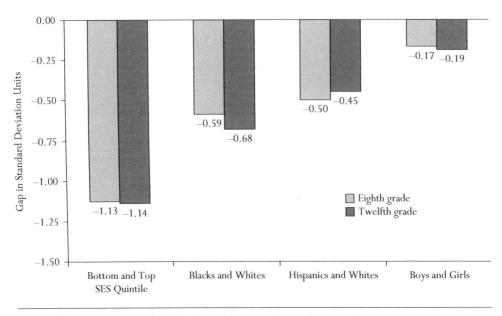

Source: Authors' calculations based on NELS88 (National Center for Education Statistics n.d.).

These figures show simple differences across groups; the online appendix tables also show counterpart differences within schools—that is, adjusting for school fixed effects.

In the case of reading and math achievement (figures 4.1 and 4.2), socioeconomic gaps are much larger than racial-ethnic and gender gaps in both eighth and twelfth grade. Comparing the first and fifth SES quintiles, the high-SES children score more than one standard deviation higher than the low-SES children in both math and reading, with the math gap being somewhat larger in twelfth grade. By contrast, the black-white gaps are about 0.6 to 0.8 of a standard deviation and the Hispanic-white gaps are about 0.5 of a standard deviation. Gender gaps are much smaller, at approximately 0.1 to 0.2 of a standard deviation, with girls higher in reading and boys higher in math. These patterns are similar to those found for kindergarten and fifth grade by Duncan and Magnuson. This suggests that where test score achievement gaps, measured in standard deviation units, are concerned, sociodemographic differences observed in kindergarten are relatively stable through twelfth grade. Further, and consistent with the theme of this volume, social-class differences in cognitive performance are very important, being much larger than those found for either race and ethnicity or gender.

Figure 4.3 shows learning behavior gaps across the sociodemographic groups in eighth and twelfth grade. These reveal both similarities and differences compared to Duncan and Magnuson's results for kindergarten and fifth grade. A major similarity is that at every time period the largest gap is associated with SES. Differences include the fact that most groups, as they move from kindergarten to fifth grade, show larger attention and engagement gaps, whereas most groups when they move from eighth to twelfth grade show modestly declining learning behavior gaps. Another difference is that we find smaller black-white and gender differences in learning behaviors in eighth and twelfth grade than Duncan and Magnuson find for kindergarten and fifth grade.

FIGURE 4.2   *Math Gaps in Eighth and Twelfth Grades*

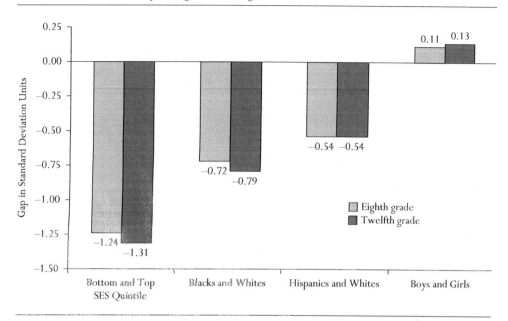

Source: Authors' calculations based on NELS88 (National Center for Education Statistics n.d.).

FIGURE 4.3   *Learning Behavior Gaps in Eighth and Twelfth Grades*

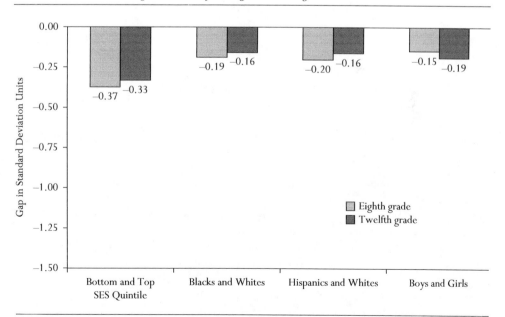

Source: Authors' calculations based on NELS88 (National Center for Education Statistics n.d.).

FIGURE 4.4   *Externalizing Behavior Problem Gaps in Eighth and Twelfth Grades*

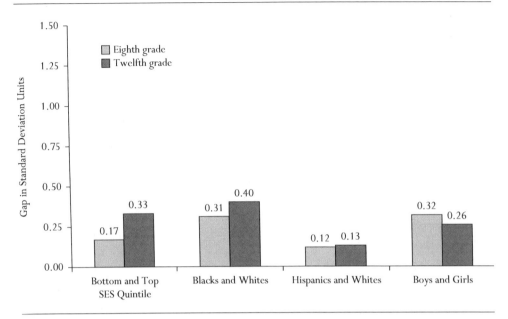

Source: Authors' calculations based on NELS88 (National Center for Education Statistics n.d.).

There are several possible explanations for these patterns. The teacher-reported measures are somewhat different across the ECLS-K (kindergarten and fifth grade) and NELS (eighth and twelfth grade) databases. However, it is also likely that the declining learning behavior gaps in twelfth grade reported in figure 4.3 indicate that learning behavior problems peak in middle school, and even among the most disadvantaged groups, these problems decline modestly by twelfth grade. (The exception is boys, whose learning behaviors are somewhat worse in twelfth grade than in eighth grade.)

Externalizing behavior problem gaps in eighth and twelfth grade are displayed in figure 4.4. They can be compared to Duncan and Magnuson's results for antisocial behavior problem gaps in kindergarten and fifth grade. Duncan and Magnuson find the largest gaps (of similar size) for the SES, black-white, and gender comparisons, with a tendency for these to increase from kindergarten to fifth grade. We too find the largest gaps for these groups in eighth and twelfth grade. In our data, both the SES and black-white externalizing gaps increase somewhat between eighth and twelfth grade, but the gender gap decreases over this time span. For internalizing problem behavior gaps, shown in online appendix table 4.A1 for eighth grade (this measure was not available for twelfth grade), only SES shows significant differences in problem behavior. This replicates Duncan and Magnuson's findings for this outcome.

In summary, in eighth and twelfth grade, SES differences are larger than racial-ethnic differences in reading and math skills and learning behaviors. This is consistent with Duncan and Magnuson's results for kindergarten and fifth grade. It is good news that these sociodemographic gaps do not generally increase between eighth and twelfth grade. The less good news is that many of these gaps are quite large. The math gaps in twelfth grade are about 1.3 standard deviations for SES, 0.8 standard deviations for the black-white gap, and 0.5 standard deviations for the Hispanic-white gap. The increased importance of social-class gaps in achievement over the

TABLE 4.1   *School-Level Concentrations of Eighth-Grade Achievement and Learning Behavior Problems*

		School Characteristics					
	All	High-Poverty Schools[b]	High-Minority Schools[c]	High-SES Schools[a]	Urban Schools	Suburban Schools	Rural Schools
Children with low test scores	20%	41%	43%	11%	24%	17%	21%
Children with low learning behaviors	20	27	26	17	23	20	19
Children with both problems	7	15	13	4	9	6	8

Source: Authors' calculations based on the 1988 National Educational Longitudinal Study (National Center for Education Statistics n.d.).
Notes: All means are weighted.
[a]Low SES is defined as the bottom 20 percent; high SES is defined as the top 20 percent.
[b]High-poverty schools are those with more than 50 percent of the students on free or reduced lunch.
[c]High-minority schools are those where more than 60 percent of the students are minorities.

past forty years (discussed by Sean F. Reardon in chapter 5 of this volume), is one of the principal themes of this volume.

School-Level Measures of Skill Distribution

Because economically disadvantaged and ethnic minority groups tend to be geographically concentrated, and since these children tend to have lower achievement and learning-related behaviors than more affluent and white children, the schools attended by these children also tend to have higher-than-average concentrations of achievement and behavior problems. Duncan and Magnuson documented this for kindergarten. Table 4.1 shows similar results for eighth grade.

We defined having a low test score in reading and math as falling in the bottom 25 percent of all scores. We used the same 25 percent cutoff to define low learning behaviors. Overall, 7 percent of all students had both problems. However, in high-poverty schools (those with more than 50 percent of their students on free or reduced lunch), 41 percent of the students had low test scores, 27 percent had low learning behaviors, and 15 percent had both problems. Similar rates of these problems are observed for schools with high minority populations. By comparison, high-SES schools average only 11 percent of students with low test scores, 17 percent with low learning behaviors, and 4 percent with both problems. Thus, as already noted by Duncan and Magnuson for kindergarten, middle schools with high levels of poverty and high minority populations have concentrations of students with problems that no doubt affect the overall learning environment in these schools.

CONSEQUENCES OF SKILLS, BEHAVIORS, ATTITUDES, AND CURRICULUM ENROLLMENT FOR SCHOOL AND EARNINGS ACHIEVEMENT AND FOR ARREST

To what extent do sociodemographics and eighth- and tenth-grade skills and learning behaviors determine high school and postsecondary education completion rates, as well as differences in arrest rates and earnings? Further, to what extent do eighth-grade attitudinal variables such as

FIGURE 4.5   *SES Gaps (First Quintile Versus Fifth Quintile) in High School Graduation,*
            Postsecondary Degree Attainment, and Earnings

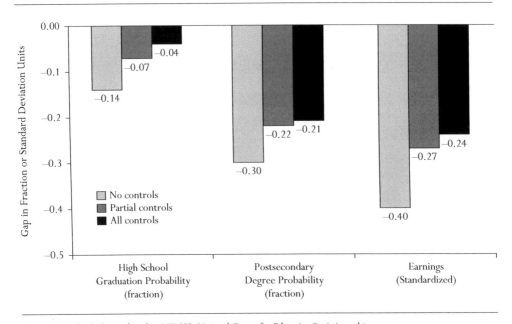

Source: Authors' calculations based on NELS88 (National Center for Education Statistics n.d.).

self-esteem and locus of control, tenth grade educational expectations, and tenth grade enrollment into a nonacademic curriculum track also affect these outcomes?

These questions are addressed in online appendix tables 4.A3 to 4.A10. In these tables, the first column shows bivariate regressions in which each variable is used by itself to predict the outcome, with no control variables. The second column shows a multivariate regression, with all the sociodemographics as predictors. The third column adds the eighth-grade test scores in reading and math, the learning behaviors, and behavior problems as predictors. The fourth column adds eighth-grade self-esteem and locus of control to the equation, and the final column adds tenth-grade nonacademic-track enrollment and educational expectations to the equation.

Some of the more noteworthy findings are summarized in figures 4.5, 4.6, and 4.7 and table 4.2. For each of three outcomes—the probability of high school graduation, the probability of attaining a postsecondary degree, and earnings at age twenty-six (in standard deviation units)— figure 4.5 shows the SES differential (first quintile/fifth quintile) in three ways: with no control variables; with a partial set of control variables, namely sociodemographics, eighth grade test scores, learning behaviors, and behavior problems; and with a full set of controls, in which attitudes, educational expectations, and enrollment into the nonacademic track have been added to the prior set of variables. (Figure 4.5 summarizes the results shown in online appendix tables 4.A3, 4.A7, and 4.A9.) Farkas (1996, table 9.2) tested for interactions in their effects on course grades of gender, poverty, and race-ethnicity, and of basic skills, absenteeism, work habits, disruptiveness, appearance and dress, and coursework mastery. Out of thirty coefficients tested, only three achieved statistical significance, suggesting that the process by which skills, behaviors, and attitudes are translated into school success is relatively uniform across sociodemographic groups.

Accordingly, the present analyses of the determinants of high school and postsecondary degree attainment are based on additive, rather than interactive, models. Similarly, Farkas (1996, table 4.3) found at most modest interactions between sociodemographics and the effects of skills, education, and experience on earnings. Thus, the equations predicting earnings in the present analysis are additive rather than interactive.

Figure 4.5 shows an overall high school graduation gap of fourteen percentage points for students in the first SES quintile compared to the fifth quintile. After controls for eighth-grade skills and behaviors are included, this declines by half, to seven percentage points. That is, middle school skills and behaviors account for about half of the SES gap in high school graduation. Adding attitudes, expectations, and curriculum-track enrollment to the equation reduces the gap to four percentage points. This is close to a further 50 percent reduction in the gap, suggesting that the attitude, expectation, and track enrollment variables play a significant role in explaining SES gaps in high school graduation, even after the effects of eighth-grade skills and behaviors have been accounted for. This supports our interest in these attitudinal and curriculum enrollment variables that play a significant role in the lives of middle and high school students.

Concerning attainment of a postsecondary degree, the SES gap is a substantial 30 percentage points. This large gap likely includes the effects of the greater ability of high-SES families to pay college tuition. After controls for skills and behaviors are included, this gap declines to twenty-two percentage points, and after additional controls for attitudes, expectations, and track enrollment are incorporated, it declines to twenty-one percentage points. These relatively modest declines after controls are added suggest that there is much about the SES gap in college degree attainment that we do not fully understand. Family finances and parental educational expectations may be important here.

The final three bars of figure 4.5 show the effects of SES on earnings (in standard deviation units) at age twenty-six. The lowest SES group earns 40 percent of a standard deviation less than the highest SES group. Controls for skills and behaviors reduce this to 27 percent of a standard deviation, and additional controls for attitudes, expectations, and curriculum-track enrollment reduce it further to 24 percent of a standard deviation. Thus, the control variables play a significant role in explaining SES differentials in earnings. However, the substantial effects that remain unexplained suggest that parental SES effects on their adult child's earnings operate through mechanisms above and beyond the child's skills, behaviors, attitudes, expectations, and track enrollment. Likely mechanisms of effect include parental and child personal and professional contacts and parental financial support.

Now we turn to the effects of test scores, behaviors, attitudes and expectations, and track enrollment on later outcomes. Detailed results are shown in online appendix tables 4.A3 to 4.A10. Highlights are shown in table 4.2 and figures 4.6 and 4.7.

Table 4.2 shows the effects of persistently (that is, occurring in both grades eight and ten) low reading and math test score achievement, persistently low learning behaviors, and persistent externalizing and internalizing behavior problems on high school graduation, postsecondary degree attainment, and earnings at age twenty-six. We see that students with persistently low reading scores had high school graduation rates approximately two percentage points lower than those of students without low test scores in either grade. Students with persistently low reading test scores also had postsecondary degree attainment rates reduced by approximately six percentage points. There were no significant effects on earnings at age twenty-six.

Effects for persistently low math scores are larger. They are associated with a rate of high school degree attainment seven percentage points lower, a rate of postsecondary degree attainment eight percentage points lower, and earnings at age twenty-six that are 13 percent of a stan-

TABLE 4.2   *Eighth and Tenth Grade Persistent and Intermittent Problems and Later Outcomes, After Controlling Other Variables*

Problem Area	Problem Frequency	High School Degree (N = 8,198)	Postsecondary Degree (N = 6,576)	Earnings (N = 6,776)
Reading	Intermittent	−0.01 (0.01)	−0.04* (0.02)	0.02 (0.04)
	Persistent	−0.02** (0.01)	−0.06** (0.02)	0.05 (0.04)
Math	Intermittent	−0.01 (0.01)	−0.04 (0.02)	−0.06 (0.04)
	Persistent	−0.07*** (0.01)	−0.08*** (0.02)	−0.13*** (0.04)
Learning behaviors	Intermittent	−0.01*** (0.003)	−0.02*** (0.01)	−0.04* (0.01)
	Persistent	−0.05*** (0.003)	−0.06*** (0.01)	−0.03* (0.02)
Externalizing behavior	Intermittent	0.001 (0.002)	−0.03*** (0.01)	0.003 (0.01)
	Persistent	−0.003 (0.002)	−0.01 (0.01)	0.03* (0.01)
Internalizing behavior	Intermittent	−0.003 (0.002)	−0.02** (0.01)	−0.03* (0.01)
	Persistent	−0.004* (0.002)	−0.01* (0.01)	−0.03* (0.01)

Source: Authors' calculations based on NELS88 (National Center for Education Statistics n.d.).
Notes: Standard errors in parentheses. "Problem" is defined as being in the worst quartile of a distribution at a given age.
$*p < 0.05$; $**p < 0.01$; $***p < 0.001$

dard deviation lower. This is consistent with Duncan and Magnuson's finding that persistently low math test scores are particularly strongly associated with later outcomes.

Table 4.2 also shows that persistent learning behavior problems are significantly associated with lower probabilities of high school and postsecondary degree attainment and lower earnings at age twenty-six. For students with learning behavior problems in both eighth and tenth grade, the probability of high school graduation declines by five percentage points; that of postsecondary degree attainment declines by six percentage points. For these students, earnings are 3 percent of a standard deviation lower. Persistent externalizing and internalizing behavior problems have some significant effects on outcomes, but these are much smaller in magnitude. (Surprisingly, persistent externalizing behavior problems are associated with earnings 3 percent of a standard deviation *higher* at age twenty-six. Perhaps aggressiveness and high energy have a positive value in the labor market.)

These results are broadly consistent with those of Duncan and Magnuson. In particular, we agree with them in finding that (1) persistent problems are much more important than intermittent problems for later outcomes, (2) the strongest effect on later outcomes is due to persistently low math test scores, with persistently low reading test scores exerting weaker effects, and (3) among behavior problems, the strongest effects are associated with persistent learning behavior problems, with externalizing and internalizing behavior problems exerting much smaller effects.

Figure 4.6 shows the association between enrollment in the nonacademic track and degree attainment and earnings. Because this enrollment is measured in tenth grade (after the measurement of eighth-grade skills and behaviors), we show the results in only two ways—with no controls and with the full set of control variables in the equation.

With no controls in the equation, nonacademic track enrollment is associated with a decrement of 14 percentage points in high school graduation, a decrement of 15.5 percentage points in postsecondary degree attainment, and a decrement of about 14 percent of a standard deviation in earnings at age twenty-six. These are substantial effects, larger than the compara-

FIGURE 4.6   *Effect of Nonacademic-Curriculum-Track Placement on High School Graduation, Postsecondary Degree Attainment, and Earnings*

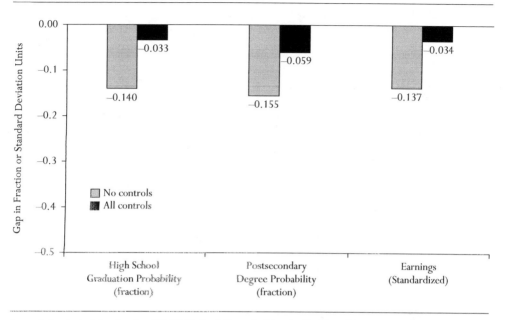

ble magnitudes for persistently low test scores, learning behavior, and externalizing behavior problems.

When the full set of control variables is added to the equation, these effects decline to about three percentage points, six percentage points, and 3 percent of a standard deviation, respectively. Although these are much smaller effects, they are similar in magnitude to the comparable effects of persistently low test scores and behavior problems. This is evidence that even after controlling for many correlated variables, nonacademic-track enrollment plays a significant role in decreasing later attainment.

Among the attitude variables, educational expectations have the most consistently significant effect on outcomes. This is particularly the case for high school and postsecondary degree attainment and is consistent with the emphasis placed on such expectations by the Wisconsin model of status attainment studies. However, as shown in figure 4.7, once all the control variables are added to the equation, the effect of an increase of one standard deviation in educational expectations declines to about three percentage points (high school or postsecondary degree attainment) or about 3 percent of a standard deviation (earnings). Thus, although higher educational expectations are associated with better outcomes, the unique effect of this variable appears to be modest in size. (For a detailed examination of the role of expectations in determining postsecondary enrollment, see chapter 7 of this volume, by Brian A. Jacob and Tamara Wilder Linkow.)

Thus far we have highlighted many of the larger effects found in the online appendix table regressions. These have been associated with SES, race and ethnicity, math and reading test scores, learning behaviors, curriculum-track enrollment, and educational expectations as predictors. Other findings are that when the full set of control variables is included in the equation, self-esteem and locus of control, measured in eighth grade, are rarely significant predictors of any of the outcomes. An exception is the significant positive effect of locus of control on earnings.

FIGURE 4.7   *Effect of a One-Standard-Deviation Increase in Educational Expectations on High School Graduation, Postsecondary Degree Attainment, and Earnings*

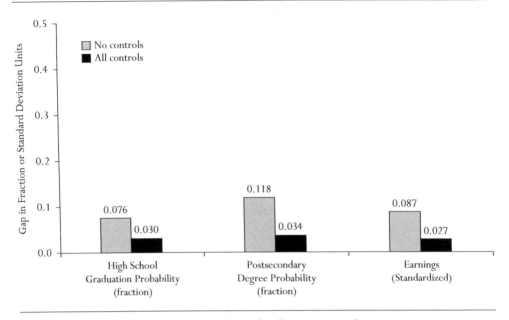

Source: Authors' calculations based on NELS88 (National Center for Education Statistics n.d.).

Our equations to predict being arrested (online appendix tables 4.A5 and 4.A6) generally show much smaller magnitudes of effect than for the other outcomes. However, the patterns are similar to those found by other researchers. Males have higher arrest rates than females. Lower test scores and higher externalizing and learning behavior problems are associated with higher arrest rates. Interestingly, we also find that a greater sense of personal control and higher educational expectations are associated with lower arrest rates.

DISCUSSION

For some years, an interdisciplinary paradigm has been emerging for the study of the school achievement of students from birth through postsecondary schooling and on into the labor market. This paradigm focuses on cognitive performance and learning-related behaviors as variables whose distributions differ across population subgroups and whose trajectories help to explain the different life outcomes experienced by these subgroups. The findings in this chapter are consistent with this paradigm. They show that by middle school, low-SES and ethnic minority students have lower test scores and learning-related behaviors than middle-class and white students, and that this fact is quite consequential for subsequent schooling and other outcomes. In particular, eighth- and tenth-grade test scores and learning behaviors play a significant role in determining high school and postsecondary degree attainment, as well as earnings at age twenty-six. Consistent with the theme of this volume, social-class differences in test score measures of cognitive performance are the largest sources of inequality in schooling and earnings achievement. Thus, the increases over time in the income-based test score gap documented by Reardon (chapter 5 of this volume) are particularly worrisome.

The results in this chapter also expand the interdisciplinary paradigm for thinking about the determinants and consequences of educational inequality. In particular, curriculum-track enrollment, but also a sense of personal control and educational expectations, are found to play a role in determining educational and earnings outcomes, even after controlling for test scores and learning-related behaviors. These variables also mediate the effects of social class and race and ethnicity on the outcomes. (For a more extensive analysis of the role of expectations in determining postsecondary enrollment, see chapter 7, in this volume.)

These findings should not be surprising. We are social beings inhabiting a social world. Everywhere in school, learning is mediated by social processes. In a recent *Science* article, the neuroscientists Andrew N. Meltzoff and colleagues (2009, 285) present "foundations for a new science of learning." Their interdisciplinary approach, drawing on neuroscience, education, psychology, and machine learning, emphasizes that learning is social and is supported by brain circuits linking perception and action. They emphasize "brain mechanisms supporting close coupling and attunement between the self and other" as a primary focus of the emerging field of social neuroscience. Curriculum-track enrollment affects the teacher and peer group "others" that the student interacts with. Educational expectations are formed by these and other interactions, in conjunction with the student's experiences, understanding of these experiences, goals, and calculations. Our results suggest that these processes of social interaction and expectation formation must be included in any comprehensive model of educational and labor market attainment.

The findings in this chapter also have implications for intervention programs aimed at improving the educational and labor-market outcomes of disadvantaged youths. A group of such interventions has focused on attempts to raise test scores, sometimes with disappointing results. Yet a recent study of career academies ("schools within a school") found that personalized social support from teachers and peers can significantly raise labor-market outcomes for at-risk males, even though no effect was observed on their test scores (Kemple 2008). This effect appears to have occurred via social interaction and attitude formation— the same types of variables that we have sought to add to the paradigm focused exclusively on test scores and learning behaviors. A rich amalgam of variables encompassing skills, behaviors, attitudes, and curriculum enrollment represents a potentially promising path toward theoretically and practically useful insights on the school and labor-market attainment process.

NOTES

Online appendix available at: http://www.russellsage.org/duncan_murnane_online_appendix.pdf.

1. See Jencks, Crouse, and Mueser (1979), chapter 5, for the use of the "noncognitive traits" label to refer to a wide-ranging set of attitudinal and behavioral variables.

2. Studies that include some but not all of these correlated variables include Rosenbaum (2001) and Downey, Ainsworth, and Qian (2009).

REFERENCES

Bandura, Albert. 1986. *Social Foundations of Thought and Action*. Englewood Cliffs, N.J.: Prentice Hall.

Blau, Peter, and Otis Dudley Duncan. 1967. *The American Occupational Structure*. New York: Wiley.

Bowles, Samuel, and Herbert Gintis. 1976. *Schooling in Capitalist America*. New York: Basic Books.

Brooks-Gunn, Jeanne, Greg Duncan, and J. Lawrence Aber. 1997. *Neighborhood Poverty: Context and Consequences for Children*. New York: Russell Sage Foundation.

Carbonaro, William. 2005. "Tracking, Student Effort, and Academic Achievement." *Sociology of Education* 78(1): 27–49.

Cunha, Flavio, and James J. Heckman. 2008. "Formulating, Identifying and Estimating the Technology of Cognitive and Noncognitive Skill Formation." *Journal of Human Resources* 43(4): 738–82.

Cunha, Flavio, James J. Heckman, Lance Lochner, and Dimitriy V. Masterov. 2006. "Interpreting the Evidence on Life Cycle Skill Formation." In *Handbook of the Economics of Education,* edited by Erik Hanushek and Finis Welch. Amsterdam: North-Holland.

Downey, Douglas B., James W. Ainsworth, and Zhenchao Qian. 2009. "Rethinking the Attitude-Achievement Paradox Among Blacks." *Sociology of Education* 82(1): 1–19.

Duncan, Greg J., and Rachel Dunifon. 1997. "Soft Skills and Long-Run Labor-Market Success." *Research in Labor Economics* 17: 1–42.

————. 1998. "Long-Run Effects of Motivation on Labor-Market Success." *Social Psychology Quarterly* 61(1): 33–48.

Duncan, Greg J., Chantelle J. Dowsett, Amy Claessens, Katherine Magnuson, Aletha C. Huston, Pamela K. Klebanov, Linda Pagani, Leon Feinstein, Mimi Engel, Jeanne Brooks-Gunn, Holly Sexton, Kathryn Duckworth, and Crista Japel. 2007. "School Readiness and Later Achievement." *Developmental Psychology* 43(6): 1428–46.

Dunifon, Rachel, Greg J. Duncan, and Jeanne Brooks-Gunn. 2001. "As Ye Sweep, So Shall Ye Reap." *American Economic Review* 91(2): 150–54.

Farkas, George. 1996. *Human Capital or Cultural Capital? Ethnicity and Poverty Groups in an Urban School District.* New York: Aldine de Gruyter.

————. 2003. "Cognitive Skills and Noncognitive Traits and Behaviors in Stratification Processes." *Annual Review of Sociology* 29: 541–62.

Farkas, George, Robert Grobe, Daniel Sheehan, and Yuan Shuan. 1990. "Cultural Resources and School Success: Gender, Ethnicity, and Poverty Groups Within an Urban School District." *American Sociological Review* 55(1): 127–42.

Gamoran, Adam, and Robert Mare. 1989. "Secondary School Tracking and Educational Inequality: Compensation, Reinforcement, or Neutrality." *American Journal of Sociology* 94(5): 1146–83.

Hallinan, Maureen. 2003. "Ability Grouping and Student Learning." In *Brookings Papers on Education Policy,* edited by Diane Ravitch. Washington, D.C.: Brookings Institution Press.

Heckman, James J., and Lance Lochner. 2000. "Rethinking Education and Training Policy: Understanding the Sources of Skill Formation in a Modern Economy." In *Securing the Future: Investing in Children from Birth to College,* edited by Sheldon Danziger and Jane Waldfogel. New York: Russell Sage Foundation.

Heckman, James J., and Yona Rubinstein. 2001. "The Importance of Noncognitive Skills: Lessons from the GED Testing Program." *American Economic Review* 91(2): 145–49.

Heckman, James J., Jora Stixrud, and Sergio Urzua. 2006. "The Effects of Cognitive and Noncognitive Abilities on Labor Market Outcomes and Social Behavior." *Journal of Labor Economics* 24(3): 411–82.

Jencks, Christopher, James Crouse, and Peter Mueser. 1979. *Who Gets Ahead? The Determinants of Economic Success in America.* New York: Basic Books.

Kemple, James. 2008. *Career Academies: Long-Term Impacts on Labor Market Outcomes, Educational Attainment, and Transitions to Adulthood.* New York: Manpower Demonstration Research Corporation.

Liu, Xiaoru, Howard B. Kaplan, and Will Risser. 1992. "Decomposing the Reciprocal Relationships Between Academic Achievement and General Self-Esteem." *Youth and Society* 24(2): 123–48.

Meltzoff, Andrew N., Patricia K. Kuhl, Javier Movellan, and Terrence J. Sejnowski. 2009. "Foundations for a New Science of Learning." *Science* 325(5938): 284–88.

Mirowsky, John, and Catherine E. Ross. 1998. "Education, Personal Control, Lifestyle and Health: A Human Capital Hypothesis." *Research on Aging* 20(4): 415–49.

Mone, Mark A., Douglas D. Baker, and Frank Jeffries. 1995. "Predictive Validity and Time Dependency of Self-Efficacy, Self-Esteem, Personal Goals, and Academic Achievement." *Educational and Psychological Measurement* 55(5): 716–27.

National Center for Education Statistics. n.d. *National Educational Longitudinal Study, 1988.* Available at: http://nces.ed.gov/surveys/nels88 (accessed May 3, 2011).

Rosenbaum, James E. 2001. *Beyond College for All: Career Paths for the Forgotten Half.* New York: Russell Sage Foundation.

Rosenberg, Morris. 1979. *Conceiving the Self.* New York: Basic Books.

————. 1989. *Society and the Adolescent Self-Image.* Middletown, Conn.: Wesleyan University Press.

Rosenberg, Morris, Carmi Schooler, and Carrie Schoenbach. 1989. "Self-Esteem and Adolescent Problems: Modeling Reciprocal Effects." *American Sociological Review* 54(6): 1004–18.

Ross, Catherine E., and Beckett A. Broh. 2000. "The Roles of Self-Esteem and the Sense of Personal Control in the Academic Achievement Process." *Sociology of Education* 73(4): 270–84.

Rotter, Julian B. 1966. "Generalized Expectancies for Internal vs. External Control of Reinforcements." *Psychological Monographs* 80(1): 1–28.

Rumberger, Russell W., and Gregory J. Palardy. 2004. "Multilevel Models for School Effectiveness Research." In *The Sage Handbook of Quantitative Methodology for the Social Sciences,* edited by David Kaplan. Thousand Oaks, Calif.: Sage.

Seeman, Melvin. 1983. "Alienation Motifs in Contemporary Theorizing: The Hidden Continuity of Classic Themes." *Social Psychology Quarterly* 46(3): 171–84.

Sewell, William H., Archibald O. Haller, and George W. Ohlendorf. 1970. "The Educational and Early Occupational Attainment Process: Replications and Revisions." *American Sociological Review* 35(6): 1014–27.

Sewell, William H., Archibald O. Haller, and Alejandro Portes. 1969. "The Educational and Early Occupational Attainment Process." *American Sociological Review* 34(1): 82–92.

Sewell, William H., and Robert M. Hauser. 1976. *Education, Occupation, and Earnings.* New York: Academic Press.

Swidler, Anne. 1986. "Culture in Action: Symbols and Strategies." *American Sociological Review* 51(2): 273–86.

Tach, Laura, and George Farkas. 2006. "Learning-Related Behaviors, Cognitive Skills, and Ability Grouping When Schooling Begins." *Social Science Research* 35(4): 1048–79.

Chapter 5

The Widening Academic Achievement Gap Between the Rich and the Poor: New Evidence and Possible Explanations

Sean F. Reardon

In this chapter I examine whether and how the relationship between family socio-economic characteristics and academic achievement has changed during the last fifty years. In particular, I investigate the extent to which the rising income inequality of the last four decades has been paralleled by a similar increase in the income-achievement gradient. As the income gap between high- and low-income families has widened, has the achievement gap between children in high- and low-income families also widened?

The answer, in brief, is yes. The achievement gap between children from high- and low-income families is roughly 30 to 40 percent larger among children born in 2001 than among those born twenty-five years earlier. In fact, it appears that the income achievement gap has been growing for at least fifty years, though the data are less certain for cohorts of children born before 1970. In this chapter, I describe and discuss these trends in some detail. In addition to the key finding that the income achievement gap appears to have widened substantially, there are a number of other important findings.

First, the income achievement gap (defined here as the income difference between a child from a family at the 90th percentile of the family income distribution and a child from a family at the 10th percentile) is now nearly twice as large as the black-white achievement gap. Fifty years ago, in contrast, the black-white gap was one and a half to two times as large as the income gap. Second, as Greg Duncan and Katherine Magnuson note in chapter 3 of this volume, the income achievement gap is large when children enter kindergarten and does not appear to grow (or narrow) appreciably as children progress through school. Third, although rising income inequality may play a role in the growing income achievement gap, it does not appear to be the dominant factor. The gap appears to have grown at least partly because of an increase in the association between family income and children's academic achievement for families above the median income level: a given difference in family incomes now corresponds to a 30 to 60 percent larger difference in achievement than it did for children born in the 1970s. Moreover, evidence from other studies suggests that this may be in part a result of increasing parental investment in children's cognitive development. Finally, the growing income achievement gap does not appear to be a result of a growing achievement gap between children with highly and less-educated parents. Indeed, the relationship between parental education and children's achievement has remained relatively stable during the last fifty years, whereas the relationship between income and achievement has grown sharply. Family income is now nearly as strong as parental education in predicting children's achievement.

The socioeconomic status of a child's parents has always been one of the strongest predictors of the child's academic achievement and educational attainment. As Greg Duncan and Katherine Magnuson point out in chapter 3 in this volume, students in the bottom quintile of family socioeconomic status score more than a standard deviation below those in the top quintile on standardized tests of math and reading when they enter kindergarten. They note that these differences do not appear to narrow as children progress through school.

Duncan and Magnuson are not the first to point out this strong association. Almost fifty years ago, in 1966, the Coleman Report famously highlighted the relationship between family socioeconomic status and student achievement (Coleman et al. 1966). The federal Head Start program was started in the 1960s as part of the War on Poverty to reduce poverty and thus to weaken the link between family poverty and children's cognitive and social development (Kagan 2002; Zigler and Muenchow 1992). The relationship between family socioeconomic characteristics and student achievement is one of the most robust patterns in educational scholarship, yet the causes and mechanisms of this relationship have been the subject of considerable disagreement and debate (see, for example, Bowles and Gintis 1976, 2002; Brooks-Gunn and Duncan 1997; Duncan and Brooks-Gunn 1997; Duncan, Brooks Gunn, and Klebanov 1994; Herrnstein and Murray 1994; Jacoby and Glauberman 1995; Lareau 1989, 2003).

An ironic consequence of the regularity of this pattern is that we tend to think of the relationship between socioeconomic status and children's academic achievement as a sociological necessity, rather than as the product of a set of social conditions, policy choices, and educational practices. As a result, much of the scholarly research on the socioeconomic achievement gradient has focused largely on trying to understand the mechanisms through which socioeconomic differences among families—in income, parental educational attainment, family structure, neighborhood conditions, school quality, and parental preferences, investments, and choices—lead to differences in children's academic and educational success. The bulk of this prior research has been based primarily on cross-sectional or single-cohort longitudinal studies. This research is less concerned with documenting the size of socioeconomic achievement gradients than with investigating the mechanisms that produce them.

As a result, we know little about the trends in socioeconomic achievement gaps over a lengthy period of time. We do not know, for example, if socioeconomic gaps are larger or smaller now than they were fifty years ago, or even twenty-five years ago. This is in contrast to what we know about the trends in racial-achievement gaps, particularly the black-white gap, which have received considerable scholarly and policy attention in the last decade or two (see, for example, Jencks and Phillips 1998; Magnuson and Waldfogel 2008). Trends in socioeconomic achievement gaps—the achievement disparities between children from high- and low-income families or between children from families with high or low levels of parental educational attainment—have received far less attention.

The question posed in this chapter is whether and how that relationship between family socioeconomic characteristics and academic achievement has changed during the last fifty years. In particular, I investigate the extent to which the rising income inequality of the last four decades has been paralleled by a similar increase in the income-achievement gradient. As the income gap between high- and low-income families has widened, has the achievement gap between children in high- and low-income families also widened?

The answer, in brief, is yes. The achievement gap between children from high- and low-income families is roughly 30 to 40 percent larger among children born in 2001 than among those born twenty-five years earlier. In fact, it appears that the income achievement gap has been growing steadily for at least fifty years, though the data are less certain for cohorts of children born before 1970. In this chapter I describe and discuss these trends in some detail. In addition to the key finding that the income achievement gap appears to have widened substantially, there are a number of other important findings.

First, the income achievement gap (defined here as the income difference between a child from a family at the 90th percentile of the family income distribution and a child from a family at the 10th percentile) is now more than twice as large as the black-white achievement gap. In contrast to this, fifty years ago the black-white gap was one and a half to two times as large as the income gap. Second, as Duncan and Magnuson (in chapter 3, this volume) note, the income achievement gap is large when children enter kindergarten and does not appear to grow (or narrow) appreciably as children progress through school. Third, although rising income inequality may play a role in the growing income achievement gap, it does not appear to be the dominant factor. The gap appears to have grown at least partly because of an increase in the association between family income and children's academic achievement for families above the median income level: a given difference in family incomes now corresponds to a 30 to 60 percent larger difference in achievement than it did for children born in the 1970s. Evidence from other studies suggests that this may be in part a result of increasing parental investment in children's cognitive development. Finally, the growing income achievement gap does not appear to be a result of a growing achievement gap between children with highly educated and less-educated parents. In fact, the relationship between parental education and children's achievement has remained relatively stable during the last fifty years, while the relationship between income and achievement has grown sharply. Family income is now nearly as strong as parental education in predicting children's achievement.

DATA

Assembling information on trends in the relationship between socioeconomic status and academic achievement requires examination of multiple sources of data. In this chapter I use data from nineteen nationally representative studies, including studies conducted by the National Center for Education Statistics (NCES), the Long-Term Trend and Main National Assessment of Educational Progress (NAEP) studies, U.S. components of international studies, and other studies with information on both family background and standardized-test scores.[1] Although these studies vary in a number of ways, each of them provides data on the math or reading skills, or both, of nationally representative samples of students, together with some data on students' family socioeconomic characteristics, such as family income, parental education, and parental occupation. Although the specific tests of reading and math skills used differ among the studies, they are similar enough to allow broad conclusions about the rough magnitude of achievement gaps. Online appendix table 5.A1 (available at: http://www.russellsage.org/duncan_murnane_online_appendix.pdf) lists the studies used here and several basic characteristics of each study, including the age and grade of students when tested, the year and subject in which they are tested, the approximate sample size, and whether or not the study includes data on family income.

Measuring Achievement Gaps

To compare the size of the achievement gap across studies, I report test-score differences between groups (for example, students from high- and low-income families) in standard-deviation units, adjusted for the estimated reliability of each test. This is standard practice when comparing achievement gaps measured with different tests (see, for example, Clotfelter, Ladd, and Vigdor 2006; Fryer and Levitt 2004, 2006; Grissmer, Flanagan, and Williamson 1998; Hedges and Nowell 1999; Neal 2006; Phillips et al. 1998; Reardon and Galindo 2009). So long as the true variance of achievement remains constant over time, this allows valid comparisons in the size of the gaps across different studies using different tests (see online appendix section 5.A2 for technical details of the computation of the achievement gaps reported here and for data on the reported reliabilities of the tests used).

Measures of Socioeconomic Status

In this chapter I rely on two key measures of socioeconomic status: family income and parental educational attainment. Each of the nineteen studies used includes information on parental educational attainment; twelve of the studies include information on family income. Nine of the studies include parent-reported family income: National Education Longitudinal Study (NELS), Education Longitudinal Study (ELS), Early Childhood Longitudinal Study, Kindergarten Cohort (ECLS-K), Early Childhood Longitudinal Study, Birth Cohort (ECLS-B), the 1979 and 1997 National Longitudinal Survey of Youth (NLSY79, NLSY97), National Longitudinal Study of Adolescent Health (Add Health), Prospects, and the Study of Early Child Care and Youth Development (SECCYD). Three include student-reported income: Project Talent, National Longitudinal Study (NLS), and High School and Beyond (HS&B).[2] In all studies, I adjust the estimated associations between family income and achievement for measurement error in family income. I do not adjust income for family size, as my interest here is in describing the simple association between family socioeconomic characteristics and student achievement, rather than an inferred association between income-to-needs ratio and achievement (though the latter is certainly worth investigating as well). Online appendix section 5.A2 describes in detail how I estimate income achievement gaps and adjust them for measurement error in family income and test scores.

Although each of the nineteen studies includes a measure of parental educational attainment, in some studies this is reported by students—National Assessment of Educational Progress, Long-Term Trends (NAEP-LTT), Main NAEP, Project Talent, NLS, Equality of Educational Opportunity study (EEO), HS&B, Trends in International Math and Science Study (TIMSS), Program for International Student Assessment (PISA), and the Progress in International Reading Literacy Study (PIRLS)—while in others it is reported by parents. Because reports of their parents' education are particularly unreliable for younger students, I include studies with student-reported parental education only if the students were in high school themselves when reporting their parents' educational attainment. As a measure of parental educational attainment, I use the maximum of the mother's and father's attainment (or the attainment of the single parent in the home if both are not present). Online appendix section 5.A2 describes how I estimate the association between parental education and achievement.

TRENDS IN SOCIOECONOMIC
STATUS-ACHIEVEMENT GRADIENTS

To begin with, consider the difference in achievement between children from high- and low-income families. One way to measure this difference is to compare the average math and reading skills of children from families with incomes at the 90th percentile of the family income distribution (about $160,000 in 2008) to those in families with incomes at the 10th percentile

FIGURE 5.1   *Trend in 90/10 Income Achievement Gap in Reading, by Birth Cohort (1943 to 2001 Cohorts)*

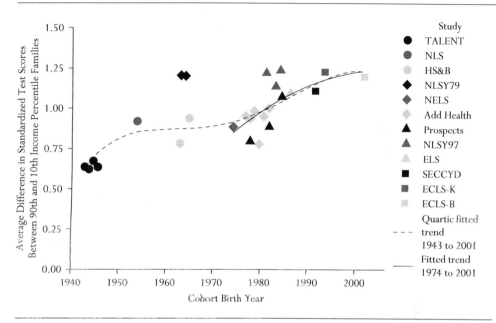

Source: Authors' compilation based on data from Project Talent (Flanagan et al. n.d.); NLS, HS&B, NELS, ELS, ECLS-K, ECLS-B (U.S. Department of Education, Center for Education Statistics 1999, 2000, 2001, 2004, 2009, 2010); Prospects (U.S. Department of Education 1995); NLSY79, NLSY97 (U.S. Bureau of Labor Statistics 1980, 1999); SECCYD (National Institute of Child Health and Human Development 2010); and Add Health (Harris 2009, reading only).
Note: See note 4 and online appendix for further details.

of the family income distribution (about $17,500 in 2008).[3] Hereafter I refer to this as the "90/10 income achievement gap."

Figures 5.1 and 5.2 present the estimated 90/10 income achievement gap for cohorts of students born from the mid-1940s through 2001.[4] These estimates are derived from the twelve nationally representative studies available that include family income as well as reading and/or math scores for school-age children.

Although the tests used are not exactly comparable across all the studies included, both figures show a clear trend of increasing income achievement gaps across cohorts born over a nearly sixty-year period. The estimated income achievement gaps among children born in 2001 are roughly 75 percent larger than the estimated gaps among children born in the early 1940s. The gap appears to have grown among cohorts born in the 1940s and early 1950s, stabilized for cohorts born from the 1950s through the mid-1970s, and then grown steadily since the mid-1970s.

There are, however, several reasons to suspect that the trend in the estimated gaps for the earliest cohorts, those born before 1970, is not as accurately estimated as the later trend. For one thing, the quality of the achievement tests used in the early studies may not have been as good as those used in the more recent studies. In addition, as I have noted, family income was reported by students rather than by a parent in three of the early studies (Project Talent, NLS, and HS&B). Furthermore, because Project Talent, NLS, and HS&B are school-based samples of students in high school, they exclude dropouts, who are disproportionately low-income and

FIGURE 5.2   *Trend in 90/10 Income Achievement Gap in Math, by Birth Cohort (1943 to 2001 Cohorts)*

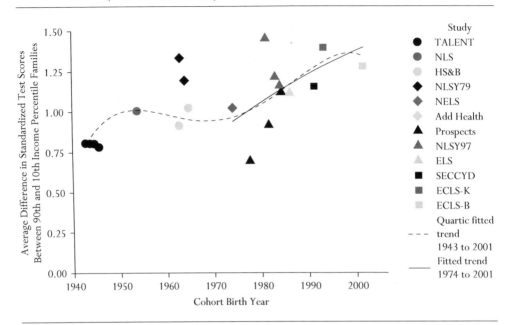

Source: Authors' compilation based on data from Project Talent (Flanagan et al. n.d.); NLS, HS&B, NELS, ELS, ECLS-K, ECLS-B (U.S. Department of Education, Center for Education Statistics 1999, 2000, 2001, 2004, 2009, 2010); Prospects (U.S. Department of Education 1995); NLSY79, NLSY97 (U.S. Bureau of Labor Statistics 1980, 1999); and SECCYD (National Institute of Child Health and Human Development 2010).
Note: See note 4 and online appendix for further details.

low-achieving students. Each of these factors might lead the gaps to be underestimated in the early cohorts relative to later cohorts.

Despite each of these concerns, there is also some evidence to suggest that they may not substantially bias the estimated trend in income achievement gaps. First, the estimated gaps are adjusted for the estimated reliabilities of the achievement test and the family income measures. Second, an assessment of the impact of excluding dropouts using data from the NELS, in which dropouts were tested, shows that excluding dropouts from the sample introduces at most a trivial amount of bias in the estimates (see online appendix section 5.A4). Third, if we focus only on the trend in the income gap in studies conducted by the National Center for Education Statistic (NCES), which use similar types of achievement tests (and many of the same test items), and ask parents to report their income in a similar way (except for NLS and HS&B, in which students reported their family income), the trend in the 90/10 achievement gap is clearly upward for cohorts born from the mid-1970s through at least the mid-1990s (see online appendix section 5.A4 and appendix table 5.A1 for details). And although the two NLSY studies suggest that the income achievement gap as measured in the NLSY97 cohort is virtually identical to the gap in the NLSY79 cohort, born twenty years earlier, the NLSY97 cohort was born in the early 1980s, just as the trend evident in the NCES studies appears to begin. Thus, the lack of an apparent trend in the income-achievement gap in the NLSY studies does not clearly contradict the evidence in the NCES studies of a rising gap among the 1980s and 1990s cohorts.

In sum, although the trend in achievement gaps prior to 1970 is somewhat unclear, the trend from the mid-1970s to 2001 appears relatively clear. Figures 5.1 and 5.2 include fitted trend lines from 1974 to 2001 (the solid lines); these indicate that the income achievement gap has grown by roughly 40 to 50 percent within twenty-five years, a very sizable increase.

One important question is whether the trend in the income achievement gap is driven by the changing racial and ethnic composition of the U.S. population. In additional analyses not shown here (see online appendix 5.A4), I find that the income achievement gap grew within the white, black, and Hispanic student populations separately, as well as within the population as a whole. For whites and Hispanics, the income achievement gap appears relatively stable through the mid-1970s and begins to grow rapidly thereafter; for blacks, the gap appears to grow steadily from the 1940s through 2001.

In chapter 6 in this volume, Martha J. Bailey and Susan M. Dynarski show that the association between family income and college completion grew very sharply between cohorts of women born in the 1960s and cohorts born in the early 1980s, but did not grow substantially among men in the same cohorts. One possible explanation for this pattern is that the association between income and achievement grew most sharply for women during this same time period. However, when I examine the income achievement gap trend separately for male and female students, I find virtually identical trends (see online appendix 5.A4). There is no evidence that the trend in the income achievement gradient varies by gender.

How Large Are These Gaps?

Figures 5.1 and 5.2 report income gaps in standard-deviation units. Although this is a metric familiar to researchers and one that is useful for comparing the size of gaps across studies using different tests, it may not be immediately obvious how large these gaps are in substantive terms. One way to get a sense of the size of the gaps is to compare them to the amount that an average student learns during the course of a year. Data from the NAEP indicate that the average student gains 1.2 to 1.5 standard deviations in math and reading between fourth and eighth grade and between 0.6 and 0.7 standard deviations in math and reading between eighth and twelfth grade.[5] Thus, a gap of 1 standard deviation is substantively very large, corresponding to roughly 3 to 6 years of learning in middle or high school.

Another way of getting a sense of how large these gaps are (and how meaningful their trend is) is to compare the income achievement gaps to contemporaneous black-white achievement gaps. The black-white achievement gap narrowed substantially among cohorts born from the mid-1950s through the mid-1970s—by roughly one-half a standard deviation—according to NAEP data (Grissmer et al. 1998; Hedges and Nowell 1998, 1999; Magnuson and Waldfogel 2008; Neal 2006). Other data show that black-white differences in IQ and adult vocabulary narrowed by a comparable amount over the same cohorts as well (Huang and Hauser 2001; Murray 2007).

Figures 5.3 and 5.4 display both the 90/10 income gaps (as shown in figures 5.1 and 5.2) and the black-white achievement gaps as estimated from the same samples.[6] In each figure the solid line indicates the fitted trend of the 90/10 income achievement gap. For comparison, the estimated black-white achievement gap from each study is displayed in the figure (the hollow circles), along with a fitted line (the dark dashed line) describing the trend in the black-white achievement gap during the same time period. For comparison, a third trend line is included in the figure—the estimated trend in black-white gaps as estimated from NAEP data. Because the NAEP-LTT tests are consistent over time (and the Main NAEP tests are relatively consistent over time), trends in the black-white gap estimated from NAEP data provide a more reliable trend than do the twelve studies that are used to estimate the income-gap trend.

FIGURE 5.3   *Comparison of Income and Black-White Reading-Gap Trends,*
1943 to 2001 Cohorts

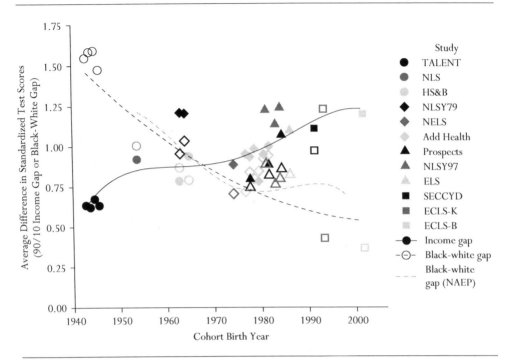

Source: Authors' compilation based on data from Project Talent (Flanagan et al. n.d.); NLS, NAEP, HS&B, NELS, ELS, ECLS-K,
ECLS-B (U.S. Department of Education, Center for Education Statistics n.d., 1999, 2000, 2001, 2004, 2005, 2009, 2010);
Prospects (U.S. Department of Education 1995); NLSY79, NLSY97 (U.S. Bureau of Labor Statistics 1980, 1999); SECCYD
(National Institute of Child Health and Human Development 2010); and Add Health (Harris 2009, reading only).
Note: Solid symbols represent 90/10 income achievement gaps; hollow symbols denote black-white achievement gaps. See note 6
and online appendix section 5.A5 for further details.

Both the NAEP data and the data from the twelve studies with income data show that the
black-white gap narrowed in reading and math for cohorts born prior to the mid-1970s. Following
the mid-1970s, the reading gap, as measured by NAEP, has remained relatively constant (see online
appendix section 5.A5 for some discussion of why the reading gap in the twelve income studies
appears to decline more in recent years than indicated by NAEP data). In math, both the NAEP
data and the data from the studies used to estimate the income gaps show a continued decline in
black-white achievement gaps among cohorts born in more recent years. The similarity of the
black-white trends estimated from NAEP and from the twelve studies used in the income-gap
analysis suggests that the tests used in the income studies are comparable to the NAEP tests, a
finding that lends increased credence to the estimated income-gap trends.

The striking feature of figures 5.3 and 5.4, however, is not so much the well-known trends
in the black-white gaps but the difference between the trends in the income gaps and the black-
white gaps. For cohorts born in the 1940s to the 1960s, the black-white achievement gap was
substantially larger than the 90/10 income achievement gap, particularly in reading. For cohorts
born in the 1970s and later, however, the opposite is true. Among children born in the last two
decades (those cohorts currently in school), the 90/10 income gap at kindergarten entry was
two to three times larger than the black-white gap at the same time.

FIGURE 5.4   *Comparison of Income and Black-White Math-Gap Trends, 1943 to 2001 Cohorts*

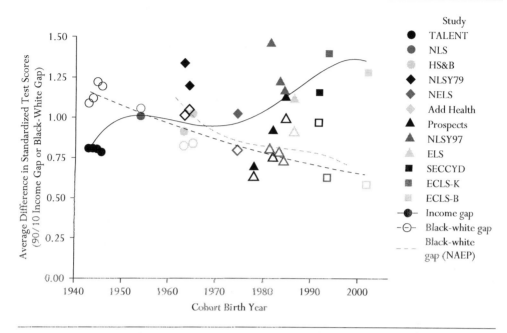

Source: Authors' compilation based on data from Project Talent (Flanagan et al. n.d.); NLS, NAEP, HS&B, NELS, ELS, ECLS-K, ECLS-B (U.S. Department of Education, Center for Education Statistics n.d., 1999, 2000, 2001, 2004, 2005, 2009, 2010); Prospects (U.S. Department of Education 1995); NLSY79, NLSY97 (U.S. Bureau of Labor Statistics 1980, 1999); SECCYD (National Institute of Child Health and Human Development 2010); and Add Health (Harris 2009, reading only).
Note: Solid symbols represent 90/10 income achievement gaps; hollow symbols denote black-white achievement gaps. See note 6 and online appendix section 5.A5 for further details.

THE DEVELOPMENT OF INCOME ACHIEVEMENT GAPS AS STUDENTS AGE

Figures 5.1 to 5.4 display the magnitude of the income achievement gaps in relation to the year students were born. The early studies focused largely on high school–age students (for example, Talent, NLS, HS&B, and NLSY79 are all high school samples). However, many of the later studies include younger students (ECLS-K, ECLS-B, SECCYD, and Prospects). As a result, it is possible that the trends displayed in figures 5.1 and 5.2 confound trends across cohorts with developmental changes as children age.

Figure 5.5 uses data from the eight cohorts of students (from six of the twelve studies) for whom longitudinal data are available to examine the extent to which the income achievement gaps change over time within individual cohorts. With the exception of the Prospects third-grade cohort, none of the samples shows evidence of a narrowing of the income achievement gap as children age. In fact, the income achievement gradient is remarkably stable across age within study samples. Figure 5.5 provides no evidence to support the hypothesis that the trends evident in figures 5.1 and 5.2 are artifacts of the inclusion of younger students in the more recent studies (this is tested more formally in online appendix section 5.A4; again there is no evidence that the varying age of the samples confounds the estimated trends).

The cohort trend in the size of the gap can be seen in the six studies with students ages fourteen to eighteen. Among these studies, the gaps are smallest in the early studies (HS&B, a cohort

FIGURE 5.5   *Income-Achievement Gradient, by Age and Subject, All Longitudinal Studies*

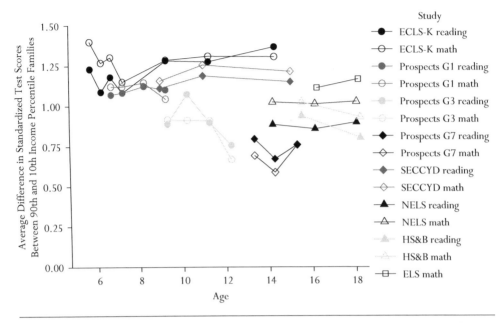

Source: Authors' compilation based on data from HS&B, NELS, ELS, ECLS-K (U.S. Department of Education, Center for Education Statistics 2000, 2001, 2004, 2010); Prospects (U.S. Department of Education 1995); and SECCYD (National Institute of Child Health and Human Development 2010).

born in 1964; NELS, a cohort born in 1974) and largest in the studies from later cohorts (ELS, a cohort born in 1986; SECCYD, a cohort born in 1990; and ECLS-K, a cohort born in 1992).[7]

WHY HAS THE INCOME ACHIEVEMENT GAP GROWN?

The evidence thus far indicates that the relationship between a family's position in the income distribution and their children's academic achievement has grown substantially stronger during the last half-century. In the following section I discuss four broad possible explanations for this increase: (1) income inequality has grown during the last forty years, meaning that the income difference between families at the 90th and 10th percentiles of the income distribution has grown; (2) family investment patterns have changed differentially during the last half-century, so that high-income families now invest relatively more time and resources in their children's cognitive development than do lower-income families; (3) income has grown more strongly correlated with other socioeconomic characteristics of families, meaning that high-income families increasingly have greater socioeconomic and social resources that may benefit their children; and (4) increasing income segregation has led to greater differentiation in school quality and schooling opportunities between the rich and the poor.

Rising Income Inequality

After decades of decline, income inequality in the United States has grown substantially in the last four decades and as of 2007 was at a level similar to the levels in 1925 to 1940, when U.S.

FIGURE 5.6   *Trends in Family-Income Inequality Among School-Age Children, 1967 to 2008 (Weighted by Number of School-Age Children)*

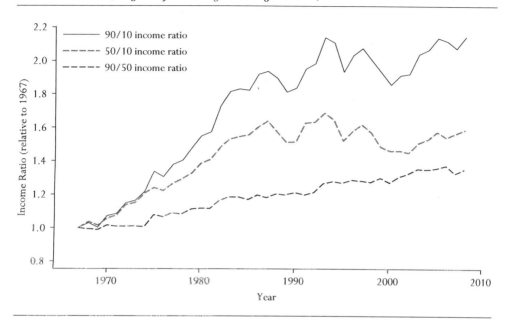

Source: Authors' calculations, based on U.S. Bureau of the Census (King et al. 2010).
Note: Each line shows the trends in the ratio of household incomes at two percentiles of the income distribution. All trends are divided by their value in 1967 in order to put the trends on a common scale.

income inequality was at its twentieth-century peak (Burkhauser et al. 2009; Piketty and Saez 2003, 2008).[8] Rising income inequality may affect income achievement gaps, though I am aware of no existing research investigating this using U.S. data (one study looking at the relationship between income inequality and educational attainment gaps in the United States is Mayer 2001). Existing cross-national studies show little or no relationship between national income inequality and socioeconomic achievement gaps, though this research typically is based on samples with little variance in income inequality and weak measures of family socioeconomic status (Dupriez and Dumay 2006; Dura-Bellat and Suchaut 2005; Marks 2005).

If rising income inequality is responsible for the growth in the income achievement gap, we would expect to see that gap grow in a pattern similar to the growth in income inequality. To investigate this, consider the trends in measures of family income inequality illustrated in figure 5.6, which shows the changes in the 90/10 family income ratio (the ratio of the family income of the child at the 90th percentile of the family income distribution to that of the child at the 10th percentile), the 90/50 family income ratio, and the 50/10 family income ratio among school-age children from 1967 to 2008.[9]

Several key trends are evident in figure 5.6. First, the 90/10 family income ratio grew rapidly from 1967 to the early 1990s, more than doubling in twenty-five years. In 1967, the family income of the child at the 90th percentile of the family income distribution was 4.6 times greater than that of the child at the 10th percentile; in 1993 this 90/10 ratio was 9.9. After 1993, the 90/10 ratio declined to 8.6 in 2000 before climbing again to 9.9 by 2005. Second, the growth in the ratio of the incomes in the 90th to those in the 10th percentiles from 1967 to 1993

FIGURE 5.7   *Trend in 90/50 and 50/10 Income Achievement Gap, Reading, by Birth Year*
                  (1943 to 2001 Cohorts)

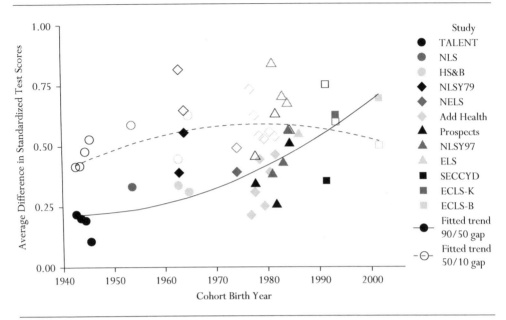

Source: Authors' compilation based on data from Project Talent (Flanagan et al. n.d.); NLS, HS&B, NELS, ELS, ECLS-K,
ECLS-B (U.S. Department of Education, Center for Education Statistics 1999, 2000, 2001, 2004, 2009, 2010); Prospects
(U.S. Department of Education 1995); NLSY79, NLSY97 (U.S. Bureau of Labor Statistics 1980, 1999); SECCYD (National
Institute of Child Health and Human Development 2010); and Add Health (Harris 2009, reading only).
Note: Solid symbols represent 90/50 income achievement gaps; hollow symbols represent 50/10 income achievement gaps.

was driven largely by a rapid increase in the 50/10 family income ratio, which grew from 2.5 in
1967 to 4.1 in 1987, a 64 percent increase in twenty years. After the late 1980s, however, the
50/10 family income ratio leveled off and then declined to 3.6 by 2002. Third, the ratio between
the 90th and the 50th family income percentiles grew steadily from the early 1970s through
2008, increasing from 1.8 in 1974 to 2.5 in 2005, an increase of 36 percent. Thus, from the late
1960s through the late 1980s, the increase in lower-tail family income inequality was largely
responsible for the increase in the ratio between the incomes of the 90th and 10th percentiles.
After the late 1980s, however, increasing upper-tail inequality and decreasing lower-tail
inequality largely offset one another for the next twenty years.

    If the increasing income achievement gap is driven by increasing income inequality, we would
expect that gap to grow most sharply between students at the 50th and 10th percentiles of the family income distribution from the 1960s through the 1980s (or for cohorts born in these years), and
then to grow among those at the high end of the income distribution after that. Moreover, because
the 50/10 ratio is larger than the 90/50 ratio, we might expect the 50/10 income-achievement gap
to be larger than the 90/50 income-achievement gap as well.[10] Figures 5.7 and 5.8 display the estimated 90/50 and 50/10 income-achievement gaps for each of the studies with income data.

    Figures 5.7 and 5.8 do not exactly conform to what we would expect if the growing income
achievement gap were simply due to rising income inequality among families with school-age
children. Although the 50/10 income achievement gap in reading is generally larger than the
90/50 income achievement gap for cohorts born before 1990, the gaps are roughly similar in
size in math, and the 90/50 gap is actually equal or larger than the 50/10 gap in the most recent

FIGURE 5.8   *Trends in 90/50 and 50/10 Income Achievement Gap in Math, by Birth Year (1943 to 2001 Cohorts)*

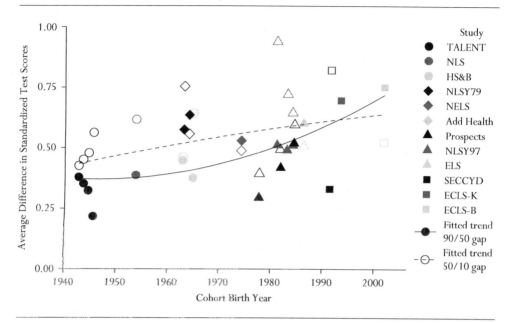

Source: Authors' compilation based on data from Project Talent (Flanagan et al. n.d.); NLS, HS&B, NELS, ELS, ECLS-K, ECLS-B (U.S. Department of Education, Center for Education Statistics 1999, 2000, 2001, 2004, 2009, 2010); Prospects (U.S. Department of Education 1995); NLSY79, NLSY97 (U.S. Bureau of Labor Statistics 1980, 1999); and SECCYD (National Institute of Child Health and Human Development 2010).
Note: Solid symbols represent 90/50 income achievement gaps; hollow symbols represent 50/10 income achievement gaps.

cohorts. Moreover, the 90/50 gap appears to have grown faster than the 50/10 gap during the 1970s and 1980s, the opposite of what we would predict on the basis of the rates of growth of the 90/50 and 50/10 income ratios (indeed, the 50/10 gap in reading appears to have been basically flat through this time period, when the 50/10 income ratio was growing most rapidly). In sum, figures 5.7 and 5.8 do not provide much support for the idea that the growing income achievement gap is attributable to rising income inequality, at least not in any simple sense. Nor, however, do they rule out the possibility that rising income inequality has contributed to the rising income achievement gap.

One complexity in investigating the relationship between income inequality and income-achievement gaps is that it is unclear how the relationships among income, achievement, and income inequality unfold through childhood and adolescence. Moreover, few of the studies I use have information on family income throughout a child's life, so I cannot disentangle the associations among family income and income inequality during childhood, family income and income inequality at the age when a child is tested, and a student's test scores. Rather, the trends described here are best understood as a set of repeated cross-sectional snapshots of the association between a child's current family income and his or her current academic achievement. Certainly, a more thorough understanding of the relationship between family income during different phases of childhood and later achievement would add to our understanding of the trends evident above, but the data available do not permit such an analysis.

In addition, the analyses presented here show the association between a child's family income rank (as opposed to income measured in dollars) and his or her academic achievement.

Given that income inequality has risen for the last thirty to forty years, a given difference in income ranks corresponds to a much larger difference in actual income (whether measured in dollars or logged dollars), as is evident in figure 5.6. Thus, if achievement were a constant function of dollars, we would expect a growing 90/10 income-achievement gap even if the association between income (measured in dollars or logged dollars) remained constant. In online appendix sections 5.A6 and 5.A7, I describe a set of analyses designed to determine to what extent the growth of the income achievement gap is due to rising income inequality and to what extent it is due to the increasing association between income and achievement. That is, I investigate whether the children of the rich score higher than the children of the poor because the income difference between the rich and poor is so much larger than it used to be, or because the relationship between achievement and dollars of income has grown stronger. Does a dollar buy more achievement than it did before, or do the rich just have more dollars than they did before?

These analyses, although not conclusive, suggest that the growth of the income achievement gap is not explained solely by rising income inequality. Rather, the association if achievement with family income (in logged dollars) has grown stronger over time, particularly among families in the upper half of the income distribution. That is, the average difference in academic achievement between two children from above-median income families whose family incomes differ by a factor of 2 has grown substantially (by 30 to 60 percent) over the last several decades. Moreover, in regression models that estimate the trend in the 90/10 income achievement gap, the time trend remains roughly constant in size, albeit with a larger standard error, regardless of whether or how I control for income inequality. Together, these analyses suggest that it is not rising income inequality per se that has caused the income-achievement gap; rather, a dollar of income (or factors correlated with income) appears to buy more academic achievement than it did several decades ago.

Differential Investments in Children's Cognitive Development

The evidence showing that the returns to income have grown, at least among higher-income families, suggests that families may be changing how they invest in their children's cognitive development. If so, this may explain some of the rising income achievement gap. Sociologists and historians of the family have argued that parents, particularly those in the middle class, have become increasingly focused on children's cognitive development during the last fifty years (Lareau 1989; Schaub 2010; Wrigley 1989). Evidence for this shift is necessarily indirect, yet it is fairly compelling. Julia Wrigley (1989), for example, examined the types of parenting advice contained in 1,017 articles published in popular magazines between 1900 and 1985 to assess whether societal notions of childhood and the role of parents had changed during the twentieth century. She found that articles published in the early part of the century were largely written by medical doctors and focused overwhelmingly on medical and nutritional advice. Prior to 1930, fewer than one in six of the articles Wrigley addressed the issue of intellectual stimulation of babies, and many of these argued that intellectual stimulation was actually harmful. Children were seen in these articles as largely "vegetative" beings, and the primary role of parents was to keep them healthy and quiet. Wrigley found that a focus on the intellectual development of children became much more prominent beginning in 1960s. Almost half of all parenting articles published in popular magazines between 1960 and 1985 discuss the intellectual development of children, more than double the proportion in the 1950s. Although some of this shift was driven by the era's interest in social inequality and the need for compensatory preschool education for poor children, Wrigley argues that children's cognitive development quickly became a concern of middle-class parents as well, as these parents increasingly saw education as essential for later economic success.

Another factor that may contribute to parents' increasing focus on their children's cognitive development is the rise of test-based accountability systems in education. Although some forms of standardized testing, including IQ tests and the SAT, have been prevalent for much of the twentieth century (Lemann 1999), standardized achievement testing has become much more common with the rise of the accountability movement following the 1983 publication of *A Nation at Risk* (National Commission on Excellence in Education 1983). The combination of the increasing importance of educational success in determining earnings (Levy and Murnane 1992) and the increasing importance of test scores in defining educational success may have caused parents to focus more on their children's cognitive development.

Although both middle-class and low-income parents may have become increasingly aware of the intellectual development of their children, Annette Lareau (1989, 2003) argues that middle- and upper-class parents engage much more commonly in what she calls "concerted cultivation"—the deliberate organization of childhood around intellectual and socioemotional development. If this concerted cultivation is effective at improving children's intellectual skills—at least, those measured by standardized tests—then this may contribute to the rising income achievement gap.

If middle- and upper-income families are increasingly likely to invest in their children's cognitive development, we would expect to see evidence of this in the trends in parental investment in children's child care, education, and education-related activities. There is, however, little available evidence with which to test this hypothesis. Studies of parental time use show that highly educated and higher-income parents spend more time in child-care activities with their children than do less-educated and lower-income children (Guryan, Hurst, and Kearney 2008; Ramey and Ramey 2010). Moreover, the amount of time parents spend in child-care activities (broadly defined) has increased from 1965 to 2008 and has increased more for college-educated parents than for less-educated parents (Bianchi 2000; Ramey and Ramey 2010). In addition, in a recent paper using data from the Consumer Expenditure Survey, Sabino Kornrich and Frank Furstenburg (2010) find that families' spending on children increased substantially from 1972 to 2007, particularly among high-income and college-educated families. Spending increases were particularly sharp among families with preschool-age children. Consistent with this is evidence that the relationship between family income and preschool enrollment among three- and four-year-old children grew from the late 1960s to the late 1980s (Bainbridge et al. 2005). These patterns are broadly consistent with the hypothesis that the rising income achievement gap is at least partly driven by the increasing investment of upper-income families in their children's cognitive development, particularly during the preschool years, though the evidence is far from conclusive on this point.

Changes in the Relationships Among Family Income, Family Socioeconomic Characteristics, and Children's Achievement

Another possible explanation for the rising income-achievement gap is that high-income families not only have more income than low-income families but also have access to a range of other family and social resources. On average, families with higher incomes tend to be those in which the parent(s) are highly educated. This has long been true, though the link between parental educational attainment and family income has grown stronger in recent decades, as the wage returns to educational attainment have increased since 1979 (Levy and Murnane 1992). Because highly educated parents are more able and more likely than less-educated parents to provide

FIGURE 5.9   *Trend in Correlation Between Parental Education and Family Income (1943 to 2001 Cohorts)*

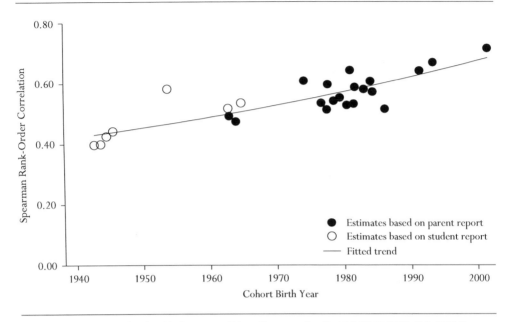

Source: Authors' compilation based on data from Project Talent (Flanagan et al. n.d.); NLS, HS&B, NELS, ELS, ECLS-K, ECLS-B (U.S. Department of Education, Center for Education Statistics 1999, 2000, 2001, 2004, 2009, 2010); Prospects (U.S. Department of Education 1995); NLSY79, NLSY97 (U.S. Bureau of Labor Statistics 1980, 1999); SECCYD (National Institute of Child Health and Human Development 2010); and Add Health (Harris 2009, reading only).
Note: See note 12 for further details.

resources and opportunities for their children to develop cognitive and academic skills in both the preschool years and the school-age years (Lareau 1989), children of parents with college degrees may have higher academic achievement, on average, than children of parents with lower levels of education, all else being equal. Thus, the income achievement gap may be partly a result of the effects of parental educational attainment.

This argument suggests two possible explanations for the rising income achievement gap. First, the trend may result from an increase in the correlation between parental educational attainment and family income—which would mean that high- and low-income families are increasingly differentiated by education levels, leading to larger differences in children's achievement. Second, the trend may derive from an increase in the achievement returns to parental education, net of income. This would mean that children of highly educated parents benefit more from their parents' educational attainment than they did in the past.

The trend in the correlation between family income and parental education is illustrated in figure 5.9, which shows a relatively unambiguous trend of increasing correlation between parental education and family income across cohorts.[11] There are several possible explanations for this trend. First, as Frank Levy and Richard Murnane (1992) point out, changes in the structure of the economy and the composition of the labor force during the 1970s and 1980s, along with declines in the real minimum wage and the weakening of unions, resulted in a decline in the real wages of those with only a high-school degree and an increase in the wage premium for a college degree. These changes would be reflected in the studies of cohorts born in the 1950s through the 1970s because these students and their parents were surveyed in the 1970s and 1980s. It is not clear, however, whether this explanation can account for the continued increase in the correlation between income and education for studies conducted after the 1980s.

A second possible reason for increasing correlation between parental education and income is the increasing polarization of families. Sara McLanahan (2004) argues that trends since 1960 in family structure and composition have led to an increasingly polarized distribution of family contexts for children—mothers with low levels of education are increasingly likely to be young, unemployed, and single or divorced; mothers with high levels of education are, conversely, increasingly likely to be older, employed, and married. As a result, the correlation of parental education and income among families with children is likely to increase with time. Moreover, McLanahan argues, this polarization in family structure implies a corresponding polarization in key resources (income, parental time) available for children, which may have important implications for the distribution of children's academic achievement.

Related to this argument is the fact that marital homogamy (the tendency for individuals to marry those with similar levels of educational attainment) has increased substantially since 1960 (Schwartz and Mare 2005). As a result, in two-parent families, the educational attainment of the higher-educated parent is increasingly predictive of the educational attainment of the less-educated spouse. This trend, coupled with the increasing disparity in single parenthood and employment between mothers with high and low levels of education described by McLanahan, and the increasing wage premium to education described by Levy and Murnane, implies that children with one highly educated parent are increasingly likely to have two highly educated, married parents and a high family income, while children with one less-educated parent are increasingly likely to live either with a single mother or with two parents, both with low levels of education and low wages.

Given the increasing correlation of parental educational attainment and family income, we might expect the association between parental education and children's achievement to grow with time in the same way that the income achievement gap does. This does not, however, appear to be the case. Online appendix section 5.A8 describes a set of analyses of the trends in the association between parental educational attainment and math and reading scores from all available studies. On the whole, the data suggest that the association between parental educational attainment and student achievement has not changed dramatically during the last fifty years, though there is some evidence that it may be increasing in recent decades.

Because income and parental education are correlated, and increasingly so with time, as shown in figure 5.9, I conduct a set of analyses to determine whether the growth in the income achievement gap is due to increases in the association between income and achievement or parental education and achievement. For each study with measures of both family income and parental education, I estimate the association between income and achievement, controlling for parental education, and the association between parental education and achievement, controlling for family income (see online appendix section 5.A8). These partial associations are shown in figures 5.10 and 5.11.

The key result evident in figures 5.10 and 5.11 is that the income coefficient grew steeply for cohorts born from the 1940s to 2000. The income coefficient for reading increased fourfold during this period, and it more than doubled for math. At the same time, the parental-education coefficient has been generally unchanged during the six decades of cohorts in the studies. Even if we focus only on the cohorts born since the mid-1970s, the income coefficient has increased substantially, more than doubling in reading and increasing more than 50 percent in math. In this same time period, the coefficient on educational attainment appears to have grown as well, albeit at a slower rate.

FIGURE 5.10   *Estimated Partial Associations Between Reading Test Scores and Both Income and Parental Education, by Birth Cohort (1943 to 2001 Cohorts)*

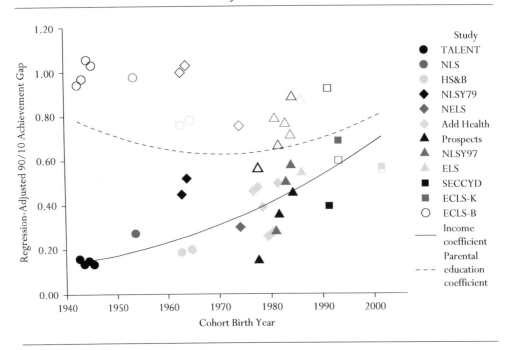

Source: Authors' compilation based on data from Project Talent (Flanagan et al. n.d.); NLS, HS&B, NELS, ELS, ECLS-K, ECLS-B (U.S. Department of Education, Center for Education Statistics 1999, 2000, 2001, 2004, 2009, 2010); Prospects (U.S. Department of Education 1995); NLSY79, NLSY97 (U.S. Bureau of Labor Statistics 1980, 1999); and SECCYD (National Institute of Child Health and Human Development 2010).
Note: Solid symbols represent regression-adjusted 90/10 income coefficients; hollow symbols represent regression-adjusted parental education coefficients. See note 12 for further details.

It is instructive to compare the trends in figures 5.10 and 5.11 with those in figures 5.1 and 5.2 and those in online appendix figures 5.A19 and 5.A20; because each of these figures reports estimated gaps between a child at the 90th and 10th percentiles of the income or educational-attainment distribution, the magnitudes of the coefficients can be directly compared. First, note that income accounts for relatively little of the gap in achievement between children from families with more- and less-educated parents (this is evident by comparing the unadjusted gaps in figures A19 and A20 to the adjusted gaps in figures 5.10 and 5.11). For cohorts from the 1940s through 2001, family income and race together account for generally less than 20 percent of the association between parental education and achievement. Parental education, however, accounts for a large proportion of the association between income and achievement in the early cohorts, but that proportion declines across cohorts (this is evident by comparing the unadjusted gaps in figures 5.1 and 5.2 to the adjusted gaps in figures 5.10 and 5.11). In reading, for example, parental education accounts for roughly 60 to 80 percent of the income-achievement gap in the studies of cohorts born in the 1940s, 1950s, and 1960s. But among cohorts born between 1980 and 2001, parental education and race explain only 40 to 60 percent of the income gap. The trend is similar, but weaker, for math. This pattern is at odds with the explanation that the growing income gap is due to the increasing correlation of income and parental education: all else being equal, we would expect the increasing correlation between the two to mean that education should explain more of the income gap over time, not less.

FIGURE 5.11   *Estimated Partial Associations Between Math Test Scores and Both Income and Parental Education, by Birth Cohort (1943 to 2001 Cohorts)*

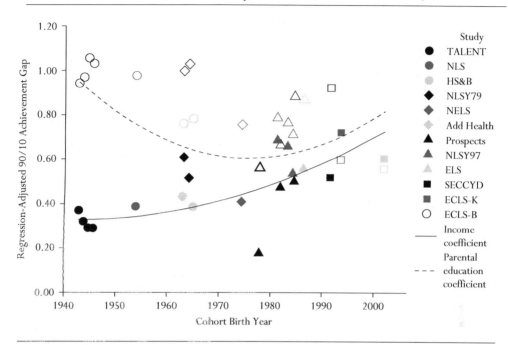

Source: Authors' compilation based on data from Project Talent (Flanagan et al. n.d.); NLS, HS&B, NELS, ELS, ECLS-K, ECLS-B (U.S. Department of Education, Center for Education Statistics 1999, 2000, 2001, 2004, 2009, 2010); Prospects (U.S. Department of Education 1995); NLSY79, NLSY97 (U.S. Bureau of Labor Statistics 1980, 1999); and SECCYD (National Institute of Child Health and Human Development 2010).

Note: Solid symbols represent regression-adjusted 90/10 income coefficients; hollow symbols represent regression-adjusted parental education coefficients. See note 12 for further details.

A second lesson evident in figures 5.10 and 5.11 is that the association between parental education and children's academic achievement, controlling for family income and race, remains larger than the association between family income and achievement, controlling for parental education and race. That is, although the association between income and achievement has grown rapidly during the last fifty years, parental educational attainment is still a more powerful predictor of student achievement than is family income.[12]

Increased Segregation by Income

A final possible explanation for the rising income achievement gap is the pattern of increasing income segregation during the last forty years. Several recent studies have found that residential segregation by income increased from 1970 to 2000, partly as a result of rising income inequality and likely partly as a result of low-income housing policy (Jargowsky 1996; Reardon and Bischoff 2011; Watson 2009). In particular, rising income inequality has led to the increasing segregation of high-income families from middle- and low-income families; high-income families increasingly live spatially far from the middle class (Reardon and Bischoff 2011). Because residential patterns are closely linked to school-attendance patterns, the rise of residential income segregation has likely led to a concurrent rise in school segregation by income, though there is little empirical evidence on this.[13] Because the growth in income segregation has been largely a result of increasing segregation of the affluent, this might explain the pattern of the rising association between income and achievement among higher-income families.

Greater residential income segregation may affect the school-quality differential between high- and low-income students, because high-income parents are better able to garner resources for their schools. Likewise, increased income segregation may lead to less variance of test scores within schools and more variance of test scores between schools, given that higher-income students generally have higher scores than lower-income students.[14]

It is not clear, however, that these factors would lead to increases in the income achievement gap. The evidence on the effects of school socioeconomic composition is somewhat weak, though a new study taking advantage of quasi-random variation in school poverty rates experienced by low-income students in Montgomery County, Maryland, finds evidence that low-income students perform better on math tests after moving to low-poverty schools (Schwartz 2010). Likewise, some studies of peer effects find evidence that the academic-achievement level of one's classmates may impact one's own achievement (for recent evidence, see Lavy, Silma, and Weinhardt 2009). Nonetheless, the evidence is far from clear if, how, and how much differences among schools in peers and school quality may affect achievement. As a result, there is little evidence to answer the question of whether rising income segregation has played a role in the increasing income achievement gap.

CONCLUSION

Most, but not all, of the evidence presented in this chapter suggests that the achievement gap between children from high- and low-income families has grown substantially in recent decades. The income achievement gap is now considerably larger than the black-white gap, a reversal of the pattern fifty years ago. In some ways, this is not surprising. The 1950s and 1960s were characterized by historically low levels of income inequality and high levels of racial inequality, not only in educational achievement and attainment but in access to educational opportunity, labor markets, housing markets, and health care. Beginning in the 1970s, this pattern began to reverse. Efforts to desegregate schools and hospitals, affirmative-action programs, enforcement of fair housing laws, and gradual but important changes in racial attitudes all led to reductions in the stark racial disparities of the 1950s and 1960s. Although racial disparities are still manifestly evident in many aspects of U.S. society, these disparities are considerably smaller in many ways than they were fifty years ago.

At the same time, however, income inequality in the United States began to grow sharply in the 1970s, a trend that continues to the present. The gap between the rich and the poor has widened significantly, particularly among families with children. Moreover, the Reagan-era changes in social policy—particularly changes in housing policies, income-support policies, and other social safety nets for low-income families (Katz 1989, 1995)—have made life much more difficult for low-income families. Not only do the poor have less money than they did before, they may have fewer social support systems as well.

It is tempting to read this chapter as evidence of a profound shift from a society in which race is more consequential than family income to one in which family income appears more determinative than race. Certainly the trends in the income- and racial-achievement gaps are consistent with this explanation. The fact that the relationship between parental education and achievement has changed relatively little during the same time period is consistent with this as well, suggesting that income, not human capital (at least as measured by parental education), is the important socioeconomic factor at work.

However, many of the other patterns in this chapter are not fully consistent with the simple explanation that income inequality has driven these trends. First, the analyses described in the chapter and the online appendix show that the income achievement gaps do not grow in the ways that would be predicted by the changes in income inequality. Although income inequality grew sharply for families with below-median incomes during the 1970s and 1980s, the income-achievement gap among children from these families was largely unchanged. The achievement gap did grow among children from above-median-income families, but this appears to be better explained by an increase in the association between income and achievement, not by increases in income inequality. Evidence from other studies suggests that parental investment in their children's cognitive development has grown during the last half-century, particularly for higher-income families, a pattern that may explain the growing returns to income during this time period.

There are a number of other possible explanations for the evident trends in the income achievement gap. Education policy increasingly focuses on standardized-test scores as outcome measures for schools; as these scores become more important, families may be increasingly likely to invest in improving their children's scores. Likewise, cultural perceptions of the role of parents have changed throughout the twentieth century to focus increasingly on early-childhood cognitive and psychological development, which may lead parents with resources to invest more in their young children's development.

In sum, the forces at work behind the rising income achievement gap are likely complex and interconnected. Certainly more research to understand the causes of these trends is necessary. Equally important, however, is research to understand the consequences of these patterns. At the same time that family income has become more predictive of children's academic achievement, so have educational attainment and cognitive skills become more predictive of adults' earnings. The combination of these trends creates a feedback mechanism that may decrease intergenerational mobility. As the children of the rich do better in school, and those who do better in school are more likely to become rich, we risk producing an even more unequal and economically polarized society.

I appreciate the thoughtful feedback and comments from Richard Murnane, Greg Duncan, Sandy Jencks, and participants in seminars at the Brookings Institution, Stanford University, University of Virginia, Teachers College (Columbia University), New York University, Northwestern University, University of Chicago, Harvard University, Georgetown University, and Johns Hopkins University. This work would not have been possible without support from the Brookings Institution, the Russell Sage Foundation, and the Spencer Foundation, as well as excellent research assistance from Demetra Kalogrides, Anna Katyn Chmielewski, Elena Grewal, and Matt Kasman. Any errors are my own.

NOTES

Online appendix available at: http://www.russellsage.org/duncan_murnane_online_appendix.pdf.
1. The included NCES studies are the National Longitudinal Study (NLS), High School and Beyond (HS&B), the National Education Longitudinal Study (NELS), the Education Longitudinal Study (ELS), the Early Childhood Longitudinal Study, Kindergarten Cohort (ECLS-K), and the Early Childhood Longitudinal Study, Birth Cohort (ECLS-B). The included international studies are the Third International Mathematics and Science Study (TIMSS), the Program of International Assessment (PISA), and the Progress in International Reading Study (PIRLS). The additional included studies are the National Longitudinal Survey of Youth: 1979 (NLSY79), the National Longitudinal Survey of Youth: 1997 (NLSY97), Prospects: The Congressionally Mandated Study of Educational Growth and Opportunity (Prospects), the National Longitudinal Study of Adolescent Health

(Add Health), the Longitudinal Survey of American Youth (LSAY), the NICHD Study of Early Child Care and Youth Development (SECCYD), the Equality of Educational Opportunity study (EEO), and Project Talent.

2. The names of these studies are provided in full in note 1. Although HS&B includes parent-reported family income for a subsample of roughly 15 percent of the full sample, the measure of family income appears highly unreliable (see online appendix 5.A2 for detail). I rely instead on the student-reported family income measure for HS&B, as described in online appendix 5.A2. NLSY79 includes parent-reported income for subjects who live with their parents; I use only the sample of sixteen- to eighteen-year-olds from NLSY79 for this reason.

3. My calculations, based on 2009 Current Population Survey data. See online appendix section 5.A3 for details.

4. Figures 5.1 and 5.2 display estimated 90/10 income achievement gaps from all available nationally representative studies that include reading- or math-achievement test scores for school-age children and family income. Labels indicate the modal grade in which students were tested in a given sample. For most of the longitudinal studies (HS&B, NELS, Prospects, ELS, and ECLS-K), only estimates from the initial wave of the study are included. ECLS-B estimates come from wave 4, when children were five years old and tested on school readiness; SECCYD come from wave 5, when children were in third grade and were first administered a broad academic-achievement test. The quartic fitted regression line is weighted by the inverse of the sampling variance of each estimate. Included studies are Project Talent, NLS, HS&B, NLSY79, NELS, Add Health (reading only), Prospects, NLSY97, ELS, SECCYD, ECLS-K, and ECLS-B. Family income is student-reported in Project Talent, NLS, and HS&B. See online appendix for details on computation of 90/10 gaps.

5. My calculations, based on Main NAEP math and reading scores. See National Center for Education Statistics website, available at: http://nces.ed.gov/nationsreportcard/naepdata/dataset.aspx (accessed March 7, 2011).

6. Figures 5.3 and 5.4 show estimated 90/10 income gaps (solid symbols) and estimated black-white gaps (hollow symbols) based on the twelve studies with family income data. The estimated trends in the income and black-white gaps are fitted lines (quartic for income gaps, quadratic for black-white gaps), weighted by the inverse of the sampling variance of each estimate. The estimated black-white gap trend from NAEP is a fitted line (quartic for reading, cubic for math) through all available NAEP-LTT and Main NAEP black-white gap estimates. The NAEP trend is adjusted for the age of the NAEP samples and the difference between Main and LTT NAEP (the line is the predicted trend for thirteen-year-old students in NAEP-LTT). See appendix section 5.A5 for details.

7. The exception here is the Prospects seventh-grade cohort (born roughly 1978), for whom the estimated gaps are much smaller than the NELS cohort (born roughly 1974), particularly in math. The magnitude of the estimated gaps from the Prospects study—especially the Prospects math gaps in the third- and seventh-grade cohorts—is generally not consistent with the size of the estimated gaps from other contemporaneous studies. Moreover, it is difficult to find documentation on the content and psychometric properties of the Prospects tests. These tests may be much less reliable than other tests; as a result, I am inclined to discount their importance in describing the trends.

8. Figure 5.A12 in the online appendix displays the trend in U.S. income inequality throughout the last century.

9. My calculations, based on Current Population Survey, 1968–2009. See appendix section 5.A3 for details.

10. We would expect this if we thought the relationship between achievement and log income was linear, which may not be the case. See online appendix section 5.A6 for discussion.

11. The same trend is evident if the correlations are plotted against the year of the study rather than against birth year. Figure 5.9 shows the Spearman rank-order correlation between parental educational attainment (coded as the maximum level of educational attainment of both parents, if two are present in the home) and family income. Because both income and parental education are measured by ordered categories in most studies (parental education is measured in four to eight categories; income in five to fifteen categories), I compute the rank-order correlation between income and parental education for each of the twelve studies with measures of both income and parental education. Correlations are disattenuated for estimated measurement error in both family income and parental educational attainment. Note that because these are rank-order correlations, they are not directly comparable to standard (Pearson) correlation coefficients.

12. The income coefficients displayed in figures 5.9 and 5.10 are roughly 20 to 40 percent the size of the parental-education coefficients in the earliest cohorts, but they are 60 to 90 percent the size of the parental-education coefficients in the later cohorts. The income coefficients here are adjusted for the estimated reliability of family income, so these differences in the magnitudes of the income and education coefficients are likely not substantially biased by the less reliable measurement of family income.

13. Because of the relatively small within-school samples in many of the studies that include measures of family income, it is difficult to assess the trends in school income segregation using the data available.

14. An examination (not shown) of the intracluster correlations of test scores from the school-based studies included in this chapter provides some evidence that the intracluster correlation has grown with time, but these estimates are very noisy because of the small sample sizes within each school in most of the studies.

REFERENCES

Bainbridge, J., M. K. Meyers, S. Tanaka, and Jane Waldfogel. 2005. "Who Gets an Early Education? Family Income and the Enrollment of Three- to Five-Year-Olds from 1968 to 2000." *Social Science Quarterly* 86(3): 724–45.

Bianchi, Susan. 2000. "Maternal Employment and Time with Children: Dramatic Change or Surprising Continuity?" *Demography* 37(4): 401–14.

Bowles, S., and H. Gintis. 1976. *Schooling in Capitalist America: Educational Reform and the Contradictions of Economic Life.* New York: Basic Books.

———. 2002. "The Inheritance of Inequality." *Journal of Economic Perspectives* 16(3): 3–30.

Brooks-Gunn, Jeanne, and Greg Duncan. 1997. "The Effects of Poverty on Children." *Future of Children* 7(2): 55–71.

Burkhauser, R. V., A. Feng, S. P. Jenkins, and J. Larrimore. 2009. "Recent Trends in Top Income Shares in the USA: Reconciling Estimates from March CPS and IRS Tax Return Data." NBER Working Paper No. 15320. Cambridge, Mass.: National Bureau of Economic Research.

Clotfelter, C. T., H. F. Ladd, and J. L. Vigdor. 2006. "The Academic Achievement Gap in Grades Three to Eight." NBER Working Paper No. 12207. Cambridge, Mass.: National Bureau of Economic Research.

Coleman, James S., Ernest Q. Campbell, Carol J. Hobson, James McPartland, Alexander M. Mood, Frederic D. Weinfeld, and Robert L. York. 1966. *Equality of Educational Opportunity.* Washington, D.C.: U.S. Department of Health, Education, and Welfare, Office of Education.

Duncan, Greg J., and Jeanne Brooks-Gunn. 1997. "Income Effects Across the Life-Span: Integration and Interpretation." In *Consequences of Growing Up Poor,* edited by Greg J. Duncan and Jeanne Brooks-Gunn. New York: Russell Sage Foundation.

Duncan, Greg J., Jeanne Brooks-Gunn, and P. K. Klebanov. 1994. "Economic Deprivation and Early Childhood Development." *Child Development* 65(2): 296–318.

Dupriez, V., and X Dumay. 2006. "Inequalities in School Systems: Effect of School Structure or of Society Structure?" *Comparative Education* 42(2): 243–60.

Dura-Bellat, M., and B. Suchaut. 2005. "Organisation and Context, Efficiency and Equity of Educational Systems: What PISA Tells Us." *European Educational Research Journal* 4(3): 181–94.

Flanagan, John C., David V. Tiedeman, William V. Clemans, and Lauress L. Wise. n.d. *Project Talent Public Use File, 1960-1976* [Computer file]. ICPSR07823-v1. Ann Arbor, Mich.: Inter-university Consortium for Political and Social Research [distributor]. Ordering information available at: http://www.projecttalent.org/contact (accessed June 24, 2011).

Fryer, R. G., and S. D. Levitt. 2004. "Understanding the Black-White Test Score Gap in the First Two Years of School." *Review of Economics and Statistics* 86(2): 447–64.

———. 2006. "The Black-White Test Score Gap Through Third Grade." *American Law and Economics Review* 8(2): 249–81.

Grissmer, D. W., A. Flanagan, and S. Williamson. 1998. "Why Did the Black-White Score Gap Narrow in the 1970s and 1980s?" In *The Black-White Test Score Gap,* edited by C. Jencks and M. Phillips. Washington, D.C.: Brookings Institution Press.

Guryan, J., E. Hurst, and M. Kearney. 2008. "Parental Education and Parental Time with Children." *Journal of Economic Perspectives* 22(3): 23–46.

Harris, Kathleen Mullan. 2009. *The National Longitudinal Study of Adolescent Health* (Add Health), Waves I & II, 1994–1996; Wave III, 2001–2002; Wave IV, 2007–2009 [machine-readable data file and documentation]. Chapel Hill, N.C.: Carolina Population Center, University of North Carolina at Chapel Hill. Ordering information available at: http://www.cpc.unc.edu/projects/addhealth/data/restricteduse (accessed June 24, 2011).

Hedges, Larry V., and A. Nowell. 1998. "Black-White Test Score Convergence Since 1965." In *The Black-White Test Score Gap,* edited by C. Jencks and M. Phillips. Washington, D.C.: Brookings Institution Press.

———. 1999. "Changes in the Black-White Gap in Achievement Test Scores." *Sociology of Education* 72(2): 111–35.

Herrnstein, R. J., and C. Murray. 1994. *The Bell Curve: Intelligence and Class Structure in American Life.* New York: Free Press.

Huang, M.-H., and R. M. Hauser. 2001. "Convergent Trends in Black-White Verbal Test-Score Differentials in the U.S.: Period and Cohort Perspectives." *EurAmerica* 31(2): 185–230.

Jacoby, R., and N. Glauberman, eds. 1995. *The Bell Curve Debate: History Documents Opinions.* New York: Random House.

Jargowsky, P. A. 1996. "Take the Money and Run: Economic Segregation in U.S. Metropolitan Areas." *American Sociological Review* 61(6): 984–98.

Jencks, C., and M. Phillips, eds. 1998. *The Black-White Test Score Gap.* Washington D.C.: Brookings Institution Press.

Kagan, J. 2002. "Empowerment and Education: Civil Rights, Expert-Advocates, and Parent Politics in Head Start, 1964–1980." *Teachers College Record* 104(3): 516–62.

Katz, M. B. 1989. *The Undeserving Poor: From the War on Poverty to the War on Welfare.* New York: Random House.

———. 1995. *Improving Poor People: The Welfare State the "Underclass" and Urban Schools as History.* Princeton, N.J.: Princeton University Press.

King, Miriam, Steven Ruggles, J. Trent Alexander, Sarah Flood, Katie Genadek, Matthew B. Schroeder, Brandon Trampe, and Rebecca Vick. 2010. *Integrated Public Use Microdata Series, Current Population Survey: Version 3.0.* [Machine-readable database]. Minneapolis: University of Minnesota.

Kornrich, Sabino, and Frank Furstenberg. 2010. "Investing in Children: Changes in Parental Spending on Children, 1972 to 2007." Unpublished manuscript.

Lareau, Annette. 1989. *Home Advantage: Social Class and Parental Intervention in Elementary Education.* London: Falmer Press.

———. 2003. *Unequal Childhoods: Class Race and Family Life.* Berkeley: University of California Press.

Lavy, V., O. Silma, and F. Weinhardt. 2009. "The Good, the Bad, and the Average: Evidence on the Scale and Nature of Peer Effects in Schools." NBER Working Paper No. 15600. Cambridge, Mass.: National Bureau of Economic Research.

Lemann, N. 1999. *The Big Test: The Secret History of The American Meritocracy.* New York: Farrar, Straus and Giroux.

Levy, Frank, and Richard J. Murnane. 1992. "U.S. Earnings Levels and Earnings Inequality: A Review of Recent Trends and Proposed Explanations." *Journal of Economic Literature* 30(3): 1333–81.

Magnuson, Katherine, and Jane Waldfogel, eds. 2008. *Steady Gains and Stalled Progress: Inequality and the Black-White Test Score Gap.* New York: Russell Sage Foundation.

Marks, G. N. 2005. "Cross-National Differences and Accounting for Social Class Inequalities in Education." *International Sociology* 20(4): 483–505.

Mayer, S. E. 2001. "How Did the Increase in Economic Inequality Affect Educational Attainment?" *American Journal of Sociology* 107(1): 1–32.

McLanahan, Sara. 2004. "Diverging Destinies: How Children Are Faring Under the Second Demographic Transition." *Demography* 41(4): 607–27.

Miller, Jon. 1994. *Longitudinal Survey of American Youth* [dataset]. Ordering information available at: http://www.lsay.org (accessed June 24, 2011).

Murray, C. 2007. "The Magnitude and Components of Change in the Black-White IQ Difference from 1920 to 1991: A Birth Cohort Analysis of the Woodcock-Johnson Standardizations." *Intelligence* 35(4): 305–18.

National Commission on Excellence in Education. 1983. *A Nation at Risk: The Imperative for Educational Reform.* Washington, D.C.: National Commission on Excellence in Education.

National Institute of Child Health and Human Development. 2010. *Study of Early Child Care and Youth Development* [dataset]. Received 2010. Ordering information available at: http://www.nichd.nih.gov/research/supported/seccyd/datasets.cfm (accessed June 24, 2011).

Neal, D. A. 2006. "Why Has Black-White Skill Convergence Stopped?" In *Handbook of the Economics of Education,* edited by E. A. Hanushek and F. Welch. Vol. 1. New York: Elsevier.

Phillips, M., Jeanne Brooks-Gunn, Greg J. Duncan, P. Klebanov, and J. Crane. 1998. "Family Background, Parenting Practices, and the Black-White Test Score Gap." In *The Black-White Test Score Gap,* edited by C. Jencks and M. Phillips. Washington, D.C.: Brookings Institution Press.

Piketty, T., and E. Saez. 2003. "Income Inequality in the United States, 1913–1998." *Quarterly Journal of Economics* 118(1): 1–39.

————. 2008. "Income Inequality in the United States, 1913–1998; Tables and Figures Updated to 2006." Available at: http://www.econ.berkeley.edu/~saez/TabFig2006.xls (accessed September 2, 2009).

Ramey, G., and V. A. Ramey. 2010. "The Rug Rat Race." Unpublished paper.

Reardon, Sean F., and K. Bischoff. 2011. "Income Inequality and Income Segregation." *American Journal of Sociology* 116(4): 1092–153.

Reardon, Sean F., and C. Galindo. 2009. "The Hispanic-White Achievement Gap in Math and Reading in the Elementary Grades." *American Educational Research Journal* 46(3): 853–91.

Schaub, M. 2010. "Parenting for Cognitive Development from 1950 to 2000: The Institutionalization of Mass Education and the Social Construction of Parenting in the United States." *Sociology of Education* 83(1): 46–66.

Schwartz, C. R., and R. D. Mare. 2005. "Trends in Educational Assortative Marriage from 1940–2003." *Demography* 42(4): 621–46.

Schwartz, H. 2010. *Housing Policy Is School Policy: Economically Integrative Housing Promotes Academic Success in Montgomery County, Maryland.* New York: Century Foundation.

U.S. Bureau of Labor Statistics. 1980. *National Longitudinal Survey of Youth, 1979* [dataset]. Available at: http://www.bls.gov/nls/nlsy79.htm (accessed June 24, 2011).

————. 1999. *National Longitudinal Survey of Youth, 1997* [dataset]. Available at: http://www.bls.gov/nls/nlsy97.htm (accessed June 24, 2011).

U.S. Department of Education. 1995. *Prospects: The Congressionally Mandated Study of Educational Growth and Opportunity* [dataset]. Ordering information available at: http://www.ed.gov/pubs/Prospects/index.html (accessed June 24, 2011).

U.S. Department of Education, Center for Education Statistics. n.d. *National Assessment of Educational Progress-Main* [dataset]. Ordering information available at: http://nces.ed.gov/nationsreportcard/researchcenter/datatools.asp (accessed June 24, 2011).

————. 1999. *National Longitudinal Study of the Class of 1972* [Computer file]. ICPSR version. Chicago, Ill: National Opinion Research Center [producer], 1992. Ann Arbor, Mich.: Inter-university Consortium for Political and Social Research [distributor]. doi:10.3886/ICPSR08085.

————. 2000. *Early Childhood Longitudinal Survey-Kindergarten (Base Year)* [dataset]. Ordering information available at: http://nces.ed.gov/ecls/kinderdatainformation.asp (accessed June 24, 2011).

————. 2001. *High School and Beyond, 1980: A Longitudinal Survey of Students in The United States* [Computer file]. 2nd ICPSR version. Chicago, Ill.: National Opinion Research Center [producer], 1980. Ann Arbor, Mich.: Inter-university Consortium for Political and Social Research [distributor]. doi:10.3886/ICPSR07896.

————. 2004. *National Education Longitudinal Study: Base Year Through Fourth Follow-Up, 1988–2000* [Computer file]. ICPSR version. Washington, D.C.: U.S. Department of Education, National Center for Education Statistics [producer], 2002. Ann Arbor, Mich: Inter-university Consortium for Political and Social Research [distributor].

————. 2005. *National Assessment of Educational Progress-Long Term Trend* [dataset]. Ordering information available at: http://nces.ed.gov/nationsreportcard/researchcenter/datatools.asp (accessed June 24, 2011).

————. 2009. *Early Childhood Longitudinal Survey-Birth Cohort (9 Month-Kindergarten)* [dataset]. Ordering information available at: http://nces.ed.gov/ecls/birthdatainformation.asp (accessed June 24, 2011).

————. 2010. *Education Longitudinal Study: Base Year Through Second Follow-Up, 2002–2006* [dataset]. Washington, D.C.: U.S. Department of Education, National Center for Education Statistics [producer], 2010. Available at: http://nces.ed.gov/surveys/els2002/orderingcds.asp (accessed June 24, 2011).

Watson, T. 2009. "Inequality and the Measurement of Residential Segregation by Income." *Review of Income and Wealth* 55(3): 820–44.

Wrigley, Julia. 1989. "Do Young Children Need Intellectual Stimulation? Experts' Advice to Parents, 1900–1985." *History of Education Quarterly* 29(1): 41–75.

Zigler, E., and S. Muenchow. 1992. *Head Start: The Inside Story of America's Most Successful Educational Experiment.* New York: Basic Books.

Chapter 6

Inequality in Postsecondary Education

Martha J. Bailey and Susan M. Dynarski

We describe changes over time in inequality in postsecondary education using nearly seventy years of data from the U.S. census and the 1979 and 1997 National Longitudinal Surveys of Youth. We find growing gaps between children from high- and low-income families in college entry, persistence, and graduation. Rates of college completion increased by only 4 percentage points for low-income cohorts born around 1980 relative to cohorts born in the early 1960s, but by 18 percentage points for corresponding cohorts who grew up in high-income families. Another striking finding is the role that gender plays in recent increases in educational inequality. Among men, inequality in educational attainment has increased slightly since the early 1980s. But among women, inequality in educational attainment has risen sharply, driven by increases in the education of the daughters of high-income parents. Sex differences in educational attainment, which were small or nonexistent thirty years ago, are now substantial, with women outpacing men in every demographic group. The female advantage in educational attainment is largest in the top quartile of the income distribution.

These sex differences present a formidable challenge to standard economic explanations for rising inequality in educational attainment. Girls are raised in the same families, live in the same neighborhoods, attend the same elementary and secondary schools, and face the same college prices as their male siblings. This means that candidate explanations for increases in the educational inequality need to explain why the same circumstances differentially affect the educational attainment of men and women or why men and women coming from the same circumstances face different incentives to invest in human capital. Because current inequalities between men and women in educational attainment were foreshadowed long ago, policymakers and researchers should look beyond current events and policies to understand today's educational inequality.

Postsecondary education is a key path to upward mobility in the United States. For this reason, understanding recent trends in college going and college graduation for children from different family backgrounds is critical to understanding how increases in family income inequality affect the life chances of children born into low-income families. In this chapter we document changes over time in inequality in educational attainment by family income, and we examine the extent to which trends vary by gender. We focus in particular on the thirty years since 1980, in which we find growing income gaps in college entry, persistence, and completion.

With regard to income gaps, we find increasing advantages for children growing up in high-income families. On all three attainment dimensions we track—college entry, persistence, and completion—cohorts born between 1979 and 1982 attained more than cohorts born between 1961 and 1964. However, the attainment advantages for the latter cohorts were larger for children raised in high- as opposed to low-income families. This is consistent with evidence presented in chapter 5 regarding growing income-based gaps in the test scores of primary and secondary school students.

A new and puzzling finding is that these increases in educational inequality are driven largely by women. Among men, inequality in educational attainment by family income has increased much less than it has among women. For example, the gap between the top and bottom quartiles in college entry increased by fifteen percentage points among women but by seven percentage points among men. This difference is driven by sharp increases in the education of daughters of high-income parents.

Sex differences in educational attainment, which were small or nonexistent thirty years ago, are now substantial, with women outpacing men in every income group. The female advantage in educational attainment is largest in the top quartile of the income distribution. These findings present a formidable challenge to standard economic explanations for rising inequality in educational attainment. Girls and boys are raised in the same families, attend the same elementary and secondary schools, and face the same college prices. Given that inequality has risen primarily among women, widening inequality in parental income, changes in school quality and organization, and rising tuition prices are candidate explanations for increases in the inequality in educational attainment if and only if these shocks differentially affect the educational attainment of men and women. An alternative (and potentially complementary) explanation is that men and women operate in segregated labor markets and asymmetric marriage markets and, therefore, face different incentives to accumulate human capital. Since current inequalities between men and women in educational attainment were foreshadowed seventy years ago, policymakers and researchers may want to look beyond current events and trends to understand today's educational inequality.

From a policy and research perspective, our main findings indicate that we cannot focus solely on the college entry margin if we wish to understand the sources of, and remedies for, inequality in postsecondary attainment. Differences in high school completion between children from low-income families and those from high-income families explain half of the gap in college entry. However, among those who enter college, children from low-income families are much less likely to get a degree. Inequality in college persistence therefore produces inequality in college completion, even if college entry rates were equal (which they are not).

HISTORICAL TRENDS IN COLLEGE ENTRY AND COMPLETION

To provide a broad historical context for our examination of trends in college going and college completion by family income, we begin by documenting changes in educational attainment between 1940 and 2007. We focus on trends in three outcomes. We define the college entry rate as the share of each birth cohort that has any college experience by age nineteen; this experience could consist of less than one year of course work. The share of a cohort that completes a bachelor's degree (B.A.) by age twenty-five is referred to as the college completion rate.[1] The college completion rate divided by the entry rate provides a measure of the share of college entrants who go on to graduate, which we refer to as the college persistence rate.

Our data sources are the U.S. decennial censuses from 1940 to 2000 and the American Community Surveys (ACS) for 2006 and 2007 (Ruggles et al. 2009). We focus on the native-born

FIGURE 6.1   *Trends in College Entry and Completion*

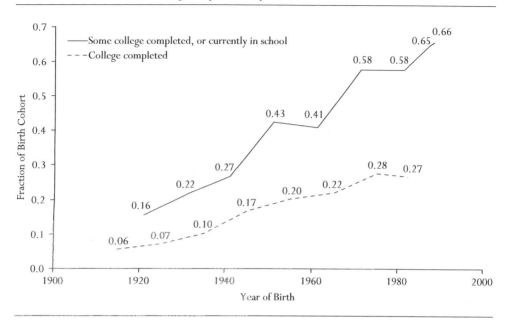

Source: Authors' calculations based on U.S. Census and the American Community Survey (Ruggles et al. 2009).

population. The census and ACS have two key advantages over other data sources. First, they provide a sixty-seven-year perspective on college entry and completion of young people. Second, they cover a broader population than, in particular, the Current Population Survey (CPS), by including residents of dormitories, barracks, and prisons. This is especially important when measuring differences across demographic groups in educational attainment, since young men, especially black men, are disproportionately likely to live in barracks and prisons. Although we can track black-white differences in educational attainment for the entire period under analysis, we can only provide reliable statistics for Hispanics as of 1980, when the census began to explicitly ask about "Hispanic origin" on the enumeration form. In any long-term analysis, changes in variable definitions can make it difficult to distinguish real changes in behavior from changes in measurement. These measurement issues are discussed in more detail in the online data appendix, available at http://www.russellsage.org/duncan_murnane_online_appendix.pdf.

Overview of College Entry and Completion Since 1940

Rates of college entry and completion increased dramatically over the last seventy years. As illustrated in figure 6.1 (top line), from 1940 to 2007 (cohorts born between 1921 and 1988), college entry increased by roughly 50 percentage points—an average of 7.6 percentage points per decade. College completion by age twenty-five among cohorts born between 1915 and 1983 more than quadrupled.[2] Whereas only 6 to 7 percent of those born in 1915 graduated from college, 28 percent of those born in 1975 would graduate by age twenty-five.[3]

The critical question for this chapter is whether the trends in college entry and completion illustrated in figure 6.1 pertain to children from low-income families as well as to children from high-income families. It is to this question that we now turn.

FIGURE 6.2   *Fraction of Students Entering College, by Income Quartile and Birth Year*

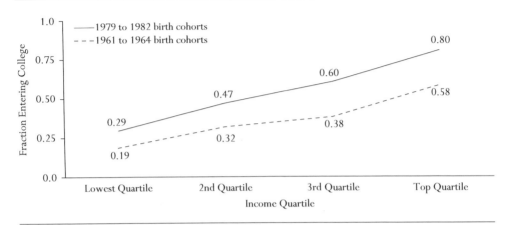

Source: Authors' calculations based on data from National Longitudinal Survey of Youth, 1979 and 1997 (U.S. Bureau of Labor Statistics 2010a, 2010b).

For this analysis, we use detailed longitudinal data from the NLSY79 and NLSY97 (National Longitudinal Survey of Youth, 1979 and 1997) and focus on educational attainment by family income quartiles for recent birth cohorts. These data sets allow us to examine the link between parental income and children's educational attainment, and how it has changed over time. We focus on two cohorts: those born in 1961 through 1964 (NLSY79, early cohort) and those born in 1979 through 1982 (NLSY97, later cohort). On-time graduation from high school for these cohorts would have been in 1979 through 1982 and 1997 through 2000, respectively. The sample is limited to respondents for whom we have information about grade attainment at both age nineteen and age twenty-five.[4]

Inequality in College Entry and Completion by Household Income

Figure 6.2 shows the college entry rates for the two cohorts, plotted separately by household-income quartile, and figure 6.3 shows the analogous college completion rates. Household income is measured at the time of each baseline survey, when children were fifteen to eighteen years old. One pattern evident in the figures is that for both cohorts, higher family income is associated with a greater probability that a child will enter and will graduate from college. Other chapters in this volume document the mechanisms that result in this pattern. For example, parents with more money can purchase better K–12 schooling for their children and can devote more resources of educational enrichment (see chapter 9).

A second pattern evident in figures 6.2 and 6.3 is that the college entry rate and the college completion rate rose between the two periods. However, of central importance to the theme of this volume, the increases were highly uneven, with gains largest at the top of the income distribution and smallest at the bottom. Philippe Belley and Lance Lochner (2007) reach a similar conclusion in their analysis of these data. Specifically, the top two quartiles boosted their college entry rates by about twenty-two percentage points, to 80 percent in the top quartile and 60 percent in the next highest quartile. In the bottom quartile, the college entry rate rose just ten percentage

FIGURE 6.3   *Fraction of Students Completing College, by Income Quartile and Birth Year*

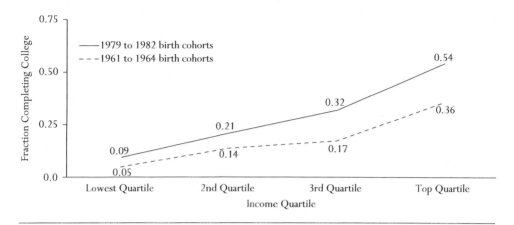

Source: Authors' calculations based on data from National Longitudinal Survey of Youth, 1979 and 1997 (U.S. Bureau of Labor Statistics 2010a, 2010b).

points, from 19 to 29 percent. A result is that the gap in the college entry rate between the bottom- and top-income quartiles increased from thirty-nine to fifty-one percentage points. The story is similar for college completion, with the top-income quartile gaining an astounding eighteen percentage points but the bottom quartile nudging up only slightly, to 9 percent from 5 percent. The product of this uneven growth was increased inequality in college outcomes during a period in which educational attainments became increasingly strong determinants of subsequent earnings.

Together these facts about college entry and completion provide insight into income differences in college persistence (figure 6.4). For both cohorts, the persistence rate rises with income, with those in the top quartile more than twice as likely to graduate as those in the bottom quartile. Persistence rates rose slightly (six percentage points) in the bottom and top two quartiles, and just one percentage point in the second quartile. The relationship between income and persistence, therefore, remained quite steep. This pattern implies that equal increases in college entry will generate highly unequal increases in college completion.

Sex Differences in Inequality in College Entry and Completion by Household Income

A striking aspect of the increase in inequality in college outcomes by income group is that it is primarily a female phenomenon. In college entry, persistence, and completion, women in the top-income quartile have pulled away from the rest of population. In the later cohort, an astounding 85 percent of women in the top quartile entered college. The gap between the top- and bottom-income quartiles in college entry rose by fifteen percentage points among women. The comparable increase for men is seven percentage points. The pattern in completion is similar, with the gap between the top and bottom quartiles rising by seventeen percentage points among women and eleven percentage points among men.

Figure 6.5 plots the difference between males and females in college completion rates by family income quartile for the two cohorts. In the early cohort, there are few differences between

FIGURE 6.4   *Fraction of Students Persisting in College, by Income Quartile and Birth Year*

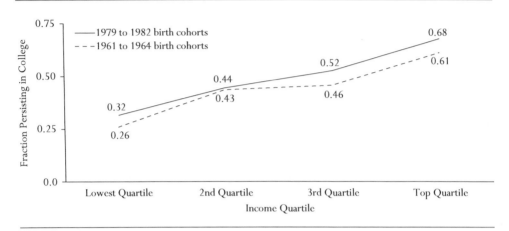

Source: Authors' calculations based on data from National Longitudinal Survey of Youth, 1979 and 1997 (U.S. Bureau of Labor Statistics 2010a, 2010b).

FIGURE 6.5   *Female Advantage in Completing College, by Income Quartile and Birth Year*

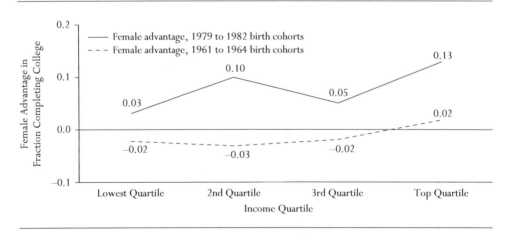

Source: Authors' calculations based on data from National Longitudinal Survey of Youth, 1979 and 1997 (U.S. Bureau of Labor Statistics 2010a, 2010b).

FIGURE 6.6   *Female Advantage in College Entry and Completion, by Birth Year*

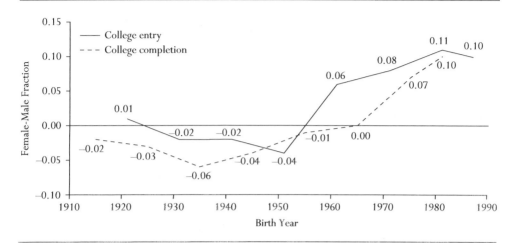

Source: Authors' calculations based on data from the U.S. Census and American Community Survey (Ruggles et al. 2009).

the sexes: there is a slight female advantage of two percentage points in the top quartile and a slight disadvantage of two to three percentage points in the bottom three quartiles. Within the later cohort, a female advantage opened in every quartile, with the largest in the top. In the top quartile, the female advantage opened to thirteen percentage points, whereas in the bottom it was just three percentage points.

The evidence from the two NLSY cohorts reveals two striking patterns. The first is that inequality in college outcomes by family income increased dramatically in recent decades. The second is that the increase in inequality is largely driven by the increase in college enrollment and completion among females from higher-income families. The female advantage in college graduation rose substantially in the top quartile, to thirteen percentage points (from two). A female disadvantage of two percentage points in the bottom quartile switched to an advantage of two percentage points. The patterns in the NLSY data sets raise two questions: When did the female advantage in achieving college outcomes begin? Is the answer different for different racial-ethnic groups? To answer these questions we return to evidence from the census.

Figure 6.6 shows the female advantage in college entry and college completion for cohorts born between 1915 and 1985. One striking pattern is that the female advantage is not a new phenomenon. In fact, the advantage in college entry is present for all cohorts born after 1950 and grew in magnitude over the last half of the twentieth century. For the most recent cohorts that have reached college-going age, the share of women who enroll in college (71 percent) is ten percentage points greater than the share of men who do so (61 percent). The female advantage in college completion evolves similarly, although starts a bit later. For cohorts born after 1965, the percentage of women who graduated college by the age of twenty-five is greater than the comparable figure for men. For the most recent cohorts, the four-year college graduation rate for women (32 percent) is ten percentage points higher than the comparable rate for males (22 percent).[5]

Figure 6.7 shows the trends in the female advantage in college completion for the major racial and ethnic groups.[6] Notice that the female advantage in college completion began much earlier for blacks than for non-Hispanic whites. In fact, for all cohorts born after 1915, the college graduation rate for black women was higher than that for black men. This female advantage in college

FIGURE 6.7   *Female Advantage in Completing College, by Race and Birth Year*

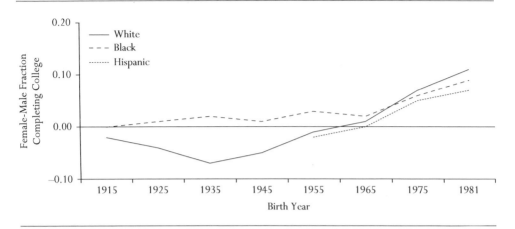

Source: Authors' calculations based on data from the U.S. Census and American Community Survey (Ruggles et al. 2009).

completion among blacks was modest (less than three percentage points) for cohorts born before 1970, but has grown markedly since then, reaching nine percentage points for cohorts born in the early 1980s. This pattern reflects the extraordinarily low college graduation rate for African American men—only 11 percent for cohorts born in the early 1980s.

The female advantage in college completion is a more recent phenomenon for white Americans than for black Americans. Among cohorts born in the first half of the twentieth century, the college graduation rate among white men was higher than that of white women. Only for cohorts born after 1960 was the pattern reversed.[7] The census data allow us to identify Hispanics as of 1980, so we are able to show completion trends for this group as of the 1955 birth cohort. We find that the female advantage in college completion has grown markedly in recent decades for Hispanic Americans. Among Hispanics born in the early 1980s, the college completion rate of women (17 percent) is six percentage points higher than that of men. The female advantage has grown most sharply among non-Hispanic whites, however, with the gap reaching more than ten percentage points for cohorts born in the early 1980s. The trend in the female advantage for Hispanic Americans is similar in recent decades to that for non-Hispanic white Americans, although the rate of increase in the female advantage is more modest.

SOME POTENTIAL EXPLANATIONS FOR INCREASED EDUCATIONAL INEQUALITY

In this section, we discuss some possible explanations for the rise in educational inequality that we have documented in the previous pages.

Inequality in High School Graduation

If students do not complete high school, they are unlikely to enter college and have little chance of earning a B.A.[8] In this sense, differences across groups in high school completion rates may "explain" some of the gaps we observe in college entry and completion. We do not mean "explain" in a causal sense. The same social and economic forces that drive the decision to complete high school may well affect the decision to enter college. That is, unobserved factors may drive both educational outcomes. In the short term, however, the stock of high school dropouts acts as a constraint on the ability of policy to increase college entry and completion: a policy to improve remedial education in college or expand financial aid will almost certainly have a near-zero effect on the schooling of a high school dropout. In the long term, by contrast, it is plausible that a more generous financial aid policy would increase high school graduation (for example, by increasing the option value of a high school degree). In this section, we calculate how much of the inequality in college entry can be "explained" by inequality in high school completion.

Inequality across income groups in high school completion was relatively stable between the two NLSY cohorts (results not shown). High school graduation rose for all income groups. The share graduating from high school rose by eight percentage points in the lowest-income quartile (from 55 to 63 percent) and by ten percentage points in the next income quartile (from 71 to 81 percent). The gap in high school graduation rates between the top and bottom quartiles shrank very slightly, from thirty-four to thirty-three percentage points. All else held constant, this would tend to slightly reduce inequality in college entry and completion.

Offsetting this is that the share of high school graduates going on to college rose dramatically, so the "penalty" for dropping out of high school also rose dramatically. Consider traditional high school graduates (who earn a standard diploma rather than a GED). In the early cohort, 52 percent of traditional high school graduates went to college, while in the later cohort the figure was 70 percent. The gap in traditional high school completion between the bottom and top quartiles was 40 percentage points for the early cohort and 37 percentage points for the later cohort. For the early cohort, the gap in high school graduation therefore "explains" 20.28 (= 0.39 × 0.52) percentage points of the gap of 36 percentage points in college entry. For the later cohort, the high school graduation gap explains 25.9 (= 0.37 × 0.70) percentage points of the gap of 51 percentage points in college entry. Differences in high school graduation therefore go a long way toward explaining differences in college entry.

Further, the "quality" of high school degrees in the bottom-income quartile is lower than that in the top. Students can complete high school in two ways: by earning a traditional diploma or by passing a test that earns them the General Educational Development credential (GED). For both cohorts, 7 percent of those in the bottom-income quartile have only a GED, compared with 2 to 3 percent in the top. Those who complete high school with a GED are less likely to go on to college than those with a traditional diploma (Cameron and Heckman 1993), and virtually no one in these data sets with a GED completes college. However, the income gap in GED receipt did not increase between the two NLSY cohorts. The GED could, therefore, explain rising inequality in college entry and completion only if the "penalty" associated with GED receipt grew worse over time—which it did. In the earlier NLSY cohort, 22 percent of GED holders went on to college, compared with 51 percent of those with a traditional high school diploma. But for the later cohort, the share of GED holders going to college dropped by nearly half (to 12 percent) while the share of traditional high school graduates entering college rose to 70 percent.

How much can inequality in GED receipt explain rising inequality in college entry and completion? A back-of-the-envelope calculation suggests "not much." For the early cohort, GED recipients are 30 percentage points less likely than traditional high school graduates to enter college (22 versus 52 percent). For the later cohort the difference is 58 percentage points (12 versus 70 percent). We can multiply the difference between quartiles in GED receipt by the GED "penalty" to get an estimate of how much of the gap in college entry is explained by differences in GED receipt. For the NLSY79 cohort, the GED explains 1.4 (= 0.047 × 0.30) percentage points of the 39-percentage-point difference in college entry between the top and bottom quartile.

For the NLSY97 cohort, the GED explains 2.4 ($= 0.042 \times 0.58$) points of the 51-percentage-point difference. Mechanically, then, the GED does not appear to explain much of the rise in or level of inequality in college entry.

Differences in Cognitive Skills

In the same sense that differences in high school graduation can "explain" gaps in college entry and completion, gaps in cognitive skills could also have explanatory power. To examine this question we regress a binary indicator for the outcome of interest (college entry or college completion) on income dummies, and examine how our estimated income gaps change when we add a measure of cognitive skills to the regression. In the NLSY, our measure of cognitive skills for both cohorts is the Armed Forces Qualification Test (AFQT). To control for AFQT, we add a set of AFQT quartile dummies to the regressions. We run regressions separately for the two NLSY panels, and for men and women.

We offer the same caveats as earlier: this is not a causal analysis. Evidence indicates that the AFQT is malleable (Cascio and Lewis 2006), and it is likely to be affected by many of the conditions that have a direct effect on college entry and completion. AFQT gaps can potentially be addressed with early childhood interventions or improved elementary schools. But a young person who arrives at college age with very low cognitive scores is unlikely, for example, to be induced by financial aid into college, so the skills acquired as of that age act as a constraint on the effectiveness of college-access policies.

For the early cohort, the gap in college entry between the bottom- and top-income quartile drops from thirty-nine to fourteen percentage points once we control for AFQT, while the gap in college completion drops from thirty-one to fourteen percentage points.[9] For the later cohort, the gap in college entry between the bottom- and top-income quartile drops from fifty-one to twenty-six percentage points once we control for AFQT, while the gap in college completion drops from forty-five to twenty-two percentage points. These regressions indicate that differences in cognitive ability explain a smaller share of the income gap for the later cohort than for the early cohort. Belley and Lochner (2007) reach a similar conclusion in their analysis of AFQT, income, and postsecondary attainment. In short, inequality by family income in postsecondary attainment has grown in recent decades. Even among those who as teenagers had the same measured cognitive skills, inequality in college entry and completion across income groups is greater today than it was two decades ago. These findings are consistent with two themes in this volume. The first is that using financial resources to develop children's cognitive skills may be one important mechanism through which high-income parents create advantages for their children in postsecondary attainment. The second is that there are many mechanisms in addition to cognitive skill development through which high-income parents may improve their children's college outcomes relative to those of children from low-income families.

EXPLAINING GROWING INEQUALITY IN COLLEGE OUTCOMES

Increasing college costs, disintegrating families, and decreasing school quality have been proposed as factors contributing to the increase in inequality in college outcomes between children from low-income families and those from high-income families. Yet all of these social concerns affect both girls and boys in a given family, of a given income. Over the sixty-seven years we have documented, sex differences in educational attainment and inequality have reversed sign. Women are more likely to enter and complete college today than men are, and inequality in educational attainment is greater among women than men. The reverse was true earlier in the twentieth century: women were less likely to enter and complete college. These findings are consistent with two main explanations: (1) Men and women may respond differently to the same family or school circumstances. (2) Differences in circumstances across women and men of the same family income and race have shaped inequality in educational attainment for some time. The social science literature provides evidence that both explanations may be at work.

Gender asymmetry in primary and secondary education and in single-parent families provides two important potential explanations of why men and women may respond differently to the same family or school circumstances. The first explanation relates to the fact that the bulk of primary and secondary schoolteachers are women. Through both "passive" (teachers provide role models to demographically similar students, or the gender or race of teachers prompts different responses from demographically similar students) and "active" teacher effects (teachers' unintended biases affect their interactions and assessments of students), boys and girls may experience and respond to the same classroom setting quite differently. The literature examining these effects has tended to focus on being assigned to a teacher of a similar race on the performance of students (Griffin and London 1979; Beady and Hansell 1981; Ferguson 1998; Ehrenberg, Goldhaber, and Brewer 1995), but Thomas S. Dee (2005) shows that both racial and gender effects are important. Using the National Educational Longitudinal Survey (1988), Dee (2005) uses a teacher fixed-effects model to show that both other race and other sex teachers are significantly more likely to rate students as disruptive and inattentive.

A second potential explanation relates to the fact that the bulk of single-parent households are headed by women and that more children in single-parent families live with their mothers. The absence of a male role model may have a differential effect on boys (see Hetherington, Bridges, and Insabella 1998 for a review of this literature). Consistent with this claim, Brian Jacob (2002) shows that college attendance was significantly lower among boys (but not girls) in single-parent households after conditioning on a rich set of covariates. Claudia Buchmann and Thomas A. DiPrete (2006) also provide supportive evidence using the Current Population Study: for birth cohorts born since 1965, sons attain less education than their sisters when the father is absent.

Complementing these forces is that the returns to higher education may have created different incentives for boys and girls to continue their education. These different incentives may arise through marriage markets (Goldin 1992; Mare 1991; Oppenheimer 1988; Lewis and Oppenheimer 2000; Schwartz and Mare 2005), labor markets (Murphy and Welch 1992; Charles and Luoh 2003), and the interaction of both with norms about household work (Chiappori, Iyigun, and Weiss 2009).

Using the sum of two spouses' earnings, Claudia Goldin (1997) estimates that the return to college rose from roughly 5 to 10 percent between cohorts born before World War I (from 1900 to 1919) to those born after World War II (from 1946 to 1965). Although the earnings-only mean returns show no consistent indication of being higher for women than men from 1963 to 2000, DiPrete and Buchmann (2006) show that the returns to college over this period rose faster for women than men when using measures that include returns through spousal income (via marriage-market educational homogamy and marriage stability) as family size.[10] These trends are reinforced by the fact that marriage rates have fallen sharply among the less-educated during the last thirty years (Qian and Preston 1993; Watson and McLanahan 2009) as the fraction of women heading single-parent households has risen (Bianchi 1999; Ellwood and Jencks 2004; McLanahan 2004). Among those marrying, the propensities of the more educated to divorce relative to the less educated has also fallen since 1980. Although it is too early to draw strong conclusions from these associations, this evidence is consistent with higher and more rapidly increasing marriage market returns to college for women.

On the labor-market side, the returns to college rose quickly for both men and women. Several studies suggest that the returns to college have increased faster for women (Murphy and Welch 1992), especially among African American women relative to African American men (Kane 1994). This may be due in part to the greater returns to a high school education among men, as skilled–blue collar professions have remained less feminized (England and Farkas 1986; Reskin and Roose 1990). This is also consistent with descriptive evidence in Jacob (2002) that boys in the NELS are more likely to explain that they will not need more education for their jobs as a reason for not attending college. In addition, Kerwin Kofi Charles and Ming-Ching Luoh (2003) point out that own earnings variability rose more quickly with schooling for men than women, which implies that education may be a less volatile investment for women. Pierre-André Chiappori, Murat Iyigun, and Yoram Weiss (2009) present a theoretical model that shows how rising labor-market returns to schooling, falling time required in home production, and changing norms about the division of labor in the household may interact to produce greater returns to education for women.

LESSONS FROM THE HISTORICAL RECORD

Our analysis shows substantial increases in college entry and college completion across income groups and across men and women. These increases reflect long-term improvements in college preparedness and increased access to postsecondary institutions. More and better high schools coupled with increasing returns to graduating led to a doubling of high school graduates from 1940 to 2007: 43 percent for the cohort of 1921 completed twelve years, compared with 89 percent of the cohort of 1988.[11] This opened the door to college for more youths.

Several lessons for researchers and policymakers emerge from our analysis. First, we have shown that inequality in high school graduation explains roughly half of income inequality in college entry. The fact that inequality in college entry can be "explained" by inequality in high school graduation has a very practical implication. Interventions that operate mainly on the college entry margin—such as scholarships, college outreach campaigns, and mentoring—can only alter the college entry decisions of those who are able to respond. Those who have already dropped out of high school, in body or spirit, cannot benefit from these interventions.

Second, we have shown that inequality in college persistence explains a substantial share of inequality in college completion. These differences in persistence may be driven by financial, academic, and social factors. Identifying these factors and coming up with effective policy responses should be a major research focus given that it is clear that inducing more low-income youth into college will not, by itself, serve to close income gaps in educational attainment. It is troubling that persistence rates among men dropped by about ten percentage points in the bottom two income quartiles while rising by more than ten percentage points among women in those same quartiles. Even if rates of college entry were miraculously equalized across income groups, existing differences in persistence would still produce large gaps in college completion.

Third, inequality in educational attainment has risen more sharply among women than among men. This is driven by rapid increases among women from upper-income families, who have pulled away from other women, and all men, in their educational attainment. This suggests that we look to institutions and factors that differentially affect women and men, especially those in the upper-income quartiles, if we want to understand the sources of increased inequality in educational attainment. Unpromising candidates are rising tuition costs and changing family structures, since these do not differ across the sexes. More promising candidates include differential interactions of boys and girls in K–12 classrooms or with a female parent or different labor- and marriage-market returns to college for men and women.

But these explanations focus on the modern era, and our time series suggest that recent changes in college entry and completion are part of a long-term historical pattern, and are not a new phenomenon. The recent reversal of the gender gap in postsecondary education was foreshadowed seventy years ago by a female advantage in high school education. Women have been more likely than men to complete high school since at least the 1940s. According to the census, 25 percent more women than men completed high school for the birth cohort of 1921. For white women, the corresponding figure is 24 percent, but black women were 67 percent more likely than black men to graduate from high school. By the 1960s, the gender gap in high school completion had narrowed to 6 percent, where it has remained. The fact that women were more likely to complete high school in an era where divorce rates were very low, childbearing rates were higher, and the labor-market prospects for women were poorer leads us to question the common current presumption that women's recent achievements reflect modern demographic developments. In addition, black women's lead of ten percentage points in college entry over black men in 1940 suggests that the recent gap between black women and men may not reflect current policies or conditions but is the legacy of something much older.

We are grateful for research assistance from Emily Beam, Nathaniel Schwartz, and Francie Streich. Rebecca Blank, Greg Duncan, Mike McPherson, Richard Murnane, and participants in the conferences on Social Inequality and Educational Disadvantage provided valuable comments.

NOTES

Online appendix available at: http://www.russellsage.org/duncan_murnane_online_appendix.pdf.

1. There is a growing divergence between completion rates at ages twenty-five and thirty-five, reflecting the increasing tendency of youths to leave college and return later to complete their B.A.s (Turner 2004). This trend is especially pronounced among women.

2. The post-1980 censuses and the ACS record whether a person has "some college" or completed a degree, but earlier censuses ask only about highest grade completed. To the extent that earlier censuses overstate college completion, this change in definition will tend to understate changes in college completion for the affected cohorts.

3. In unreported results, we find that the March Current Population Survey (CPS) matches the census closely: the CPS understates college completion by age twenty-five by less than one and a half percentage points; graduation by age thirty-five is identical for the 1955 cohort forward. The NLSY, however, appears to overstate college completion slightly: graduation rates by age twenty-five are three percentage points higher for the 1965 cohort in the NLSY79 and six percentage points for the 1982 cohort in the NLSY97.

4. In NLSY79, 89 percent of those providing grade-attainment information at age nineteen also do so at twenty-five. For NLSY97, the figure is 95 percent.

5. For more details on the recent sex-based gaps in college outcomes, see Goldin, Katz, and Kuziemko (2006).

6. Although we can track black-white differences in educational attainment for the entire period under analysis, for Hispanics we can provide reliable statistics for Hispanics only as of 1980, when the census began to explicitly ask about "Hispanic origin" on the enumeration form.

7. The reversal would have taken place a decade earlier if the Vietnam War had not resulted in a temporary jump in the college-entry rate for males.

8. In the NLSY, about 5 percent of those with no high school degree show some postsecondary experience, and near zero have a B.A. It is possible to attend community college and many certificate programs without a high school degree, and this may explain the 5 percent figure.

9. These specifications include the black and Hispanic dummies, so the stated income gaps do not correspond to those in the graphs. Pedro Caneiro and James J. Heckman (2002) and David Ellwood and Thomas J. Kane (2000) explore the relationship between AFQT, income, and college attainment.

10. They use both a standard of living and insurance against deprivation measure. Standard of living is measured as the natural log of the sum of own and family income divided by the square root of family size. Insurance against deprivation is measured as being roughly at a middle-class standard of living: family income in pretax dollars of at least $16,000 for one person, $23,000 for two people, $28,000 for a family of three, and $32,000 for a family of four.

11. GED recipients are counted as high school graduates in the figures reported in this paragraph.

REFERENCES

Beady, Charles H., and Stephen Hansell. 1981. "Teacher Race and Expectations for Student Achievement." *American Educational Research Journal* 18(2): 191–206.

Belley, Philippe, and Lance Lochner. 2007. "The Changing Role of Family Income and Ability in Determining Educational Achievement." *Journal of Human Capital* 1(1): 37–89.

Bianchi, Susan M. 1999. "Feminization and Juvenilization of Poverty: Trends, Relative Risks, Causes and Consequences." *Annual Review of Sociology* 25: 307–33.

Buchmann, Claudia, and Thomas A. DiPrete. 2006. "The Growing Female Advantage in Higher Education: The Role of Parental Resources and Academic Achievement?" *American Sociological Review* 71(4): 515–41.

Cameron, Stephen V., and James J. Heckman. 1993. "The Nonequivalence of High School Equivalents." *Journal of Labor Economics* 11(1): 1–47.

Caneiro, Pedro, and James J. Heckman. 2002. "The Evidence on Credit Constraints in Post-Secondary Schooling." *Economic Journal* 112(482): 705–34.

Cascio, Elizabeth, and Ethan Lewis. 2006. "Schooling and the AFQT: Evidence from School Entry Laws." *Journal of Human Resources* 41(2): 294–318.

Charles, Kerwin Kofi, and Ming-Ching Luoh. 2003. "Gender Differences in Completed Schooling." *Review of Economics and Statistics* 85(3): 559–77.

Chiappori, Pierre-André, Murat Iyigun, and Yoram Weiss. 2009. "Investment in Schooling and the Marriage Market." *American Economic Review* 99(5): 1689–1713.

Dee, Thomas S. 2005. "A Teacher Like Me: Does Race, Ethnicity, or Gender Matter?" *American Economic Review* 95(2): 158–65.

Ehrenberg, Ronald G., Dan D. Goldhaber, and Dominic J. Brewer. 1995. "Do Teachers' Race, Gender and Ethnicity Matter? Evidence from the National Educational Longitudinal Study of 1988." *Industrial and Labor Relations Review* 48(3): 547–61.

Ellwood, David T., and Christopher Jencks. 2004. "The Uneven Spread of Single-Parent Families: What Do We Know? Where Do We Look for Answers?" In *Social Inequality,* edited by Kathryn M. Neckerman. New York: Russell Sage Foundation.

Ellwood, David, and Thomas J. Kane. 2000. "Who Is Getting a College Education?" In *Securing the Future: Investing in Children from Birth to College,* edited by Sheldon Danziger and Jane Waldfogel. New York: Russell Sage Foundation.

England, Paula, and George Farkas. 1986. *Households, Employment and Gender: A Social, Economic and Demographic View.* New York: Aldine.

Ferguson, Ronald F. 1998. "Teachers' Perceptions and Expectations and the Black–White Test Score Gap," In *The Black-White Test Score Gap,* edited by Christopher Jencks and Meredith Phillips. Washington, D.C.: Brookings Institution Press.

Goldin, Claudia. 1992. "The Meaning of College in the Lives of American Women: The Past 100 Years." NBER Working Paper No. 4099. Cambridge, Mass.: National Bureau of Economic Research.

———. 1997. "Career and Family: College Women Look to the Past." In *Gender and Family Issues in the Workplace,* edited by Francine D. Blau and Ronald G. Ehrenberg. New York: Russell Sage Foundation.

Goldin, Claudia, Lawrence Katz, and Ilyana Kuziemko. 2006. "The Homecoming of American College Women: The Reversal of the College Gender Gap." *Journal of Economic Perspectives* 20(4): 133–56.

Griffin, Albert R., and Clement B. G. London. 1979. "Student Relations Among Inner-City Teachers: A Comparative Study by Teacher Race." *Education* 101(2): 139–47.

Hetherington, E. Mavis, Margaret Bridges, and Glendessa M. Insabella. 1998. "What Matters? What Does Not? Five Perspectives on the Association Between Marital Transitions and Children's Adjustment." *American Psychologist* 53(2): 167–84.

Jacob, Brian. 2002. "Where the Boys Aren't: Non-Cognitive Skills, Returns to School, and the Gender Gap in Higher Education." *Economics of Education Review* 21: 589–98.

Kane, Thomas. 1994. "College Entry by Blacks Since 1970: The Role of College Costs, Family Background and the Returns to Education." *Journal of Political Economy* 102(5): 878–911.

Lewis, Susan K., and Valerie K. Oppenheimer. 2000. "Educational Assortative Mating Across Marriage Markets: Non-Hispanic Whites in the United States." *Demography* 37(1): 29–40.

Mare, Robert D. 1991. "Five Decades of Educational Assortative Mating." *American Sociological Review* 56(1): 15–32.

McLanahan, Sara S. 2004. "Diverging Destinies: How Children Are Faring Under the Second Demographic Transition." *Demography* 41(4): 607–27.

Murphy, Kevin M., and Finis Welch. 1992. "The Structure of Wages." *Quarterly Journal of Economics* 107(1): 215–36.

Oppenheimer, Valerie K. 1988. "A Theory of Marriage Timing." *American Journal of Sociology* 94(3): 563–91.

Qian, Zhenchao, and Sam H. Preston. 1993. "Changes in American Marriage, 1972 to 1987: Availability and Forces of Attraction by Age and Education." *American Sociological Review* 58(4): 482–95.

Reskin, Barbara F., and Patricia A. Roose. 1990. *Job Queues, Gender Queues: Explaining Women's Inroads into Male Occupations.* Philadelphia: Temple University Press.

Ruggles, Steven, Matthew Sobek, Trent Alexander, Catherine A. Fitch, Ronald Goeken, Patricia Kelly Hall, Miriam King, and Chad Ronnander. 2009. *Integrated Public Use Microdata Series: Version 4.0* [Machine-readable database]. Minneapolis: Minnesota Population Center.

Schwartz, Christine R., and Robert D. Mare. 2005. "Trends in Educational Assortative Mating from 1940 to 2003." *Demography* 42(4): 621–46.

Turner, Sarah. 2004. "Going to College and Finishing College: Explaining Different Educational Outcomes." In *College Choices: The Economics of Where to Go, When to Go, and How to Pay for It,* edited by Caroline Hoxby. Chicago: University of Chicago Press.

U.S. Bureau of Labor Statistics, U.S. Department of Labor. 2010a. *National Longitudinal Survey of Youth 1979 Cohort, 1979–2008* (rounds 1–20) [computer file]. Produced and distributed by the Center for Human Resource Research, Ohio State University, Columbus, Ohio.

———. 2010b. *National Longitudinal Survey of Youth 1997 Cohort, 1997–2008* (rounds 1–12) [computer file]. Produced by the National Opinion Research Center, the University of Chicago, and distributed by the Center for Human Resource Research, Ohio State University, Columbus, Ohio.

Watson, Tara, and Sara McLanahan. 2009. "Marriage Meets the Joneses: Relative Income, Identity, and Marital Status." NBER Working Paper No. 14773. Cambridge, Mass.: National Bureau of Economic Research, March.

Chapter 7

Educational Expectations and Attainment

Brian A. Jacob and Tamara Wilder Linkow

Researchers, educators, and policymakers have frequently looked to the educational expectations of young people—that is, their beliefs about their likely educational attainment—to gauge their future success. Although there is no convincing evidence that expectations influence attainment in a causal sense, many still believe that inspiring students to attend college will result in a more highly educated population. There is very little evidence on how expectations have evolved over the past fifteen years, a period during which educational attainment has become even more important for disadvantaged youth.

In this chapter we examine the role of educational expectations in the educational attainment process. Specifically, we investigate how family experiences, school qualities, and knowledge of labor-market pathways affect a student's educational expectations and how these expectations may in turn influence eventual educational outcomes. We utilize data from a variety of data sets, including three longitudinal National Center for Education Statistics (NCES) data sets—the High School and Beyond survey (HS&B), the National Education Longitudinal Study of 1988 (NELS), and the Education Longitudinal Study of 2002 (ELS)—in addition to the Monitoring the Future survey (MTF).

We document that expectations increased rapidly from the 1970s through the mid-1990s and somewhat less rapidly (but nonetheless steadily) from the mid-1990s through 2006. The expectations gap between more and less advantaged students has narrowed substantially over this time period. Expectations of girls grew much faster than those of boys, particularly in more disadvantaged families.

We find that students' expectations in tenth grade are strong predictors of enrollment, even after controlling for a host of individual, family, and school characteristics, although they appear to have become somewhat less predictive of attainment over the past several decades. The expectations themselves are positively associated with student academic ability and socioeconomic status.

Turning to the alignment between student expectations and actual attainment, we find greater misalignment among disadvantaged students. The vast majority of variance in such misalignment is within rather than between high schools. The data demonstrate that the majority (about 60 percent) of students update their expectations at least once between eighth grade and eight years post high school. Updating appears to be based in part on the acquisition of new information about academic ability.

INTRODUCTION

Education has become an increasingly important determinant of labor-market success in the United States over the past several decades. The economic returns to a college degree have jumped dramatically. For example, between 1980 and 2005 the weekly earnings of workers with exactly a B.A. degree increased by roughly 22 percent relative to workers with only a high school diploma (Goldin and Katz 2007). At the same time, rates of college completion have increased across all racial, ethnic, and socioeconomic groups during this period. Yet economically disadvantaged groups still lag behind their more-advantaged peers in terms of educational attainment. According to the U.S. Census, 37 percent of white, non-Hispanic twenty-five- to twenty-nine-year-olds had at least a B.A. degree in 2008, compared with only 21 percent and 12 percent of African Americans and Hispanics respectively (U.S. Bureau of the Census 2008).

Researchers, educators, and policymakers have frequently looked to the educational expectations of young people—that is, their beliefs about their likely educational attainment—to gauge their future success. During the 1960s, William H. Sewell, Otis D. Duncan, and their colleagues produced seminal research demonstrating a strong positive correlation between expectations and educational and occupational attainment. This research spurred almost fifty years of inquiry into the effects of expectations on attainment. Although there is no convincing evidence that expectations influence attainment in a causal sense, many still believe that inspiring students to attend college will result in a more highly educated population.

In this chapter we examine the role of educational expectations in the education-attainment process. Specifically, we investigate how family experiences, school functioning, and knowledge of labor-market pathways affect educational outcomes by means of expectations. We begin by documenting the trends in educational expectations between 1980 and the early 2000s, highlighting how these trends have changed differentially across racial-ethnic and socioeconomic groups. Although considerable literature on expectations in the 1980s and 1990s exists, there is very little evidence on how expectations have evolved over the past fifteen years, arguably a period during which educational attainment has become even more important for disadvantaged youths.[1]

To document these trends we combine data from three longitudinal National Center for Education Statistics (NCES) data sets: the High School and Beyond survey (HS&B), the National Education Longitudinal Study of 1988 (NELS), and the Education Longitudinal Study of 2002 (ELS). In addition, we use data from Monitoring the Future (MTF), a rich source of information on a nationally representative set of high school students beginning in the mid-1970s that is not often used in studies of educational expectations (the exception is Reynolds et al. 2006). Our trend analysis pays particular attention to the gap between expectations and actual attainment.

Next, we examine how expectations are related to attainment. Earlier research documents that, conditional on a number of family, neighborhood, individual, and school characteristics, higher expectations are associated with higher attainment. However, the growing gap between expectations and actual attainment suggests that this relationship has weakened over time. Our analysis focuses on how the relationship between expectations and attainment has changed over time for various groups.

We will examine how, if at all, students update their expectations in response to additional information about costs and benefits of college for themselves. Prior work has documented this updating among college students (Stinebrickner and Stinebrickner 2009), but there is no evidence on whether high school students or young adults in the labor force update their educational expectations. Understanding the process by which students form expectations and how they update these expectations is critical to understanding variation in educational attainment. We use data on a nationally representative set of eighth-grade students in 1988 from NELS to explore how young people update their expectations during high school and to determine whether high school experiences and college costs affect students' development and maintenance of expectations.

In the second section of the chapter we lay out the conceptual framework for how expectations affect attainment. In the third section we describe the data used in our analysis. In the fourth section we document the trends in educational expectations and actual attainment from the late 1970s through the early 2000s, highlighting differences across racial/ethnic and socioeconomic groups. In the fifth section, we analyze the relationship between expectations and attainment. In the sixth section, we develop a measure of the alignment between expectations and predicted attainment and investigate the determinants of misalignment in high school. Delving into the black box of expectations in the seventh section, we document whether and when students update their expectations and analyze how schools and states' higher education policies can influence students' expectations. In the final section we discuss the implications of our findings and our conclusions.

CONCEPTUAL FRAMEWORK

Since the 1970s much research has focused on the link between educational expectations and educational attainment, with a focus on determining what factors influence the development of educational expectations. Much of the early literature in this area uses the terms "expectations" and "aspirations" interchangeably, but in fact these two concepts are quite distinct. Expectations are what individuals think will happen, whereas aspirations are what they hope will happen. In this chapter we focus on expectations for several reasons. First, historically aspirations are higher than expectations, perhaps because they are more heavily influenced by societal norms, but given today's mantra of college for all, aspirations and expectations are virtually indistinguishable. According to MTF data, 85.1 percent of the class of 2007 aspired to attain a B.A. or higher degree, and 84.8 percent of the class of 2007 expected at least a B.A. Second, expectations should be more amenable to rational updating than aspirations, as a result of the acquisition of new information. In this sense, expectations are the more appropriate target of social policies designed to increase educational attainment among young people.

The vast majority of the research on expectations was conducted by sociologists and psychologists, who view formation of expectations as a social process whereby individuals draw on the experiences and expectations of those around them. Figure 7.1 displays the potentially complex relationship between expectations and attainment.

The rectangles on the left side of the figure contain the determinants of educational expectations. Solid lines indicate relationships we hypothesize to be unidirectional, and dashed lines indicate potentially bidirectional relationships. Some of the determinants, such as family factors and college costs, are exogenous to the individual. Other factors, such as an individual's academic achievement and the attitudes and behaviors of one's peers, can vary with time and are likely both to influence and to be influenced by one's own expectations.[2] For example, family socioeconomic status (SES) affects a student's expectations, but the student's expectations are not likely to influence the family's SES. However, the high school program a student is placed in affects the student's expectations—but the expectations may also affect the program in which the guidance counselor or administrator places the student.

Many factors that affect expectations are also determinants of attainment, as shown by the curved arrows in figure 7.1. Because expectations and attainment share many determinants, untangling the effect of expectations on attainment is difficult. It may be that any relationship between expectations and attainment is merely correlational, and the expectations merely mediate the relationship between various individual, family, neighborhood, school, and cost factors and attainment.

FIGURE 7.1   *Relationship Between Educational Expectations and Educational Attainment*

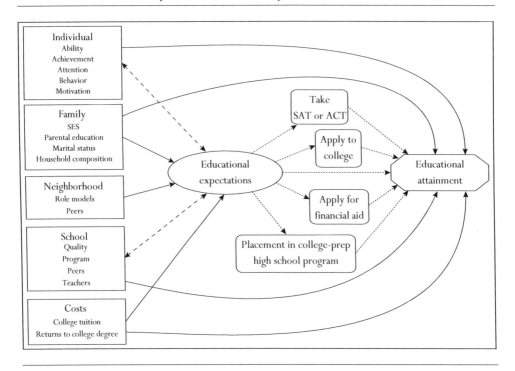

Source: Authors' figure.

Yet a substantial body of literature leads one to believe that the arrow between expectations and attainment does exist. Expectations might influence attainment through a variety of mechanisms. For example, a student who expects to attend college may make a point of signing up for college entrance exams or researching financial aid options. Similarly, upon entering high school a student with college expectations may be placed in the college-prep program as opposed to the general program. These mechanisms are shown with dotted arrows in figure 7.1. This chapter investigates the relationships outlined in figure 7.1 to better understand how expectations might influence educational attainment.

DATA

The analysis in this chapter draws on several data sets. To provide a consistent picture of educational expectations over a long time period, we utilize data from the MTF survey. Funded by the National Institute on Drug Abuse and conducted at the University of Michigan's Survey Research Center, MTF collects data on student attitudes, behaviors, and beliefs. Since 1976, MTF has collected data annually on a nationally representative sample of twelfth-graders and has consistently asked twelfth-grade students about their educational expectations. MTF began surveying eighth- and tenth-graders in 1991, asking them similar questions.

To more carefully investigate the determinants of educational expectations, we utilize data from three longitudinal surveys conducted by the NCES: HS&B, NELS, and ELS. These surveys are longitudinal, following the high school sophomore classes of 1980, 1990, and 2002 into adulthood, thus documenting changes in expectations over time.

Each NCES survey follows students from the beginning of high school through entry into their young-adult lives. Included in each survey are data gathered from students and their parents, teachers, and schools, and administrative data such as high school transcripts. Because the goal of each survey is similar—to monitor students' academic experiences and educational and occupational expectations to better understand the transition from high school to young adult life—the questions pertaining to educational expectations are consistently asked throughout each survey. Although previous research has used both HSB and NELS to investigate educational expectations, our study links these two surveys to the most recent data from the ELS. This is our contribution to the literature.

In addition to information on individual, family, and school characteristics, these data sets include demographic and local labor-market data from the U.S. Census that is matched to the respondent's county of residence in the corresponding census year.[3] Finally, to measure the cost of postsecondary education for each respondent, we created county-level measures of tuition and room and board costs at all degree-granting Title IV institutions using data from the Higher Education General Information Survey (HEGIS) and Integrated Postsecondary Education Data System (IPEDS). In our analysis we use the minimum in-state tuition and room and board data for 2007.

To compare trends across all three files, in one of our analyses we focused solely on students from tenth grade through two years following their expected high school graduation. In all three data sets, this entailed tracking a nationally representative set of tenth-graders for four years, even if they left school. To facilitate our analysis, we excluded students with missing data on tenth-grade expectations or key demographic variables such as race, gender, socioeconomic status, and test scores. This resulted in dropping 15 percent of students in the HS&B, 18 percent of students in the NELS, and 13 percent of students in the ELS. Data in all the analyses were weighted to be nationally representative.

Table 7.A1 in the online appendix (available at http://www.russellsage.org/duncan_murnane_online_appendix.pdf) presents the summary statistics from this three-cohort analysis sample.[4] Several facts are worth noting. First, the expectations of attaining at least some college education increase sharply between 1980 and 1990 but change little from 1990 to 2002. In contrast, expectations regarding B.A. completion jumped considerably in all periods. Second, parental education increased over this period, particularly from 1980 to 1990. Last, the percentage of students enrolling in four-year postsecondary institutions increased by nearly 50 percent between 1980 and 2002.

In addition to the three-cohort panel, we also utilized the full NELS panel to more carefully examine how students update their expectations. This panel tracks a nationally representative set of eighth-graders in 1988 for twelve years, with the final survey administered in 2000, when this cohort was eight years beyond their expected high school graduation date. Online appendix table 7.A2 presents summary statistics for this sample. Note that the sample size varies across waves and outcomes, as not all respondents have data for each variable in each wave.

TRENDS IN EDUCATIONAL EXPECTATIONS

To begin, we present data on how educational expectations have evolved over the past several decades. As noted, most prior research has used survey data from high school students in the early 1980s (HS&B) and early 1990s (NELS). In figure 7.2 we present similar data on educational expectations from MTF, which has regularly surveyed nationally representative cohorts of students

FIGURE 7.2   *Students Expecting a B.A., by Grade and Year*

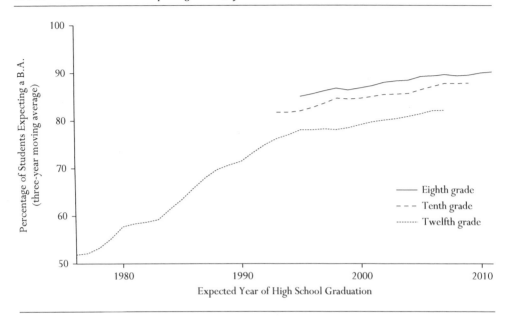

Source: Authors' calculations based on the Monitoring the Future study (Johnston et al. n.d.).

since 1976. These data not only allow us to extend our analysis beyond the scope of HS&B and NELS but also to provide a useful cross-check on the reliability of the expectations data. To minimize the impact of sampling variability, we present three-year moving averages.

In figure 7.2, we see that in 1976, roughly 52 percent of high school seniors expected to complete a B.A. degree. Expectations increased rapidly from the 1970s through the mid-1990s and somewhat less rapidly, but nonetheless steadily, from the mid-1990s through the present. At the same time we see that on average, students lower their expectations between eighth and twelfth grade. Among the class of 2006, for example, roughly 90 percent of students believed as eighth-graders that they would complete a B.A., but by the time this cohort reached twelfth grade, only slightly more than 80 percent expected to attain a B.A.

The trend is quite similar for expectations of at least some college (see online appendix figure 7.A1). In 1976, roughly 77 percent of high school seniors expected to complete at least some college. This fraction rose dramatically until the late 1990s, at which point about 93 percent of seniors expected to complete at least some college. Comparing the trends for eighth- and tenth-graders with those for twelfth-graders, we see that on average, students' expectations with respect to completing some college did not change during high school.

Comparing these trends to the statistics shown in online appendix table 7.A1 reveals a relatively good correspondence between the various data sets. Roughly 80 percent of the HS&B cohort believed they would attend at least some college, compared with about 85 percent in MTF, but only 40 percent believed they would attain a B.A., compared with 58 percent in MTF. Among the ELS cohort, who were high school seniors in 2004, 94 percent expected at least some college and 75 percent expected to earn a B.A. (compared with about 95 percent and 80 percent in the MTF data).

FIGURE 7.3   *Twelfth-Graders Expecting a B.A., by Gender and Parents' Education*

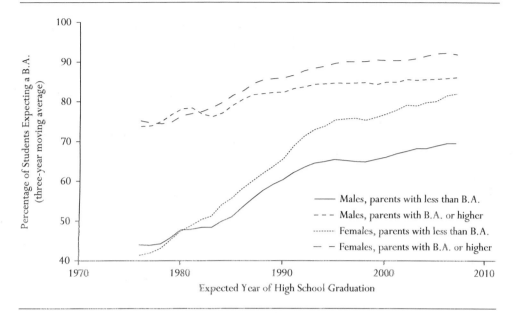

Source: Authors' calculations based on the Monitoring the Future study (Johnston et al. n.d.).

The next figures explore trends in educational expectations by socioeconomic status. Because MTF does not have data on parental income, figure 7.3 shows trends by gender and parental education (online appendix figure 7.A2 documents the trends in expectations of some college among the same subgroups). Figure 7.4 uses data from the HS&B, the NELS, and the ELS to show how expectations have changed for male and female students in quintiles of the SES distribution, as measured by the composite SES in these datasets.

Several interesting patterns emerge. First, the expectations gap between more- and less-advantaged students has narrowed substantially over this time period. In the mid-1970s, students whose parents had a B.A. degree had substantially higher educational expectations than their peers; about 75 percent of males and females with college-educated parents expected to attain a B.A., whereas only 41 percent of females and 45 percent of males whose parents had less than a B.A. expected to do so. By the mid-2000s, expectations among all groups had risen, although the largest increases were among more disadvantaged families. About 92 percent of females and 86 percent of males with college-educated parents expected to attain a B.A., while 82 percent of females and 70 percent of males whose parents had less than a B.A. expected to do so.

Second, expectations have grown much faster among females than among males. For example, the percentage of females expecting to earn a B.A. whose parents had less than a B.A. doubled between the mid-1970s and mid-2000s, increasing from 41 percent to 82 percent, compared to a change of twenty-five percentage points, from 45 percent to 70 percent, among males from similar households.

Third, the evolution of expectations displays interesting interactions between socioeconomic status and gender. The data in figure 7.4 indicate that the growth of female expectations relative to male expectations was greater in more disadvantaged households. For example, figure 7.4

FIGURE 7.4   *Tenth-Graders Expecting a B.A., by Gender and SES*

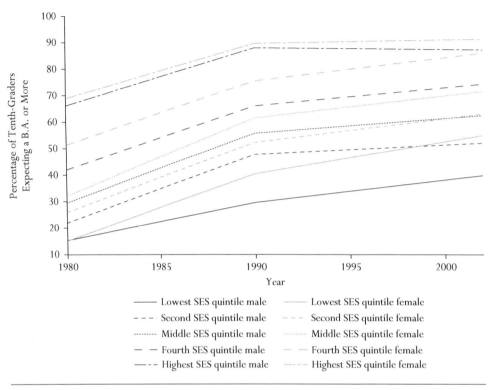

Source: Authors' calculations based on the National Education Longitudinal Study, High School and Beyond, and Education Longitudinal Study (National Center for Education Statistics 2003, 1995, 2007).

shows that in 1980 there was not a gender gap in expectations among bottom-quintile households, but by 2002 there was a gender gap of fifteen percentage points, while the corresponding gender gap for top-quintile households increased by only one percentage point from 1980 to 2002.

Interestingly, the particularly rapid increase in expectations among females from disadvantaged households differs from the trends in educational attainment. As Martha J. Bailey and Susan M. Dynarski document in chapter 6 of this volume, females in higher-SES families have experienced larger growth in postsecondary attainment than females in lower-SES families over roughly the same period. One explanation for the more modest gains in expectations among females from more-advantaged families is a ceiling effect—that is, these female students already reported extraordinarily high expectations. For example, by the mid-1990s almost all advantaged females expected to attain a B.A., thus limiting the potential size of the gender gap in expectations among advantaged students.

THE RELATIONSHIP BETWEEN EDUCATIONAL EXPECTATIONS AND ACTUAL ENROLLMENT

Researchers in the 1970s identified educational expectations as an important predictor of educational and occupational attainment (Duncan, Featherman, and Duncan 1972; Sewell, Haller, and Ohlendorf 1970; Sewell, Haller, and Portes 1969; Sewell and Hauser 1972).[5] Even after conditioning on an extensive set of family background characteristics, educational expectations are strongly correlated with educational attainment (Duncan, Featherman, and Duncan 1972; Sewell and Hauser 1972; Sewell, Hauser, and Wolf 1980; Sewell and Shah 1967).[6]

Of course, this correlation does not necessarily imply that expectations have a causal impact on attainment. The positive correlation may simply reflect the fact that individuals have better information about their future paths than can be captured with the measures commonly available in researchers' data. For example, money available from a relative for college might not show up in family income measures available in standard data sets. Alternatively, some students with mediocre grades and test scores undoubtedly have greater academic potential than others with similar high school performance. If those with greater "unobserved potential" indicate higher educational expectations, one would find a positive correlation due to the presence of this unobserved factor and not because of the independent causal power of expectations themselves. In the analyses that follow, we not only document the relationship between expectations and attainment but also take considerable pains to assess, as well as possible, whether the documented relationship is causal or not.

To examine the relationship between expectations and enrollment, in table 7.1 we present results from regressions of postsecondary enrollment on tenth-grade expectations and other background variables. The top section of the table presents ordinary least-squares (OLS) estimates where the dependent variable is enrollment in any postsecondary institution; the bottom section presents estimates where the dependent variable is enrollment in a four-year institution. Columns 1 to 3 show estimates in which the only predictors are tenth-grade expectations. Columns 4 to 6 present estimates from a model that includes as predictors all family background variables, student demographics, and school and county characteristics.

We see in columns 1 to 3 that tenth-grade expectations are indeed strong predictors of enrollment. For example, in the 2002 cohort of tenth-graders, students who expected to attain at least some college were twenty-three percentage points more likely to be enrolled in postsecondary education than their peers who expected to attain at most a high school degree. Interestingly, however, nearly 27 percent of students who as tenth-graders did not expect to attain any college were enrolled in college within two years of their expected high school graduation. Similarly, students in this cohort who expected to attain a B.A. degree were roughly forty-one percentage points more likely to be enrolled in a four-year college. Again, it is interesting to note that roughly 7 percent of students with no expectations of college report being enrolled in a four-year college in the second follow-up survey.

Even after we control for a host of individual, family, and school characteristics, tenth-grade expectations are strongly predictive of eventual enrollment (columns 4 to 6). For example, among the 2002 cohort of tenth-graders, students who expected to attain at least some college were about fourteen percentage points more likely to be enrolled in postsecondary education than their peers who expected to attain at most a high school degree. Similarly, students in this cohort who expected to attain a B.A. degree were roughly sixteen percentage points more likely to be enrolled in a four-year college.

Although these results indicate that expectations remain strong predictors of attainment above and beyond other standard determinants of schooling, the data also reveal that expectations have become somewhat less predictive of attainment over the past several decades. In the 1980 cohort, tenth-grade expectations explained roughly 25 percent of the variation in postsecondary enrollment. This figure decreased to roughly 20 percent for the 1990 cohort and to roughly 15 percent in the 2002 cohort. The pattern is similar for B.A. attainment. One reason for the decreasing explanatory power of expectations is that the variance of expectations decreased by about one-third between 1980 and 2002.

TABLE 7.1   OLS Estimates of the Relationship Between Educational Expectations and Actual Enrollment, Sophomore Cohorts

Dependent Variable: Enrollment in any Postsecondary Institution Within Two Years of Expected High School Graduation

	Sophomores in 1980	Sophomores in 1990	Sophomores in 2002	Sophomores in 1980	Sophomores in 1990	Sophomores in 2002
	(1)	(2)	(3)	(4)	(5)	(6)
Expectation of some college or more, grade ten	0.309***	0.294***	0.231***	0.193***	0.201***	0.142***
	(0.016)	(0.019)	(0.025)	(0.016)	(0.019)	(0.023)
Expectation of B.A. or more, grade ten	0.297***	0.325***	0.326***	0.144***	0.157***	0.144***
	(0.013)	(0.014)	(0.018)	(0.014)	(0.015)	(0.018)
Variance of expectation of at least some college, grade ten	0.183	0.082	0.067	0.183	0.082	0.067
Variance in linear measure of educational expectations	2.907	2.138	1.969	2.907	2.138	1.969
Controls	No	No	No	Yes	Yes	Yes
N	11,498	11,857	12,174	11,498	11,857	12,174
R^2	0.247	0.205	0.155	0.336	0.311	0.320
Mean of dependent variable	0.632	0.712	0.76	0.632	0.712	0.76
Mean of dependent variable for students with expectations of less than college	0.25	0.241	0.273	0.25	0.241	0.273

Dependent Variable: Enrollment in a Four-Year College Within Two Years of Expected High School Graduation

	Sophomores in 1980	Sophomores in 1990	Sophomores in 2002	Sophomores in 1980	Sophomores in 1990	Sophomores in 2002
	(1)	(2)	(3)	(4)	(5)	(6)
Expectation of some college or more, grade ten	0.139***	0.098***	0.066***	0.032***	0.019	−0.19
	(0.010)	(0.010)	(0.015)	(0.010)	(0.010)	(0.015)
Expectation of B.A. or more, grade ten	0.411***	0.398***	0.414***	0.223***	0.176***	0.163***
	(0.013)	(0.012)	(0.014)	(0.014)	(0.012)	(0.015)

Variance of expectation of at least some college, grade ten	0.248	0.235	0.142	0.248	0.235	0.142
Variance in linear measure of educational expectations	2.907	2.138	1.969	2.907	2.138	1.969
Controls	No	No	No	Yes	Yes	Yes
N	11,498	11,857	12,174	11,498	11,857	12,174
R^2	0.264	0.186	0.127	0.381	0.353	0.374
Mean of dependent variable	0.364	0.379	0.513	0.364	0.379	0.513
Mean of dependent variable for students with expectations of less than college	0.054	0.031	0.072	0.054	0.031	0.072

Source: Authors' calculations based on High School and Beyond, National Education Longitudinal Study, and Educational Longitudinal Study (National Center for Education Statistics 1995, 2003, 2007).

Notes: Standard errors clustered at the school level.

Data are weighted to be nationally representative.

Data on applying and enrolling in college are based on self-reports.

To be enrolled in a postsecondary institution, students had to finish high school with either a regular diploma or a GED.

Data on tenth-graders in 1980 are from High School and Beyond.

Data on tenth-graders in 1990 are from National Education Longitudinal Study.

Data on tenth-graders in 2002 are from Education Longitudinal Study.

Control variables include SES, gender, race-ethnicity, siblings, tenth-grade GPA, number of students per guidance counselor, high school program, percentage of high school's previous graduating class going on to college, percentage of students eligible for free and reduced-priced lunch at high school, county unemployment rate, county per capita income, county minimum in-state tuition, and county minimum room and board.

***$p < 0.001$

However, determining the causality in this association is difficult. Omitted variables such as family wealth, personal connections, intrinsic motivation, or talent (athletic, musical, artistic) may drive the apparent relationship between expectations and attainment. Additionally, the potential for reverse causality between expectations and the predictors is strong. For example, student grades directly affect both expectations and attainment, but expectations may also affect grades such that as expectations increase, students earn higher grades. The causal loop between expectations and grades makes it difficult to determine the primary mechanism (that is, grades or expectations) through which these two variables affect attainment.

To further examine the relationship between expectations and enrollment and attainment, we estimate increasingly comprehensive specifications for attainment using data from the sophomore class of 1990. These results, shown in tables 7.2 and 7.3, come from OLS regressions. Table 7.2 documents the effects of expectations on enrollment, and table 7.3 shows how expectations affect attainment. The coefficients on the expectations variables in the enrollment regressions (table 7.2) are larger than those in the attainment regressions (table 7.3), but expectations remain strong predictors of attainment. Within each panel, each successive column includes additional predictors to demonstrate the robustness of the expectations effect. The inclusion of family background and individual demographics in column 2 of each panel reduces the effect of expectations on both enrollment and attainment only slightly. The inclusion of high school achievement measures in column 3, however, dramatically reduces the coefficients on the expectations variables in each of the panels. Interestingly, the inclusion of nonachievement measures (column 4) including personality characteristics such as self-esteem and locus of control as well as behavioral measures (for example, TV watching, homework completion, suspensions, and so forth) has very little, if any, effect on the relationship between expectations and enrollment and attainment. This result is somewhat surprising, given the extensive psychological literature on the importance of self-regulation and intrinsic motivation—two related characteristics—on academic achievement and attainment (Benware and Deci 1984; Deci et al. 1991; Grolnick and Ryan 1987; Grolnick, Ryan, and Deci 1991; Ryan and Deci 2000; Zimmerman, Bandura, and Martinez-Pons 1992). The limited mitigating effect that personality characteristics have on the expectations-attainment relationship suggests that expectations are separate from internal student characteristics and may, instead, be developed more through social experiences.

Similarly, the coefficients on expectations decrease only slightly when measures of school characteristics (column 6) or school fixed effects (column 5) are added. County-level demographics and college cost variables (column 7) also do not influence the relationship between expectations and attainment. The fact that the inclusion of an increasingly rich set of observable characteristics does not change the relationships between expectations and enrollment and expectations and attainment lends credence to the view that expectations themselves may directly influence attainment.

In a further attempt to dissect the relationship between expectations and attainment, online appendix table 7.A3 shows results from OLS regressions of various tenth-grade behaviors on eighth-grade expectations. If expectations had a causal impact on attainment, one would expect them to also predict a host of mediating mechanisms, such as high school grade-point average and time spent on homework. Of course, the existence of a relationship between early expectations and subsequent behaviors associated with schooling success does not by any means prove that expectations influence attainment. But the absence of such relationships would be troubling. The results in table 7.A3 show that college expectations are positively associated with academic outcomes such as GPA, hours of homework per week, and type of high school program but are not related to self-reported absenteeism, self-reported TV watching, parent-reported behavior problems, or personality measures, such as self-esteem and locus of control. Although the results are somewhat mixed overall, the GPA and homework results are consistent with expectations' having a causal impact on achievement and attainment. The results presented in tables 7.1, 7.2, 7.3, and 7.A3 are, however, merely suggestive of a causal relationship between expectations and college enrollment and completion.

UNDERSTANDING THE GAP BETWEEN EXPECTATIONS AND ATTAINMENT

Prior literature has documented a substantial gap between the expectations and actual attainment of young people. Figure 7.5 documents the trends, by race and gender, in both expectations for and attainment of a B.A. (figure 7.A4 in the online appendix shows trends in expecting and attaining some college).[7] Although expectations of a B.A. degree steadily increased from about 60 percent in the early 1970s to over 80 percent by 2000, attainment of such a degree did not rise accordingly for blacks or whites. In fact, the percentage of blacks and males completing a B.A. has remained fairly constant over this time period. A greater proportion of females and whites have completed a B.A. today than in the early 1970s, but the rising trend has not kept pace with increases in expectations. (For a more detailed discussion of the trends in educational attainment, see chapter 6, in this volume).

Understanding why students' educational expectations are much higher than their actual attainment is important if we desire to change individuals' expectations in an effort to attain more optimal outcomes. The first step in doing this is to understand how young people form educational expectations. Expectation formation is a complex process; individuals do not have access to the same information and likely weight various factors differently in determining expectations (Manski 1993).

DETERMINANTS OF EDUCATIONAL EXPECTATIONS

Prior research documents a variety of factors associated with educational expectations, including children's own abilities and school experiences (Duncan, Featherman, and Duncan 1972; Hoelter 1982; Reynolds et al. 2006; Rosenbaum 2001; Sewell, Haller, and Portes 1969; Teachman and Paasch 1998), family characteristics such as parental educational attainment and income (Duncan, Featherman, and Duncan 1972; Goyette 2008; Kao and Tienda 1998; Sewell, Haller, and Ohlendorf 1970; Sewell, Haller, and Portes 1969; Teachman and Paasch 1998), and neighborhood characteristics (Teachman and Paasch 1998). One means by which parental income likely influences children's educational expectations is by the ability to pay for postsecondary education (Astone and McLanahan 1991; McLanahan and Bumpass 1988). Parental involvement—as evidenced by activities such as monitoring children's homework, offering encouragement about school-related activities, and providing academic enrichment materials at home—is positively related to expectations (Astone and McLanahan 1991; Kao and Tienda 1998; Schneider and Stevenson 1999). Additionally, parents' educational expectations for their children affect the children's educational expectations (Davies and Kandel 1981; Schneider and Stevenson 1999).[8]

Much of the literature focuses on the influence of teacher encouragement and expectations and peer expectations, finding significant positive effects of both on expectations (Davies and Kandel 1981; Duncan, Featherman, and Duncan 1972; Hoelter 1982; Kiuru et al. 2007; Schneider and Stevenson 1999; Sewell, Haller, and Ohlendorf 1970; Sewell, Haller, and Portes 1969). Other research demonstrates that when neighborhoods are socially, economically, and racially segregated, expectations may be depressed. Children growing up in neighborhoods of concentrated disadvantage likely do not have exposure to individuals similar to themselves and their families who have high levels of educational attainment. Consequently, children lack information about

(Text continues on p. 149.)

TABLE 7.2   *OLS Estimates of the Relationship Between Educational Expectations and Enrollment, 1990 Sophomore Cohort*

	Enrolled in Any Postsecondary Institution Within Two Years of Expected High School Graduation				
	(1)	(2)	(3)	(4)	(5)
Expectation of some college or more, grade ten	0.233*** (0.018)	0.227*** (0.018)	0.183*** (0.018)	0.178*** (0.018)	0.157*** (0.014)
Expectation of B.A. or more, grade ten	0.244*** (0.014)	0.192*** (0.015)	0.104*** (0.016)	0.104*** (0.016)	0.084*** (0.010)
Student characteristics		X	X	X	X
Family characteristics		X	X	X	X
Academic achievement characteristics			X	X	X
Nonachievement characteristics				X	X
School characteristics					
County characteristics					
Tenth-grade school fixed effects					X
R^2	0.108	0.136	0.169	0.173	0.373
N	15,803				
F-statistic for fixed effect					3.112
Degrees of freedom for absorbed fixed effect					1,466
Residual degrees of freedom					14,294
Probability for F-statistic of joint significance					0.000
Mean of dependent variable	0.539				
Mean of dependent variable for students with expectations of less than college	0.215				

Source: Authors' calculations based on data from the National Education Longitudinal Study (National Center for Education Statistics 2003).

Notes: Standard errors clustered at the school level.

Data are weighted to be nationally representative.

Data on applying and enrolling in college are based on self-reports.

To be enrolled in a postsecondary institution, students had to finish high school with either a regular diploma or a GED.

Student characteristics are SES quartile in grade eight, gender, and race-ethnicity.

Family characteristics are siblings in grade eight, household composition in grade eight, and number of sibling dropouts as of grade ten.

Academic achievement characteristics are combined grade-eight math and reading test score quartiles, high school program, and grade-ten GPA.

Nonachievement characteristics are locus of control in grade ten, school suspensions in grade ten, days absent in grade ten, hours of TV per week in grade ten, and hours of homework per week in grade ten.

School characteristics are private school in grade ten, school size in grade ten, percent of previous year's graduates attending college, percent of students eligible for free and reduced-priced lunch in grade ten, and number of students per guidance counselor.

County characteristics are percentage of population unemployed in grade ten, county per capita income in grade ten, minimum postsecondary education in-state tuition in grade twelve, and minimum postsecondary education room and board costs in grade twelve.

X indicates that this set of variables was included in the model.

***$p < 0.001$

(6)	(7)	Enrolled in a Four-Year College Within Two Years of Expected High School Graduation						
		(1)	(2)	(3)	(4)	(5)	(6)	(7)
0.178***	0.169***	0.068***	0.051***	0.006	0.003	0.010	0.007	0.005
(0.018)	(0.017)	(0.009)	(0.008)	(0.009)	(0.009)	(0.013)	(0.009)	(0.009)
0.096***	0.096***	0.310***	0.240***	0.125***	0.124***	0.122***	0.113***	0.113***
(0.016)	(0.016)	(0.011)	(0.011)	(0.011)	(0.011)	(0.009)	(0.011)	(0.011)
X	X		X	X	X	X	X	X
X	X		X	X	X	X	X	X
X	X			X	X	X	X	X
X	X				X	X	X	X
X	X					X	X	X
	X							X
						X		
0.185	0.193	0.127	0.171	0.244	0.246	0.429	0.265	0.268
		15,803						
						3.13		
						1,466		
						14,294		
						0.000		
		0.286						
		0.041						

TABLE 7.3   *OLS Estimates of the Relationship Between Educational Expectations and Attainment, 1990 Sophomore Cohort*

	Dependent Variable: Attainment of at Least Some College				
	(1)	(2)	(3)	(4)	(5)
Expectation of some college or more, grade ten	0.114***	0.100***	0.057***	0.053***	0.045**
	(0.015)	(0.015)	(0.016)	(0.016)	(0.014)
Expectation of B.A. or more, grade ten	0.209***	0.147***	0.058***	0.055***	0.040***
	(0.013)	(0.012)	(0.013)	(0.013)	(0.010)
Student characteristics		X	X	X	X
Family characteristics		X	X	X	X
Academic achievement characteristics			X	X	X
Nonachievement characteristics				X	X
School characteristics					
County characteristics					
Tenth-grade school fixed effects					X
R^2	0.065	0.106	0.143	0.146	0.341
N	15,803				
F-statistic for fixed effects					2.875
Degrees of freedom for absorbed fixed effect					1,466
Residual degrees of freedom					14,294
Probability for F-statistic of joint significance					0.000
Mean of dependent variable	0.337				
Mean of dependent variable for students with expectations of less than college	0.113				

Source: Authors' calculations based on National Education Longitudinal Study (National Center for Education Statistics 2003).

Notes: Standard errors clustered at the school level.

Data are weighted to be nationally representative.

Data on applying and enrolling in college are based on self-reports.

To be enrolled in a postsecondary institution, students had to finish high school with either a regular diploma or GED.

Student characteristics are SES quartile in grade eight, gender, and race-ethnicity.

Family characteristics are siblings in grade eight, household composition in grade eight, and number of sibling dropouts as of grade ten.

Academic achievement characteristics are combined grade-eight math and reading test score quartiles, high school program, and grade-ten GPA.

Nonachievement characteristics are locus of control in grade ten, school suspensions in grade ten, days absent in grade ten, hours of TV per week in grade ten, and hours of homework per week in grade ten.

School characteristics are private school in grade ten, school size in grade ten, percent of previous year's graduates attending college, percent of students eligible for free and reduced-priced lunch in grade ten, and number of students per guidance counselor.

County characteristics are percent of population unemployed in grade ten, county per capita income, in grade ten, minimum postsecondary education in-state tuition in grade twelve, and minimum postsecondary education room and board costs in grade twelve.

X indicates that this set of variables was included in the model.

***$p < 0.001$

		Dependent Variable: Attainment of a B.A. or More						
(6)	(7)	(1)	(2)	(3)	(4)	(5)	(6)	(7)
0.055***	0.051***	0.048***	0.030***	−0.008	−0.010	−0.014	−0.005	−0.006
(0.015)	(0.015)	(0.007)	(0.006)	(0.007)	(0.008)	(0.012)	(0.008)	(0.008)
0.048***	0.048***	0.281***	0.203***	0.103***	0.102***	0.096***	0.092***	0.092***
(0.013)	(0.013)	(0.010)	(0.009)	(0.009)	(0.009)	(0.008)	(0.009)	(0.009)
X	X		X	X	X	X	X	X
X	X		X	X	X	X	X	X
X	X			X	X	X	X	X
X	X				X	X	X	X
X	X					X	X	X
	X							X
						X		
0.155	0.159	0.115	0.180	0.240	0.242	0.416	0.252	0.254
		15,803						
						2.903		
						1,466		
						14,294		
						0.000		
		0.240						
		0.027						

educational and occupational opportunities and may be unaware of the economic benefits of educational attainment (Ogbu 1991; Stewart, Stewart, and Simons 2007; Streufert 1991; Wilson 1987).

Although the prior literature has documented strong correlations between individual, family, and neighborhood characteristics and children's educational expectations, one should not necessarily interpret these relationships as causal. For many of the reasons previously discussed, factors omitted from the statistical models may explain the observed relationship. For example, the value parents place on higher education influences the neighborhood in which a child lives and the schools he or she attends, and may explain a child's expectations. But it may be hard to observe parents' value of education, which is likely manifest in numerous ways, making it seem as though other correlated observables such as neighborhood explain a child's expectations.

Table 7.A4 in the online appendix presents the determinants of tenth-grade expectations for the NELS sophomore cohort. The results generally confirm the findings in the literature. SES and academic ability are the strongest predictors of expectations. Both SES and academic ability are positively related to expectations such that higher-SES students have higher expectations than lower-SES students, and students with higher test scores and higher GPAs have higher expectations than students with lower test scores and GPAs. The only school-level variable that affects expectations is enrollment in a private school, and this is particularly true when looking at expectations of a B.A. or more.

DETERMINANTS OF MISALIGNMENT

With a general understanding of what determines expectations, we can begin to investigate potential explanations for the gap between expectations and attainment. Researchers have posited mul-

FIGURE 7.5A   *Blacks' Expectations and Attainment of B.A.*

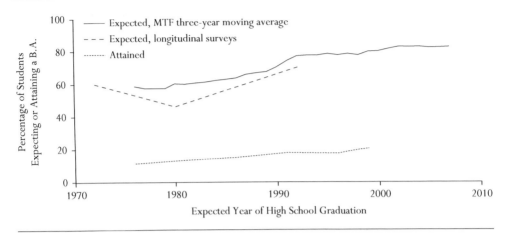

Source: Authors' calculations based on the National Education Longitudinal Study (National Center for Education Statistics 2003).

FIGURE 7.5B   *Whites' Expectations and Attainment of B.A.*

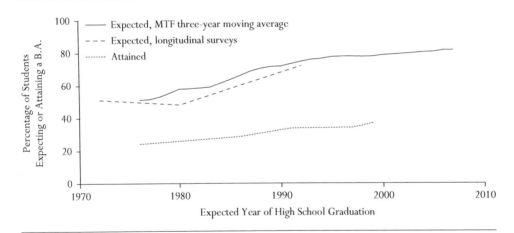

Source: Authors' calculations based on the National Education Longitudinal Study (National Center for Education Statistics 2003).

tiple explanations for the gap between expectations and attainment. In general, the gap exists because students' expectations are too high. Expectations are a student's best guess of his or her eventual attainment given ability, family background, school quality, and neighborhood—all factors that determine attainment. Hence, the expectations-attainment gap implies inappropriate or "irrational" expectations, given a student's fixed characteristics and experiences.

Researchers often describe the gap as a problem in course selection or preparation. Although these factors do influence attainment, they do not technically explain the gap given our definition of expectations: a student's best estimate of attainment using available information. If the question is how to help students attain their expectations, then these are reasonable paths to pursue, but they do not reveal the causes of the expectations-attainment gap. The gap has two potential causes: (1) students have misinformation about costs or requirements of college (that is, students expect to be able to pay for college and easily complete the coursework), or (2) an

FIGURE 7.5C   *Females' Expectations and Attainment of B.A.*

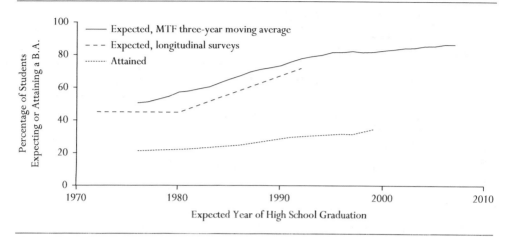

Source: Authors' calculations based on the National Education Longitudinal Study (National Center for Education Statistics 2003).

FIGURE 7.5D   *Males' Expectations and Attainment of B.A.*

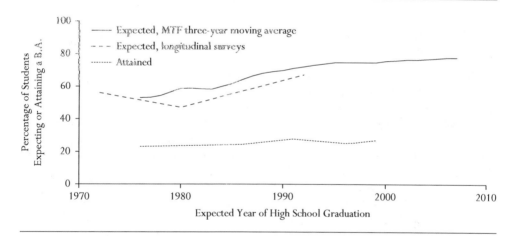

Source: Authors' calculations based on the National Education Longitudinal Study (National Center for Education Statistics 2003).

unexpected shock occurs after students form their expectations, which prevents them from attending. Shocks such as changes in family income or illness can be positive as well as negative, which would drive the gap in different directions, resulting in minimal net change; however, the data do not show this pattern, making random shocks an unlikely cause of the gap. The fact that most students attain less education than they expect (that is, the expectations-attainment gap is negative) suggests that misinformation causes the gap. Students have misinformation about the cost of college, the preparation they will need, and the difficulty of completing college. Even with adequate preparation and available funding, students may simply realize that college is not a good match for them (Orfield and Paul 1994; Schneider and Stevenson 1999).

When a student has expectations based on misinformation or the student is unprepared to meet his or her expectations, sociologists call the student's expectations misaligned. Aligned expectations fit with other life goals and ability and are stable throughout high school (Schneider and Stevenson 1999). Economists use slightly different terminology, typically speaking of "rational" expectations or expectations that would result in the largest economic gain for the individual, given his or her affinity for schooling (Manski 1993).

Previous research suggests that some groups are more likely to have misaligned expectations than others. For example, a study of middle school students in two Massachusetts schools showed that urban students had less alignment between their educational expectations and their educational preparation (for example, college-prep track versus vocational track) and their other life plans (for example, age of marriage and age of pregnancy and starting a family) (Malcolmson 2007).

In table 7.4 we develop a measure of alignment and attempt to discern which students are more or less likely to have aligned expectations. We measure alignment in twelfth grade as the predicted probability of reaching one's twelfth-grade expectations on the basis of observable twelfth-grade characteristics. Specifically, for each student we determined the probability that the student would attain each level of education (less than high school degree, high school degree, some college, and college degree or more). The predicted probabilities were estimated through four regression models, one for each dichotomous dependent variable for each level of attainment regressed on a host of student, family, school, and neighborhood factors measured as of twelfth grade. Using these regression coefficients for each student, we predicted the probability that each level of attainment was the highest level reached by 2000.

Next, we created the probability-of-alignment variable using only the predicted probability estimate for the student's expected education level in twelfth grade. For example, if a student expected a high school degree, we used the predicted probability of that student's attaining a high school degree in the probability-of-alignment variable, but for a student expecting a college degree we used the predicted probability of that student's receiving a college degree by 2000. If a student only expected to complete some college, we used the predicted probability that he or she would attain at least some college as the measure of alignment. (Note that in this way we consider misalignment in a positive direction—when a student is predicted to attain more education than expected—the same as alignment.) Students with a higher value of our alignment measure are more likely to reach their expectations, and low alignment values correspond to a low probability of reaching one's expectations and greater misalignment.[9] If a student expected to attain a B.A. but the predicted probability of this is only 0.36, the student's expectations are not particularly well aligned.

Table 7.4 displays the results of a series of multilevel models estimating what affects expectation alignment in twelfth grade. With the full set of predictors (column 4), the results show that lower-SES students are less likely to reach their expectations and high-achieving students are more likely to reach their expectations. Not surprisingly, students in larger schools and those with greater proportions of students eligible for free and reduced-price lunches are less likely to reach their expectations, and as the average test score in a school rises, so does the likelihood that students within that school will reach their expectations. Positively, students with more aligned expectations—higher predicted probabilities of reaching their expectations—in eighth grade are more likely to reach their twelfth-grade expectations. This finding highlights the importance of students' developing realistic and informed expectations early in their academic careers.

Perhaps schools can play a role in solidifying the link between expectations and attainment. Running the random-effects model estimated in table 7.4 without any predictors indicates that about 30 percent of the variance in the probability of students' reaching expectations that they held in the twelfth grade can be explained by schools. Yet once student characteristics such as demographics, family background variables, and academic ability are added to the model, schools explain only 7 percent of the variance in misalignment (see the bottom of column 1 in table 7.4). Observable school characteristics such as the percentage of students eligible for free and

TABLE 7.4   *Determinants of Aligned Educational Expectations in Twelfth Grade,*
NELS Eighth-Grade Cohort

	Student Predictors, School Random Effects	Student and School Predictors, School Random Effects	Student, School, County Predictors, School Random Effects	Student, School, County, School Average GPA Predictors, School Random Effects
	(1)	(2)	(3)	(4)
Student characteristics				
Alignment of eighth-grade educational expectations[a]	0.376***	0.366***	0.366***	0.363***
	(0.014)	(0.014)	(0.014)	(0.014)
Expectation of less than high school, grade eight	0.041*	0.044*	0.045*	0.046*
	(0.021)	(0.021)	(0.021)	(0.021)
Expectation of high school, grade eight	−0.083***	−0.078***	−0.077***	−0.075***
	(0.010)	(0.010)	(0.010)	(0.010)
Expectation of B.A. or more, grade eight	−0.021***	−0.022***	−0.021***	−0.022***
	(0.004)	(0.004)	(0.004)	(0.004)
Academic GPA, grade eight (0–4 scale)	0.032***	0.035***	0.036***	0.036***
	(0.003)	(0.003)	(0.003)	(0.003)
Living with two parents, grade eight	0.024***	0.018***	0.019***	0.018***
	(0.004)	(0.003)	(0.003)	(0.003)
Locus of control, grade eight (standardized)	0.007*	0.006*	0.006*	0.006
	(0.003)	(0.003)	(0.003)	(0.003)
Self-concept, grade eight (standardized)	0.000	−0.001	−0.001	−0.000
	(0.003)	(0.003)	(0.003)	(0.003)
Lowest SES quintile female, grade eight	−0.067***	−0.055***	−0.054***	−0.050***
	(0.009)	(0.009)	(0.009)	(0.009)
Second SES quintile female, grade eight	−0.088***	−0.078***	−0.077***	−0.075***
	(0.008)	(0.008)	(0.008)	(0.008)
Third SES quintile female, grade eight	−0.060***	−0.052***	−0.051***	−0.049***
	(0.007)	(0.007)	(0.007)	(0.007)
Fourth SES quintile female, grade eight	−0.022**	−0.016*	−0.015*	−0.013
	(0.007)	(0.007)	(0.007)	(0.007)
Highest SES quintile female, grade eight	0.067***	0.067***	0.067***	0.068***
	(0.007)	(0.006)	(0.006)	(0.006)
Lowest SES quintile male, grade eight	−0.096***	−0.084***	−0.083***	−0.080***
	(0.009)	(0.009)	(0.009)	(0.009)
Second SES quintile male, grade eight	−0.103***	−0.095***	−0.094***	−0.092***
	(0.008)	(0.008)	(0.008)	(0.008)
Third SES quintile male, grade eight	−0.091***	−0.083***	−0.083***	−0.080***
	(0.008)	(0.008)	(0.008)	(0.008)
Fourth SES quintile male, grade eight	−0.063***	−0.058***	−0.057***	−0.056***
	(0.007)	(0.007)	(0.007)	(0.007)
Hispanic, grade eight	−0.010	0.004	0.001	0.002
	(0.006)	(0.006)	(0.006)	(0.006)
Black, grade eight	−0.024***	−0.015*	−0.016**	−0.012*
	(0.006)	(0.006)	(0.006)	(0.006)
Other, grade eight	0.015*	0.023***	0.021***	0.021***
	(0.006)	(0.006)	(0.006)	(0.006)
One sibling, grade eight	0.026***	0.028***	0.029***	0.029***
	(0.006)	(0.006)	(0.006)	(0.006)

(Table continues on p. 154.)

TABLE 7.4   *Continued*

	Student Predictors, School Random Effects	Student and School Predictors, School Random Effects	Student, School, County Predictors, School Random Effects	Student, School, County, School Average GPA Predictors, School Random Effects
	(1)	(2)	(3)	(4)
Two siblings, grade eight	−0.012	−0.010	−0.009	−0.009
	(0.007)	(0.007)	(0.007)	(0.006)
Three or more siblings, grade eight	−0.013*	−0.011	−0.011	−0.011
	(0.007)	(0.007)	(0.006)	(0.006)
Lowest-quartile combined math and reading test score, grade eight	−0.101***	−0.097***	−0.097***	−0.092***
	(0.006)	(0.006)	(0.006)	(0.006)
Second-quartile combined math and reading test score, grade eight	−0.112***	−0.109***	−0.109***	−0.105***
	(0.006)	(0.005)	(0.005)	(0.005)
Third-quartile combined math and reading test score, grade eight	−0.075***	−0.073***	−0.073***	−0.071***
	(0.005)	(0.005)	(0.005)	(0.005)
High school academic program	0.024***	0.020***	0.019**	0.019***
	(0.004)	(0.006)	(0.006)	(0.006)
High school vocational program	−0.015**	−0.021*	−0.019*	−0.019*
	(0.005)	(0.009)	(0.009)	(0.009)
School characteristics				
Private school, grade twelve		0.072***	0.006	−0.001
		(0.007)	(0.011)	(0.011)
School size, grade twelve		−0.001***	−0.001***	−0.001***
		(0.000)	(0.000)	(0.000)
Percentage of previous year's graduates in four-year college, grade ten		0.048***	0.037**	0.018
		(0.012)	(0.012)	(0.012)
Percentage of students eligible for free- and reduced-price lunch students, grade ten		−0.094***	−0.087***	−0.074***
		(0.012)	(0.013)	(0.013)
Students per guidance counselor, grade ten, in hundreds		−0.003	−0.002	−0.002
		(0.001)	(0.001)	(0.001)
Students per guidance counselor * high school academic program		0.000	0.000	0.000
		(0.001)	(0.001)	(0.001)
Students per guidance counselor * high school vocational program		0.002	0.002	0.002
		(0.002)	(0.002)	(0.002)
School average combined test score, grade twelve				0.035***
				(0.006)
County characteristics				
Percentage of county population unemployed, grade ten			0.386**	0.411***
			(0.126)	(0.124)
County per capita income, in thousands, grade ten			0.003***	0.002***
			(0.001)	(0.001)
County minimum postsecondary education in-state tuition, in thousands, grade twelve			0.002*	0.002*
			(0.001)	(0.001)
County minimum postsecondary education room and board costs, in thousands, grade twelve			0.001	0.001
			(0.002)	(0.002)
Variance explained by schools	0.005	0.003	0.003	0.002

TABLE 7.4   *Continued*

	Student Predictors, School Random Effects	Student and School Predictors, School Random Effects	Student, School, County Predictors, School Random Effects	Student, School, County, School Average GPA Predictors, School Random Effects
	(1)	(2)	(3)	(4)
Residual variance	0.030	0.029	0.029	0.029
Proportion of total variance explained at school level	0.070	0.038	0.036	0.034
N	14,403			
Mean of dependent variable	0.415			
Variance of dependent variable	0.075			

Source: Authors' calculations based on the National Education Longitudinal Study (National Center for Education Statistics 2003).

Notes: Data are weighted to be nationally representative. Multilevel models with random effects at school level.

[a] Predicted probability of eventually attaining eighth grade self-reported educational expectations.

$*p < 0.05$; $**p < 0.01$; $***p < 0.001$

reduced-price lunches, school size, and the number of students per guidance counselor account for about 3 percent of school-level explained variance, leaving about 4 percent of the total variance in alignment unexplained at the school level. Schools appear to be only minimally capable of helping students develop aligned expectations. Students' own characteristics, particularly SES and academic ability, explain misalignment much more than the characteristics of their high schools. Economically disadvantaged students and those in the bottom three test score quartiles consistently have greater misalignment than do their more economically and academically advantaged peers.

INFORMED EDUCATIONAL EXPECTATIONS

Much of the literature on expectations is concerned with the students' abilities to develop informed expectations, arguing that individuals often do not have the information needed to form aligned expectations or to accurately calculate the returns on schooling (Manski 2004; Orfield and Paul 1994; Rosenbaum 2001; Schneider and Stevenson 1999). However, recent research suggests that college students may indeed update their expectations on the basis of knowledge about their academic ability gained during school (Stinebrickner and Stinebrickner 2009; Zafar 2009). Todd Stinebrickner and Ralph Stinebrickner (2009) follow Berea College students from entrance through each semester of college attendance, tracking their expected and actual performance. They find that students update their expectations on the basis of their actual grade performance, so that students whose performance is significantly lower than expected are more likely to drop out than students whose performance is as expected or better than expected. Basit Zafar (2009) studied the expectations of college students at Northwestern University and found evidence of updating consistent with that of Stinebrickner and Stinebrickner (2009). Specifically, Zafar found that students revise their expectations of future GPAs in light of their prior GPAs. Perhaps more interesting, he found that individuals are more likely to revise expectations that involve higher degrees of uncertainty, such as workplace outcomes, than they are to revise expectations initially held with certainty, such as parental approval and college completion.

To date, the literature has not investigated how high school students update their expectations. The data presented in figure 7.2 showing that students lower their expectations of B.A. completion between eighth and twelfth grade provide some evidence that students do change expectations as they move through the educational process, acquiring new information. If high school students do update their expectations on the basis of new information, policy interventions designed to help high school students develop rational or realistic expectations may be successful. In this section, we analyze NELS data to determine if, when, and why high school students update their expectations.[10]

Figure 7.6 and online appendix table 7.A5 provide descriptive statistics on updating. In figure 7.6, we see that 61 percent of students changed expectations at least once between 1988 and 2000, with 24 percent changing exactly twice and 14 percent changing three or more times. (Note that students were surveyed in five years—1988, 1990, 1992, 1994, and 2000—so a maximum of four changes can be captured in this data. To the extent that students update more frequently, we may be understating the extent of instability in expectations.) Perhaps not surprisingly, considerably more students lowered their expectations between 1988 and 2000 (29 percent) than raised their expectations (13 percent; see table 7.A5). Nearly all students who changed over the entire period did so at least once in the first six years, from 1988 to 1994. This makes sense insofar as one might expect that students learn a great deal about their potential success in college during and immediately after high school.

Given that students frequently change their expectations during high school and that updating is not a random process (students are more likely to update downward than upward), we examine the nature of updating. We first explore whether students in certain schools are more likely to update than others. Online appendix table 7.A6 presents results from OLS regressions of updating on various individual characteristics. We include high school fixed effects so that we

FIGURE 7.6   *Students Changing Expectations over Time, NELS Data, 1988 to 2000*

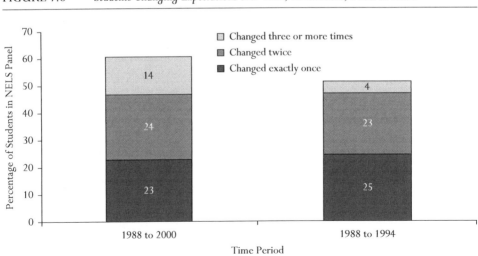

Source: Authors' calculations based on the National Education Longitudinal Study (National Center for Education Statistics 2003).

identify the relationships between updating and student characteristics from the variation within each of the 1,016 schools included in the NELS eighth grade survey.[11]

SES and academic achievement are the strongest predictors of updating of expectations. Eighth-graders in the lower SES quintiles update their expectations more often than students in the highest SES quintile, and males update more often than females. In fact, students in the lowest SES quintile are about 50 percent more likely to have updated their expectations than students in the highest SES quintile. Lower-achieving students are also predicted to update more often than higher-achieving students. More disadvantaged youth (in terms of family income and academic achievement) update their expectations more often than peers. These socioeconomically and academically disadvantaged students start out with extremely high expectations and in general lower them during high school. Interestingly, the F-test for joint significance of the school fixed effects shows that schools seem to matter in terms of updating expectations at least once between eighth and twelfth grade but do not matter for updating twice. This result suggests that serial updaters—those updating twice between eighth and twelfth grade—are influenced more by individual student and family characteristics than by schools.

Next, we investigate whether or not students update in a systematic way on the basis of the acquisition of new information. To do so we estimate the determinants of updating with panel data models and student fixed effects. These models essentially examine whether within-student changes in factors such as academic performance are systematically associated with within-student changes in educational expectations. The results in table 7.5 demonstrate that changes in GPA are positively associated with changes in expectations but that changes in test scores and SES are not associated with changes in expectations.[12] The limited effect of changes in test scores on expectations may be due to the fact that students are not aware of their scores on the NELS achievement tests. Having a child is a strong predictor of decreasing expectations.[13]

Online appendix table 7.A7 presents results separately for a variety of subgroups. Interestingly, students in the two lowest SES quintiles do not seem to update expectations on the basis of changes in GPA. Yet increases in GPA are positively associated with changes in expectations for students in the three highest SES quintiles (the third, fourth, and fifth) and minority students. Having a child is negatively related to changes in expectations for both males and females, and the magnitude of the negative effect on males and females is comparable. Although negatively associated with the expectations of all groups, having a child is particularly detrimental to the overall expectations of minorities, those in the middle SES quintile, and those in the highest test score quartile.

The bottom of table 7.A7 displays the results of changing academic and family characteristics on the expectation of earning a B.A. by subgroups. The results are generally similar to those reported in the top panel, but a few differences are noteworthy. In general, almost all groups seem to update in the predicted directions on the basis of changes in GPA and changes in parent status, but some groups are more affected by these changes than others. Students in the middle of the SES distribution (that is, in the third and fourth quintiles) and students in the tails of the test score distribution seem to be the most influenced by changes in academic achievement. These results lend support to the conclusion that students rely upon their own academic achievement to determine their college expectations. Yet many students still do not fulfill their expectations, suggesting that the updating that takes place during high school on the basis of academic achievement is not sufficient to link expectations to attainment.

Misunderstandings with regard to the costs of college may contribute to the observed expectations-attainment gap. Although economic circumstances have not played a large role in the models thus far, college costs are the focus of many studies investigating barriers to college entry and completion, and states have control over the costs of their public higher education institutions. Beginning in the early 1990s, states began adopting broad-based merit aid programs

TABLE 7.5   Changing Expectations, NELS Panel Data

	Linear Expectations as Dependent Variable				Expectation of Four-Year College as Codependent Variable			
	1988 to 1990	1990 to 1992	1988 to 1992	1988 to 1994	1988 to 1990	1990 to 1992	1988 to 1992	1988 to 1994
Standardized academic GPA	0.093**	0.041*	0.058*	0.066***	0.047**	0.032**	0.034**	0.034***
	(0.030)	(0.017)	(0.025)	(0.018)	(0.016)	(0.011)	(0.011)	(0.009)
Standardized combined test score	0.051	0.023	0.039	0.015	0.047	0.031	0.038**	0.022*
	(0.057)	(0.031)	(0.025)	(0.013)	(0.034)	(0.023)	(0.015)	(0.010)
Standardized SES	-0.681	4.575	-0.860	0.009	-0.673	2.066	-0.748	-0.005
	(1.619)	(5.313)	(1.265)	(0.011)	(1.018)	(3.178)	(0.745)	(0.008)
Have children				-0.155***				-0.112***
				(0.036)				(0.022)
1990	-0.090*		-0.093*	-0.168*	-0.072**		-0.073***	-0.106
	(0.044)		(0.042)	(0.082)	(0.022)		(0.017)	(0.067)
1992		0.140	-0.003	-0.059		0.080	-0.027**	-0.050
		(0.109)	(0.020)	(0.074)		(0.067)	(0.011)	(0.067)
1994				0.000				0.016
				(0.000)				(0.067)
N	21,322	19,710	30,387	40,932	21,322	19,710	30,387	40,932
R^2	0.771	0.860	0.715	0.662	0.752	0.821	0.689	0.633
Mean of dependent variable	2.530	2.561	2.565	2.583	0.648	0.654	0.665	0.679

Source: Authors' calculations based on the National Education Longitudinal Study (National Center for Education Statistics 2003).
Notes: Models include student fixed effects.
Standard errors clustered at the school level.
Data are weighted to be nationally representative.
*p < 0.05; **p < 0.01; ***p < 0.001

that award tuition and fees to student residents who meet a fairly low threshold of academic achievement, such as a high school GPA of 3.0 (Dynarski 2004). The adoption of statewide merit aid programs was a dramatic shift from prior aid programs that at the federal level consisted mostly of need-based aid (Pell Grants and Stafford Loans) and at the state level mainly provided subsidies to public universities to keep tuition and fees low (Dynarski 2004).[14] Research suggests that broad-based statewide merit aid programs have the potential to increase college enrollment. The literature concludes that a $1,000 decrease in college tuition is associated with about a 3.5 percent increase in enrollment (Dynarski 2003; Kane 1995; Leslie and Brinkman 1987).

Expectations may be a mediating factor between state merit aid programs and college enrollment. For this reason, online appendix table 7.A8 demonstrates the effects of state-run, broad-based merit scholarship programs on the expectations of two cohorts, the sophomore classes of 1990 and 2002. Controlling for state fixed effects, changes in the cost of college that are based on the implementation of a statewide merit aid program do not appear to influence student expectations for college. Because almost all sophomores in 1990 and 2002 expected to attend at least some college, the statewide merit aid program may have provided the impetus for more of these students to act upon their high expectations and enroll in college, instead of raising the expectations of the 10 percent of students who did not expect to pursue any postsecondary education.

CONCLUSION

Expectations increased substantially starting in the early 1980s but seem to have leveled off since then; now almost everyone expects to attend at least some college. Individual, family background, and school characteristics have become less predictive of student expectations over time. Yet the data demonstrate a persistent link between socioeconomic inequality and differences in expectations. Although expectations have become somewhat less predictive of attainment, they remain strong predictors of attainment above and beyond other standard determinants of schooling. Expectations, determined largely by factors outside of the school walls, do appear to have an important influence on college enrollment and persistence. More than 60 percent of students update their expectations at least once between eighth grade and eight years post–high school. Updating seems to be based somewhat on acquisition of new information, particularly ability, especially for marginal students in terms of college entry. Early alignment of expectations is predictive of greater likelihood of reaching later expectations. Demographic characteristics of students and schools explain a substantial portion of the between-school variation in the likelihood of students' reaching their expectations. State policies to decrease the costs of college do not seem to influence student expectations.

These results suggest that to generate a cohort of students with expectations likely to lead to enrollment and persistence in postsecondary education, policies should be directed at helping middle school students attain their maximum academic potential. Students rely on knowledge of their own academic ability to develop and maintain their expectations. They lower their expectations when presented with indicators of lower academic ability and raise them when presented with evidence of their higher academic ability.

NOTES

Online appendix available at: http://www.russellsage.org/duncan_murnane_online_appendix.pdf.

1. For research on expectations in the 1980s using the High School and Beyond survey (HS&B), see Nan M. Astone and Sara S. McLanahan (1991), Sandra L. Hanson (1994), James Rosenbaum (2001), and Jay D. Teachman and Kathleen Paasch (1998). For research on expectations in the 1990s, see Grace Kao and Marta Tienda (1998), Shouping Hu (2003), Graziella P. McCarron and Karen K. Inkelas (2006), and John Reynolds et al. (2006). For research on expectations in the 2000s, see Kimberly A. Goyette (2008).

2. A related set of factors likely to influence and be influenced by expectations are students' self-efficacy and intrinsic and extrinsic motivations toward educational attainment. A body of literature exists in the field of psychology on how students develop motivation to achieve their goals and how their experiences and environments can increase and decrease both their intrinsic and extrinsic motivation for educational attainment (see, for example, Skinner, Wellborn, and Connell 1990; Deci 1971; Deci et al. 1991; Grolnick, Ryan, and Deci 1991; Zimmerman, Bandura, and Martinez-Pons 1992).

3. In HS&B, census data were matched by NCES to the county in which the student's tenth grade high school is located, in the NELS the census data was matched to the student's twelfth grade high school, and in the ELS the census data are matched to the county in which the student's tenth grade high school is located. The HS&B incorporates data from the 1980 census, the NELS incorporates 1990 census data, and the ELS incorporates 2000 census data.

4. All figures and tables labeled with an A are found in the online appendix, http://www.russellsage.org/duncan_murnane_online_appendix.pdf.

5. Although our analysis explicitly investigates expectations and outcomes, much of the prior research in this area blurs the distinction between the concepts of expectations and aspirations. Because of ambiguity in the literature, unless the authors explicitly define aspirations as hopes for educational attainment, we use the term "expectations" instead of "aspirations," even in cases where the original researcher used "aspirations."

6. The unconditional correlation between educational expectations and educational attainment tends to be on the order of 0.6 to 0.7 (Sewell, Hauser, and Wolf 1980; Teachman 1987).

7. Attainment data were collected from the U.S. Bureau of the Census.

8. However, the effect of parental expectations on children's expectations can easily be overstated when parental expectations are measured via the child's perception, not the parent's reported expectations (Davies and Kandel 1981). Perceived parental expectations in part represent the expectations they are supposed to predict.

9. We truncated the predicted probability to fall between zero and 1.

10. Because the NELS is the most longitudinally comprehensive of the NCES surveys, spanning from eighth grade to eight years after expected high school graduation, we rely exclusively on the NELS to analyze updating behavior among students.

11. On average there are eighteen students per school. The minimum number of students at a school is one, and the maximum number of students is fifty-eight. Schools at the 25th percentile have fourteen students, and schools at the 75th percentile have twenty-two students.

12. The models only include students from the NELS 1988-to-2000 panel with data at each time point. The NELS achievement tests are designed to measure student growth and as such are vertically equitable.

13. To check the panel analysis assumptions, we ran the 1988-to-1990 full model with the cross-sectional data and found even stronger statistically significant relationships between expectations and GPA and expectations and test scores.

14. Merit aid programs did exist at both the federal and state levels prior to the early 1990s, but these programs, such as the National Merit Scholarship Program, were very small and were targeted at the very best-performing students.

REFERENCES

Astone, Nan M., and Sara S. McLanahan. 1991. "Family Structure, Parental Practices, and High School Completion." *American Sociological Review* 56(3): 309–20.

Benware, Carl A., and Edward L. Deci. 1984. "Quality of Learning with an Active Versus Passive Motivational Set." *American Educational Research Journal* 21(4): 755–65.

Davies, Mark, and Denise B. Kandel. 1981. "Parental and Peer Influences on Adolescents' Educational Plans: Some Further Evidence." *American Journal of Sociology* 87(2): 363–87.

Deci, Edward. 1971. "Effects of Externally Mediated Rewards on Intrinsic Motivation." *Journal of Personality and Social Psychology* 18(1): 105–15.

Deci, Edward L., Richard J. Vallerand, Luc G. Pelletier, and Richard M. Ryan. 1991. "Motivation and Education: The Self-Determination Perspective." *Educational Psychology* 26(3–4): 325–46.

Duncan, Otis D., David L. Featherman, and Beverly Duncan. 1972. *Socioeconomic Background and Achievement.* New York: Seminar Press.

Dynarski, Susan M. 2003. "Does Aid Matter? Measuring the Effect of Student Aid on College Attendance and Completion." *American Economic Review* 93(1): 279–88.

————. 2004. "The New Merit Aid." In *College Choices: The Economics of Where to Go, When to Go, and How to Pay for It,* edited by Caroline M. Hoxby. Chicago: University of Chicago Press.

Goldin, Claudia D., and Lawrence F. Katz. 2007. "Long-Run Changes in the Wage Structure: Narrowing, Widening and Polarizing." *Brookings Papers on Economic Activity* 38(2): 135–68.

Goyette, Kimberly A. 2008. "College for Some to College for All: Social Background, Occupational Expectations, and Educational Expectations over Time." *Social Science Research* 37(2): 461–84.

Grolnick, Wendy S., and Richard M. Ryan. 1987. "Autonomy in Children's Learning: An Experimental and Individual Difference Investigation." *Journal of Personality and Social Psychology* 52(5): 890–98.

Grolnick, Wendy S., Richard M. Ryan, and Edward L. Deci. 1991. "The Inner Resources for School Achievement: Motivational Mediators of Children's Perceptions of their Parents." *Journal of Educational Psychology* 83(4): 508–17.

Hanson, Sandra L. 1994. "Lost Talent: Unrealized Educational Aspirations and Expectations Among U.S. Youths." *Sociology of Education* 67(3): 159–83.

Hoelter, Jon W. 1982. "Segregation and Rationality in Black Status Aspiration Processes." *Sociology of Education* 55(1): 31–39.

Hu, Shouping. 2003. "Educational Aspirations and Postsecondary Access and Choice: Students in Urban, Suburban, and Rural Schools Compared." *Education Policy Analysis Archives* 11(14). Available at: http://epaa.asu.edu/ojs/article/view/242 (accessed July 30, 2008).

Johnston, Lloyd D., Jerald G. Bachman, Patrick M. O'Malley, and John E. Schulenberg. n.d. *Monitoring the Future: A Continuing Study of American Youth, 1976–2007.* Ann Arbor, Mich.: Inter-university Consortium for Political and Social Research (ICPSR).

Kane, Thomas J. 1995. "Rising Public College Tuition and College Entry: How Well Do Public Subsidies Promote Access to College?" NBER working paper 5164. Cambridge, Mass.: National Bureau of Economic Research.

Kao, Grace, and Marta Tienda. 1998. "Educational Expectations of Minority Youth." *American Journal of Education* 106(3): 249–384.

Kiuru, Noona, Kaisa Aunola, Jukka Vuori, and Jari-Erik Nurmi. 2007. "The Role of Peer Groups in Adolescents' Educational Expectations and Adjustment." *Journal of Youth and Adolescence* 36(8): 995–1009.

Leslie, Larry L., and Paul T. Brinkman. 1987. "Student Price Response in Higher Education: The Student Demand Studies." *Journal of Higher Education* 58(2): 181–204.

Malcolmson, Carole N. 2007. "Neighborhood, Parents, No One: Home Networks Inform Young Adolescents' Status Attainment Goals." Ph.D. dissertation, Harvard University.

Manski, Charles F. 1993. "Adolescent Econometricians: How Do Youth Infer the Returns to Schools?" In *Studies of Supply and Demand in Higher Education,* edited by Charles Clotfelter and Michael Rothschild. Chicago: University of Chicago Press.

————. 2004. "Measuring Expectations." *Econometrica* 72(5): 1329–76.

McCarron, Graziella P., and Karen K. Inkelas. 2006. "The Gap Between Educational Aspirations and Attainment for First Generation College Students and the Role of Parental Involvement." *Journal of College Student Development* 47(5): 534–49.

McLanahan, Sara S., and Larry Bumpass. 1988. "Intergenerational Consequences of Family Disruption." *American Journal of Sociology* 94(1): 130–52.

National Center for Education Statistics. 1995. *High School & Beyond: 1992 (Restricted) Data File.* Washington: U.S. Department of Education, Institute of Education Sciences.

————. 2003. *National Education Longitudinal Study: 88/2000 Restricted Use Data Files and Electronic Codebook.* Washington: U.S. Department of Education, Institute of Education Sciences.

————. 2007. *Education Longitudinal Study of 2002/06: Restricted Use Second Follow-up Data Files, Data File Documentation, and Electronic Codebook System.* Washington: U.S. Department of Education, Institute of Education Sciences.

————. n.d. *Integrated Postsecondary Education Data System Data Center.* Available at: http://nces.ed.gov/ipeds/datacenter (accessed July, 2009).

Ogbu, John U. 1991. "Low School Performance as an Adaptation: The Case of Blacks in Stockton, California." In *Minority Status and Schooling: A Comparative Study of Immigrant and Involuntary Minorities,* edited by Margaret A. Gibson and John U. Ogbu. New York: Garland.

Orfield, Gary, and Faith G. Paul. 1994. *High Hopes, Long Odds: A Major Report on Hoosier Teens and the American Dream.* Indianapolis: Indiana Youth Institute.

Reynolds, John, Michael Stewart, Ryan Macdonald, and Lacey Sischo. 2006. "Have Adolescents Become Too Ambitious? High School Seniors' Educational and Occupational Plans, 1976 to 2000." *Social Problems* 53(2): 186–206.

Rosenbaum, James. 2001. *Beyond College for All: Career Pathways for the Forgotten Half.* New York: Russell Sage Foundation.

Ryan, Richard M., and Edward L. Deci. 2000. "Intrinsic and Extrinsic Motivations: Classic Definitions and New Directions." *Contemporary Educational Psychology* 25(1): 54–67.

Schneider, Barbara, and David Stevenson. 1999. *The Ambitious Generation: America's Teenagers, Motivated But Directionless.* New Haven, Conn.: Yale University Press.

Sewell, William H., Archibald O. Haller, and George W. Ohlendorf. 1970. "The Educational and Early Occupational Status Attainment Process: Replication and Revision." *American Sociological Review* 35(6): 1014–27.

Sewell, William H., Archibald O. Haller, and Alejandro Portes. 1969. "The Educational and Early Occupational Attainment Process." *American Sociological Review* 34(1): 82–92.

Sewell, William H., and Robert M. Hauser. 1972. "Causes and Consequences of Higher Education: Models of the Status Attainment Process." *American Journal of Agricultural Economics* 54(5): 851–61.

Sewell, William H., Robert M. Hauser, and Wendy C. Wolf. 1980. "Sex, Schooling and Occupational Status." *American Journal of Sociology* 86(3): 551–83.

Sewell, William H., and Vimal P. Shah. 1967. "Socioeconomic Status, Intelligence, and the Attainment of Higher Education." *Sociology of Education* 40(1): 1–23.

Skinner, Ellen A., James G. Wellborn, and James P. Connell. 1990. "What It Takes to Do Well in School and Whether I've Got It: A Process Model of Perceived Control and Children's Engagement and Achievement in School." *Journal of Educational Psychology* 82(1): 22–32.

Stewart, Endya B., Eric A. Stewart, and Ronald L. Simons. 2007. "The Effect of Neighborhood Context on the College Expectations of African American Adolescents." *American Educational Research Journal* 44(4): 896–919.

Stinebrickner, Todd, and Ralph Stinebrickner. 2009. "Learning About Academic Ability and College Drop-Out Decision." NBER working paper 14810. Cambridge, Mass.: National Bureau of Economic Research.

Streufert, Peter. 1991. "The Effect of Social Isolation on Schooling Choice." Working paper. Madison, Wis.: Institute for Research on Poverty.

Teachman, Jay D. 1987. "Family Background, Educational Resources, and Educational Attainment." *American Sociological Review* 52(4): 548–57.

Teachman, Jay D., and Kathleen Paasch. 1998. "The Family and Educational Expectations." *Journal of Marriage and the Family* 60(3): 704–14.

U.S. Bureau of the Census. 2008. Educational Attainment. See "Detailed Educational Attainment Tables (ACS 2008)." Available at: http://www.census.gov/population/www/socdemo/education/cps2008.html (accessed March 28, 2011).

Wilson, William J. 1987. *The Truly Disadvantaged: The Inner City, the Underclass, and Public Policy.* Chicago: University of Chicago Press.

Zafar, Basit. 2009. "How Do College Students Form Expectations?" Working paper. New York: Federal Reserve Bank of New York.

Zimmerman, Barry J., Albert Bandura, and Manuel Martinez-Pons. 1992. "Self-Motivation for Academic Attainment: The Role of Self-Efficacy Beliefs and Personal Goal Setting." *American Educational Research Journal* 29(3): 663–76.

Part III

The Family

Chapter 8

Educational Mobility in the United States Since the 1930s

Michael Hout and Alexander Janus

Educational mobility has declined in the United States in recent decades. Only 40 percent of young men who turned twenty-five in the past decade achieved more education than their fathers did, compared with 67 percent of men who matured in the 1960s and 1970s. Women's upward educational mobility declined less; 52 percent are upwardly mobile now compared with 65 percent in the 1960s and 1970s. Meanwhile, downward mobility increased. In the past decade, 18 percent of men and 13 percent of women finished their schooling with less education than their same-sex parent.

Yet paradoxically, today's college-educated parents are no better at passing on their advantages to their children now than in the past, nor are parents with no educational credentials more of a hindrance now than they used to be. In other words, the correlation between young people's educational attainments and their parents' is no stronger for recent cohorts than it was in the past, and it may be somewhat weaker.

The combination of worsening mobility and stable intergenerational correlations is, at first, a puzzle. The solution is the realization that mobility trends depend as much on institutional growth as on the correlation between people's achievements and their parents'. Expansion of educational capacity is powerful. In previous generations, many states required that students complete more secondary education by raising the minimum age at which they could leave school. They built new public colleges and universities and expanded existing ones. These requirements and investments created a rising educational tide that lifted all boats. Most people were upwardly mobile, even though people with better-educated parents gained the most education and those with the least-educated parents achieved the least. Now, however, states invest less. Without expansion of educational capacity, fewer people experience upward mobility, and more experience downward mobility.

Racial disparities changed significantly in the last fifty years. During the 1950s and 1960s, African Americans from all family backgrounds improved their educational attainments faster than other young people did, closing the gap between themselves and white Americans. Since the 1980s, however, African Americans have lost most of the ground they gained in the civil rights era. Meanwhile, Asian Americans have rapidly moved up the educational ladder, catching up to and passing white Americans in educational attainment.

Family breakup contributes to racial disparities and has some independent role in educational mobility as well. Increased divorce has exposed more young people to the negative consequences of family breakup, and there is some evidence that the "penalty" for growing up in a single-parent family has increased recently, though statistical tests of that change are inconclusive.

The persistence of advantages and disadvantages from generation to generation is driven by parental education, income, family structure, and patterns of racial inequality in complicated ways. Some of these factors help or hinder young people more or less directly. About half the correlation between young adults' education and that of their parents, though, depends on the American pattern of residential and school segregation. Past statistical models and some new calculations in this chapter indicate that eliminating segregation and making school experiences completely homogeneous across secondary schools would reduce the intergenerational correlation of educational attainment by 40 to 50 percent.

Current social and economic conditions could threaten the United States' enviable record of social mobility. For most of the nation's history upward mobility has exceeded downward mobility by a large margin. Our calculations show that among young people leaving education in the quarter-century from 1951 to 1975, 59 percent had more education than their parents and just 9 percent had less. Similar calculations indicate that 45 percent of the men from those cohorts had more desirable jobs than their fathers, and 26 percent had less desirable jobs (Beller and Hout 2006, table 4).[1]

The United States sustained growth in its educational institutions from roughly 1870 to 1975 while, to varying degrees, fostering openness and access (Goldin and Katz 2007). Scholars of social mobility (for example, Blau and Duncan 1967; Sobel, Hout, and Duncan 1985) identify these two factors—growth and openness—as the keys to mobility. Growth in education fosters mobility by increasing the number and variety of positions in educational institutions; it increases every young person's chances of educational advancement by increasing the capacity of educational institutions themselves. Openness in education fosters mobility by removing some of the barriers in the way of young people whose parents lack education or by removing some of the advantages that young people whose parents were highly educated get. Offering scholarships for first-generation college students is an example of removing a barrier; abolishing special admissions for the offspring of alumni is an example of removing an advantage.

Economic inequality, family disruption, housing segregation, and limited public revenues make it harder to maintain growth and openness in secondary and higher education. Inequality reduces affluent people's incentive to support public institutions. Affluent parents can afford to pay for their child's education even if the state fails to provide it, eroding their support for the public schools that educate other people's children. Family disruption often reduces the contact and contribution of one or both parents to a young person's development. Residential segregation coupled with local funding of public education sequesters resources in some communities, effectively denying them to others. Curtailing public financing invites the colleges and universities that can do so to replace state support with private tuition money; without adequate financial aid, this practice can allow the affluent to purchase advantages that the poor cannot afford. Unchecked by adequate responses in educational institutions, these problems of our time will result in less growth, less openness, or both. Less growth or less openness will reverse upward educational mobility and replace it with downward mobility.

We show in this chapter that the mix of upward and downward educational mobility in the United States has, in fact, worsened since the 1970s. A majority of America's young people still leave school with more education than their parents had, but although the upwardly mobile were a strong and unmistakable majority in 1975, since 1990 they have become less of a majority. Slow growth, and not an increase in the intergenerational correlation, is the culprit. High school and college graduation rates are only a few percentage points higher than where they were in 1975. Without growth to sustain it, upward mobility becomes less common and downward mobility becomes more common. And that is exactly what has happened in the United States since 1975. Openness, fortunately, has not been compromised yet. Even though there is cause for concern, the local control, institutional competition, easy access, and egalitarian values that promoted openness in the past (Goldin and Katz 2007) remain important today. The clearest overall sign of institutional openness—the correlation between a young adult's education and that of his or her parents—is still what it was in the 1960s (about 0.4 on a scale from zero to 1). That correlation is significantly stronger than the null correlation that would indicate equity and probably is also higher than efficiency demands, but equality of educational opportunity is not worsening by this bottom-line measure.[2]

In the sections that follow, we briefly outline how openness and growth contribute to mobility, describe the data we use, show the trends in mobility and attainment for men and women, evaluate the evidence for stability and change in openness, and consider the implications of differences in racial ancestry and family disruption for our conclusions. We focus on simple results that can be displayed in graphs, but all of the trends we show are robust to statistical controls for the factors shown in the other graphs as well as for other important factors such as immigration, segregation, and test scores. In our last substantive section, we introduce school-based panel studies that allow us to make preliminary estimates of how much of the intergenerational correlation reflects the sorting of college-educated and less-educated parents' children into different secondary schools and how much is attributable to factors outside the school environment.

We have relatively little to say about family income in this chapter. Ideally, we would have a dataset that accurately measured it over a fifty-year or longer period to fulfill our charge from the editors to take the long view of educational mobility. Unfortunately, national data correlation between family income and educational success start in 1972, and that study sampled high school graduates; therefore, its educational variation was all related to postsecondary education. Longitudinal studies begun in 1979 and 1980 offered the first look at the national correlation between family income and the high school dropout rate. We make some use of the 1972 and 1980 data late in the chapter. But for the long view, we rely on data about parents' educations to study mobility in the United States since the 1930s.

Nonetheless we have confidence in the value of our contribution to the understanding inequality of educational opportunity, because comparisons of the relative effects of parents' educations and incomes show that parents' educations affect their children's educational success far more than the parents' incomes do (see, for example, Fischer et al. 1996, 77–91). A common observation in inequality studies is that "like goes with like" across generations. The most important family factor in a study of income inequality is the parents' incomes, the most important family factor in a jobs study is the parents' jobs, and the most important family factor in an educational study like this one is the parents' educations.

MOBILITY, GROWTH, AND OPENNESS

Social scientists have been studying American social mobility since the early 1900s. Pitirim A. Sorokin summarized nineteen academic mobility studies in his 1927 classic, *Social Mobility*. The heyday for this type of research was the 1970s, when the Census Bureau provided a wealth of high-quality, nationally representative data by including questions about family background—such as father's education and occupation, family structure, nativity—on the March 1962 and March 1973 Current Population Surveys (CPSs, the monthly unemployment surveys). *The American Occupational Structure,* by Peter M. Blau and Otis Dudley Duncan (1967), was the most important of these studies. Blau and Duncan, in addition to producing the key results from the 1962 CPS, proposed a theoretical model of intergenerational correlations that guided future research by sociologists and economists alike (see Becker and Tomes 1979). The Blau-Duncan model put education in the middle of a socioeconomic life course that began in the family and moved outward to the school and labor market. An individual's background included his or her father's education and occupation, race, and family structure, each of which influenced the individual's educational achievements, which in turn affected the quality of his or her first and current occupation and earnings.[3] The model was laid out in a series of equations that rendered social mobility as part of the path from family background to accomplishments in the labor market (see online appendix at http://www.russellsage.org/duncan_murnane_online_appendix.pdf). Gary Becker and Nigel Tomes (1979) added family wealth as a crucial background characteristic and advanced the theory by viewing educational achievements as human-capital investments. Dozens of subsequent studies drew on the Blau-Duncan model and documented important changes over time, integrated women into the analysis, and detailed subgroup differences.[4]

The four main insights from this literature that inform this chapter are as follows:

1. Growth (often called "structural mobility") promotes social mobility by increasing the supply of the kinds of positions, in college or the job market, that people desire most.

2. Openness (sometimes called "exchange mobility") promotes mobility by limiting the ways that privileged people can hand off advantages to their offspring at the expense of less advantaged competitors.

3. Education can preserve privilege from one generation to the next if educational achievements depend heavily on family background because education is so central to rewards in the job market.

4. Education can be a channel of mobility if most of the variation in educational achievement is independent of family background.

Blau and Duncan (1967) made all four of these points, and the subsequent literature validated their insights or rediscovered them. A fifth point, attributed to Michael E. Sobel, Hout, and Duncan (1985)—implicit in prior work (for example, Duncan 1966; Featherman and Hauser 1978, chapter 2)—is that growth completely determines the relative frequency of upward and downward mobility. In the absence of growth, openness operating alone implies equal numbers of upward and downward moves. Only if growth creates more top destinations will mobility be, on net, upward. Although not yet documented, the opposite would also be true: the creation of more positions low in the hierarchy could yield more downward than upward moves. The first page of our online appendix presents a few equations that illustrate these key results.

Comparisons of mobility over time and between countries find more variation in the growth component than in openness (see Beller and Hout 2006 for a review). The historic rise of manufacturing and the concomitant disappearance of family farms generated tremendous mobility in the United States and Europe. Subsequent postindustrial development of the service economy occasioned even more. Meanwhile, openness—gauged by the correlation between people's characteristics and their parents'—varies much less. The analysis in this chapter shows that American educational mobility since the 1930s fits that pattern. Most of the increasing mobility from 1930 to 1975 reflected the growth and expansion of educational institutions, not an increase in openness. The subsequent slowdown in mobility from 1975 to the present reflects the stasis in educational institutions. The correlation between young people's education and that of their parents has changed little if at all since 1930.

DATA

We use three data sources: a very large collection of surveys from the U.S. Bureau of the Census and the Bureau of Labor Statistics that provides the basic time series of educational attainment across cohorts, a series of much smaller surveys that parallels the big one but adds the crucial data on parents' educations and where people grew up (to tie individuals to their family backgrounds and the U.S. educational system), and a shorter time series that includes data on test scores and secondary schools.

Our initial descriptive data on growth of education come from the CPS March supplements from 1962 to 2009. This large database—based on annual household surveys of 30,000 to 45,000 households covering up to 60,000 adults—gives us very precise statistical estimates of each cohort's high school and college graduation rates. We drop people younger than twenty-seven years old because the education of eighteen- to twenty-six-year-olds understates the education of their cohort; many of the people who eventually have the most education are still pursuing advanced degrees into their late twenties. We also drop people age sixty-five and older because education correlates with mortality (see, for example, Preston and Elo 1995); the educational attainment of those who survive to be interviewed as seniors consequently overstates the whole cohort's educational attainment. The CPS excludes institutionalized individuals, which introduces an upward bias. It also fails to distinguish diplomas earned from high schools from those earned through tests (GEDs), furthering the upward bias (see Heckman and LaFontaine 2007). Nonetheless, the CPS offers the best coverage and largest numbers of respondents available for this time span. Unfortunately, only the March 1962 and 1973 CPSs include questions about parents—and then only for men. We use the CPS data to describe the trend in educational attainment and turn to other data to study mobility.

The General Social Survey (GSS) is our primary data source for information about family background. Since 1972, the National Opinion Research Center at the University of Chicago has conducted the GSS. They interview representative samples of American adults on a broad array of issues. From 1972 to 1994, the GSS was fielded almost every year, and the size of the main samples averaged 1,400 interviews.[5] Since 1994, the GSS has been fielded in even-numbered years with sample sizes averaging 2,850 interviews. Beginning in 2006, GSS respondents could choose between being interviewed in Spanish or English. Most interviews are face-to-face. The GSS maintains a very high response rate, averaging more than 75 percent from 1972 to 1998. Design changes in 2000 lowered the minimum response target to 70 percent; the actual response rate has been between 70 and 72 percent in each survey since then (see Davis, Smith, and Marsden 2008, appendix A, available at: http://www.norc.org/GSS+Website/Documentation; accessed March 14, 2011).

We picked the GSS because it parallels the sampling frame of the CPS and adds crucial measures of family background. The full GSS covers cohorts born over a one-hundred-year span. Samples of people twenty-seven to sixty-four years old leave us with data covering conditions in secondary education from 1930 to 2000 and higher education from 1938 to 2008. No other data set with information on people's education and that of their parents covers that broad a time span. The GSS also contains data on where people lived when they were sixteen years old. That allows us to exclude people who were not in the United States, ensuring that inferences pertain to American education and are not confounded by immigration. Most important, the GSS includes information on a broad array of family-background variables in addition to parents' education. We know whether people were living with both, one, or neither parent, father's occupation for all cohorts, and mother's occupation for cohorts born since 1930 (finishing their educations in the post–World War II period). Data are weighted to correct for design effects in the sampling design and nonresponse patterns (see Davis, Smith, and Marsden 2008, appendix A).

Some cases in the GSS are incomplete. Many people cannot say or decline to say how much education one or both of their parents had. Missing data is particularly prevalent for the missing parent in one-parent families. Other data are missing more or less at random. Ignoring missing data can lead to incorrect inferences. We used multiple imputation methods to construct twenty independent data sets composed of all the observed data and an imputation for each missing case (Rubin 1987; Treiman 2008). The figures display the averages across the twenty imputed data sets; the coefficients for statistical models are the mean of the twenty independent estimates, and their standard errors adjust for the imprecision of the individual estimates and variation from imputation to imputation.

An ideal data set would add test scores to the GSS data. Ideal data do not exist. We approach the role of test scores less formally here using some calculations from panel studies conducted by the National Center for Educational Statistics (NCES). (Sean F. Reardon makes more extensive use of the NCES panels; see chapter 5 for details about scope and comparability of those data sets). We used multiple imputation methods to correct the NCES data for missing data with the added complication that the respondents are nested within schools; multilevel multiple imputation models are described by Sophia Rabe-Hesketh and Anders Skrendel (2008).

EDUCATIONAL ATTAINMENT BY COHORT

The story of America's educational expansion is well known. The slowdown in attainment (Hout 1995; Fischer and Hout 2006; Goldin and Katz 2007; Heckman and LaFontaine 2007; see also chapter 6 in this volume, by Martha J. Bailey and Susan M. Dynarski) is less broadly known. Figure 8.1 shows the trend as revealed in the CPS data. High school and college graduation rates are arrayed by year of birth plus eighteen (labeled "high school graduation cohort") and gender for cohorts born between 1900 and 1982; they were old enough to graduate from high school between 1917 and 2000.

The trend in high school graduation shows a steep rise from 28 percent in the World War I era to 88 percent in 1968, when progress stopped suddenly. There is no net change in the last thirty years of the time series. Men lagged a few years behind women in the early years and since 1980, but the gender difference is small enough to pale in comparison with the overall trends.

The trend in college graduation rose more slowly, from 7 percent to 28 percent between the high school class of 1917 and that of the late 1960s.[6] College trends differed significantly for men and women. Men led women for roughly thirty years. Then men's graduation rates declined and women's continued upward, and today's women will have a graduation rate about 5 percentage points higher than men's (see DiPrete and Buchmann 2006 for detailed analysis).

The leveling off of high school and college graduation rates represents a near halt in educational growth. The percentage of young adults attaining some college has continued to rise, so total years of schooling completed by recent cohorts is higher than the figure for the late 1960s high school classes. The growing tendency to substitute a GED for a regular high school diploma and the fact that data for prison inmates are excluded from the samples might be enough to off-set even that apparent increase (Heckman and LaFontaine 2007).

Similar graduation rates during a thirty-year period—roughly the length of a generation—mean that the most recent cohorts probably have the same prevalence of high school and college

FIGURE 8.1   *Percentage Graduating from High School and College, by High School Graduating Class and Gender; Persons Twenty-Seven to Sixty-Four Years Old at Time of Interview*

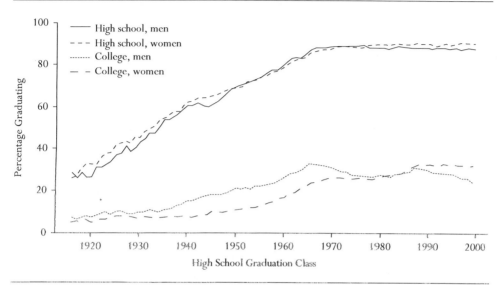

Source: Authors' calculations based on King et al. (2010).
Notes: High school graduating class is year of birth plus eighteen for all persons, regardless of when they actually left high school. The data refer to percentage of each cohort that graduated from high school or college; college graduation is for the entire cohort and is not restricted to those completing high school. The CPS does not interview people in institutions, so the data cover household residents only.

diplomas as their parents. This educational stasis presages a decline in educational mobility. We turn to that subject now.

EDUCATIONAL MOBILITY

Educational mobility is defined as young people's education relative to that of their parents. Upwardly mobile people attained more education than their parents did; downwardly mobile people attained less than their parents did. Overall current trends in education imply that a slowdown in educational mobility is occurring. The rapid spread of secondary and then higher education in the United States from 1875 to 1975 pretty much guaranteed that each generation had more education than the previous one, but the flat trends in high school and college graduation rates since 1975 make it far less likely that a young person's education will exceed his or her parents' today.

The parents of one generation were students in a previous generation. Upward mobility will eventually wane if growth in education stops. We have taken the first step in mobility analysis by documenting the progress of each cohort; now we take the second step and examine trends in parents' educational attainments. Figure 8.2 shows the proportion of adults in each cohort whose father and mother both had a high school diploma and those whose parents both had a college degree.[7] The trends echo the trends in figure 8.1 with a lag of twenty to twenty-five years. Because less-educated women and men have more children, the peak percentages are lower for parents than for the young people in figure 8.1. Seventy-seven percent of American adults born between 1970 and 1980, who turned twenty-five recently, have a high school–educated mother;

FIGURE 8.2   *Trends in Family Background as Indicated by Percentage of Parents Graduating from High School and College, by Respondent's Year Turned Twenty-Five and Parent's Gender: U.S.-Educated Persons, Twenty-Seven to Sixty-Four Years Old at Time of Interview*

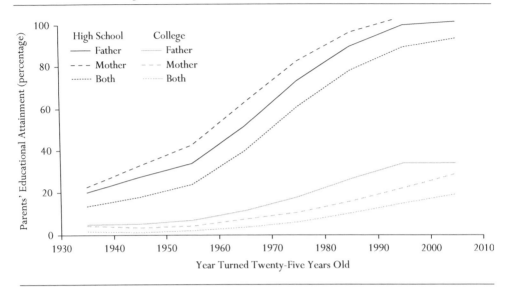

Source: Authors' calculations based on Smith et al. (2008).
Notes: U.S.-educated is defined as living in the United States at age sixteen. The educational attainments are those of parents, but they are used to indicate the family backgrounds of the cohorts in question. So, for example, among young people leaving high school around 2005, 77 percent had a high school–educated mother, 75 percent had a high school–educated father, 24 percent had a college–educated mother, and 23 percent had a college–educated father.

75 percent have a high school–educated father; 67 percent have two high school–educated parents. Twenty-five percent of young people from recent cohorts have college-educated fathers, 23 percent have college-educated mothers, and 13 percent have two college-educated parents. These figures are all significantly higher than the percentages for older cohorts. For cohorts that reached maturity during the Great Depression, the high school numbers more closely resemble today's college numbers than today's high school numbers: 20 percent had a high school–educated mother, 19 percent had a high school–educated father, and 11 percent had two high school–educated parents; less than 5 percent had a college-educated parent.

Educational mobility depends on both the growth of the educational system and its openness as reflected in the correlation between people's educational attainments and their parents' educations. Growth alone determines the balance of upward and downward mobility. If the average person has more education than his or her parents, then upward mobility will exceed downward, and vice versa. Figure 8.3 shows the trends in upward and downward mobility for Americans reaching age twenty-five between 1935 and 2005. For each person who grew up living with two parents, we had to choose a basis of comparison: the same-sex parent, the better-educated parent, or the average of the two parents. We chose same-sex parent so that the trends could show the impact of continuing growth in women's education but the relative stagnation for men.

One-third of men who turned twenty-five years old during the Great Depression were upwardly mobile, and one-half of men who turned twenty-five in the 1940s and 1950s were. Men's upward mobility peaked in the 1960s and 1970s, when almost two-thirds were upwardly

FIGURE 8.3   *Percentage Upwardly and Downwardly Mobile by Year Turned Twenty-Five and Gender: U.S.-Educated Persons, Twenty-Seven to Sixty-Four Years Old at Time of Interview*

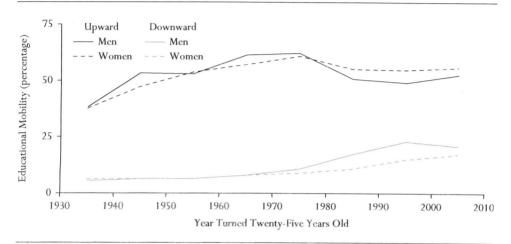

Source: Authors' calculations, based on Smith et al. (2008).

mobile. Since then, men's upward mobility has slipped below 50 percent. That is still a very significant amount of upward movement; it appears to be modest only in relation to the very high rates of the 1960s and 1970s. Women's upward mobility is not significantly different from men's through the 1970s, but after that, women have been more upwardly mobile than men, as admission to public universities became more competitive and private universities that once were all-male opened their doors to women. Downward mobility for men and women increased substantially, from 5 percent to 18 percent of men and 5 percent to 13 percent of women.

Downward mobility is more prevalent both because the slowdown in educational expansion has removed the support for upward relative to downward mobility and because the correlation between people's education and their that of their parents is moderately strong (r = .4). A stronger correlation would reduce both kinds of mobility, and a weaker correlation would increase both kinds of mobility (Sobel, Hout, and Duncan 1985).

These trends bring the consequences of slowed educational growth into focus. Slower growth in educational institutions makes it harder for young people to outpace their parents' achievements. Upward mobility has decreased twelve percentage points for men and eight points for women since the late 1970s. Twenty-five percent of men in the late 1990s and 20 percent of men and women in the last decade were downwardly mobile, despite sharp increases in the college aspirations, expectations, and preparation of young people (Schneider and Stevenson 1999; see also Jacob and Linkow, chapter 7, this volume). Young people have heard the message from their elders and the labor markets that higher education is their key to a secure future. But states invest less than they used to, squeezing out aspiring, able young people (Hout 2009; Bound, Herschbein, and Long 2009).

THE CORRELATION BETWEEN GENERATIONS

To track exactly how a person's education correlates with that of his or her parents, we examine trends in high school and college graduation for those whose educational credentials differ from their parents'. For simplicity, we show four lines: both parents have no credentials, both parents

FIGURE 8.4A   *Percentage Graduating from High School, by Year Turned Twenty-Five, Parental Education, and Gender: U.S.-Educated Persons, Twenty-Seven to Sixty-Four Years Old at Time of Interview*

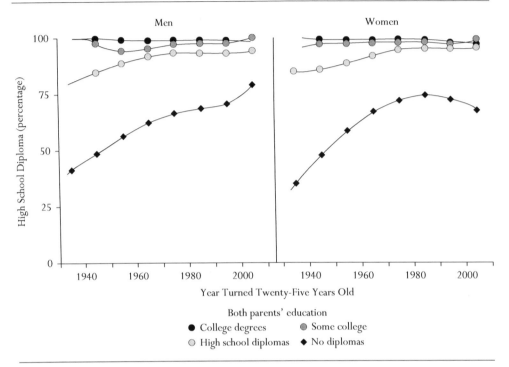

Source: Authors' calculations, based on Smith et al. (2008).
Notes: Data smoothed by locally esimated (loess) regression.

have high school diplomas, both parents have some college, and both parents have college degrees (see figure 8.4A). The trends for people whose parents mixed different credentials fit in among these trend lines: for example, the lines for people who have one parent with a high school diploma and one parent with some college fit between those who have two high school—graduate parents and those who have two parents with some college.

As far back as the 1930s, more than 90 percent of people with high school—graduate parents earned high school diplomas themselves. People whose parents had no credentials saw their chances of high school graduation rise sharply from 1935 to 1970 (as did those who had one parent with a high school diploma and one without, though that group is not shown in the figure). Apportioning the rise in overall high school rates to differences among parental-education categories and trends within parental-education categories, we find that rising parental education accounts for almost 60 percent of the overall increase in high school graduation through 1970. That is, the momentum of earlier improvements carried forward into the lives of the succeeding generation, pushing high school graduation upward until 1970 or 1975. Since the late 1970s, however, the fortunes of people with less-educated parents have not improved any further. High school graduation remains at 75 percent for the sons and daughters of high school—dropout parents.

College graduation overall rose between 1935 and 1970, then leveled off, as we saw in figure 8.1. Within social classes defined by parents' educations, however, we see more decline than

FIGURE 8.4B   *Percentage Graduating from College, by Year Turned Twenty-Five, Parental Education, and Gender: U.S.-Educated Persons, Twenty-Seven to Sixty-Four Years Old at Time of Interview*

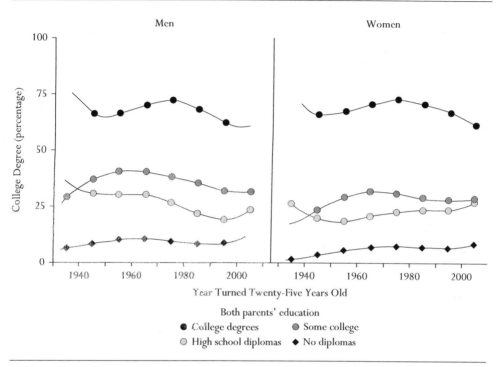

Source: Authors' calculations, based on Smith et al. (2008).
Notes: Data smoothed by locally esimated (loess) regression.

increase (see figure 8.4B) This is especially true for men, but it is quite clear for women as well. The probability that the son of a high school graduate would earn a college degree decreased steadily from the 1950s onward. So, too, did the probability that the son of parents with some college would earn a college degree. Even sons of college graduates are doing worse now than in the 1950s, though their decreases started roughly twenty-five years later, in the mid-1970s.

For women, the declines are substantial only for the daughters of college-educated parents. Statistical uncertainties make the separate percentage estimates somewhat uncertain, but the evidence of more decreases than increases is very strong. The size of the decreases is about ten percentage points. For the last thirty years or so, men's family-background resources, reflected in their parents' educations, have been improving, while men's rate of achieving a college diploma has changed little if at all. That implies the pattern we see in figure 8.4B: decline within each category of parental education. Women's college graduation rate has been improving overall, so we see less evidence of decline for them, although a twelve-percentage-point decrease for women with college-graduate parents is quite substantial.

The educational trajectories of women and men through both the secondary- and higher-education systems diverged after the late 1970s (DiPrete and Buchmann 2006; see also chapter 6, this volume). During the 1980s and early 1990s, losses among men offset every gain by women. Both show progress overall in the most recent cohorts, but men's improvements are mostly in

FIGURE 8.5   *Coefficients for Parental Education, by Year Turned Twenty-Five and Gender:*
U.S.-Educated Persons, Twenty-Seven to Sixty-Four Years Old at Time of Interview

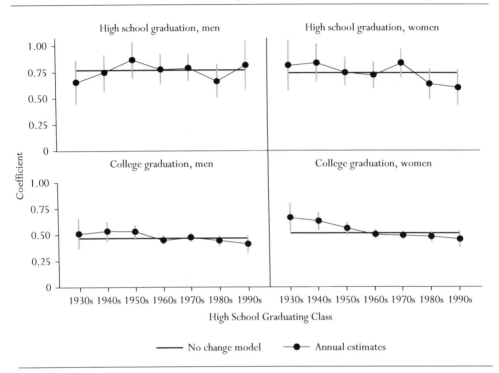

Source: Authors' calculations, based on Smith et al. (2008).
Notes: No change model fit to all data with dummies for high school graduating class; annual estimates fit to each class separately.
Vertical lines show 95 percent confidence intervals of annual estimates.

getting some college education but no degree, so these improvement do not show in our charts, of diplomas and degrees gained. This gender disparity, reversing long-standing male dominance, is very widespread, showing up in data on medical and law students and Ph.D. programs in the humanities. Multivariate analyses confirm impressions based on graphs. Coefficients representing men's high school diplomas and college degree trends point downward with time, after the models adjust the data for regional differences and the effects of family size, divorce or death of a parent, racial ancestry, and immigrant status.

The motivation for this analysis is the prospect that changes in the economy and family life may have increased the correlation between educational attainment and family background. The data in figures 8.4A and 8.4B are germane to this question. Increasing correlations would show up in those figures as diverging trend lines; in other words, the evidence of increased correlation would be a wider gap between people whose parents were college graduates and people whose parents were high school dropouts. In fact, what we see is the opposite. The gaps decreased if they changed at all. Multivariate analyses confirm that impression. Statistical coefficients that capture the degree to which educational advancement depends on parents' educations show slight downward trends (see figure 8.5). The change in coefficients with time is statistically significant for women but not for men. Yet each cohort's coefficient for men is not significantly different from that for women in the same cohort, so the men might be changing. The evidence is not precise enough to say with confidence whether correlation of education across generations decreased for everyone or just for women. But this much is clear: the intergenerational correlations did not increase. The figures indicate that most of the change is due to the at one time rising and now stalled progress toward high school graduation among students whose parents did not themselves graduate from high school. While the fortunes of dropouts' offspring improved, socioeconomic inequality declined. But that trend stalled before 1980, and we see no other evidence of changing inequality of opportunity.

Some of what appears to be high school graduation in these data is actually high school dropout followed by a GED. The data cannot separate diplomas given by schools from GEDs. More young people are taking the GED route to credentials in recent cohorts (Heckman and LaFontaine 2007). If students earning GEDs disproportionately come from families with high school–dropout parents, then the GED trend could mask some of the effect of parents' educations on young people's own attainments. The GSS lacks the data necessary to distinguish between diplomas granted by high schools and those earned as GEDs, but the National Educational Longitudinal Survey (NELS) begun in 1988 contains a reliable categorization into school—granted and GED credentials of people whose highest credential is a high school diploma. If the father's and mother's education affect school-granted diplomas more than GEDs, then regressing a dummy variable for that distinction on parents' education will return positive coefficients for the father's and mother's education. It does not. A logistic regression model with parents' educational level as the only independent variables returned coefficients of 0.06 for the father's education and −0.08 for the mother's education (with standard errors of 0.11 and 0.09, respectively). More complete models that included a wide array of family and school variables (shown in the online appendix table 8.A1) returned similar negligible results; only being in a vocational track in high school helped predict which students got diplomas from high school and which ones earned GEDs. Thus we conclude that knowing which students graduated from high school and which subsequently earned GEDs would not alter our estimates of how much parents' educations matter and our conclusion that the effect of parents may have decreased, but definitely did not increase, since the 1950s and probably since the 1930s.

Thus, all available evidence contradicts fear of rising socioeconomic advantage in educational opportunity. Scholars (for example, Ehrenberg 2002) and journalists (for example, Ferguson 2011) have asked if growing economic inequality might mix with rising tuition at colleges and universities to make it easier for affluent parents to give their children educational advantages that other young people lack. These data show that among the offspring of the most educated parents of the last generation, college-going was actually less prevalent. Their sons' and daughters' fortunes are, in fact, worse than they were when college-going was less prevalent. Although we have serious worries that college opportunity is insufficient overall (Hout 2009), at least it is not disproportionately excluding the disadvantaged. These results imply that colleges and universities are, on the whole, sufficiently egalitarian institutions to offset the inegalitarian pressures of increasing economic inequality and falling public support. Policies such as need-blind admissions and widespread financial aid are probably key to the trends. Most students' education is subsidized in one way or another. Grants and scholarships are based largely on need and ability to pay, though competition among colleges is pushing them to use more test-based scholarships to lure top-scoring students. On net, though, the two kinds of financial aid still put the disadvantaged students who are admitted at less of a disadvantage.[8]

FIGURE 8.6   *Percentage of All Young People Graduating from College, by Year Turned Twenty-Five and Racial Ancestry: U.S.-Educated Women, Twenty-Seven to Sixty-Four Years Old at Time of Interview*

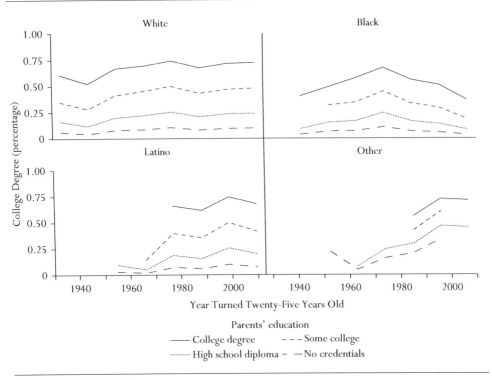

Source: Authors' calculations, based on Smith et al. (2008).
Notes: Data smoothed by locally estimated (loess) regression. Data refer to all members of a cohort whether they graduated from high school or not.

RACIAL ANCESTRY, FAMILY STRUCTURE, AND NATIVITY

Family background is more than just how much education parents have. Money matters (see Hout 2004), but we lack high-quality data on this. What we do have is evidence that African Americans closed the gap between themselves and whites between the 1950s and 1980s but have subsequently lost most of the ground they gained. Asian Americans have made steady progress and now have the highest educational attainment among the four large, broad racial ancestries we can identify in the GSS. Family-structure disparities changed little, but more young people than ever are exposed to the negative treatment of family disruption. Immigrants began arriving in larger numbers after 1965, and immigration accelerated after 1985. In this section, we discuss these and other disparities in educational attainment.

Other chapters in this volume discuss racial disparities in educational attainment in depth (see, for example, chapters 6, 12, and 23). We focus on differences in educational attainment by racial ancestry, by comparing parents with equal amounts of education but different racial ancestry. Among whites we would see a trend in college graduation rates much like that for the whole population (figure 8.1) if we ignored parents' educations. In the upper left panel of figure 8.6, we draw separate trend lines for four combinations of parents' educations: both with no credentials, both with a high school diploma, both with some college, and both with a college degree. The trend lines are surprisingly flat. College graduation rates have not increased significantly for whites, once the educations of their parents are held constant. Among Latinos, shown in the lower left panel, we see pretty much the same pattern. The trend lines are shorter because the data set contains too few U.S.-educated Latinos in the early cohorts. But where the data are sufficient, the pattern for Latinos is not statistically significantly different from that for whites. Latinos are less likely to graduate from college than are whites, overall, but that difference goes away when we control for parents' educations. Among blacks, the percentage earning a college degree rose from the 1950s to the late 1970s and then fell to significantly lower levels through the 1980s, 1990s, and 2000s. The trend is sharpest for the young people whose parents earned college degrees. Compared to whites and Latinos with the same levels of parental education, blacks were significantly less likely to get a college degree in the 1950s, as likely to get one in the 1970s, and significantly less likely to get one since then. Asians and others are shown in the lower right. Their educational progress sweeps across all categories of parental education. Since the 1990s they have had the highest percentages earning college degrees among these four groups.

Family stability is a very important factor in educational inequality (Beller 2009; see also chapter 11, this volume). Much of the difference between the education of people whose parents divorced and that of those whose parents stayed married is attributable to parental education. To a fairly accurate approximation, the effect of an absent father in particular is roughly equivalent with the gap between a high school—graduate and a high school—dropout father. Figure 8.7 (panel a) shows that from the 1950s on, the percentage of men graduating from high school if their mothers graduated from high school is uniformly lower, by about 7 percentage points, for men from a one-parent home than for men from a two-parent home. Yet an absent father was even more consequential in the 1930s and 1940s: 50 percent of men from one-parent families who came of age in the Great Depression graduated from high school compared with 77 percent of men from two-parent families.

College graduation trends among sons of college-educated women differ markedly depending on whether the father was living with them. Since the 1970s, young men from single-parent homes became increasingly disadvantaged relative to young men from two-parent homes. The college graduation rate for the sons of college-educated single mothers has decreased from 50 percent to 25 percent since 1975, whereas the college graduation rate for the sons of partnered college-graduate mothers has not deviated significantly since 1975 from its average of 66 percent.

Immigration has accelerated since 1965. Immigrants have a bimodal educational distribution according to our calculations, based on the CPS data. High school dropouts and college graduates are both more prevalent among immigrants than among the native-born. Immigrants are both less likely to have high school diplomas and more likely to have college diplomas than people who grew up in the United States. Eighty percent of male immigrants who were educated in the 1960s and 1970s completed high school, but new waves of unskilled immigrants have brought that proportion down to 50 percent of the most recent, youngest arrivals. The rising premium for college—widely documented; see, for example, Fischer and Hout 2006, figure 5.4)—attracts skilled labor from abroad. The U.S. government also issues special visas for people with rare skills and for students to get advanced degrees. The patterns for women are similar to those for men, except that immigrant women have more education than immigrant men. Thus, one-third of immigrant men have college degrees earned abroad, as compared to one-fourth of native-educated men. Educated immigrant men are also more likely than U.S.-educated men to have advanced degrees, reflecting both U.S. labor-market conditions and U.S. immigration policy.

FIGURE 8.7   *Percentage Completing as Much or More Education as Mother, by Year Turned Twenty-Five, Level of Education, Mother's Highest Degree, and Family Structure at Age Sixteen: Men Twenty-Seven to Sixty-Four Years Old at Time of Interview*

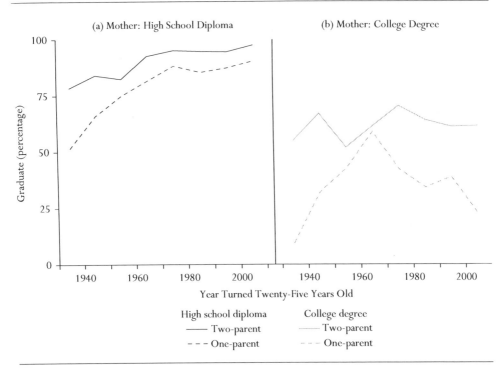

Source: Authors' calculations, based on Smith et al. (2008).
Notes: Men whose mothers either dropped out of high school or completed some college are not shown; women are not shown.

SCHOOL-RELATED FACTORS

Policies and practices in high schools and colleges in the United States contribute to the persistent inequalities we have documented. As addressed in chapters 5 and 13 in this volume, more-educated parents send their children to better schools than do less-educated parents. Residential segregation by wealth, income, and education contributes to disparities in the quality of public schools. And the 10 percent of families headed by two college graduates are the most likely to send their children to private schools.

We leave it to our colleagues to present the details of these patterns. For us, the key questions are whether differences among schools account for all of the disparities by parental education and the degree to which learning differences that follow from having more-educated parents or attending better schools mediate the effects of parents and schools.

Answering these questions is more difficult that it ought to be. The National Center for Educational Statistics (NCES) has mounted four significant cohort studies to answer similar kinds of questions. Unfortunately, differences in design—including differences in the starting point of the study, how schools were chosen, which tests were administered, how long students were followed, and how much of the data were released to researchers—all make exact comparisons from study to study impossible. Although we could not conduct a full analysis of trends, we could assess

TABLE 8.1   *Logistic Regression Coefficients for Selected Variables in Three Models of High School Graduation, by High School Graduating Class*

	High School Class of 1992		
	Model 0	Model 1	Model 2
Father's education[a]	0.465*	0.265	0.034
	(0.071)	(0.152)	(0.114)
Mother's education[a]	0.174*	−0.120	0.091
	(0.064)	(0.165)	(0.118)
Intact family[b]	—	1.905*	0.840*
		(0.435)	(0.363)
Educational expectations[a]	—	0.605*	0.318*
		(0.169)	(0.106)
Other individual-level variables[b]	No	Yes	Yes
School-level variables	No	No	Yes

Source: Authors' calculations based on U.S. Department of Education, National Center for Education Statistics (1996).
Note: Standard errors in parentheses.
[a]Centered: high school graduate.
[b]Centered: grand mean.
*$p \leq 0.05$

the robustness of the educational-mobility conclusions we reached using the GSS data. On that score, the NCES panels are reassuring. We find no evidence of change with time in the effects of mothers' and fathers' education in the limited comparisons the data allow.

Our method of decomposing the observed correlations between young people's education and their parents' is to compare models that have no controls with models that control for other measurable features of family background, school differences, and test scores (see tables 8.1 and 8.2). Table 8.1 shows coefficients of parents' educations from logistic regressions in which the dependent variable is graduation from high school or higher educational attainment versus less than that, and table 8.2 shows similar results, this time for graduating from college versus having a lower level of education. Descriptive statistics and full regression results are shown in appendix tables 8.A1 to 8.A3 online.

Our high school analysis is limited to the high school class of 1992. The gross effects of parents' educations are familiar. Father's and mother's educations were strongly associated with their children's probability of graduating from high school. Each parental credential increased the probability of the child's graduating by two to eleven percentage points, depending on the baseline graduation rate.[9] Adding individual-level controls, including family structure and test scores, results in a coefficient for father's education that is 43 percent smaller than the baseline effect and a negative coefficient for mother's education. Thus, much of what parents do to advance their children through high school is tied to what those students learn, though, as the very large coefficient for family stability in the table shows, it is also important to have both parents present. Educated parents promote learning by helping with homework, supporting academic activities at school and at home, and, perhaps most importantly, reinforcing lessons learned in school when school is not in session (Downey, Von Hippel, and Broh 2006). Also critically important is the degree to which the student internalizes parental and school influences through her or his own educational expectations. Adding school characteristics to the model explains most of the remaining parental influence on high school graduation. Thus the influence of parental education on high school graduation

TABLE 8.2   *Logistic Regression Coefficients for Selected Variables in Three Models of College Graduation by Model*

	High School Class of 1972			High School Class of 1992		
	Model 0	Model 1	Model 2	Model 0	Model 1	Model 2
Father's education[a]	0.209*	0.067*	0.060*	0.265*	0.101*	0.080*
	(0.012)	(0.021)	(0.019)	(0.018)	(0.024)	(0.018)
Mother's education[a]	0.186*	0.085*	0.072*	0.173*	0.047	0.052*
	(0.014)	(0.023)	(0.021)	(0.019)	(0.026)	(0.019)
Intact family[b]	—	0.267*	0.276*	No	0.584*	0.537*
		(0.097)	(0.086)		(0.094)	(0.069)
Educational expectations[b]	—	0.593*	0.590*		0.423*	0.396*
		(0.032)	(0.026)		(0.029)	(0.023)
Other individual-level variables[b]	No	Yes	Yes	No	Yes	Yes
School-level variables	No	No	Yes	No	No	Yes

Sources: Authors' calculations based on U.S. Department of Education, National Center for Education Statistics (1992, 1996).
[a]Centered: high school graduate.
[b]Centered: grand mean.
*$p < 0.05$

is largely indirect. Parents with more education tend to inculcate learning habits and educational values in their children that are very important in any school context; they also choose secondary schools for their children that facilitate their children's success.

Parents' educations exert a somewhat more direct effect on college graduation. About one-fourth of the total association between father's and mother's educations and the student's college graduation is evident (and statistically significant) after controlling for individual and school variables. Thus, parents continue to shape their children's education after they go off to college, though most of their influence is indirect, through the student's own attributes and those of the secondary school the student attended. There is no evidence in the comparison between the classes of 1972 and 1992 that these relationships changed over time.

Our results also confirm the conclusions that Robert Hauser, Shuling Tsai, and William H. Sewell (1983) reached almost thirty years ago. The path from parents' status to students' attainments is largely mediated by the students' own orientations and school-related experiences. Having college-educated parents leads to educational advantages over and above the contributions that educated parents make to a young person's chances of attending the better high schools and learning school material at home, but the residual advantages are effective only if the student internalizes and acts on them.

CONCLUSIONS

Inequality of educational opportunity in the United States is substantial and persistent. Parents' education contributes to young people's success as much now as it did fifty years ago. In those fifty years, the nation and its states reformed many practices and made many changes in how schools operate and who attends them. Yet the inequalities persist.

Social and economic trends raise a number of concerns about access and opportunity. Although rising inequality could be exacerbating educational stratification, we find no evidence to support that conjecture. Persisting differences in high school and college graduation rates among people whose parents differ in education point on one hand to the tenacity of inequality and on the other to the effectiveness of some mechanisms in offsetting the pressures of rising inequality. Samuel R. Lucas (2001) called it "effectively maintained inequality." The precise mechanisms shift—he cites the consequences of increasing, then decreasing, the rigidity of curriculum stratification in high schools for graduation rates. But the total effects of educational inequality do not change.

We do find that overall educational mobility has decreased significantly since the 1970s. The primary cause is the lack of progress in high school and college graduation rates. Young people in the 2000s are just about as likely to graduate from college as the young people of the 1970s were. Women have caught up to men, but the overall college graduation rate was about 27 percent in the 1970s and is the same now. The parents of today's college-age youth were themselves educated in the years when college opportunities quit expanding, and educational growth has stopped being a factor in upward educational mobility. Downward educational mobility actually increased in recent years as the enrollment capacity of colleges and universities failed to keep up with population growth and rising aspirations (Hout 2009).

In any era, expansion drives the balance of upward and downward mobility. In an era such as the present one, the absence of expansion curtails upward mobility and leads to more downward mobility. To restart the engine of upward mobility, the United States will have to build more colleges and universities, substantially expand the capacity of today's colleges and universities, or improve the productivity of those colleges and universities.

Social mobility features prominently in current policy discussions. William G. Bowen, Matthew M. Chingos, and Michael S. McPherson (2009) discuss one of the core concerns here: the inefficiency of the system represented by students' dropping out of college. Any attempt to increase educational mobility should aim to reduce the dropout rate. The high school dropout rate is equally important. James Heckman and Paul A. LaFontaine (2007) identified flagging high school graduation rates as contributors to the slow rate of progress in overall educational attainment. The recession of 2007 to 2009 may have deepened the problem by having a negative impact on state financing of education. In the long term, however, expanding educational opportunity will contribute to economic growth.

NOTES

Online appendix available at: http://www.russellsage.org/duncan_murnane_online_appendix.pdf.

1. Emily Beller and Hout (2006) restricted attention to men because they lacked data on mothers' occupations.
2. Some evidence indicates that family income affects attending college more than it used to (Karen 2002; Hout 2005).
3. A serious limitation of these CPS studies was their exclusion of women.
4. Harry B. G. Ganzeboom, Donald J. Treiman, and Ruud Luijkx (1991), Hout (2004), and Samuel Bowles and Herbert Gintis (2002) review these studies.
5. Oversamples of African Americans made 1982 and 1987 bigger than other surveys in the 1980s. Random sampling within the survey makes the number of observations for some items smaller than the overall sample size, but education and parents' characteristics are universal items not subject to the sampling.
6. To clarify: We use the high school graduation cohort as a way of making uniform comparisons over time, but we do not limit our calculations to high school graduates. These data show the percentage of the whole cohort that earned a college or higher degree.
7. The father's education is attributed in 20 percent of cases, and the mother's, in 8 percent of cases. We used twenty multiple imputations and averaged across all of them. The 3 percent of cases with missing data on both parents' educational levels received no imputation and are thus excluded from the analysis.
8. We recognize that money is not the only source of advantage for people with college-educated parents. College-educated parents provide cultural opportunities, books, and help with homework (Coleman and Hoffer 1987;

Bowles and Gintis 2002) and tend to have more effective interactions with teachers (Lareau 1987). All of these things add to the financial benefits that flow from parents' financial returns to their own education.

9.   The relationship between independent variables and the probability of success in logistic regression models is non-linear; effects are largest when the baseline probability of success is near 50 percent. In that case, the students whose parents did not graduate from high school have about a 64 percent probability of graduating from high school themselves. The difference between their expected probability of graduating from high school and that of a student whose mother was a high school graduate but whose father was not was 75 percent. Similar calculations comparing students whose parents had some college with students who had one parent with some college and the other with a degree indicate just a two-percentage-point difference (a baseline of 92 percent and a higher 94 percent with one college-graduate parent).

REFERENCES

Becker, Gary, and Nigel Tomes. 1979. "An Equilibrium Theory of the Distribution of Income and Intergenerational Mobility." *Journal of Political Economy* 87(6): 1153–89.

Beller, Emily. 2009. "Bringing Intergenerational Social Mobility Research into the Twenty-First Century: Why Mothers Matter." *American Sociological Review* 74(4): 507–28.

Beller, Emily, and Michael Hout. 2006. "Intergenerational Social Mobility: The United States in Comparative Perspective." *Future of Children* 16(2): 19–36.

Blau, Peter M., and Otis Dudley Duncan. 1967. *The American Occupational Structure.* New York: Free Press.

Bound, John, Brad Herschbein, and Bridget Terry Long. 2009. "Playing the Admissions Game: Student Reactions to Increasing College Competition." *Journal of Economic Perspectives* 23(4): 119–46.

Bowen, William G., Matthew M. Chingos, and Michael S. McPherson. 2009. *Crossing the Finish Line: Completing College at America's Public Universities.* Princeton, N.J. : Princeton University Press.

Bowles, Samuel, and Herbert Gintis. 2002. "The Inheritance of Inequality." *Journal of Economic Perspectives* 16(3): 3–30.

Coleman, James S., and Thomas Hoffer. 1987. *Public and Private High Schools: The Impact of Communities.* New York: Basic Books.

Davis, James A., Tom W. Smith, and Peter V. Marsden. 2008. General Social Surveys, 1972 to 2008. Machine-readable data file. Chicago: National Opinion Research Center, producer, distributed by University of Connecticut, Roper Center for Public Opinion Research, Storrs, Conn. Also available at: Inter-university Consortium for Political and Social Research, www.icpsr.umich.edu/icpsrweb/ICPSR/studies?archive=ICPSR&q=General+Social+Surveys (accessed March 14, 2011).

DiPrete, Thomas A., and Claudia Buchmann. 2006. "Gender Specific Trends in the Value of Education and the Emerging Gender Gap in College Completion." *Demography* 43(1): 1–24.

Downey, Douglas B., Paul T. Von Hippel, and Beckett Broh. 2006. "Are Schools the Great Equalizer? School and Non-School Sources of Inequality in Cognitive Skills." *American Sociological Review* 69(5): 613–35.

Duncan, Otis Dudley. 1966. "Methodological Issues in the Analysis of Social Mobility." In *Social Structure and Economic Development,* edited by Neil J. Smelser and Seymour Martin Lipset. Chicago: Aldine.

Ehrenberg, Ronald G. 2002. *Tuition Rising.* Cambridge, Mass.: Harvard University Press.

Featherman, David L., and Robert M. Hauser. 1978. *Opportunity and Change.* New York: Academic Press.

Ferguson, Andrew. 2011. *Crazy U: One Dad's Crash Course in Getting His Kid into College.* New York: Simon and Schuster.

Fischer, Claude S., and Michael Hout. 2006. *Century of Difference: How American Changed Over the Past One Hundred Years.* New York: Russell Sage Foundation.

Fischer, Claude S., Michael Hout, Martín Sánchez Jankowski, Samuel R. Lucas, Ann Swidler, and Kim Voss. 1996. *Inequality by Design.* Princeton, N.J.: Princeton University Press.

Ganzeboom, Harry B. G., Donald J. Treiman, and Ruud Luijkx. 1991. "Comparative Intergenerational Stratification Research: Three Generations and Beyond." *Annual Review of Sociology* 17: 277–302.

Goldin, Claudia, and Lawrence F. Katz. 2007. *The Race Between Education and Technology.* Cambridge, Mass.: Harvard University Press.

Hauser, Robert M., Shuling Tsai, and William H. Sewell. 1983. "A Model of Stratification with Response Error in Social and Psychological Variables." *Sociology of Education* 56(1): 20–46.

Heckman, James J., and Paul A. LaFontaine. 2007. "The American High School Graduation Rate: Trends and Levels." NBER Working Paper No. 13670. Cambridge, Mass.: National Bureau of Education Research.

Hout, Michael. 1995. "The Politics of Mobility." In *Generating Social Stratification,* edited by Alan C. Kerckhoff. Boulder, Colo.: Westview.

———. 2004. "Social Mobility and Inequality: A Review and an Agenda." In *Social Inequality,* edited by Kathryn Neckerman. New York: Russell Sage Foundation.

———. 2005. "Educational Progress for African-Americans and Latinos in the United States from the 1950s to the 1990s: The Interaction of Ancestry and Class." In *Ethnicity, Social Mobility and Public Policy,* edited by Glenn C. Loury, Tariq Modood, and Steven Michael Teles. Cambridge: Cambridge University Press.

———. 2009. "Rationing College Opportunity." *American Prospect,* November, pp. A8–A10.

Karen, David. 2002. "Changes in Access to Higher Education in the United States, 1980–1992." *Sociology of Education* 75(3): 191–210.

King, Miriam, Steven Ruggles, J. Trent Alexander, Sarah Flood, Katie Genadek, Matthew B. Schroeder, Brandon Trampe, and Rebecca Vick. 2010. *Integrated Public Use Microdata Series, Current Population Survey: Version 3.0.* [Machine-readable Data File]. Minneapolis: University of Minnesota.

Lareau, Annette. 1987. "Social Class Differences in Family-School Relationships: The Importance of Cultural Capital." *Sociology of Education* 60(2): 2–85.

Lucas, Samuel R. 2001. "Effectively Maintained Inequality: Education Transitions, Track Mobility, and Social Background Effects." *American Journal of Sociology* 106(6): 1642–90.

Preston, Samuel H., and Irma Elo. 1995. "Are Educational Differentials in Adult Mortality Increasing in the United States?" *Journal of Aging and Health* 7(4): 476–96.

Rabe-Hesketh, Sophia, and Anders Skrendel. 2008. *Multilevel and Longitudinal Data Analysis.* 2d ed. College Station, Texas: Stata Press.

Rubin, Donald. 1987. *Multiple Imputation for Nonresponse in Surveys.* New York: Wiley.

Schneider, Barbara, and David Stevenson, 1999. *The Ambitious Generation.* New Haven, Conn.: Yale University Press.

Smith, Tom W., James A. Davis, and Peter V. Marsden. 2008. *General Social Surveys, 1972–2008.* [machine-readable data file]. Chicago: National Opinion Research Center.

Sobel, Michael E., Michael Hout, and Otis Dudley Duncan. 1985. "Exchange, Structure, and Symmetry in Occupational Mobility." *American Journal of Sociology* 91(02): 359–72.

Sorokin, Pitirim A. 1927. *Social Mobility.* New York: Harper & Bros.

Treiman, Donald J. 2008. *Quantitative Data Analysis.* San Francisco: Jossey-Bass.

U.S. Department of Education, National Center for Education Statistics. 1992. *National Longitudinal Study of the Class of 1972* [Machine Readable Data File]. ICPSR version. Chicago, Ill.: National Opinion Research Center [producer], 1992. Ann Arbor, Mich.: Inter-university Consortium for Political and Social Research [distributor], 1999. doi:10.3886/ICPSR08085.

———. 1996. *National Education Longitudinal Study: Base Year Through Third Follow-up, 1988–1994* [Machine Readable Data File]. ICPSR version. Washington: U.S. Department of Education, National Center for Education Statistics [producer], 1996. Ann Arbor, Mich.: Inter-university Consortium for Political and Social Research [distributor], 1999. doi:10.3886/ICPSR06961.

Chapter 9

How Is Family Income Related to Investments in Children's Learning?

Neeraj Kaushal, Katherine Magnuson, and Jane Waldfogel

In this chapter we explore the extent to which families' investments in items and activities related to children's learning differ by income. The analysis relies on the Consumer Expenditure Survey (CEX) and the Early Childhood Longitudinal Study, Kindergarten Cohort (ECLS-K). The data span from 1997 to 2006, and include family expenditures on education-related items and activities such as music and art lessons, children's books and toys, sports equipment and classes, and tutoring. Although descriptive, our analyses shed light on the links between income and family investments and also suggest some directions for further research and policy.

Our analyses from the CEX data suggest that as family expenditures (our rough proxy of permanent income) rise, so too does spending on items of enrichment. This pattern is present not only at one point in time (via cross-sectional data) but also over time (via longitudinal data) as expenditures on enrichment activities change when family financial resources change. This latter finding supports the proposition that providing low-income families with more resources could increase the amount of money spent on enrichment items and activities for children.

Because the CEX does not contain data on children's actual access to or participation in particular investments, we turn to another data set to examine the links between family income and children's exposure to several education-related items and activities. Our analysis of the ECLS-K indicates that the learning-related items children possess and the enrichment activities in which they participate vary considerably by family income, with higher-income families providing substantially more enriching environments and activities for their children than low-income families.

Thus, both data sets point to substantial income-related gaps in education-related items and activities. To the extent that such investments matter for child outcomes, economic inequality among families, and the associated differences in such investments, may contribute to future inequality.

Parents supplement children's in-school educational activities and promote children's learning through a wide variety of investments. For preschool-age children, family income may be invested in early care and education programs as well as enrichment activities and items such as books and toys, computers, and music and art lessons. For school-age children and adolescents, family income may be used to purchase after-school tutoring programs, enrichment activities such as music and art lessons, summer camp programs, family or educational travel, extracurricular activities, and, ultimately, higher education.

Parental investments are central to theoretical models of child development. In particular, economic household production theory argues that time and money are the two basic resources that parents invest in children, and that such investments in combination with children's endowments are formative in shaping children's outcomes (Becker 1991). Parents' preferences, such as the importance they place on education and their orientation toward the future, shape the extent and form of these investments, as do children's endowments and characteristics (Becker 1991; Foster 2002). For example, if a young child is talkative and enthusiastic about learning, parents are more likely to purchase children's books or take the child to the library (Raikes et al. 2006). Or if a child appears to be lagging in development, parents may make investments, in extra lessons or tutoring, to compensate.

Of course, one of the strongest determinants of parents' investments is their access to economic resources. As a result, the role of budget constraints looms large in such theoretical models. Household production theory suggests that children from low-income families trail behind their economically advantaged counterparts because their parents have fewer resources to invest in them (Becker 1991). Compared with more affluent parents, low-income parents are less able to purchase items and environments for their children, including books and educational materials at home, high-quality child-care settings and schools, and safe neighborhoods (Danziger and Waldfogel 2000; Kalil and DeLeire 2004). Economically disadvantaged parents may also have less time to invest in children, owing to the higher prevalence of single-parenthood, nonstandard work hours, and inflexible work schedules (Smolensky and Gootman 2003). However, it is the limited financial resources they have to spend on their children, particularly during the early-childhood years, that remains one of the central explanations for why poor children lag behind their peers (Duncan and Brooks-Gunn 1997; Haveman and Wolfe 1994).

Studies of family expenditures have documented clear gaps between lower- and higher-income families in spending and ownership of durable goods (see, for example, Lino and Carlson 2009). Yet relatively few studies have focused specifically on learning-related items, activities, and goods. Focusing specifically on such items is important because income-related gaps in spending may not be constant across items. Low-income families may prioritize child-related items, such that spending gaps on those are smaller than for other items. Alternatively, lower-income families may have other characteristics that are associated with preferences for less spending on learning-related items (low levels of parental education, for instance), and thus may spend relatively less on such items even when their incomes increase (Chin and Phillips 2004; Lareau 2003). Studies have documented income-related differences in particular types of investments in isolation, for example, early education programs or after-school activities (Bainbridge et al. 2005; Meyers et al. 2004; Smolensky and Gootman 2003). This approach is also unsatisfying, as it provides a piecemeal view of parental investments.

Showing that income is associated with learning-related investments does not establish the extent to which increasing families' incomes would lead to greater investments. As just noted, families' investment decisions are driven not just by budget constraints but also by their preferences and other characteristics, as well as the characteristics and preferences of children (Chin and Phillips 2004; Lareau 2003). Nevertheless, prior studies do provide some evidence that when low-income families receive additional income, they increase their spending on learning-related items and activities. For instance, in the New Hope antipoverty experiment, families used their additional income to enroll children in child care, after-school activities, and other enrichment programs (Duncan, Huston, and Weisner 2007). Nonexperimental analyses of recent antipoverty reforms in the United Kingdom found that low-income families used their additional income to increase their spending on items of enrichment and other items for children (Gregg, Waldfogel, and Washbrook 2005, 2006).

Documenting that such investments matter for child development is equally challenging. In this chapter we do not analyze this question but instead briefly review prior evidence on it. Presumably, parental investments in out-of-school learning materials and activities complement students' in-school learning by teaching them diverse skills and by providing positive peer socialization contexts and experiences that broaden children's horizons. Parental investments in children's activities also create forums for the socialization of cultural knowledge and practices (Rogoff 1990). Psychologists argue that one of the key developmental tasks of middle childhood is building a sense of competence (Eccles 1999; Erikson 1959), and to the extent that parental investments provide enriching contexts and opportunities to gain such competencies and develop talents, such investments will improve child well-being. In addition, parental investments may be protective in middle childhood, keeping children from spending unsupervised time in potentially dangerous neighborhood or peer environments (Morris and Kalil 2006; McHale, Crouter, and Tucker 2001).

Thus, parental investments come in several forms, and we focus on the following heuristic categories in this study: extracurricular activities (lessons or participation in organized activities such as athletics and Boy Scouts, which do not provide an explicitly academic content); home learning materials (books, computers); and school-related investments (preschool, tutors, and private school attendance). Although theory suggests that extracurricular activities, home learning materials, and school-related investments should be positively associated with children's achievement and behavior, the empirical evidence for causal connections is inconclusive. In the case of extracurricular activities, studies do find positive links between such activities and children or adolescents' school-related outcomes (Mahoney, Larson, and Eccles 2005), particularly for low-income youths (Posner and Vandell 1994, 1999). However, the effects differ across activities and outcomes, and with the level of children's participation (Morris and Kalil 2006; Ripke, Huston, and Casey 2006).[1]

Home learning–related materials are rarely the sole subject of study; rather, such items are more often part of a more general measure of learning opportunities and literacy experiences that contribute to the quality of cognitive stimulation in the home environment (Bradley et al. 2001a). Studies consistently find that these broader measures of home environment are linked with higher levels of children's achievement (Bradley et al. 2001b) and that such associations may explain at least part of the associations between poverty and child outcomes (Duncan and Brooks-Gunn 2000). Finally, the literature on parents' school-related investments is vast, but again such investments are typically studied in isolation. Attending preschool and private schools is generally associated with improved school performance, although effects differ by the type of preschool and private school children attend (Magnuson, Ruhm, and Waldfogel 2007; Lubienski and Lubienski 2006).[2] Parents also use higher incomes to purchase housing in districts with better public schools.

A large concern with all of these research areas is the inability to say decisively that these factors cause improved performance, given that few studies have used rigorous methods that adequately account for the potential for omitted variable biases. Children and families "select into" certain activities, and estimates that do not take this selection into account will be biased. Only a few studies have been able to persuasively demonstrate that reducing family poverty or improving family incomes affects children's well-being. These studies take advantage of changes in policies and programs that provide families with additional income. For example, the only large-scale randomized interventions to alter family income directly were the Negative Income

Tax Experiments, conducted between 1968 and 1982 with the primary goal of identifying the influence of guaranteed income on parents' labor-force participation. Using information from those sites that also collected data on child achievement and attainment, researchers found that elementary school children in the experimental group (whose families gained $2,000 per year from the program, about a 50 percent increase in income) had higher early academic achievement and better school attendance (Maynard and Murnane 1979). The study found no test score differences for adolescents, although youths in the experimental group did have higher rates of high school completion and educational attainment (Salkind and Haskins 1982).

More recently, studies of experimental welfare reform and antipoverty policies (Morris, Duncan, and Clark-Kauffman 2005), the expansion of the Earned Income Tax Credits (Dahl and Lochner 2008), and the distribution of Native American Indian casino earnings (Akee et al. forthcoming) all point to a similar conclusion: increasing family incomes improves children's outcomes. It is important to note, however, that these studies do not indicate how increased incomes led to improved outcomes for children through, for example, increased expenditures for child investments or improvements in other aspects of family life, such as parents' mental health (Magnuson and Votruba-Drzal 2009).

INCOME INEQUALITY AND INVESTMENTS IN CHILDREN

Recent increases in income inequality may be associated with increased inequality of investments in children (discussed in chapter 1 of this volume). Analyses of investments in children between 1972 and 2006 show that such investments have increased much more rapidly among high-income families than among their low-income peers (see chapter 1, figure 1.6; see also Kornrich and Furstenberg 2010).

Our goal in this chapter is to produce and bring together new evidence on current income-related differences in parental investments in children. Using two large, nationally representative data sets, we explore the extent to which families' investments in enrichment items and activities differ by income. These descriptive analyses shed light on the links between income and family investments in educational items and activities.

We begin with analyses of the Consumer Expenditure Survey (CEX), a repeated cross-sectional survey that contains detailed data on family income and expenditures. In particular, we take advantage of its detailed information about expenditures on education-related items and activities such as music and art lessons, children's books and toys, sports equipment and classes, and tutoring (see online appendix table 9.A1).[3] We use CEX data from 1997 to 2006 to describe how spending on items and activities that might supplement children's learning varies across income groups. We then use the CEX data to estimate models for how expenditures on such items change as families' total expenditure changes.

The CEX does not contain data on children's actual access to nor participation in particular investments, and thus we turn to another data set, the Early Childhood Longitudinal Study, Kindergarten Cohort (ECLS-K), to examine the links between family income and children's exposure to several education-related items and activities. The ECLS-K follows a large and nationally representative sample of children first assessed at the start of kindergarten in fall 1998, and collects data on their academic and behavioral outcomes, as well as learning materials in the home and the child's involvement in learning-related activities outside of school (see online appendix table 9.A2 for information on the variables in the ECLS-K). Sizable income-related gaps in child academic and behavioral outcomes are apparent in the ECLS-K at both kindergarten and fifth grade. We use the ECLS-K data to examine to what degree investments in child learning vary by family income (by quintile) at those two points.

CONSUMER EXPENDITURE SURVEY

In this section, we describe the CEX data, our empirical approach to the CEX analyses, and the results of those analyses.

Data

The CEX provides detailed information on expenditures among a sample of consumer units (we use the terms "family" and "consumer unit" interchangeably in referring to our sample). A unit is defined as all members of a housing unit related by blood, marriage, adoption, or some other legal arrangement; or two or more persons living together who use their incomes to make joint expenditures; or a single person who is living with others but is financially independent (U.S. Bureau of Labor Statistics 2005). We restrict the analysis to families with children, where the mother is age eighteen to fifty-four.

The CEX provides detailed demographic information on each consumer unit, including respondent's age, education level, marital status, race and ethnicity, family size, number of children and their ages, and number of elderly persons (age sixty-five and above) in the family. We first classify quarterly expenditures into ten major categories: housing and utilities, food, alcohol and tobacco, clothing and footwear, transportation, health, leisure, personal care, education (including reading), and miscellaneous. The CEX also provides data on expenditures on narrower categories. We use these detailed items to select eleven different categories of expenditures that potentially represent investments in children's learning: books and magazines, school supplies and books, college tuition and books,[4] noncollege tuition and private bus, computer, electronics, recreation lessons and activities, entertainment, sports, trips, and child care. We also compute a composite category combining these eleven items as a summary measure of expenditures on items and activities of enrichment. A detailed description of the data is provided in the online appendix (available at: http://www.russellsage.org/duncan_murnane_online_appendix.pdf).

Empirical Model

Our objective is to understand the relationship between permanent family incomes, and expenditures on items of enrichment and developmental activities for children. Our analysis is guided by Milton Friedman's permanent-income hypothesis, which states that families base their consumption on what they consider their permanent or expected incomes, and not their current incomes. Thus, the transitory changes in incomes that families experience have little effect on their consumption expenditures (Friedman 1957). The CEX data provide information on the current annual income of families, which includes a transitory component (unexpected or temporary gain or loss) as well. Therefore, following previous research, we use total expenditures as a proxy for permanent income and compute expenditure elasticities (Archibald and Gillingham 1981; Deaton and Muellbauer 1980; Massell, 1969; Ogaki 1992; Wagner and Mokhtati 2000). A second reason for estimating expenditure (rather than income) elasticities is the poor quality of income data in the CEX (see Wagner and Mokhtati 2000 for a detailed discussion; see also Meyer and Sullivan 2003). Nevertheless, in supplementary analysis, we also compute income elasticities.

We begin with a simple reduced-form equation,

(9.1)
$$E_{ict} = \alpha_m + \alpha_t + \beta TE_{ct} + \Gamma X_{ct} + u_{it}$$

where E_{ict} is the quarterly annualized expenditures on item i by consumer unit c in year t, which is predicted by total family expenditures in year t, (TE_{ct}), and family characteristics (X_{ct}) namely: mother's age (denoted by a set of dummy variables for age groups: 18 to 22; 23 to 27; 28 to 32; 33 to 37; 38 to 42; 43 to 48; and 49 to 54); mother's education (less than a high school degree, high school degree, some college, B.A. or higher degree); race-ethnicity (non-Hispanic white, non-Hispanic black, Hispanics, and others); number of adults in the family (other than the reference person); number of children in the family; number of persons over age sixty-four living in the family; and whether the family lives in an urban area. α_m denotes month effects that adjust for seasonal changes in expenditures, and α_t estimates year effects adjusting for time-varying factors such as national-level changes in prices, tastes, and preferences, and policies. The coefficient β estimates the marginal propensity to spend on item i. To adjust for potential non-independence among observations belonging to the same family, standard errors are computed by clustering at the family unit.

Equation 9.1 estimates a linear association between expenditures on item i and total family budget. To allow for a less restrictive association between the two, we estimate equation 9.1 by stratifying families into quintiles according to total family expenditures relative to their needs. We compute the "budget to needs" ratio as total expenditures of a consumer unit divided by the poverty threshold corresponding to the unit's family size and structure. The data on poverty thresholds are taken from the Census Bureau (U.S. Bureau of the Census n.d.). Although stratifying the sample in this manner permits a less restrictive functional form, using family budgets to stratify data in a study of the association between family budgets and expenditures on items of enrichment is potentially problematic and may yield biased estimates. To overcome this limitation we also stratify families by mother's education into four categories: less than high school, high school, some college, and B.A. degree or higher, and estimate equation 9.1 for each group separately.

It is also of interest whether the association between expenditures on items of enrichment and family budgets differs for families with preschool children versus families with school-aged children, given that expenditures on such items may well vary by the age of the children. We investigate this by stratifying our sample as: families with preschool children only (all children younger than age six); families with school-age children only (all children age six or higher); and families with both preschool and school-age children.

Coefficient β in equation 9.1 estimates the association between family budgets and spending on children's enrichment and developmental activities. Ideally we would like to estimate causal links, if any, between family budgets and expenditures on enrichment items. Estimating a causal relationship, however, would require that variation in total budgets is unrelated to other unobserved factors that influence family spending patterns. It is unlikely that such random variation exists in our cross-sectional data. Thus, it is quite possible that the cross-sectional findings are biased by the presence of omitted variables.

Fortunately we can take advantage of the panel feature of the CEX data and adopt a second approach to estimating the associations between total expenditures and expenditures on education-related items. Each family in the CEX is interviewed for five consecutive quarters. We use the longitudinal aspect of the CEX to examine the association between changes in total expenditures and expenditures on items of enrichment within a family unit. Mathematically, our second approach can be described by equation 9.2:

$$(9.2) \qquad E_{ict} = \alpha_c + \alpha_m + \alpha_t + \beta TE_{ct} + X_{ct}\Gamma + u_{it}$$

where α_c denotes family-specific effects. We estimate the longitudinal analyses using fixed-effects models. These models are useful in reducing omitted variable bias because any perma-

FIGURE 9.1   *Expenditures on Enrichment Items, by Expenditure Quintiles (Mean Annualized Expenditure, Equivalized for Family Size)*

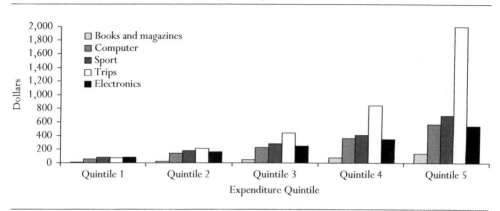

Source: Authors' estimates based on data from the Consumer Expenditure Survey (U.S. Bureau of Labor Statistics 1997–2006).

nent family-level confounds are removed, although bias due to time-varying confounds will likely remain. We also conduct these analyses across subgroups defined by expenditure quintiles, mother's education, and children's age.

Results

We begin with analyses of families' mean annualized expenditures on items and activities of enrichment (details available in online appendix table 9.A3). Families' spending patterns may differ in two ways. First, they may differ because the amount of resources available to be spent differs. Second, families may allocate resources differently across categories of spending, even if their total amount of spending is similar. For this reason, we present both total amount of expenditures for each category as well as spending in specific categories as a proportion of all expenditures. In supplemental analyses we also report mean annualized total expenditures and expenditures on the major ten categories for the full sample and for subsamples defined by expenditure quintiles, race-ethnicity, family type, mother's education, and children's age, but for brevity we do not discuss them here (details in online appendix table 9.A4).

We find that the share of total expenditures allocated to items of enrichment rises with each expenditure quintile (quintile 1 represents families with the lowest expenditures, while quintile 5 represents families with the highest; details in online appendix table 9.A3). Families in the bottom quintile (quintile 1) allocate 3 percent of their total expenditures to enrichment items; families in the top two quintiles (4 and 5) spend 9 percent on items of enrichment. The gap in absolute expenditures on items of enrichment is wider (see figures 9.1 and 9.2, showing family-level and child-level items, respectively). In dollar terms, families in quintile 1 spend almost one-third of what families in quintile 2 spend and almost one-fifth of what families in quintile 3 spend on items of enrichment.[5]

A similar gap emerges when the sample is divided by mother's education. However, when the sample is stratified by mother's race-ethnicity, family type (single mother versus two-parent families), or child's age, the gap in the proportion of spending on items of enrichment is relatively modest, suggesting that most of the difference in absolute spending on enrichment activities

FIGURE 9.2   *Expenditures on Children's Enrichment, by Expenditure Quintiles (Mean Annualized Expenditure per Child)*

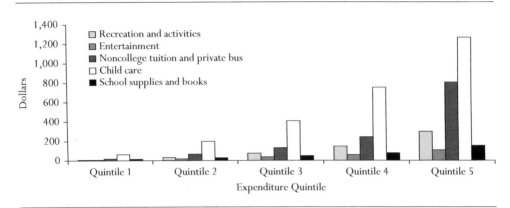

Source: Authors' estimates based on data from the Consumer Expenditure Survey (U.S. Bureau of Labor Statistics 1997–2006).

among these groups is likely attributed to the size of their total budget, rather than the allocation of resources across budget categories.

In the bottom quintile, 86 percent of the expenditures on items of enrichment goes to sports, family trips, electronics, child care, and computers. Families in higher quintiles allocate a somewhat larger proportion on other items of enrichment, such as books and magazines, education (college, noncollege, and school supplies), recreation activities and lessons, and entertainment. A similar story emerges when the sample is stratified by mother's education: more educated families allocate a larger proportion on the previously mentioned other items of enrichment than do less educated families. As expected, families with only preschool children spend a relatively large proportion on child care (45 percent of their total expenditures on items of enrichment), whereas families with only school-age children spend relatively more on school supplies, noncollege tuition (including private buses), recreation lessons and activities, and books and magazines.

Multivariate Results: Cross-Sectional Estimates of the Association Between Total Expenditures and Expenditures on Items of Enrichment

We estimate the association between total expenditures and expenditures on items of enrichment based on the model described in equation 9.1 that adjusts for a rich set of demographic variables (results shown in online appendix table 9.A5). We first do the analysis using the full sample of families, and then stratify families using three different kinds of categories: quintiles of expenditure-to-needs ratio (adjusting for family size and structure), levels of mother's education, and children's age.[6] Standard errors clustered on consumer units are reported in parentheses, and expenditure elasticities computed at the mean expenditure are in straight brackets.[7] Note that we use the term "elasticity" for convenience. Because total expenditure is not exogenous, our measure of elasticity does not necessarily suggest any causal association between total expenditures and expenditures on items of enrichment.

Estimates for the full sample show that a $1,000 increase in family expenditures (as a rough proxy for a $1,000 increase in permanent income) is associated with a $91 increase in expendi-

FIGURE 9.3　　*Change in Spending on Enrichment Items as Family Budgets Increase by $1,000, by Expenditure Quintile*

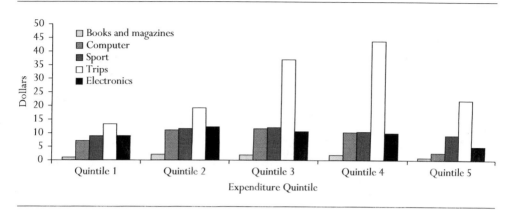

Source: Authors' estimates based on regression analysis in online appendix table 9.A5, adjusting for demographic characteristics, using data from the Consumer Expenditure Survey (U.S. Bureau of Labor Statistics 1997–2006).

FIGURE 9.4　　*Changes in Spending on Children's Enrichment Items as Family Budgets Increase by $1,000, by Expenditure Quintile*

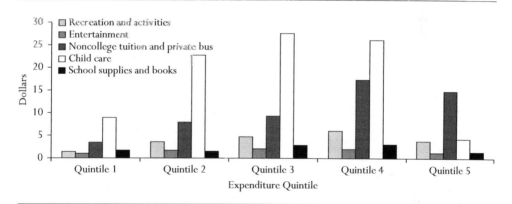

Source: Authors' estimates based on regression analysis in online appendix table 9.A5, adjusting for demographic characteristics, using data from the Consumer Expenditure Survey (U.S. Bureau of Labor Statistics 1997–2006).

tures on items of enrichment (online appendix table 9.A5, row 1). The estimated elasticity for expenditures on enrichment items is 1.1, suggesting that as income increases, the proportion of income devoted to items of enrichment increases by a somewhat higher proportion. The bulk of the increase is in expenditures on trips, followed by expenditure on noncollege tuition and private buses, and child care. The elasticity of expenditures is less than 1.0 for books and magazines, computers, electronics, child care, and school supplies and books, and more than 1.0 for the other five items.

As mentioned earlier, it may be that increases in income and expenditure may have different effects at different points in the income and expenditure distribution (see figures 9.3 and 9.4). Accordingly, we estimate similar models by expenditure quintile. The results indicate that estimates of elasticities for items of enrichment for quintiles 1 to 4 are greater than 1.0 for the combined

FIGURE 9.5   *Change in Spending on Enrichment Items as Family Budgets Increase by $1,000, by Mother's Education Group*

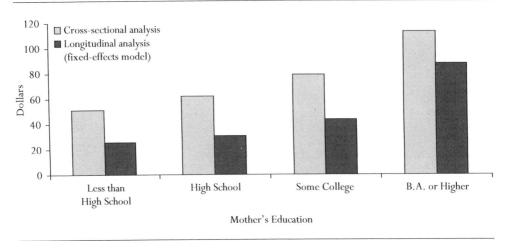

Source: Authors' estimates based on regression analysis in online appendix table 9.A5, adjusting for demographic characteristics, using data from the Consumer Expenditure Survey (U.S. Bureau of Labor Statistics 1997–2006).

category of items of enrichment and for each individual item, with the exception of the elasticity of expenditure on books and magazines for the fourth quintile). This result suggests that families in the bottom four quintiles of the expenditure distribution allocate a higher proportion of their budgets to items of enrichment as budgets grow. Families in the top quintile, in contrast, spend a relatively smaller proportion of their budget on items of enrichment as income rises. In terms of spending on specific items, families in the top quintile have elasticities of expenditure lower than 1.0 for all items of enrichment, except sports and noncollege tuition and private buses.

As mentioned, the analyses by expenditure quintiles suffer from the fact that we have used a right-hand-side variable to stratify the data, so the resulting estimates are likely to be biased. For instance, any increase (or decrease) in total family expenditures that occurs above (below) the expenditure cut-off for a given quintile is not captured by our quintile-level estimates. Therefore, we next estimate the marginal propensity to spend and elasticities for families stratified by mother's education (see figure 9.5, cross-sectional analysis results). Among families in the lowest-education group, a $1,000 increase in total expenditures is associated with a $51 increase in expenditures on items of enrichment. A $1,000 increase in total expenditures is associated with a $62 increase in spending on items of enrichment for families with high-school-graduate mothers, a $79 increase in families with mothers who have some college education, and a $113 increase in families with college-graduate mothers. For all groups, the expenditure elasticity of enrichment items (all items combined) is more than 1.0.

In terms of detailed items, families with children have much higher elasticities for noncollege tuition and private buses than for the other items of enrichment, irrespective of mother's education. Interestingly, the expenditure elasticity of computers is more than 1.0 for only the least educated families, and the elasticity of expenditure on sports is more than one for only the most educated families. For all other items, elasticities do not differ much by mother's education.

We next consider estimates for families stratified by children's age (see figure 9.6 and online appendix table 9.A5). The expenditure elasticity is estimated to be somewhat less than one for families with preschool children only and somewhat higher than one for families with school-aged

FIGURE 9.6   *Change in Spending on Enrichment Items as Family Budgets Increase by $1,000, by Age of Children*

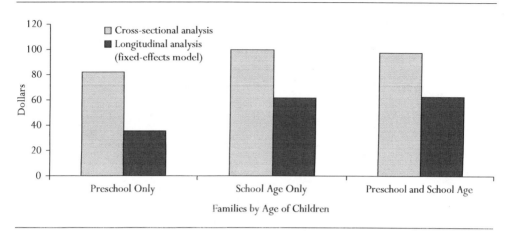

Source: Authors' estimates based on regression analysis cross-sectional models in online appendix table 9.A5, and longitudinal models in online appendix table 9.A8, using data from the Consumer Expenditure Survey (U.S. Bureau of Labor Statistics 1997–2006).

children (this is true both for those with only school-aged children and those with both preschool and school-aged children). In the detailed item-wise analyses as well, point estimates show that families with only preschool children have lower elasticities of spending on most items except for child care and electronics than families with school-aged children only. Similarly, point estimates show that families with both preschool and school-aged children have higher elasticity of spending on most items of enrichment than families with preschool-aged children only.

Multivariate Results: Longitudinal Analyses of the Association Between Changes in Total Expenditures and Changes in Expenditures on Enrichment Items

The next set of models estimates the marginal propensities to spend and elasticities, taking advantage of the longitudinal aspect of the data (details in online appendix table 9.A8). The results from these fixed-effects models suggest that a $1,000 increase in total expenditures is associated with a $59 increase in expenditures on items of enrichment. This point estimate is about one-third lower than the estimated marginal propensity in the cross-sectional analysis. The fixed-effects models yield an expenditure elasticity of 0.75, again lower than the estimate from the cross-sectional analysis. As in the cross-sectional analysis, the elasticity is more than 1.0 for families in the bottom four quintiles, and less than 1.0 for families in the top quintile. Again, these estimates may be biased given that the data are stratified by family expenditures, the key right-hand-side variable for our analyses. We therefore also estimate these models stratifying families by mother's education.

The fixed-effects models, stratified by mother's education, estimate the elasticity of enrichment expenditure to be less than 1.0 for all families, irrespective of mother's education, and point estimates indicate the elasticity for the most highly educated families (families in which mothers are college graduates) to be higher than those of other groups (also see marginal propensity estimates in figure 9.5). When we re-estimate the models stratifying by the children's age (also see marginal propensity estimates in figure 9.6), point estimates indicate that families with only preschool-age children have much lower elasticities of enrichment items than families with school-age children. This indicates that families are more likely to increase their financial spending on children as the children grow older.

To sum up, our analyses using the cross-sectional as well as longitudinal data suggest that families increase expenditures on items of enrichment as their budgets increase. The estimate of the marginal propensity to spend on items of enrichment from fixed-effects models (longitudinal analysis), however, is about two-thirds of the estimates from the cross-sectional data. This is true of the estimates for the full sample and for samples stratified by mother's education and child's age. That the associations between permanent income and expenditures on enrichment items are smaller in the fixed-effects models suggest that at least a portion of these associations reflect unobserved differences between lower- and higher-income families, which may be confounded with increases in expenditures. Nevertheless, even the reduced associations in the fixed-effects models indicate that as family incomes rise, expenditures on items of enrichment rise as well.

EARLY CHILDHOOD LONGITUDINAL STUDY, KINDERGARTEN COHORT OF 1998 TO 1999

How do these expenditures relate to children's actual experiences of such items and activities? Our analyses of the CEX data can tell us what families are purchasing, but they do not tell us who in the family is consuming those items. We therefore turn to analyses of our second data set, the ECLS-K.

Data

The data for this portion of the analysis come from the ECLS-K cohort of 1998 to 1999, a nationally representative sample of children attending kindergarten in fall 1998. We use information from fall 1998 (kindergarten fall), spring 1999 (kindergarten spring), spring 2000 (for most children, first grade), spring 2002 (for most children, third grade), and spring 2004 (for most children, fifth grade). The ECLS-K includes academic assessments; child, parent, teacher and school administrator surveys; and observational ratings of school environments.

We use two samples of children from these data. The sample used for our kindergarten analysis includes some 19,805 children with valid reading or math outcomes in kindergarten spring. The sample used in our fifth-grade analysis includes 10,985 children who had valid math or reading outcomes in kindergarten spring and fifth-grade spring. Nonresponse and missing data are prevalent. For example, of children with valid achievement assessments in kindergarten spring, about 14 percent had parents who did not complete the kindergarten fall parent interview, and 8 percent had parents who did not complete the kindergarten spring parent interview. Some attrition in the later years was due to study design. In particular, the study followed only a portion of children who changed schools. To handle missing data on the investment variables, we used multiple imputation techniques using Stata's software (ICE) to create and analyze five data sets.

Children's Academic Achievement and Behavior

We assessed children's math and reading skills with instruments created for the ECLS-K by a team of experts, with some items adapted from existing tests. Reported reliabilities for the tests were quite high for all assessments (Tourangeau et al. 2006). The math and reading outcomes are transformations of latent ability scores into standardized t-scores that have a mean of 50 and standard deviation of 10 (based on the full-sample distribution).[8] Consequently, the scores should be interpreted as indicating children's ability relative to their peers, and gaps can be translated into effect sizes by dividing by 10.

Teacher reports of children's externalizing and internalizing behavior measure children's classroom behavior.[9] Externalizing problem behavior refers to aggressive behavior as indicated by a five-item scale measuring how frequently the child fights, argues, gets angry, acts impulsively, or disturbs ongoing activities. The internalizing items tap teachers' perceptions of the child's anxiety, loneliness, and sadness. These scores were standardized (for the full sample) to have a mean of 0 and a standard deviation of 1. As such, gaps in scores can be interpreted as effect sizes.

Family Investments

Our key variables measure, or proxy for, parents' investments in children.[10] These measures fall into several rough categories: lessons (foreign language instruction, crafts, drama, art, music, and dance) and participation in organized activities (athletics, performing arts, and clubs); schooling (preschool attendance, private school attendance); and learning materials in the home (audio CDs, books, computer). (Means and standard errors for these variables are provided in online appendix table 9.A9. for imputed data, and additional descriptive details about these measures can be found in online appendix table 9.A10.)

The set of items we use differ slightly in kindergarten and later years. For the kindergarten analysis, almost all of the information we use is reported by parents during the kindergarten spring. For the fifth-grade sample we use additional information reported by parents at later waves (first-, third-, and fifth-grade spring), although several items are only asked in kindergarten fall (drama and craft lessons; number of audio CDs; preschool attendance, and foreign-language instruction). For items that are repeated we averaged values across the kindergarten, first-grade, third-grade, and fifth-grade data. In addition, we included two items that were only asked of parents in third-grade spring (newspaper receipt and magazine receipt). We also use measures of total household income in our analyses. Total household income is reported by parents in the fall or spring of kindergarten. We use this information to code families into five income quintiles.

Descriptive Analyses: ECLS-K

Our analyses are designed to better understand the extent to which reading and math skills and classroom behavior differ by family income, and the extent to which family investments in learning-related items and activities vary by family income. We present two sets of descriptive data. First, we report average levels of child outcomes and family investments during the kindergarten year, by income quintile. Second, we report average child outcomes and cumulative family investments by fifth grade, again by income quintile.

Descriptive statistics for the ECLS-K sample display income gradients in math and reading achievement and classroom behavior (see online appendix table 9.A9). On average, kindergarteners in the lowest family income quintile 1 have reading and math scores of approximately 45. This compares with scores of approximately 50 for children from the middle-income quintile, quintile 3, and approximately 55 for children from the top income quintile, quintile 5. Because these scores have a mean of 50, and a standard deviation of 10, the gap between the bottom and middle income quintiles—1 and 3—represents 0.5 standard deviations, whereas the gap between the bottom and the top income quintiles—1 and 5—represents a gap of 1.0 standard deviation (figure 9.7).

FIGURE 9.7   *Income-Related Differences in Children's Achievement and Behavior*

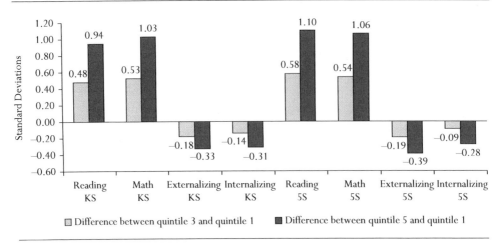

Source: Authors' estimates based on data from the Early Childhood Longitudinal Study, Kindergarten Cohort (U.S. Department of Education n.d.).

Notes: Quintile 1 includes families with the lowest incomes, and quintile 5 includes families with the highest incomes. KS = kindergarten spring; 5S = fifth-grade spring.

Patterns for behavior-problem scores, where a higher score indicates more problems, also display a gradient, although the total size of the gap is considerably smaller. Kindergarteners from the lowest income quintile have average scores greater than 0.15. This compares with scores of approximately zero for the middle income quintile, quintile 3, and approximately –0.15 for the top income quintile. Because these scores are standardized to have mean of 0 and standard deviation of 1, these bottom-to-middle and bottom-to-top gaps represent 0.15 and 0.30 standard deviations, respectively (see figure 9.7).

The descriptive statistics also indicate gradients in family investments in the set of enrichment items and activities. In some cases, investments increase in a roughly linear fashion as family income rises (see, for example, the family's report in the kindergarten survey of the number of CDs or children's books in the home in figure 9.8). In other cases, however, these investments do not differ much across the lower and middle income quintiles, but are sharply higher for the top income quintile (see, for example, the family's report in the kindergarten survey as to whether the child receives music lessons).

Overall, the descriptive statistics suggest that children in lower-income families have both poorer outcomes and lower levels of family investments in enrichment items and activities, but they cannot tell us whether these differences account for any of the differences in children's outcomes. As discussed earlier, estimating the causal effects of such investments is challenging, and carrying out such estimates is beyond the scope of the present study. Nevertheless, these ECLS-K results echo those found in the CEX, pointing to gaps in family investments the consequences of which should be further explored in future research.

CONCLUSION

This chapter provides some new evidence on how family investments in learning-related items and activities vary across the income distribution. The results from the CEX suggest that families increase expenditures on items of enrichment as their overall expenditures (our rough proxy

FIGURE 9.8   *Income-Related Differences in the Percentage of Children Experiencing Enrichment Activities*

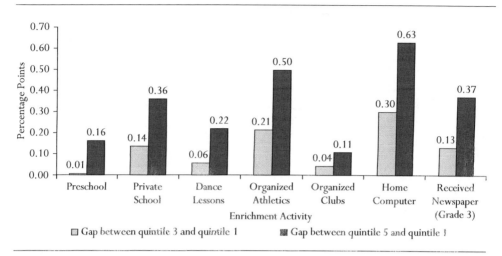

Source: Authors' estimates based on data from the Early Childhood Longitudinal Study, Kindergarten Cohort (U.S. Department of Education n.d.).

Notes: Quintile 1 includes families with the lowest incomes, and quintile 5 includes families with the highest incomes. All items are measured during kindergarten unless otherwise noted.

of permanent income) rise. This is true both in cross-sectional estimates and longitudinal estimates, which examine changes in family expenditures over time. Estimates of the marginal propensity to spend on items of enrichment from our fixed-effects longitudinal analysis, however, are about two-thirds of the estimates arising from our cross-sectional analysis. This is true for the full sample as well for samples stratified by mother's education and child's age. The fact that the associations between total expenditure and expenditures on enrichment items are smaller in the fixed-effects models suggest that at least a portion of these associations reflect unobserved heterogeneity between lower- and higher-income families. This in turn indicates that at least some the association is spurious rather than causal. Nevertheless, even the reduced associations in the fixed-effects models suggest that as family incomes rise, expenditures on items of enrichment rise as well.

Our analysis, like any analysis based on consumer expenditures, is constrained by the fact that we only measure the money families invest in children's enrichment activities, and not the quality of the services they purchase. In addition, some of the other investments that families make may indirectly affect their investments in children. For instance, as incomes rise, families may move to better neighborhoods in search of better schools or more sports clubs for their children. In our analysis this will be reflected as an increase in expenditure on housing, while in effect some of the increased expenditure on housing in response to an increase in income may be incurred to access better-quality services for children.

Our analyses of the CEX data are further limited in that we cannot tell which individual(s) within the family are accessing or using the items that have been purchased. Our analyses of data from the ECLS-K cohort of 1998 to 1999 address this particular limitation by providing information about the items and activities that children possess and participate in, although we still do not know who has paid for the investments. These analyses confirm sizable income-related gaps in children's enrichment items and activities. These gaps exist alongside substantial income-related gaps in reading and math skills, as well as in externalizing and internalizing behavior.

There are however also several key limitations to our ECLS-K analyses. First, although the ECLS-K is unusually rich in some areas, it does not provide comprehensive or detailed information on the full range of family investments that may be of interest. For example, we do not have any information on family vacations and travel. Nor do we have any information about the quality of the extracurricular activities or intensity of students' involvement in these activities. Although there is some information about school quality, presumably an important aspect of parental investment during middle childhood, it is not straightforward to measure it with the available survey data. More intensive studies with better information about particular types of investments are likely needed to improve our understanding of how family investments differ by income and how they might influence children's development.

In addition, this study was unable to study investments that families made during early childhood, given that the data available from the ECLS-K primarily cover investments during middle childhood only. The omission of early-childhood investments is important given that much of the literature points to family investments mattering most during early childhood (Duncan and Brooks-Gunn 1997).

Despite these limitations, our results confirm that the gaps in school achievement between children of varying incomes are already large at school entry, and show little sign of diminishing as children move through school. Even if family investments contribute only a small share to such gaps, it is worth understanding that contribution and the role that community or school policies might be able to play in leveling the playing field.

How consequential are the gaps in family investments in accounting for the gaps in children's cognitive and behavioral development, and how far could additional income, or direct provision of additional items and activities of enrichment, go in improving outcomes for low-income children? Although the present study could not answer these questions, they are important topics for further research. As discussed earlier, there have been few rigorous studies that examine the effects of income supplements on child outcomes, and even fewer that rigorously evaluate the effects of enrichment items and activities. Given the pronounced income-related gaps that exist in both enrichment items and activities and outcomes, and the fact that such gaps appear to be growing over time as income inequality increases, further experimentation with policies that would boost incomes and enrichment items and activities for low-income children would be very worthwhile, although we note that it is unlikely that family investments will account for all of the differences between the outcomes of poor and those of more affluent children.

We received helpful comments from the volume editors as well as Rebecca Blank, Julie Cullen, and Christopher Jencks. We also gratefully acknowledge the assistance of Nathan Hutto with the analyses of the CEX data, and of Daniel Miller and Yougeon Lee with the ECLS-K.

NOTES

Online appendix available at: http://www.russellsage.org/duncan_murnane_online_appendix.pdf.

1. A distinct but related literature considers children's learning over the summer—what has been termed the "summer learning gap." Although nearly all studies document that lower-socioeconomic-status students lose ground during the summer months when compared with their more advantaged peers (Alexander, Entwisle, and Olson 2007; Downey, von Hippel, and Broh 2004), evidence suggests that parental investments per se may explain only a modest portion of such losses (Burkham et al. 2004).

2. The literature on effects of private school attendance is vast and diverse, with attention given to how effects differ across type of private school (religious schools, charter schools, and schools funded by vouchers) as well as student characteristics (ethnic/racial minority or poverty).

3. Although the CEX collects data on a very extensive set of expenditures, it does not capture all the investments families might make in learning-related activities and programs. For example, it does not collect data on expenditures on overnight camps, nor does it capture contributions parents make to their children's schools through charitable foundations.

4. We do not present the income and expenditure elasticity of college tuition and books because items under this category are not directly consumed by children younger than eighteen. These elasticities can be obtained on request.

5. In supplemental analyses, not shown but available on request, we checked the sensitivity of our results for the bottom quintile by repeating the analysis for families at the 5th to 20th percentile (dropping those below the 5th percentile) and found that the results are similar.

6. A similar analysis of the association between income and expenditure on items of enrichment is presented in online appendix table 9.A6. Appendix table 9.A7 reports the description of the sample used in the analysis in appendix table 9.A6.

7. Elasticity is defined as the percentage change in expenditure on an item divided by the percentage change in total expenditure. An elasticity greater than one indicates that the percentage change in expenditures on an item is greater than the associated percentage change in total expenditures; an elasticity less than 1.0 indicates that the percentage change in expenditures on an item is less than the associated percentage change in total expenditures.

8. The skills tests were conducted in two steps. Children were first given common questions. The second set of questions differed in difficulty, depending on their performance in answering the first set of questions. Because children did not answer the same questions, the scores were calculated using Item Response Theory (IRT), which uses patterns of right, wrong, and missing answers and the difficulty of questions to place each child on a continuous ability scale. The resulting score is an estimate of the number of questions the child would have correctly answered had he or she been asked all available questions.

9. These are adapted from the Social Rating System (SRS) (Gresham and Elliot 1990).

10. We recognize that some of these items or activities may be provided by communities, but we nevertheless view them as parental investments given that parents have some control over the community their family lives in and also over whether they enroll their child in offered activities.

REFERENCES

Akee, Randall, William Copeland, Gordon Keeler, Adrian Angold, and Jane Costello. Forthcoming. "Parents' Incomes and Children's Outcomes: A Quasi-Experiment." *American Economic Journal: Applied Economics.*

Alexander, Karl, Doris Entwisle, and Linda Olson. 2007. "Lasting Consequences of the Summer Learning Gap." *American Sociological Review* 72(April): 167–80.

Archibald Robert, and Robert Gillingham. 1981. "A Decomposition of the Price and Income Elasticities of the Consumer Demand for Gasoline." *Southern Economic Journal* 47(4): 1021–31.

Bainbridge, Jay, Marcia Meyers, Sakiko Tanaka, and Jane Waldfogel. 2005. "Who Gets an Early Education? Family Income and the Gaps in Enrollment of 3–5 Year Olds from 1968 to 2000." *Social Science Quarterly* 86(3): 724–45.

Becker, Gary Stanley. 1991. *A Treatise on the Family.* Cambridge, Mass.: Harvard University Press.

Bradley, Robert, Robert Corwyn, Harriet McAdoo, and Cynthia Garcia Coll. 2001a. "The Home Environments of Children in the United States, Part I: Variations by Age, Ethnicity, and Poverty Status." *Child Development* 72(6): 1844–67.

Bradley, Robert, Robert Corwyn, Margaret Burchinal, Harriet McAdoo, and Cynthia Garcia Coll. 2001b. "The Home Environments of Children in the United States, Part II: Relations with Behavioral Development Through Age Thirteen." *Child Development* 72(6): 1868–86.

Burkham, David, Douglas Ready, Valerie Lee, and Laura LoGerfo. 2004. "Social-Class Differences in Summer Learning Between Kindergarten and First Grade: Model Specification and Estimation." *Sociology of Education* 77(1): 1–31.

Chin, Tiffany, and Meredith Phillips. 2004. "Social Reproduction and Child-Rearing Practices: Social Class, Children's Agency, and the Summer Activity Gap." *Sociology of Education* 77(3): 185–210.

Dahl, Gordon and Lance Lochner. 2008. "The Impact of Family Income on Child Achievement." NBER Working Paper No. 14599. Cambridge, Mass.: National Bureau of Economic Research.

Danziger, Sheldon, and Jane Waldfogel, eds. 2000. *Securing the Future: Investing in Children from Birth to College.* New York: Russell Sage Foundation.

Deaton, Angus, and John Muellbauer. 1980. "An Almost Ideal Demand System." *American Economic Review* 70(3): 312–26.

Downey, Douglas, Paul von Hippel, and Beckett Broh. 2004. "Are Schools the Great Equalizer? Cognitive Inequality During the Summer Months and the School Year." *American Sociological Review* 69(5): 613–35.

Duncan, Greg, and Jeanne Brooks-Gunn. 1997. *Consequences of Growing Up Poor.* New York: Russell Sage Foundation.

———. 2000. "Family Poverty, Welfare Reform, and Child Development." *Child Development* 71(1): 188–96.

Duncan, Greg, Aletha Huston, and Thomas Weisner. 2007. *Higher Ground: New Hope for the Working Poor and Their Children.* New York: Russell Sage Foundation.

Eccles, Jacquelynne. 1999. "The Development of Children Ages 6 to 14." *Future of Children* 9(2): 30–44.

Erikson, Erik. 1959. *Childhood and Society.* New York: Norton.

Foster, E. Michael. 2002. "How Economists Think About Family Resources and Child Development." *Child Development* 73(6): 1904–14.

Friedman, Milton. 1957. *A Theory of the Consumption Function.* Princeton, N.J.: Princeton University Press.

Gregg, Paul, Jane Waldfogel, and Elizabeth Washbrook. 2005. "That's the Way the Money Goes: Expenditure Patterns as Real Incomes Rise for the Poorest Families with Children." In *A More Equal Society? New Labour, Poverty, Inequality and Exclusion,* edited by John Hills and Kitty Stewart. Bristol, U.K.: Policy Press.

———. 2006. "Family Expenditures Post–Welfare Reform in the UK: Are Low-Income Families with Children Starting to Catch Up?" *Labour Economics* 13(6): 721–46.

Gresham, Frank M., and Stephen N. Elliot. 1990. *The Social Skills Rating System.* Circle Pines, Minn.: American Guidance Systems.

Haveman, Robert H., and Barbara Wolfe. 1994. *Succeeding Generations: On the Effects of Investment in Children.* New York: Russell Sage Foundation.

Kalil, Ariel, and Thomas DeLeire, eds. 2004. *Family Investments in Children's Potential: Resources and Parenting Behaviors that Predict Children's Success.* Mahwah, N.J.: Lawrence Erlbaum.

Kornrich, Sabino, and Frank Furstenberg. 2010. "Investing in Children: Changes in Parental Spending on Children, 1972 to 2007." Unpublished paper. Juan March Foundation, Center for Advanced Studies in the Social Sciences.

Lareau, Annette. 2003. *Unequal Childhoods: Class, Race, and Family Life.* Berkeley: University of California Press.

Lino, Mark, and Andrea Carlson. 2009. *Expenditures on Children by Families. 2008.* Washington: U.S. Department of Agriculture. Also available at: http://www.cnpp.usda.gov/Publications/CRC/crc2008.pdf (accessed March 28, 2011).

Lubienski, Sarah, and Christopher Lubienski. 2006. "School Sector and Academic Achievement: A Multilevel Analysis of NAEP Mathematics Data." *American Educational Research Journal* 43(4): 651–98.

Magnuson, Katherine, Christopher Ruhm, and Jane Waldfogel. 2007. "Does Prekindergarten Improve School Preparation and Performance?" *Economics of Education Review* 26(1): 33–51.

Magnuson, Katherine and Elizabeth Votruba-Drzal. 2009. "Enduring Influences of Childhood Poverty." In *Changing Poverty,* edited by Maria Cancian and Sheldon Danziger. New York: Russell Sage Foundation.

Mahoney, Joseph, Reed Larson, and Jacquelynne Eccles. 2005. *Organized Activities as Contexts of Development: Extra-Curricular Activities, After-School, and Community Programs.* Mahwah, N.J.: Lawrence Erlbaum.

Massell, Benton. 1969. "Consistent Estimation of Expenditure Elasticities from Cross-Section Data on Households Producing Partly for Subsistence." *Review of Economics and Statistics* 51(2): 136–42.

Maynard, Rebecca, and Richard Murnane. 1979. "The Effects of a Negative Tax on School Performance: Results of an Experiment." *Journal of Human Resources* 14(4): 463–76.

McHale, Susan, Ann Crouter, and Corinna Tucker. 2001. "Free-Time Activities in Middle Childhood: Links with Adjustment in Early Adolescence." *Child Development* 72(6): 1764–78.

Meyer, Bruce, and James X. Sullivan. 2003. "Measuring the Well-Being of the Poor Using Income and Consumption." *Journal of Human Resources* 38(Spring): 1180–1220.

Meyers, Marcia, Dan Rosenbaum, Christopher Ruhm, and Jane Waldfogel. 2004. "Inequality in Early Childhood Education and Care: What Do We Know?" In *Social Inequality,* edited by Kathryn Neckerman. New York: Russell Sage Foundation.

Morris, Pamela, Greg J. Duncan, and Elizabeth Clark-Kauffman. 2005. "Child Well-Being in an Era of Welfare Reform: The Sensitivity of Transitions in Development to Policy Change." *Developmental Psychology* 41(6): 919–32.

Morris, Pamela, and Ariel Kalil. 2006. "Out-of-School Time Use During Middle Childhood in a Low-Income Sample: Do Combinations of Activities Affect Achievement and Behavior?" In *Developmental Contexts in Middle Childhood*, edited by Aletha Huston and Marika Ripke. New York: Cambridge University Press.

Ogaki, Masao. 1992. "Engel's Law and Cointegration." *Journal of Political Economy* 100(5): 1027–46.

Posner, Jill, and Deborah Vandell. 1994. "Low-Income Children's After School Care: Are There Beneficial Effects to After School Programs?" *Child Development* 65(2): 440–56.

———. 1999. "After-School Activities and the Development of Low-Income Urban Children: A Longitudinal Study." *Developmental Psychology* 35(3): 868–79.

Raikes, Helen, Gayle Luze, Jeanne Brooks-Gunn, H. Abigail Raikes, Barbara Alexander Pan, Catherine S. Tamis-LeMonda, Jill Constantine, Louisa Banks Tarullo, and Eileen T. Rodriguez. 2006. "Mother-Child Book Reading in Low-Income Families: Correlates and Outcomes During the First Three Years of Life." *Child Development* 77(4): 924–53.

Ripke, Marika, Aletha Huston, and David Casey. 2006. "Low-Income Children's Activity Participation as a Predictor of Psychosocial and Academic Outcomes in Middle Childhood and Adolescence." In *Developmental Contexts in Middle Childhood*, edited by Aletha Huston and Marika Ripke. New York: Cambridge University Press.

Rogoff, Barbara. 1990. *Apprenticeship in Thinking.* New York: Oxford University Press.

Salkind, Neil J., and Ron Haskins. 1982. "Negative Income Tax: The Impact on Children from Low-Income Families." *Journal of Family Issues* 3(2): 165–80.

Smolensky, Eugene, and Jennifer A. Gootman, eds. 2003. *Working Families and Growing Kids: Caring for Children and Adolescents.* Washington, D.C.: National Academies Press.

Tourangeau, Karen, Christine Nord, Thanh Lê, Judith M. Pollack, and Sally Atkins-Burnett. 2006. *Early Childhood Longitudinal Study, Kindergarten Class of 1998–99 (ECLS-K), Combined User's Manual for the ECLS-K Fifth-Grade Data Files and Electronic Codebooks* (NCES 2006–032). Washington, D.C.: National Center for Education Statistics.

U.S. Bureau of the Census. n.d. *Poverty Thresholds.* Available at: http://www.census.gov/hhes/www/poverty/data/threshld/index.html (accessed April 30, 2011).

U.S. Bureau of Labor Statistics. 1997–2006. *Consumer Expenditure Survey, Public use Microdata, Interview Survey, 1997–2006.* Available at: http://www.bls.gov/cex/csxmicro.htm (accessed April 30, 2011).

———. 2005. "2003 Consumer Expenditure Interview Survey Public Use Microdata Documentation." Available for download at: http://www.bls.gov/cex/csxintvw.pdf (accessed June 27, 2011).

U.S. Department of Education, Institute of Education Sciences, National Center for Education Statistics. n.d. *Early Childhood Longitudinal Study Kindergarten Class of 1998–1999* (ECLS-K). Available at: http://nces.ed.gov/ecls/kindergarten.asp (accessed May 2, 2011).

Wagner, Janet, and Manouchehr Mokhtati. 2000. "The Moderating Effect of Seasonality on Household Apparel Expenditure." *Journal of Consumer Affairs* 34(2): 314–29.

Chapter 10

Parenting, Time Use, and Disparities in Academic Outcomes

Meredith Phillips

African American, Latino, and low-income children enter school less well prepared, on average, than their white, Asian American, and middle-class counterparts. Because these large ethnic and socioeconomic disparities in academic skills originate before children enter school, these gaps undoubtedly arise, at least in part, from disparities in children's experiences during their infant, toddler, and preschool years. Once children enter school, disparities in children's experiences outside the classroom continue to play a role in their academic performance.

This chapter begins with a review of the extensive social science literature on the importance of time use for child development. Probably the most enduring and consistent finding in the time-use literature is that reading to young children is positively associated with children's verbal skills. The literature also suggests that adult-child conversation influences children's verbal development, and that particular contexts—such as novel environments, mealtimes, and book reading—may generate conversation that is especially educationally productive.

The chapter then describes socioeconomic and racial disparities in the types of time use thought to be most educationally productive. It draws on a unique national data set, the Panel Study of Income Dynamics Child Development Supplement, which used time diaries to record how young children and elementary school–age children spent their time, and with whom, on a randomly sampled weekday and weekend day.

The analyses reveal stark social-class and racial disparities in some types of time use. For example, the estimates imply that between birth and age six, children from high-income families will have spent about 1,300 more hours in nonroutine contexts than children from low-income families. Similarly, before school entry, white children will have spent about 1,300 more hours engaged in conversation with adults than their African American counterparts. Less dramatic, but possibly more critical to future academic success, by the time they enter school, high-income or white children will have spent over 400 more hours in literacy activities than their low-income or African American peers.

I conclude with a brief summary of some interventions that have tried to alter the processes that generate academic inequality. This literature convinces me that targeted programs can enhance the educational content of children's everyday experiences and thus have the potential to reduce ethnic and socioeconomic disparities in children's school readiness and academic progress.

School readiness differs markedly among children from different racial, ethnic, and socioeconomic groups. For example, three-quarters of white and Asian American children can identify all their upper- and lower-case letters at kindergarten entry, compared to around half of African American and Latino children. Similarly, nearly 50 percent of kindergartners with college-educated mothers start school able to identify the beginning sounds that letters make, compared to just 20 percent of children with high school–educated mothers (West, Denton, and Germino-Hausken 2000).

Disparities in children's experiences during their infant, toddler, and preschool years undoubtedly contribute to these gaps in academic skills at school entry (Brooks-Gunn and Markman 2005). Moreover, differential experiences outside the classroom continue to play a role in students' academic performance after they enter school. For example, the literature on children's experiences during summer vacation highlights the role of out-of-school experiences in exacerbating achievement gaps across the school years (see Alexander, Entwisle, and Olson 2007; Chin and Phillips 2004; Downey, von Hippel, and Broh 2004; Entwisle, Alexander, and Olson 1997; Heyns 1978).

In this chapter I describe socioeconomic and racial disparities in how young children spend their time. I begin by discussing the empirical literature on the association between time use and academic skills. Time-use studies fall into two main categories: those that focus on proxies for time use, such as mothers' employment or family size, and those that measure time inputs directly. My review of the literature leads me to conclude that certain types of time use, such as exposure to adult speech and book reading, influence children's academic skills and that the quality of engagement by both adults and children probably moderates the educational productivity of these activities (see also Leibowitz 1977; Chin and Phillips 2003).

In the empirical section of the chapter I present descriptive evidence on social class and racial disparities in some of the dimensions of parenting and time use that the literature suggests may be important for the development of academic skills. I find stark social-class and racial disparities in some types of time use, in particular time spent in non-routine contexts, engaged in conversation with adults, and notable gaps in time spent engaged in literacy activities with adults. I do not estimate how much these parenting and time-use disparities matter for children's academic outcomes because nonexperimental estimates of these associations are undoubtedly biased in an unknown direction and to an unknown degree (see discussion in section 10.A1 of the online appendix, available at: http://www.russellsage.org/duncan_murnane_online_appendix.pdf). Instead, I conclude with a brief summary of some interventions that have attempted to change parenting practices and children's time use. That literature suggests to me that interventions targeted at improving specific aspects of children's experiences have the potential to narrow school-readiness gaps and help all children start school on more equal footing.

BACKGROUND

Numerous social scientists have theorized that how children spend their time—and, in particular, how parents spend time with their young children—influences children's future academic success. For example, the Nobel Prize–winning economist Gary Becker argues that "children from successful families are more likely to be successful themselves by virtue of the additional time spent on them and also [of] their superior endowments of culture and genes" (1981, 179). Similarly, James Coleman (1988), an eminent sociologist, posits that social interaction within families—family social capital, to use his term—influences children's academic development over and above hered-

FIGURE 10.1   *Associations Among Structural Characteristics of Families, Time Use, and Children's Outcomes*

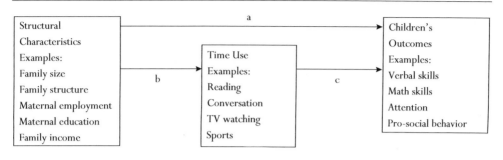

Source: Authors' diagram.

ity and parents' educational background. Using John Stuart Mill's upbringing to illustrate his argument about the central role of social capital in the development of human capital, Coleman (1988, S110) writes:

> John Stuart Mill, at an age before most children attend school, was taught Latin and Greek by his father, James Mill, and later in childhood would discuss critically with his father and with Jeremy Bentham drafts of his father's manuscripts. John Stuart Mill probably had no extraordinary genetic endowments, and his father's learning was no more extensive than that of some other men of the time. The central difference was the time and effort spent by the father with the child on intellectual matters.

Theories like these about the importance of adult-child interaction for child development have produced extensive empirical literatures in sociology, psychology, and economics. In economics and sociology, this literature has tended to focus on how particular social or demographic variables that may proxy for time-use quality or quantity—what Urie Bronfenbrenner and Anne Crouter (1983) call "social address" variables—are linked to time spent in particular activities and to children's academic outcomes. In psychology, this literature has tended to focus more on measuring adult-child interaction directly and linking it to children's academic outcomes. Figure 10.1 shows these associations and helps to organize the literature I review.

Structural Proxies for Time Use

A vast and varied social science literature provides indirect estimates of the importance of the amount and quality of time that adults devote to children. Some studies examine whether structural characteristics of families that, at least in theory, should reduce the quantity of time adults can devote to children are negatively associated with children's educational success (see path a in figure 10.1). Examples of such studies include those of the effects of family size, birth order, growing up in a single-parent family, and mothers' employment on student achievement. Another set of studies examines whether characteristics that should enhance the quality of children's time use, such as mothers' years of schooling or test scores, are positively associated with children's educational success.[1]

Much of the literature in both areas focuses on whether differences in family characteristics genuinely cause disparities in educational outcomes or whether these family characteristics merely proxy for the real causes of disparities in educational outcomes. But even when studies produce reasonably convincing causal evidence that structural characteristics matter, the mechanisms underlying these effects often remain unclear.

Studies that measure mechanisms bring us closer to understanding whether time use mediates the association between structural contexts and children's outcomes (paths b and c in figure 10.1). In the area of birth order and family size, for example, studies from several disciplines suggest that time use is an important mediator. In economics, Joseph Price (2008) shows that a likely mechanism for why first-born children have better educational outcomes than their later-born counterparts (see, for example, Black, Devereux, and Salvanes 2005) is that firstborn children experience more interactive time with their parents than second-born children do. In sociology, Brian Powell and Lala Carr Steelman (1993) and Douglas B. Downey (1995) suggest that how much parents talk to their children about school helps explain some of the association between family size and children's grades, test scores, and educational attainment. And in psychology, Celeste Pappas Jones and Lauren B. Adamson (1987) show that mothers talk less, and differently, to second-born children, and that both of these factors are associated with the development of children's verbal skills.

The literature is less clear on whether time use mediates the associations between family structure or maternal employment and children's outcomes. Single mothers spend less total time, and less interactive time, with their children than do married mothers. But these differences disappear after controlling for socioeconomic background (Kendig and Bianchi 2008). Children in single-parent families also spend slightly less time doing art, playing sports, doing homework, and reading than their counterparts in two-parent families, and more time watching TV, but these time-use differences do not take into account the substantial socioeconomic differences between single- and two-parent families (Bianchi, Robinson, and Milkie 2007; see also Asmussen and Larson 1991).

Other things equal, mothers' employment seems to have a small negative impact on children's achievement.[2] The effect is probably small because working mothers protect time with their children, especially "quality time," by taking less time for themselves and doing less housework (Bianchi 2000; Bianchi, Robinson, and Milkie 2007). For example, John F. Sandberg and Sandra L. Hofferth (2005) show that working mothers spend about eight fewer hours per week in the presence of their three- to twelve-year-old children than their stay-at-home counterparts, but spend only about two fewer hours per week directly interacting with their children. The children of working mothers do, however, seem to spend their time in somewhat different ways than the children of stay-at-home mothers. For example, the children of working mothers read slightly less than the children of stay-at-home mothers, and they spend more time outdoors, playing sports, and attending events (Bianchi, Robinson, and Milkie 2007).

Parents' education serves as a proxy for both the quantity and quality of parent-child interaction. Early time-use studies showed that highly educated mothers spent more time caring for their children, and more time doing educational activities with them, than their less well educated counterparts did (Leibowitz 1974a, 1974b, 1977). Contemporary studies replicate these results, both in the United States and across a large set of countries (Guryan, Hurst, and Kearney 2008). And recent work indicates that the child-care time gap between college-educated and less educated parents doubled during the late 1990s, with college-educated mothers now spending somewhere between four and six more hours per week caring for their children than their less-educated counterparts (Ramey and Ramey 2010). College-educated parents not only spend more time with their children, but they also spend more time reading to them and less time watching television with them (Bianchi and Robinson 1997; Hofferth and Sandberg 2001). Compared to less well educated parents, college-educated parents also talk more to their children, use more varied vocabulary in their speech, provide more relevant replies to children's questions, ask children more questions, and use less speech that directs children's behavior (Hart and Risley 1995; Hoff 2003, 2006; Hoff-Ginsberg 1991).

Some studies explicitly examine whether time use mediates the association between parents' education and children's verbal skills. This literature indicates that parents' reading time, warmth, and verbal responsiveness account for some of the association between parents' education and children's verbal skills (Davis-Kean 2005; Leibowitz 1977; Magnuson et al. 2009).

Direct Measures of Time Use

Other studies, many of them in psychology, focus on measuring parents' or children's time use directly and examining the association between time use and academic outcomes (path c in figure 10.1). These studies use a wide range of methods. Some rely on survey questions that ask parents or children how often they do particular activities. Others use evidence from time diaries that ask parents or children to report chronologically on the duration and type of children's activities over a twenty-four-hour day. Still others ask children to wear pagers and report on their activities when the pagers buzz. And some collect audio or video recordings of social interactions within families.

The most enduring and consistent finding in the time-use literature is that reading to young children is positively associated with children's verbal skills (Leibowitz 1977; Scarborough and Dobrich 1994; Snow, Burns, and Griffin 1998; Storch and Whitehurst 2001). Older children who spend more time reading for pleasure also tend to have higher verbal skills than children who spend less time reading for pleasure, even when comparing children who had similar verbal skills earlier in their lives (Hofferth and Sandberg 2001; Jencks and Phillips 1999; Phillips 2008; Storch and Whitehurst 2001). Younger children who are read to more often also tend to have better verbal skills than children who are read to less often, even when comparing children from households in which the mothers have similar verbal skills (Phillips et al. 1998). Using a contemporary national sample and propensity score-matching techniques, Joseph Robinson (2008) estimates that about a third of the association between parental reading and the cognitive skills of toddlers is causal.

The time-use literature also suggests that adult-child conversation influences children's verbal development. Children have larger vocabularies and learn new vocabulary words faster when they hear more words, or more different words, spoken by their parents (Hart and Risley 1995; Huttenlocher et al. 1991; Pan et al. 2005). Children also seem to reach verbal developmental milestones more quickly when their mothers are more responsive to their speech (Tamis-LeMonda, Bornstein, and Baumwell 2001).[3] Some of these associations persist even after accounting for differences in mothers' verbal skills (Pan et al. 2005).

Finally, certain activities seem to elicit higher-quality conversation, which may help explain why these activities tend to be associated with positive child outcomes. For example, families' mealtime conversations tend to stimulate the use of relatively complex language structures, as well as sophisticated vocabulary (Dickinson and Tabors 2001; Snow and Beals 2006). Likewise, book reading provides a context in which parents talk more, use a more varied vocabulary, ask more questions, and use fewer words telling children what to do (Hoff 2006; Hoff-Ginsberg 1991; Weizman and Snow 2001).

Other types of time use show less robust associations with educational outcomes. For example, among demographically similar children, watching more television is not associated with lower math or verbal test scores (Hofferth and Sandberg 2001). But demographically similar children who spend more time playing sports or participating in structured activities do tend to have higher math scores and fewer behavior problems than their less involved counterparts (Hofferth and Sandberg 2001; Mahoney, Harris, and Eccles 2006).

Racial and Ethnic Disparities in Time Use

Although a large literature indicates that social class, especially mothers' education, is associated with the quantity and quality of time devoted to children, the literature on ethnic disparities in time use and parenting is less extensive. And much of this literature does not adequately examine the extent to which ethnic differences in time use actually reflect socioeconomic differences among families from different ethnic groups. Nonetheless, Jeanne Brooks-Gunn and Lisa Markman (2005) review the literature on ethnic disparities in parenting and conclude that African American mothers rank lower than white mothers on most measures of effective parenting. Black and Latino mothers read less to their children than white parents do (Brooks-Gunn and Markman 2005; Hofferth 2006). Black parents also sometimes score lower than white parents on measures of warmth and sensitivity (Brooks-Gunn and Markman 2005). Black and white parents also differ in their disciplinary practices, with black parents more likely to spank their children and white parents more likely to reason with their children (Brooks-Gunn and Markman 2005). Some of these parenting and time-use disparities help explain ethnic differences in academic skills among young children (Brooks-Gunn and Markman 2005; Phillips et al. 1998), even after adjusting for many other differences between black and white families.

Black children also watch considerably more television than their white counterparts (Thernstrom and Thernstrom 2003), but disparities in TV watching do not seem to contribute to academic disparities (Hofferth and Sandberg 2001; Phillips 2008). Some studies indicate that white children spend more time reading for pleasure than do black and Latino children (Hofferth and Sandberg 2001), which is probably both a consequence and a cause of reading disparities. In contrast, black and Latino children seem to spend a little more time doing homework than their white counterparts (Ainsworth-Darnell and Downey 1998; Hofferth and Sandberg 2001).[4]

We know very little, however, about ethnic differences in the quantity and quality of parent-child verbal interaction and its association with children's academic skills. Many studies of parent-child conversation involve nearly entirely white samples (see, for example, Pan et al. 2005), and others rely on very small samples, in which race and social class are confounded (see, for example, Hart and Risley 1995). Because these small studies do not to have the statistical power to separate the effects of race and social class, we do not know the extent of ethnic disparities in parent-child verbal interaction or whether those disparities influence ethnic disparities in children's academic skills.

METHODS

Scholars face numerous challenges when trying to estimate how much time use matters for children's development. (See section 10.A1 of the online appendix for a discussion of these challenges.) Because of these substantial difficulties in using nonexperimental data to estimate the effects of time use on children's outcomes, this chapter simply describes social-class and ethnic disparities in the aspects of parent-child interaction and time use that prior studies suggest may be important for the development of children's academic skills. I strongly caution readers not to assume that the time-use disparities I describe here explain why lower-income or African American children tend to have worse academic outcomes than their middle-class or white peers. At most, this chapter simply adds to an already large literature showing that children from different social-class and racial backgrounds experience quite different home environments (see, for example, Brooks-Gunn and Markman 2005; Chin and Phillips 2004; Hart and Risley 1995; Lareau 2003).

Readers should also bear in mind that although some activities are undoubtedly more educationally productive than others, even nominally similar activities, such as reading, are quite heterogeneous. This heterogeneity arises from several sources, including the extent and quality of adults' participation, children's own temperaments, and the extent to which social contexts change the nature of activities (see Chin and Phillips 2003). Unfortunately, existing large-scale data sources tell us very little about disparities in the *quality* of time spent in any particular activity.

Data

This chapter uses data from the Panel Study of Income Dynamics (PSID) Child Development Supplement (hereafter CDS). The CDS is a nationally representative sample of 3,653 children who were first studied in 1997, when they were zero to thirteen years old. These children have been followed up twice since (in 2002–3 and 2007–8), although this chapter, because it focuses on young children, does not use those longitudinal data. I restrict the sample to white and African American children because the samples of children from other ethnic groups are too small to calculate reliable estimates, especially for specific age groups.

What distinguishes the CDS from other data sets on children and their families is that the CDS collected time-diary information about how children spent their time on one randomly sampled weekday and one randomly sampled weekend day. Respondents (typically parents, or children and parents together) initially received a diary in the mail, with instructions to complete it prior to the interview. Trained interviewers then reviewed and edited the diaries with the respondents, either in person or over the phone. The diaries asked respondents to report, in chronological sequence starting at midnight of the diary day, what their child was doing, the duration of the activity, where the child was, who was doing the activity with the child, who else was there but not directly involved, and what else the child was doing at the same time. (See section 10.A3 of the online appendix for details on the analytic sample used in this chapter.)

Measures

I measure children's academic outcomes and environments using a wide range of variables constructed from the time diaries, surveys, in-home interviews, and individually-administered tests.

Academic Skills and Behaviors   Although I do not link time use to academic outcomes, I nonetheless describe socioeconomic and racial disparities in four school-related measures. I measure children's verbal and math skills with two subtests from the Woodcock-Johnson Psycho-Educational Battery—Revised (WJ-R). The Letter-Word Identification subtest asks children to identify letters and read words. The Applied Problems subtest asks children to analyze and solve math problems. I measure children's attention difficulties using a scale composed of four parent-reported items about the extent to which their child has difficulty concentrating, is easily confused, cannot sit still, and does careful work. I measure antisocial behavior using a scale composed of twelve parent-reported items about the extent to which their child lies, argues, is mean to others, disobeys, is impulsive, loses his or her temper easily, and destroys things. The CDS measured academic skills and behaviors only in children who were at least three years old.

Time Diaries   Respondents provided time-diary data for one weekday and one weekend day. I multiplied the weekday estimate by 5 and the weekend estimate by 2, and then summed those measures to estimate weekly time spent in an activity. For each time period, respondents reported what their child was doing (the "primary" activity) and what else their child was doing at the same time (the "secondary" activity). For example, a child's primary activity might be listening to a story and her secondary activity might be talking. For all time-diary measures reported in this chapter, I summed up time in both primary and secondary activities to create a measure of time spent doing a particular activity. For example, if a parent reported that her child was eating (primary) and talking (secondary) during one fifteen-minute period and talking (primary) and watching television (secondary) during another fifteen-minute period, the child would be coded as talking for thirty minutes. This decision to combine primary and secondary activities is particularly important for measures such as time spent in conversation, because conversation frequently occurs in conjunction with another primary activity (such as eating or travel). For many of the activities, I counted time only if it occurred when an adult was participating. Readers should note that the time diaries do not provide details on children's activities while they are in day care or at school. As a result, children who spend less time in day care or school will by definition spend more time in the activities described in this chapter. (See section 10.A2 of the online appendix for a discussion of other methodological limitations of the time-diary data.)

Time-Use Measures   I constructed several measures of time spent in certain contexts that may be especially likely to stimulate productive conversation or analytical thinking: nonroutine locations (including indoor recreation places, outdoor recreation places, churches, and businesses or other non-school and non-day-care institutions); meals with adults (including eating at home, at others' homes, and at restaurants); and interactive play with adults (including playing pretend and dress-up, playing educational games, and doing puzzles).

I also constructed measures of adult-child conversation and parents' verbal responsiveness. Conversation includes time spent visiting with others, socializing, talking on the phone, and face-to-face conversation, but only when at least one adult is participating. Parents' verbal responsiveness is the average of the interviewer's response to two survey questions regarding the extent to which the "primary caregiver spontaneously spoke to or conversed with (CHILD)" and the extent to which the "primary caregiver responded verbally to (CHILD's) speech, questions, or request" during the interviewer's home visit.

Finally, I created measures of the time children spent listening to stories, read or told by adults, as well as the time they spent in a wider range of literacy activities, including being read to or told a story, but also including surfing the Internet; using a computer to look up information; looking at books; reading books, magazines, or newspapers; and writing of any type.

Control Variables   Some studies indicate that disparities in social class, neighborhood safety, and maternal mental health contribute to racial disparities in parenting practices (see, for example, Ceballo et al. 2008; Hill and Herman-Stahl 2002; Phillips et al. 1998). Because of those associations, and because both child and parent health may affect how parents spend time with their children, I describe racial disparities in time use after adjusting for some of these variables. The set of child health variables includes measures of the child's birth weight, the primary caregiver's rating of the child's health at birth, and the primary caregiver's rating of the child's current health. The set of parent health variables includes the primary caregiver's ratings of her own health, as well as measures of her depression and anxiety, self-esteem, and self-efficacy. The set of family background variables includes the primary caregiver's educational attainment, the natural log of family income averaged over the previous five years, family structure, the number of children in the household, the primary caregiver's work status, the primary caregiver's parents' average educational attainment, and a "safe neighborhood" index composed of the primary caregiver's rating of the neighborhood as a good place to raise children, its safety after dark, and whether he or she leaves the doors to the house or car unlocked when at home. (Section 10.A3 of the online appendix describes these measures in more detail.)

Analysis   Because child age tends to be the best predictor of the amount of time parents spend with their children (Zick and Bryant 1996), when possible I display comparisons for three groups: zero- to two-year-olds, three- to five-year-olds, and children who are already in school (I refer to this last category as children who are six or older but about 6 percent of these students are younger than six but have already started kindergarten or first grade). Because the background for this edited volume is widening income inequality, I use income as the main indicator for social class in the chapter's graphs.[5] Yet because the time-use literature focuses so heavily on the association between parents' education and time use, and because parents' education is more highly correlated with children's achievement than income is (see, for example, chapter 5 in this volume), I also discuss descriptive results for education in the prose and provide graphs displaying those results in section 10.A4 of the online appendix.

RESULTS

I begin by displaying income and race gaps for the four measures of academic skills and behaviors. I then show income and race gaps for the time-use variables, estimated from regressions of each time-use variable on the child's age in months at the time of the parent interview and the child's gender. For the analysis of racial disparities, I also present gaps that are adjusted not only for age and gender but also for all of the control variables taken together. When independent variables are missing, I impute an arbitrary value for them and include a missing-data indicator variable in the regression. I weight all estimates with the 1997 child weight and adjust the standard errors for the clustering of children within families.

Most of the time-use variables are quite right-skewed (a few children spend a lot of time in a particular activity). The results were somewhat sensitive to the inclusion of these extreme values, and the estimates tended to be more precise and usually a little smaller in magnitude when I excluded these values. As a result, I excluded the top 1 percent of children with extreme values on each of the time-use variables derived from the time diaries.

Social Class and Racial Disparities in Academic Skills and Behaviors

Figures 10.2 and 10.3 describe disparities in verbal and math skills, attention difficulties, and antisocial behavior for preschool- and school-age children from different income and racial groups. Low-income children have considerably fewer verbal and math skills, and more attention difficulties and behavior problems, than higher-income children. School-age children from the bottom 20 percent of the income distribution score more than one standard deviation lower than children from the top 20 percent of the income distribution, on both reading and math tests, with only slightly smaller disparities among preschool-age children. Children from the highest- and lowest-income quintiles differ by about a half a standard deviation in their attention difficulties and behavior problems. Test score and behavior disparities are similarly large when children whose mothers completed college are compared to children whose mothers did not finish high

FIGURE 10.2   *Income Disparities in Academic Skills and Behaviors, by Age*

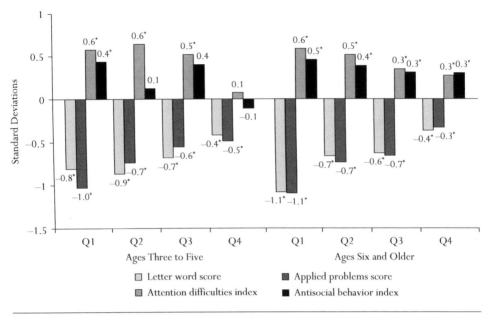

Source: Authors' calculations based on Panel Study of Income Dynamics (2009).
Notes: Estimates are adjusted for child's age in month and gender. Bars show difference relative to children whose family income is in the top quintile.
*Denotes statistically significant difference at *p* < 0.05 level.

FIGURE 10.3   *Black-White Disparities in Academic Skills and Behaviors, by Age*

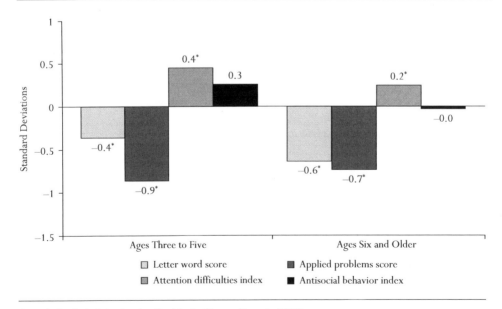

Source: Authors' calculations based on Panel Study of Income Dynamics (2009).
Notes: Estimates are adjusted for child's age in month and gender.
*Denotes statistically significant difference at *p* < 0.05 level.

FIGURE 10.4　　*Income Disparities in Weekly Time Spent in Novel Places, by Age*

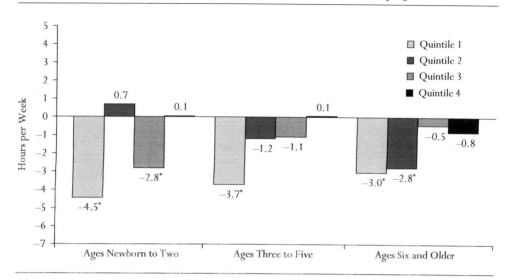

Source: Authors' calculations based on Panel Study of Income Dynamics (2009).
Notes: Estimates are adjusted for child's age in month and gender. Bars show difference relative to children whose family income is in the top quintile.
*Denotes statistically significant difference at $p < 0.05$ level.

school (see figure 10.A1 in the online appendix). African American children also have fewer verbal and math skills, and more attention difficulties, than white children, on average (figure 10.3), but the black-white gap in academic and behavioral skills is smaller than the gap between the top and bottom income quintiles. These estimates reinforce results from numerous previous studies that have shown strong associations between social class and race on the one hand and children's academic skills and behavior on the other (see, for example, Duncan et al. 2007 and Farkas 2003).

Social Class and Racial Disparities in Time Spent in Contexts and Activities

Research suggests that time spent in particular contexts (such as novel environments) or in particular activities (such as mealtimes or interactive play) may be especially educational. Figures 10.4 and 10.5 show disparities in the amount of time that children spend in nonroutine or "novel" places (that is, not at home or at school and not being cared for by another parent or a day-care provider). Infants, toddlers, and preschoolers from the top and bottom income quintiles differ considerably in their exposure to novel places (figure 10.4). Infants and toddlers from high-income families spend around 4.5 additional hours per week in indoor or outdoor recreation places, at church, or at businesses or other institutions relative to infants and toddlers from low-income families. The disparity for preschoolers is similar (3.7 hours per week). Taken together, these estimates imply that high-income children spend nearly 1,300 more hours in novel places between birth and age six than their low-income counterparts. Disparities in exposure to novel contexts are even larger when the young children of high school dropouts are compared to those of college graduates (see figure 10.A2 in the online appendix). After children start school, high-income children and children with college-educated mothers continue to spend about three more hours per week in novel contexts than their counterparts in low-income and less-educated families. Racial disparities in

FIGURE 10.5   *Black-White Disparities in Weekly Time Spent in Novel Places, by Age*

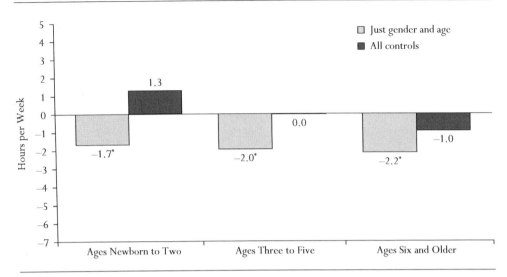

Source: Authors' calculations based on Panel Study of Income Dynamics (2009).
Notes: Controls include measures of child health, parent health, and socioeconomic status. See text and online appendix for more details.
*Denotes statistically significant difference at the $p < 0.05$ level.

exposure to novel environments are smaller (about one and a half to two hours a week) and are statistically indistinguishable from zero for black and white children from similar family backgrounds (figure 10.5).

Social-class and racial disparities in the time children spend eating meals with adults or playing with them are smaller and less consistent. Family income is not strongly associated with adult-child mealtime (see figure 10.A3 in the online appendix), and the association between race and adult-child mealtimes may vary with age. Black infants and toddlers spend about two fewer hours per week eating with adults than white infants and toddlers do, and these disparities persist even among young children from similar socioeconomic backgrounds. Among older children, however, the disparities reverse, with white school-age children spending about one fewer hour per week eating with adults than socioeconomically similar black children (see figure 10.A4 in the online appendix).

Family income is also not associated with the amount of time that children spend in interactive play with adults, although the estimates are imprecise (figure 10.A6 in the online appendix). Race may, however, be associated with interactive play, with white preschool-age children spending about an hour more per week in this type of play—or about 150 more hours between the ages of three and six—than their African American counterparts (figure 10.A7 in the online appendix).

Social Class and Racial Disparities in Adult-Child Verbal Interaction

Figures 10.6 and 10.7 describe how much time children from different family backgrounds spend talking with adults. Among school-age children, low-income children seem to talk about three hours less per week with their parents than high-income children do (figure 10.6). Otherwise, however, family income is not consistently associated with the quantity of adult-child conversation.

FIGURE 10.6   *Income Disparities in Weekly Time Spent in Conversation with Adults, by Age*

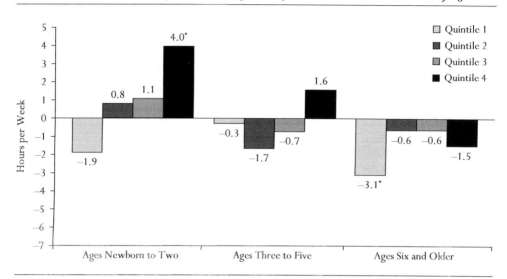

Source: Authors' calculations based on Panel Study of Income Dynamics (2009).
Notes: Estimates are adjusted for child's age in month and gender. Bars show difference relative to children whose family income is in the top quintile.
*Denotes statistically significant difference at the $p < 0.05$ level.

FIGURE 10.7   *Black-White Disparities in Weekly Time Spent in Conversation with Adults, by Age*

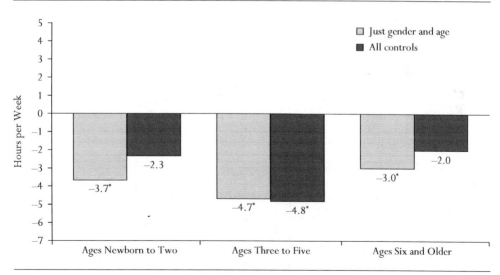

Source: Authors' calculations based on Panel Study of Income Dynamics (2009).
Notes: Controls include measures of child health, parent health, and socioeconomic status. See text and online appendix for more details.
*Denotes statistically significant difference at the $p < 0.05$ level.

FIGURE 10.8   *Income Disparities in Primary Caregivers' Verbal Responsiveness, by Age*

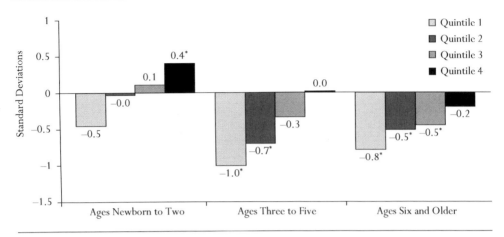

Source: Authors' calculations based on Panel Study of Income Dynamics (2009).
Notes: Estimates are adjusted for child's age in month and gender. Bars show difference relative to children whose family income is in the top quintile.
*Denotes statistically significant difference at the $p < 0.05$ level.

Children with college-educated parents may spend more time conversing with adults than their counterparts from less-educated families, but those associations are not statistically significant (figure 10.A9 in the online appendix).

Racial disparities in adult-child conversation, on the other hand, are large and potentially important. In the infant, toddler, and preschool years, black children spend about four fewer hours per week conversing with adults than white children (figure 10.7). Cumulatively, between birth and age six, these estimates imply a black-white gap in adult-child conversation of about 1,300 hours. Racial disparities in conversation are smaller and statistically insignificant among black and white infants and toddlers from similar family backgrounds. But large black-white disparities in adult-child conversation persist among preschoolers from similar family backgrounds. School-age children also experience a racial gap in adult-child conversation of about three hours per week, but that gap is smaller, and statistically insignificant, among children from similar family backgrounds. (Note that when I define adult-child conversation as mother-child conversation only, the raw black-white gap among the zero- to two-year-olds is somewhat smaller than in figure 10.7 but remains substantial—about 2.7 hours per week—and is statistically significant among children from similar family backgrounds. Among preschool-age and school-age children, however, the raw gaps in mother-child conversation are smaller than the gaps in adult-child conversation, and none remains large or statistically significant among children from similar family backgrounds.)

Unfortunately, the CDS tells us far more about the quantity of time use than its quality. Although the interviewer's rating of the primary caregiver's verbal responsiveness during the interviewer's visit to the child's home is an imperfect proxy for the quality of adult-child conversation, is better than nothing. Interviewers rate lower-income primary caregivers of preschool-age and school-age children as substantially less verbally responsive than high-income primary caregivers (figure 10.8). The same pattern holds for parental education, even in the youngest age group (figure 10.A10 in the online appendix). Interviewers also rate black primary caregivers of children of all ages as substantially less verbally responsive than white primary caregivers (figure 10.9).

FIGURE 10.9   *Black-White Disparities in Primary Caregivers' Verbal Responsiveness, by Age*

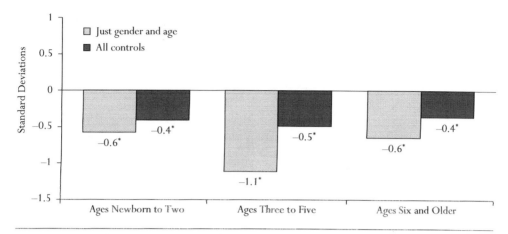

Source: Authors' calculations based on Panel Study of Income Dynamics (2009).

Notes: Controls include measures of child health, parent health, and socioeconomic status. See text and online appendix for more details.

*Denotes statistically significant difference at the $p < 0.05$ level.

Among children from similar backgrounds, black-white gaps in verbal responsiveness are smaller (0.4 to 0.5 standard deviations) but still statistically significant.

Social Class and Racial Disparities in Literacy Activities

Figures 10.10 and 10.11 show social class and racial disparities in the time that children spend in a broad set of literacy-related activities. High-income children of all ages spend around one and half more hours per week engaged in literacy activities than their low-income counterparts (figure 10.10). These results imply that between birth and age six, low-income children spend around 400 fewer hours of time on literacy activities than their high-income counterparts. Literacy time disparities are equally large when the children of college graduates are compared to the children of high school dropouts (figure 10.A11 in the online appendix).

The black-white gap in literacy time among younger children is similar in size to the income gap, but the black-white gap among school-age children is smaller (figure 10.11). Preschool-age and school-age black and white children from similar family backgrounds spend similar amounts of time in literacy activities. Between birth and age two, however, black children spend 140 fewer hours in literacy activities than white children, even when children from similar family backgrounds are compared.

Social-class and racial gaps in adult-child reading time are smaller than gaps in general literacy time. High-income infants and toddlers spend about 24 more minutes per week reading with adults than their low-income counterparts (figure 10.A12 in the online appendix). Similarly, preschool children of college graduates spend about forty more minutes per week reading with adults than children of high school dropouts (figure 10.A13 in the online appendix). Black infants, toddlers, and preschoolers are read to somewhere between twenty and thirty minutes less per week than their white counterparts (figure 10.A14 in the online appendix), but these reading disparities shrink to statistical insignificance when comparing black and white children from similar family backgrounds. Nonetheless, seemingly small black-white

FIGURE 10.10   *Income Disparities in Weekly Time Spent in Literacy Activities, by Age*

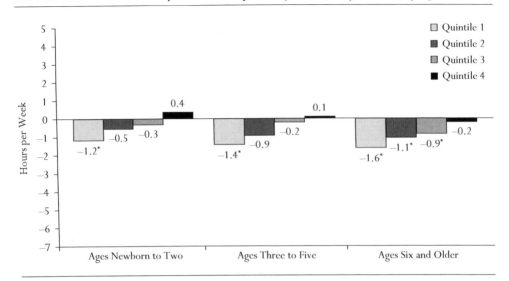

Source: Authors' calculations based on Panel Study of Income Dynamics (2009).
Notes: Estimates are adjusted for child's age in month and gender. Bars show difference relative to children whose family income is in the top quintile.
*Denotes statistically significant difference at the $p < 0.05$ level.

FIGURE 10.11   *Black-White Disparities in Weekly Time Spent in Literacy Activities, by Age*

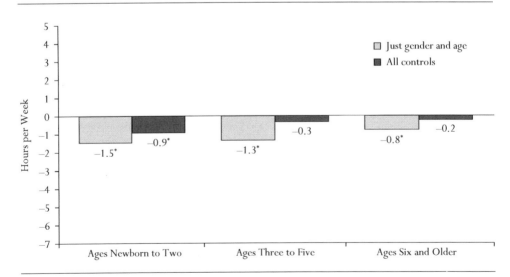

Source: Authors' calculations based on Panel Study of Income Dynamics (2009).
Notes: Controls include measures of child health, parent health, and socioeconomic status. See text and online appendix for more details.
*Denotes statistically significant difference at the $p < 0.05$ level.

disparities in weekly reading imply a black-white gap of over 100 hours of reading exposure by the time children enter school.

DISCUSSION

In this chapter I suggest that the everyday family experiences of young children from different socioeconomic and racial backgrounds differ in ways that probably contribute to socioeconomic and racial disparities in academic success. Small-scale observational and ethnographic studies have previously uncovered important differences in the lives of children from disparate family backgrounds that probably generate skill and behavioral inequality (see, for example, Chin and Phillips 2003; Hart and Risley 1995; Lareau 2003). This chapter shows that some of these disparities in children's lives appear in a large national sample and thus are probably systematic and widespread.

As many previous studies have shown, social-class gaps in academic skills and related behaviors are large before children enter school and remain large after school entry. Racial gaps in academic skills and related behaviors are also substantial and troubling before school entry and during school; but in these data, racial gaps are not as large as income gaps.

In some respects, the descriptive results in this chapter are unsurprising. For example, social class is more strongly related to the amount of time children spend in novel places than is ethnicity. We should of course expect income to be related to time spent outside the home because families with higher incomes have more money to spend on activities such as eating meals in restaurants, shopping, going to movies, and so on. Although I do not in this chapter investigate the link between time spent in novel locations and children's outcomes, it seems probable that certain nonroutine activities—especially those that stimulate children's senses, encourage analytic thinking, or result in extended conversations among participants—contribute to children's cognitive development.

Other results are more unexpected. For example, in their study of parent-child speech, Betty Hart and Todd R. Risley (1995) argue that social-class differences, rather than racial differences, explain the large disparities in the quality and quantity of speech they recorded during their extensive longitudinal home visits to a relatively small sample of families. In contrast, the results reported in this chapter suggest that racial differences in adult-child conversation may be larger than social-class differences, and that some of these racial differences persist even among children from similar family backgrounds.

The results for verbal responsiveness, on the other hand, support Hart and Risley's (1995) argument that middle-class parents tend to be more verbally responsive to their children than are lower- or working-class parents. However, the results also reveal important racial differences in verbal responsiveness, not all of which can be attributed to racial differences in family background (or at least not to the family background variables included in this chapter's models).

The data on income and racial gaps in time spent reading to children reveal gaps that readers may perceive as relatively small, on the order of twenty to thirty minutes per week. These gaps are small because, on average, adults report reading to young children only about forty-five minutes per week. This average is low because a large fraction of children are not read to at all—or at least were not read to on the two sampled diary days in the CDS. These reading-time estimates may be too low because the time-diary methodology probably understates activities that are short-lived or not part of a regular routine, and thus that are unlikely to be remembered and recorded by tired parents (probably an accurate characterization of much of the reading that happens with infants and toddlers). Nonetheless, the data reveal potentially important disparities in reading exposure on the two diary days. For example, 34 percent of young white children were read to by adults on at least one of those days, compared to only

14 percent of black children. Similarly, 39 percent of young children in the top income quintile were read to on at least one of those days, compared to only 20 percent of children in the bottom income quintile (results not shown). These disparities suggest that interventions designed to increase reading time among poor families or among African American families could potentially reduce social-class and racial gaps in reading time, and thus potentially narrow gaps in school readiness.

But do we have evidence that such interventions can be effective? Unfortunately, most studies designed to change children's time use or parent-child interaction do not involve representative groups of families and children, and thus it is difficult to know how generalizable intervention results are. In addition, most intervention studies lack long-term follow-ups, so it is impossible to know the extent to which their effects persist. Frank F. Furstenberg reviews the evidence on the effectiveness of parenting interventions in this volume (see chapter 22) and concludes that micro-level parenting interventions have at best modest effects and are unlikely to improve children's social mobility dramatically. He argues instead for macro-level interventions that provide children with high-quality day care, preschool, summer programs, and schools.

Perhaps because I focus more on younger children than Furstenberg does, I am more sanguine about the potential of parent and child interventions to reduce academic inequality. For example, numerous programs have tried to teach parents how to respond more appropriately to their children's negative behavior, and some of these programs seem to have reduced children's behavior problems (see, for example, Dishion et al. 2008; Leung et al. 2003; Miller-Heyl, MacPhee, and Fritz 1998).

Other studies have evaluated the effects of programs designed to change how often parents read to their children. These studies suggest that providing books and information to parents about the importance of reading can affect how much parents enjoy reading to their children (Jones et al. 2000), how often they read to their children (Golova et al. 1999), and their children's measured verbal skills (High et al. 2000). Studies with elementary school–age children have shown that providing books to children over the summer, along with encouragement to practice reading with family members or incentives to encourage children to read books and answer comprehension questions about them, can improve students' test scores (Kim 2006; Fryer 2010).

Finally, although I am unaware of interventions specifically intended to change the quantity or quality of parent-child conversation, Grover J. Whitehurst and his colleagues (1994) have shown that parents and preschool teachers can be taught to engage in higher-quality conversations while reading with three-year-olds, and that such a program can lead to improvements in children's vocabulary skills.

These studies, taken together, suggest to me that programs, whether micro or macro, that are targeted at the specific mechanisms generating academic inequality—especially programs designed to enhance the quantity and quality of reading and conversation in young children's lives—have the potential to enhance the educational content of children's everyday experiences, thereby reducing ethnic and socioeconomic disparities in children's school readiness and academic progress. I look forward to the continued refinement, implementation, and high-quality evaluation of such programs so that policymakers can learn more about their relative cost-effectiveness. This work cannot happen too soon, especially because family income has become more strongly associated with children's academic achievement than it was in the past (see chapter 5 in this volume) and because the social-class gap in the time that parents spend with children seems to have increased even since the data used in this chapter were collected (Ramey and Ramey 2010). This growing social inequality implies that the large disparities in children's time use described in this chapter may well understate inequalities in the experiences of today's children.

I am grateful to the Russell Sage Foundation and the Spencer Foundation for their financial support of this work via the Social Inequality and Educational Disadvantage (SIED) project; Rebecca Blank, Greg Duncan, Richard Murnane, Angel Harris, and the other participants at the SIED conference for their helpful advice about this work; and Sarah Shoff and Mary Zavala for their research assistance.

NOTES

Online appendix available at: http://www.russellsage.org/duncan_murnane_online_appendix.pdf.

1. Although this chapter focuses on time use in families, an analogous literature has arisen in education. That literature examines whether reducing the child-teacher ratio in a class, or improving teachers' education or test scores, improves children's academic skills (see, for example, Blau 1997; Ehrenberg and Brewer 1995; Ferguson 1998; Goldhaber 2002; Krueger 1999; Rowan, Chiang, and Miller 1997).

2. The most consistent result in the maternal-employment literature is that mothers' full-time work in the first year after the birth of a child may be somewhat detrimental to the child's academic skills (see, for example, Hill et al. 2005). These results imply that the time that working mothers would otherwise spend with their infants is more educationally productive, on average, than the time substitute caregivers spend with those infants. In addition, Christopher Ruhm (2008) finds that maternal employment may be especially detrimental to the academic skills of children from higher-social-class backgrounds. These results suggest that the time children of well-educated mothers spend with them is more educationally productive, on average, than the time children of less-educated mothers spend with their mothers.

3. Analogously, in the education literature, teachers' responsiveness seems to be an important dimension of high-quality child care (Blau and Currie 2006).

4. Note, however, that white adolescents are more likely than black adolescents to do large amounts of homework (Cook and Ludwig 1998).

5. I calculated income quintiles using the weighted full sample of children. Children in the lowest income group come from families with average incomes of approximately $21,000 or less (in 1997 dollars) during the previous five years. Children in the highest income group come from families with average incomes of approximately $71,000 or more (in 1997 dollars) during the previous five years.

REFERENCES

Ainsworth-Darnell, James W., and Douglas B. Downey. 1998. "Assessing the Oppositional Culture Explanation for Racial/Ethnic Differences in School Performance." *American Sociological Review* 63(4): 536–53.

Alexander, Karl L., Doris R. Entwisle, and Linda Steffel Olson. 2007. "Lasting Consequences of the Summer Learning Gap." *American Sociological Review* 72(2): 167–80.

Asmussen, Linda, and Reed Larson. 1991. "The Quality of Family Time Among Young Adolescents in Single-Parent and Married-Parent Families." *Journal of Marriage and Family* 53(4): 1021–30.

Becker, Gary S. 1981. *A Treatise on the Family*. Cambridge, Mass.: Harvard University Press.

Bianchi, Suzanne M. 2000. "Maternal Employment and Time with Children: Dramatic Change or Surprising Continuity?" *Demography* 37(4): 401–14.

Bianchi, Suzanne M., and John Robinson. 1997. "What Did You Do Today?: Children's Use of Time, Family Composition, and the Acquisition of Social Capital." *Journal of Marriage and Family* 59(2): 332–44.

Bianchi, Suzanne M., John P. Robinson, and Melissa A. Milkie. 2007. *Changing Rhythms of American Family Life*. New York: Russell Sage Foundation.

Black, Sandra E., Paul J. Devereux, and Kjell G. Salvanes. 2005. "Why the Apple Doesn't Fall Far: Understanding Intergenerational Transmission of Human Capital." *American Economic Review* 95(1): 437–49.

Blau, David M. 1997. "The Production of Quality in Child Care Centers." *Journal of Human Resources* 32(2): 354–87.

Blau, David, and Janet Currie. 2006. "Preschool, Day Care and After School Care: Who's Minding the Kids?" In *Handbook of the Economics of Education*, edited by Eric Hanushek and Finis Welch. Vol. 2. Amsterdam: North-Holland.

Bronfenbrenner, Urie, and Anne Crouter. 1983. "The Evolution of Environmental Models in Developmental Psychology." In *Handbook of Child Psychology.* Vol. 1, *History, Theory and Methods,* 4th ed., edited by Paul H. Mussen (series editor) and William Kessen (volume editor). New York: John Wiley.

Brooks-Gunn, Jeanne, and Lisa Markman. 2005. "The Contribution of Parenting to Ethnic and Racial Gaps in School Readiness." *Future of Children* 15(1): 139–68.

Ceballo, Rosario, Ruth Chao, Nancy E. Hill, Huynh-Nhu Le, Velma McBride Murry, and Ellen E. Pinderhughes. 2008. "Excavating Culture: Summary of Results." *Applied Developmental Science* 12(4): 220–26.

Chin, Tiffani, and Meredith Phillips. 2003. "Just Play? A Framework for Analyzing Children's Time Use." In *Sociological Studies of Children and Youth,* edited by Katherine Brown Rosier and David Kinney. Vol. 9. Oxford: JAI/Elsevier.

———. 2004. "Social Reproduction and Child-Rearing Practices: Social Class, Children's Agency, and the Summer Activity Gap." *Sociology of Education* 77(3): 185–210.

Coleman, James S. 1988. "Social Capital in the Creation of Human Capital." *American Journal of Sociology* 94(supp.): S95–S120.

Cook, Phillip J., and Jens Ludwig. 1998. "The Burden of 'Acting White': Do Black Adolescents Disparage Academic Achievement?" In *The Black-White Test Score Gap,* edited by Christopher Jencks and Meredith Phillips. Washington, D.C.: Brookings Institution.

Davis-Kean, Pamela E. 2005. "The Influence of Parent Education and Family Income on Child Achievement: The Indirect Role of Parental Expectations and the Home Environment." *Journal of Family Psychology* 19(2): 294–304.

Dickinson, David K., and Patton O. Tabors, eds. 2001. *Beginning Literacy with Language: Young Children Learning at Home and School.* Baltimore: Brookes.

Dishion, Thomas J., Daniel Shaw, Arin Connell, Frances Gardner, Chelsea Weaver, and Melvin Wilson. 2008. "The Family Check-Up with High-Risk Indigent Families: Preventing Problem Behavior by Increasing Parents' Positive Behavior Support in Early Childhood." *Child Development* 79(5): 1395–414.

Downey, Douglas B. 1995. "When Bigger Is Not Better: Family Size, Parental Resources, and Children's Educational Performance." *American Sociological Review* 60(5): 746–61.

Downey, Douglas B., Paul T. von Hippel, and Beckett A. Broh. 2004. "Are Schools the Great Equalizer? Cognitive Inequality During the Summer Months and the School Year." *American Sociological Review* 69(5): 613–35.

Duncan, Greg J., Chantelle J. Dowsett, Amy Claessens, Katherine Magnuson, Aletha C. Huston, Pamela Klebanov, Linda S. Pagani, Leon Feinstein, Mimi Engel, Jeanne Brooks-Gunn, Holly Sexton, Kathryn Duckworth, and Crista Japel. 2007. "School Readiness and Later Achievement." *Developmental Psychology* 43(6): 1428–46.

Ehrenberg, Ronald G., and Dominic J. Brewer. 1995. "Did Teachers' Verbal Ability and Race Matter in the 1960s? Coleman Revisited." *Economics of Education Review* 14(1): 1–21.

Entwisle, Doris R., Karl L. Alexander, and Linda Steffel Olson. 1997. *Children, Schools, and Inequality.* Boulder, Colo.: Westview.

Farkas, George. 2003. "Cognitive Skills and Noncognitive Traits and Behaviors in Stratification Processes." *Annual Review of Sociology* 29: 541–62.

Ferguson, Ronald F. 1998. "Can Schools Narrow the Black-White Test Score Gap?" In *The Black-White Test Score Gap,* edited by Christopher Jencks and Meredith Phillips. Washington, D.C.: Brookings Institution.

Fryer, Roland G., Jr. 2010. "Financial Incentives and Student Achievement: Evidence from Randomized Trials." NBER Working Paper No. 15898. Cambridge, Mass.: National Bureau of Economic Research.

Goldhaber, Dan. 2002. "The Mystery of Good Teaching." *Education Next* 2(1): 50–55.

Golova, Natalia, Anthony J. Alario, Patrick M. Mivier, Margarita Rodriguez, and Pamela C. High. 1999. "Literacy Promotion for Hispanic Families in a Primary Care Setting: A Randomized Controlled Trial." *Pediatrics* 103(5): 993–97.

Guryan, Jonathan, Erik Hurst, and Melissa Kearney. 2008. "Parental Education and Parental Time with Children." *Journal of Economic Perspectives* 22(3): 23–46.

Hart, Betty, and Todd R. Risley. 1995. *Meaningful Differences in the Everyday Experience of Young American Children.* Baltimore: Brookes.

Heyns, Barbara. 1978. *Summer Learning and the Effects of Schooling.* New York: Academic Press.

High, Pamela C., Linda LaGasse, Samuel Becker, Ingrid Ahlgren, and Adrian Gardner. 2000. "Literacy Promotion in Primary Care Pediatrics: Can We Make a Difference?" *Pediatrics* 105(S4): 927–34.

Hill, Nancy E., and Mindy A. Herman-Stahl. 2002. "Neighborhood Safety and Social Involvement: Associations with Parenting Behaviors and Depressive Symptoms Among African American and Euro-American Mothers." *Journal of Family Psychology* 16(2): 209–19.

Hill, Jennifer L., Jane Waldfogel, Jeanne Brooks-Gunn, and Wen-Jui Han. 2005. "Maternal Employment and Child Development: A Fresh Look Using Newer Methods." *Developmental Psychology* 41(6): 833–50.

Hoff, Erika. 2003. "The Specificity of Environmental Influence: Socioeconomic Status Affects Early Vocabulary Development via Maternal Speech." *Child Development* 74(5): 1368–78.

———. 2006. "How Social Contexts Support and Shape Language Development." *Developmental Review* 26(1): 55–88.

Hoff-Ginsberg, Erika. 1991. "Mother-Child Conversation in Different Social Classes and Communicative Settings." *Child Development* 62(4): 782–96.

Hofferth, Sandra L. 2006. "Response Bias in a Popular Indicator of Reading to Children." *Sociological Methodology* 36(1): 301–15.

Hofferth, Sandra L., and John F. Sandberg. 2001. "How American Children Spend Their Time." *Journal of Marriage and the Family* 63(2): 295–308.

Huttenlocher, Janellen, Wendy Haight, Anthony Bryk, Michael Seltzer, and Thomas Lyons. 1991. "Early Vocabulary Growth: Relation to Language Input and Gender." *Developmental Psychology* 27(2): 236–48.

Jencks, Christopher, and Meredith Phillips. 1999. "Aptitude or Achievement: Why Do Test Scores Predict Educational Attainment and Earnings?" In *Earning and Learning: How Schools Matter,* edited by Susan E. Mayer and Paul E. Peterson. Washington, D.C.: Brookings Institution.

Jones, Celeste Pappas, and Lauren B. Adamson. 1987. "Language Use in Mother-Child and Mother-Child-Sibling Interactions." *Child Development* 58(2): 356–66.

Jones, V. Faye, Sofia M. Franco, Sharon C. Metcalf, Robert Popp, Susan Staggs, and Amy E. Thomas. 2000. "The Value of Book Distribution in a Clinic-Based Literacy Intervention Program." *Clinical Pediatrics* 39(9): 535–41.

Kendig, Sarah M., and Suzanne M. Bianchi. 2008. "Single, Cohabitating, and Married Mothers' Time with Children." *Journal of Marriage and Family* 70(5): 1228–40.

Kim, James S. 2006. "Effects of a Voluntary Summer Reading Intervention on Reading Achievement: Results from a Randomized Field Trial." *Educational Evaluation and Policy Analysis Winter* 28(4): 335–55.

Krueger, Alan B. 1999. "Experimental Estimates of Education Production Functions." *Quarterly Journal of Economics* 114(2): 497–532.

Lareau, Annette. 2003. *Unequal Childhoods: Class, Race, and Family Life.* Berkeley: University of California Press.

Leibowitz, Arleen. 1974a. "Education and Home Production." *American Economic Review* 64(2): 243–50.

———. 1974b. "Home Investments in Children." *Journal of Political Economy* 82(S2): S111–S131.

———. 1977. "Parental Inputs and Children's Achievement." *Journal of Human Resources* 12(2): 242–51.

Leung, Cynthia, Matthew Sanders, Shirley Leung, Rose Mak, and Joseph Lau. 2003. "An Outcome Evaluation of the Implementation of the Triple P-Positive Parenting Program in Hong Kong." *Family Process* 42(4): 531–44.

Magnuson, Katherine A., Holly R. Sexton, Pamela E. Davis-Kean, and Aletha C. Huston. 2009. "Increases in Maternal Education and Young Children's Language Skills." *Merrill-Palmer Quarterly* 55(3): 319–50.

Mahoney, Joseph L., Angel L. Harris, and Jacquelynne S. Eccles. 2006. "Organized Activity Participation, Positive Youth Development, and the Over-Scheduling Hypothesis." *Social Policy Report of the Society for Research in Child Development* 20(4): 1–31.

Miller-Heyl, Jan, David MacPhee, and Janet Fritz. 1998. "DARE to Be You: A Family-Support, Early-Prevention Program." *Journal of Primary Prevention* 18(3): 257–85.

Pan, Barbara Alexander, Meredith L. Rowe, Judith D. Singer, and Catherine E. Snow. 2005. "Maternal Correlates of Growth in Toddler Vocabulary Production in Low-Income Families." *Child Development* 76(4): 763–82.

Panel Study of Income Dynamics. 2009. *Child Development Supplement* [public-use dataset]. Institute for Social Research Survey Research Center, University of Michigan, Ann Arbor [producer and distributor].

Phillips, Meredith. 2008. "Culture and Stalled Progress in Narrowing the Black-White Test Score Gap." In *Steady Gains and Stalled Progress: Inequality and the Black-White Test Score Gap,* edited by Katherine Magnuson and Jane Waldfogel. New York: Russell Sage Foundation.

Phillips, Meredith, Jeanne Brooks-Gunn, Greg J. Duncan, Pamela Klebanov, and Jonathan Crane. 1998. "Family Background, Parenting Practices, and the Black-White Test Score Gap." In *The Black-White Test Score Gap,* edited by Christopher Jencks and Meredith Phillips. Washington, D.C.: Brookings Institution.

Powell, Brian, and Lala Carr Steelman. 1993. "The Educational Benefits of Being Spaced Out: Sibship Density and Educational Progress." *American Sociological Review* 58(3): 367–81.

Price, Joseph. 2008. "Parent-Child Quality Time: Does Birth Order Matter?" *Journal of Human Resources* 43(1): 240–65.

Ramey, Garey, and Valerie A. Ramey. 2010. "The Rug Rat Race." *Brookings Papers on Economic Activity.* Spring: 129–76.

Robinson, Joseph. 2008. "Essays on the Effectiveness of Policies and Practices for Reducing Cognitive Gaps Between Linguistic Groups and Socioeconomic Groups." Ph.D. diss. Stanford University.

Rowan, Brian, Fang-Shen Chiang, and Robert J. Miller. 1997. "Using Research on Employees' Performance to Study the Effects of Teachers on Students' Achievement." *Sociology of Education* 70(4): 256–84.

Ruhm, Christopher. 2008. "Maternal Employment and Adolescent Development." *Labour Economics* 15(5): 958–83.

Sandberg, John F., and Sandra L. Hofferth. 2005. "Changes in Children's Time with Parents: A Correction." *Demography* 42(2): 391–95.

Scarborough, Hollis S., and Wanda Dobrich. 1994. "On the Efficacy of Reading to Preschoolers." *Developmental Review* 14(3): 245–302.

Snow, Catherine E., and Diane E. Beals. 2006. "Mealtime Talk That Supports Literacy Development." *New Directions for Child and Adolescent Development* 2006(111): 51–66.

Snow, Catherine E., M. Susan Burns, and Peg Griffin, eds. 1998. *Preventing Reading Difficulties in Young Children.* Washington, D.C.: National Academy Press.

Storch, Stacey A., and Grover J. Whitehurst. 2001. "The Role of Family and Home in the Literacy Development of Children from Low-Income Backgrounds." *New Directions for Child and Adolescent Development* 2001(92): 53–72.

Tamis-LeMonda, Catherine S., Marc H. Bornstein, and Lisa Baumwell. 2001. "Maternal Responsiveness and Children's Achievement of Language Milestones." *Child Development* 72(3): 748–67.

Thernstrom, Abigail, and Stephan Thernstrom. 2003. *No Excuses: Closing the Racial Gap in Learning.* New York: Simon and Schuster.

Weizman, Zehava Oz, and Catherine E. Snow. 2001. "Lexical Output as Related to Children's Vocabulary Acquisition: Effects of Sophisticated Exposure and Support for Meaning." *Developmental Psychology* 37(2): 265–79.

West, Jerry, Kristin Denton, and Elvira Germino-Hausken. 2000. "America's Kindergartners." NCES report 2000-070. Washington, D.C.: U.S. Department of Education, National Center for Education Statistics.

Whitehurst, Grover J., David S. Arnold, Jeffery N. Epstein, Andrea L. Angell, Meagan Smith, and Janet E. Fischel. 1994. "A Picture Book Reading Intervention in Day Care and Home for Children from Low-Income Families." *Developmental Psychology* 30(5): 679–89.

Zick, Cathleen D., and W. Keith Bryant. 1996. "A New Look at Parents' Time Spent in Child Care: Primary and Secondary Time Use." *Social Science Research* 25(3): 260–80.

Chapter 11

Family-Structure Instability and Adolescent Educational Outcomes: A Focus on Families with Stepfathers

Megan M. Sweeney

The declining proportion of children sharing a household with their two biological parents has been called the most profound change in American families within the past four decades (Amato 2005). This demographic shift is of concern to scholars, educators, and policymakers because families contribute in important ways to shaping youth outcomes. Indeed, evidence suggests that family-based factors may more strongly influence adolescent achievement and behavior than do neighborhoods or schools (Duncan, Boisjoly, and Harris 2001). Family structure change has not occurred uniformly across the population, but rather growth in single-parent families is concentrated among the most disadvantaged mothers. Because children living with a single parent tend to have fewer material and parenting resources relevant to supporting educational success than do children living with two parents, recent shifts in family structure may both exacerbate existing inequalities and contribute to reproducing patterns of inequality across generations (McLanahan and Percheski 2008; Western, Bloome, and Percheski 2008).

A large body of research documents that children who live apart from their biological fathers tend to perform less well in school, have lower academic confidence, and attain fewer total years of education than children who live with both biological parents (for a recent review, see Sigle-Rushton and McLanahan 2004). The underlying reason(s) for these associations, however, remain insufficiently understood. Moreover, although estimates suggest that 30 percent of children spend some time living in a married or cohabiting stepfamily (Bumpass, Raley, and Sweet 1995), the experiences of youths living with a stepparent remain relatively neglected. Yet attention to stepfamilies highlights issues of instability in children's family environments, the importance of marital status and biology for defining ties between adults and children, and the potential for pre-existing selectivity in the characteristics of individuals entering families of various types. In short, the study of stepfamilies offers strategic opportunities to address many key concerns regarding the broader consequences of family structure and family instability for youths' well-being.

Chapter 11 begins with a broad overview of the recent contours of change and diversity in U.S. family structures. It highlights the declining share of youths living with two biological parents, owing both to high rates of marital instability and to growth in the proportion of births to unwed mothers. It also reviews major explanations for observed associations between family structure and youth well-being, including differences between family types in economic and parenting resources and the lingering effects of family instability. It discusses the possibility that variability in well-being in different family types may result from preexisting differences in characteristics of adults and children rather than from causal effects of family structure itself.

Finally, the chapter uses data from a large and nationally representative sample of adolescents to empirically investigate how family structure and family transitions are associated with a variety of indicators of adolescent educational well-being. With the exception of school engagement, findings reveal that relatively poorer educational well-being associated with having experienced a recent family transition is largely attributable to selective preexisting characteristics of parents and children. No evidence emerges that living in a stably married stepfamily is associated with poorer educational outcomes than living with two biological parents. Nor is there evidence of any reduction in educational well-being associated with transitioning from a solo-mother family to a married stepfamily.

The analysis uncovers some evidence of a reduction in educational well-being associated with the dissolution of a stepfamily, but only when stepfamilies are formed through marriage. Considered in the context of broader debates about the benefits of marriage, these findings remind us that encouraging marriage for all parents may not always be in children's best interest and suggests that policies encouraging mothers to enter relatively unstable marriages have the potential to do more harm than good.

CHANGE AND DIVERSITY IN U.S. FAMILY STRUCTURES

Shifting patterns of childbearing and intimate partnership have fundamentally reshaped American family environments in recent decades, with growing numbers of children spending at least some time living with a single parent. Most often this parent is a child's mother, although the proportion of children living with a single father has also steadily increased over time. These trends are broadly illustrated by data from the U.S. Census and the Current Population Survey (CPS) shown in figure 11.1. Whereas 85 percent of children were living with two parents in 1970, this was true of only about two-thirds of children in 2007. During this same period, the share of children living with a single parent more than doubled, rising from roughly 12 to 29 percent.

The share of African American children living apart from one or both parents is particularly high—more than 56 percent lived with a single parent and only 37 percent lived with two parents in 2007. The share of single-parent families is highest, and has grown most rapidly over the past forty years, among mothers with the least education (Ellwood and Jencks 2004).

The high prevalence of single-parent families in the contemporary United States is driven both by marital instability and the increasing share of births to unmarried mothers. Approximately half of recent first marriages are expected to end in separation or divorce (Raley and Bumpass 2003). Whereas unmarried mothers accounted for roughly 11 percent of births in 1970, they accounted for nearly 40 percent of all births in 2007 (Hamilton, Martin, and Ventura 2009; Ventura and Bachrach 2000). Again, we see variability in these patterns across race and educational groups, with rates of divorce and unmarried childbearing highest among black women and those with the least education (Raley and Bumpass 2003; Sweeney and Phillips 2004; Ventura 2009).

When we consider these trends it is important to keep in mind that many children living with an unmarried parent today also share a home with their parent's intimate partner. Rates of

FIGURE 11.1   *Percentage of U.S. Children Under Eighteen Years Old Living in Various Family Types, by Year and Race-Ethnicity*

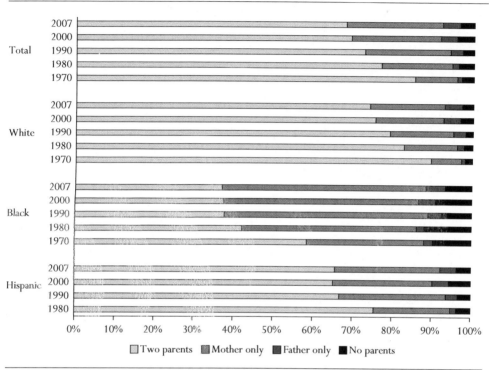

Source: Authors' calculations based on U.S. Bureau of the Census (2009, tables ch-1, ch-2, ch-3, ch-4).

nonmarital cohabitation have grown dramatically in recent decades, and cohabiting unions are increasingly likely to involve children. Recent estimates suggest that close to half of all children will spend some time in a cohabiting family before age sixteen (Kennedy and Bumpass 2008). Fully 18 percent of all births in recent years, and more than half of births to unmarried women, occurred within the context of a nonmarital cohabiting relationship (Kennedy and Bumpass 2008). These figures stand in stark contrast to data from the early 1980s, when only 6 percent of all births were to cohabiting but not married mothers (Bumpass and Lu 2000). Young people may also enter cohabiting families later in childhood when their parent moves in with an unmarried partner. Adolescents are more likely than relatively younger children to enter cohabiting families in this way and less likely to live with their two unmarried biological parents (Kreider and Elliot 2009), in part reflecting the relatively low stability of cohabiting relationships (Kennedy and Bumpass 2008).

Finally, when we consider aggregate trends in family structure, it is also important to keep in mind that many youths in "two-parent" families do not live with both biological parents but rather one of the parents is a stepparent who may or may not be married to the child's biological parent. In 2004, 5.3 million children, or 7.2 percent of all children, lived with one biological parent and a stepparent (Kreider 2008). This represents a small increase since 1996, when 6.6 percent of all children lived with a biological parent and stepparent. White children are more likely than black or Hispanic children to live with a stepparent (7.7 versus 5.4 and 5.6 percent, respectively) (Kreider 2008). Stepfamily scholars also increasingly highlight diversity in the relationships among children sharing a household. For example, in the early 2000s 11.7 percent of children lived with at least one half sibling and 1.7 percent lived with at least one stepsibling (Kreider 2008). The implication of complex sibling relationships for youths' well-being in stepfamilies—closely tied to broader discussions of multipartnered fertility—remains an important area of investigation (see, for example, Hetherington and Kelly 2002).

FAMILY STRUCTURE AND YOUTHS' EDUCATIONAL WELL-BEING

The increasing diversity of children's family environments, along with the concentration of growth in single parenthood among disadvantaged families, elevates the importance of understanding how family structure influences youths' well-being. The majority of research in this area compares outcomes among youths living with two married biological parents to those living with a single mother. With respect to a wide array of educational outcomes—including measures of school engagement, school performance, school-related behavior problems, and completed years of schooling—youths living with two biological parents tend to display higher well-being than those living with a single mother (Acs 2007; Brown 2004; Deleire and Kalil 2002; Manning and Lamb 2003; McLanahan and Sandefur 1994; Nelson, Clark, and Acs 2001; Painter and Levine 2000). For example, adjusting for child's age, race, and sex, Susan L. Brown (2004) finds that adolescents living with a single mother display levels of school engagement just under half of a standard deviation lower than those living with two married biological parents. Thomas Deleire and Ariel Kalil (2002) find that 90 percent of youths who lived with two married biological parents in the eighth grade eventually graduated from high school, compared with 69 percent of youths who lived with a never-married solo mother and 75 percent of youths who lived with a divorced solo mother.

A growing body of research also examines how stepfamilies affect children's well-being, although it is important to note that the question itself is not well defined. A stepfamily can include a number of different living arrangements and has more than one possible counterfactual comparison group (for example, two-biological-parent versus single-parent families, cohabiting versus married stepfamilies). Most work on the well-being of youths in stepfamilies continues to emphasize comparisons between youths living with a stepparent and those living with both biological parents. Relative to living with two married biological parents, living with a married or cohabiting stepparent is generally associated with lower well-being on a wide array of educational and cognitive outcomes (for example, Deleire and Kalil 2002; Fomby and Cherlin 2007; Hofferth 2006; Manning and Lamb 2003). Such comparisons provide only limited insight into the pathways through which stepfamilies affect children's well-being, however, given that much distinguishes these two groups beyond the exchange of a biological parent for a stepparent in the home—often (but not always) including the experience of marital disruption and time spent living with a single parent.

Many theoretical explanations of how stepfamilies might matter for offspring's well-being speak more directly to the question of how well-being ought to change as a young person transitions from a single-parent family into a stepfamily, or vice versa (see also Sweeney 2010b). Studies that directly investigate such change, or that compare outcomes among youths living with a stepparent to those living with a single parent, tend to identify fewer differences between groups, although results vary across studies and the specific domain of well-being considered (Ganong and Coleman 2004). The relatively limited work to date that directly compares the educational or behavioral well-being of youths living with a stepparent to those living with a single parent has produced mixed results (Aughinbaugh, Pierret, and Rothstein 2005; Hawkins, Amato, and King 2007; Manning and Lamb 2003). Several recent studies point to relatively lower behavioral and educational well-being among youths living with cohabiting stepfather than either those living with a single mother or those living with a married stepfather, although findings vary across specific outcomes considered (Bulanda and Manning 2008; Manning and Lamb 2003; Raley, Frisco, and Wildsmith 2005; Tillman 2007).

Explanations for Family-Structure Differences in Child Well-Being

Scholars offer a number of possible explanations for the ways family structure might be associated with youths' well-being. For example, many scholars point to the ways economic or parenting resources vary across family structures. In addition, social scientists increasingly attempt to account for the potentially selective processes associated with entering families of various structures. Finally, growing attention has been devoted to the possibility that observed associations between family structure and outcomes for youths may reflect legacies of family instability rather than casual effects of the composition of families per se.

A primary explanation for differences in children's well-being across family structures is variation in economic resources. Family-structure differences in economic well-being are well documented, with married two-biological-parent families tending to display greater economic well-being than single-parent or stepparent families (Manning and Brown 2006). Moving from a single-parent family to a stepfamily is associated with increased family economic resources, although stepfamilies are associated with better long-run economic prospects when they are formed through marriage rather than through cohabitation (Morrison and Ritualo 2000). Family-type differences may also exist in the ways in which parents use the money they have. For example, cohabitors are more likely than married people to spend money on alcohol or tobacco and less likely to spend money on children's education (Deleire and Kalil 2005).

Other work emphasizes the role played by differences across family types in parenting behaviors. A (step)father may contribute directly to child care, may allow a mother to spend more time parenting by taking over other responsibilities, or may provide an additional positive adult role model within the household (but see Thomson et al. 2001). With respect to comparisons between stepfather and two-biological-parent families, an evolutionary perspective on child rearing suggests that parents may be more strongly motivated to invest in biological children than stepchildren. When differences are found regarding average levels of children's involvement with resident biological fathers versus stepfathers, these differences tend to diminish when background factors are controlled, such as through comparisons of half siblings living in the same household (Hofferth and Anderson 2003). Marital status seems to matter more than biology, however, as cohabiting biological fathers tend to be less involved with children than married biological fathers even when extensive background factors are controlled (Berger et al. 2008; Hofferth and Anderson 2003).

A major challenge faced by social scientists is to determine how much of the observed association between family structure and youths' well-being reflects the selective nature of processes governing entry into families of various types. Indeed, preexisting selectivity in the characteristics of parents and children observed in various family types is important to consider, as such unobserved characteristics potentially create a spurious (or noncausal) association between family structure and children's well-being. For example, a mother's poor mental health or relationship skills might reduce her likelihood of remarriage after divorce, but such characteristics of mothers may also directly affect the well-being of children.

Some studies attempt to adjust for such selectivity by explicitly controlling background characteristics of parents or children in models estimating family-structure effects (for example, see Painter and Levine 2000). Another approach is to use statistical techniques to control for unobserved factors that may bias estimates of the association between family structure and offspring well-being. Much of this work relies on fixed-effects models—most often taking advantage of study designs that sample multiple siblings within a household—to investigate whether unmeasured characteristics of families might explain relatively worse outcomes among youths in stepfamilies compared with those in two-biological-parent families (for example, Case, Lin, and McLanahan 2001; Evenhouse and Reilly 2004; Gennetian 2005; Ginther and Pollak 2004).

Results to date are mixed, however, and little of this work considers stepfamilies formed through nonmarital cohabitation. In addition, such studies generally provide little insight into what specific mechanisms might be responsible for potential family-structure effects and rely on often untestable assumptions about the determinants of children's well-being.[1] Taken together, research suggests that preexisting selectivity of children and parents explains some but not all of the observed differences in youths' well-being across family types, but this remains an active area of investigation.

Finally, a growing number of scholars ask whether family-structure differences in youths' well-being might be better understood as the result of family instability rather than intrinsic differences in the resources available to children within families of varying types. This possibility is of particular concern given that children in the United States are considerably more likely than children in other industrialized countries to experience three or more maternal co-residential partnerships before reaching their eighteenth birthday (Cherlin 2009). A stress-and-instability perspective suggests that changes in family structure disrupt the equilibrium of family environments; the resulting stress leads to conflict within families or interrupts effective parenting behaviors (Wu and Martinson 1993).

Several recent empirical studies investigate the association between family-structure instability and youths' well-being. Given that much instability in children's family environments is missed when only marital transitions are considered (Raley and Wildsmith 2004), it is not surprising that most of this work considers turnover of marital as well as nonmarital relationships. Results indicate that family instability is associated with outcomes such as problem behavior, early childbearing, and low cognitive and academic achievement (Bulanda and Manning 2008; Carlson and Corcoran 2001; Cavanagh, Crissey, and Raley 2008; Cavanagh and Huston 2006, 2008; Fomby and Cherlin 2007; Magnuson and Berger 2009; Manning and Lamb 2003).

Yet this emerging area of work remains limited in a number of important respects. For example, efforts to determine the extent to which the association between children's well-being and family instability might be attributable to unobserved characteristics have been limited, although some evidence suggests that selective characteristics of parents may explain this association more for cognitive than for behavioral outcomes (Fomby and Cherlin 2007). Furthermore, little research to date has considered whether effects of instability might differ depending on what type of family-structure transition is experienced, such as whether a transition leads to the formation versus dissolution of couple relationships or whether effects of such transitions differ when marriage versus cohabitation is involved.

In a recent analysis of data from the National Longitudinal Study of Adolescent Health (Add Health), Susan L. Brown (2006) investigates how adolescent family-structure transitions involving marital and cohabiting relationships affect a variety of outcomes, while also controlling for child well-being and family economic and parenting resources measured before such transitions occurred. For those transitioning from a single-mother family to a stepfamily, entering a cohabiting stepfamily is associated with a larger drop in school engagement than entering a married stepfamily. Yet Brown does not directly test whether school-engagement outcomes for either of these groups differ significantly from those displayed by youths remaining in stable single-mother families. At the same time, Brown finds that the dissolution of a cohabiting stepfamily is associated with some increase in school engagement—that is, improved well-being—compared with those remaining in a stable cohabiting stepfamily. Although offering an important contribution to the study of family transitions, this work remains limited in a number of respects. For example, Brown relied on school engagement as her sole measure of educational well-being, did not limit the Add Health's school-based sample by age to minimize bias from pre-transition school dropout, and relied on potentially problematic child reports to infer whether stepfamilies were formed through marriage or cohabitation. These limitations are described in greater detail below.

In my analysis I use data from the Add Health study to reconsider the association between recent family-structure transitions and well-being during early adolescence, with a particular interest in the educational outcomes among youths who experience transitions into or out of stepfamilies between study waves. To assess the sensitivity of estimates of the association between family structure and educational outcomes to selectivity in the types of children and parents who enter and exit stepfamilies, I follow the approach used in a number of recent studies and control for theoretically significant characteristics of children and their parents measured before family-structure transitions occur (see also Brown 2006; Fomby and Cherlin 2007; Painter and Levine 2000). I also include a wider array of indicators of educational well-being than much prior work, carefully consider transitions involving married versus cohabiting stepfamilies as well as transitions leading to the formation versus the dissolution of stepfamilies, and attend to measurement problems associated with distinguishing stepfamilies formed through cohabitation versus marriage in the Add Health data. Finally, I use a counterfactual perspective to guide comparisons of family-structure groups. Like most research in this area, I initially emphasize comparisons between youths living in stable two-biological-parent families with various family-structure groups, but then move on to consider more theoretically appropriate comparisons between youths living with a solo single parent versus a married or cohabiting stepparent.

Data and Methods

Data for this analysis are drawn from the National Longitudinal Study of Adolescent Health (Add Health) and the Adolescent Health and Academic Achievement transcript study (AHAA). The Add Health is a school-based sample with information on adolescents' school performance and behavior as well as family structure and processes. In-home interviews were conducted with a core nationally representative sample of over 12,000 adolescents in grades seven through twelve in 1995 (Wave 1) and also oversamples of select groups of particular interest such as black youths from well-educated families. In addition, interviews were conducted with a parent of the adolescent respondent during this first study wave. The sample was subsequently re-interviewed in 1996 (Wave 2) and 2001 to 2002 (Wave 3).[2] Response rates for these surveys ranged from 77.4 percent to 88.2 percent (Harris et al. 2009). Approximately 91 percent of Wave 3 respondents also completed a valid transcript release form, and for these individuals the AHAA study gathered supplemental information from official high school transcripts.

I applied a number of restrictions to the study sample for the current analysis. First, I limited the sample to adolescents who participated in Waves 1 through 3 of the Add Health study and who had valid sampling weights (n = 10,828). Second, since adolescents had to be currently enrolled in school to participate in the initial Add Health interview, I further limited the analytic sample to youths who were between the ages of twelve and fifteen at the time of the Wave 1 interview (n = 5,594). This restriction is necessary given considerably higher rates of school

TABLE 11.1   *Family-Structure Patterns Between Add Health Wave 1 (1995) and Wave 2 (1996)*

	N	Percentage
Transition	252	6.0
Two biological parents to single mother	65	1.4
Single mother to stepfamily (either type)	109	2.6
Married stepfamily to single mother	33	0.7
Cohabiting stepfamily to single mother	45	1.3
No transition	3,999	94.0
Two biological parents	2,751	66.0
Single mother	796	16.8
Married stepfamily	345	8.6
Cohabiting stepfamily	107	2.6
Total	4,251	100.0

Source: Authors' calculations based on data from the National Longitudinal Study of Adolescent Health (Add Health; Harris 2009).
Note: Frequency counts are unweighted and percentages are weighted. Percentages do not sum to 100 because of rounding. Sample is limited to Add Health Wave 3 respondents who were between the ages of twelve and fifteen at the Wave 1 interview, as described in the text.

dropout during later adolescence than early adolescence and a well-documented association between dropout risk and measures of in-school attainment and behavior.[3] I also dropped a small number of youths under age twelve at the first study wave from the analytic sample because of the selectivity associated with enrollment at or beyond the seventh grade at these ages.

Next, given that youths who live apart from their mothers remain a relatively select group (Cancian and Meyer 1998), I limited the sample to adolescent respondents who lived with their biological mother at both Wave 1 and Wave 2 and whose biological mother or father responded to the parent interview (n = 4,584). I also limited the sample to youths who experienced one of the family-structure trajectories listed in table 11.1 (n = 4,492), because of the relatively small numbers of youths in other groups. Finally, I limited the sample to respondents with valid data on most independent variables and all outcomes in the study.[4]

Together, these restrictions led to final sample sizes of 4,251 adolescents for the analysis of school engagement and high school graduation (both self-reported in the Add Health study) and 3,390 adolescents for the analysis of grade point average (GPA) and advanced math course completion (on the basis of AHAA transcript data). I applied appropriate sampling weights to all regression analyses, and corrected standard errors for design effects using Stata.

Measures

Next I turn to educational well-being, family structure, and other independent variables.

Dependent Variables   I consider four educational outcomes in the current analysis to reflect the concepts of school-related achievement, behavior, and attainment. First, I constructed a measure of school engagement based on a three-item scale, tapping how often in the past year the adolescent had skipped school and had had trouble paying attention or getting homework done (see Brown 2006; Johnson, Crosnoe, and Elder 2001). The scale is based on self-reported information provided by adolescents at the time of the Wave 2 interview and ranges from zero to four, with the top end of the scale capturing the highest level of school engagement.

Second, I constructed a binary measure of high school graduation, coded one if the respondent reported having graduated from high school at the time of the Add Health Wave 3 interview and zero otherwise. Because General Educational Development (GED) recipients do not experience the same benefits or later attainment as those with a traditional high school diploma (Heckman and LaFontaine 2006), these individuals were not counted as high school graduates for the purpose of the current analysis.

Third, I constructed a measure of overall GPA during the 1996 to 1997 school year from information from the students' official high school transcripts. Finally, I constructed a dichotomous measure of whether students completed an advanced math course before the end of high school, coded 1 if they completed algebra II or higher and 0 otherwise. Math courses tend to be arranged in a hierarchical sequence during high school, where access to more advanced courses requires completion of specific earlier offerings (Cavanagh, Schiller, and Riegle-Crumb 2006). The last two outcome measures were based on high school transcript data gathered as part of the supplementary AHAA study.

Family Structure   Information about children's family structure at the first wave of the Add Health study can be gleaned either from questions about parental "marriage" and "marriage-like" relationships, asked during the parent interview, or from adolescent self-reports of household membership. A number of prior analyses of Add Health data classify youths who report sharing a household with their "mother's partner" as living in a cohabiting stepfamily and those who report sharing a household with their "mother's husband" or a "stepfather" as living in a married stepfamily (for example, Brown 2006; Brown and Manning 2009). Yet there are a several reasons why this approach may not accurately distinguish married from cohabiting stepfamilies. For example, only 39 percent of young adolescents whose mothers report an ongoing "marriage-like" relationship report sharing a household with their "mother's partner," whereas another 34 percent of these adolescents report living with a "stepfather" or "other nonrelative" who is an adult male (Sweeney 2010a). Other research indicates that "unmarried partner" is not a phrase easily understood by cohabitors, as many consider it to refer to same-sex couples or to nonexclusive sexual partners (Manning and Smock 2005).

Two key lessons can be drawn from these findings. First, relying on adolescent reports of co-residence with their "mother's partner" seems likely to result in an undercount of the number of cohabiting stepfamilies. Second, the term "stepfather" may sometimes be used by adolescents to refer to married stepfathers and sometimes to refer to cohabiting stepfathers. For these reasons, I relied on parents' reports of relationship status rather than household rosters reported by adolescents to distinguish married from cohabiting stepfamilies in the Add Health data.

With these issues in mind, I constructed two measures of family structure that capture stability and change in adolescents' family environments between the first two waves of the Add Health study. My first measure distinguishes youths experiencing a family-structure transition between Waves 1 and 2 from those remaining in stable two-biological-parent families, stable single-mother families, stable married stepfamilies, and stable cohabiting stepfamilies. I relied on adolescent household rosters at Waves 1 and 2 to distinguish two-biological-parent families from single-mother families and stepfamilies, and information from the parent interview to distinguish cohabiting from married stepfamilies at Wave 1.[5] My second family-structure measure disaggregates the major types of family-structure transition experienced, separately classifying transitions from two-biological-parent to single-mother families, single-mother families to stepfamilies (married or cohabiting), married stepfamilies to single-mother families, and cohabiting stepfamilies to single-mother families. Unfortunately, parent interviews were not conducted at the second wave of the study, and thus I only distinguish married from cohabiting stepfamilies at Wave 1 of the study for the reasons previously described.

The distribution of family-structure experiences between the first two waves of the Add Health data is displayed in table 11.1. Six percent of adolescents experienced a family-structure transition during this period. Of these, the most common transition was moving from a single-mother family to a stepfamily (2.6 percent), followed by moving from a family with two biological parents to a single-mother family (1.4 percent), cohabiting stepfamily to single-mother family (1.3 percent), and married stepfamily to single-mother family (0.7 percent). Consistent with prior findings on the relatively lower stability of cohabiting than married relationships (for example, Bumpass and Lu 2000), it is worth noting that a substantially higher fraction of Wave 1 cohabiting than married stepfamilies has dissolved by Wave 2. Another 16.8 percent of adolescents lived in a stable single-mother family at both study waves, compared with 8.6 percent who lived with a stable married stepfamily and 2.6 percent who lived in a stable cohabiting stepfamily. Just under two-thirds of adolescent respondents lived with two biological parents at both Waves 1 and 2 of the study.

Independent Variables   I constructed a series of variables to reflect pretransition levels of adolescent educational well-being and the potentially selective characteristics of parents. First, I constructed a measure of Wave 1 school engagement based on the same set of questions previously described for the Wave 2 school-engagement measure. I also constructed a measure GPA at Wave 1, based on self-reported average GPA during the most recent grading period in English and language arts, math, history and social studies, and science. As previously noted, GPA information from official transcripts is only available in the AHAA data for years that adolescents were in high school, and a nontrivial portion of my analytic sample was not yet in high school at the time of the Wave 1 interview.

Next, I considered a series of measures of family economic resources. I constructed a measure of the income-to-needs ratio, defined as total gross family income in the 1994 calendar year relative to the official U.S. government poverty threshold for a given family composition (U.S. Bureau of the Census 1996). To allow for nonlinear effects of family income, I employed a categorical specification of this variable, with categories for income-to-needs ratios of less than one, greater than or equal to one but less than two, greater than or equal to two but less than four, and greater than or equal to four. Family income was reported during the parent interview. Because education can powerfully shape a family's long-run economic stability, I also constructed a measure of mother's years of schooling. Finally, because women who have early births may be disadvantaged both in the labor market and the marriage market (McLanahan and Percheski 2008), I also measured the mother's age at the birth of the adolescent respondent.

Next I created several measures of parenting on the basis of information provided by the adolescent respondents at Wave 1. I first constructed a measure of whether a resident parent is usually present when the child leaves for school, returns from school, eats dinner, and goes to bed. I defined this as more than five days per week in the case of eating dinner and "most of the time" or "always" responses to questions about the other three activities.[6] Scores on this measure of parental presence range from zero to four, the highest score indicating that a parent is usually present at all of these times. I also construct separate measures of the biological mother's and biological father's involvement with the adolescent.[7] These measures are based on a composite index of whether the adolescent has engaged in each of a total of nine activities with his or her mother or father in the past month, such as shopping, going to a religious service, or talking about schoolwork or grades. These measures of involvement range from zero to nine, where the higher end of the scale indicates a relatively greater level of involvement.

Finally, I constructed a series of control measures for factors potentially associated with the educational outcomes considered here. These include race, child's age, child's gender, and whether child was born outside the United States or lived in an urban area (at Wave 1). Basic descriptive statistics for all variables used in the analysis are displayed in online appendix tables 11.A1 and 11.A2 (available online at http://www.russellsage.org/duncan_murnane_online_appendix.pdf).

Analytic Techniques

I used ordinary least-squares (OLS) regression models for the analysis of school engagement and GPA and logistic regression models for the analysis of the completion of advanced math courses and high school graduation. For each outcome I estimated a series of nested models. First, I separately regressed each outcome on family structure and my series of control variables (race-ethnicity, age, sex, nativity status, and whether the respondent lived in an urban area). During this first stage of the analysis I consider only the simplified measure of family structure that aggregates all types of family-structure transitions. In addition to testing differences between each family-structure category and living with two biological parents at both waves, I also used Wald statistical tests to assess the significance of differences between other family-structure categories and having experienced a family-structure transition between survey waves. Because views vary on the single best way to adjust significance thresholds for multiple comparisons, I provided specific (uncorrected) p values for these tests in the text as appropriate. For ease of presentation, I display key results as differences across family-structure groups in predicted values of the outcomes based on setting continuous variables to the sample mean and categorical variables to the sample mode.

Next, to investigate whether preexisting levels of child educational well-being can explain associations between family structure and educational outcomes, I added the best available parallel measure of youth educational well-being at Wave 1 to the previously described model specifications (Model 2). For the analysis of Wave 2 school engagement, this is the measure of self-reported school engagement at the time of the Wave 1 interview. The analysis of GPA in 1996 and 1997 relies on the self-reported measure of average GPA reported at Wave 1. Analyses of advanced math course completion and high school graduation include controls for both prior school engagement and GPA reported at the time of the Wave 1 interview. Finally, I added to the model measures of the potentially selective characteristics of parents—including economic resources and parenting—which are all assessed at the time of the Wave 1 interview (Model 3).

In the last stage of the analysis I expanded the previously described family-structure measure to distinguish among the various types of family-structure transitions made. Because my particular interest here lies in stepfamilies, I tested the significance of differences between a number of theoretically interesting comparison groups, including stable married stepfamily versus transition from a married stepfamily to a single-mother family, stable cohabiting stepfamily versus transition from cohabiting stepfamily to single-mother family, and stable single-mother family versus transition from single-mother family to stepfamily. Again, to facilitate flexibility in applying statistical corrections for multiple comparisons, specific p values associated with these tests are reported in the text as appropriate.

RESULTS

I first considered the association between family structure and adolescent school engagement using my constrained measure of family structure, with results displayed in figure 11.2 (see also online appendix table 11.A3). The baseline model (Model 1) regresses school engagement on family-structure and control variables. Results suggest that living with two biological parents at

FIGURE 11.2   *Predicted Level of School Engagement (Wave 2), by Family Type*

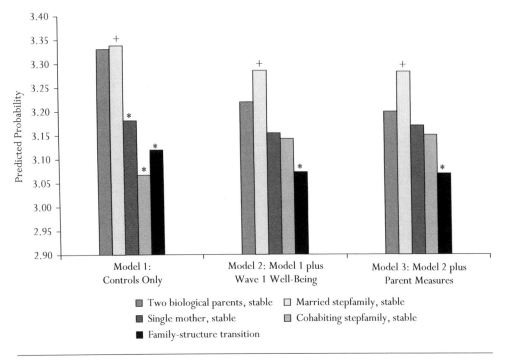

Source: Authors' calculations based on regression models shown in online appendix table 11.A3, based on data from the National Longitudinal Study of Adolescent Health (Harris 2009).
* Differs significantly from two biological parents ($p < 0.05$).
\+ Differs significantly from transition group ($p < 0.05$).

both Waves 1 and 2 is associated with relatively higher school engagement than experiencing a family-structure transition between waves or living in a stable single-mother family or a stable cohabiting stepfamily.

However, I find no significant difference in school engagement associated with living with two biological parents as compared to a stably married stepfamily. As observed for stable two-biological-parent families, living in a stably married stepfamily is associated with significantly higher levels of school engagement than is experiencing a family structure transition between Waves 1 and 2 ($p = 0.005$). As the vast majority of adolescents living with their two biological parents are living with married parents,[8] these findings suggest that a stable marriage may matter more than biological ties to children in creating youths' stronger school engagement.[9]

I next asked whether adjusting for preexisting characteristics of children and their parents can explain these observed family-structure differentials in school engagement (Model 2). Although differences in school engagement at Wave 1 appear to explain the relatively lower levels of Wave 2 school engagement among adolescents living with a stable single or cohabiting mother relative to those living with two biological parents, pretransition school engagement cannot explain the relatively lower well-being associated with having experienced a recent family-structure transition. Adding further controls for selective characteristics of parents and the parent-child relationship (Model 3) similarly fails to explain the relatively lower school engagement associated with experiencing a recent family-structure transition.

It is also worth noting that even after adjusting for preexisting characteristics of parents and children (Model 3), experiencing an inter-wave family structure transition is associated with relatively lower levels of school engagement than living in a stably married stepfamily ($p = 0.016$). Levels of school engagement remain statistically indistinguishable for youth who at both waves lived in a stably married stepfamily or with two biological parents. In short, with respect to school engagement, stable family-structure environments are associated with relatively higher levels of school engagement, both only when those stable environments involve marriage or biological ties between children and two residential parents.

I next move on to consider results for my three other schooling outcomes: GPA, completion of advanced math courses, and high school graduation. Key results for these outcomes are displayed graphically in figures 11.3 to 11.5 (see also online appendix tables 11.A4 to 11.A6 online). A few points about these findings are worth emphasizing. First, as found for school engagement, in no case is educational well-being significantly poorer for adolescents living in stably married stepfamilies than in families headed by two biological parents. Only in the case of high school graduation, however, do I find any evidence that those in stably married stepfamilies are better off than those experiencing an inter-wave family-structure transition ($p = 0.046$, Model 1, figure 11.5).

Second, as again found for school engagement, results from the baseline model for all three outcomes (Model 1, figures 11.3 to 11.5) suggest that lower well-being is associated with living

FIGURE 11.3   *Predicted GPA (1996 to 1997), by Family Type*

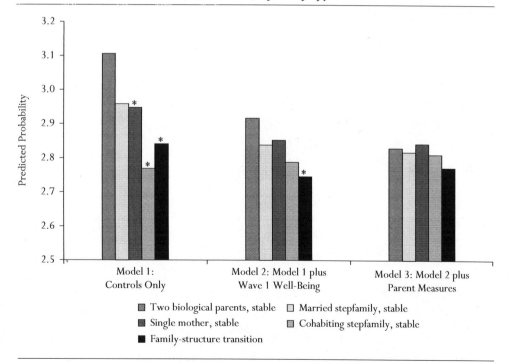

Source: Authors' calculations based on regression models shown in online appendix table 11.A4, based on data from the National Longitudinal Study of Adolescent Health (Harris 2009).
* Differs significantly from two biological parents ($p < 0.05$).
+ Differs significantly from transition group ($p < 0.05$).

FIGURE 11.4   *Predicted Probability of Completing an Advanced Math Course, by Family Type*

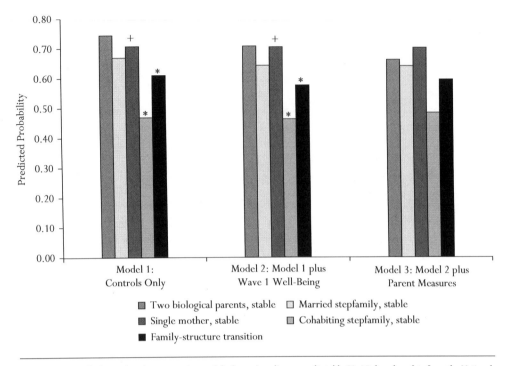

Source: Authors' calculations based on regression models shown in online appendix table 11.A5, based on data from the National Longitudinal Study of Adolescent Health (Harris 2009).
* Differs significantly from two biological parents ($p < 0.05$).
+ Differs significantly from transition group ($p < 0.05$).

in a stable cohabiting stepfamily or experiencing an interwave family-structure transition than living with two biological parents at both waves. With respect to GPA and high school graduation, I also find significantly lower well-being associated with living in a stable single-parent family than a stable two-biological-parent family.

Third, in no case do these family-structure differences remain statistically meaningful once controlling for preexisting characteristics of children and their parents (Models 2 and 3, figures 11.3 to 11.5). In other words, unlike findings for school engagement, differences in GPA, advanced-math-course completion, and high school graduation across family-structure type and stability groups appear largely attributable to the selective characteristics of these groups.

Does the Type of Family Transition Matter?

Results thus far indicate that preexisting characteristics of children and parents can explain the relatively low well-being associated with experiencing a recent family-structure transition with respect to all educational outcomes except school engagement. Yet, these analyses did not distinguish among the specific types of family-structure transitions that an

FIGURE 11.5   *Predicted Probability of High School Graduation, by Family Type*

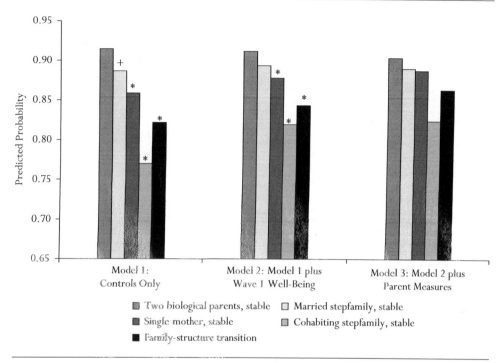

Source: Authors' calculations based on regression models shown in online appendix table 11.A6, based on data from the National Longitudinal Study of Adolescent Health (Harris 2009).
* Differs significantly from two biological parents (p <0.05).
+ Differs significantly from transition group (p <0.05).

adolescent may have experienced between the first two waves of the Add Health study. In a final set of models, I expanded my measure of family structure to disaggregate transitions of different types. Among these groups, I emphasize the previously described theoretically relevant comparisons for understanding children's experiences in stepfamilies. Key results from these models are displayed graphically in figures 11.6 to 11.9 (see also online appendix table 11.A7).

Taken together, a few points about these results are worth emphasizing. First, in no case are differences statistically significant between stable single-mother families and transitions from single-mother families to stepfamilies (see online appendix table 11.A7). In other words, I find no evidence that experiencing the formation of a new stepfamily during early adolescence is associated with poor educational outcomes as compared to remaining with a solo mother.

Second, with respect to three out of four of the educational outcomes considered here (school engagement, advanced-math-course completion, and high school graduation), I find at least some evidence that transitioning from a married stepfamily to a single-mother family is associated with relatively poorer well-being than is remaining in a stably married stepfamily (see figures 11.6 to 11.9 and online appendix table 11.A7). These family-structure differences are not explained by the set of preexisting characteristics of children or parents considered here.[10]

FIGURE 11.6   *Predicted Level of School Engagement (Wave 2), by Detailed Family Type*

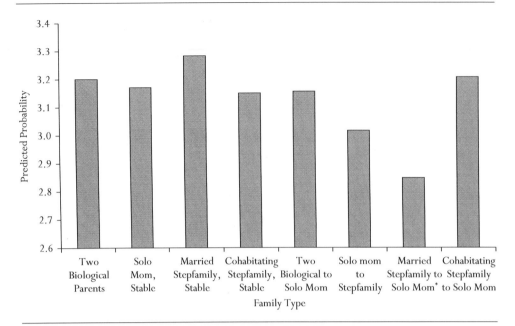

Source: Authors' calculations based on regression models shown in online appendix table 11.A7, based on data from the National Longitudinal Study of Adolescent Health (Harris 2009).
Note: Models include Wave 1 well-being and parent selectivity (see online appendix table 11.A7).
*Transition from married stepfamily to solo mom differs significantly from stable married stepfamily ($p < 0.5$).

FIGURE 11.7   *Predicted Grade-Point Average (1996 to 1997), by Detailed Family Type*

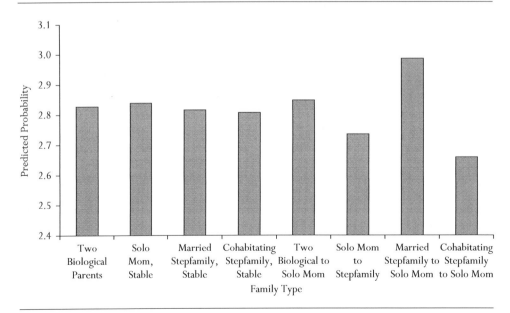

Source: Authors' calculations based on regression models shown in online appendix table 11.A7, based on data from the National Longitudinal Study of Adolescent Health (Harris 2009).
Note: Models include Wave 1 well-being and parent selectivity (see online appendix table 11.A7).

FIGURE 11.8   *Predicted Probability of Advanced Math Course Completion, by Detailed Family Type*

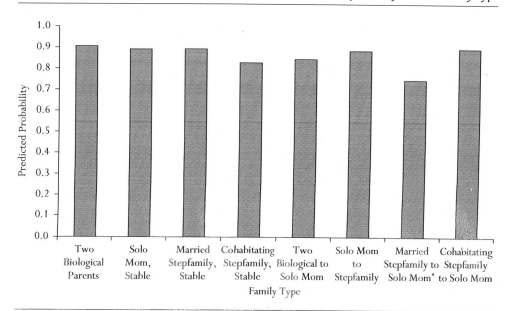

Source: Authors' calculations based on regression models shown in online appendix table 11.A7, based on data from the National Longitudinal Study of Adolescent Health (Harris 2009).
Note: Models include Wave 1 well-being and parent selectivity (see online appendix table 11.A7).
*Transition from married stepfamily to solo mom differs significantly from stable married stepfamily ($p < 0.5$).

FIGURE 11.9   *Predicted Probability of High School Graduation, by Detailed Family Type*

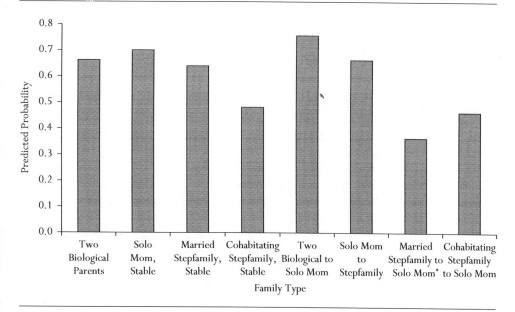

Source: Authors' calculations based on regression models shown in online appendix table 11.A7, based on data from the National Longitudinal Study of Adolescent Health (Harris 2009).
Note: Models include Wave 1 well-being and parent selectivity (see online appendix table 11.A7).
*Transition from married stepfamily to solo mom differs significantly from stable married stepfamily ($p < 0.5$).

In no case, however, do I find evidence that experiencing the dissolution of a mother's cohabiting relationship is associated with significantly lower well-being than remaining in a stable cohabiting stepfamily (see online appendix table 11.A7). This intriguing result warrants further study, but it suggests that experiencing the breakup of a stepfamily may be more detrimental for adolescent well-being when a union was formed through marriage than cohabitation.

DISCUSSION

With a particular focus on stepfamilies, this study set out to better understand how youth educational outcomes are influenced by family structure and family-structure transitions. A few key points are worth emphasizing from the current findings. Stable family environments are associated with relatively higher levels of well-being with respect to school engagement than experiencing a family-structure transition, but only when those stable environments involve marriage or biological ties between children and two residential parents. These differences are not explained by pretransition levels of adolescent school engagement or background characteristics of parents. Yet evidence for a negative effect of experiencing a family transition between survey waves is weaker with respect to GPA, advanced math course completion, and high school graduation, and observed differences in these outcomes that do exist are fully explained by background characteristics of children or their parents. It is also worth noting that even for the outcome where family-structure differentials tend to be strongest—that is, school engagement—I find no evidence that living in a stably married stepfamily is associated with relatively lower well-being than living with two biological parents. This suggests that, in the case of school engagement, benefits associated with marriage are conferred regardless of whether biological ties exist between residential fathers and adolescents.

The variability in my findings suggests that it is important to consider how school engagement differs from other types of outcomes that reflect educational achievement or attainment. Why might school engagement be particularly sensitive to family instability? In addition, however, the variability demonstrates that social scientists must look beyond school engagement to garner a more comprehensive picture of the association between family structure and educational outcomes. A number of recent studies do not include direct measures of achievement or attainment when documenting the association between family structure and youths' educational well-being (for example, Brown 2006; Teachman 2008). On the other hand, the different educational outcomes considered here varied somewhat in their measurement timing; thus, future work should also consider how changes in educational well-being following a family-structure transition may tend to evolve or dissipate over time.

This study also asked whether the type of family-structure transition mattered for children's educational well-being. Although I find no evidence of a reduction in adolescent educational well-being associated with entering a stepfamily compared to remaining in a single-mother family, my results do suggest that transitions out of married (but not cohabiting) stepfamilies may be associated with relatively lower well-being with respect to school engagement, advanced-math-course completion, and high school graduation. Although a large body of evidence has documented the relatively lower stability of cohabiting families than that of married families (Bumpass and Lu 2000; Manning, Smock, and Majumdar 2004), my results suggest that marital instability may be relatively more disruptive than instability of cohabiting relationships to the educational trajectories of youth. This interesting finding warrants further attention in future work, but may in part reflect the more dramatic drop in economic well-being experienced by women upon ending marriages than by entering cohabiting unions (Avellar and Smock 2005).

This study also suggests a number of other important directions for future work. For example, given substantial variability in children's family-structure experiences across race, ethnic, and economic groups, an obvious next step in this research will be to consider whether and how the current findings vary across demographic subpopulations. Such work will further improve our understanding of how family structure and family instability contribute to exacerbating and reproducing patterns of income inequality. It is also important to keep in mind that this analysis considered only family-structure transitions experienced during early adolescence—a life-course stage during which, some evidence suggests, it may be particularly difficult for youths to experience a parent's remarriage (Hetherington and Kelly 2002). Whether findings vary meaningfully for transitions experienced at other stages of childhood remains largely an open question. In addition, a growing body of work points to the importance of sibling composition for youth outcomes and for understanding youths' well-being in stepfamilies (Gennetian 2005; Tillman 2008). This avenue, too, will be an important one to pursue in future work.

Finally, this analysis considered direct effects of families on youths' educational outcomes, but it is important to keep in mind that at a more aggregate level, family structure may also indirectly affect youths' educational outcomes by changing the ways schools or neighborhoods function. For example, a larger proportion of single-parent families at a school may translate into less supervision of children at home, which could have spillover effects in terms of disruptive behavior problems in the classroom or high rates of absenteeism or mobility of student populations, requiring teachers to repeat material often. The collective family-structure composition of students in a school may also serve a role-modeling effect, influencing individual students' expectations for the future (Harris, Duncan, and Boisjoly 2002). Some evidence suggests that attending a school with a high concentration of children from single-parent families or stepfamilies is indeed associated with reduced student achievement, even after adjusting for children's own family structures (Pong 1997). Research further indicates that two-biological-parent families display higher levels of involvement with schools—such as attending school events and participating in parent-teacher associations—than do single-parent families or stepfamilies (Pong 1997, 1998; Zill 1994).

The extent to which these associations reflect true causal effects of family structure rather than artifacts of social-class differences or other aspects of selectivity remains insufficiently understood. Furthermore, theoretical mechanisms for school-level spillover effects associated with high concentrations of stepfamilies are less clear than those associated with high concentrations of single-parent families. Greater attention to these questions, however, may contribute to a deeper understanding of multifaceted ways in which families influence youth educational outcomes.

In conclusion, this study offers a number of key lessons for broader efforts to understand how family contexts contribute to youth educational outcomes. My results highlight the importance of considering multiple indicators of educational well-being to understand the consequences of family-structure instability. Relying on school engagement alone may tend to overstate the overall association between family structure and educational well-being. Although youths experiencing a family-structure transition display lower levels of school engagement than do those living in a stably married stepfamily or with two biological parents, these differences are explained by the pretransition characteristics of children and parents with respect to GPA, advanced-math-course completion, and high school graduation.

In addition, despite some suggestions that the formation of stepfamilies may be particularly stressful for youths (Cherlin 1978), I find no evidence that living in a stably married stepfamily is associated with relatively worse educational outcomes than living with two biological parents, nor do I find evidence of a reduction in educational well-being associated with transitioning from a solo-mother family to a stepfamily. Finally, I find evidence of some reduction in educational well-being associated with experiencing the dissolution of a stepfamily, but only among stepfamilies formed through marriage. This finding suggests that broader debates about the observed benefits of marriage should also take into account the possibility that in cases where relationships end, marriage may be associated with greater costs for young people than other relationship forms. This finding has clear policy implications for marriage-promotion efforts aimed at couples who are otherwise unlikely to marry.

This material is based on research supported by the National Science Foundation under grant no. 0137182 and by a Scholars Award from the William T. Grant Foundation. The AHAA study was funded by a grant from the National Institute of Child Health and Human Development under grants 01 HD40428-02 to the Population Research Center, University of Texas at Austin; Chandra Muller (principal investigator) and from the National Science Foundation under grant REC-0126167 to the Population Research Center, University of Texas at Austin; Chandra Muller and Pedro Reyes (co–principal investigators). Additionally, this research uses data from Add Health, a program project directed by Kathleen Mullan Harris and designed by J. Richard Udry, Peter S. Bearman, and Kathleen Mullan Harris at the University of North Carolina at Chapel Hill, and funded by grant P01-HD31921 from the Eunice Kennedy Shriver National Institute of Child Health and Human Development, with cooperative funding from twenty-three other federal agencies and foundations. Special acknowledgment is due to Ronald R. Rindfuss and Barbara Entwisle for assistance in the original design. Information on how to obtain the Add Health data files is available on the Add Health website (http://www.cpc.unc.edu/addhealth; accessed June 27, 2011). No direct support was received from grant P01-HD31921 for this analysis. Any opinions, findings, conclusions, or recommendations expressed in this material are those of the author.

NOTES

Online appendix available at: http://www.russellsage.org/duncan_murnane_online_appendix.pdf.

1. Furthermore, studies based on comparisons of half siblings within a household may have limited generalizability to larger populations of children, as children living with a half sibling tend to be unusually disadvantaged regardless of the nature of biological ties to adults in the home (Ginther and Pollak 2004).

2. Add Health respondents were also re-interviewed in 2007 and 2008, although these data are not used in the current analysis.

3. In 1995, when the Wave 1 Add Health data were collected, roughly 12 percent of black youths and 8.6 percent of white youths age sixteen to twenty-four were not enrolled in school and had not earned a high school diploma or equivalency credential (U.S. Department of Education 2009). Citing a 2003 paper by Richard J. Udry and Kim Chantala published in *Social Science Research,* some prior researchers (for example, Heard 2007) suggest that omission of school dropouts from the Add Health sample does not bias estimates of children's educational outcomes. It is important to keep in mind, however, that Udry and Chantala (2003) do not look specifically at educational outcomes but rather at risk behaviors related to exercise and diet, sexual behavior, emotional distress, exposure to violence, and substance abuse. The omission of older high school dropouts in the initial Add Health sample may be relatively more consequential when one looks specifically at school-related outcomes, as dropout risk is known to be associated with course performance and school engagement (Tyler and Lofstrom 2009).

4. Because of the relatively large amount of missing information on family income, I make a separate category for missing data on this measure. Substantive conclusions do not change, however, when these cases are instead dropped from the analysis.

5. Although some cohabiting mothers at Wave 1 will have married their partners by Wave 2, these transitions will not be captured in my analysis because parents of primary Add Health respondents were only interviewed at Wave 1 of the study. In addition, a recent analysis suggests that adolescents in the Add Health study may

sometimes describe a mother's cohabiting partner as an "other nonrelative" when completing a household roster (Sweeney 2010a). Unfortunately, without corroborating evidence from another source (for example, the mother), it is not possible to determine which reports of other nonrelatives in the home are meant to refer to a mother's romantic partner. My measure of stepfamily membership at Wave 2 is thus likely to somewhat underrepresent youths living with their mother and her cohabiting partner.

6.   Or responses of "she [or he] takes me to school" or "she [or he] brings me home from school" in the case of the two school-related items.

7.   Although measures of involvement with a stepfather would also be desirable, this information is not consistently gathered for cohabiting stepfathers in the Add Health.

8.   Mothers report being currently married for more than 98 percent of children coded as living with two biological parents in my analytic sample.

9.   Conclusions regarding any apparent benefits of marriage should not be generalized to same-sex couples, however, who in most U.S. states do not have the same legal opportunity to marry as heterosexual couples and whose experiences are not directly considered in this analysis.

10.   In Model 3 (figures. 11.6 to 11.9), p values from Wald tests of the significance of differences between stably married stepfamilies and transitions from married stepfamilies to single-mother families are 0.016 for school engagement, 0.042 for advanced math course completion, and 0.026 for high school graduation.

REFERENCES

Acs, Gregory. 2007. "Can We Promote Child Well-Being by Promoting Marriage?" *Journal of Marriage and Family* 69(5): 1326–44.

Amato, Paul R. 2005. "The Impact of Family Formation Change on the Cognitive, Social, and Emotional Well-Being of the Next Generation." *Future of Children* 15(2): 75–96.

Aughinbaugh, Alison, Charles R. Pierret, and Donna S. Rothstein. 2005. "The Impact of Family Structure Transitions on Youth Achievement: Evidence from the Children of the NLSY79." *Demography* 42(3): 447–68.

Avellar, Sarah, and Pamela J. Smock. 2005. "The Economic Consequences of the Dissolution of Cohabiting Unions." *Journal of Marriage and the Family* 67(2): 315–27.

Berger, Lawrence M., Marcia J. Carlson, Sharon H. Bzostek, and Cynthia Osborne. 2008. "Parenting Practices of Resident Fathers: The Role of Marital and Biological Ties." *Journal of Marriage and the Family* 70(3): 625–39.

Brown, Susan L. 2004. "Family Structure and Child Well-Being: The Significance of Parental Cohabitation." *Journal of Marriage and the Family* 66(2): 351–67.

———. 2006. "Family Structure Transitions and Adolescent Well-Being." *Demography* 43(3): 447–61.

Brown, Susan L., and Wendy D. Manning. 2009. "Family Boundary Ambiguity and the Measurement of Family Structure: The Significance of Cohabitation." *Demography* 46(1): 85–101.

Bulanda, Ronald E., and Wendy D. Manning. 2008. "Parental Cohabitation Experiences and Adolescent Behavioral Outcomes." *Population Research and Policy Review* 27(5): 593–618.

Bumpass, Larry L., and H.-H. Lu. 2000. "Trends in Cohabitation and Implications for Children's Family Contexts in the United States." *Population Studies* 54(1): 29–41.

Bumpass, Larry L., R. Kelly Raley, and James A. Sweet. 1995. "The Changing Character of Stepfamilies: Implications of Cohabitation and Nonmarital Childbearing." *Demography* 32(3): 425–36.

Cancian, Maria, and Daniel R. Meyer. 1998. "Who Gets Custody?" *Demography* 35(2): 147–57.

Carlson, Marcia J., and Mary E. Corcoran. 2001. "Family Structure and Children's Behavioral and Cognitive Outcomes." *Journal of Marriage and the Family* 63(3): 779–92.

Case, Anne, I-Fen Lin, and Sara McLanahan. 2001. "Educational Attainment of Siblings in Stepfamilies." *Evolution and Human Behavior* 22(4): 269–89.

Cavanagh, Shannon E., Sarah R. Crissey, and R. Kelly Raley. 2008. "Family Structure History and Adolescent Romance." *Journal of Marriage and the Family* 70(3): 698–714.

Cavanagh, Shannon E., and Althea C. Huston. 2006. "Family Instability and Children's Early Problem Behavior." *Social Forces* 85(1): 551–81.

———. 2008. "The Timing of Family Instability and Children's Social Development." *Journal of Marriage and Family* 70(5): 1258–70.

Cavanagh, Shannon E., Kathryn S. Schiller, and Catherine Riegle-Crumb. 2006. "Marital Transitions, Parenting, and Schooling: Exploring the Link Between Family-Structure History and Adolescents' Academic Status." *Sociology of Education* 79(4): 329–54.

Cherlin, Andrew J. 1978. "Remarriage as an Incomplete Institution." *American Journal of Sociology* 84(3): 634–50.

————. 2009. The Marriage-Go-Round: The State of Marriage and the Family in America Today. New York: Alfred A. Knopf.

Deleire, Thomas, and Ariel Kalil. 2002. "Good Things Come in Threes: Single-Parent Multigenerational Family Structure and Adolescent Adjustment." *Demography* 39(2): 393–413.

————. 2005. "How Do Cohabiting Couples with Children Spend Their Money?" *Journal of Marriage and Family* 67(2): 286–95.

Duncan, Greg J., Johanne Boisjoly, and Kathleen Mullan Harris. 2001. "Sibling, Peer, Neighbor, and Schoolmate Correlations as Indicators of the Importance of Context for Adolescent Development." *Demography* 38(3): 437–47.

Ellwood, David T., and Christopher Jencks. 2004. "The Uneven Spread of Single-Parent Families: What Do We Know? Where Do We Look for Answers?" In *Social Inequality,* edited by Kathryn Neckerman. New York: Russell Sage Foundation.

Evenhouse, Eirik, and Siobhan Reilly. 2004. "A Sibling Study of Stepchild Well-Being." *Journal of Human Resources* 39(1): 248–76.

Fomby, Paula, and Andrew J. Cherlin. 2007. "Family Instability and Child Well-Being." *American Sociological Review* 72(2): 181–204.

Ganong, Lawrence H., and Marilyn Coleman. 2004. Stepfamily Relationships: Development, Dynamics, and Interventions. New York: Kluwer Academic/Plenum.

Gennetian, Lisa A. 2005. "One or Two Parents? Half or Step Siblings? The Effect of Family Structure on Young Children's Achievement." *Journal of Population Economics* 18(3): 415–36.

Ginther, Donna K., and Robert A. Pollak. 2004. "Family Structure and Children's Educational Outcomes: Blended Families, Stylized Facts, and Descriptive Regressions." *Demography* 41(4): 671–96.

Hamilton, Brady E., Joyce A. Martin, and Stephanie J. Ventura. 2009. "Births: Preliminary Data for 2007." *National Vital Statistics Reports* 57, no. 12 (March 18). Available for download at: http://www.cdc.gov/nchs/data/nvsr/nvsr57/nvsr57_12.pdf (accessed on July 20, 2010).

Harris, Kathleen Mullan. 2009. The National Longitudinal Study of Adolescent Health (Add Health), Waves I & II, 1994–1996; Wave III, 2001–2002; Wave IV, 2007–2009 [machine-readable data file and documentation]. Chapel Hill, N.C.: Carolina Population Center, University of North Carolina at Chapel Hill. Ordering information: http://www.cpc.unc.edu/projects/addhealth/data/restricteduse (accessed May 4, 2011).

Harris, Kathleen Mullan, Greg J. Duncan, and Johanne Boisjoly. 2002. "Evaluating the Role of 'Nothing to Lose' Attitudes on Risky Behavior in Adolescence." *Social Forces* 80(3): 1005–39.

Harris, Kathleen Mullan, Carolyn T. Halpern, Eric Whitsel, Jon Hussey, Joyce Tabor, Pamela P. Entzel, and J. Richard Udry. 2009. "The National Longitudinal Study of Adolescent Health: Research Design." Available for download at: http://www.cpc.unc.edu/projects/addhealth/design (accessed March 18, 2010).

Hawkins, Daniel N., Paul R. Amato, and Valarie King. 2007. "Nonresident Father Involvement and Adolescent Well-Being: Father Effects or Child Effects?" *American Sociological Review* 72(6): 990–1010.

Heard, Holly E. 2007. "The Family Structure Trajectory and Adolescent School Performance." *Journal of Family Issues* 28(3): 319–54.

Heckman, James J., and Paul A. LaFontaine. 2006. "Bias-Corrected Estimates of GED Returns." *Journal of Labor Economics* 24(3): 661–700.

Hetherington, E. Mavis, and John Kelly. 2002. For Better or for Worse: Divorce Reconsidered. New York: Norton.

Hofferth, Sandra L. 2006. "Residential Father Family Type and Child Well-Being: Investment Versus Selection." *Demography* 43(1): 53–77.

Hofferth, Sandra L., and Kermyt G. Anderson. 2003. "Are All Dads Equal? Biology Versus Marriage as a Basis for Paternal Investment." *Journal of Marriage and the Family* 65(1): 213–32.

Johnson, Monica K., Robert Crosnoe, and Glen H. Elder. 2001. "Students' Attachment and Academic Engagement: The Role of Race and Ethnicity." *Sociology of Education* 74(4): 318–40.

Kennedy, Sheela, and Larry Bumpass. 2008. "Cohabitation and Children's Living Arrangements: New Estimates from the United States." *Demographic Research* 19(47):1663–92.

Kreider, Rose M. 2008. *Living Arrangements of Children: 2004.* Washington, D.C.: U.S. Bureau of the Census.

Kreider, Rose M., and Diana B. Elliot. 2009. *American's Families and Living Arrangements: 2007.* Washington, D.C.: U.S. Bureau of the Census.

Magnuson, Katherine, and Lawrence M. Berger. 2009. "Family Structure States and Transitions: Associations with Children's Well-Being During Middle Childhood." *Journal of Marriage and Family* 71(3): 575–91.

Manning, Wendy D., and Susan Brown. 2006. "Children's Economic Well-Being in Married and Cohabiting Parent Families." *Journal of Marriage and Family* 68(2): 345–62.

Manning, Wendy D., and Kathleen A. Lamb. 2003. "Adolescent Well-Being in Cohabiting, Married, and Single-Parent Families." *Journal of Marriage and Family* 65(4): 876–93.

Manning, Wendy D., and Pamela J. Smock. 2005. "Measuring and Modeling Cohabitation: New Perspectives from Qualitative Data." *Journal of Marriage and the Family* 67(4): 989–1002.

Manning, Wendy D., Pamela J. Smock, and Debarun Majumdar. 2004. "The Relative Stability of Cohabiting and Marital Unions for Children." *Population Research and Policy Review* 23(2): 135–59.

McLanahan, Sara, and Christine Percheski. 2008. "Family Structure and the Reproduction of Inequalities." *Annual Review of Sociology* 34(1): 257–76.

McLanahan, Sara, and Gary Sandefur. 1994. *Growing Up with a Single Parent: What Hurts, What Helps.* Cambridge, Mass.: Harvard University Press.

Morrison, Donna R., and Amy Ritualo. 2000. "Routes to Children's Economic Recovery After Divorce: Are Cohabitation and Remarriage Equivalent?" *American Sociological Review* 65(4): 560–80.

Nelson, Sandi, Rebecca L. Clark, and Gregory Acs. 2001. *Beyond the Two-Parent Family: How Teenagers Fare in Cohabiting Couple and Blended Families.* New Federalism: National Survey of America's Families, publication no. B-31. Washington, D.C.: Urban Institute. Available for download at: http://www.urban.org/publications/310339.html (accessed on July 20, 2010).

Painter, Gary, and David I. Levine. 2000. "Family Structure and Youths' Outcomes: Which Correlations Are Causal?" *Journal of Human Resources* 35(3): 524–49.

Pong, Suet-Ling. 1997. "Family Structure, School Context, and Eighth-Grade Math and Reading Achievement." *Journal of Marriage and the Family* 59(3): 734–46.

———. 1998. "The School Compositional Effect of Single Parenthood on 10th-Grade Achievement." *Sociology of Education* 71(1):23–41.

Raley, R. Kelly, and Larry L. Bumpass. 2003. "The Topography of the Divorce Plateau: Levels and Trends in Union Stability in the United States After 1980." *Demographic Research* 8(8): 245–59.

Raley, R. Kelly, Michelle L. Frisco, and Elizabeth Wildsmith. 2005. "Maternal Cohabitation and Educational Success." *Sociology of Education* 78(2): 144–64.

Raley, R. Kelly, and Elizabeth Wildsmith. 2004. "Cohabitation and Children's Family Instability." *Journal of Marriage and the Family* 66(1): 210–19.

Sigle-Rushton, Wendy, and Sara McLanahan. 2004. "Father Absence and Child Well-Being: A Critical Review." In *The Future of the Family,* edited by Daniel Patrick Moynihan, Timothy M. Smeeding, and Lee Rainwater. New York: Russell Sage Foundation.

Sweeney, Megan M. 2010a. "Boundary Ambiguity and Cohabiting Stepfamilies in the United States." Paper presented at the 2010 annual meeting of the Population Association of America. Dallas (April 15–17).

———. 2010b. "Remarriage and Stepfamilies: Strategic Sites for Family Scholarship in the 21st Century." *Journal of Marriage and Family* 72(4): 805–27.

Sweeney, Megan M., and Julie A. Phillips. 2004. "Understanding Racial Differences in Marital Disruption: Recent Trends and Explanations." *Journal of Marriage and the Family* 66(3): 639–50.

Teachman, Jay D. 2008. "The Living Arrangements of Children and Their Educational Well-Being." *Journal of Family Issues* 29(6): 734–61.

Thomson, Elizabeth, Jane Mosley, Thomas L. Hanson, and Sara S. McLanahan. 2001. "Remarriage, Cohabitation, and Changes in Mothering Behavior." *Journal of Marriage and the Family* 63(2): 370–80.

Tillman, Kathryn Harker. 2007. "Family Structure Pathways and Academic Disadvantage Among Adolescents in Stepfamilies." *Sociological Inquiry* 77(3): 383–424.

———. 2008. "'Non-Traditional' Siblings and the Academic Outcomes of Adolescents." *Social Science Research* 37(1): 88–108.

Tyler, John H., and Magnus Lofstrom. 2009. "Finishing High School: Alternative Pathways and Dropout Recovery." *Future of Children* 19(1): 77–103.

Udry, Richard J., and Kim Chantala. 2003. "Missing School Dropouts in Surveys Does Not Bias Risk Estimates." *Social Science Research* 32(2): 294–311.

U.S. Bureau of the Census. 1996. "Income, Poverty, and Valuation of Noncash Benefits: 1994." In *Current Population Reports,* Series P60-189. Washington, D.C.: U.S. Government Printing Office.

————. 2009. "Living Arrangements of Children under 18 Years Old: 1960 to Present." Available at: http://www.census.gov/population/socdemo/hh-fam/html (accessed on September 12, 2009).

U.S. Department of Education, National Center for Education Statistics. 2009. *The Condition of Education 2009.* NCES 2009-081, table A-20-2. Washington, D.C.: National Center for Education Statistics.

Ventura, Stephanie J. 2009. "Changing Patterns of Nonmarital Childbearing in the United States." NCHS data brief, no. 18. Hyattsville, Md.: National Center for Health Statistics.

Ventura, Stephanie J., and Christine A. Bachrach. 2000. "Nonmarital Childbearing in the United States, 1940–99." *National Vital Statistics Report* 48, no. 16 (October 18). Hyattsville, Md.: National Center for Health Statistics.

Western, Bruce, Deirdre Bloome, and Christine Percheski. 2008. "Inequality Among American Families with Children, 1975 to 2005." *American Sociological Review* 73(6): 903–20.

Wu, Lawrence L., and Brian C. Martinson. 1993. "Family Structure and the Risk of a Premarital Birth." *American Sociological Review* 58(2): 210–32.

Zill, Nicholas. 1994. "Understanding Why Children in Stepfamilies Have More Learning and Behavior Problems than Children in Nuclear Families." In *Stepfamilies: Who Benefits? Who Does Not?,* edited by Alan Booth and Judy Dunn. Hillsdale, N.J.: Lawrence Erlbaum.

Part IV

Neighborhoods

Chapter 12

Converging Evidence for Neighborhood Effects on Children's Test Scores: An Experimental, Quasi-Experimental, and Observational Comparison

Julia Burdick-Will, Jens Ludwig, Stephen W. Raudenbush,
Robert J. Sampson, Lisa Sanbonmatsu, and Patrick Sharkey

Rising income inequality has been found to be associated with rising segregation at the neighborhood level, generating concern about whether neighborhood environments themselves may influence children's life chances, independent of other individual child and family characteristics. Because poor and minority Americans are overrepresented in our most disadvantaged neighborhoods, any "neighborhood effects" on children may contribute to persistent disparities in overall schooling outcomes along race and class lines in the United States.

A large body of nonexperimental research dating back to the Coleman Report in 1966 has produced evidence consistent with the idea of large neighborhood effects on children's schooling outcomes. However, drawing causal inferences from these studies is complicated by the fact that the attributes of a neighborhood in which a family lives is likely correlated with characteristics of the family that predict schooling outcomes. These studies are therefore vulnerable to selection bias. The one formal randomized experiment in this literature is the five-city Moving to Opportunity (MTO) experiment, data from which suggests no statistically significant impacts, on average, on reading or math test scores for children in MTO measured four to seven years after baseline. How one should weight the findings from the MTO experiment versus the larger body of nonexperimental research remains the topic of ongoing debate within the research and policy communities.

In this chapter, we try to reconcile the experimental, quasi-experimental, and observational research regarding neighborhood effects on children, and we argue that the available findings are more convergent than many people believe. Drawing on a number of recent and unusually high-quality quasi-experimental and observational studies, together with a reexamination of MTO findings across the individual MTO demonstration sites, we believe that the available evidence allows us to reject the null hypothesis that neighborhood environments *never* matter for children's outcomes. Yet at the same time, the data also do not support the hypothesis that neighborhoods *always* matter.

In our view, the key question for research and public policy is to learn more about the conditions under which neighborhoods matter for children's academic outcomes and why. Our ability to answer this question in the present chapter is restricted by the limited number of studies that have employed sufficiently strong research designs to support inferences about neighborhood effects on children's outcomes, and by the fact that a disproportionate share of the studies that meet this research-design threshold have been carried out in a single city (Chicago).

With these important qualifications in mind, we believe that there is at least a suggestive case to be made that children's test scores may be most strongly affected by community violence or may respond nonlinearly to concentrated neighborhood disadvantage or community violence. Put differently, what may matter most for children's cognitive development is to avoid living in the most severely economically distressed or dangerous neighborhoods in the country, neighborhoods that are found in Baltimore and Chicago but, surprisingly, are less prevalent even in other major urban areas such as Boston, Los Angeles, and New York. Given the limitations of the available evidence, we offer these as hypotheses to be tested further rather than as strong conclusions.

Recent evidence indicates that the rise in income inequality has led to an associated rise in the sorting of families into neighborhoods that are increasingly segregated by race and by class (Reardon and Bischoff 2011; Watson 2009). The potential consequences of these trends become clear when one considers the dramatic variation in educational outcomes across neighborhoods in America. For example, in the Chicago suburb of Wilmette, where the median home value is $441,000, almost everyone graduates from high school and a majority go on to attend, and complete, college. In contrast, in Chicago's public high schools the dropout rate is around 44 percent (Allensworth and Easton 2001)[1] and is much higher still in some of the city's most disadvantaged neighborhoods.

This variation in schooling achievement and other outcomes has generated concern about whether neighborhood environments influence children's life chances, independent of other individual child and family characteristics. Concern is greatest when one focuses on the nation's poorest neighborhoods. Despite a decline during the 1990s in the number of people living in some of the most distressed census tracts (poverty greater than 40 percent), a total of 8 million people still lived in such areas in 2000, nearly twice the number as in 1970 (Jargowsky 2003). Because poor and minority Americans are overrepresented in our most disadvantaged neighborhoods, any neighborhood effects on children may contribute to persistent disparities in overall schooling outcomes that follow race and class lines in the United States.

One reason why neighborhood of residence might affect children's schooling outcomes is through variation among neighborhoods in the quality of local public schools. Another plausible explanation focuses on the social environment. Exposure to more pro-social, higher-achieving peers may provide stronger social support for academic achievement, enable children to participate in more developmentally productive study groups, and allow teachers to better present classroom instruction and spend less time dealing with disruptive students. Adults may vary across neighborhoods in their capacity and willingness to help monitor local children and enforce community norms, or in their ability to signal the value of staying in school. And exposure to high rates of crime and violence may cause stress, trauma, or other mental health problems that negatively affect children's schooling outcomes, might make children more reluctant to go to school or participate in developmentally enriching after-school activities, could hamper the ability of local schools to attract and retain high-quality teachers, and might entice youth to leave school early to earn money in the underground economy or to join street gangs for protection against criminal victimization. For policy purposes, distinguishing the causal effects of schools from the effects of the social environment is important because in principle the former could be directly affected by education policy without having to either change the qualities of neighborhood environments outside of schools or else to relocate low-income families into new neighborhoods.

Empirical claims for the effect of neighborhood context on children's schooling outcomes dates back at least to the Coleman Report, which argued that "attributes of other students account for far more variation in the achievement of minority group children than do any attributes of school facilities and slightly more than do attributes of staff" (Coleman et al. 1966, 302). These findings, if taken at face value, would seem to imply powerful neighborhood effects on children's learning, given that school composition is determined in large part by neighborhood composition. However, drawing causal inferences from the Coleman Report and most of the subsequent research on peer or neighborhood effects is complicated by the fact that the attributes leading families to select specific types of neighborhoods may be the same attributes that predict schooling outcomes among children. Because researchers are not always able to capture and control for all of the relevant attributes of a family that influence neighborhood selection, estimates of neighborhood on educational outcomes may be systematically biased. Put differently, educational outcomes could vary between neighborhoods because of the different types of families living in different types of areas, rather than because of any direct causal effects of neighborhood environments on children's outcomes.

The one formal randomized experiment that has been conducted to date to test whether neighborhood environments affect children's life chances is the U.S. Department of Housing and Urban Development's (HUD) Moving to Opportunity (MTO) residential mobility experiment. MTO has been in operation since 1994 in five cities (Baltimore, Boston, Chicago, Los Angeles, and New York City) and has enrolled a total of 4,600 mostly minority families with children that live in public housing. Via random lottery, some families but not others were offered the chance to use a housing voucher to relocate to low-poverty census tracts. Random assignment helps solve the selection-bias concern with observational studies by generating differences in average neighborhood environments between otherwise similar groups of families, so that any difference we observe in average outcomes across groups can be attributed to the differences in neighborhood trajectories that families experience. Data from the MTO interim study find no statistically significant impacts, on average, on reading or math test scores for children in MTO as measured four to seven years after baseline (Sanbonmatsu et al. 2006). The interim data did show positive and statistically significant effects on reading scores for African Americans in the experimental group. However, due to the number of subgroups examined, it is unclear whether this subgroup effect reflects differential treatment impacts across subgroups or reflects sampling variability. Moreover, the effect observed for African Americans was driven by just two of the five MTO sites, Baltimore and Chicago.

How should one weight the findings from the randomized MTO experiment in relation to the larger body of nonexperimental research, much of which has shown strong neighborhood effects on educational outcomes? This question remains the topic of ongoing discussion (and some disagreement) within the research and policy communities (see, for example, Clampet-Lundquist and Massey 2008; Ludwig et al. 2008; Sampson 2008). Some have interpreted the MTO findings as providing sufficient evidence to conclude that neighborhood environments per se are not very important for children's schooling outcomes. Others have been reluctant to draw this conclusion, in part because of the sizable body of observational and quasi-experimental research suggesting important neighborhood effects and the uncertainty about the practical importance of any selection-bias concerns with these studies. Moreover, some critics have expressed skepticism about whether MTO generated sufficiently large changes in neighborhood environments, particularly in racial composition, to adequately test the neighborhood-effects hypothesis.

In this chapter we try to reconcile the experimental, quasi-experimental, and observational research regarding neighborhood effects on children, and we argue that the available findings may be more convergent than many people believe. Drawing on a number of recent high-quality quasi-experimental and observational studies and on a reexamination of MTO findings across the MTO demonstration sites, we believe the evidence allows us to reject the null hypothesis that neighborhood environments never matter for children's outcomes—although the data also do not support the hypothesis that neighborhoods always matter. In our view, the key question for research and public policy is to learn more about the conditions under which neighborhoods matter for children's academic outcomes and why—either-or hypotheses are unlikely to capture the complex realities of social life, and indeed the data do not support them.

Our ability to answer the questions posed in this chapter is restricted by the limited number of studies that have employed sufficiently strong research designs to support inferences about neighborhood effects on children's outcomes, and by the fact that a disproportionately large share of the studies that meet this research-design threshold have been carried out in a single city, Chicago. With these qualifications in mind, we believe there is at least a suggestive case to be made that children's test scores may be most strongly affected by community violence or may respond nonlinearly to levels of concentrated neighborhood disadvantage or community violence. In other words, what may matter most for children's cognitive development is to avoid living in the most severely economically distressed or dangerous neighborhoods in the country—neighborhoods that are found in cities like Baltimore and Chicago but are less prevalent even in other major American cities such as Boston, Los Angeles, and New York City. Given the limitations of the available evidence, we offer these as hypotheses to be tested further, rather than as strong conclusions.

In the next section we review literature on neighborhood effects on children's academic outcomes, focusing mostly on the studies that employ strong research designs. The third section explores candidate explanations for why neighborhood environments might matter more for some children in certain circumstances than others. The fourth section discusses potential implications of our hypotheses about what features of neighborhood environments might be most relevant for children's academic outcomes.

NEIGHBORHOOD EFFECTS AND EDUCATION-RELATED OUTCOMES

The causal effects of different aspects of the neighborhood environment on schooling outcomes among children remain a subject of disagreement (Dietz 2002; Ellen and Turner 1997; Leventhal and Brooks-Gunn 2000; Sampson, Morenoff, and Gannon-Rowley 2002). Families choose their places of residence under more or less severe constraints, given family size, income, local housing prices, and varied levels of racial or other kinds of discrimination in the housing market. As a result of these differential constraints and family preferences, family characteristics are systematically associated with place of residence. Disentangling the causal effects of neighborhood environments from those difficult-to-measure attributes that may be relevant for both residential selection and the key behavioral outcomes of interest is a major challenge for this empirical literature. In light of these methodological concerns, and given the large number of good reviews of the neighborhood-effects literature that are already in circulation, we provide here a more selective discussion of particularly influential national studies of neighborhood effects on educational outcomes. We then focus on a more recent set of unusually strong observational or quasi-experimental studies, which happen to have all been carried out in Chicago, and the five-city HUD-funded MTO randomized housing mobility experiment.

Neighborhood Correlations on Schooling Outcomes

Two studies conducted with data from the Panel Study of Income Dynamics (PSID) provide evidence for strong neighborhood effects on children's test scores and schooling outcomes, while a third using the same data set but different methods finds null effects. David J. Harding (2003) uses the PSID data to compare outcomes of children who are matched with respect to their family background characteristics but who are living in different types of neighborhoods, and he finds strong evidence for important neighborhood effects. For blacks and nonblacks, there are only very slight differences in school dropout rates between youth living in low-poverty tracts (less than 10 percent poor) versus moderate poverty rates (10 to 20 percent poor) during adolescence. On the other hand, he finds large differences in dropout rates between those living in low- versus high-poverty (greater than 20 percent poor) census tracts during adolescence; these effects are equal to around twelve percentage points for both blacks and nonblacks, which are very large compared with the baseline dropout rate of 20 to 25 percent for youth in low-poverty tracts. Similarly, in a highly influential early study of neighborhood effects, Jeanne Brooks-Gunn and her colleagues (1993) find evidence that it is the absence of affluent adults within a census tract, rather than the presence of disadvantaged neighbors, that is most strongly predictive of children's test scores (see also Brooks-Gunn, Duncan, and Aber 1997a, 1997b).

The results from these studies contrast with the findings from Robert D. Plotnick and Saul Hoffman (1999), who use sibling fixed effects to study neighborhood effects on educational attainment, among other outcomes. Using variation in neighborhood characteristics among siblings in the PSID to estimate the effects of neighborhoods on the probability of receiving postsecondary education, the results show null effects for each measure of neighborhood disadvantage examined. This is one of several studies that have questioned the presence of neighborhood effects on methodological grounds, an issue we return to later.

Observational and Quasi-Experimental Findings from Chicago

To date four major studies of neighborhood effects on children's schooling outcomes have been carried out in Chicago. Three of the four studies find evidence of large gains in children's academic outcomes from living in less rather than more distressed neighborhoods. The one study that yields contradictory findings follows a sample of families who were involuntarily displaced by public-housing demolitions, which raises the possibility that whether families benefit from living in less distressed areas may depend on whether they want to live in such areas.

Perhaps the most extensive observational study of neighborhood effects to date is the Project on Human Development in Chicago Neighborhoods (PHDCN), which followed a racially and socioeconomically mixed sample of children ages zero to eighteen and living in Chicago as of 1995 (see table 12.1). A random sample of about six thousand children and their primary caregivers were interviewed from 1995 to 1997, and then again from 1997 to 1999 and 1999 to 2002.

Three of the authors (Sampson, Sharkey, and Raudenbush 2008) analyzed verbal cognitive ability among African American children living in neighborhoods that vary with respect to an index of neighborhood concentrated disadvantage.[2] This index is a weighted average of six census-tract characteristics: share of residents who receive welfare, share who are poor, share who are unemployed, share with female-headed households, share that are African American, and share that are under eighteen years old. The analysis compares outcomes for African American children living in census tracts that fall in the top quarter of the concentrated-disadvantage distribution (N = 237, average concentrated-disadvantage index value of 2.52) versus the rest of the sample (N = 543, average index value of 1.58). A key strength of the PHDCN design is that it follows children over

TABLE 12.1 Comparing Study Samples' Baseline Characteristics

	Gautreaux	Public-Housing Demolitions	PHDCN: African American	PHDCN: Hispanic	CHAC: Public Housing	CHAC: in MTO Tract at Baseline	MTO: Full Sample	MTO: Chicago Only	MTO: Chicago, Baltimore Only	MTO: NY, LA, Boston
Child age	8.47	10.34 (4.01)	9.01 (2.52)	8.93 (2.49)	7.76 (2.21)	7.67 (2.25)				
Household Head Characteristics										
Age	36.06		36.83 (9.30)	35.34 (6.93)	30.51 (6.64)	30.05 (6.33)	34.09 (9.08)	32.49 (8.78)	32.91 (8.78)	34.81 (9.18)
African American	1.00	1.00	0.98 (0.13)	0.01 (0.09)	0.98 (0.13)	0.99 (0.08)	0.67 (0.40)	0.99 (0.09)	0.99 (0.12)	0.47 (0.50)
Hispanic			0.00 (0.04)	0.95 (0.22)	0.01 (0.09)	0.00 (0.03)	0.29 (0.45)	0.01 (0.08)	0.01 (0.11)	0.46 (0.50)
Employed			0.53 (0.50)	0.52 (0.50)	0.35 (0.48)	0.33 (0.47)	0.27 (0.43)	0.27 (0.43)	0.26 (0.43)	0.27 (0.44)
Receiving welfare	50.03		0.48 (0.50)	0.23 (0.42)	0.83 (0.38)	0.85 (0.36)	0.74 (0.43)	0.81 (0.39)	0.81 (0.39)	0.71 (0.45)
Neighborhood Characteristics										
Tract poverty rate		0.84 (0.11)	0.27 (0.13)	0.22 (0.10)	0.61 (0.19)	0.71 (0.11)	0.50 (0.14)	0.66 (0.10)	0.58 (0.15)	0.45 (0.12)
Tract-share black			0.76 (0.29)	0.13 (0.18)	0.89 (0.24)	0.99 (0.06)	0.59 (0.33)	0.99 (0.04)	0.90 (0.23)	0.39 (0.21)
Concentrated-disadvantage index			2.20 (1.11)	0.70 (0.85)	3.00 (0.77)	3.39 (0.33)	2.18 (0.72)	3.16 (0.29)	2.74 (0.71)	1.84 (0.46)
Concentrated-disadvantage index (without percentage black)			1.93 (1.18)	0.84 (0.87)	2.25 (0.61)	2.56 (0.31)	1.69 (0.51)	2.34 (0.27)	1.99 (0.55)	1.51 (0.38)

Sources: Authors' compilation based on data from Jacob (2004), Ludwig et al. (2010), Rubinowitz and Rosenbaum (2000), Sampson, Sharkey, and Raudenbush (2008); and Sanbonmatsu et al. (2006).

Notes: This table reports baseline household and neighborhood characteristics for the different studies that we review: Gautreaux (Rubinowitz and Rosenbaum 2000); Chicago public-housing demolition study (Jacob 2004); Project on Human Development in Chicago Neighborhoods (PHDCN) (Sampson, Sharkey, and Raudenbush 2008); Chicago CHAC voucher study for families living in public housing at baseline (Ludwig et al. 2010); and results from the Moving to Opportunity (MTO) study for different cities (Sanbonmatsu et al. 2006). The concentrated-disadvantage index is a weighted average of several different census tract-level characteristics, including tract-share poor, tract-share black, tract-share unemployed, tract-share households headed by a female, tract-share on welfare, and share of the tract's population that is under age eighteen.

time, meaning the analysis can control for past residence within a high- or low-disadvantage neighborhood. The estimated effect of living in concentrated disadvantage is driven in large part by comparing the outcomes of children who stay in such neighborhoods over time with those of other children who move from very disadvantaged into less disadvantaged areas, or vice versa (that is, children who begin in low-disadvantage neighborhoods and move to high-disadvantage neighborhoods).[3]

The analysis suggests that living in the most disadvantaged quarter of Chicago neighborhoods (statistically, this is associated with roughly a one-standard-deviation difference in the scale of concentrated disadvantage) reduces children's verbal test scores by around one-quarter of a standard deviation (see figure 12.1). This effect size is roughly equivalent to missing one or two years of schooling. There is also some evidence of an age interaction, such that the influence of concentrated disadvantage may be greatest for younger children (Sampson 2008).

Although the PHDCN findings have been influential within the social sciences, at least as important for housing policy have been the findings from the Gautreaux mobility program in Chicago. This program was named after the plaintiff Dorothy Gautreaux in a 1966 racial discrimination lawsuit filed against the Chicago Housing Authority (CHA) and HUD. The lawsuit charged discrimination on the basis of the heavy concentration of African American families in public-housing projects located in high-poverty areas. The U.S. Supreme Court agreed in 1976 and ordered the CHA to provide housing vouchers to African American public-housing residents that could be used only in neighborhoods in the city or suburbs that were less than 30 percent black. Units were assigned to eligible families on a waiting list of approximately two thousand families a year (Rubinowitz and

FIGURE 12.1   *Summary of Effects of Different Studies on Children's Verbal Test Scores*

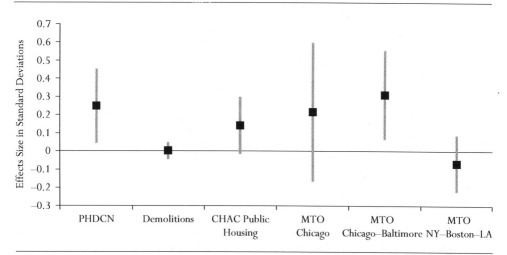

Source: Authors' compilations based on data from Jacob (2004), Ludwig et al. (2010), Sampson, Sharkey, and Raudenbush (2008), and Sanbonmatsu et al. (2006).
Notes: The X-axis lists the name of each study: Project on Human Development in Chicago Neighborhoods (PHDCN) (Sampson, Sharkey, and Raudenbush 2008); Chicago public-housing demolition study (Jacob 2004); Chicago CHAC voucher study for families living in public housing at baseline (Ludwig et al. 2010); and results from the Moving to Opportunity (MTO) study for different cities (Sanbonmatsu et al. 2006). The Y-axis shows the estimated effect of changing neighborhoods on children's verbal test scores in each of the studies, expressed as an effect size (share of a standard deviation in the test score distribution, so that an effect size of 0.2 means children living in less distressed areas have average scores about one-fifth of a standard deviation higher than children living in more distressed areas). For the mobility studies, we are presenting effects of actually moving through the program (the effects of treatment on the treated, or TOT).

Rosenbaum 2000). Some of those apartments were in areas of Chicago that were poor and segregated, but improving, while other apartments were located in low-poverty, predominantly white or integrated suburban areas (Mendenhall, DeLuca, and Duncan 2006).

A 1988 follow-up survey of 342 families who used Gautreaux vouchers found that moving to the Chicago suburbs versus other parts of the city was associated with significant improvements in young adults' later educational attainment. Compared with the surveyed students who remained in the city of Chicago, suburban movers were four times less likely to have dropped out of school (5 percent versus 20 percent); more likely to be in a college track in high school (40 percent versus 24 percent); twice as likely to attend any college (54 percent versus 21 percent); and almost seven times as likely to attend a four-year college (27 percent versus 4 percent). The only measure for which the suburban students did not appear to be doing significantly better than the city students was their grade-point average, which could reflect higher grading standards in suburban schools (Rubinowitz and Rosenbaum 2000, 134–36).

Although the Gautreaux program has been extremely influential, the study was nevertheless not a true randomized experiment. Families may have had some choice in whether they accepted the first apartment offered to them, and indeed there is some evidence that the baseline characteristics of families who ended up in the suburbs are systematically different from those who ended up in the city (Mendenhall, DeLuca, and Duncan 2006; Votruba and Kling 2009). This has made researchers nervous that the Gautreaux city and suburban movers may have been different with respect to preexisting unobserved characteristics as well, which could lead analysts to confound the causal effects of suburban moves with the influence of these unmeasured attributes that may affect outcomes as well as the likelihood of moving to the suburbs.

However, a more recent experimental study of Chicago's housing voucher program, which relies on true random assignment of families to different neighborhood environments, seems to support the basic conclusion from Gautreaux (Ludwig et al. 2010). In July 1997 the private firm running the city's voucher program, CHAC, Inc., opened the city's housing-voucher program wait list for the first time in a dozen years. A total of 82,607 income-eligible households, almost all of whom were black (see table 12.1 and, for more details, online appendix table 12.A1[4]), applied and were then randomly assigned to the program wait list. Starting in August 2007, the families were offered vouchers in order of their wait-list position. Roughly 4,625 families were offered vouchers in the first year of the program, and by May 2003 around 18,110 families had been offered housing vouchers, at which point CHAC was over-leased and stopped offering vouchers.

Jens Ludwig and his colleagues (2010) focus on families who were living in public housing at the time they applied to CHAC for a voucher; the analytic sample is composed of children who are four to eleven years old at baseline. Families who received a voucher experienced changes in neighborhood environments that are fairly similar to those observed among MTO families, a point that we discuss in more detail later. These voucher-supported moves increased children's achievement test scores in reading and math on the Iowa Tests of Basic Skills (ITBS). The effect of being offered a housing voucher, known in the program evaluation literature as the intent to treat (ITT) effect, was equal to around 0.05 and 0.08 standard deviations for reading and math scores, respectively. Given that only approximately one-quarter of CHAC families with children relocated using a voucher, the effects of actually leasing up with a voucher (the effects of treatment on the treated, or TOT) and the effects of voucher receipt are on the order of 0.2 and 0.3 standard deviations for reading and math, respectively (see figures 12.1 and 12.2).

Brian A. Jacob (2004) uses variation in neighborhood conditions generated by the demolition of public housing in Chicago and finds little systematic evidence of any achievement test score changes among children. His analytic sample consists of around 10,500 mostly African American children living in Chicago public housing in the mid-1990s, when the CHA began to use federal

FIGURE 12.2   *Summary of Effects of Different Studies on Children's Math Test Scores*

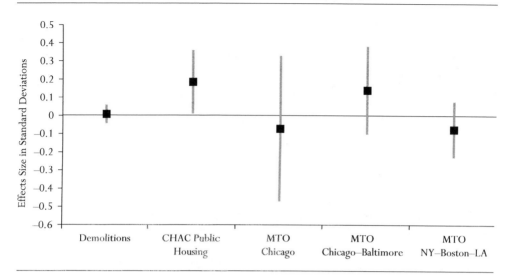

Source: Authors' compilations based on data from Jacob (2004), Ludwig et al. (2010), and Sanbonmatsu et al. (2006).
Notes: The X-axis lists the name of each study: Chicago public-housing demolition study (Jacob 2004); Chicago CHAC voucher study for families living in public housing at baseline (Ludwig et al. 2010); and results from the Moving to Opportunity (MTO) study for different cities (Sanbonmatsu et al. 2006). The Y-axis shows the estimated effect of changing neighborhoods on children's math test scores in each of the studies, expressed as an effect size (share of a standard deviation in the test score distribution, so that an effect size of 0.2 means children living in less distressed areas have average scores about one-fifth of a standard deviation higher than children living in more distressed areas). For the mobility studies, we are presenting effects of actually moving through the program (the effects of treatment on the treated, or TOT).

funding to demolish housing projects. Jacob argues that the timing of which projects were demolished first was driven by random events at the projects (for example, broken pipes and so on). Public-housing demolitions led children to move into census tracts with poverty rates that were about fifteen percentage points lower than those of children who stayed in public housing (and who have an average tract poverty rate of 68 percent). Yet the difference in reading and math scores on the Iowa tests for children who did versus who did not move is less than 0.01 standard deviations. The 95 percent confidence interval around this estimate enabled Jacob to rule out impacts that are any larger than about 0.05 standard deviations (figures 12.1 and 12.2).

One candidate explanation for why the children in Jacob's sample do not show the same gains in test scores as children in the other three Chicago studies noted here could be that only families who want to live in less economically distressed areas may benefit. Data from the MTO study discussed next reveal that only around one-quarter of eligible public-housing families volunteered for that mobility program (Goering, Feins, and Richardson 2003), which suggests that a majority—perhaps a large majority—of families who were displaced by public-housing demolitions may not have wanted to move. Of course, in any comparison of results across such a small number of studies, alternative explanations for differences in study findings are also possible.

Moving to Opportunity (MTO)

Motivated by the suggestive findings of Chicago's Gautreaux mobility program, in the early 1990s HUD decided to fund a large-scale randomized housing-mobility experiment known as Moving to

Opportunity (MTO). Eligibility for MTO was limited to families living at baseline in public housing in selected high-poverty census tracts in five U.S. cities (Baltimore, Boston, Chicago, Los Angeles, and New York City). Starting in 1994, HUD began randomly assigning eligible low-income families with young children who volunteered to participate in MTO into three different groups: the experimental group was offered a housing voucher that could only be used in neighborhoods where the poverty rate was 10 percent or less according to the 1990 census and was given relocation counseling assistance; the Section 8 housing voucher group was offered standard housing vouchers that could be used for any unit that met basic standards but were not restricted geographically; and a control group, which did not receive any special MTO funding but could receive any of the regularly available social services for which they would have been eligible.

In total, 4,600 families signed up between 1994 and 1997 to be randomly assigned to one of the three groups. Of households assigned to the MTO experimental group, 47 percent used an MTO voucher to relocate to a low-poverty census tract, while 62 percent assigned to the regular Section 8 housing voucher group relocated through MTO. Compliance rates vary across MTO cities.

The interim MTO study found no overall statistically significant impacts on either broad reading or broad math scores on the Woodcock-Johnson Revised tests measured four to seven years after baseline (Sanbonmatsu et al. 2006). Data on risky behaviors, delinquency, and other youth outcomes revealed sharp gender differences in MTO impacts (Kling, Liebman, and Katz 2007; Kling, Ludwig, and Katz 2005). MTO moves generated beneficial changes for females and, on balance, adverse behavioral changes for males. For test scores, there were no statistically significant changes for either boys or girls (Sanbonmatsu et al. 2006). There were also no statistically significant differences in MTO impacts on test scores by age overall, although the youngest MTO children who were under age six at baseline were only beginning their school years.

However, when we look separately at Chicago combined with the one other almost entirely black demonstration site in MTO, Baltimore, there is some evidence of impacts of neighborhood changes on children's achievement test scores. Researchers are usually (and appropriately) cautious about estimating too many subgroup effects because of concerns about false positives—if one generates estimates for, say, twenty independent subgroups, one would expect to see an estimated effect for at least one subgroup that is statistically significant at the usual 5 percent (that is, one-in-twenty) level purely by chance. But there is an important substantive justification for looking separately by site in MTO, given the evidence noted previously for neighborhood effects in Chicago (at least from three of the four Chicago studies). When we generate separate estimates for the set of African American children enrolled in the Baltimore and Chicago demonstration sites, the treatment on the treated (TOT) effect is equal to 0.3 standard deviations in reading, with mixed results in math (see figures 12.1 and 12.2).[5] That the impacts are more pronounced in reading than math is itself interesting, given that most studies of school-based interventions tend to find larger impacts on math than on reading.

UNDERSTANDING VARIATION IN NEIGHBORHOOD EFFECTS ON CHILDREN

The research literature summarized in the previous section enables us to reject the null hypothesis that neighborhoods never matter. But the mixed pattern of findings across studies seems to also allow us to reject the alternative null hypothesis that neighborhoods always matter. In our view, a key question for both social science and public policy is why and for whom neighborhood environments seem to matter for academic outcomes, and what the implications of that variation in treatment effects might be for policy efforts designed to improve the life chances of some of our nation's most disadvantaged children.

In this section we try to narrow down the set of candidate explanations for the variation documented in the previous section in findings about when and how neighborhoods affect children's reading or math achievement test scores. Our ability to convincingly determine which explanations are most important is limited by the small number of very strong study findings and the even smaller number of study sites and independent data samples from which results have been generated.

Before presenting a new analysis that attempts to adjudicate among different potential explanations, we begin by highlighting some basic evidence that runs counter to several plausible candidate explanations for why results might vary across studies. Variation in findings does not seem to rest with methodological problems such as selection bias in observational studies, given that we find support for neighborhood effects on children's test scores even in studies that use random assignment of families to different mobility conditions. Study results do not seem likely to vary because of slight differences in the age of the samples being studied, given that there is considerable overlap in the age of the different study samples and because age differences in responses to neighborhood environments are not large enough to explain the differences across studies. An alternative explanation is that just a few particularly distressed public-housing projects might be responsible for all the findings of neighborhood effects on children's test scores, yet the PHDCN provides evidence for neighborhood effects among a sample that includes few public-housing families. It would be surprising if the private-market housing in which these families lived was of lower quality than the public housing in which control families were living in the Boston, Los Angeles, and New York City demonstration sites. A more subtle hypothesis is that differences in findings within MTO could stem from variation across sites in how the experiment was carried out, but this explanation also does not seem to fit the data very well.[6]

In what follows, we show that the variation across studies in findings does not seem to be due to differences in neighborhood effects on children according to race or ethnic group, nor to differences across studies in the size of the changes that children experience with respect to potentially key neighborhood attributes, including local school quality, racial composition, and concentrated disadvantage more generally. The evidence we produce does not allow us to rule out the possibility that there may be nonlinearities in the relationship between concentrated neighborhood disadvantage and children's academic outcomes, meaning that the effect of a given unit change in neighborhood disadvantage may be greater for children whose starting position is a relatively more disadvantaged neighborhood environment. We also cannot rule out the possibility that different study samples experience differently sized changes in neighborhood violence rates or that there are nonlinearities in the relationship between children's test scores and exposure to violence in the community.

Variations in Vulnerability Across Demographic Groups

One candidate explanation for the apparent discrepancy in results across studies is differences in study populations. Table 12.1 shows that all of the Chicago samples are almost entirely African American, as is the set of MTO families in the Baltimore site (the one other MTO city besides Chicago where we find evidence that moving to less distressed areas increases children's test scores). Put differently, some of the strongest empirical evidence for neighborhood effects on children's test scores comes from studies of African American samples, who might be more vulnerable to neighborhood influences than Hispanic or white families, perhaps because of higher rates of single-parent households.[7] In the MTO study, the proportion of never-married adults at baseline was higher in Baltimore and Chicago (68.5 to 72.7 percent) than in the other three sites (54.5 to 57.2 percent). Two-parent households may mitigate any adverse influences of living in a distressed neighborhood by providing more parental supervision, which could reduce exposure to neighborhood influences (if children who are more supervised are subject to earlier or stricter curfews) or ameliorate adverse neighborhood influences by, for example, intervening at the first sign of trouble and providing academic or social support. Note that although African Americans in Chicago and Baltimore are similar with respect to marital status to African Americans at the other MTO sites, there are differences in baseline characteristics, suggesting that African Americans in Baltimore and Chicago were slightly more disadvantaged than African Americans at the other three sites in terms of work status, teen parenting, and welfare receipt (see also online appendix table 12.A1).

We can test and reject this hypothesis with the MTO data by pooling data from the three MTO sites where there is racial and ethnic diversity in the program populations—Boston, Los Angeles, and New York City—and by examining whether there is evidence for MTO effects on test scores for African Americans in these cities but not for Hispanic children. We find that there is no evidence for test score gains for either blacks or Hispanics in these three MTO cities. A different way to test this hypothesis is to use the PHDCN data, which—unlike samples studied in the Chicago MTO site, the Chicago CHAC voucher study, or the Chicago public-housing demolition study—does sample Hispanics as well as African Americans. Within the Chicago PHDCN data, we find at least suggestive evidence that living in a disadvantaged neighborhood may have adverse impacts on the verbal scores for Hispanic as well as African American children (see online appendix figure 12.A1).

Local School Quality

Because most public schools draw their students from the local community, it is plausible that much or even most of the variation in test scores of children who live in different neighborhoods could be due to variation in the quality of schools. Neighborhoods might vary in the quality of their local schools because of differences in political power in securing resources from centralized public school bureaucracies or because many teachers tend to prefer teaching at schools that serve more affluent student bodies (Hanushek, Kain, and Rivkin 2004; Hanushek and Rivkin 2007), which might make it hard to recruit and retain the best teachers in high-poverty areas.

One hypothesis to explain differences in study findings, then, is differences in the degree to which variation in neighborhood environments is associated with the underlying quality of the schools that children attend. Attention to this hypothesis is motivated in part by the fact that the Gautreaux mobility program sent some families to the suburbs, where schools are thought to be much better than Chicago public schools, while table 12.2 shows that the children who moved to less distressed areas with MTO vouchers still attended struggling schools. For example, in the full MTO sample, children in the treatment group who moved using a voucher on average attended schools in the 25th percentile of the statewide ranking. This is around eight percentage points higher than we estimate their schools would have been had they not moved, but it still suggests that these children were attending fairly low-performing schools. The minimal change in school quality induced by MTO led Will Dobbie and Roland G. Fryer (2009, 22) to conclude, "A better community, as measured by poverty rate, does not significantly raise test scores if school quality remains essentially unchanged."

Table 12.2 shows that children in MTOs Chicago and Baltimore samples experienced larger changes in the socioeconomic and racial composition of their schools than did children in Boston, Los Angeles, and New York City, but they did not experience larger gains in the one measure of school quality available—the statewide ranking of schools on reading and math tests.[8] In the Chicago CHAC voucher study, children who moved to a less distressed area had higher test scores than the control group despite no gains in the share of children scoring above national norms.

TABLE 12.2   *Control Means and Effects of Voucher-Assisted Residential Mobility at Follow-Up on Average School Characteristics*

	CHAC: Public Housing at Baseline	CHAC: In MTO Census Tract at Baseline	MTO: Full Sample	MTO: Chicago Only	MTO: Chicago and Baltimore Only	MTO: NY, LA, and Boston
Percent black						
Control mean	0.899	0.954	0.557	0.914	0.902	0.343
Impact of voucher move	−0.048	−0.022	−0.049*	−0.082	−0.096*	−0.032
	(0.025)	(0.027)	(0.022)	(0.062)	(0.041)	(0.023)
Percent Hispanic						
Control mean	0.075	0.031	0.307	0.042	0.029	0.479
Impact of voucher move	0.034	0.009	−0.053*	0.013	0.004	−0.076*
	(0.020)	(0.016)	(0.017)	(0.035)	(0.020)	(0.023)
Percent receiving free lunch						
Control mean	0.929	0.936	0.726	NA	0.699	0.733
Impact of voucher move	−0.373*	−0.035*	−0.093*	NA	−0.191*	−0.068*
	(0.008)	(0.010)	(0.021)	NA	(0.041)	(0.023)
Percent at or above national norms (CHAC) and state percentile rankings (MTO)						
Control mean	0.304	0.282	0.169	0.104	0.128	0.194
Impact of voucher move	−0.021	0.014	0.075*	0.080*	0.066*	0.085*
	(0.013)	(0.021)	(0.018)	(0.038)	(0.029)	(0.022)

Source: Authors' compilation based on data from Ludwig et al. (2010) and Sanbonmatsu et al. (2006).
Notes: This table reports the effects of relocating using a housing voucher on different school characteristics reported at left; that is, each cell in the table represents the difference in average school characteristics for children who moved with a voucher versus the average for children in the control group who would have moved had their families been assigned a voucher (the effect of treatment on the treated, or TOT). The voucher effect cells report the difference in average characteristics with the standard error underneath reported in parentheses. Each column reports results for a different study or sample within a study: Chicago CHAC voucher study for families living in public housing at baseline (Ludwig et al. 2010); and results from the Moving to Opportunity (MTO) study for different cities (Sanbonmatsu et al. 2006).
*Statistically significant at the 5 percent level.

Recognizing the limitations of this school quality measure, the results in table 12.2 taken at face value would nevertheless seem to argue against the hypothesis by Dobbie and Fryer (2009) that absent changes in school quality, test scores are unresponsive to changes in neighborhood environments.

Neighborhood Racial Composition

A different hypothesis for the variation in impacts on children's test scores comes from differences revealed by the studies in the change that families experienced in neighborhood racial segregation. Perhaps most famously, the Gautreaux mobility program in Chicago was required to move families into racially mixed neighborhoods. In contrast, MTO focused on moving families into lower-poverty areas, which it did. MTO did not induce major changes in neighborhood racial composition among participating families (table 12.3; see also web appendix table 12.A3).

Some have argued that the lack of change in neighborhood racial segregation undermines the MTO study's capacity to provide a rigorous test of the neighborhood-effects hypothesis, given that racial composition might itself be a crucial aspect of a child's neighborhood (Clampet-Lundquist

TABLE 12.3   *Control Means and Effects of Voucher-Assisted Mobility at Follow-Up—*
Neighborhood Characteristics

	CHAC: Public Housing at Baseline	CHAC: In MTO Census Tract at Baseline	MTO: Full Sample	MTO: Chicago Only	MTO: Chicago and Baltimore Only	MTO: NY, LA, and Boston
Tract poverty rate						
Control mean	0.481	0.467	0.392	0.419	0.387	0.394
Impact of voucher move	−0.274*	−0.336	−0.190*	−0.183*	−0.140*	−0.213*
	(0.094)	(0.259)	(0.019)	(0.069)	(0.041)	(0.018)
Tract share black						
Control mean	0.837	0.912	0.548	0.857	0.848	0.371
Impact of voucher move	0.028	−0.112	−0.022	0.038	−0.059	−0.009
	(0.091)	(0.287)	(0.028)	(0.086)	(0.057)	(0.029)
Concentrated-disadvantage index						
Control mean	2.057	2.170	1.869	2.307	2.192	1.678
Impact of voucher move	−0.548*	−1.012	−0.488*	−0.404	−0.397*	−0.528*
	(0.258)	(0.809)	(0.067)	(0.240)	(0.143)	(0.064)
Concentrated-disadvantage index (without percentage black)						
Control mean	1.357	1.408	1.409	1.59	1.482	1.366
Impact of voucher move	−0.572*	−0.918	−0.465*	−0.436	−0.348*	−0.516*
	(0.215)	(0.648)	(0.052)	(0.189)	(0.110)	(0.051)

Source: Authors' compilation based on data from Ludwig et al. (2010) and Sanbonmatsu et al. (2006).
Notes: This table reports the effects of relocating using a housing voucher on different neighborhood characteristics reported at left; that is, each cell in the table represents the difference in average neighborhood characteristics for children who moved with a voucher versus the average for those children in the control group who would have moved had their families been assigned a voucher (the effect of treatment on the treated, or TOT). The voucher effect cells report the difference in average characteristics with the standard error underneath reported in parentheses. Each column reports results for a different study and/or sample within a study: Chicago CHAC voucher study for families living in public housing at baseline (Ludwig et al. 2010); and results from the Moving to Opportunity (MTO) study for different cities (Sanbonmatsu et al. 2006). The concentrated-disadvantage index is a weighted average of several different census tract-level characteristics including tract-share poor, tract-share black, tract-share unemployed, tract-share households headed by a female, tract-share on welfare, and share of the tract's population that is under age eighteen.
*Statistically significant at the 5 percent level.

and Massey 2008).[9] However, the MTO experiment had little effect on racial composition anywhere. Table 12.3 shows that families in the MTO Chicago and Baltimore sites did not experience significantly greater changes in neighborhood racial segregation, despite starting in neighborhoods with much higher concentrations of African Americans, than did families in the other three MTO sites. In those other three sites, children did not experience any gains in achievement test scores as a result of their MTO moves. Since the MTO experiment had little effect on racial composition anywhere, it cannot explain site differences. Table 12.3 also shows that the share of the census tract that is black did not decline for families in the Chicago CHAC voucher study when compared to controls (nor did the share of the census tract that is minority, broadly defined), and yet these moves were still sufficient to increase children's achievement test scores. Although we do not have a great many data points, the available evidence suggests that changes in neighborhood racial composition are not necessary for improved educational outcomes and do not explain the divergent findings across sites.

Comparing black to black *black*

Concentrated Neighborhood Disadvantage

Although differences in the size of the changes in neighborhood racial segregation do not seem to explain variation across studies in achievement-test-score gains, other aspects of neighborhood disadvantage may. What can be inferred from table 12.1 is that almost all of the best empirical evidence to date for neighborhood effects on children's learning comes from studying African American families living in neighborhoods that are much more disadvantaged than what we see in other cities. The next-to-last row of table 12.1 shows, for each of our study samples, the values of the concentrated-disadvantage index used by Sampson, Sharkey, and Raudenbush (2008). This measures a weighted average of a neighborhood's poverty, the percentage of residents who are black, the percentage adults who are unemployed, the percentage of households with a female head, the percentage residents on welfare, and the percentage of residents under age eighteen (see online appendix table 12.A1 for details). We focus on the concentrated-disadvantage index in order to have a consistent measure of neighborhood environments in different studies. We note that the neighborhood concentrated-disadvantage index has a strong negative correlation with the presence of affluent residents, which is the neighborhood measure that seems particularly predictive of youth outcomes in the analyses by Brooks-Gunn and her colleagues (1993).[10]

The mean value of the neighborhood concentrated-disadvantage index for the public-housing families in the new Chicago housing voucher sample studied by Ludwig et al. (2010) was 3.39, 3.16 for the Chicago MTO sample, and 2.74 for the pooled samples of families in the Baltimore and Chicago MTO sites. By comparison, the average value of the concentrated-disadvantage index in the three other MTO sites (Boston, Los Angeles, and New York City) was just 1.84, and it was 2.20 for the African American PHDCN sample. Much, but certainly not all, of the difference in concentrated disadvantage in Baltimore and Chicago is due to the substantially greater level of racial segregation in those cities. This can be seen in the last row in table 12.1, where we recalculate the concentrated neighborhood disadvantage by excluding the measure of the percentage of black residents in the census tract.

Table 12.3 shows that samples that experienced the largest changes in achievement test scores did not experience unusually large changes in concentrated disadvantage. Figures 12.1 and 12.2 show that achievement-test score gains are largest for families in the Baltimore and Chicago MTO sites, families in the new Chicago housing voucher study, and African American families in the PHDCN. The changes in the concentrated neighborhood disadvantage scale experienced by families in these three samples are −0.397, −0.548, and −0.935, respectively (second-to-last row, table 12.3). The first two numbers are not substantially different from what we see in Boston, Los Angeles, and New York City, the three MTO sites, where there are no detectable test score impacts (−0.528). The fact that Baltimore and Chicago appear different from our other study samples with respect to baseline concentrated-disadvantage levels but not changes leads to a hypothesis that neighborhood effects on children's outcomes may be nonlinear. The web appendix discusses several statistical tests that we have carried out to formally test for nonlinearities. Although our analyses do not yield clear, convincing evidence for such nonlinearities, it is important to note that our tests have relatively weak statistical power.

little effect

Exposure to Violent Crime in the Community

In addition to the possibility of nonlinearities between concentrated neighborhood disadvantage and children's test scores, we cannot reject another possible explanation for variation in impacts: exposure to community violence. The two MTO cities in which we find evidence for neighborhood effects on children's outcomes, Baltimore and Chicago, have greatly elevated levels of crime and violence compared with the other three MTO cities. For example, 1998 homicide rates per 100,000 were 47.1 in Baltimore and 25.6 in Chicago, compared with 6.1 in Boston, 11.8 in Los Angeles, and 8.6 in New York City (see the web appendix for additional details). This raises the possibility that, as with concentrated disadvantage, there may be a nonlinear relationship between exposure to extremely violent neighborhood settings and children's test scores. Unfortunately, it is even more difficult to test for nonlinearity in the effects of crime or violence because of data limitations and the associated difficulty in making comparisons of crime data across cities. Cities vary considerably in how they measure crime rates: for Baltimore the data are from 9 police beats, from 11 for Boston, from 18 for Los Angeles, from 76 for New York City, and from 279 for Chicago.[11]

Bearing these differences in mind, it is possible to examine how changes in exposure to area-level crime rates relates to changes in test scores. Figure 12.3 plots the averages of both measures separately for each MTO site and each randomized mobility group (experimental, Section 8, and control).[12] All statistical analyses of MTO data always compare the average outcomes of the randomized mobility groups within sites (that is, control for site-fixed effects). Therefore, for each data point, we have subtracted the overall mean of beat-level violence in that MTO city. The line fit through these data points in the figure shows the correlation between beat-level violence and children's test scores, and shows that there is a negative relationship between beat-level violent crime and children's test scores, that this negative relationship is larger for reading than for math, and that this relationship is driven by the Baltimore and Chicago sites (as seen by the regression lines that are fitted by dropping data from those two MTO sites).[13]

Sharkey's (2009) analysis of data from the PHDCN provides some confirming support for the link between neighborhood violence and achievement using variation between Chicago neighborhoods at different points in time. He compares the outcomes of children in the PHDCN within the same neighborhood who were interviewed and tested at different times, and he finds that African American children interviewed within a week of a homicide in their neighborhood had achievement test scores around one-half standard deviation lower than other children, suggesting a large acute effect of violence on achievement scores. Because these analyses compare outcomes for children living in the same neighborhood (that is, from models that control for neighborhood fixed effects), the results are not simply picking up the fact that test scores are generally lower in some neighborhoods than others within the city of Chicago.[14] Additional support comes from Jeffrey T. Grogger's (1997) analysis of High School and Beyond, which suggests that high school graduation rates are lower in schools in which principals report serious problems with crime and violence.

CONCLUSION

Most of the empirical evidence supporting neighborhood effects on children's educational outcomes came from observational studies such as the PHDCN, which follow families wherever they wind up living, or quasi-experimental studies of government mobility programs such as Gautreaux. In contrast, the one randomized mobility study, HUD's MTO demonstration, found no detectable evidence on children's achievement test scores, on average, across the five program sites (Baltimore, Boston, Chicago, Los Angeles, and New York City).

This has led to a variety of different hypotheses that seek to reconcile the apparently conflicting evidence. Since the Gatureaux and PHDCN studies show large gains in educational outcomes when comparing families who live in neighborhoods with different levels of racial as well as economic segregation, but the MTO housing vouchers did not result in large changes in racial segregation, some researchers conclude that the most important feature of neighborhood environments for children's learning must be racial segregation. Since many of the MTO examined in the five-year follow-up were already of school age when their families relocated, other researchers hypothesize

FIGURE 12.3   *Relationship Between Beat-Level Violent Crime and Children's Reading and Math Test Scores in MTO Demonstration Cities and Randomized Mobility Groups*

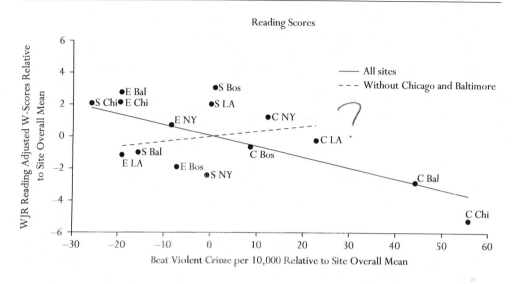

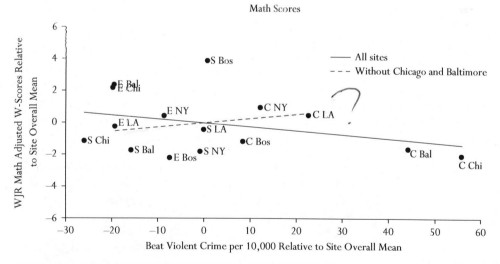

Source: Authors' compilations based on Sanbonmatsu (2006), and Ludwig and Klein (2007).

Notes: The figures plot the average beat- or district-level violent crime rate (X-axis) and average Woodcock-Johnson Revised reading score (top panel) or math score (bottom panel) for MTO families broken out by whether families were assigned to the MTO experimental, Section 8 only, or control groups, and by site (Baltimore, Boston, Chicago, Los Angeles, and New York City). We rescale each group's test score and beat violent crime rate by subtracting off the average values for test scores and beat violent crime rates within that MTO site. The solid lines in each figure show the correlation between beat violent crime rates and test scores implied by the fifteen data points (that is, the regression line fit through these points), while the dashed line in each figure shows what happens to this relationship when we drop the data points for the Baltimore and Chicago sites.

3 hypotheses

that these children may be unresponsive to changes in neighborhood environments once they are no longer at a young age. A third hypothesis stems from the observation that the MTO program led to relatively little change in school characteristics and suggests the possibility that neighborhood environments by themselves may not have much affect on children's achievement-test scores.

Our reexamination of the available data plus results from a new housing-voucher lottery in Chicago lead us to reject the hypothesis that neighborhood environments have no effect on children's achievement-test scores. Our reading of the evidence suggests (1) that moving children to a different neighborhood can improve their achievement-test scores even if there are no changes in the level of neighborhood racial segregation or in school quality, and (2) that even children who have already spent many years living in segregated, economically distressed, and dangerous neighborhoods can experience gains in cognitive outcomes from moving.

But moving to a less distressed neighborhood does not inevitably produce this outcome—treatment-by-city interactions seem to be an important part of the story. Namely, moves to less distressed areas in Chicago and Baltimore appear to improve children's test scores, but that does not appear to be the case in the other three MTO sites of Boston, Los Angeles, and New York City. This does not mean neighborhood effects in general are not present in the latter three cities; it may be that the kinds of changes in neighborhood environments that MTO fostered did not significantly change educational test scores but did affect other outcomes.

One possible explanation for this pattern is nonlinearity in the relationship between neighborhood concentrated disadvantage and children's achievement-test scores. This hypothesis is bolstered by the observation that baseline levels of concentrated disadvantage are much higher in Baltimore and Chicago than in the other three cities (though the treatment dose in terms of the change in neighborhood attributes does not systematically vary from city to city). Our direct tests of the nonlinearity hypothesis have relatively low statistical power. Consequently, our argument for that explanation is mostly circumstantial. We can also circumstantially argue that exposure to violence explains variation in children's academic achievement; Baltimore and Chicago have much higher rates of violence than the other three MTO cities, and the MTO treatment group assignment generates larger changes in exposure to violence in Baltimore and Chicago as well, although from much higher levels to begin with. In addition, the PHDCN study provides evidence that test scores are lower for children tested within a week of a homicide in their neighborhood than are those of children from the same neighborhood assessed a longer time after the most recent local homicide.

It is hoped that the evidence presented here will provoke a change in the conversation around neighborhood effects on children's learning and refocus attention away from a narrow examination of the role of schools and neighborhood racial segregation, toward a broader examination of the reasons that neighborhood influences might vary across cities. Of particular importance is the possibility that neighborhood effects on children are nonlinear or may be related to community violence.

If future research supports the importance of community violence or the existence of a nonlinear relationship between community disadvantage and children's school performance, a potential recommendation would be for policymakers to focus scarce housing resources on trying to deconcentrate neighborhoods in the United States, of the sort found in Baltimore and Chicago, that show the most severe concentrated disadvantage. The existence of nonlinear relationships between concentrated disadvantage and children's outcomes suggests that moving poor children out of concentrated-disadvantage neighborhoods would lead to an increase in their overall average achievement. This would be consistent with Jonathan Guryan's (2004) finding that court-ordered school desegregation, which started in the late 1960s, led to declines in black dropout rates with no detectable changes in schooling outcomes for whites. If more were known about the specific aspects of concentrated disadvantage that were most harmful to children, then in principle community-development strategies or mixed-income housing as well as residential mobility strategies could be employed to help improve the life chances of poor children in these areas. Such policies might also require subsidies, either to nonpoor families in exchange for their living alongside poor families in mixed-income developments, or to poor families in exchange for their making relatively longer-distance moves into lower-poverty neighborhoods. In any case, evidence for nonlinearities in neighborhood effects would suggest the great importance of prioritizing the use of the most scarce housing-policy resources in the most distressed areas At present, just 28 percent of income-eligible poor families receive assistance under existing means-tested housing programs (Olsen 2003).

If community violence is confirmed as a key contributor to children's cognitive development, one implication might be that policymakers interested in children's cognitive development and success in school should expand their focus outside of the school setting and consider policies relating to the provision of effective policing and the provision of safe community environments for children. Shifts in police practices or increased policing, done well, may achieve short-term changes in the developmental quality of some of our nation's most disadvantaged neighborhoods (Evans and Owens 2007; Sherman 2003). John J. Donohue and Ludwig (2007) argue that each additional dollar spent on policing generates from four to six dollars in benefits to society just from the increase in well-being of community residents, setting aside the possibility of any developmental benefits to children. Interventions designed to provide safe and enriching environments for children, both within and outside the schools, also represent promising policy options. The Harlem Children's Zone is the best-known example of a program that has attempted to provide a "conveyor belt" of services that would enhance the environment for an entire community of children, but only the school component of the program has been evaluated at this point (Dobbie and Fryer 2009; see also Tough 2008). But perhaps the main point, and a key theme underlying this entire volume, is that some promising ways to improve children's schooling outcomes may have little to do with schools directly.

This chapter was prepared for the Brookings Institution's Project on Social Inequality and Educational Disadvantage: New Evidence on How Families, Neighborhoods, and Labor Markets Affect Educational Opportunities for American Children, with support from the Russell Sage Foundation and Spencer Foundation. Thanks to Julian Betts, Rebecca Blank, Greg Duncan, Lawrence Katz, Jeffrey Kling, Richard Murnane, Steven Rivkin, and seminar participants at the Brookings Institution for helpful comments. Thanks also to Ryan Gillette and Matt Sciandra for terrific research assistance. Data for the Moving to Opportunity (MTO) analyses were provided by the U.S. Department of Housing and Urban Development (HUD). The contents of this chapter are the views of the authors and do not necessarily reflect the views or policies of HUD or the U.S. government. The authors are listed in alphabetical order; all opinions, and any errors, are of course our own.

NOTES

Online appendix available at: http://www.russellsage.org/duncan_murnane_online_appendix.pdf.

1. There is some controversy about how to measure school dropout rates. The figure we cite is calculated as the fraction of students enrolled in school at age thirteen who go on to drop out of school by age nineteen (see also Allensworth and Easton 2001).

2. This measure of verbal cognitive ability is a composite of the Wechsler Intelligence Scale for Children vocabulary test and the Wide Range Achievement Test reading examination. Math ability was not assessed in the PHDCN.

3. All of the time-varying covariates in the PHDCN analysis are controlled using inverse probability of treatment weighting (IPTW) as introduced by James M. Robins, Miguel Ángel Hernan, and Babette Brumback (2000) and extended to the multilevel setting by Guanglei Hong and Stephen W. Raudenbush (2008). Like related

forms of propensity-score matching, inverse probability of treatment may be susceptible to bias from unobserved characteristics, but it has the advantage over standard least-squares regression of being less sensitive to assumptions about the functional form of the relationship between the observable covariates and the outcomes of interest. IPTW gives relatively low weight in the analysis to people who receive the "treatment" (concentrated neighborhood disadvantage) that they are predicted to have a very high likelihood of receiving. Previous residence in a concentrated-disadvantage neighborhood is a very strong predictor for future residence in such a neighborhood, so that the observations that receive the largest weights in the analysis are of children who were living in concentrated-disadvantaged neighborhoods in a previous wave of the PHDCN but who moved to a less distressed neighborhood in a subsequent wave of the survey, or vice versa.

4. Online appendix available at: http://www.russellsage.org/duncan_murnane_online_appendix.pdf.

5. The reading and math achievement levels of MTO participants were measured in 2002 by Abt Associates using the Woodcock-Johnson Revised (WJ-R) instrument. The WJ-R scores have been adjusted for interviewer effects (see Sanbonmatsu et al. 2006, appendix 1, for additional details). We estimate the effect on treatment compliers (TOT effect) using a two-stage least-squares regression controlling for a series of baseline covariates (see Orr et al. 2003, p. B-15, for a complete list). MTO children ranged from roughly ages six to twenty at the time of testing.

6. We might worry that in demonstration sites where the housing-search assistance was least effective, only the most motivated families would relocate as part of the MTO treatment. If more motivated families benefited more from changing neighborhoods, then differences at the sites in the composition of who moves through MTO could explain differences among cities in the size of the estimated effects of TOT for children's test scores. But there is no clear relationship between the size of the MTO impact on test scores and the MTO treatment-compliance rates. Relative to the other MTO cities, Baltimore has a relatively high compliance rate among experimental group families (57 percent) and Chicago has a relatively low compliance rate for the experimental group (34 percent). There is also no clear relationship between the size of the impacts and responses rates by site or by treatment group within site.

7. In a nationally representative sample of kindergarten students conducted in 1998, 15 percent of white students, 50 percent of black students, and 24 percent of Hispanic students were living in single-parent households (Duncan and Magnuson 2005).

8. Note that this story would not be likely to change much if we used our data to calculate some sort of school value-added measure that adjusted schoolwide average test scores for the sociodemographic composition of the school's student body. If the MTO mobility treatment caused children to move into schools serving relatively more disadvantaged student bodies compared with the schools of the control group children, then we might worry that what looks like a fairly modest difference between the average treatment versus control school in the share of children meeting national norms might actually reflect large differences in underlying schools that are value added to student learning, given that the treatment schools in this case would be achieving slightly better average student outcomes among a more disadvantaged student population. But there is unlikely to be any hidden value-added advantage to the schools serving MTO-treatment-group children because these schools are serving slightly less disadvantaged student bodies compared with control group schools and are achieving only slightly better average student outcomes.

9. Susan Clampet-Lundquist and Douglas S. Massey (2008, 115–16) argue: "Because of the history of segregation and continuing barriers to realizing residential preferences . . . relative to areas inhabited by middle-class whites, Asians, or Latinos, those inhabited by the black middle class exhibit lower property values, higher crime rates, lower employment rates, higher levels of unwed childbearing, poorer schools, lower educational achievement, and higher rates of welfare dependency. . . . Even though middle-class black areas may not themselves display concentrated poverty, because of racial segregation they tend to be located adjacent to or very near areas of concentrated deprivation and often share common service catchment areas."

10. In Chicago our concentrated-disadvantage index has a correlation of −0.83 with the share of families in the tract with incomes of at least $30,000; the correlation is quite similar for national data, −0.82.

11. In some cities these police department administrative units are districts or areas instead of beats, although for convenience we refer to all of these areas as "beats." What we mean is the smallest geographic area for which we were able to obtain crime data for the cities and years that were relevant for the MTO study.

12. See online appendix figure 12.A4 for raw score differences, available at: http://www.russellsage.org/duncan_murnane_online_appendix.pdf.

13. Fitting a regression line through these means of MTO site groups is essentially equivalent to generating instrumental variables estimates for the relationship between beat-level violent crime and children's test scores using interactions of indicators for MTO-treatment-group assignment and MTO site as instruments for local violent crime (Kling, Liebman, and Katz 2007; Ludwig and Kling 2007).

14. We have also tried to carry out other within-city analyses by examining whether children in the Chicago CHAC voucher study who lived in more violent baseline neighborhoods—and so presumably experienced the largest changes in beat-level violent crime—experienced the largest test score changes. Unfortunately, these results are not very informative because they are relatively imprecisely estimated. For example, for a one-standard-deviation change in beat-level violent crime rates (around 68 per 10,000), we could not rule out a relationship that is as large (in absolute value) as around −0.15 standard deviations in reading or math achievement-test scores.

REFERENCES

Allensworth, Elaine, and John Q. Easton. 2001. "Calculating a Cohort Dropout Rate for the Chicago Public Schools: A Technical Research Report." Chicago: Consortium on Chicago School Research. Available at: http://ccsr.uchicago.edu/publications/p0a01.pdf (accessed July 20, 2010).

Brooks-Gunn, Jeanne, Greg J. Duncan, Pamela Kato Klebanov, and Naomi Sealand. 1993. "Do Neighborhoods Influence Child and Adolescent Development?" *American Journal of Sociology* 99(2): 353–95.

Brooks-Gunn, Jeanne, Greg J. Duncan, and J. Lawrence Aber, eds. 1997a. *Neighborhood Poverty.* Vol. 1: *Context and Consequences for Children.* New York: Russell Sage.

———, eds. 1997b. *Neighborhood Poverty,* Vol. 2: *Policy Implications in Studying Neighborhoods.* New York: Russell Sage Foundation.

Clampet-Lundquist, Susan, and Douglas S. Massey. 2008. "Neighborhood Effects on Self-Sufficiency: A Reconsideration of Moving to Opportunity Experiment." *American Journal of Sociology* 114(1): 107–43.

Coleman, James S., Ernest Q. Campbell, Carol J. Hobson, James McPartland, Alexander M. Mood, Frederic D. Weinfeld, and Robert L. York. 1966. *Equality of Educational Opportunity.* Washington, D.C.: Government Printing Office.

Dietz, Robert D. 2002. "The Estimation of Neighborhood Effects in the Social Sciences: An Interdisciplinary Approach." *Social Science Research* 31(4): 539–75.

Dobbie, Will, and Roland G. Fryer Jr. 2009. "Are High-Quality Schools Enough to Close the Achievement Gap? Evidence from a Bold Social Experiment in Harlem." Working paper. Harvard University, Department of Economics.

Donohue, John J., and Jens Ludwig. 2007. "More COPS." Policy Brief No. 158. Washington, D.C.: Brookings Institution.

Duncan, Greg, and Katherine Magnuson. 2005. "Can Family Socioeconomic Resources Account for Racial and Ethnic Test Score Gaps?" *Future of Children* 15(1): 35–54.

Ellen, Ingrid Gould, and Margery Austin Turner. 1997. "Does Neighborhood Matter? Assessing Recent Evidence." *Housing Policy Debate* 8(4): 833–66.

Evans, William, and Emily Owens. 2007. "COPS and Crime." *Journal of Public Economics* 91(1–2): 181–201.

Goering, John, Judith D. Feins, and Todd M. Richardson. 2003. "What Have We Learned about Housing Mobility and Poverty Deconcentration?" In *Choosing a Better Life? Evaluating the Moving to Opportunity Social Experiment,* edited by John Goering and Judith D. Feins. Washington, D.C.: Urban Institute Press.

Grogger, Jeffrey T. 1997. "Local Violence and Educational Attainment." *Journal of Human Resources* 32(4): 659–82.

Guryan, Jonathan. 2004. "Desegregation and Black Dropout Rates." *American Economic Review* 94(4): 919–43.

Hanushek, Eric A., John F. Kain, and Steve G. Rivkin. 2004. "Why Public Schools Lose Teachers." *Journal of Human Resources* 39(2): 326–54.

Hanushek, Eric A., and Steve G. Rivkin. 2007. "Pay, Working Conditions and Teacher Quality." *Future of Children* 17(1): 69–86.

Harding, David J. 2003. "Counterfactual Models of Neighborhood Effects: The Effect of Neighborhood Poverty on Dropping Out and Teenage Pregnancy." *American Journal of Sociology* 109(3): 676–719.

Hong, Guanglei, and Stephen W. Raudenbush. 2008. "Causal Inference for Time-Varying Instructional Treatments." *Journal of Educational and Behavioral Statistics* 33(3): 333–62.

Jacob, Brian A. 2004. "Public Housing, Housing Vouchers and Student Achievement: Evidence from Public Housing Demolitions in Chicago." *American Economic Review* 94(1): 233–58.

Jargowsky, Paul A. 2003. *Stunning Progress, Hidden Problems: The Dramatic Decline of Concentrated Poverty in the 1990s.* Living Cities Census series. Washington, D.C.: Brookings Institution.

Kling, Jeffrey R., Jeffrey B. Liebman, and Lawrence F. Katz. 2007. "Experimental Analysis of Neighborhood Effects." *Econometrica* 75(1): 83–119.

Kling, Jeffrey R., Jens Ludwig, and Lawrence F. Katz. 2005. "Neighborhood Effects on Crime for Female and Male Youth: Evidence from a Randomized Housing Voucher Experiment." *Quarterly Journal of Economics* 120(1): 87–130.

Leventhal, Tama, and Jeanne Brooks-Gunn. 2000. "The Neighborhoods They Live In: The Effects of Neighborhood Residence on Child and Adolescent Outcomes." *Psychological Bulletin* 126(2): 309–37.

Ludwig, Jens, Brian A. Jacob, Michael Johnson, Greg J. Duncan, and James E. Rosenbaum. 2010. "Neighborhood Effects on Low-Income Families: Evidence from a Randomized Housing Voucher Lottery." Working paper. University of Chicago.

Ludwig, Jens, and Jeffrey Kling. 2007. "Is Crime Contagious?" *Journal of Law and Economics* 50(3): 491–518.

Ludwig, Jens, Jeffrey Liebman, Jeffrey Kling, Greg J. Duncan, Lawrence F. Katz, Ronald C. Kessler, and Lisa Sanbonmatsu. 2008. "What Can We Learn About Neighborhood Effects from the Moving to Opportunity Experiment? A Comment on Clampet-Lundquist and Massey." *American Journal of Sociology* 114(1): 144–88.

Mendenhall, Ruby, Stefanie DeLuca, and Greg Duncan. 2006. "Neighborhood Resources and Economic Mobility: Results from the Gautreaux Program." *Social Science Research* 35(4): 892–923.

Olsen, Edgar O. 2003. "Housing Programs for Low-Income Households." In *Means-Tested Transfer Programs in the United States,* edited by Robert A. Moffitt. Chicago: University of Chicago Press.

Orr, Larry, Judith D. Feins, Robin Jacob, Erik Beecrof, Lisa Sanbonmatsu, Lawrence Katz, Jeffrey Liebman, and Jeffrey Kling. 2003. *Moving to Opportunity Interim Impacts Evaluation.* Washington, D.C.: U.S. Department of Housing and Urban Development, Office of Policy Development and Research.

Plotnick, Robert D., and Saul Hoffman. 1999. "The Effect of Neighborhood Characteristics on Young Adult Outcomes: Alternative Estimates." *Social Science Quarterly* 80(1): 1–18.

Reardon, Sean F., and Kendra Bischoff. 2011. "Income Inequality and Income Segregation." *American Journal of Sociology* 116(4): 1092–153.

Robins, James M., Miguel Ángel Hernan, and Babette Brumback. 2000. "Marginal Structural Models and Causal Inference in Epidemiology." *Epidemiology* 11(5): 550–60.

Rubinowitz, Leonard S., and James E. Rosenbaum. 2000. *Crossing the Class and Color Lines.* Chicago: University of Chicago Press.

Sampson, Robert J. 2008. "Moving to Inequality: Neighborhood Effects and Experiments Meet Social Structure." *American Journal of Sociology* 114(1): 189–231.

Sampson, Robert J., Jeffrey D. Morenoff, and Thomas Gannon-Rowley. 2002. "Assessing 'Neighborhood Effects': Social Processes and New Directions in Research." *Annual Review of Sociology* 28: 443–78.

Sampson, Robert J., Patrick Sharkey, and Stephen W. Raudenbush. 2008. "Durable Effects of Concentrated Disadvantage on Verbal Ability Among African American Children." *Proceedings of the National Academy of Sciences* 105(3): 845–53.

Sanbonmatsu, Lisa, Jeffrey R. Kling, Greg J. Duncan, and Jeanne Brooks-Gunn. 2006. "Neighborhoods and Academic Achievement: Results from the MTO Experiment." *Journal of Human Resources* 41(4): 649–91.

Sharkey, Patrick. 2009. "The Acute Effect of Local Homicides on Children's Cognitive Performance." *Proceedings of the National Academy of Sciences* 107 (26): 11733–38.

Sherman, Lawrence W., ed. 2003. "Misleading Evidence and Evidence-Led Policy: Making Social Science More Experimental." *Annals of the American Academy of Political and Social Science* 589(1): 6–19.

Tough, Paul. 2008. *Whatever It Takes: Geoffrey Canada's Quest to Change Harlem and America.* New York: Houghton Mifflin Harcourt.

Votruba, Mark Edward, and Jeffrey R. Kling. 2009. "Effects of Neighborhood Characteristics on the Mortality of Black Male Youth: Evidence from Gautreaux, Chicago." *Social Science and Medicine* 68(5): 814–23.

Watson, Tara. 2009. "Inequality and the Measurement of Residential Segregation by Income in American Neighborhoods." *Review of Income and Wealth* 55(3): 820–44.

Chapter 13

Unpacking Neighborhood Influences on Education Outcomes: Setting the Stage for Future Research

David Harding, Lisa Gennetian, Christopher Winship,
Lisa Sanbonmatsu, and Jeffrey Kling

The link between rising income inequality and rising residential segregation by income suggests that, if neighborhood environments affect educational outcomes, diverging educational outcomes may be due in part to the increasing numbers of youths growing up in neighborhoods of concentrated poverty or concentrated affluence. Most existing social science research on neighborhoods conceptualizes neighborhood effects at the macro-level, hypothesizing how general neighborhood characteristics such as the poverty rate affect a variety of individual and family outcomes. Contemporary research on this topic has largely failed to recognize the diverse types of families living in poor neighborhoods or the potentially wide variety of ways that they may respond to a given set of neighborhood conditions. Our core argument is that future neighborhood research must seriously consider this diversity both conceptually and methodologically.

Our hypothesis is that there is considerable heterogeneity in the experiences of youths in the same neighborhood that might vary by their personal or family resources, their ability to cope with or navigate neighborhood circumstances, and the decisions that youths and their family make about how, with whom, and where their time is spent. Depending on these and other factors, different youths may get a different "dose" of their neighborhood. This heterogeneity can generate substantial variation in how a given neighborhood characteristic affects any one youth. Youths who live in the same neighborhood may experience it in different ways, leading to effect heterogeneity: neighborhood effects of different direction or magnitude for different youths.

Effect heterogeneity is the core of our argument. We therefore motivate future neighborhood research using a simple model that considers youths' educational outcomes as a function of neighborhood context, neighborhood exposure, individual vulnerability to neighborhood effects, and non-neighborhood educational inputs. Moving this research agenda forward requires three steps. First, researchers need to shift focus away from broad theories of neighborhood effects and examine the specific mechanisms through which the characteristics of a neighborhood might affect an individual. By "mechanisms," we mean the social, economic, and cultural processes that create associations between the compositional or demographic characteristics of neighborhoods, such as neighborhood poverty, and individual educational outcomes, such as achievement scores or educational attainment.

Second, neighborhood research desperately needs new and far more nuanced data. In particular, we need data that measure how individuals and families of different types allocate their time between different places, the extent of exposure to different people and locations, and the consequent influences on individual behavior.

Third, we advocate for research designs that can unpack the causal effects, if any, of specific neighborhood characteristics as they operate through well-specified mechanisms. Much current neighborhood research estimates the reduced form or total neighborhood effect. The bane of this literature has been the problem of selection—whether differences in outcomes are due to the neighborhoods themselves or instead reflect differences in the characteristics of individuals who live in different types of neighborhoods. Rather than trying to assess the overall effect of living in a particular type of neighborhood, researchers should strive to examine discrete mechanisms in ways that account for effect heterogeneity.

In the first section of this chapter we introduce our conceptual framework; in the second section we argue for a shift from general theories to concrete specifications of mechanisms and sources of effect heterogeneity. In the third section we describe the need for new, detailed data on social interactions, both neighborhood- and non-neighborhood-based (including schools) that allow for measurement of responses and exposure to people and places. In the fourth section we discuss the types of research designs that might profitably be employed to estimate the effects of such interactions on educational outcomes. In the fifth section we present a substantive example through which we illustrate one possible research design.

Rising income inequality has led to rising residential segregation by income, especially among blacks. Changes in income inequality have particularly increased the spatial segregation of the affluent from middle-class and lower-income families (Reardon and Bischoff 2011). These trends suggest that diverging educational outcomes by family income (see chapters 3 and 5 in this volume) may be due in part to the increasing numbers of youths growing up in neighborhoods characterized by either concentrated poverty or concentrated affluence. These impacts depend on both the nature and magnitude of the effects of concentrated-poverty neighborhoods and concentrated-affluence neighborhoods on educational outcomes. These impacts may also depend on the timing of exposure to different neighborhood environments by developmental stage and the cumulative effects of sustained exposure over time.

Our goal in this chapter is to set the stage for future research—its opportunities as well as challenges—to better understand the influence of neighborhood social settings on youths' educational outcomes. For the purposes of this chapter, we intentionally define a neighborhood social setting broadly: a setting that is outside home and school. We differentiate social settings according to the characteristics of the place, the types of people with whom the individual interacts, and how time is spent there. Our definition casts a wide net so that consideration may be given to a range of youths' experiences, whether time spent in an after-school program, hanging out at a basketball court or the local mall, or staying at home.

Because neighborhood context is the most frequently discussed social setting, we ground our discussion in neighborhood effects on education. Our analysis is driven by a simple yet novel conceptual framework in which a youths' educational outcome (Y) is a multiplicative function of the neighborhood context (N), individual exposure to that neighborhood context (E), and individual vulnerability to the effects of the neighborhood context (V) as well as other variables (X). $Y = f(N, E, V, X) = (N \times E \times V) + X$, where each quantity potentially has multiple dimensions. The prior literature has primarily focused on estimating the effects of compositional measures of N (such as neighborhood poverty rate) and on the methodological challenges of identifying the effect of N, particularly separating the effects of neighborhood context from the preexisting differences between residents of different neighborhoods (X).

Although selection bias remains a central issue worthy of further research, we argue that the literature has too often ignored several other key research problems that are captured in our model. The first is the mechanisms, or social processes, by which neighborhood context (N) affects individual outcomes (Y). The second is effect heterogeneity, or differences between individuals in the effects of N on Y. This heterogeneity is driven by both E and V. Different youths living in the same neighborhood will have different histories of exposure (E) to the people, places, and activities that drive neighborhood effects. In other words, E can be thought of as the "dose" of different neighborhood characteristics that an individual receives. E may vary by cumulative time exposed to a neighborhood environment or by differential exposure to specific mechanisms. As Patrick Sharkey (2006) argues, individuals to some degree determine their level of exposure to different neighborhood characteristics through the decisions they (and their parents) make about where, how, and with whom to spend their time. Though the neighborhood-effects literature has focused on the selection of individuals and families into neighborhoods, the selection of exposure to different neighborhood characteristics presents a second identification problem, what we might call "within-neighborhood selection bias." The social and economic processes that create differential exposure are worthy of study from both a methodological and a substantive perspective. Effect heterogeneity may also be generated by differences in the vulnerability (V) or susceptibility of youths to the effects of the neighborhood (N). This variation in vulnerability may be driven by differences in individual and family characteristics that make some youths more or less susceptible to neighborhood-effects mechanisms.[1] One source of difference in vulnerability is age-specific developmental needs, but other factors such as parenting decisions and family resources may also play a role. For example, consider the possible responses to neighborhood violence among parents of male adolescents. Some parents may require their sons to stay inside. For some, this will mean more time studying; for others, more time watching *TV*. For the first individual, the effect of neighborhood violence will be to increase educational attainment; for the second, the effect will be neutral or to decrease educational attainment. Considerably more theorizing is needed to understand the processes behind effect heterogeneity due to both E and V.

Although policy recommendations are not explicitly advanced in this chapter, we think the agenda put forth here is an important step toward building evidence to inform public policy. In conceptualizing neighborhood effects, it is helpful to differentiate between interventions that are designed to affect residential mobility and interventions that are designed to directly change a place or neighborhood. In the former, an individual's neighborhood environment changes because his or her family moves to a new neighborhood, as in the Gautreaux project and the Moving to Opportunity (MTO) housing mobility experiment. In the latter, the characteristics of the social setting or environment that the neighborhood provides for children is targeted for change (Sampson 2008). As we think about estimating neighborhood effects on education, we will return throughout the chapter to these two types of policy interventions. In the example study design described later in this chapter (see "An Illustrative Example), we describe an intervention that changes individual exposure to the neighborhood.

CONCEPTUALIZING EFFECTS OF SOCIAL SETTINGS ON EDUCATIONAL OUTCOMES

In this section we motivate our critique of traditional neighborhood research by describing various mechanisms that might affect individual outcomes and, in appropriate cases, why these effects might differ across families or individuals.

Environment and Health   Some of the processes through which neighborhood context may affect educational outcomes occur because of geographic location or physical proximity, rather than through local social interactions. One such mechanism operates through environmental or health effects. For example, a neighborhood adjacent to a major highway may expose children to high levels of particulate-matter pollution that leads to asthma and therefore to more school absences.

Spatial Mismatch   Another mechanism is proximity to jobs, or "spatial mismatch" (Jencks and Mayer 1990; Mouw 2000). A neighborhood located near an abundance of job opportunities may affect the way that individual youths think about the rewards of their own education and future opportunities (Anderson 1999).

Violence   Neighborhood violence may affect the amount of time youths spend on homework if going outside means risking an experience with violence or victimization. Witnessing frequent acts of violence may lead to post-traumatic stress disorder or biological responses to stress that can also interfere with learning (Massey 2001, 2004).

Neighborhood Resources   Neighborhoods certainly differ in their institutions and other resources or resource brokers. For example, one neighborhood may have an after-school program that provides homework help, and another may not. One neighborhood may be near a community center that provides a safe, supervised space for teens to hang out, and another may not. We are only beginning to understand which resources are more or less abundant in different neighborhoods (Small 2006, 2009; Small and McDermott 2006; Small and Stark 2005). Mario L. Small and Monica McDermott (2006) find that, on average, poor neighborhoods actually have slightly more commercial establishments such as pharmacies, grocery stores, and child-care centers, but that poor black neighborhoods with declining population density have fewer such establishments. Neighborhood resources can also fluctuate with the residential mobility of middle-class families, who disproportionately sustain community institutions and organizations (Wilson 1987).

Culture   Cultural mechanisms may also be important, as posited by, for example, social isolation theory (Wilson 1987; Massey and Denton 1993). According to this theory, poor, inner-city black neighborhoods are thought to be socially isolated from "mainstream" or middle-class individuals and institutions (particularly the labor market). This leads to cultural isolation and the development of a "ghetto-specific" culture, which orients young people away from schooling by reinforcing norms and values that denigrate the value of education. A similar formulation is Signithia Fordham and John Ogbu's (1986) oppositional culture theory (see also Ogbu 2004), according to which behaviors that promote academic achievement—such as speaking standard English, doing homework, and engaging in class discussion—in poor black communities become defined as "acting white" in response to discrimination, inferior schools, and blocked labor-market opportunities (see also Massey and Denton 1993). However, subsequent examinations have found no evidence for the core claim that black students are disproportionately sanctioned by their peers for academic effort (Cook and Ludwig 1998; Ainsworth-Darnell and Downey 1998; Harris 2006; Carter 2005). One exception is Roland Fryer (2006), who finds that black students who get good grades are less popular than whites who get good grades, but only in racially mixed public schools. When students' experiences with oppositional culture are investigated, we begin to see why. Prudence L. Carter (2005) finds that notions of "acting white" among poor black and Latino youths have more to do with musical tastes, fashion, and speech patterns than with academic performance or effort.

An alternative perspective on the cultural context of poor neighborhoods emphasizes the cultural heterogeneity of such neighborhoods. Instead of a distinct subculture, neighborhood cultural context can be conceptualized as culturally heterogeneous, incorporating competing and conflicting cultural models, some of which are shared across society more broadly and some of which are locally developed alternatives (Harding 2007, 2010). For example, Carter (2005) argues that poor youths have a "continuum of cultural attachments" available to them, which different youths embrace to differing degrees. For young people enmeshed in this heterogeneous cultural environment, creating and sustaining strategies for career and school success are major challenges (Harding 2010). When multiple educational and career pathways are locally available and socially supported, some adolescents may jump to alternative pathways when one pathway becomes challenging, whether or not they have full information about the risks and benefits of new strategies or the financial and cultural resources to successfully implement them.

Social Organization

Social organization theory focuses on the capacity of neighborhood residents to regulate behavior that occurs within the neighborhood. It is relevant to another set of neighborhood mechanisms, including school-related behaviors, such as truancy. Much of the current emphasis on the capacity of neighborhoods is on behavior that occurs in public spaces, particularly crime and violence. Collective efficacy, defined as "social cohesion among neighbors combined with their willingness to intervene on behalf of the common good" (Sampson, Raudenbush, and Earls 1997), mediates the relationship between compositional neighborhood characteristics (residential instability, ethnic or racial heterogeneity, and poverty) and crime rates. When parents in a community are connected to one another, what James S. Coleman (1988) calls "intergenerational closure," they are thought to be better able to present adolescents with a consistent set of cultural ideals regarding education, which leads to more school effort. They should also be better able to monitor and control their children's education-related behaviors, such as school attendance. However, when the idea of intergenerational closure has been applied to schools, it has not always met with consistent empirical support (see, for example, Morgan and Sørensen 1999), which raises the question of whether, how, or under what circumstances socially connected parents can indeed enforce common educational ideals, and whether only pro-schooling cultural ideals are strengthened by intergenerational closure. It is also unclear what proportion of the parents in a community need to be well connected in order for the community to effectively monitor adolescent behavior. Such tipping points or thresholds remain relatively unexamined.

Local Incentives

Local incentives refers to an economic perspective on social interactions by individuals as agents responding to incentives provided by the local environment and shaped by their time and money resources (Manski 2000). For example, living in a neighborhood in which many students drop out of high school might reduce the stigma of dropping out and thus increase a student's preference for doing so. Such a preference depends on the actions of other individuals. In another neighborhood, observing neighbors who attend college and obtain high-paying jobs may increase expectations about the benefits of attending college, but one negative consequence of this increase may be a reduced number of spots in advanced-placement courses, reducing the availability of such courses. But in the long run it might also stimulate the development of additional courses to meet the new demand. The difficulty is that such empirical patterns can be generated by many different interaction processes, or even by individuals acting in isolation. In the absence of measurement of expectations and preferences, researchers are left to infer the presence of interactions from observations of outcomes.

The mechanisms we have discussed often work in tandem. For example, high collective-efficacy neighborhoods may be more effective at securing outside resources, such as police protection or the resources to build and maintain a community center. Because institutions provide social contexts for the creation and maintenance of social ties, the presence of such institutions may affect the nature and extent of neighborhood social interactions. Small's research on child-care centers in New York City finds, contrary to social isolation and deinstitutionalization theories, that poor neighborhoods have as many child-care centers as wealthier neighborhoods, that centers in poor neighborhoods have more organizational ties to key resources, and that centers are key sites for social interaction, the creation of social ties, and resource brokering in poor neighborhoods (Small, Jacobs, and Massengill 2008; Small 2009).

It should also be noted that mechanisms often operate through parents rather than directly on children. The neighborhood environment may affect parental employment, marital decisions, parenting practices, and psychological or physical health, and any of these can influence their children's development (for example, see Leventhal and Brooks-Gunn 2000). Parents coping with violent environments may be more likely to use physical forms of discipline because of the heightened dangers that come with misbehavior or because of the stress of living in a violent neighborhood, or parents may take cues from their neighbors when judging the academic achievement of their children. Presumably, most of any neighborhood effect on young children would operate through parenting practices or environmental mechanisms, since children's direct exposure to neighborhood social interactions are likely to be minimal.

EFFECT HETEROGENEITY

These theoretical perspectives provide broad outlines of how neighborhood effects on educational outcomes might work, but none of these frameworks adequately considers how these effects might vary with differences in the daily experiences of youths. These differences, $E,$ in our conceptual model described earlier, are potentially important but largely uninvestigated sources of effect heterogeneity (see also Small 2004).

One possible source of neighborhood-effect heterogeneity is differences among individuals in social networks. Though interaction-based neighborhood-effects theories implicitly assume that neighborhoods play some role in structuring the social networks of their residents, we actually know little about whether—or, more important, for whom—this is the case, particularly among youths. Social networks are one of the key conduits (but by no means the only one) through which information and cultural frames or scripts are transmitted. Social networks of similar-age youths—peer networks—have received considerable attention in the literature (for example, Anderson 1999). Such peer networks may play important roles as cultural conduits, as most theories of peer effects assume, but our theories need to be more specific about who those peers are, which peer attachments are more common among young people in poor neighborhoods, and what is transmitted through peer networks. David Harding (2009b, 2010) argues that older adolescents and young adults on the street in poor, violent neighborhoods have considerable cultural power and play an important role in socializing younger adolescents by exposing them to local cultural frames and scripts regarding schooling and sexual behavior.

A second source of effect heterogeneity is different behavioral adaptations to the challenges of daily life in poor neighborhoods. A focus on behavioral adaptations explicitly considers the individual as an actor who can adapt in different ways to mitigate or overcome challenges faced in different neighborhoods. The distinction developed by Sharkey (2006) between "imposed" environments (everything present in the neighborhood where an individual lives) and "selected" environments (the people and institutions with whom he or she interacts) highlights the idea that youths living in the same neighborhood may choose very different social environments for themselves. Different choices or adaptations can have different consequences. For example, violent neighborhoods provide particular challenges to adolescents. In order to feel safe, some adolescents may spend as little time as possible in public spaces, thus limiting their exposure to their neighborhood's violence. Others, however, may engage in behaviors such as demonstrating their toughness, forming strong bonds of mutual protection with friends, or relying on older individuals for protection in order to avoid victimization (Anderson 1999; Harding 2009b, 2010). For the latter group, these behaviors may have unforeseen educational consequences because such adolescents can be viewed as resistant or disruptive by teachers (Dance 2002). Another example is provided by Carter (2005), who argues that "cultural authenticity" among ethno-racial minority groups, in the form of speech styles, clothing, music, and other tastes, can have positive payoffs in terms of group membership and solidarity (what Carter calls "nondominant cultural capital") but also can be misinterpreted by white middle-class teachers as oppositional or resistant. Parents may also adapt their parenting practices to the neighborhood environment by, for example, limiting their children's interactions with neighbors (Furstenberg et al. 1999; Jarrett 1997a, 1997b).

A third potential source of neighborhood-effect heterogeneity is variation in family characteristics and the interaction between family characteristics and the properties of social settings. Here, effect heterogeneity is driven less by differences in social interactions and more by differences between individuals and families in their capacity to access resources and to insulate their children from negative aspects of their neighborhood and, as a result, their susceptibility to neighborhood effects (or V in our conceptual model). (Our online appendix provides a detailed example of family-based effect heterogeneity, available at: http://www.russellsage.org/duncan_murnane_online_appendix.pdf.) Finally, differences in cities' economic, social, and geographic characteristics may also be important sources of heterogeneity in neighborhood effects (Small 2007).

WHO, WHEN, WHERE, AND WHAT: THE NEED FOR NEW DATA AND METHODS

In order to incorporate the mechanisms and effect heterogeneity just described into neighborhood-effects research, measures of exposure and vulnerability are required. With the easy availability of census data, early sociological research on neighborhood effects (for example, Brewster 1994a, 1994b; South and Crowder 1999; South and Baumer 2000) often relied on compositional measures of neighborhood characteristics as indicators of emergent properties (for example, the percentage of single-mother families as a measure of cultural norms regarding nonmarital childbearing). Economists drew liberally from these sociological roots, continuing the tradition of using compositional measures. These various compositional measures (for example, poverty rate, unemployment rate, rates of welfare receipt) tend to be fairly strongly correlated with one another.

Using compositional measures of neighborhood characteristics as proxies for emergent cultural characteristics assumes a tight connection between culture and behavior, exposure, networks, and interactions, when (1) this assumption is probably incorrect and (2) the connection is something we should be investigating. For example, if we observed high rates of high school dropout in poor neighborhoods, would we assume that neighborhood norms and culture did not place a high value on education? Research suggests that the poor, particularly African American poor, actually place a very high value on education (Solorzano 1992; Goldenberg et al. 2001; Carter 2005; Young 2004; Newman 1999). More recent research has focused on developing noncompositional measures using "ecometric" methods (Sampson Raudenbush, and Earls 1997; Raudenbush and Sampson 1999). Ecometric methods are an important advance, allowing us to measure the social and cultural characteristics of neighborhoods.

Measuring Emergent Properties

Because our theories are often about emergent properties of neighborhoods rather than neighborhood composition, we must measure emergent properties. The development of constructs and methods of data collection should be guided by relatively detailed questions such as the following:

> What are some of the dimensions that determine social-interaction exposures?

> Where is a youth spending his or her time: inside the home, in the neighborhood, at school, or outside the neighborhood? When is the youth spending time in this environment?

> How long is the youth there, and where could he or she otherwise spend time? Is the youth studying, watching TV, playing sports, participating in an organized activity, or hanging out with family or friends?

> Whom is the youth interacting with or observing: family, friends, or unrelated adults?

> What are the characteristics, experiences, attitudes, and behaviors of the people with whom the youth is interacting?

> What is the youth's relationship with or attitude toward these individuals (close or trusted friend, casual acquaintance, authority figure, negatively perceived)?

Qualitative, Time-Use, and Social-Network Methods

Developing methods for measurement is as important as conceptualizing what to measure. Qualitative methods are especially well suited to understanding social processes and day-to-day behaviors, particularly when the key dimensions the analyst might consider are not clear at the outset. By interacting with individuals in their natural social contexts or talking to them at length about their experiences and perceptions of those contexts, the ethnographer or interviewer can understand in detail how neighborhoods structure the who, when, where, and what of daily life and the content of the messages or ideas that youths encounter in these contexts.

We see three roles for qualitative methods in research on contextual effects. First, ethnographic participant observation or in-depth, unstructured interviews can be used in the pilot or exploratory phase of a project to generate hypotheses, inform the development of survey measures, or understand the boundaries of a social context in question. Second, qualitative methods can be embedded in a mixed-method study in order to understand the mechanisms by which quantitatively measured effects are operating and to inform the interpretation of estimates from statistical models. One recent example of the utility of qualitative research is the mixed-methods work in the MTO evaluation. Quantitative data showed that MTO improved the outcomes of female youths, particularly their mental health, but had unfavorable effects on male youths (Kling, Liebman, and Katz 2007). The qualitative research revealed that boys in the experimental group were more socially isolated than girls in their new low-poverty neighborhoods, that boys in the control group experienced greater contact with father figures, and that boys generally experienced more negative peer effects. These mechanisms would have been virtually impossible to uncover with the quantitative data alone, but because qualitative data collection occurred after the quantitative work, qualitative researchers had the opportunity to explore through open-ended interviews why MTO had disparate effects.[2]

Third, stand-alone qualitative studies can illuminate social organization and daily life in poor communities and inform theorizing about how contextual effects operate, develop evidence for or against hypotheses on the basis of prior research or theorizing, or complicate previous theoretical accounts. For example, Small (2004) shows that neighborhood poverty does not always lead to social disorganization, and he explores the conditions under which poor communities can develop and deploy social capital. A long history of ethnographic research in urban sociology has developed the "stylized facts" that now inform much of the current neighborhood-effects research (for example, Anderson 1999; Hannerz 1969; Suttles 1968; Whyte 1943; Young 2004).

Time diaries and social-network analysis methods are additional tools for gathering data that can detail how, where, and with whom time is spent. These methods hold considerable potential for measuring an individual's involvement in or exposure to neighborhood social processes (see, for example, Fu 2005, 2007, on network data). Traditional time-use measurement studies (Juster and Stafford 1985; Robinson 1977; Csikszentmihalyi and Larson 1987; Larson 1989; American Time Use Survey [Bureau of Labor Statistics 2009]) ask individuals to report on what they are doing either retrospectively, using a time diary, or at the moment, using experience sampling methods. Often data are also gathered on secondary activities (for example, monitoring children, watching television), others present, and where the individual is (home, school, work, store, park, and so on), yet when locations are requested, they are of generic form (for example, grocery store, friend's house) and do not include geographic information that would allow researchers to measure distances or locations. Time-use and social-network data collection can be expensive and therefore must be weighed against other data-collection needs in any particular study. However, measures of social interaction in and outside of the neighborhood are critical to measuring neighborhood exposure, and data-collection efforts can be efficiently tailored to these purposes.

Recent work in criminology offers a promising example of how time-diary methods can measure where, how, and with whom adolescents spend their time. Motivated by both a concern with neighborhoods and crime and the routine-activity theory of crime, which posits that much crime is based on spur-of-the-moment calculations related to opportunity, potential victims or targets, and likelihood of apprehension (Cohen and Felson 1979), the criminologist Per-Olof Wikström and David A. Butterworth (2006) collected time-use data on a subsample of adolescents in the Peterborough Youth Study (United Kingdom) using "space-time budgets." They asked respondents to report their primary activity for each hour during the previous seven days. For each activity, respondents also reported where they were (type of location and geographic location), who else was present (number of friends, other peers, family, nonfamily adults, teachers, and so on), whether they had consumed alcohol or drugs, whether they were engaging in crime, whether they were carrying a weapon, and whether the situation involved elements that might increase the risk of offending or victimization, such as threats, arguments, or harassment (Wikström and Butterworth 2006; Wikström et al. 2010). Even this relatively simple form of data collection led to new descriptive information on adolescent criminal involvement and its relation to neighborhood context. For example, even the most frequent offenders spend very little time during the week offending; offenses most often occurred with peers and in risky situations, and youths in disadvantaged neighborhoods were exposed to more risky situations. This example suggests that neighborhood-effects researchers might profitably adopt and extend this form of data collection in order to examine time-use and social interactions. For instance, by gathering data on the characteristics of others with whom a youth spends time, researchers can gauge exposure to local socialization.

Physical environment [handwritten marginalia, rotated]

Measuring Institutional Resources

Place can influence whom individuals are interacting with and how much time they spend there (that is, how desirable or appealing it is to engage in interactions), and it can serve as a setting for the transfer of information and resources. Traditional methods to measure availability of institutions rely on geographic mapping to measure distance to supermarkets, or more intensive neighborhood-observation checklists that systematically ask observers to rate neighborhoods on items such as presence of public playgrounds and the condition of such playgrounds (graffiti, trash, barbed wire, and so on). Such methods have grown in sophistication as technologies such as Google Earth have vastly lowered the cost of assembling this type of information. As a result, researchers have used these methods to answer a variety of public-health questions about the role of social and physical environments in health outcomes among individuals living in disadvantaged communities (for example, see Ponce et al. 2005; Zenk et al. 2005).

Although mapping or collecting rater observations (also called "Systematic Social Observation") is a good strategy for documenting the number and proximity of these types of neighborhood institutions, these methods, as Sampson, Jeffrey D. Morenoff, and Thomas Gannon-Rowley (2002) argue, do not capture the quality and diversity of available institutions—such as gathering places, trusted pharmacies, or safe parks—or the ubiquity and acceptance of their use by residents. For example, recently those working in public health who have examined supermarket availability in impoverished neighborhoods have concluded that travel time may be a better indicator of accessibility than physical distance (Zenk et al. 2005). A fuller understanding of institutional resources can complement how well researchers understand where and how time is spent and how to characterize place. Retrieving this type of data may require a hybrid model that combines low-cost methods (mapping and counting) with more resource-intensive but tailored methods, such as neighborhood-observation checklists along with individual qualitative assessments of institutions (via a subsample of survey respondents or respondents to more in-depth open-ended interviews).

ESTIMATION STRATEGIES: EFFECTS OF CAUSES, EFFECT HETEROGENEITY, AND MECHANISMS

Selection-bias problems present themselves when families and individuals have some control over where they live, with whom they interact, and where they spend their time. Individuals make decisions about the social settings they occupy on the basis of a variety of factors, from preferences to personal resources and other constraints; but because researchers cannot always observe or measure these factors, selection bias may result. This means that individual or family characteristics may confound the estimates of social setting on youth outcomes because the associations we observe between a social setting such as neighborhood context and educational outcomes may be due to unobserved differences in individual or family characteristics in different neighborhoods and not to the effects of residing in different neighborhoods. The magnitude of the bias will depend on two quantities: the association between the confounder and the social setting, and the association between the confounder and the outcome.

A useful way of conceptualizing this identification problem is to consider the sources of variation in social settings experienced by different youths. Take, for example, neighborhood context. One type of variation, endogenous variation, refers to the confounders that produce the selection bias just discussed. The second type of variation is exogenous variation in neighborhood context, variation that is produced by economic or social processes that do not directly affect individual outcomes. For example, a change in public policy may move some families out of public housing into neighborhoods with lower poverty rates without directly affecting outcomes of interest.

Solving the selection-bias problem requires finding and measuring those exogenous sources of variation. In searching for such exogenous variation in neighborhood contexts, researchers have focused on two types of processes that lead to variation in neighborhood characteristics experienced by different individuals: (1) residential mobility, the movement of families from one neighborhood to another, and (2) changes in neighborhood conditions over time—place-based change. Since both sources of variation can be endogenous or exogenous, both present identification challenges. Regarding moving, we need to understand why some families move to or stay in disadvantaged neighborhoods while others do not. We must also consider the potential negative effects of residential mobility itself, which could dilute the positive effects of an improved neighborhood context (Sampson 2008).[3] Regarding changes in neighborhood conditions, we need to understand why some neighborhoods change and some do not, and we may also worry about why some families move in response to changes in their neighborhoods and others do not. If these reasons are also causally related to the outcomes, selection bias is introduced. Finally, note that these two types of interventions typically will not estimate the same quantity. Residential mobility manipulates an entire set of linked neighborhood characteristics, while a place-based intervention typically manipulates a single key feature (or small number of key features) of the neighborhood context. A place-based intervention will therefore more often provide a narrow test of a specific neighborhood-effects mechanism. For this reason, and because we have already learned much from residential mobility studies such as MTO and Gautreaux, we support the development of place-based interventions for studying neighborhood effects. Key challenges in developing such interventions include designing interventions that are strong enough to produce detectable effects and specific enough to reveal the importance of a single mechanism.

Identifying the Effects of Specific Mechanisms

Focusing on mechanisms introduces an additional set of complications to research designs that rely on harnessing exogenous variation in social settings. Though it is not cast precisely in terms of mechanisms, it is helpful to start with Charles F. Manski's (1993, 1995) discussion of identification problems in neighborhood-effects research, for his framework is well known and the fundamental problems of interpreting associations between contextual characteristics and individual outcomes are especially relevant in identifying mechanisms.

Manski describes three sources of association between neighborhood characteristics and individual outcomes. First, "endogenous effects" are the effects of group-level values on individual values on the same variable such as time spent studying. Contagion or peer-effects theories propose that individuals are more likely to do what others around them are doing. A child will spend more time studying when he sees his peers spending more time studying. Endogenous effects generate a social multiplier because they amplify any direct effect of an intervention. These types of effects are particularly challenging to identify because of direction of causality, or what Manski calls the "reflection problem." Is directionality from the group to the child or vice versa?

Second, in "contextual effects," individual behavior varies with other characteristics of the group, such as when achievement varies with neighborhood socioeconomic composition. A child may spend more time studying when he observes adults in the neighborhood who have benefited from high levels of education. Third are "correlated effects," which is simply another name for selection bias.

If we want to identify the total effect of exposure to one neighborhood rather than another, it is not necessary to distinguish between endogenous and contextual effects with respect to the mechanisms that they specify. The main concern is selection bias at the neighborhood level, as previously discussed. (Note, however, that even if we were able to deal with the selection-bias problem and obtain a causal estimate of the effect of, say, neighborhood poverty on an educational outcome, this would not distinguish between the effects of neighborhood poverty and other neighborhood characteristics correlated with it.)

The reflection problem emerges whenever we are interested in endogenous effects of social settings, but it is not the same identification problem as the selection-bias problem that researchers face when trying to estimate total effects. The reflection problem can be understood as a failure to specify, measure, and manipulate (or find an instrument for) one particular mechanism, the average value of the outcome among a group with whom one interacts. The only other option is to draw on theory to invoke strong identifying assumptions that specify the direction of causality. For instance, perhaps older friends' actions affect younger friends' actions, but not the reverse. The key point is that the reflection problem is not an inherent intractable problem in the estimation of neighborhood effects but rather results from failure to conceptualize mechanisms and develop strategies for identifying their effects.

We now return to the selection-bias problem but consider it in the context of identifying the role of mechanisms. Even if there is a source of random variation in neighborhood context, the selection-bias problem reemerges when mechanism variables are considered, as self-selection into the mechanisms may no longer be random with respect to the outcomes. Identifying the effects of mechanisms on an outcome will require multiple sources of exogenous variation. Consider figure 13.1, which diagrams a simplified research design in which there are three hypothesized mechanisms (*M1, M2, M3*) for the effect of N (a neighborhood characteristic) on Y (the outcome). For example, N might be the amount of violence in the neighborhood, and Y might be educational achievement. The three mechanisms might be (*M1*) leveling of educational expectations through a focus on safety, (*M2*) exposure to violence affecting cognitive development through post-traumatic stress disorder, and (*M3*) joining a gang for protection, which leads to less time for studying.[4] *U* represents a set of unobserved X variables that are uncorrelated with Z (it was randomly assigned) but are correlated with neighborhood violence (*N*), the outcome (*Y*), and the mechanisms (*M*'s).[5]

If we are interested in the total effect of neighborhood violence (*N*) on educational achievement (*Y*), we can use instrumental variables to estimate the effect. This approach involves find-

FIGURE 13.1   *Identifying the Effects of Multiple Mechanisms*

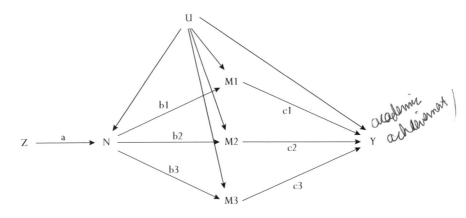

ing another variable (*Z*) that is correlated with neighborhood violence (*N*) and uncorrelated with the unobserved variables (*U*). *Z* is the source of exogenous variation in our neighborhood characteristic (*N*). For example, the city might randomly assign an antiviolence program to some neighborhoods and not others. Referred to as an instrument, *Z* is used to purge *N* of the portion of its variation that is correlated with the unobservables. The exogenous portion of *N*'s variation—that is, the uncorrelated portion that remains—is then used to estimate the effect of *N* on *Y*. Intuitively, this means that our analysis is using only the variation in neighborhood violence created by the antiviolence program to identify the effects of violence. Because the antiviolence program is randomly assigned, the communities that did not get the antiviolence program are similar in observed and unobserved ways to the communities that did. We can use a similar procedure to identify the effect of the neighborhood characteristic (*N*) on each of the mechanisms. For example, *b1* can be estimated as the association between the antiviolence program (*Z*) and educational expectations (*M1*) divided by the effect of the program on neighborhood violence (*a*).

The difficulty is that as long as each of the mechanisms (*M*'s) is associated with the outcome *Y* through the unobserved variables (*U*), we have no way to identify the effects of these mechanisms on educational achievement without more instruments, that is, without sources of exogenous variation in the mechanisms. Moreover, if the mechanisms are causally related to one another, then even if we could measure all the *U*'s, we would also have to assume that we have measured all the mechanisms as well, lest our estimate of the effect of any one mechanism on *Y* be biased by its association with an unobserved mechanism. If we thought that violence also directly reduced school attendance and that educational expectations are correlated with school attendance, but we did not observe school attendance, we might attribute some of the effects that operate solely through school attendance to educational expectations. One way to create the additional exogenous variation necessary to identify the effects of specific mechanisms (*c*'s) is to design an experiment with multiple treatment arms that produce exogenous random variation in both *N* and the *M*'s across the treatment arms.

Another general approach in an experimental setting is to examine patterns of effects on mediating mechanisms by subgroups. This can be useful when the experiment is not designed with multiple treatment arms for the various mechanisms and can be done by dividing the sample into subgroups for which theory and previous evidence suggest that treatment effects of *N* on *Y* may differ. A review of the overall pattern of results can provide some evidence to support a theoretical framework by testing, in part, the hypothesized relationships between mechanisms and outcomes across treatment categories and subgroups. The advantage of this type of experimental approach is that the source of variation in the social setting (for example, from something like randomly assigned rent subsidies that affect residential location) is clear, so we can be confident that changes in the mechanisms are causally related to residential location. However, without an exogenous source of variation in the mechanisms, the mechanisms may be spuriously correlated with the outcomes through unobservables.

Focusing on mechanisms can also strengthen our confidence in causal claims. Consider again figure 13.1 in which there are three mechanisms (*M*'s) and some set of unobserved confounders (*U*). If any one of the observed mechanisms is uncorrelated with *U*, then we can identify the portion of the effect of the treatment (*N*) on the outcome (*Y*) that operates through that mechanism. For example, if we can assume that the "joining gangs" mechanism (*M3*) is not affected by unobservables (*U*), then the arrow between *U* and *M3* disappears from the diagram. When *M3* is not affected by *U* and when we can observe the other mechanisms, both the effect (*b3*) of the treatment on joining gangs and the effect (*c3*) of joining gangs on achievement can now be identified even if there is no instrument. The effect of the neighborhood violence (*N*) on achievement (*Y*) that operates through joining gangs (*M3*) can be calculated as the product of *b3* and *c3*. Although this does not provide us with an unbiased estimate of the total effect of *N* on *Y*, if *b3* × *c3* is nonzero, it does provide evidence that there is some nonzero effect of *N* on *Y*.[6]

Complications Introduced by Effect Heterogeneity

In the previous example, the subgroups are observed and effect heterogeneity is harnessed to provide further information. The possibility of heterogeneity in effects also introduces complications, particularly when the subgroups cannot be identified in the data. The first complication has already been discussed in the methodological literature on instrumental-variables estimation—that is, unless the treatment effect can be assumed to be the same for all units of analysis, an instrument identifies the local average treatment effect (LATE) (Angrist and Krueger 2001; Angrist, Imbens, and Rubin 1996; and see Gennetian et al. 2005, for a less technical exposition). It answers the question: What is the average effect of the treatment among those who were actually induced to take the treatment by the instrument? The conventional solution to the LATE problem is to use multiple instruments (see applications by Gennetian, Magnuson, and Morris 2008; Kling, Liebman, and Katz 2007). If different LATE estimates from different instruments operate in the same direction and are of similar magnitude, then we can be more confident that the effect of the treatment is not specific to particular subgroups.

A second complication arises because estimating the role of a particular mechanism in the effect of a neighborhood characteristic (N) on an educational outcome (Y) requires identifying both the effect of X on the mechanism and the effect of the mechanism on Y. When there is treatment-effect heterogeneity, it is possible to produce an estimate of the role of the mechanism that applies to none of the cases if some cases experience effects of N on the mechanism and other cases experience an effect of the mechanism on Y (see also Bullock and Ha 2010). In technical terms, this means that the LATE for the effect of N has a different group of compliers than the LATE for the effect of M.

This problem highlights the importance of specifying and measuring sources of effect heterogeneity. It is particularly important to choose exogenous family or child characteristics, lest subgroup membership be a product of the treatment. Ideally, one might also purposely stratify one's sample to ensure a sufficient sample size in each subgroup. Our discussion thus far suggests a number of other family or child characteristics on which one might focus. Our emphasis on family capacity or family resources suggests that family income, family structure, number of children, or access to transportation may determine the strength of a neighborhood effect. Our emphasis on social ties and interactions in the neighborhood suggests that proximity to extended kin, parents' social ties to the neighborhood, or parental employment outside the neighborhood may determine the strength of the neighborhood effect. Many of these characteristics are both determinants and effects of the treatment. Further ethnographic work may be required to better understand these and other sources of effect heterogeneity.[7] We emphasize as well that an exhaustive search for effect heterogeneity may lead to multiple testing problems through the mining of sample data for statistical significance. Sources of effect heterogeneity should be closely informed by theory and prior research, and any analyses should be preceded by a clear set of hypotheses limiting the number of subgroups to be examined.

AN ILLUSTRATIVE EXAMPLE

Because violence is spatially concentrated in poor neighborhoods, it may be an important mechanism linking neighborhood poverty to school outcomes. In this section we sketch an example study that examines whether the observed correlation between neighborhood violence and unfavorable schooling outcomes (for example, Harding 2009a) is causal by manipulating exposure to neighborhood violence through youths' time use. Suppose we observe that youths living in more violent neighborhoods have lower school attendance and graduation rates, high rates of suspensions, and poorer math achievement. One can try to test the neighborhood-violence hypothesis by estimating the relationship between an individual's time spent on the streets in a violent neighborhood and educational achievement using a regression model, but this estimate will be susceptible to within-neighborhood selection bias (different youths choosing to spend their time in different places, in different ways, and with different people). An alternative is to identify this effect by generating exogenous variation in youths' time use through random assignment.

We can manipulate the amount of time that youths spend in areas of higher neighborhood violence under the hypothesis that such time use affects exposure to violence. Randomization ensures that individuals assigned to different locations are the same in both observed and unobserved characteristics, except for chance variation, so any differences in outcomes across groups can be attributed to the planned variation in exposure to violence.

Details of this example study can be found in the online appendix. Briefly, the design is the following: In the first stage, we select a target set of neighborhoods with high neighborhood violence and match each of them to neighborhoods that are comparable in terms of poverty, race, and educational levels but have lower neighborhood violence (see Seith et al. 2003 on the feasibility of matched-neighborhood designs). An intervention would be designed that is nonacademic but involves engagement with the neighborhood, such as working on a local clothing drive. For the study we would recruit individuals from the neighborhoods with higher levels of neighborhood violence, so that the neighborhoods where subjects are placed through the intervention are all less risky than their own neighborhoods. We would randomly assign these youths to teams in different locations outside of their own neighborhoods, some of which would have lower neighborhood violence than others.

With this type of random-assignment study design, we can learn about the effect of exposure to neighborhood violence by comparing the educational outcomes of youths in the different intervention groups. Although we do not directly manipulate exposure to violence, we can estimate the intervention's impact on educational outcomes and the intervention's impact on exposure to violence. For example, we hypothesize that youths working in less violent neighborhoods would experience more beneficial educational effects than those working in more violent neighborhoods. The benefits of the interventions may vary at the individual level by pre-intervention exposure and vulnerability to neighborhood violence, as determined by family connections to resources outside of the neighborhood, parenting skills, parental motivation and capacity to seek positive alternative environments for children, and the youth's own social relationships and decisions about how to use his or her time.

Measures of youths' time use, neighborhood characteristics and exposure to violence, and a range of information about families and their youths can be collected through surveys. With these data we can also check for any other important differences in youth experiences that arise during the study that may be correlated with exposure to violence. Survey data can be complemented by in-depth qualitative interviews with a small subsample of youths in both the experimental and control groups to better understand aspects of youth time use and exposure to violence that are difficult to detect or measure through a survey.

CONCLUSION

Our aim in this chapter has been to set the stage for future research—its opportunities as well as challenges, both conceptually and empirically—whose purpose is to better understand the influence of neighborhood social settings on youth educational outcomes. Conceptually, we argue that the field is ready to move away from estimating the effects of compositional properties of neighborhoods and toward an analysis of specific mechanisms and effect heterogeneity. A new focus on mechanisms, exposure, and vulnerability can only be achieved with more nuanced data. Our recommendation is to build on the successes of prior efforts and invest in new, mixed-methods data-collection strategies that can measure individual interactions, networks, and time use, and provide reliable assessments of neighborhood resources, cultural contexts, and physical conditions. We see particular promise in adapting time-use and social-network data-collection methods to assess exposure to the social and cultural processes that produce contextual effects. Finally, we point to both across-neighborhood and within-neighborhood selection biases as long-standing challenges in identifying neighborhood effects, and we illustrate some promising approaches for designing studies to identify mechanisms and assess effect heterogeneity. Although we tailor our discussion to social settings outside of the school and home, much of what we discuss might also be applied to school settings or home environments.

Neither neighborhoods nor individual residential decisions are static. Our proposed framework recognizes this to some extent by highlighting the importance of effect heterogeneity. Differences in cumulative exposure to advantaged or disadvantaged neighborhoods as well as differences in exposure depending on children's developmental stage may also be important sources of effect heterogeneity. We have not examined other forms of neighborhood dynamics. Neighborhoods change over time as residents move in and out, and community investment increases or decreases. When families move in response to changes in the neighborhoods around them or in response to the outcomes experienced by their children as a result of neighborhood context, more sophisticated statistical methods, such as marginal structural models or inverse probability of treatment weighting (Robins, Hernan, and Brumback 2000), are required to estimate unbiased causal effects, even when all sources of selection bias are accurately measured (Sampson, Sharkey, and Raudenbush 2008; Sharkey and Sampson 2010; Sharkey and Elwert forthcoming).

Identifying mechanisms and the types and extent of effect heterogeneity might uncover influences that contribute to income inequality as well as disparate educational outcomes. We have discussed identification of mechanisms for neighborhood effects without regard to the absolute magnitude of these effects, to their relative magnitudes compared with the effects of schools or of families, or to their resulting policy significance. Policy trade-offs between housing vouchers that offer the opportunity to move compared with place-based neighborhood investment (such as building a community center or clinic) are best informed by quantifying the size of effects and comparing costs and benefits. Mechanisms by which neighborhoods can have their effects are particularly important in considering these types of policy trade-offs. For example, if the mix of peers in neighborhood-based after-school activities is an important predictor of youths' math achievement, policymakers can evaluate the size of this beneficial peer effect (and any spillover effects) compared with the cost of busing disadvantaged youths to programs that offer this same mix of peers, or the cost of offering an equivalent program in the schools attended by disadvantaged youths.

Heterogeneous treatment effects are equally important in considering policy trade-offs. Policy interventions that primarily benefit only some subgroups may be more or less appealing. For example, an intervention with a large effect on a small group of youths may be more or less appealing than an intervention with a small effect on a very large group of youths.

We thank Greg Duncan, Richard Murnane, Rebecca Blank, Robert Sampson, Steve Raudenbush, Patrick Sharkey, Susan Clampet-Lundquist, Tama Leventhal, Larry Katz, Robert Moffitt, and participants at the Social Inequality and Educational Disadvantage conferences and the University of Michigan Robert Wood Johnson Health Policy Seminar for helpful comments on previous drafts of this paper. The views expressed here are those of the authors and should not be interpreted as those of the Congressional Budget Office.

NOTES

Online appendix available at: http://www.russellsage.org/duncan_murnane_online_appendix.pdf.

1. V may therefore be a subset of X.
2. In addition to the promise of MTO qualitative research for uncovering potential mechanisms, the MTO follow-up surveys collected data on items that also provide some supporting evidence for particular pathways by which MTO affected outcomes. Although the MTO study was primarily designed to answer questions about the causal effects of housing vouchers and neighborhoods and not to identify specific mechanisms, one method of gleaning possible mediating mechanisms is to examine the pattern of MTO's experimental effects on outcomes (such as math achievement) and mediators (such as school discipline) to see if the effects align with hypotheses.
3. Michael Sobel (2006) discusses another identification problem in mobility experiments, interference between units that we do not fully describe here. This is a particular challenge in this context because encouraging and succeeding in changing residential mobility inherently can have possible confounding effects on the families in the receiving neighborhood as well as those in the neighborhood left behind.
4. Note that one might further theorize the existence of mechanisms for these mechanisms. The level of detail in the specification of mechanisms depends on one's substantive and policy goals. See Stephen L. Morgan and Christopher Winship (2007, chapter 8) for a discussion of this issue.
5. For simplicity, we omit the observed X's from the figure. The discussion in this section will assume conditioning on observed X variables.
6. This discussion is an example of identification through what Judea Pearl (2000) calls his "front door" criterion. See Winship and Harding (2008) for an example and further details.
7. One might also consider family type to be a latent class and conduct a latent class analysis.

REFERENCES

Ainsworth-Darnell, James, and Douglas Downey. 1998. "Assessing the Oppositional Culture Explanation for Racial/Ethnic Differences in School Performance." *American Sociological Review* 63(4): 536–53.

Anderson, Elijah. 1999. *Code of the Street: Decency, Violence, and the Moral Life of the Inner-City*. New York: Norton.

Angrist, Joshua, and Alan Krueger. 2001. "Instrumental Variables and the Search for Identification: From Supply and Demand to Natural Experiments." *Journal of Economic Perspectives* 15(4): 69–85.

Angrist, Joshua, Guido Imbens, and Donald Rubin. 1996. "Identification of Causal Effects Using Instrumental Variables." JASA Applications Invited paper, with comments and authors' response. *Journal of the American Statistical Association* 91(434): 444–55.

Brewster, Karin L. 1994a. "Neighborhood Context and the Transition to Sexual Activity Among Young Black Women." *Demography* 31(4): 603–14.

———. 1994b. "Race Differences in Sexual Activity Among Adolescent Women: The Role of Neighborhood Characteristics." *American Sociological Review* 59(3): 408–24.

Bullock, John G., and Shang E. Ha. 2010. "Mediation Analysis Is Harder Than It Looks." In *Cambridge Handbook of Experimental Political Science*, edited by James N. Druckman, Donald P. Green, James H. Kuklinski, and Arthur Lupia. New York: Cambridge University Press.

Bureau of Labor Statistics. 2009. *American Time Use Survey User's Guide*. Available at: http://www.bls.gov/tus/atususersguide.pdf (accessed on February 25, 2010).

Carter, Prudence L. 2005. *Keepin' It Real: School Success Beyond Black and White*. New York: Oxford University Press.

Cohen, Lawrence E., and Marcus Felson. 1979. "Social Change and Crime Rate Trends: A Routine Activity Approach." *American Sociological Review* 44(4): 588–608.

Coleman, James S. 1988. "Social Capital in the Creation of Human Capital." *American Journal of Sociology* 94(supplement): S95–S120.

Cook, Philip, and Jens Ludwig. 1998. "The Burden of 'Acting White': Do Black Adolescents Disparage Academic Achievement?" In *The Black White Test Score Gap*, edited by Christopher Jencks and Meredith Phillips. Washington, D.C.: Brookings Institution.

Csikszentmihalyi, Mihaly, and Reed Larson. 1987. "Validity and Reliability of the Experience Sampling Method." *Journal of Nervous and Mental Disease* 175(9): 526–36.

Dance, L. Janelle. 2002. *Tough Fronts: The Impact of Street Culture on Schooling*. New York: Routledge Falmer Press.

Fordham, Signithia, and John Ogbu. 1986. "Black Students' School Success: Coping with the Burden of 'Acting White.' " *Urban Review* 18(3): 176–206.

Fryer, Roland G. 2006. " 'Acting White': The Social Price Paid by the Best and Brightest Minority Students." *Education Next* 6(1): 53–59.

Fu, Yang-chih. 2005. "Measuring Personal Networks with Daily Contacts: A Single-Item Survey Question and the Contact Diary." *Social Networks* 27(3): 169–86.

———. 2007. "Contact Diaries: Building Archives of Actual and Comprehensive Personal Networks." *Field Methods* 19(2): 194–217.

Furstenberg, Frank F., Thomas D. Cook, Jacquelynne Eccles, Glen H. Elder Jr., and Arnold Sameroff, eds. 1999. *Managing to Make It: Urban Families and Adolescent Success.* Chicago: University of Chicago Press.

Gennetian, Lisa, Katherine Magnuson, and Pamela Morris. 2008. "Statistical Association to Causation: What Developmentalists Can Learn from Instrumental Variables Techniques Coupled with Experimental Data." *Developmental Psychology* 44(2): 381–94.

Gennetian, Lisa, Pamela Morris, Johannes Bos, and Howard Bloom. 2005. "Coupling the Nonexperimental Technique of Instrumental Variables with Experimental Data to Learn How Programs Create Impacts." In *Moving to the Next Level: Combining Experimental and Non-Experimental Methods to Advance Employment Policy Research,* edited by Howard Bloom. New York: Russell Sage Foundation.

Goldenberg, Claude, Ronald Gallimore, Leslie Reese, and Helen Garnier. 2001. "Cause or Effect?: A Longitudinal Study of Immigrant Latino Parents' Aspirations and Expectations, and Their Children's School Performance." *American Educational Research Journal* 38(3): 547–82.

Hannerz, Ulf. 1969. *Soulside: Inquiries into Ghetto Culture and Community.* New York: Columbia University Press.

Harding, David J. 2007. "Cultural Context, Sexual Behavior, and Romantic Relationships in Disadvantaged Neighborhoods." *American Sociological Review* 72(3): 341–64.

———. 2009a. "Collateral Consequences of Violence in Disadvantaged Neighborhoods." *Social Forces* 88(2): 757–82.

———. 2009b. "Violence, Older Peers, and the Socialization of Adolescent Boys in Disadvantaged Neighborhoods." *American Sociological Review* 74(3): 445–64.

———. 2010. *Living the Drama: Community, Conflict, and Culture Among Inner-City Boys.* Chicago: University of Chicago Press.

Harris, Angel L. 2006. "I (Don't) Hate School: Revisiting Oppositional Culture Theory of Blacks' Resistance to Schooling." *Social Forces* 85(2): 797–834.

Jarrett, Robin L. 1997a. "African American Family and Parenting Strategies in Impoverished Neighborhoods." *Qualitative Sociology* 20(2): 275–88.

———. 1997b. "Bringing Families Back In: Neighborhood Effects on Child Development." In *Neighborhood Poverty.* Vol. 2: *Policy Implications in Studying Neighborhoods,* edited by Jeanne Brooks-Gunn, Greg J. Duncan, and J. Lawrence Aber. New York: Russell Sage Foundation.

Jencks, Christopher, and Susan E. Mayer. 1990. "Residential Segregation, Job Proximity, and Black Job Opportunities: The Empirical Status of the Spatial Mismatch Hypothesis." In *Inner-City Poverty in the United States,* edited by Lawrence Lynn Jr. and Michael G. H. McGeary. Washington, D.C.: National Academy of Sciences Press.

Juster, F. Thomas, and Frank P. Stafford, eds. 1985. *Time, Goods, and Well-Being.* Ann Arbor: University of Michigan, Institute for Social Research.

Kling, Jeffrey R., Jeffrey B. Liebman, and Lawrence Katz. 2007. "Experimental Analysis of Neighborhood Effects." *Econometrica* 75(1): 83–119.

Larson, Reed. 1989. "Beeping Children and Adolescents: A Method for Studying Time Use and Daily Experience." *Journal of Youth and Adolescence* 18(6): 511–30.

Leventhal, Tama, and Jeanne Brooks-Gunn. 2000. "The Neighborhoods They Live In: The Effects of Neighborhood Residence upon Child and Adolescent Outcomes." *Psychological Bulletin* 126(2): 309–37.

Manski, Charles F. 1993. "Identification of Endogenous Social Effects: The Reflection Problem." *Review of Economic Studies* 60(3): 531–42.

———. 1995. *Identification Problems in the Social Sciences.* Cambridge, Mass.: Harvard University Press.

———. 2000. "Economic Analysis of Social Interactions." *Journal of Economic Perspectives* (14)3: 115–36.

Massey, Douglas S. 2001. "Segregation and Violent Crime in Urban America." In *Problem of the Century: Racial Stratification in the United States,* edited by Elijah Anderson and Douglas S. Massey. New York: Russell Sage Foundation.

———. 2004. "Segregation and Stratification: A Biosocial Perspective," *Du Bois Review* 1(1): 7–25.

Massey, Douglas S., and Nancy Denton. 1993. *American Apartheid: Segregation and the Making of an Underclass.* Cambridge, Mass.: Harvard University Press.

Morgan, Stephen L., and Aage B. Sørensen. 1999. "Parental Networks, Social Closure, and Mathematics Learning: A Test of Coleman's Social Capital Explanation of School Effects." *American Sociological Review* 64(5): 661–81.

Morgan, Stephen L., and Christopher Winship. 2007. *Counterfactuals and Causal Inference: Methods and Principles for Social Research.* Cambridge: Cambridge University Press.

Mouw, Ted. 2000. "Job Relocation and the Racial Gap in Unemployment in Detroit and Chicago, 1980 to 1990." *American Sociological Review* 65(5): 730–53.

Newman, Katherine S. 1999. *No Shame in My Game: The Working Poor in the Inner-City.* New York: Vintage Books/ Russell Sage Foundation.

Ogbu, John U. 2004. "Collective Identity and the Burden of 'Acting White' in Black History, Community, and Education." *Urban Review* 36(1): 1–35.

Pearl, Judea. 2000. *Causality: Models, Reasoning, and Inference.* Cambridge: Cambridge University Press.

Ponce, Ninez A., Katherine J. Hoggatt, Michelle Wilhelm, and Beate Ritz. 2005. "Preterm Birth: The Interaction of Traffic-Related Air Pollution with Economic Hardship in Los Angeles Neighborhoods." *American Journal of Epidemiology* 162(2): 140–48.

Raudenbush, Stephen W, and Robert J. Sampson. 1999. "Ecometrics: Toward a Science of Assessing Ecological Settings, with Application to the Systematic Social Observation of Neighborhoods." *Sociological Methodology* 29(1): 1–41.

Reardon, Sean F., and Kendra Bischoff. 2011. "Income Inequality and Income Segregation." *American Journal of Sociology* 116(4): 1092–153.

Robins, James A., Miguel A. Hernan, and Babette Brumback. 2000. "Marginal Structural Models and Causal Inference in Epidemiology." *Epidemiology* 11(5): 550–60.

Robinson, John P. 1977. *How Americans Used Time in 1965.* Ann Arbor: University of Michigan, Institute for Social Research.

Sampson, Robert J. 2008. "Moving to Inequality: Neighborhood Effects and Experiments Meet Social Structure." *American Journal of Sociology* 114(1): 189–231.

Sampson, Robert J., Jeffrey D. Morenoff, and Thomas Gannon-Rowley. 2002. "Assessing Neighborhood Effects: Social Processes and New Directions in Research." *Annual Review of Sociology* 28: 443–78.

Sampson, Robert, Stephen Raudenbush, and Felton Earls. 1997. "Neighborhoods and Violent Crime: A Multilevel Study of Collective Efficacy." *Science* 277(5328): 918–24.

Sampson, Robert J., Patrick Sharkey, and Stephen Raudenbush. 2008. "Durable Effects of Concentrated Disadvantage on Verbal Ability Among African-American Children." *Proceedings of the National Academy of Sciences* 105(3): 845–52.

Seith, David C., Nandita Verma, Howard S. Bloom, and George C. Galster. 2003. "Exploring the Feasibility and Quality of Matched Neighborhood Research Designs." MDRC Working Papers on Research Methodology. New York: MDRC.

Sharkey, Patrick T. 2006. "Navigating Dangerous Streets: The Sources and Consequences of Street Efficacy." *American Sociological Review* 71(6): 826–46.

Sharkey, Patrick T., and Robert J. Sampson. 2010. "Destination Effects: Residential Mobility and Trajectories of Adolescent Violence in a Stratified Metropolis." *Criminology* 48(3): 639–81.

Sharkey, Patrick T., and Felix Elwert. Forthcoming. "The Legacy of Disadvantage: Multigenerational Neighborhood Effects on Cognitive Ability." *American Journal of Sociology.*

Small, Mario L. 2004. *Villa Victoria: The Transformation of Social Capital in a Boston Barrio.* Chicago: University of Chicago Press.

———. 2006. "Neighborhood Institutions as Resource Brokers: Childcare Centers, Inter-Organizational Ties, and Resource Access Among the Poor." *Social Problems* 53(2): 274–92.

———. 2007. "Is There Such a Thing as 'The Ghetto'?: The Perils of Assuming That the South Side of Chicago Represents Poor Black Neighborhoods." *City* 11(3): 413–21.

————. 2009. *Unanticipated Gains: Origins of Network Inequality in Everyday Life.* New York: Oxford University Press.

Small, Mario Luis, Erin M. Jacobs, and Rebekah P. Massengill. 2008. "Why Organizational Ties Matter for Neighborhood Effects: A Study of Resource Access through Childcare Centers." *Social Forces* 87(1): 387–414.

Small, Mario L., and Monica McDermott. 2006. "The Presence of Organizational Resources in Poor Urban Neighborhoods: An Analysis of Average and Contextual Effects." *Social Forces* 84(3): 1697–724.

Small, Mario L., and Laura Stark. 2005. "Are Poor Neighborhoods Resource-Deprived?: A Case Study of Childcare Centers in New York." *Social Science Quarterly* 86(s1): 1013–36.

Sobel, Michael. 2006. "What Do Randomized Studies of Housing Mobility Demonstrate? Causal Inference in the Face of Interference." *Journal of the American Statistical Association* 101(476): 1398–407.

Solorzano, Daniel G. 1992. "An Exploratory Analysis of the Effects of Race, Class and Gender on Student and Parent Mobility Aspirations." *Journal of Negro Education* 61(1): 30–44.

South, Scott J., and Eric P. Baumer. 2000. "Deciphering Community and Race Effects on Adolescent Premarital Childbearing." *Social Forces* 78(4): 1379–407.

South, Scott J., and Kyle D. Crowder. 1999. "Neighborhood Effects on Family Formation: Concentrated Poverty and Beyond." *American Sociological Review* 64(1): 113–32.

Suttles, Gerald. 1968. *The Social Order of the Slum: Ethnicity and Territory in the Inner City.* Chicago: University of Chicago Press.

Whyte, William. 1943. *Streetcorner Society.* Chicago: University of Chicago Press.

Wikström, Per-Olof H., and David A. Butterworth. 2006. *Adolescent Crime: Individual Difference and Lifestyles.* Cullompton, U.K.: Willan.

Wikström, Per-Olof H., Vania Ceccato, Beth Hardie, and Kyle Treiber. 2010. "Activity Fields and the Dynamics of Crime: Advancing Knowledge About the Role of the Environment in Crime Causation." *Journal of Quantitative Criminology* 26(1): 55–87.

Wilson, William Julius. 1987. *The Truly Disadvantaged: The Inner-City, the Underclass, and Public Policy.* Chicago: University of Chicago Press.

Winship, Christopher, and David J. Harding. 2008. "A General Strategy for the Identification of Age, Period, Cohort Models: A Mechanism Based Approach," *Sociological Methods and Research* 36(3): 362–401.

Young, Alford A., Jr. 2004. *The Minds of Marginalized Black Men: Making Sense of Mobility, Opportunity, and Life Chances.* Princeton, N.J.: Princeton University Press.

Zenk, Shannon N., Amy J. Schulz, Barbara A. Israel, and Sherman A. James. 2005. "Neighborhood Racial Composition, Neighborhood Poverty, and the Spatial Access." *American Journal of Public Health* 95(4): 660–67.

Part V

Labor Markets

Chapter 14

The Effects of Local Employment Losses on Children's Educational Achievement

Elizabeth O. Ananat, Anna Gassman-Pines, and Christina M. Gibson-Davis

As the United States closes out the first decade of the twenty-first century, it is experiencing its worst economic crisis since the Great Depression. Rising unemployment and associated increases in poverty have highlighted the importance of understanding the linkages between economic downturns and child well-being, as even temporary income losses are strongly correlated with negative outcomes for children (Duncan and Brooks-Gunn 1997). Moreover, the destruction of blue-collar U.S. jobs through globalization and technological growth has meant that job loss is much more likely to hit families and communities in which adults have low education (Autor 2010); impacts of downturns thus tend to concentrate among children who already face disadvantage, as outlined in the other chapters of this volume.

Identifying the causal effects of economic losses on children, however, is difficult because in most instances there are likely to be unmeasured or unobserved characteristics that affect both a given family's financial status and the family's well-being. For example, in families facing health or substance-use problems, parents may be less likely to maintain employment and children may also have less school success than in other families. Using other methods of accounting for this omitted variable bias, such as creating an instrument for parental job loss, may miss effects of local economic crises on children that come through channels other than parental unemployment. Such channels could include increased stress among parents and teachers, declines in the tax base that reduce school resources, or spillover effects in the classroom from peers whose parents lose jobs.

In chapter 15 of this volume, Phillip Levine focuses on the impact of individual-level parental job loss, from many different sources, on families. In this chapter, we complement his approach by examining the impact of community-level job losses caused by business closings and layoffs on communities' student test scores. Using plausibly exogenous variation in business closings permits us to identify the causal effect of an economic downturn on students overall and on vulnerable subgroups of students in particular, and can provide insight to policy makers and researchers seeking solutions to cope with the effects of the current economic crisis.

We use data from North Carolina, which has experienced significant ongoing job losses from globalization that began well before the 2008 to 2009 downturn. Over the past twenty years, the furniture and textile industries, once important foundations of the state's economy, have largely collapsed, and newer economic drivers such as microchip manufacturing have been subject to significant fluctuations as well. Using data from 1997 to 2007, we link information on a county's business closings and layoffs to data on the end-of-grade test scores of fourth- and eighth-graders for that county. In addition to identifying the reduced-form effect of closings on test scores, our analysis enables us to explore many potential mechanisms that allow us to peek inside the "black box" to determine *how* community economic losses affect children.

We find that community-level job losses lower test scores; effects are stronger for older children and are concentrated among children in the lower middle of the test-score distribution. Job losses have immediate effects on children from families with low socioeconomic status (SES) but take longer to affect children from high-SES families. It appears that the lower test scores are not the product of structural changes, such as reduced school resources, or of selective migration of high-achieving students. Instead, our results suggest that short-term psychological responses such as stress, including the spillover of stress onto children whose families are not directly affected by unemployment, most likely account for much of the observed negative impacts.

A broad consensus now exists that business closings can be viewed as exogenous shocks to workers and communities adjusting for counties' pre-existing characteristics (Jacobson, LaLonde, and Sullivan 1993; Stevens 1997) and that effects on workers and communities subsequent to closings can therefore be interpreted as causal effects of job loss.

BACKGROUND

One literature in this area has concentrated on the effects of community-level job losses (the total number of jobs lost in a community) on community-wide outcomes such as levels of employment or welfare receipt. A separate literature has looked at the effects of an individual-level job loss (the loss of a job by the household head in a family as a result of a factory closing, regardless of how many others in the community are affected) on family-level outcomes such as income, parenting practices, or children's test scores. To complement this work, we use a different strategy, one in which we examine the effect of the number of jobs lost in the community on community-wide measures of children's achievement. This strategy allows us to identify effects on children that do not come solely through their parents' employment status. In the following section we discuss the community-level and individual-level literatures on the effect of job loss and use their results to generate hypotheses on why communitywide job losses might affect aggregate levels of child well-being.

Evidence of Effects of Community-Level Job Losses

Several papers coming from the field of economics have measured the causal effects of job loss on community-level employment, earnings, and public-assistance receipt. A set of studies by Dan A. Black (2005a, 2005b), and Black, Terra G. McKinnish, and Seth G. Sanders (2003) examined booms and busts in the steel and coal industries in the 1970s and 1980s and found that downturns led to lower employment not only within but also outside of the initially affected industries. Downturns resulted in lower aggregate earnings in affected counties and to higher rates of receipt of Disability Insurance and Aid to Families with Dependent Children. Both lower income and higher rates of public-assistance receipt might augur worse outcomes for children, including children whose parents were not directly affected by a business closure but were affected by related job loss in other industries. Timothy J. Bartik (1993) found that the employment and wages of minorities and low-skilled workers were particularly affected by changes in the rate of local job growth, which raises the possibility that children from disadvantaged families in particular may have lower test scores in the wake of job losses.

Other research has examined the effects of relative job losses on community characteristics, such as property values. Michael Greenstone and Enrico Moretti (2004) found that when counties that were finalists to receive a new plant were compared, the county that did not win the plant experienced lower property-value growth than did its winning counterpart. Lower property values imply a lower overall quality of life in a community, but Greenstone and Moretti did not identify in what specific ways residents are worse off. Greenstone, Richard Hornbeck, and Moretti (2008) explored wages and employment and found evidence that both are partial causes for the difference in property values. However, it is plausible that a poorer educational environment for children is another cause of lower property values. Furthermore, decreased property values by themselves can cause a decline in the level of financial resources and thus a potential decline in the quality of a community's public-education system (Ludwig and Bassi 1999).

Finally, qualitative work has found increases in community-level stress from the shutdown of large local firms. Allison Zippay (1991) detailed how displaced steelworkers in a Pennsylvania community were required to rely on family, friends, and neighbors for economic and social support. If enough people in a community experience job loss after a business closes, it is quite likely that the aggregate level of stress may increase among family, friends, and neighbors, and thereby affect families that do not directly experience unemployment. Teacher stress might also increase and alter the educational environment of schools.

Evidence also suggests that there may be "silver linings" for communities from business closings, however. The studies of steel and coal communities by Dan A. Black and colleagues (2005a, 2005b) found that downturns led to reductions in school dropout rates, as people looked to education to improve their job-market prospects. Increased parental education might portend better outcomes for children (Oreopoulos, Page, and Stevens 2006), and older children may also respond to a changing job market by investing more in their own education. In addition, fewer opportunities in the local private labor market may increase teacher retention, which has been linked with higher student achievement (Rockoff 2004).

Evidence for Individual-Level Losses

The most immediate individual-level effect of losing one's job through a business closing is unemployment. Psychologists have found that unemployment has strong links to reduced individual well-being in many domains, including economic and also physical health (Sullivan and von Wachter 2009), psychological health (McKee-Ryan et al. 2005), and one's sense of satisfaction and accomplishment (Blustein 2008). Job loss also leads to lower earnings over the longer term because people who lose their jobs as a result of industry downturns must start over in new firms and new industries (Jacobson, LaLonde, and Sullivan 1993; Stevens 1997).

Individual unemployment is associated with decreased functioning of families and child well-being. Job loss can lead to higher levels of parental depression and anxiety, and thereby impair parent-child interactions (Conger and Elder 1994; Jones 1988; McLoyd et al. 1994). Parental mental health and parent-child interactions have both been strongly linked to child adjustment and school achievement (Elder et al. 1995; McLoyd 1998). In particular, recent research has shown that parental unemployment resulting from business closings has negative effects on children's grade completion (Stevens and Schaller 2011), test scores (Rege, Telle, and Votruba 2007), and reduced later acquisition of human capital, such as lower earnings and greater receipt of public assistance in adulthood (Oreopoulos, Page, and Stevens 2008). Even after parents return to the workforce, permanently lower earnings can affect children; parental income and material resources are critical to child well-being and in particular to school achievement (Dahl and Lochner 2008).

HYPOTHESES

The consensus that business closings have negative impacts on communities beyond just individual impacts (through job losses in related industries, declining property values, increased community stress, and the like) coupled with the consensus that parental job loss harms children's development suggests that there may be multiple impacts of business closings in a community on aggregate child academic achievement. In this chapter, we test this question by examining whether community-level job losses induced by firm closings cause decreases in test scores among local fourth- and eighth-graders.[1]

We hypothesize that business closings will affect test scores both through lower achievement among children whose parents lose jobs and through additional community-level mechanisms. We do not, therefore, expect that the relationship between community job losses and community average test scores will be simply the relationship between individual-level job loss and child tests scores identified in earlier papers (Oreopoulos, Page, and Stevens 2008; Stevens and Schaller 2011), scaled by the size of the total job loss in relation to the size of the community. Whether the relationship at the community level is more or less negative than the relationship at the family level depends on whether potential negative effects of job losses on communities (declining tax base, increased stress) or potential "silver linings" (increased teacher retention, increased expected returns to education) dominate.

Our data set does not allow us to observe whether each child has experienced job loss at the family level, but using demographic information on children, we are able to identify subgroups of children whose families are likely to have been directly affected by job losses and to compare their outcomes with those of demographic subgroups whose families likely did not lose jobs. In this way we are able to gauge the extent to which community-level job losses affect members of the community who both do and who do not experience individual losses.

Further, we build on previous research by examining a variety of potential mechanisms for changes in child test scores. We test for effects on both reading and math scores, as math scores might more strongly reflect school inputs, whereas reading scores might more strongly reflect family inputs. We look for changes in peer composition after plant closings and for peer effects through spillovers from affected to unaffected groups of children. We test for impacts through strategic educational investments by examining whether children respond more strongly to changes in employment within their own gender. We examine whether the demographic makeup of the industries affected by job loss affects our results, by testing whether job losses that disproportionately impact women lead to different child outcomes than job losses that disproportionately impact men. We test for differences in impacts on test scores for children from low-education and high-education families. In the conclusion, we discuss fruitful areas for future research, including increased attention to measuring both family- and community-level processes.

TABLE 14.1   *Student Demographics*

	Eighth Grade (N = 1,054,642)	Fourth Grade (N = 1,075,670)
	Percentage of Total	Percentage of Total
Ethnicity		
Black	29.12	28.99
White	62.26	60.27
Hispanic	4.14	5.34
American Indian	1.39	1.44
Asian	1.79	1.81
Multiracial or other	1.30	2.15
Gender		
Female	49.65	49.36
Male	50.35	50.64
Parents' education (SES proxy)		
Neither parent has more than a high school diploma	56.46	56.26
At least one parent has some higher education	43.54	43.74
Reading score	Mean	Mean
Overall	212.3	197.4
Parent low-education subgroup	209.5	192.5
Parent high-education subgroup	215.9	203.6
Math score		
Overall	256.2	236.8
Parent low-education subgroup	252.2	231.8
Parent high-education subgroup	261.5	243.2

Source: Authors' calculations based on data from North Carolina Education Research Data Center (n.d.).

DATA

Data for this chapter come from three sources:

1. Student achievement data from the North Carolina School Administrative Records database

2. An array of publicly available county-level, time-varying characteristics

3. The Business Closings Database, an in-house database that uses industry information obtained from the North Carolina Employment Security Commission

The North Carolina School Administrative Records database contains detailed information for all 115 public school districts in North Carolina. Data are available at the district, school, teacher, and student levels, and incorporate a wide variety of measures, including school demographic composition, teacher performance and experience, and student achievement. These data are collected by the North Carolina Department of Public Instruction and housed at the North Carolina Education Research Data Center (NCERDC) at Duke University. Data are currently available from 1997 to 2007. Table 14.1 presents demographic data on students, including race and gender composition and also reports a proxy for students' socioeconomic background: the highest education level either of their parents has achieved. Although the education categories vary from year to year in the data, it is always possible to distinguish parents with more than a high school education from parents who are high school graduates or dropouts. In the text that follows, we refer to children in families whose parents have a high school diploma or less as the low socio-economic status (SES) group. Slightly more than one-half of North Carolina students (56 percent) fall into the low-SES group.

The measures of achievement data that we use are end-of-grade (EOG) tests in reading comprehension and math. Tests are taken by all fourth- and eighth-graders in North Carolina public schools. End-of-grade tests in reading comprehension measure the ability to demonstrate understanding of a written passage and knowledge of vocabulary. End-of-grade tests in math measure proficiency in five areas: numbers and operations, measurement, geometry, data analysis and probability, and algebra. We choose to examine tests taken by eighth-graders because such tests are unlikely to be affected by dropout rates. In addition, these tests, unlike tests taken in later grades, are required of all eighth-graders, regardless of their curriculum or track. To understand how responses to job losses may vary by developmental stage, we also examine the test scores of fourth-graders.

Because the scoring of tests has varied over time, we standardize each year's scores to have a mean of 0 and a standard deviation of 1. We then take the mean standardized score within each of one hundred counties for each of eleven years. We use data from just over one million tests in reading comprehension and in math for both fourth- and eighth-graders. Table 14.1 presents raw test-score summary statistics for the universe of students. Students with at least one parent who has more than a high school degree have average math and reading scores about 20 percent of a standard deviation higher than students whose parents have a terminal high school diploma or less.

The second data set is an array of publicly available county-level time-varying characteristics. Data provided at the county level include size of the working-age population (U.S. Census Bureau), unemployment rate (U.S. Bureau of Labor Statistics), and tax revenue per capita (North Carolina Treasury). We also present county-level schools data. Most of the one hundred counties in North Carolina contain exactly one school district, and for the handful of counties that contain more than one school district, we make county-level measures using the pupil-weighted average of district characteristics. The schools measures, all from the NCERDC database, include the one-year teacher turnover rate, student severe behavioral offenses, student year-over-year attrition from the sample, per-pupil expenditures, student racial composition, and within-district racial segregation.[2] Summary statistics for these measures are presented in online appendix table 14.A1 (available at http://www.russellsage.org/duncan_murnane_online_appendix.pdf).

The third data set is the Business Closings Database, an in-house database that uses industry information obtained from the North Carolina Employment Security Commission. The state Employment Security Commission provides information on any business that shuts down or lays off workers. On the basis of this information, we have constructed, for all one hundred counties and for the years 1997 to 2007 a database that includes the company name, the type of business (using the North American Industry Classification System, or NAICS), whether the business is closing or laying off workers, the number of workers affected, the date of employment termination, and the reason for the closing or layoff (for example, business relocation, branch closure and consolidation, and so on). Although the economics literature has typically treated job losses and job gains as parallel processes, we focus on losses, because policy concerns center on remedying harm caused by unemployment, and behavioral economics research suggests that losses may have stronger impacts than gains (Kahneman and Tversky 1979). We create measures of job losses by quarter, scaled by the working-age (age twenty-five to sixty-four) population in that county.

By combining the NAICS code associated with the closing or layoff with data from the decennial U.S. Census, we identify the national age, gender, race, and education composition of the industry in which workers lost jobs. This information allows us more precision in matching job

FIGURE 14.1   *Maximum Share of Workers Affected by Closings or Layoffs in a Month, by County, 1997 to 2007*

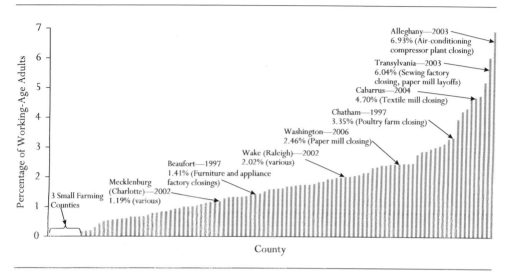

Source: Authors' calculations based on data from North Carolina Employment Security Commission (n.d.).

losses to pupils whose parents' earning prospects are likely to have been impacted by the event. We compile these job losses at the county level by quarter and calculate the share of all potential employment in the county that is lost in that quarter due to the closing.

As illustrated by figure 14.1, the measure of job losses derived using the Business Closings Database generates good variation both across counties and over time. Figure 14.1 displays the maximum share of jobs lost to closings in a month in each county over the period under observation. Losses range from zero for three small farming communities to 6.9 percent of the working-age population in Alleghany County, where a large air-conditioning plant closed. Other large business closings include a textile plant in Cabarrus County (4.7 percent of the working-age population lost jobs) and a poultry farm in Chatham County (3.4 percent). Online appendix figure 14.A1 displays the variation within and between years and counties in the intensity of job losses. Job losses were generally most intense prior to 2003, when textile, tobacco, and manufacturing were experiencing severe declines, though losses continued throughout the study period.

Our data on job losses strongly predict unemployment. As an illustration, figure 14.2 displays graphically the relationship between overall losses at the state level and North Carolina's residual unemployment relative to national trend over time; the two lines co-vary visibly. Within counties, a job loss impacting 1 percent of a county's working-age population leads to an increase in unemployment of 0.86 percent (standard error = 0.095) the following quarter; the effect fades in the next quarter, causing an increase in unemployment relative to baseline of 0.73 percent (standard error = 0.075). It continues to fade subsequently.

METHODS

We estimate the effect of the number of jobs recently lost to closings and layoffs in a given county in a given year on the test scores for that county in that year. In some regressions, instead of examining the effect of job losses on test scores, we examine the effect on another county-year outcome,

FIGURE 14.2   *Quarterly Residual Unemployment and Percentage of Affected Workers for North Carolina, 1997 to 2007*

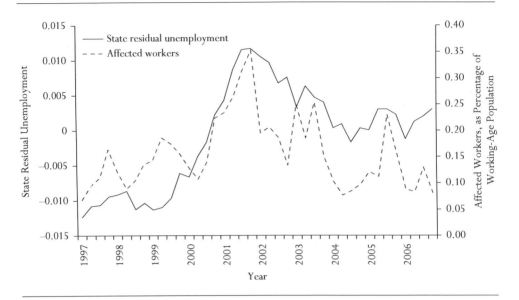

Source: Authors' calculations based on data from North Carolina Employment Security Commission (n.d.).

such as student attrition or school-reported student behavior offenses. When measuring these effects we control for the following: persistent differences between counties; any events that may have affected all counties in the state in any given year; and different over-time trends within each county. Using this approach means that our estimates isolate the effect of job losses that are "shocks" to a county, relative to the county's typical economic situation, the overall economy in the state that year, and the county's own gradually evolving labor market. Likewise, our estimates isolate test-score "jumps" in a county relative to the county's typical test scores, the overall test performance of students across the state that year, and the county's own gradually evolving test-score performance. We then measure the relationship of job-loss shocks to jumps in test scores in order to identify the effects of job losses on achievement. The approach rules out a great deal of alternate explanations that might otherwise prevent us from making causal claims. For example, our results cannot be due to stable county characteristics, such as a more disadvantaged population, that might be related both to a county's likelihood of losing jobs and its students' test scores. Our results also cannot be attributed to statewide changes in a given year, such as the creation of a new education or business policy, which could affect both job losses and test scores across the state. Finally, our results cannot be due to county-specific trends over time, such as declining school quality in a given county, leading companies to leave town. As discussed in more detail later, we also formally test to see whether changes in test scores precede job losses and find that they do not.

Ultimately the definition of "recent" is arbitrary when we create the measure of jobs recently lost in the county. One option is to include separate measures of job losses that have occurred in each period prior to the test (all the way back to the beginning of the panel); however, estimates for effects three or more quarters prior to the test are never statistically significant, so for elegance and clarity we include measures only for the last four quarters, and in the tables report the coefficients only for the last two quarters.

As an illustrative example, consider a county with 100,000 adults age twenty-five to sixty-four that experienced exactly one job loss in April of the year prior to the test. If that job loss affected 1,000 individuals, then the value of our job-loss measure for that county in that year would be 1,000/100,000, or 1 percent, in the quarter of the test. If we estimate a relationship between job losses in the quarter of the test and normalized reading test scores of −0.1, this can be interpreted to mean that a county that experienced a job loss to 1 percent of its working-age population in that quarter had reading scores one-tenth of a standard deviation lower than would otherwise be expected, given that county's typical test scores and recent trend in scores.

In some cases we use an alternative measure of job losses that represents the share of losses attributable to a given demographic group, such as high school graduates, women, or African Americans. When using this measure, if the county in the example just described experienced the loss in an industry that employs 50 percent women and 30 percent African Americans nationally, and the county has 50,000 women and 10,000 African Americans, then our job-loss measure in the quarter of the test would be 0.5 × 1,000/50,000, or 1 percent, for women, and 0.3 × 1,000/10,000, or 3 percent, for African Americans.

RESULTS

Table 14.2 reports the results from estimating the relationship of job losses in the quarter of the test and the previous quarter to county average test scores (measures for the third and fourth previous quarters are included in the regressions, but their estimated coefficients are not displayed, as they are never statistically significant). When estimating the relationship across the entire population of eighth- or fourth-graders, the coefficients are negative and estimated effects of a loss of jobs to 1 percent of the working-age population range from 0.4 to 1.4 percent of a standard deviation (SD) in student test scores, but the results are not consistently significant.

However, students whose parents have a high school diploma or less have significantly lower scores immediately after a job loss. A loss of jobs to 1 percent of the county's working-age population in the same quarter as the test leads to a significant decline among eighth-graders from low-SES backgrounds in both math and reading scores of over 1.3 percent SD. A loss leads to a marginally significant decline among fourth-graders from low-SES backgrounds in reading of 1.1 percent SD, and a nonsignificant decline of 0.7 percent SD in math. In all cases, the effects weaken in the quarters further from the test; losses that occurred more than two quarters ago (in December or earlier, for tests taken in June) have no effect on test scores.

By contrast, the impact of job loss on children from higher-education families appears to lag the job-loss event by one quarter. In the quarter of the test itself (that is, losses occurring between April and June), there is no effect on test scores. Losses occurring one quarter prior, however (that is, between January and March, for tests taken in June), have a negative and significant impact on eighth-grade test scores of 1.5 percent SD for reading. Results for math are also negative (2.2 percent SD) but not significant. Results for fourth-graders are also negative but not significant. Again, in all cases, the effects weaken in the third quarter; losses that occurred more than two quarters ago (in December or earlier) have no effect on test scores.

Because of this finding that job losses affect children from low-education households differently than they affect those from high-education households, in the rest of the chapter we perform parallel analyses of the two groups.

TABLE 14.2   *Regressions on Math and Reading Scores*

	Eighth-Graders		Fourth-Graders	
Sample universe	Reading Coefficient (Standard Error)	Math Coefficient (Standard Error)	Reading Coefficient (Standard Error)	Math Coefficient (Standard Error)
All				
Losses$_q$	−0.0054	−0.0065	−0.0100[†]	−0.0051
	(0.0052)	(0.0060)	(0.0053)	(0.0068)
Losses$_{q-1}$	−0.0114[†]	−0.014	−0.0049	−0.0043
	(0.0061)	(0.0091)	(0.0065)	(0.0064)
By education[a]				
High school or less				
Losses$_q$	−0.0135*	−0.0133*	−0.0110[†]	−0.0066
	(0.0059)	(0.0061)	(0.0065)	(0.0068)
Losses$_{q-1}$	−0.0108†	−0.013	−0.0026	0.0007
	(0.0058)	(0.0090)	(0.0066)	(0.0078)
More than high school				
Losses$_q$	0.0056	0.0012	−0.0075	−0.0005
	(0.0073)	(0.0088)	(0.0068)	(0.0097)
Losses$_{q-1}$	−0.0151[†]	−0.0218	−0.0054	−0.0082
	(0.0087)	(0.0133)	(0.0084)	(0.0090)

Source: Authors' calculations based on North Carolina Education Research Data Center (n.d.) and North Carolina Employment Security Commission (n.d.).
Note: Losses defined as number of workers who lost jobs among population ages twenty-five to sixty-four.
q refers to the quarter when test was taken.
All regressions include controls for losses in q−2 and q−3; coefficients are suppressed.
[a]Refers to the educational attainment of the student's parents.
†$p < 0.10$, *$p < 0.05$

In addition to examining effects of job losses on mean test scores, we also estimated effects of job losses across the entire distribution of outcomes. (Regressions are presented in online appendix table 14.A5; each pair of coefficients in table 14.A5 represents estimates from a different linear probability model, with an indicator that a student has scored below a given percentile on the end-of-year tests as the outcome.) In eighth grade, students from low-education backgrounds in communities with downturns in the most recent quarter are less likely to score above every percentile between the 10th and the 90th; the effects are statistically significant at the 10th and 20th percentiles for math. In fourth grade, estimates for students from low-education families are suggestive that job losses in the most recent quarter lower test scores in the bottom half of the test-score distribution and are marginally significant for reading at the 10th and 20th percentiles.

Among children from high-education households, eighth-graders in communities with downturns in the previous quarter are less likely to score above every percentile between the 10th and the 90th; the effect is statistically significant at the 20th and 50th percentiles for reading and at the 20th, 30th, 40th, 50th, 60th, and 90th percentiles for math. For fourth-graders, however, effects are small and insignificant throughout the distribution for both math and reading.

We also considered how job-loss impacts varied by subgroup. In online appendix table 14.A2, we consider the demographic characteristics of the child (labeled "student characteristics"). In online appendix table 14.A3, we consider characteristics of both students and of the workers most likely affected by job loss (labeled "affected worker characteristics"). For girls, effects do not appear to differ from overall patterns by grade and parent education. Results for boys are less precise but generally follow the overall pattern; however, there is evidence that eighth-grade boys from low-education backgrounds continue to experience negative effects from job losses after a one-quarter lag. In addition, there is no evidence that losses to female-dominated industries have a different impact on test scores than do losses to male-dominated industries, or that children are more sensitive to job losses within their gender.

When the sample is split by race and ethnicity, the trends are quite clear that job losses in both the quarter of the test and the prior quarter are harmful to educational achievement in eighth grade—although the estimates are less precise. The results show negative coefficients on twenty-one of the twenty-four race splits for eighth-graders. For fourth-graders, for whom effects of job losses appear to be weaker overall, estimates from racial splits are uninformative.

Online appendix table 14.A6 (middle panel) presents a check for whether our main results are driven by migration of high-performing low-SES students out of counties where there have been plant closings. We match each student to the county in which he or she was first observed—usually in third grade—and use closings in that county during eighth grade to predict students' eighth-grade test scores, or during fourth grade to predict fourth-grade test scores. Although this test allows us to avoid the possibility that changes in county-level test scores merely reflect student mobility, it necessarily introduces measurement error, as any students who moved counties between third and seventh grade were not actually exposed to the closings to which we match them. Using closings in the county in which students were originally observed does, as expected, increase the standard errors of our estimates. However, the coefficients attenuate only slightly and remain significant in most cases. This check gives us confidence that our main results are not driven by selective moving of students between counties but rather by treatment effects of local closings on individual students' test scores. Similarly, when we group geographically proximate small counties together (the top panel of online appendix table 14.A6), the coefficients change very little; this check gives us confidence that our main results are not driven by unusual events in small counties.

The bottom panel of online appendix table 14.A6 presents a falsification check in which we use next year's job losses to predict current test scores. Significant estimates from this regression would cast doubt on our identifying assumption that job losses can be viewed as exogenous shocks to communities; instead, such results would suggest that counties that experience closings already had differential trends in test scores. However, the estimates are very small and generally statistically insignificant; although three of the sixteen coefficients are marginally significant, one is in the unexpected direction. These estimates lend support to the assumption that changes in test scores do not occur in counties until after closings occur, and hence the relationship between job losses and test scores can be interpreted as causal.

Having validated our finding that job losses cause declines in test scores, we sought to examine the extent to which these declines may be attributable to changes in the school environment. We had hypothesized a priori that changes in the school environment—in funding, demographic composition, and teacher turnover—might explain associations between job losses and student test scores. We found immediate effects on test scores that attenuate within six months, whereas changes in the school environment, even in response to job losses, are likely to occur more slowly. Therefore, we do not believe that changes in the school environment can account for the effects of job losses on test scores.

We had hypothesized that student migration might help explain effects of job loss on student achievement. However, as shown in online appendix table 14.A4, we find no evidence that job losses lead to an exodus of those with better prospects that is quick enough to explain declines in average test scores among those who remain. All of the estimates on attrition from the sample—

defined as the share of students observed in the previous grade who do not take the state EOG tests in the current year—are small and insignificant, and seven of the twelve are actually negative. Although families may in the long run relocate after a job loss, it appears that they do not do so prior to the end of their child's school year, so attrition cannot account for our findings.

In contrast, the behavior of students within schools may help account for the changes in test scores we observe (these results are shown in online appendix table 14.A4). To parallel our analysis of the subgroup of children from low-education families, we examine the subgroup of counties with high proportions of students from low-education families. It is plausible that one reason job losses have a different pattern of effects on disadvantaged students is that schools with concentrated disadvantaged populations experience more structural change. The "disadvantaged" subsample consists of thirty-four counties (374 observations) in which at least two-thirds of the students come from low-education backgrounds. Our measure of student behavior is a count of the number of legally reportable offenses (LROs) committed in the county that year. These offenses consist of a set of seventeen serious in-school disciplinary problems, including drug and alcohol infractions, assaults, and possession of weapons. Job losses increase LROs slightly but nonsignificantly overall; but they do significantly increase LROs in disadvantaged counties (see online appendix table 14.A4). Among the disadvantaged counties, job losses to 1 percent of the working-age population are associated with an increase of 0.17 LROs per 1,000 students. Unfortunately, because these offenses are reported at the district level, we cannot analyze them separately by grade. However, such serious offenses likely are committed by older students, which would be consistent with the pattern of stronger effects on test scores for older students.

DISCUSSION

Our results show that community-level job losses affect the achievement test scores of children, particularly those in eighth grade. We find similar impacts on both reading and math scores. Although we are unable to conclusively describe the mechanisms whereby job losses affect test scores, taken together our results suggest both direct effects on children whose parents lost jobs as well as indirect peer and teacher effects, either compositional or behavioral.

Peer effects could help explain how test scores fall even for those students whose parents remain employed. First, parents' job loss would cause some children to act out in school (Kalil and Ziol-Guest 2008), which can disrupt the learning of other students (Figlio 2003). It is possible that behavioral changes among existing peers lead to lower test scores for all children; our estimate that job losses increase LROs in disadvantaged counties is consistent with this possibility. Future research should examine this mechanism by measuring the relationship of community-level job losses to classroom- and school-level behavior problems and associated test-score changes.

Second, some students might move out of the area or not move into the area. Peer effects of migration on student test scores will be negative if the share of high-achieving students declines (Imberman, Kugler, and Sacerdote 2009). We find no evidence consistent with this pathway. Job losses do not predict the likelihood that a student who took EOG tests in seventh grade did not take them in eighth grade.

Finally, average test scores may decrease as a result of declining achievement among children whose parents lose jobs. Our results are consistent with this scenario. If we assume, however, that the aggregate relationship between job losses and test scores is driven entirely by a change in outcomes for children whose parents become unemployed, with zero impact on the test scores of other children, our results seem implausibly large. If our effects were driven entirely by children whose parents lost jobs, the 1.3 percent of an SD fall in test scores in response to a 1 percent job loss that we measure must reflect a 1.3 SD fall in test scores among the 1 percent of children whose

TABLE 14.3   *Calibration: Combinations of Direct and Indirect Effects Consistent with a Population Average Effect of 0.013 Standard Deviation*

Spillover[a]	Direct Effect on 1 Percent of Population	Indirect Effect on 99 Percent of Population	Measured Direct Effect When Assuming Spillover = 0	Share of Population Effect Missed When Assuming Spillover = 0
0.00	1.300	0.000	1.300	0.000
0.01	0.653	0.007	0.647	0.503
0.05	0.218	0.011	0.208	0.840
0.10	0.119	0.012	0.107	0.917
0.15	0.082	0.012	0.070	0.946
0.20	0.063	0.013	0.050	0.962
0.50	0.026	0.013	0.013	0.990
0.80	0.016	0.013	0.003	0.998
1.00	0.013	0.013	0.000	1.000

Source: Authors' calculations.
[a]Spillover defined as percentage of measured direct effect that is due to effects on children of unaffected workers.

parents lose employment. Such an effect is substantially larger than those measured in studies of parental job loss (Oreopoulos, Page, and Stevens 2008; Stevens and Schaller 2011; see also chapter 15 in this volume). It is possible that our effect is larger because of the population under study or the measures used. It is also plausible that our estimates reflect negative effects on workers and families who maintain employment but are affected by their friends' and neighbors' job loss and the resulting changes to their communities, as shown in table 14.3.

For example, suppose that children whose parents are not directly affected by job loss, but who are indirectly affected either at home or at school, experience test score declines that are 10 percent of the magnitude of the decline experienced by students whose parents lost jobs. In that case, a 0.119 SD decrease among directly affected students would imply a 0.0119 SD decrease among other students, and the combination of these effects would produce a 0.013 SD decrease in the county (and a 0.107 SD decrease using the typical methodology in prior studies, that focus on parental unemployment and assume no effects on other; see also the work described in chapter 15, in this volume, by Philip B. Levine).

In addition, we find that the effect of job losses on the test scores of children from high-education families is delayed. It is possible that high-education parents, who typically have more savings, are able to buffer their children from stress for a while, but that as job loss persists (recall that the effect of loss on unemployment falls little between the first and second quarter), these children show signs of stress. It is also possible that stress within the school environment—such as from increased disciplinary problems, which are unlikely to manifest immediately—is what drives test-score declines among children from high-education backgrounds. That hypothesis is consistent with our result that children from these backgrounds experience larger losses in math than in reading scores, unlike children from low-education backgrounds. It is possible that math scores are relatively more affected by the in-school environment than are reading scores. Much more work is needed to understand what drives these divergent patterns.

Aggregate changes in family stress and psychological resources, which we are unable to measure, may also help explain the effects of community economic downturns on youth school achievement. More work is needed in order to understand the ways in which large local job losses may impact children whose parents do not lose their jobs but who are exposed to the resulting downturn in other ways.

CONCLUSION

Overall we find evidence that community-level job losses affect the academic achievement of children in those communities, but not all children's academic achievement is equally affected by job losses. Older children appear to be more harmed by job losses than younger children, either because they are developmentally more vulnerable or because families are better able to shield younger children from the effects of job losses. In addition, effects appear to differ by family socioeconomic status.

Research using new measures of family- and communitywide stress and potential interventions to moderate it are an important and promising area for future study. In particular, understanding why more advantaged families are able to temporarily buffer their children can shed light on how resources affect family processes, an essential issue for understanding the effects of income inequality on children's educational achievement. In addition, economists predict that future job losses will concentrate in less-skilled industries (Autor 2010), implying that children of less-skilled parents and children living in communities with fewer skilled workers are likely to continue to struggle against these shocks even after the Great Recession fades. Thus, identifying interventions to ameliorate these effects will be important for fighting educational inequality.

The authors would like to thank Dania V. Francis for her outstanding research assistance and Dorothyjean Cratty for her expert analytical support. They gratefully acknowledge the support of the Spencer Foundation, the Russell Sage Foundation, and the Smith Richardson Foundation. Ananat acknowledges the support of the Brookings Institution; Gibson-Davis acknowledges the support of the William T. Grant Foundation; and Gassman-Pines acknowledges the support of the Foundation for Child Development. Helpful comments were provided by members of the Smith Richardson research team at Duke University.

NOTES

Online appendix available at: http://www.russellsage.org/duncan_murnane_online_appendix.pdf.

1. Our measure of job loss includes both closings and layoffs, but for ease of explication, we refer to both types of losses as closings. Robustness checks indicated that our results do not differ by the type of job loss considered.

2. Calculated by the authors from school-level racial composition using the formula for a standard dissimilarity index.

REFERENCES

Autor, David. 2010. "The Polarization of Job Opportunities in the U.S. Labor Market: Implications for Employment and Earnings." White paper. Washington, D.C.: Brookings Institution.

Bartik, Timothy J. 1993. "Who Benefits from Local Job Growth, Migrants or the Original Residents?" *Regional Studies* 27(4): 297–311.

Black, Dan A. 2005a. "The Economic Impact of the Coal Boom and Bust." *Economic Journal* 115(503): 449–76.

———. 2005b. "Tight Labor Markets and the Demand for Education: Evidence from the Coal Boom and Bust." *Industrial & Labor Relations Review* 59(1): 3–15.

Black, Dan A., Terra G. McKinnish, and Seth G. Sanders. 2003. "Does the Availability of High-Wage Jobs for Low-Skilled Men Affect Welfare Expenditures? Evidence from Shocks to the Steel and Coal Industries." *Journal of Public Economics* 87(9–10): 1921–42.

Blustein, David L. 2008. "The Role of Work in Psychological Health and Well-Being." *American Psychologist* 63(4): 228–40.

Conger, Rand, and Glen H. Elder Jr. 1994. *Families in Troubled Times*. New York: Walter de Gruyter.

Dahl, Gordon, and Lance Lochner. 2008. "The Impact of Family Income on Child Achievement: Evidence from the Earned Income Tax Credit." NBER Working Paper No. 14599. Cambridge, Mass.: National Bureau of Economic Research.

Duncan, Greg J., and Jeanne Brooks-Gunn. 1997. *Consequences of Growing Up Poor*. New York: Russell Sage Foundation.

Elder, Glen H., Jacquelynne S. Eccles, Monika Ardelt, and Sarah Lord. 1995. "Inner-City Parents Under Economic Pressure: Perspectives on the Strategies of Parenting." *Journal of Marriage and the Family* 57(3): 771–84.

Figlio, David. 2003. "Boys Named Sue: Disruptive Children and Their Peers." Unpublished paper. Gainesville: University of Florida.

Greenstone, Michael, Richard Hornbeck, and Enrico Moretti. 2008. "Identifying Agglomeration Spillovers: Evidence from Million Dollar Businesses." NBER Working Paper No. 55. Cambridge, Mass.: National Bureau of Economic Research.

Greenstone, Michael, and Enrico Moretti. 2004. "Bidding for Industrial Businesses: Does Winning a 'Million Dollar Business' Increase Welfare?" Unpublished paper. Cambridge, Mass.: Massachusetts Institute of Technology.

Imberman, Scott, Adriana D. Kugler, and Bruce Sacerdote. 2009. "Katrina's Children: Evidence on the Structure of Peer Effects from Hurricane Evacuees." NBER Working Paper No. 15291. Cambridge, Mass.: National Bureau of Economic Research.

Jacobson, Louis S., Robert J. LaLonde, and Daniel G. Sullivan. 1993. "Earnings Losses of Displaced Workers." *American Economic Review* 83(4): 685–709.

Jones, Loring P. 1988. "The Effect of Unemployment on Children and Adolescents." *Child and Youth Services Review* 10(3): 199–215.

Kahneman, Daniel, and Amos Tversky. 1979. "Prospect Theory: An Analysis of Decision Under Risk." *Econometrica* 47(2): 263–92.

Kalil, Ariel, and Kathleen M. Ziol-Guest. 2008. "Parental Employment Circumstances and Children's Academic Progress." *Social Science Research* 37(2): 500–515.

Ludwig, Jens, and Laurie Bassi. 1999. "The Puzzling Case of School Resources and Student Achievement." *Educational Evaluation and Policy Analysis* 21(4): 385–403.

McKee-Ryan, Frances E., Zhaoli Song, Connie R. Wanberg, and Angelo J. Kinicki. 2005. "Psychological and Physical Well-Being During Unemployment: A Meta-Analytic Study." *Journal of Applied Psychology* 90(1): 53–76.

McLoyd, Vonnie C. 1998. "Socioeconomic Disadvantage and Child Development." *American Psychologist* 53(2): 185–204.

McLoyd, Vonnie C., Toby Jayaratne, Rosario Ceballo, and Julio Borquez. 1994. "Unemployment and Work Interruption Among African American Single Mothers: Effects on Parenting and Adolescent Socioemotional Functioning." *Child Development* 65(2): 562–89.

North Carolina Education Research Data Center. n.d. *North Carolina School Administrative Records Database*. Durham, N.C.: Duke University. Available at: http://www.childandfamilypolicy.duke.edu/project_detail.php?id=35 (accessed April 13, 2011).

North Carolina Employment Security Commission. n.d. *Announced Business Closings and Permanent Layoffs*. Raleigh, N.C.: North Carolina Employment Security Commission. Available at: http://eslmi23.esc.state.nc.us/masslayoff/ (accessed April 13, 2011).

Oreopoulos, Philip, Marianne E. Page, and Ann Huff Stevens. 2006. "The Intergenerational Effects of Compulsory Schooling." *Journal of Labor Economics* 24(4): 729–60.

———. 2008. "The Intergenerational Effects of Worker Displacement." *Journal of Labor Economics* 26(3): 455–83.

Rege, Mari, Kjetil Telle, and Mark Votruba. 2007. "Parental Job Loss and Children's School Performance." Discussion paper no. 517. Oslo: Statistics Norway.

Rockoff, Jonah E. 2004. "The Impact of Individual Teachers on Student Achievement: Evidence from Panel Data." *American Economic Review Proceedings* 94(2): 247–52.

Stevens, Ann Huff. 1997. "Persistent Effects of Job Displacement: The Importance of Multiple Job Losses." *Journal of Labor Economics* 15(1): 165–88.

Stevens, Ann Huff, and Jessamyn Schaller. 2011. "Short-Run Effects of Parental Job Loss on Children's Academic Achievement." *Economics of Education Review* 30(2): 289–99.

Sullivan, Daniel, and Till von Wachter. 2009. "Average Earnings and Long-Term Mortality: Evidence from Administrative Data." *American Economic Review: Papers & Proceedings* 99(2): 133–38.

U.S. Bureau of Labor Statistics. n.d. *Local Area Unemployment Statistics* [database]. Washington: U.S. Bureau of Labor Statistics. Available at: http://www.bls.gov/lau/ (accessed April 13, 2011).

Zippay, Allison. 1991. *From Middle Income to Poor: Downward Mobility Among Displaced Steelworkers*. New York: Praeger.

Chapter 15

How Does Parental Unemployment Affect Children's Educational Performance?

Phillip B. Levine

Does children's growing up in households with unemployed parents alter their educational outcomes? The answer to this question is not obvious; parental unemployment could help children or it could hurt them. If parents are unemployed, they have the opportunity to spend more time with their children. Alternatively, parents' unemployment may add a dimension of stress to the household that may hinder children's development. The actual impact of parental unemployment is an empirical question and is the focus of this chapter.

To answer this question, this study relies on microdata from the 2003 through 2007 American Time Use Survey (ATUS) and the 1979 cohort of the National Longitudinal Surveys of Youth (NLSY79). The ATUS analysis examines time spent with children among parents in different labor-market categories. The NLSY79 is used to link test scores to parents' labor-market activity. Careful attention is paid to the issue that any observed relationship between parental unemployment and children's educational outcomes may be attributable to a third set of factors that are unobservable to the researcher and that drive both variables. Where possible, I implement empirical methods to correct for this problem and generate causal estimates of the impact of parental unemployment on children's outcomes.

The results do not support the notion that differences in parental labor-market activity have much of an impact on children's educational performance, as measured by their scores on tests of cognitive ability. Broader movements in labor-market conditions as measured by the unemployment rate in the local area also are not found to have a sizable impact on children's test scores. Many factors may contribute to this finding; this analysis considers the role that time use may play. Differences in time spent with children by mothers and fathers of different labor-market status are not large, particularly when one considers only time spent in activities related to education.

One explanation for these findings is that all forms of unemployment have been treated as having the same impact. The definition of unemployment, however, includes very different labor-market experiences. Individuals may be looking for work because they lost their job, because they are on temporary layoff with an expected recall date, or because they were unhappy in their previous position and quit. The impact on family dynamics associated with these different types of unemployment could vary dramatically. Except during severe recessions like one from 2007 to 2009, relatively few unemployed workers suffer stressful job losses that may translate to negative experiences for their children. We may have learned from this exercise that the forms of unemployment that are more routinely experienced are not deleterious to children's educational performance.

A child's education plays a major role in determining his or her subsequent economic well-being. The debate among researchers exclusively focuses on just how large the effect really is. Given that education is so important, the pressing question becomes what factors determine educational outcomes. Clearly there are strong linkages across generations such that parents who did well in school have children who do better in school than children of parents who did not excel in school, but what other factors alter educational outcomes? In particular, what role do parents have in affecting these outcomes? Common areas of concern include parents' marital status, parents' age at the child's birth, the amount and type of the child's television viewing, and the parents' work, among other factors. This study assesses the role that parents' labor-market activities play in determining educational performance, as measured by scores on cognitive ability tests.

The importance of this topic is highlighted by recent labor-market developments that have led to a dramatic increase in parental unemployment. The unemployment rate has more than doubled in the current recession; many more children are now living in households where parents are unemployed. If children grow up in households with unemployed parents, does this alter their educational outcomes?

The answer to this question is not obvious; parental unemployment could help children or it could hurt them. If parents are unemployed, they have the opportunity to spend more time with their children. This additional time may help, regardless of how it is spent, or parents may be able to dedicate more time to education-related activities (reading, helping with homework, and so forth) that may have a direct impact on educational outcomes. Alternatively, having unemployed parents may add stress to the household that may hinder children's development. Parents' preoccupation with their financial difficulties may reduce the level or quality of time spent with children, increase the stress that children face in their daily lives, and hinder children's educational performance. The actual impact of parental unemployment is an empirical question and is the focus of this chapter.

To address this question, I rely on microdata from the 2003 through 2007 American Time Use Survey (ATUS) and the 1979 cohort of the National Longitudinal Surveys of Youth (NLSY79). The ATUS is a supplement to the Current Population Survey (CPS). Its data describe how much time individuals spend per day in a wide variety of tasks, including spending time with children. I use these data to provide a descriptive analysis of time spent with children among parents in different labor-market categories. The NLSY79 data began tracking individuals between the ages of fourteen and twenty-one in 1979 and has followed them since then. Beginning in 1986 it also began tracking children of the female respondents and has administered tests of cognitive ability biennially to those under age fifteen. I link these test scores to parents' labor-market activity in the preceding year as well as the years since the child was born.

An important shortcoming in an analysis attempting to determine the relationship between parental unemployment and children's educational outcomes is the possibility that factors unobservable to the researcher drive both variables. Hardworking, motivated, success-oriented parents are less likely to be unemployed and more likely to make investments in their children that will make them successful as well. These other attributes, not their labor-market status, may generate their children's outcomes. Any analysis attempting to uncover a causal impact of parental unemployment needs to take this issue into consideration. In this chapter, some of the results I present need to be interpreted as purely descriptive because of this problem. On the other hand, for some results I implement fixed-effects methods that can address the issue of unobservable heterogeneity, if perhaps imperfectly.

The results do not support the notion that differences in parental labor-market activity have much of an impact on children's educational performance, as measured by their scores on tests of cognitive ability. This result holds regardless of whether the mother's or father's activity is considered, and it holds for differences in employment, unemployment, and labor-force participation. Broader movements in labor-market conditions, as measured by the unemployment rate in the local area, are also not found to have a sizable impact on children's test scores. Although many factors may contribute to this finding, this analysis considers the role that time use may play. I detect differences in time spent with children by mothers and fathers of different labor-market status, but these differences are not large, particularly when one considers time spent in activities related to education. Although I am unable to detect any impact of differential patterns of labor-market activity on children's educational performance in this analysis, I also offer conjectures that may help reconcile these findings with other work in the literature and in this volume.

LITERATURE REVIEW

Although little previous research has evaluated the particular issues of this analysis, closely related topics have been studied. This section reviews these other areas of the literature.

Research in Developmental Psychology

Previous research in the field of developmental psychology provides us with some perspective regarding the mechanisms by which changes in parental labor-market activity may alter children's outcomes.[1] Empirical research in this area has been rather limited, but this research provides a useful perspective to help interpret the work that I report in this chapter. In this review, I focus on the role that parental unemployment can play in altering children's outcomes.[2] The family stress model is one perspective for viewing a link between parental unemployment and children's outcomes. Such a relationship may result from altered parenting practices, behaviors, and emotions of the unemployed parent. The impacts of job loss and income loss are not distinguished. This work was originally based on Glen Elder's analysis of children raised in the Great Depression and the impact that economic hardship and parental job loss had on their development (see Elder 1974; Elder, Nguyen, and Caspi 1985). When a father lost his job, he became irritable and less nurturing, which led to greater social and emotional problems among his children. The impact would diminish if the child's mother had a warm and affectionate relationship with the child. More recent research has found similar results for maternal job loss in a more contemporary setting (Christoffersen 2000; McLoyd et al. 1994).

Alternative perspectives that relate parental unemployment to children's outcomes exist as well. Children's dependency on the unemployed parent's emotions is a framework related to the family stress model (Harris 1994). From this viewpoint, it is not the parenting behavior per se that changes as a result of job loss, but the child's perceptions of the parent's emotional stress. The ABC-X model (Voydanoff 1983) also draws a link between parental unemployment and children's outcomes. In this model, children from less cohesive families with poorer coping mechanisms are differentially adversely affected by parental unemployment.

For the present purposes, the literature has some important limitations. First, its primary focus is on the psychological well-being of the children of unemployed parents. Certainly children's educational outcomes may be altered if their social and emotional development is hindered, but that is a further step away from the source. At some point the effect may sufficiently dissipate. Second, empirical studies in the literature have a limited ability to distinguish causal effects; with no counterfactual, it is difficult to determine what outcomes would have occurred otherwise.

Impact of Maternal Employment

The economics literature has largely ignored the role of parental unemployment on childhood outcomes, but it has explored the related issue of maternal employment. The studies of Christopher J. Ruhm (2004, 2008) exemplify this approach. Not surprisingly, the theoretical underpinnings of this research are very different from that in other disciplines. In particular, children's outcomes are viewed as the result of a "production function" that includes various inputs. Parents "invest" in their children through the resources they devote to them, which may include a parent's time as well as earnings from work. Consequently, it is difficult to determine theoretically the impact of parental labor-force status on children's outcomes. Having a parent at home increases time that can be invested in children but decreases monetary investments. Economists also focus on the attributes with which children are "endowed," which also contribute to their outcomes. Although this discussion focuses on employment, it can be modified to include unemployment as well with similar implications for children's outcomes.

Each of these factors contributes to the difficulty of determining the causal impact of changes in parental labor-force status on children's outcomes. First, no theoretically consistent impact exists since the predicted effects of earnings and time spent with children counteract each other. The answer becomes strictly empirical. Second, the role played by endowments complicates empirical estimation because they are likely to be both unobserved and correlated with decisions regarding labor-market behavior. As a result, identifying the causal impact of employment and unemployment is difficult. The limited available solutions to resolve this problem have not been widely implemented, suggesting that this question has not clearly been answered by previously conducted research.

Ruhm (2008) provides a useful example of empirical research approaches designed to overcome the problem of unobservable heterogeneity. He uses an extensive set of control variables, propensity-score matching, and sibling fixed-effects models to estimate the relationship between maternal employment and children's cognitive development (along with childhood obesity, which is a not a focus of this work) at ages ten and eleven. Defining "advantage" as socioeconomic status (SES), he finds that "more advantaged" children of mothers who work experience lower test scores than children of mothers who do not work. "Less advantaged" children are either unaffected or perhaps helped by having a mother who works. The net results indicate little overall effect.

Ruhm's (2008) study is useful partly because much of the literature examining the impact of maternal employment focuses on the mother's labor-market status in the child's very early life, such as under age one or age three (Hill et al. 2005; Ruhm 2004; Waldfogel, Han, and Brooks-Gunn 2002). This work typically finds that maternal employment in the child's first year of life is linked to subsequent test scores lower than those of children whose mothers do not work, but the impact of employment beyond the first year is less clear. Less research credibly addresses the impact of maternal employment for school-age children, with Ruhm's (2008) study reflecting a valuable exception.

Impact of Income

Another related area of inquiry is the impact of income on a child's achievement. Although a parent's decision to work rather than not work is endogenous, a spell of unemployment may at least partially result in a shock to a family's income. If low income has a causal (presumably negative) impact on children's outcomes, then children may suffer if one parent loses a job. The difficulty in identifying whether income has a causal impact on children's outcomes, however, presents an obstacle that has rarely been overcome (Duncan and Brooks-Gunn 1997; Mayer 1997).

One contribution to the literature does a nice job of addressing this causal link. Gordon B. Dahl and Lance Lochner (2005) use legislated changes to Earned Income Tax Credits (EITCs) to identify the impact of changes in income on children's outcomes. Some of those changes increased family incomes by as much as 20 percent for some families but not for others in a plausibly exogenous manner. Dahl and Lochner use the same NLSY79 data that I use and a child fixed-effects framework similar to mine. They also supplement this approach with the exogenous variation in EITC eligibility to instrument family income with changes in EITC policies. The results of this analysis indicate that a $1,000 increase in family income leads to improvements of 2.1 and 3.6 percent of a standard deviation in math and reading test scores, respectively.

To simulate how this estimate may be translated into the impact of job loss, consider the typical worker who makes around $700 per week in 2008 who is unemployed for ten weeks, the approximate median duration of an unemployment spell in that year. Total earnings loss would amount to $7,000. Some of this may be replaced by unemployment insurance. If we assume a 50 percent benefit replacement rate (which assumes that the state formula has a 50 percent replacement rate, as most states do, and that this worker is below the maximum benefit amount, which would be true in many states), then the income loss would amount to $3,500. For complete accuracy other changes would need to be incorporated (a reduction in income taxes, potentially greater expenditures on health care, and so forth), but this amount serves as a satisfactory ballpark figure. As such, Dahl and Lochner's estimates indicate that the income loss associated with unemployment would reduce math and reading test scores respectively by 7.4 percent and 12.6 percent of a standard deviation.

The impact of money falling from the sky (or the loss of that money), however, would not necessarily be the same as the income loss associated with unemployment. The stress associated with the job loss and the additional time available to spend with kids is not present with the money drop. Although informative, the evidence from Dahl and Lochner's study is not sufficient to draw strong conclusions regarding the impact of unemployment.

Direct Evidence on the Impact of Parental Unemployment

A reasonably small literature regarding the impact of job loss on children has recently emerged and may usefully inform the analysis reported here. This research differs from mine because it more narrowly targets the impact of worker displacements and plant closures.[3] The advantage of this narrower focus, though, is that worker displacements and plant closures provide a potentially exogenous shock to the family's income that may translate into alterations in children's educational outcomes. Mari Rege, Kjetil Telle, and Mark Votruba (2007) focus specifically on the impact of parents' exposure to plant closings on their children's GPA in high school using Norwegian administrative data. They find that grades suffer when fathers' plants close if the family lives in a location with a weak job market. Ann Huff Stevens and Jessamyn Schaller (2009) investigate the impact of job loss on grade retention using data from three waves of the Survey of Income and Program Participation (SIPP) in the United States. Their results suggest that grade retention increases in response to job loss using a child fixed-effects methodology similar to what I report here. The impact is concentrated among children of less-educated parents.

Some research also focuses on outcomes such as children's earnings when they grow up rather than educational outcomes, although it certainly seems likely that these outcomes are related. Philip Oreopoulos, Marianne Page, and Ann Huff Stevens (2008) and Espen Bratberg,

Øivind Anti Nilsen, and Kjell Vaage (2008) focus on subsequent earnings for the child. Bratberg, Nilsen, and Vaage find no significant effect on earnings in the next generation using Norwegian data, whereas Oreopoulos, Page, and Stevens find that children of displaced workers in Canada did suffer lower earnings. In the latter case, the effect was stronger among children of less-educated parents, which is consistent with the results of Stevens and Schaller. Although these valuable studies contribute to our knowledge, the literature addressing the effect of parental unemployment on children's educational outcomes is still at a very early stage. Additional work is required to better understand the nature of the relationship.

TIME USE AND PARENTAL LABOR-MARKET ACTIVITY

The first part of the empirical analysis in this chapter explores the time that parents spend with their children as a function of parents' current labor-market status.[4] I use data from the 2003 through 2007 American Time Use Survey (ATUS), a supplement to the monthly Current Population Survey (CPS) that is administered to a subsample of respondents. The CPS is the main source of data on labor-market activity in the United States, including data on labor-force status, hours worked, earnings, and the like.[5] In this analysis I classify workers into four separate categories: employed full-time (thirty-five or more hours per week), employed part-time (fewer than thirty-five hours), unemployed (looking for work or on layoff), and out of the labor force.

The CPS also provides the necessary demographic information to identify an individual's gender, own age, age of the youngest child in the household, and marital status. I focus on respondents between the ages of twenty-five and fifty-four who have children under age six and under age thirteen in the household. I distinguish respondents by marital status and gender, although I exclude unmarried men because so few of them have young children in their household.

The primary advantage of the ATUS is that it contains time-diary data for each respondent that quantifies the number of minutes spent in a wide array of activities. One set of those activities represents time that respondents spend with their children. In my analysis I total all time spent with children and separately consider four subcategories: basic care (physical care, looking after children, caring for children, organizing and planning for children), recreation (playing, sports, arts and crafts, talking and listening, attending events, waiting, picking up and dropping off), education-related (reading, homework, meetings and school conferences, homeschooling, waiting associated with education, other education-related activities), and health-related (providing and obtaining medical care, waiting associated with health, other health-related activities). Because time spent with children is likely to differ between weekdays and weekends, I further restrict the sample to those who completed the time diary on a weekday. The results of this analysis are presented in tables 15.1 (for children under age thirteen) and 15.2 (for children under age six). In table 15.1, the ATUS provides data on 4,602 married women, 1,863 unmarried women, and 4,000 married men. In each demographic group, and especially married men, the largest number of respondents is employed full-time, but each labor market category, including unemployed, still has more than one hundred individuals. Sample sizes for those with a youngest child in the house under age six (table 15.2) are smaller and some of the subcategories contain well under one hundred respondents, somewhat reducing the power of these reported statistics. Nevertheless, I report them because children younger than age six are a group of special focus and because it is easier to abstract from time spent in school, which somewhat complicates the interpretation for older children. The results in table 15.1 show a clear relationship between time spent with children and labor-market status.[6] Married women who are out of the labor force spend about three hours per day caring for their children. Those who are unemployed are similar to those who work part-time, spending a little more than two hours with their children per

TABLE 15.1   *Time Spent with Children (Youngest Child Under Age Thirteen), by Labor-Market Category and Demographic Characteristics*

	Employed Full-Time	Employed Part-Time	Unemployed	Out of the Labor Force
Married women (N = 4,602)				
Total time	90	140	121	184
Basic care	27	49	36	61
Recreation	46	67	56	90
Education-related	12	20	22	27
Health-related	4	5	7	5
Sample size	1,926	1,106	143	1,427
Unmarried women (N = 1,863)				
Total time	76	101	97	145
Basic care	25	32	32	39
Recreation	36	49	50	78
Education-related	12	13	14	24
Health-related	3	7	1	4
Sample size	1,077	325	131	330
Married men (N = 4,000)				
Total time	54	67	98	111
Basic care	24	33	37	42
Recreation	23	22	41	47
Education-related	7	12	20	18
Health-related	1	1	1	4
Sample size	3,615	139	110	136

Source: Authors' calculations based on data from the 2003–2007 American Time Use Survey (Abraham et al. 2008).
Notes: Cell entries represent minutes per day on a weekday. Each subsample is restricted to those between the ages of twenty-five and fifty-four with a child in the house younger than age thirteen. Full-time employment is defined as thirty-five or more hours per week. There are too few unmarried men in some of these categories to be reported. All estimates represent weighted means. Time categories are defined as follows: basic care (physical care, looking after children, caring for children, organizing and planning for children); recreation (playing, sports, arts and crafts, talking and listening, attending events, waiting, picking up and dropping off); education-related (reading, homework, meetings and school conferences, homeschooling, waiting associated with education, other education-related activities); health-related (providing and obtaining medical care, waiting associated with health, other health-related activities).

day. Married women who work full-time spend ninety minutes per day caring for their children. Interestingly, married women spend relatively little time with their children in education-related activities. Those who are out of the labor force spend twenty-seven minutes and those who work full-time spend twelve minutes in these activities. Again, unemployed women and those who work part-time are comparable to each other and to the other two groups.

These findings can be interpreted as consistent with the penalty associated with having a working mother. Women who work full-time spend half the amount of time with their children as women who do not work at all. If this additional time contributes to educational performance, it could help explain a causal finding between maternal labor-market activity and children's test scores. On the other hand, the differences in time spent on education-related activities call this interpretation into question. Women who work full-time clearly spend less time on education-related activities than women who do not work at all, but the difference simply is not large in absolute magnitude. If the overall time that mothers spend with their children is what matters,

TABLE 15.2   *Time Spent with Children (Youngest Child Under Age Six), by Labor-Market Category and Demographic Characteristics*

	Employed Full-Time	Employed Part-Time	Unemployed	Out of the Labor Force
Married women (N = 2,579)				
Total time	118	180	150	218
Basic care	35	63	47	74
Recreation	67	94	75	114
Education-related	11	17	15	25
Health-related	4	7	13	6
Sample size	962	588	79	950
Unmarried women (N = 819)				
Total time	94	124	126	173
Basic care	33	38	42	47
Recreation	50	65	71	106
Education-related	8	9	11	16
Health-related	3	11	2	4
Sample size	419	157	62	181
Married men (N = 2,365)				
Total time	67	71	109	122
Basic care	29	35	48	49
Recreation	31	24	48	55
Education-related	6	11	12	13
Health-related	1	1	1	5
Sample size	2,141	90	65	69

Source: Authors' calculations based on data from the 2003–2007 American Time Use Survey (Abraham et al. 2008).
Notes: Cell entries represent minutes per day on a weekday. Each subsample is restricted to those between the ages of twenty-five and fifty-four with a child in the house younger than age thirteen. Full-time employment is defined as thirty-five or more hours per week. There are too few unmarried men in some of these categories to be reported. All estimates represent weighted means. Time categories are defined as follows: basic care (physical care, looking after children, caring for children, organizing and planning for children); recreation (playing, sports, arts and crafts, talking and listening, attending events, waiting, picking up and dropping off); education-related (reading, homework, meetings and school conferences, homeschooling, waiting associated with education, other education-related activities); health-related (providing and obtaining medical care, waiting associated with health, other health-related activities).

maybe this finding can explain differences in educational outcomes. If time spent on education-related activities is what matters, the absolute difference across groups is relatively small and unlikely to matter much.

Table 15.1 also presents this analysis for unmarried women and married men. In most labor-market categories, married men spend considerably less time with their children than married women; unmarried women fall between the two groups. Regardless of the overall time spent with children, though, the patterns across labor-market categories are similar. Those who do not work spend considerably more time with their children, but the absolute difference in education-related activities is small. Table 15.2 presents the same analysis for women and married men with children under the age of six. Aside from the higher across-the-board mean values of minutes spent with these younger children, all the other patterns described previously hold here as well.

I also attempt to determine the extent to which observable differences in personal characteristics (mainly demographics and educational attainment) can account for the observed differences

TABLE 15.3   *Regression-Adjusted Estimates of Time Spent with Children, by Labor-Market Category and Demographic Characteristics*

	Married Women	Unmarried Women	Married Men
No covariates			
Employed full-time	−93.99	−69.42	−57.53
	(4.20)	(6.66)	(7.16)
Employed part-time	−43.03	−43.85	−44.52
	(4.89)	(8.15)	(9.74)
Unemployed	−62.43	−47.99	−12.92
	(9.95)	(10.73)	(7.02)
Full set of covariates			
Employed full-time	−85.79	−70.01	−66.63
	(3.94)	(6.53)	(6.93)
Employed part-time	−42.20	−45.80	−51.90
	(4.53)	(7.72)	(9.40)
Unemployed	−42.02	−45.08	−17.22
	(9.05)	(10.11)	(10.24)

Source: Authors' calculations based on data from the 2003–2007 American Time Use Survey (Abraham et al. 2008).
Notes: All estimates reflect differences from time use of individuals out of the labor force in the relevant demographic group and are reported in minutes per day on a weekday. Each three-cell column block represents the results from a separate regression. Covariates include educational attainment, race, ethnicity, parent's age and age squared, and the age of the youngest child in the household. Each subsample is restricted to those between the ages of twenty-five and fifty-four with a child in the house younger than age thirteen. Full-time employment is defined as thirty-five or more hours per week. There are too few unmarried men in some of these categories to be reported. Sample weights are used in all regression models. Standard errors in parentheses.

in time spent with children among men and women in different labor-market categories and different gender and marital status groups. The results of this analysis are reported in table 15.3. This table reports coefficients for indicator variables reflecting full-time employment, part-time employment, and unemployment; these coefficients should be interpreted as the difference in time spent with children between individuals in each of these groups and those who are out of the labor force. Subcategories of time use within the broader heading of time spent with children are not reported here for expediency, but the qualitative findings for these subcategories are similar to those described here. For similar reasons, I focus just on individuals in households with a child under the age of thirteen.

The first section of table 15.3 replicates the findings in table 15.1 in regression format; it does not include any additional control variables beyond the labor-market status indicators. We learn from these regressions that raw time-use differences between categories are mainly strongly statistically significant. In the second section of the table, I include the parents' demographics (race, ethnicity, age and age squared, and the age of the youngest child in the house) along with their educational attainment, measured as indicators for highest degree attained. These results suggest that little, if any, of the differences in time use between categories of labor-market and gender and marital status are attributable to differences in observable characteristics of the parents. As a descriptive statement, individuals who work full-time spend the least time with their children, those who are not in the labor market spend the most time with their children, and those who work part-time and those who are unemployed are between these two groups and similar to each other.

I conduct one additional analysis with the ATUS data that is designed to test the sensitivity of time spent with children to broader labor-market conditions. In theory, if the results from

TABLE 15.4   *Impact of Labor-Market Conditions on Time Spent with Children,*
by Demographic Characteristics

	Married Women	Unmarried Women	Married Men
Unemployment rate	5.19	−1.39	3.88
	(5.12)	(7.25)	(3.98)

Source: Authors' calculations based on data from the 2003–2007 American Time Use Survey (Abraham et al. 2008).
Notes: All estimates reflect coefficients on the state and year unemployment rate. Other covariates include educational attainment, race, ethnicity, parent's age and age squared, the age of the youngest child in the household, and state and year fixed effects. Each subsample is restricted to those between the ages of twenty-five and fifty-four with a child in the house younger than age thirteen. There are too few unmarried men in some of these categories to be reported. Sample weights are used in all regression models. Standard errors in parentheses.

the preceding analyses have any causal component, one might expect increases in the unemployment rate to generate an increase in time spent with children, particularly if workers move from full-time employment to another labor-market status. Using state identifiers in these data along with the year in which the survey was conducted, I assign the state-level and year-specific unemployment rate to each individual respondent and regress time use against the unemployment rate, including the same additional control variables as described in the preceding analysis. Sampling weights are used to correct for heteroskedasticity since some states have many more observations than others. This exercise is somewhat limited by the relatively short sampling window and reasonably stable labor-market conditions over the period from 2003 through 2007 (there were no recessions), but no other data were available at the time of analysis.

The results of this analysis, reported in table 15.4, provide no support for cyclical variations in time spent with children. None of the unemployment rate coefficients for any gender or marital status groups are statistically significant. Two of them are positive and actually quite large. If married women spend an extra five minutes with their children for each point increase in the unemployment rate, then the roughly five-point increase in the unemployment in the current recession would generate an estimate of twenty-five additional minutes per day spent with children. This is quite a large increase considering that the vast majority of working, married women would keep their jobs. Nevertheless, the standard error is large enough that we cannot reject the null hypothesis of no effect, suggesting that it is difficult to draw strong conclusions from this exercise due to limited power.

ANALYSIS OF NLSY79 DATA

Now, I turn to the NLSY79 data used in my analysis and provide a characterization of the econometric methods that I used. The descriptive statistics presented in this section will enable one to get a sense of the information that can be gleaned from the data, and the formal results of my econometric analysis are presented as well.

Description of the Data

The 1979 cohort of the NLSY79 initially surveyed 12,686 respondents born between 1957 and 1964 (age fourteen to twenty-two) in the initial survey year. Since then, respondents have been interviewed each year through 1994 and then every other year after that. The most recent data available at the time of this analysis were from 2006. Beginning in 1986, a biennial data collection effort began for the children of the 6,283 original female respondents. Through the 2006 survey, 11,469 children were born to these women and are included in the sample.

The NLSY79 is well known for the wealth of data it collects for those who respond to the survey. Two elements of the data are important for this study. First, the survey conducted tests of cognitive ability for each child of the original female respondents between age four or five and age fourteen. This means that children may have up to five test scores over a ten-year interval. The specific tests I use in this analysis are the Peabody Individual Achievement Test (PIAT) in math, reading comprehension, and reading recognition and the Peabody Picture Vocabulary Test (PPVT). I also explore one other outcome measure that is collected in the NLSY79, the Behavior Problems Index (BPI). The BPI is designed to distinguish those who have received clinical treatment focusing on antisocial behavior, depression, aggressiveness, and the like.

Second, the survey collects very detailed work information for each respondent, which has been used to create work histories indicating whether an individual was employed, unemployed, or out of the labor force week by week since January 1, 1978, when respondents were thirteen to twenty years old. I use these data to create the percentage of weeks mothers spent in each labor-market state in the year before each test was taken by the child and the percentage of weeks spent in each state since the child's birth (or January 1, 1978, whichever is later).[7] The survey also collects data on the labor-market activity of spouses or partners, although these data are more limited. I use reported information on weeks spent in each labor-market state in the calendar year preceding the child assessments to measure the employment history of the respondent's spouse or partner. Since the survey became biennial in 1994, tracking a complete labor-market history is not possible for the spouses.

Methodology

The purpose of this analysis is to assess the relationship between parental labor-market activity and children's performance on cognitive assessments. The simplest approach to assess this relationship is to estimate a regression model where the child's test score is the dependent variable and measures of parental labor-market activity are included as explanatory variables along with other demographic and family background variables. As alluded to earlier, however, this approach is open to the possibility of omitted variable bias. Labor-market histories are not assigned randomly to different parents. The different attributes that determine success in the labor market may also determine the transmission of knowledge to one's children and their performance on tests of cognitive ability. If all these attributes could be observed, they could be included as explanatory variables in the regression. In all likelihood, however, some (many?) of them are not observable and omitting them from the regression would generate bias. This bias would likely go in the direction of suggesting a positive relationship between labor-market success (more employment, less unemployment) and children's test scores.

One alternative approach that researchers have adopted to deal with this problem is to estimate family fixed-effects models. Because the NLSY79 includes assessments of each child born to the original female survey respondents, all siblings are present in the data. This approach is the equivalent of including dummy variables for each family so that the estimated impact of parents' labor-market activity is determined on the basis of within-family differences. In essence it compares siblings' test scores of at different times when their parents may have had different labor-market outcomes. Do children within the household do better or worse during the periods in which their parents are working or are unemployed relative to when their parents are not working? The limitation of this approach is that parental labor-market activity may be affected by the children. If one child in the house is struggling in school or requires extra attention for an issue like poor health, then parents may work less, lose their jobs because they have been missing work, or stop working for some other reason. Regardless of the reason, this possibility means that bias still may be present using this estimation method.

Similar to the previous approach, I also estimate child fixed-effects models. Because each child may have been assessed up to five times, I can include in the regression model the equivalent of a dummy variable for each child. In this approach, I compare the same child's test scores over time as a function of changes in his or her parents' labor-market activity. The approach improves upon a family fixed-effects model because it avoids the issue of different allocations of time to different siblings with different issues that may affect test performance and parental labor-market activity. On the other hand, it is still subject to the criticism that parents may change their labor-market activity in response to changes in their children's lives that may affect the children's test scores. Although this method is not a perfect way to identify a causal effect, it is a substantial improvement over traditional regression methods.

I also explore one additional estimation strategy that can potentially answer a somewhat different question. One way to help correct for the unobservable heterogeneity problem would be to find an instrumental variable that is correlated with the parents' labor-market outcomes but unrelated to residuals in test scores. The local area unemployment rate is a potential candidate. It certainly would be related to the likelihood that parents would be unemployed, and it would be unrelated to family-specific factors that may alter children's test scores. On the other hand, certain attributes of the unemployment rate reduce its value as an instrument. Local labor-market conditions may impact educational outcomes in ways that may not be transmitted solely through the parents' unemployment experiences. Stress in the community may affect kids. Lack of tax revenue may hinder school operations. These and other reasons violate the notion that the unemployment rate would be unrelated to residuals in test scores.

Instead, we estimate a "reduced form" version of this model, including just the unemployment rate as the key explanatory variable, replacing the direct measures of parental labor-market activity. This model captures the overall impact of changes in aggregate labor-market conditions through parental labor-market behavior, community factors, and other factors on test scores. I estimate and report models of this form as well.

Descriptive Analysis

Before reporting the results of this econometric analysis, I present in table 15.5 the results of a descriptive analysis that simply compares test scores across children who differ according to their parents' labor-market activities. In this analysis, children are categorized according to their mother's and her husband's or partner's employment and unemployment experiences in the past year (mother) or past calendar year (husband/partner). Unemployment categories include no unemployment, less than 20 percent of the year unemployed, and more than 20 percent of the year unemployed. Employment categories include none, full-year, and part-year.

The results show a clear pattern that test scores rise and behavior problems fall with labor-market success for the child's mother and her spouse or partner. Children in households in which the mother and her spouse or partner experience less unemployment or work more score higher on each of these measures and exhibit fewer behavior problems. For instance, children of mothers experiencing no unemployment in the past year received average math percentile scores of 57.9, compared to 49.9 for children of mothers who experienced a relatively small amount of

TABLE 15.5   Mean Child Test Scores by Maternal Labor-Force Status in Past Year

Fraction of Weeks	Percentage of Mothers or Spouses or Partners	PIAT Math Percentile	PIAT Reading Comprehension Percentile	PIAT Reading Recognition Percentile	PPVT Percentile	BPI Percentile
Mother's unemployment experience in past year						
None	87.1	57.9	58.1	63.1	45.7	57.3
Positive but less than 0.2	8.2	49.9	51.7	55.8	36.2	65.2
Between 0.2 and 1	4.7	46.8	49.6	53.5	32.2	65.6
Sample size		30,548	25,728	30,420	18,473	34,418
Mother's employment experience in past year						
None	22.8	53.2	55.5	59.3	40.4	58.4
Between 0 and 1 (exclusive)	28.1	54.7	56.1	60.2	42.4	60.8
Full year	49.1	59.5	58.5	64.5	47.4	56.9
Sample size		30,548	25,728	30,420	18,473	34,418
Spouse's or partner's unemployment experience (if available) in last calendar year						
None	90.0	59.9	60.1	65.0	48.8	55.8
Positive but less than 0.2	3.6	54.9	57.8	60.7	42.9	65.1
Between 0.2 and 1	5.4	53.0	54.6	58.1	37.1	62.8
Sample size		21,214	17,824	21,121	12,824	24,324
Spouse's or partner's employment experience (if available) in last calendar year						
None	1.8	44.5	46.2	48.7	31.3	64.5
Between 0 and 1 (exclusive)	24.8	58.3	59.8	63.3	46.8	59.4
Full year	73.4	60.4	60.4	65.6	48.9	55.1
Sample size		20,632	17,348.0	20,580	12,632	23,744

Source: Authors' calculations, based on data from the 1986–2006 extracts from the 1979 National Longitudinal Surveys of Youth (U.S. Bureau of Labor Statistics 2010).
Notes: Percentage of mothers is based on women whose children have available PIAT math scores. These data are available for 30,548 mother or child test score observations. Sample sizes are somewhat smaller for other test scores.

unemployment and 46.8 for children of mothers who experienced more unemployment. The gap between the no-unemployment and high-unemployment groups is more than ten percentage points. Similar patterns emerge for mother's employment and for the employment and unemployment experiences of her spouse or partner.

These results show a very strong positive association between labor-market success and children's test scores; behavior problems and labor-market success are negatively correlated. Nevertheless, one must keep in mind that these associations do not necessarily identify a causal impact. Because labor-market outcomes are not randomly assigned, and no other method is used to hold constant other differences across families, the potential for these results to be biased is quite high. The remainder of this discussion presents my attempt to substantially reduce this problem.

Econometric Analysis

The estimation results from these models are reported in tables 15.6 through 15.8. The first section of table 15.6 presents ordinary least-squares (OLS) regression estimates that include the fraction of weeks the mother was unemployed and employed in the year preceding the child's assessment along with the same measures for the "father" (really the spouse or partner of the mother) in the calendar year preceding the assessment.[8] Additional control variables in these regressions include the mother's age, race, ethnicity, marital status, educational attainment, and Armed Forces Qualification Test (AFQT) score; child's age, birth order, and an indicator for being firstborn; and missing variable indicators marking when mothers' or fathers' labor-market activity is missing. The omitted labor-market category is fraction of weeks out of the labor force, so these results can be interpreted as the impact of having a working or unemployed mother or father relative to having one out of the labor force.

The results from these models confirm a strong association between parental labor-market activity and children's outcomes. Father's employment, in particular, is found to be strongly related to test scores. Children of fathers who work the full year score about three to five percentile points higher on these tests of cognitive ability than children of fathers who do not work at all. Mother's employment is similarly positively linked to test scores, although the effect is smaller. A plausible alternative interpretation of these findings is that mother's and father's employment are strongly linked to income, and higher-income families have children who perform better on these exams. This may not be a causal link, however. Mother's and father's unemployment similarly are found to reduce test scores (for those tests where the results are statistically significant), which is consistent with this alternative interpretation.

The remainder of the table reports the results of mother fixed-effects and child fixed-effects models that are designed to substantially reduce the unobservable heterogeneity problem. In terms of income, these fixed effects difference out permanent income, so these methods should help overcome the apparent problems observed in OLS estimation. It also controls for other unobservable factors that are fixed within households or even within the child, although it does not completely eliminate the possibility that some unobservable heterogeneity remains. Once these fixed effects are included, virtually all the coefficients for parental labor-market activity become insignificant. The fact that we cannot statistically distinguish these coefficients from zero, however, does not enable us to conclude that there is no effect. It could be that a sizable effect is present, but our standard errors are sufficiently large that we cannot rule out a zero effect. In other words, this could simply be a test that lacks power.

My interpretation of these findings, however, is not consistent with this view. Most standard errors on both maternal and paternal unemployment in both types of fixed-effects specifications are in the range of about 1.2 to 2.4. To reject the null hypothesis at the 5 percent level would require coefficients in the range of roughly 2.4 to 4.8 (in absolute value). The exercise that this coefficient reflects, however, is the impact of moving from no unemployment over the course of the past year (or calendar year) to a full year of unemployment. This is a huge increase in unemployment exposure, and one could reject the null hypothesis of no effect if the estimate were above 2.4 to 4.8, depending on the specific specification. Recall that mean test scores are in the vicinity of 50 (see table 15.4), which means we would be able to reject effects that are 5 to 10 percent of that score in response to a dramatic change in unemployment exposure. An alternative way to view this is to note that a typical standard error for these test scores is in the vicinity of 28 to 30. A 2.4 to 4.8 percentile estimate would reflect, say, 0.1 to 0.15 standard deviations.

My interpretation is that this test may not be the most powerful, but it is not weak, either. We can rule out modest or larger effects of parental labor-market activity on children's test

TABLE 15.6   *Estimated Relationship Between Parental Labor-Force Status in Past Year and Children's Test Scores (Standard Errors in Parentheses)*

Variable	PIAT Math	PIAT Reading Comprehension	PIAT Reading Recognition	PPVT	BPI
Sample size	29,315	24,699	29,199	17,689	32,838
Ordinary least squares					
Mother's unemployment	−0.978	1.154	0.320	−3.273	6.203
in past year	(1.356)	(1.495)	(1.468)	(1.605)	(1.503)
Mother's employment	1.608	0.840	1.412	0.378	0.131
in past year	(0.579)	(0.598)	(0.626)	(0.679)	(0.661)
Father's unemployment	−1.025	−3.346	−0.601	−5.290	0.069
in past calendar year	(2.036)	(2.046)	(2.050)	(2.599)	(2.041)
Father's employment	4.146	2.577	4.683	4.924	−6.013
in past calendar year	(1.551)	(1.578)	(1.668)	(1.800)	(1.466)
Mother fixed effects					
Mother's unemployment	0.091	1.477	3.196	−0.019	−0.309
in past year	(1.260)	(1.607)	(1.311)	(1.653)	(1.144)
Mother's employment	−0.340	−1.121	−0.903	−0.909	0.813
in past year	(0.597)	(0.630)	(0.557)	(0.797)	(0.524)
Father's unemployment	−0.152	−2.146	−0.778	−0.866	0.316
in past calendar year	(1.779)	(1.729)	(1.559)	(2.320)	(1.545)
Father's employment	1.980	0.564	1.298	2.502	0.894
in past calendar year	(1.501)	(1.522)	(1.357)	(1.882)	(1.197)
Child fixed effects					
Mother's unemployment	−0.390	1.600	2.857	0.457	−0.376
in past year	(1.418)	(1.907)	(1.421)	(2.161)	(1.319)
Mother's employment	0.073	−0.677	−0.492	−0.425	0.819
in past year	(0.661)	(0.744)	(0.593)	(1.092)	(0.583)
Father's unemployment	0.468	−0.433	−0.897	−0.583	1.170
in past calendar year	(1.978)	(1.956)	(1.582)	(3.200)	(1.727)
Father's employment	1.906	0.711	0.641	1.027	0.920
in past calendar year	(1.653)	(1.680)	(1.319)	(2.527)	(1.367)

Source: Authors' calculations based on data from the 1986–2006 extracts from the 1979 National Longitudinal Surveys of Youth (U.S. Bureau of Labor Statistics 2010).
Notes: Regressions are weighted and include the following covariates (some of which drop out in the fixed-effects models): the mother's age, race, ethnicity, marital status, educational attainment, and AFQT score; child's age, birth order, and an indicator for being firstborn; and missing variable indicators for spouse's or partner's labor force status. Standard errors are clustered on the child identifier.

scores based on this analysis. An analogous analysis of parental employment effects goes even more strongly in this direction because standard errors are typically in the 0.5 to 1 range. These tests are even more powerful than those for parental unemployment. Taken as a whole, these results provide little evidence that parental labor-market activity alters children's test scores. One limitation of this exercise is that it focuses on transitory changes in labor-market status. Fixed-effects models, for instance, are identified based on the percentage of the year employed or unemployed compared to the percentage of a different year in those different states. It may be that transitory changes in labor-market activity have no impact but long-standing differences are more meaningful. To examine this issue, I also include a measure of mother's employment and unemployment since the child's birth (or since data collection began on January 1, 1978).[9] I am unable to do this for the child's father because complete labor-market histories are not available. These measures are then included in the same specifications as estimated previously, except that child fixed-effects specifications are no longer identified. Mother fixed-effects specifications can be identified because of the difference in lifetime labor-market activity generated during the period after one child is born and before another is born.

The results of this exercise are reported in table 15.7. In OLS models, mother's unemployment since birth provides reasonably consistent evidence of a negative association with children's cognitive test scores. Interestingly, mother's employment since child's birth shows no such association. Once family fixed effects are included, however, these results disappear again as we are left with smaller and mainly statistically insignificant coefficients. Standard errors are larger than those described earlier, which may lead one to question the power of this analysis. On the other hand, the thought experiment of moving from an entire life with, say, no unemployment to an entire life of all unemployment is also a vastly larger change in behavior. On that basis, the somewhat larger standard errors compared to those found for transitory changes in labor-market activity seem in keeping with the notion that this test is reasonably powerful. I would again conclude that there is not much evidence to support the notion that parental labor-market activity has any impact on children's test scores.

Similar to my earlier investigation using ATUS data, I also conduct one additional analysis to test the sensitivity of children's test scores to broader labor-market conditions. To investigate this question, I use geographic identifiers that can be obtained for the NLSY79.[10] With these data, I link the local unemployment rate for each mother in the survey to her record along with that of her children, which includes the test score data that I have been using. Using these data, I estimate regression models of test scores against the local unemployment rate, including the same additional control variables as described in the preceding analysis along with state and year fixed effects. The results of this analysis are reported in table 15.8. The first section of the table presents the results for all children and shows no statistically significant impact of these broad labor-market conditions on children's test scores.

One possible shortcoming in this analysis as well as those previously reported is that there may be heterogeneity in the impact of experiencing unemployment. A family with greater resources, for example, may find it much easier to weather the storm without the children being affected. The impact on less advantaged families may be different. The analysis reported so far aggregates all families and children into one category, but different effects across families in different socioeconomic groups may occur. In fact, some earlier studies suggest that such differences may occur (Ruhm 2008).

Distinguishing families in different socioeconomic groups in these data is somewhat complicated by the fact that family income is altered if unemployment occurs. A more permanent measure of SES would be desirable. To test this hypothesis, I distinguish families according to the mother's level of educational attainment, separately considering those who dropped out of high school, those who have a high school degree, and those who attended college (regardless of whether or not they graduated). Then I reestimate all the regressions reported earlier according to SES. In those specifications that regress test scores against mother's and father's labor-market experiences over the past year and since birth, I am unable to identify any statistically significant impacts for any of the three SES groups.[11]

On the other hand, in examining the impact of the aggregate unemployment rate on test scores, I do find a pattern. Lower-SES groups appear to experience reductions in test scores in some instances in response to higher unemployment. For instance, children of mothers who dropped out of high school are estimated to face about a half-percentage-point deficit for every

TABLE 15.7   *Estimated Relationship Between Parental Labor-Force Status in Past Year, Mother's Labor-Force History Since Child's Birth, and Children's Test Scores*

Variable	PIAT Math	PIAT Reading Comprehension	PIAT Reading Recognition	PPVT	BPI
Sample size	29,315	24,699	29,199	17,689	32,838
Ordinary least squares					
Mother's unemployment	0.351	2.564	2.123	0.056	2.022
in past year	(1.527)	(1.693)	(1.603)	(1.928)	(1.606)
Mother's unemployment	−5.612	−6.304	−7.396	−10.545	15.686
since child's birth	(3.994)	(4.183)	(4.372)	(4.333)	(4.354)
Mother's employment	1.395	0.858	1.372	1.365	−0.176
in past year	(0.729)	(0.750)	(0.770)	(0.915)	(0.808)
Mother's employment	0.378	−0.031	0.078	−1.589	0.488
since child's birth	(1.066)	(1.070)	(1.146)	(1.288)	(1.234)
Father's unemployment	−0.874	−3.200	−0.404	−5.097	−0.345
in past calendar year	(2.030)	(2.049)	(2.055)	(2.597)	(2.055)
Father's employment	4.101	2.536	4.642	4.943	−5.942
in past calendar year	(1.553)	(1.579)	(1.671)	(1.770)	(1.476)
Mother fixed effects					
Mother's unemployment	0.280	1.334	2.149	0.242	0.611
in past year	(1.340)	(1.711)	(1.411)	(1.810)	(1.249)
Mother's unemployment	−1.675	1.476	9.464	−1.633	−7.069
since child's birth	(5.477)	(5.902)	(5.906)	(5.169)	(4.679)
Mother's employment	−0.222	−0.884	−0.349	−0.805	1.245
in past year	(0.652)	(0.671)	(0.609)	(0.890)	(0.591)
Mother's employment	−0.740	−1.954	−4.180	−0.427	−2.245
since child's birth	(1.779)	(1.950)	(1.941)	(2.028)	(1.636)
Father's unemployment	−0.132	−2.155	−0.787	−0.857	0.387
in past calendar year	(1.778)	(1.728)	(1.567)	(2.322)	(1.542)
Father's employment	1.986	−2.155	1.381	2.498	0.910
in past calendar year	(1.503)	(1.728)	(1.359)	(1.883)	(1.195)

Source: Authors' calculations based on data from the 1986–2006 extracts from the 1979 National Longitudinal Surveys of Youth (U.S. Bureau of Labor Statistics 2010).
Notes: Standard errors in parentheses. Regressions are weighted and include the following covariates (some of which drop out in the fixed-effects models): the mother's age, race, ethnicity, marital status, educational attainment, and AFQT score; child's age, birth order, and an indicator for being firstborn; and missing variable indicators for spouse's/partner's labor force status. Standard errors are clustered on the child identifier.

one-point increase in the unemployment rate. This deficit is not present for children of mothers who attended college. Although children of high school graduates do not appear to do worse on math tests during recessions, they appear to do worse on reading exams, as do children of high school dropouts. All the coefficients on the unemployment rate in models estimated for children of mothers who attended college are fairly close to zero—in fact, three of the four point estimates are positive. This evidence is consistent with the notion that families with greater resources are better able to weather the storm of unemployment.

The magnitude of the impact for the lower-SES children, however, is not large. In a severe recession where the unemployment rate spikes by 5.0 percentage points, math test scores for

TABLE 15.8   *Estimated Relationship Between Unemployment Rate and Children's Test Scores*

Variable	PIAT Math	PIAT Reading Comprehension	PIAT Reading Recognition	PPVT	BPI
All children					
Local unemployment rate	−0.0426	−0.0259	−0.096	0.035	−0.032
	(0.100)	(0.105)	(0.120)	(0.142)	(0.177)
Sample size	29,635	29,521	24,970	17,776	33,183
Children of mothers who dropped out of high school					
Local unemployment rate	−0.464	−0.208	−0.694	−0.137	0.373
	(0.218)	(0.312)	(0.324)	(0.295)	(0.317)
Sample size	5,076	5,065	4,125	3,326	5,616
Children of mothers who are high school graduates					
Local unemployment rate	−0.129	−0.422	−0.261	−0.067	−0.050
	(0.211)	(0.175)	(0.114)	(0.190)	(0.259)
Sample size	13,337	13,264	11,243	8,115	14,917
Children of mothers who attended college					
Local unemployment rate	−0.021	0.085	0.258	0.058	−0.094
	(0.158)	(0.137)	(0.146)	(0.220)	(0.342)
Sample size	11,222	11,192	9,602	6,335	12,650

Source: Authors' calculations based on 1986–2006 extracts from the 1979 National Longitudinal Surveys of Youth.
Notes: Regressions are weighted and include the following covariates: the mother's age, race, ethnicity, marital status, educational attainment, and AFQT score; child's age, birth order, and an indicator for being firstborn; and state and year fixed effects. Standard errors are clustered on the state of residence.

children of high school dropouts would be estimated to fall by 2.3 percentage points, which is about 0.08 of a standard deviation. Although this impact is statistically significant, its economic meaning is limited.

DISCUSSION AND CONCLUSIONS

This study examines the potential of parental unemployment to alter children's educational performance, as measured by their scores on tests of cognitive ability. The perspective of developmental psychology along with that offered by economists on this issue both suggest that a link could exist. The direction of the link is unclear, however, so the question is an empirical one. My analysis focuses on examining whether parental unemployment alters time spent with children and whether it has an ultimate impact on test scores.

Taken as a whole, the results provide little support for such a link. My analysis of time use is largely descriptive in nature and inadequate to draw strong causal conclusions. This analysis shows that unemployed parents do spend more time with their children than employed parents. The differences, however, are not that large, particularly when I examine the use of time specifically dedicated to education-related activities. Moreover, the statistical biases inherent in this descriptive analysis probably go in the direction of the true effects' being smaller than those reported here. My impression from this analysis is that the return on time spent with children would have to be quite large for differences of this magnitude to matter. The remainder of this chapter uses NLSY79 data to estimate the relationship between parental labor-market status and children's test scores in a way that more definitely (if not perfectly) can be thought of as causal. That analysis provides little

TABLE 15.9   *Reasons Workers Are Unemployed at Peaks and Troughs of the Business Cycle*

	2000	2003	2006	2009
On layoff	15.0%	12.8%	13.2%	11.4%
Permanent job loss	19.6	32.4	24.1	43.0
Temporary job ended	9.6	9.9	10.2	9.8
Job leaver	13.7	9.3	11.8	6.2
Reentrant	34.5	28.2	32.0	22.3
New entrant	7.6	7.3	8.8	7.3
Unemployment rate	4.0	6.0	4.6	9.3

Source: Authors' compilation based on data from U.S. Bureau of Labor Statistics (various years).

evidence that such a link exists. The one area where I identify any type of relationship involves the link between local labor-market conditions and test scores among low-SES households. In that exercise, I find that a higher unemployment rate is linked to lower test scores among low-SES households, but the estimated effect is so small that it has little economic meaning.

One reason why I may not have been able to identify an effect is that I treat all unemployment as having the same impact. The definition of unemployment, however, includes those whose labor-market experiences may be very different. Individuals may be looking for work because they lost their jobs, because they are on temporary layoff with an expected recall date, or because they were unhappy in their previous position and quit. They may not even have left a job prior to their unemployment spell. Individuals who are searching for work because they have entered the labor-market for the first time or because they are reentering after a prolonged absence (after raising children?) are included among the count of the unemployed as long as they are searching for work.

The impact on family dynamics associated with these different types of unemployment could vary dramatically. The view from the psychology literature focuses on the stress that unemployment may generate within the family. That stress may be greater if the unemployment spell is attributable to a sudden and unexpected job loss compared to one that may be more readily anticipated (new or reentrant) or less traumatic, financially or otherwise (temporary layoff). Of greatest concern during the current economic downturn is the issue of permanent job loss. Although this type of unemployment is considerably more common now, it still reflects no more than about half of total unemployment. Table 15.9 displays the breakdown of these different causes of unemployment in years that exemplify peaks and troughs of the labor market. In 2009, when the unemployment rate neared its post–World War II high, 43 percent of unemployed workers reported a permanent job loss and another 11.4 percent reported a layoff with an expectation of recall. In 2000, the unemployment rate hit its post–World War II low and still 19.6 percent of the unemployed suffered a permanent job loss and 15 percent more reported a layoff.

An exercise like the one I conduct here using nationally representative data over this period may not be sufficiently narrowly focused on the traumatic types of unemployment experiences that may impact children. From this exercise we may learn that the more routinely experienced forms of unemployment are not deleterious to children's educational performance. An alternative exercise that focuses more specifically on labor-market shocks that generate more extreme forms of job loss may better gauge the impact of the current economic crisis. The research conducted by Elizabeth O. Ananat, Anna Gassman-Pines, and Christina M. Gibson-Davis that is reported in chapter 14 of this volume accomplishes this goal. Most likely this difference explains the differences in our findings.

I would like to thank Becky Blank, Greg Duncan, and Dick Murnane, as well as participants in the preconference and at the American Time Use Research Conference held at the University of Maryland for their useful comments. Thanks also to Eric Dearing and Tracey Lund for sharing their expertise in developmental psychology and to Samantha Heep for providing valuable research assistance.

NOTES

Online appendix available at: http://www.russellsage.org/duncan_murnane_online_appendix.pdf.

1. I am grateful to Eric Dearing and Tracey Lund, developmental psychologists at Boston College, for their contributions to this section.
2. See Ruhm (2004, 2008) for multidisciplinary reviews of the literature on the impact of maternal employment.
3. This work is perhaps more directly linked to the issue of mass layoffs, which is discussed in chapter 14 of this volume, by Elizabeth O. Ananat, Anna Gassman-Pines, and Christina M. Gibson-Davis.
4. Jonathan Guryan, Erik Hurst, and Melissa Kearney (2008) report similar statistics that relate time spent with children to employment status as well as educational attainment. Parents' labor-market activity is divided into working and not working, though, and my work in this chapter emphasizes that unemployment is a diverse labor-market state.
5. In theory, one would be able to use these data to further segment unemployed individuals according to the reason their spell of unemployment began. In practice, however, this exercise is difficult to implement because the reason for unemployment is asked in a different survey month than the time-use question. In fact, they could be up to five months apart. Since unemployment spells typically do not last that long, a large number of the unemployed people in the time-use part of the survey were not unemployed in the part of the CPS where I can identify the reason for unemployment.
6. For purposes of presentation, I have chosen not to include test statistics designed to determine which measures are statistically different from each other. F-tests designed to determine whether time use differs among all labor-market activity categories indicate that we are generally able to reject this null hypothesis. Otherwise, as a broad characterization, all observed pairwise comparisons that appear sizable in magnitude are significantly different.
7. Some research on brain development suggests that early-life experiences may have long-lasting effects (see Nelson and Sheridan 2009). In this context, I have also experimented with measures of parental labor-market activity in the child's first three years of life. The findings I obtain using early-life experiences are qualitatively similar to those regarding parental labor-market activity since birth.
8. I will subsequently refer to the respondent's spouse or partner as the child's father for ease of exposition, but that certainly does not need to be the case.
9. As described earlier, I have also conducted this analysis examining the impact of parental labor-market activity in the child's first three years of life.
10. These identifiers are available with the permission of the U.S. Department of Labor. Thus, I cannot share these data for replication purposes.
11. These results are not reported here but are available upon request.

REFERENCES

Abraham, Katharine G., Sarah M. Flood, Matthew Sobek, and Betsy Thorn. 2008. *American Time Use Survey Data Extract System:* Version 1.0 [Machine-readable database]. Maryland Population Research Center, University of Maryland, College Park, Maryland, and Minnesota Population Center, University of Minnesota, Minneapolis, Minnesota. Available at: http://www.atusdata.org (accessed April 27, 2011).

Bratberg, Espen, Øivind Anti Nilsen, and Kjell Vaage. 2008. "Job Losses and Child Outcomes." *Labour Economics* 15(4): 591–603.

Christoffersen, Mogens Nygaard. 2000. "Growing Up with Unemployment: A Study of Parental Unemployment and Children's Risk of Abuse and Neglect Based on National Longitudinal 1973 Birth Cohorts in Denmark." *Childhood* 7(4): 421–38.

Dahl, Gordon B., and Lance Lochner. 2005. "The Impact of Family Income on Child Achievement." NBER Working Paper No. 11279. Cambridge, Mass.: National Bureau of Economic Research.

Duncan, Greg J., and Jeanne Brooks-Gunn. 1997. *Consequences of Growing Up Poor.* New York: Russell Sage Foundation.

Elder, Glen H., Jr. 1974. *Children of the Great Depression.* Chicago: University of Chicago Press.

Elder, Glen H., Jr., Tri Van Nguyen, and Avshalom Caspi. 1985. "Linking Family Hardship to Children's Lives." *Child Development* 56(2): 361–75.

Guryan, Jonathan, Erik Hurst, and Melissa Kearney. 2008. "Parental Education and Parental Time with Children." *Journal of Economic Perspectives* 22(3): 23–46.

Harris, Paul L. 1994. "The Child's Understanding of Emotion: Developmental Change and the Family Environment." *Journal of Child Psychology and Psychiatry* 35(1): 3–28.

Hill, Jennifer L., Jane Waldfogel, Jeanne Brooks-Gunn, and Wen-Jui Han. 2005. "Maternal Employment and Child Development: A Fresh Look Using Newer Methods." *Developmental Psychology* 41(6): 833–50.

Mayer, Susan. 1997. *What Money Can't Buy: Family Income and Children's Life Chances.* Cambridge, Mass.: Harvard University Press.

McLoyd, Vonnie C., Toby Epstein Jayaratne, Rosario Ceballo, and Julio Borquez. 1994. "Unemployment and Work Interruption Among African American Single Mothers: Effects on Parenting and Adolescent Socioemotional Functioning." *Child Development* 65(2): 562–89.

Nelson, Charles A., and Margaret Sheridan. 2009. "Lessons from Neuroscience Research for Understanding Causal Links Between Family and Neighborhood Characteristics and Educational Outcomes." Unpublished paper. Harvard Medical School.

Oreopoulos, Philip, Marianne Page, and Ann Huff Stevens. 2008. "The Intergenerational Effects of Worker Displacement." *Journal of Labor Economics* 26(3): 455–83.

Rege, Mari, Kjetil Telle, and Mark Votruba. 2007. "Parental Job Loss and Children's School Performance." Statistics Norway Research Department discussion paper 517. Kongsvinger, Norway: Statistics Norway.

Ruhm, Christopher J. 2004. "Parental Employment and Child Cognitive Development." *Journal of Human Resources* 39(1): 155–92.

———. 2008. "Maternal Employment and Adolescent Development." *Labour Economics* 15(5): 958–83.

Stevens, Ann Huff, and Jessamyn Schaller. 2009. "Short-Run Effects of Parental Job Loss on Children's Academic Achievement." Unpublished paper. University of California, Davis.

U.S. Bureau of Labor Statistics. Various years. *The Employment Situation.* Washington, D.C.: Bureau of Labor Statistics.

U.S. Bureau of Labor Statistics, U.S. Department of Labor. 2010. *National Longitudinal Survey of Youth 1979 cohort, 1979–2006* [computer file]. Produced and distributed by the Center for Human Resource Research, Ohio State University, Columbus, Ohio.

Voydanoff, Patricia. 1983. "Unemployment: Family Strategies for Adaptation." In *Stress and the Family: Coping with Catastrophe,* edited by Hamilton I. McCubbin and Charles R. Figley. New York: Brunner/Mazel.

Waldfogel, Jane, Wen-Jui Han, and Jeanne Brooks-Gunn. 2002. "The Effects of Early Maternal Employment on Child Cognitive Development." *Demography* 39(2): 369–92.

Part VI

Schools

Chapter 16

The Role of Family, School, and Community Characteristics in Inequality in Education and Labor-Market Outcomes

Joseph G. Altonji and Richard K. Mansfield

This chapter assesses the relative importance of families, neighborhoods, and high schools in explaining variation in high school completion, college attendance, and labor-market success for U.S. students over the past four decades. It finds that families are much more influential than schools and communities in producing successful students, but that school- and community-based factors also make a big difference. The study draws on data from three large national surveys: the National Longitudinal Study of the High School Class of 1972, the National Educational Longitudinal Study: 1988, and the Education Longitudinal Study: 2002.

For all three cohorts, differences between high schools in the average student and family background of their students can account for large disparities in high schools' average outcomes, even if the student and parent composition of schools has no influence on school quality and community resources and average peer effects are small. Such sorting increased significantly between 1972 and 1990 but changed little after 1990. This process contributed to an increase in the variance among schools' college attendance rates between 1972 and the early 1990s. There are also large differences in student characteristics within schools, and overall much more of the variation in high school graduation rates, four-year college attendance rates, and labor-market earnings of American youth can be explained by variables associated with students and their families than by school-based influences.

Nonetheless, we find that moving a student from a school and associated community at the 10th percentile of quality to one at the 90th percentile would increase the student's predicted high school graduation probability by eight to ten percentage points. School and community matter even more for four-year college enrollment. Moving a high school senior in 1972 from a school and community at the 10th percentile of the quality distribution to one at the 90th percentile would increase the probability of enrolling in a four-year college by 19 to 23 percentage points, a very substantial change. The estimates are even larger for the more recent cohorts, in line with evidence for rising social inequality that is summarized in the introduction to this volume. We also find a substantial effect of school and community on adult wage rates.

Parents agonize over which school and community will be best for their children. Government recognizes this concern. A number of state and federal policies have aimed to close, reform, and provide alternatives to "failing" schools. These policies include greater school choice within and between school districts, charter school programs, and holding schools accountable under the No Child Left Behind Act of 2001. At the neighborhood level, federal, state, and local programs to replace large public housing projects with Section 8 vouchers that families can use anywhere are motivated in part by the belief that concentrations of poverty harm children (see, for example, Kling, Katz, and Liebmen 2007; Oreopoulos 2003).

But how much difference do schools and communities make? Although there is a large literature examining the impact of school, family, community, and peer inputs on test scores and delinquency (see, for example, Coleman 1966; Hanushek et al. 2003; Hoxby 2000; Goldhaber and Brewer 1997), less is known about their effects on later outcomes of arguably greater concern: high school completion, college attendance, and especially permanent wage rates (see Speakman and Welch 2006 on school quality and wages). How segregated are schools in terms of race and ethnicity, parental characteristics, prior educational achievement, and other factors that influence adult outcomes in American society? How much of the impact that parents have on their child's outcomes is independent of the school? How much occurs indirectly via their choice of the child's community, school, and peer environment? How much do the differences between schools and communities matter for educational attainment and wages? Has the degree of segregation and the relative importance of student and family characteristics versus school and community factors changed since the early 1970s?

The answers to these questions have important policy implications. On the one hand, suppose parental characteristics predict child outcomes primarily because they predict the quality of the schools their children attend. If so, then interventions to provide some children with a supportive family environment will not result in major aggregate education or wage gains because, to the extent that these children benefit, they do so by taking spots at more effective schools from other students (unless the better schools have room to grow). Finding ways to improve schools could have a big payoff in this context. On the other hand, suppose that most of the impact of family environment on child outcomes comes from crafting better child behavior, raising child expectations, or directly fostering intellectual development, and that the school a child attends predicts his or her eventual outcomes primarily because it reflects the child's probable family environment. Then, school-level interventions such as changes in administrative personnel or class sizes are unlikely to improve child outcomes.[1]

Information about changes in the importance of student-level and school- and community-level factors is key to understanding trends in educational attainment. Have there been changes in the amount of variation in family-background characteristics across students and schools, perhaps as a result of changes in marriage and fertility patterns or changes in the distribution of education and income? Or instead, do family, peer, and school characteristics now matter more (or less) than they once did, perhaps as a result of changes in residential segregation and school reforms?

In this chapter we provide evidence that addresses these questions, drawing heavily on Joseph G. Altonji and Richard K. Mansfield (2010). To do so, we use three rich panel data sets. Each data set samples multiple students from each of a large number of schools and, importantly, tracks outcomes for several years past high school. The National Longitudinal Study of the High School Class of 1972 (NLS72) follows twelfth-graders in 1972. The National Educational Longitudinal Study: 1988 (NELS88) starts with eighth-graders in 1988 and provides information about tenth-graders in 1990. The Education Longitudinal Study: 2002 (ELS02) tracks tenth-graders in 2002. The outcomes considered are high school graduation (NELS88 and ELS02), enrollment in a four-year college in the second year after the normal high school graduation date for the cohort (all three data sets), years of completed postsecondary education (NLS72 only), and adult wages (NLS72 only). We standardize the set of variables used in the three data sets so that we can examine trends in the relative importance of observable and unobservable student- and school-level inputs.

Following a number of previous studies, we exploit the fact that the samples are clustered at the school level to decompose the variance in outcomes into the contributions of observed and unobserved student and family characteristics that vary both within and between schools, and observed and unobserved school and neighborhood variables that vary only between schools (see Jencks and Brown 1975; Altonji 1988; Bryk and Raudenbush 1988, among others). We use variation within schools to estimate the direct effect of observed student and family characteristics (such as race and parental education) on the outcomes of students, controlling for the high school and associated community characteristics. Then we use the remaining variation between schools to identify the combined effects of peer characteristics and other school and community characteristics, such as the student-teacher ratio, teacher salary levels, and school type. We use these estimates to calculate the average effect on educational attainment and wage rates of moving a child from a school and associated community that is at roughly the 10th percentile of the "quality" distribution to one at the 90th percentile, holding student-specific characteristics fixed. We emphasize the results obtained using a baseline specification that excludes test scores, measures of educational expectations, and behaviors that may have been influenced by the school and community. We also present results with test scores added to the baseline model as well as results with a more full set of student, family, and school characteristics.

Although we employ a rich set of student, family, and school and community characteristics in our models, we do not identify the causal effects of particular variables. Chapters 3 and 4 in this volume, by Greg Duncan and Katherine Magnuson, and George Farkas, respectively, investigate the predictive power of individual student behavioral measures and family-background measures in greater detail, including the question of when in a child's development differences in these measures start to create performance disparities among students. Instead, we focus on providing an overall assessment of the extent to which students with common observed or unobserved characteristics cluster in the same high schools, and the degree to which disparities in average educational outcomes simply reflect such clustering, as opposed to the causal effects of particular high school and associated community factors.

In the next section we present our econometric model of education outcomes. We then discuss our estimation methodology, the data, and results.

A MODEL OF EDUCATIONAL ATTAINMENT AND WAGE RATES

Here we explain the underlying econometric model of adult outcomes that provides the basis for the variance decompositions that we present. We use Y_{si} to refer to the outcome of student i from high school s. In our application, the outcomes are high school graduation, attendance at a four-year college, a measure of years of postsecondary education, and the permanent wage rate. In the case of wages and years of postsecondary education, Y_{si} is the actual outcome and is determined according to

$$(16.1) \qquad Y_{si} = X_{si}B + Z_sG + m_s + v_s + v_{si}$$

In the case of high school graduation and attendance at a four-year college, which take on the values 0 or 1, Y_{si} is a continuous "latent" variable. The student graduates high school if Y_{si} is greater than 0. College graduation also depends on whether Y_{si} is positive. Naturally, the coefficients B and G and the error components in equation 16.1 depend on the specific outcome under consideration.

The variable X_{si} is a set of observable student and family characteristics that have a causal impact on student i's educational attainment and wages. Examples include race, gender, immigrant status, and parental education, income, and employment. The error component $v_s + v_{si}$ reflects student and family influences that are unrelated to X_{si}. There are many characteristics of the student (for example, physical attractiveness and temperament) and parents (for example, parenting skill and time allocation during early childhood) that we do not measure at all. Furthermore, we measure child and family variables only at a single point in time, rather than at various stages of the child's life. The component v_s is the mean at high school s of unobserved characteristics that affect the outcome, while v_{si} reflects student-specific variation around the mean. The term v_{si} also captures variation in environmental influences among students who attend the same school. Importantly, $X_{si}B + v_s + v_{si}$ affects the outcome of student i regardless of the average characteristics of the school and neighborhood the student attends and lives in.

The vector Z_s is a set of school and neighborhood influences that are common to students who attend school s. It comprises two components: school-level averages of the individual observable characteristics X_{si} (for example, average parent income) and other school- and neighborhood-level inputs (for example, student-teacher ratio or city-size indicators). The error component m_s is an index of unobserved school and community characteristics that influence the outcomes of students who attend school s but are unrelated to Z_s. These include the school mean of relevant unobserved peer characteristics as well as the component of the quality of the school principal and teachers that is unpredictable based on Z_s.

The coefficient vector B is composed of two parts. The first is made up of the causal effects of X_{si} as well as part of the effects of omitted student and family characteristics, to the extent that these observed and omitted characteristics covary within a school. We do not make any attempt to interpret individual components of the coefficient vectors B, and thus we do not tease apart the distinct influences of student characteristics, family characteristics, and early childhood schooling inputs, respectively. But given that B reflects in part the direct effects of both observed and unobserved characteristics, a student's value of $X_{si}B$ provides a useful summary of the impact of his or her background and prior schooling on the outcomes we measure. Furthermore, removing average values of $X_{si}B$ at each school (which we denote X_sB) when comparing average school outcomes allows us to better isolate differences in the quality of the high schools and associated communities themselves. Because X_sB does not fully capture student and family influences, the residual differences in school outcome means ($Y_s - X_sB$) will still reflect (via v_s) differences in background characteristics and prior school quality of student populations that are impervious to high school–level interventions, in addition to true differences in the school's ability to change student outcomes (via Z_s and m_s).

The second component of B is an indirect effect. This component corresponds to the influence of X_{si} on the part of the child's school and community experience that is not shared by others at his or her school. Examples include variation in the trustworthiness of immediate neighbors and specific courses taken in school. The magnitude of this component is determined by the extent to which the differences in the micro environment of the student within a school or school neighborhood are predictable based on variables such as race, parental education, student aptitude and achievement, and so forth that are part of X_{si}. Consequently, the links will depend on how families in general, and students in particular, are stratified within communities and high schools. They also depend to some degree on policies such as zoning, housing policy, and curriculum tracking that were in place at the time. The presence of the indirect component in B will bias upward the estimates of the importance of differences *between* schools in the index of average student characteristics X_sB and bias downward the estimates of the importance of Z_sG.[2]

G captures the direct influence of the elements of Z_s, but it will also pick up part of the effect of school characteristics that we do not control for. As with $X_{si}B$, our aim is not to interpret individual elements of G, but instead to capture the collective impact of a number of school and community characteristics. This avoids attributing the variation to differences in student background and gives an overall sense of how much of the differences in school performance are predictable based on their characteristics. Of course, gaps in performances across schools may be difficult to close even if they are predictable, and some of these characteristics may be beyond the school's control (for example, crime in the neighborhood).

ESTIMATION OF MODEL PARAMETERS

In the case of years of postsecondary academic education and wages, we estimate B by controlling for all high school variables with a school-specific fixed effect (a separate constant term for each high school). This is a standard procedure in the education production function literature.[3] We estimate G by applying least-squares regression to

$$Y_{si} - X_{si}\hat{B} = \overline{Z}_s G + e_{si},$$

where $\hat{B}$ is the estimate of B and we have replaced Z_s with $\overline{Z}_s$ to reflect the fact that we must estimate the components of Z_s corresponding to schoolwide averages of the variables in X_{si} using averages for the sample members from each school. Because the school samples are relatively small, this introduces measurement error. Measurement error is a source of downward bias in the estimate of $Var(Z_sG)$ and upward bias in the estimate of the importance of the unobserved school and community factors ($Var(m_s)$).

For high school graduation and college attendance, we estimate G and B from a probit regression on the variables in X_{si} and $\overline{Z}_s$.

DECOMPOSING THE VARIANCE IN EDUCATIONAL ATTAINMENT AND WAGES

In this section we discuss an analysis of variance based on equation 16.1 that can be used to measure the importance of factors that are common to students from the same school. We also consider estimation of the effect of a shift in school and community quality from the tenth to the ninetieth percentile.

One may decompose $Var(Y_{si})$ into its within- and between-school components using

$$Var\left(Y_{si}\right) = Var\left(Y_{si} - Y_s\right) + Var\left(Y_s\right),$$

where $(Y_{si} - Y_s)$ is the part of Y_{si} that varies across students in school s and Y_s is the average outcome for students from s. We focus much of our attention on the ratio $Var(Y_s)/Var(Y_{si})$ which is the fraction of the total variance that is across schools. This ratio is also known as the "intraclass correlation," where the class is the school. Using equation (16.1) and the fact that B and G are defined so that the errors in the model are unrelated to X and Z, $Var(Y_{si})$ may be decomposed as:

$$(16.2) \qquad Var\left(Y_{si}\right) = Var\left(\left(X_{si} - X_s\right)B\right) + Var\left(v_{si}\right) + Var\left(X_s B\right) + Var\left(v_s\right) + 2Cov\left(X_s B, Z_s G\right)$$
$$+ 2Cov\left(v_s, m_s\right) + Var\left(m_s\right) + Var\left(Z_s G\right)$$

Note that $Var(X_sB)$ and $Var(v_s)$ are part of the between-school variance $Var(Y_s)$ even though these components do not represent the influence of student-body composition or other aspects of a particular high school and community. Rather, they simply reflect the fact that average outcomes will vary between high schools if average characteristics of the students in the high schools vary. Consequently, they should not be counted as neighborhood or school influences. It is unclear whether one should attribute the two covariance terms to the contribution of individual characteristics or to high school– and community-level factors. Given this ambiguity and the fact that we cannot distinguish the contribution of m_s from that of v_s, we define an "upper-bound" estimate of the fraction of the variance attributable to high school and community factors as $Var(Z_sG) + Var(m_s + v_s) + 2Cov(X_sB, Z_sG)$. Our "lower-bound" estimate is just $Var(Z_sG)$. We present results based on these two extreme assumptions. As detailed in Altonji and Mansfield (2010), we use quotation marks because these "bounds" may not represent true inviolable bounds.

We use appropriate sample variances and covariances and estimates of B and G to estimate the variance and covariance terms in equation 16.2. The estimates of the impact of school and community essentially come from a comparison of how much more alike the outcomes of those who attended the same school are than the outcomes of individuals with the same characteristics who attended different schools. The details of how we estimate the variance terms depend on whether the outcome is binary, such as high school graduation, or continuous, such as years of educational attainment and wages. For wages, we decompose the permanent component of wages, which we isolate from transitory disturbances in wages by using covariances between observations at two points in time, both for the same individual and for different individuals from the same school. See Altonji and Mansfield (2010) for the details.

The variance decompositions provide a good indication of the importance of school and community factors relative to student-specific factors. However, the effect of a shift from the left tail of the distribution of school and community quality to the right tail might be socially significant even if most of the outcome variability is student-specific. This is particularly true in the case of binary outcomes such as high school graduation. Below we report the effect of a shift in the school community index $Z_sG + m_s$ from 1.28 standard deviations below the mean to 1.28 standard deviations above the mean on education and wages, holding the distributions of X and v constant. This would correspond to a shift from the 10th percentile to the 90th percentile if $Z_sG + m_s$ has a normal distribution. We provide lower-bound estimates based on setting $Var(m_s)$ to 0 and $Var(v_s)$ to $\widehat{Var}(m_s + v_s)$ and upper-bound estimates based on setting $\widehat{Var}(m_s)$ to $Var(m_s + v_s)$ and $Var(v_s)$ to 0. That is, the upper-bound attributes all of the variance of the unobserved factors that vary at the school level to school and community factors rather than to differences in the average unobserved characteristics of the students and their families.

DATA

The NLS72, NELS88, and ELS02 span more than thirty years and display a set of common properties that make them well suited for our analysis. First, each source selects a sample of an entire cohort of American students to survey. The cohorts are students who were in twelfth grade in 1972 in the case of NLS72, eighth grade in 1988 (tenth grade in 1990) for NELS88, and tenth grade in 2002 for ELS02. Second, each source is based on a stratified sample design in which a representative sample of American high schools or eighth grades is selected, and then samples of students are selected within each school. This design has the virtue that the entire universe of schools is represented (public, Catholic, other private, and charter). Also, a sizable number of individuals are sampled from each school, permitting us to construct estimates of the school means of a large array of student-specific variables and providing sufficient within-school variation to support a between- and within-school variance decomposition. Third, all three surveys collect information from school administrators as well as from sampled students at each school. This provides rich sets of individual-level and school-level variables to examine, allowing a meaningful decomposition of observable versus unobservable variation at both levels of observation. Fourth and most critically, each survey collects follow-up information from each student past high school graduation, facilitating analysis of the impact of high school environment on a number of the outcomes social scientists and policy makers care most about: the high school graduation rate, college enrollment, and wages.

Although these common properties led us to choose the three data sets for our analysis, each survey displays idiosyncratic features that complicate comparisons over time. In the baseline specification, we only use variables that are available and measured consistently across all three data sets. Also, the baseline set of variables is limited to student-level characteristics that are unlikely to be affected by the high school the student attends. However, we also provide decompositions that include in X_s scores from standardized tests taken by students in high school as proxies for ability, in specifications labeled "w/tests." These scores may be influenced directly by high school inputs, so including them could cause an underestimate of the contribution of school-level inputs. However, excluding them could instead cause an overestimate of the contribution of school-level inputs, given that we would run the risk of understating the extent of ability differences among students who attend different schools.

Restricting our analysis to measures that are common across data sets prevents us from exploiting the full power of these rich data sets to explain the distribution of an important set of outcomes, particularly in the case of NELS88 and ELS02. For these data sets, we also work with a larger set of common variables, which we label our "full" specification. It includes measures of student behavior and parental expectations that, like test scores, are not clearly exogenous but may allow one to more accurately characterize differences in the backgrounds of students attending different schools. Table 16.1 lists the individual-level and school-level explanatory measures used for each data set.[4]

The outcome variables are defined as follows. The measure of college attendance is an indicator for whether the student is enrolled in a four-year college in the second year beyond the high school graduation year of his or her cohort. It is available in each data set.[5] We also examine high school graduation rates in NELS88 and ELS02. The measure of high school graduation is an indicator of whether a student has a high school diploma (not including a GED) as of two years after the high school graduation year of his or her cohort. Notice, though, that since ELS02 first surveys students in tenth grade, it misses a substantial fraction of the early dropouts. Indeed, in NELS88, about one-third of the 16 percent who eventually drop out do so before the first follow-up survey in the middle of tenth grade. Since NLS72 first surveys students in twelfth grade, we cannot properly examine dropout behavior in this data set.[6] However, because NLS72 resurveys individuals in 1979 and 1986 (when respondents are around twenty-five and thirty-two years old), we can analyze completed years of postsecondary education and adult wages. For the wage analysis, we include only respondents who report wages in both 1979 and 1986.[7]

RESULTS

We now turn to the empirical findings, beginning with estimates of the degree to which the characteristics of students vary between schools. We then address the importance of school and community factors for educational attainment and wages.

TABLE 16.1   *Variables Used in Baseline and Full Specifications**

	Variables
Student characteristics	Female, black, Hispanic, Asian, *immigrant*
Student ability	*Math standardized score*, reading standardized score**
Student behavior	*Hours per week spent on homework, parents often check homework, hours per week spent on leisure reading, hours per week spent watching TV, often arrives at class without a pencil, physical fight this year*
Family background	Standardized SES number of siblings, both biological parents present, mother and male guardian present, father and female guardian present, mother only present, father only present, father's years of education, mother's years of education, mother's years of education missing, English spoken at home, log(family income), *immigrant mother, immigrant father, employed mother, employed father, parents are married*
Parental expectations	*Mother's desired years of education, father's desired years of education*
School characteristics	School is Catholic, school is private non-Catholic, student-teacher ratio, percentage teacher turnover since last year, percentage on college prep. track, percentage of teachers with master's degrees or more, average percentage daily attendance, school percentage minority, school teacher percentage minority, total school enrollment, *log(minimum teacher salary), school percentage free–reduced price lunch, school percentage LEP, school percentage special education, school percentage remedial reading, school percentage remedial math*
Neighborhood characteristics	School in urban area, school in suburban area, school in rural area, school in northeast region of United States, school in south region of United States, school in midwest region of United States, school in west region of United States

Source: Authors' compilation.
Note: Italics represent full specifications.
*Standardized test scores are also included in the tests specifications, along with all of the baseline variables.

How Much Do Students in Different Schools Vary?

We start by examining whether schools vary in the composition of their student bodies along the observable dimensions that best predict future outcomes. We approach this question by first studying the distribution of particular student-level variables such as mother's education and then considering a more comprehensive index of student characteristics.

We find a moderate degree of segregation of students across schools along the lines of parental education, parental income, and test scores. Column 3 of table 16.2 reports the fraction of the variance in each variable that is between schools (the intraclass correlation). For 2002 tenth-graders, the value is 0.24 for family income. For 1990 tenth-graders, there is slightly less total variance in family income (standard deviation of 0.85 versus 0.96) but a greater fraction that is between schools (0.27). There is less total variation as well as a smaller fraction between schools in 1972, reflecting a more equitable distribution of family income both within and between schools and communities. Mother's years of education shows the same pattern of an increase in total and between-school variation between 1972 and 1990, followed by a leveling off between 1990 and 2002 (although the mean value of mother's education has continued to increase). The intraclass correlation for whether the student lives with both biological parents is between 0.07 and 0.09 in all three data sets, but the mean has declined substantially since the early 1970s.

Not surprisingly, indicators for race-ethnicity and whether English is spoken at home all show large intraclass correlations. For example, the intraclass correlation for black is 0.73 in 1972, 0.70 in 1990, and 0.53 in 2002. The value for English spoken at home is only 0.12 in NLS72 but is 0.49 in both NELS88 and ELS02.

TABLE 16.2   *Summary Statistics for Selected Demographic Characteristics by Data Source*

	1972 12th Grade (National Longitudinal Study of the High School Class of 1972)			
Variable Name	Sample Mean (1)	Standard Deviation (2)	Between Variance/ Total Variance (3)	Between-School Standard Deviation (4)
Black	0.08	0.28	0.73	—
Hispanic	0.03	0.18	0.61	—
Math standard score	0.02	1.00	0.13	0.36
Log(family income)	10.90	0.71	0.21	0.33
Mother's years of education	12.33	2.05	0.12	0.72
Both biological parents present	0.77	0.42	0.07	—
English spoken at home	0.92	0.27	0.12	—

	1988 8th Grade (National Educational Longitudinal Study, 1988)			
Variable Name	Sample Mean (1)	Standard Deviation (2)	Between Variance/ Total Variance (3)	Between-School Standard Deviation (4)
Black	0.10	0.30	0.70	—
Hispanic	0.09	0.29	0.61	—
Math standard score	0.15	1.00	0.20	0.45
Log(family income)	10.94	0.85	0.27	0.44
Mother's years of education	13.05	2.21	0.20	1.00
Both biological parents present	0.69	0.46	0.08	—
English spoken at home	0.92	0.28	0.49	—

	2002 10th Grade (Education Longitudinal Study, 2002)			
Variable Name	Sample Mean (1)	Standard Deviation (2)	Between Variance/ Total Variance (3)	Between-School Standard Deviation (4)
Black	0.14	0.35	0.53	—
Hispanic	0.15	0.36	0.44	—
Math standard score	0.05	1.00	0.21	0.46
Log(family income)	10.92	0.96	0.24	0.47
Mother's years of education	13.52	2.28	0.18	0.97
Both biological parents present	0.59	0.49	0.09	—
English spoken at home	0.90	0.30	0.49	—

Source: Authors' calculations based on NLS72, NELS88, and ELS02 (National Center for Education Statistics 1994, 1996, 2007).
Note: Between school variances group using the grade 10 school (NELS88 and ELS02) or grade 12 school (NLS72). Between variance/Total variance is the fraction of the variance of the variable that is between schools. This value is also known as the intraclass correlation.

FIGURE 16.1   *Estimated Difference Between the 10th and 90th Percentiles of School Averages of*
Student Characteristics

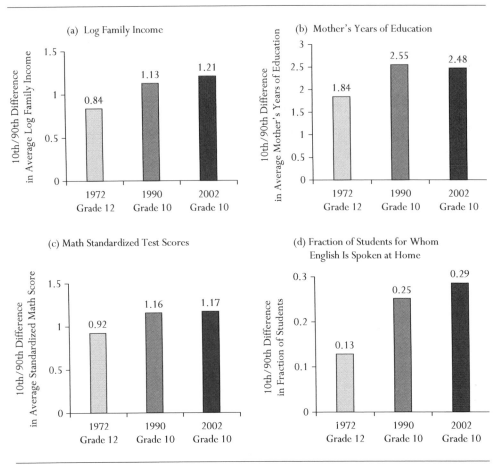

Source: Authors' calculations based on NLS72, NELS88, and ELS02 (National Center for Education Statistics 1994, 1996, 2007).

To provide a better sense of the extent to which the values of these student-background variables vary between schools, figure 16.1 displays the estimated difference between the 10th and 90th percentiles of the school averages for a few of these variables for seniors in 1972 and sophomores in 1990 and 2002. The height of the bar indicates the size of the differential.[8] The gap in the log of family income is 0.84 in 1972, 1.13 in 1990, and 1.21 in 2002. These imply ratios of average family incomes at the 90th versus 10th percentile schools of 2.31, 3.10, and 3.35, respectively. The gap in the school averages of mother's education rose from 1.84 in 1972 to 2.55 in 1990 and 2.48 in 2002. The 10-90 gap in school averages of the math test increased from 0.92 standard deviations in 1972 to 1.16 in 1990 to 1.17 in 2002, while the corresponding gap for the fraction of students for whom English is the predominant language spoken at home increased from 0.13 to 0.25 to 0.29.[9]

Finally, for NELS88 and ELS02, Altonji and Mansfield (2010) examine the distributions of student behavior and parental expectations measures that are included in the full specification but not the baseline specification. In general, they do not find much clustering at the school level in the measures of student behavior and expectations. For example, they find that very little of the variation in the indicator for whether parents check homework, the indicator for whether the student engaged in a physical fight in the past year, and mother's desired years of education for the student is between schools (between 2 percent and 9 percent). Moreover, the small changes between 1990 and 2002 in the differences in means between the tenth and ninetieth percentile schools for these measures are driven primarily by more desirable overall sample means for each measure. If few students are fighting in any school, for example, there will not be much within- or between-school variation, independent of the extent to which the few fights are clustered at the same schools.

To provide a more comprehensive assessment, we examine the distribution of students' backgrounds using the index $X_s B$. This index weights observed student and family characteristics such as family income, parental education, race-ethnicity, and family structure by how much they matter for a particular outcome. The coefficients depend on the outcome, so we construct separate indices for each one. They also depend on whether we use the baseline specification, the baseline specification plus tests, or the full specification in selecting the components of X_s. For college attendance, the fraction of the variance in the student-background index that is between schools ranges from 0.19 for the 1972 cohort to 0.28 for the 1990 cohort to 0.29 for the 2002 cohort. The values for high school graduation are 0.28 for the 1990 cohort and 0.24 for 2002. The estimates are smaller when we add test scores to the baseline model or use the full set of student-level variables.[10] The NLS72 results for years of postsecondary education are similar to the results for four-year college enrollment. In the case of log wages, the value for both the baseline and full specifications is 0.25. Overall, the index results indicate a substantial degree of sorting across schools on the basis of student background.

In figure 16.2, panel a, we use the student-background index to investigate the degree to which some high schools have higher graduation and college attendance rates simply because they have advantaged students who would obtain more schooling regardless of which high school they attend. Specifically, the figure displays the difference between what the high school graduation rate would be for high schools ranked at the 10th percentile versus schools at the 90th percentile of the distribution of the between-school component of the student-background index. These calculations hold fixed the distributions of all observed and unobserved school-quality variables. In particular, we are holding the distribution of peer effects constant even though we are shifting $X_s \hat{B}$ and the components of X_s are a subset of the school variables Z_s.

Using our baseline set of explanatory variables, the difference is 0.07 for 1990 sophomores and 0.08 for 2002 sophomores. This is large relative to the mean dropout rates of 0.09 for the 1990 sophomores and 0.10 for 2002 sophomores. The values are substantially higher if we cluster on the eighth grade rather than tenth grade, primarily because a substantial fraction of dropouts occur prior to tenth grade.

Figure 16.2, panel b, reports the corresponding difference in the fraction of students who are enrolled in a four-year college in the second year after they should have graduated from high school. The 10th-90th percentile differential in the college enrollment rate is 0.16 for 1972 seniors, 0.25 for 1990 sophomores, and 0.25 for 2002 sophomores. The differentials are large relative to the enrollment rates of 0.27, 0.34, and 0.37 for the three cohorts, respectively. The differential in average adult wage rates is about 16 percent for 1972 seniors (figure 16.2, panel c). For all the outcomes, the differentials are larger if we include test scores.

To sum up, the results for the individual background variables show a moderate amount of clustering at the school level by family income and parental education and a much more substantial clustering by race-ethnicity and assimilation measures. The degree of clustering in other

FIGURE 16.2 *Effect on School Outcomes of a Shift of the School Average of the Student Background Index (X_sB) from the 10th to the 90th Percentile*

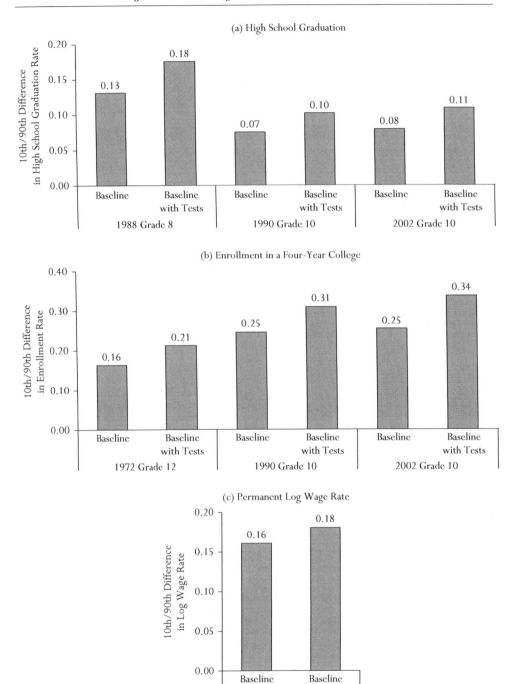

(a) High School Graduation

(b) Enrollment in a Four-Year College

(c) Permanent Log Wage Rate

Source: Authors' calculations based on NLS72, NELS88, and ELS02 (National Center for Education Statistics 1994, 1996, 2007).

student-level characteristics that are likely to influence educational attainment and wages is more modest. We tend to observe an increase in the grouping of students with similar backgrounds at the same high schools between 1972 and 1990, but no further increase between 1990 and 2002. This increase is reflected in greater clustering in test scores. The analysis of the student-background index indicates that there is enough clustering of students at the high school level to account directly for substantial differences in high schools' average outcomes, even if there are no peer effects and even if the student and parent composition of schools has no influence on school quality and community resources. These results also show an increase in the grouping of students with similar backgrounds at the same high schools between 1972 and 1990, but no further increase between 1990 and 2002. The increase in the early period is consistent with other evidence in the volume, suggesting an increase in social stratification along dimensions that matter for adult outcomes.

How Much Do Schools and Communities Matter for Educational Attainment and Wages?

We now decompose the variance of educational attainment and wages into observed and unobserved characteristics of the student and observed and unobserved characteristics of the school and community. For the binary outcomes, high school graduation and college attendance two years after the graduation year, the variance decompositions refer to the corresponding continuous latent variable that determines them.

The height of the bars in figure 16.3, panel a, indicates the fraction of the variance in the latent variable for high school graduation that is between schools. The value is about 0.15 for 1990 tenth graders and about 0.125 for 2002 tenth-graders. For college attendance, the estimates are 0.141 for 1972 twelfth-graders and about 0.21 for both 1990 and 2002 tenth-graders (figure 16.3, panel b). The value for the permanent wage rate (figure 16.3, panel c) is about 0.165. Thus, most of the variation in education outcomes and wages is between students who attend the same schools rather than across schools. Within-school variation in unobserved student-level characteristics ($Var(v_{si})$) is typically considerably more important than variation in observed student-level characteristics ($Var((X_{si} - X_s)B)$). The value of the latter is larger when we include test scores or use the full set of student characteristics. For example, $Var((X_{si} - X_s)B)$ and $Var(v_{si})$ contribute 0.161 and 0.630 of the variance in college attendance in the baseline model for 1990 tenth graders and 0.306 and 0.480 in the model with tests. The relative contributions for the other cohorts are similar.

The bars in the three graphs making up figure 16.3 break down the between-school variation in each outcome into the fractions of $Var(Y_s)$ contributed by the various components. The top section of each bar corresponds to $Var(X_sB)$. In keeping with the results in the prior section, the figures show that for all outcomes and all three cohorts, a substantial part of the between-school variation in outcomes is due to the direct effects of student-background characteristics. For example, for both NELS88 and ELS02 tenth-graders, $Var(X_sB)$ accounts for about 0.064 of the total variance in college attendance when we use the baseline specification and 0.107 when we use the full specification. The importance of $Var((X_{si} - X_s)B)$ and $Var(X_sB)$ relative to $Var(Z_sG)$ indicates that most of the effect of observed parental characteristics on education and wages either is direct or operates by influencing the environment of the student within a school and community rather than through choice of school and community.

The lengths of the lower sections of the bars in figure 16.3 correspond to $Var(Z_sG)$, $2Cov(X_sB, Z_sG)$ and variation among schools in unobservable student and school factors ($Var(v_s + m_s)$), measured as a fraction of the total variance in the outcome. They are the basis for the approximate

FIGURE 16.3   *Decomposition of the Between-School Variance, by Outcome*

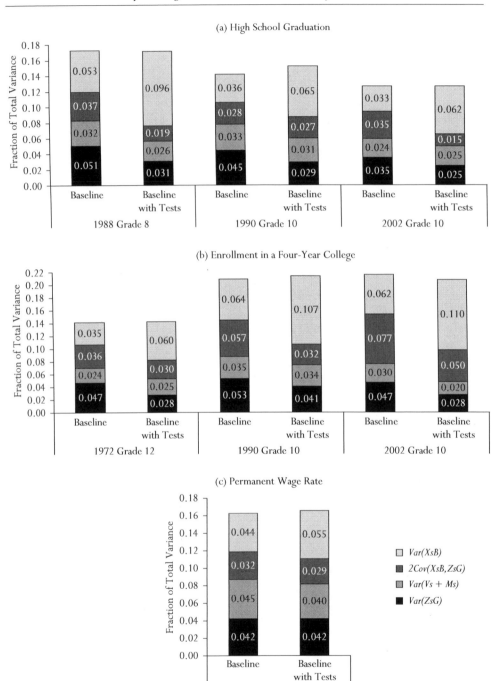

lower and upper bounds for the contribution of school and community factors to the variance in the outcomes.

There are two ways to view our results. On one hand, the percentage of the variance in educational attainment and in wages that is due to observed and unobserved school characteristics is only modest. Figure 16.4 implies that the upper-bound estimates lie between 6.1 and 12 percent for high school graduation, 8.2 and 15.4 percent for college attendance, and 11.0 and 11.9 percent for adult wage rates, with the specific value depending on the cohort data and explanatory variables used. The values for years of postsecondary education are 4.4 and 6.4 percent. Furthermore, the upper-bound estimates are probably overstated, although our estimates of the variances of student-specific and school-level factors are subject to biases in both directions, as is explained in detail in Altonji and Mansfield (2010).[11] The lower-bound estimates are typically considerably smaller.

On the other hand, even the lower-bound estimates of the variance of observed and unobserved school characteristics translate into substantial effects of schools on their students' graduation and college attendance rates. Figure 16.5, panel a, shows that the average effect on the probability of graduating high school of switching students from a school and community at the 10th percentile of quality (in terms of factors that matter for the particular outcome) to one at the 90th percentile is considerable. The light bar displays the lower bound, and the grey bar displays the upper bound. For both the 1990 and 2002 sophomore cohorts, the lower-bound estimate of the difference in graduation rates is about 0.08, and the upper-bound estimate is about 0.11. The figures are higher for 1988 eighth graders: 0.13 and 0.17. These larger numbers are primarily because students who drop out prior to tenth grade are included in the eighth-grade samples.

Figure 16.5, panel b, presents the effect of a 10th-to-90th-percentile shift in school quality on college attendance rates. The lower-bound estimate is 0.188 for 1972 seniors. The estimate is higher for later cohorts: about 0.22 for 1990 and 2002 sophomores. The upper-bound estimates are about 0.29 for both of the more recent cohorts. Figure 16.5 also shows that the estimates are smaller when we add test scores to the list of student characteristics. Results are similar when we use a full set of student characteristics that includes educational expectations and student behavior (not reported). Thus, a sizable fraction of students appear to be sufficiently close to the margin for high school graduation and for college attendance for the difference between a weak school and community and a strong one to be decisive.[12]

We also find a substantial effect of a 10th-to-90th-percentile shift in school and community quality on adult log wage rates. The lower-bound estimate is 0.16 and the upper-bound estimate is 0.23, which correspond to wage increases of about 17 and 26 percent, respectively.

Like our analysis of the between-school variation in background characteristics, these results suggest that the school and community factors that matter for college attendance grew in importance in the 1970s and 1980s but have remained constant since then. Restricting NELS88 and ELS02 to students who made it to twelfth grade does not significantly affect the comparison between time periods. The high school graduation results are also remarkably similar for the 1990 and 2002 cohorts of sophomores.

CONCLUSION

In a nutshell, our main results are as follows. First, we find a moderate degree of segregation of students across schools along the lines of parental education and income and in test scores and much more segregation by race-ethnicity. There is enough clustering of similar students at the high school level to account directly for substantial differences in average outcomes across high schools even if there are no peer effects.

FIGURE 16.4   *Fraction of Variance of Education and Log Wages Attributable to School or Community Environment*

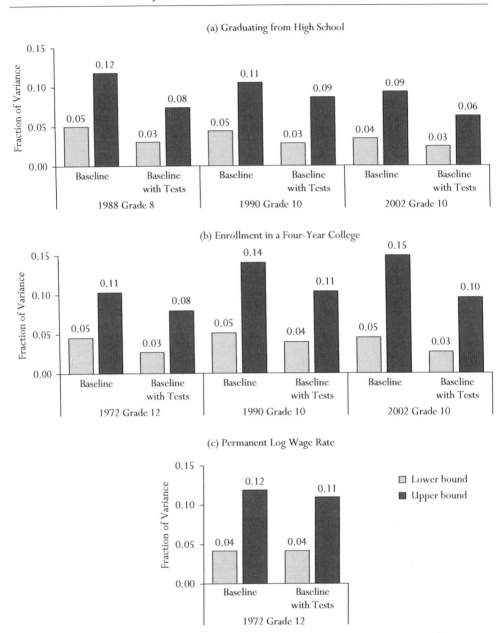

Source: Authors' calculations based on NLS72, NELS88, and ELS02 (National Center for Education Statistics 1994, 1996, 2007).

FIGURE 16.5   *Effect of a Shift from the 10th to 90th Percentile of School or Community Quality* $(Z_sG + M_s)$ *on Education and Log Wages*

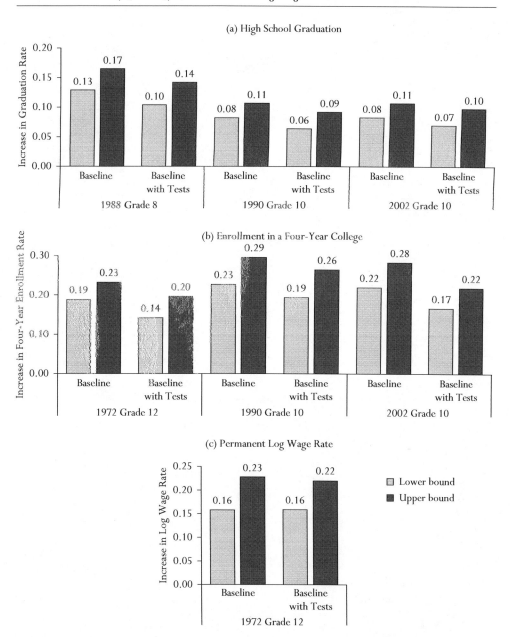

(a) High School Graduation

(b) Enrollment in a Four-Year College

(c) Permanent Log Wage Rate

Source: Authors' calculations based on NLS72, NELS88, and ELS02 (National Center for Education Statistics 1994, 1996, 2007).

Second, for the most part, parents influence the outcomes of their children either directly or by influencing the environment of the student within a school and community rather than through choice of school and the associated community.

Third, the estimates of the percentage of the variance in education and in wages that is due to observed and unobserved school characteristics, including peer effects, are only modest. Our upper-bound estimates lie between 6.1 and 12 percent for high school graduation, 8.2 and 15.4 percent for college attendance, and 11.0 and 11.9 percent for wages, with the specific value depending on the data set and explanatory variables used. The lower-bound estimates are often considerably smaller. However, the average effect on high school graduation rates, college attendance, and permanent wage rates of switching students from a school and community at the 10th percentile of the quality distribution to one at the 90th percentile is substantial. For 1990 and 2002 sophomores, even the lower-bound estimates indicate that such a shift boosts the high school graduation rate by about eight percentage points and the college attendance rate by about twenty percentage points.

Fourth, we observe an increase in the grouping of students with similar backgrounds at the same high schools between 1972 and 1990, but no further increase of such grouping between 1990 and 2002. The importance of factors at the high school and community levels for college attendance also increased between 1972 and 1990 but not between 1990 and 2002.

We close on a cautionary note. Our assessment of the role of family background, schools, and community factors in educational attainment and wages is subject to a number of limitations discussed in detail in Altonji and Mansfield (2010). First, we lack complete personal histories of school, community, and family characteristics. Second, we do not directly measure all important factors at the student level and the school and community level, and nonrandom sorting is evident. This might lead to an overstatement of school and community effects from unobserved variation in student variables across schools. Third, parental characteristics and other student characteristics influence the environment within a school. As a result, the importance of school and community factors may be understated, although other biases go in the opposite direction. Finally, differences in the data sets could affect comparisons between different points in time. Clearly, there is more work to be done.

We thank Rebecca Blank, Greg Duncan, Richard Murnane, Lawrence Katz, Jesse Rothstein, and participants at the conferences for helpful comments. This chapter is a nontechnical summary of research reported in Joseph G. Altonji and Richard K. Mansfield (2010). We are responsible for any shortcomings of the chapter.

NOTES

Online appendix available at: http://www.russellsage.org/duncan_murnane_online_appendix.pdf.

1. Of course, finding that school-level characteristics do not explain variation in student outcomes (conditional on the direct effect of student-level characteristics) would not imply that schools are unimportant or that some potential school interventions might not still be successful. It would, however, suggest that the current disparities in school characteristics are not driving the outcome gaps we observe, so that attempts to mitigate these disparities are unlikely to bear fruit. Instead, school-level interventions would need to focus on changing features of schools that are common to all schools.

2. To better understand what the elements of B capture, consider the coefficient on parental education. It captures not only the direct effect of parental education (holding the other variables in X, such as race-ethnicity and family income, constant), but also the influence of parental education on school and neighborhood environment conditional on the choice of school, the association between parental education and the child's school and neighborhood environment

before high school, and the association between parental education and other parental attributes (such as genetic endowment) that are not controlled for in the regression.

3. In the case of wages, we control for the effects of labor-market experience and economywide time trends by including them along with X when we estimate B. Our variance decompositions exclude the influence of these variables. See Altonji and Mansfield (2010).

4. Altonji and Mansfield (2010) report summary statistics of these measures, including the within-school and between-school fractions of each variable's variance.

5. However, in NLS72, enrollment status is reported in January to March of the second full school year after graduation, whereas in NELS88 and ELS02 it is reported in October.

6. Altonji and Mansfield (2010) show that the comparisons with NLS72 are robust to restricting NELS88 and ELS02 to students who are enrolled in twelfth grade.

7. Details on the selection of the samples and imputation of missing data are in Altonji and Mansfield (2010). All of the analyses use sample weights.

8. It is an increasing function of both the fraction of the variance that is between schools and the total variance. In the case of binary variables, it also is larger when the mean of the variable for the cohort is closer to 0.5.

9. The 10-90 differentials for fraction black are 0.29 for seniors in 1972, 0.35 for sophomores in 1990, and 0.42 for sophomores in 2002. The corresponding differentials for fraction Hispanic are 0.09, 0.30, and 0.41. Part of the change over time reflects the larger fractions of blacks and Hispanics in the later years. The specific estimates should be taken with a big grain of salt, because the normality assumption underlying them is unlikely to hold. The 10-90 differentials for both biological parents present are 0.21, 0.26, and 0.31. These values are affected by the decline in the mean of the variable as well as growth in the intraclass correlation.

10. For example, in the case of college enrollment for the 2002 cohort, the between-school fraction is 0.26 when test scores are added and 0.25 for the full set of controls.

11. Sampling errors reported in Altonji and Mansfield (2010) are generally small.

12. The contrast between the seemingly modest variance contribution of school and community factors and the substantial effect of a shift from the 10th to the 90th percentile echoes the evidence from Gary Solon, Marianne Page, and Greg Duncan (2000). They find that common neighborhood influences, including schools, explain only about 10 percent of the variance in educational attainment, but they also point out that the effect of a 1 standard deviation shift in the common component is economically significant.

REFERENCES

Altonji, Joseph G. 1988. "The Effects of Family Background and School Characteristics on Education and Labor Market Outcomes." Unpublished manuscript. Yale University. Available at: www.econ.yale.edu/~jga22/website/research_papers/FamSchoolCharacteristics_Altonji_1988.pdf (accessed March 18, 2011).

Altonji, Joseph G., and Richard K. Mansfield. 2010. "The Contribution of Family, School, and Community Characteristics to Inequality in Education and Labor Market Outcomes." Unpublished manuscript. Yale University, November. Available at: http://www.econ.yale.edu/~jga22/website/research_papers/Altonji and Mansfield 2010.pdf (accessed March 18, 2011).

Bryk, Anthony, and Stephen Raudenbush. 1988. "Toward a More Appropriate Conceptualization of Research on School Effects: A Three Level Hierarchical Linear Model." *American Journal of Education* 97(November): 65–108.

Coleman, James S. 1966. *Equality of Educational Opportunity*. Washington, D.C.: U.S. Government Printing Office.

Goldhaber, Dan, and Dominic Brewer. 1997. "Why Don't Schools and Teachers Seem to Matter? Assessing the Impact of Unobservables on Educational Productivity." *Journal of Human Resources* 32(3): 505–23.

Hanushek, Eric A., John F. Kain, Jacob M. Markman, and Steven G. Rivkin. 2003. "Does Peer Ability Affect Student Achievement?" *Journal of Applied Econometrics* 18(5): 527–44.

Hoxby, Caroline. 2000. "Peer Effects in the Classroom: Learning from Gender and Race Variation." NBER Working Paper No. 7867. Cambridge, Mass.: National Bureau of Economic Research.

Jencks, Christopher S., and Marsha D. Brown. 1975. "Effects of High Schools on Their Students." *Harvard Educational Review* 45(August): 273–324.

Kling, Jeffrey, Lawrence Katz, and Jeffrey Liebman. 2007. "Experimental Analysis of Neighborhood Effects." *Econometrica* 75(January): 83–119.

National Center for Education Statistics. (1996). *National Education Longitudinal Study of 1988* (NELS88), 1988–94 Data Files and Electronic Codebook System. Washington: U.S. Department of Education, Institute of Education Sciences. Available at: http://nces.ed.gov/surveys/nels88/ (accessed May 2, 2011).

———. (1994). *The National Longitudinal Study of the High School Class of 1972* (NLS72), Data Files and Documentation. Washington: U.S. Department of Education, Institute of Education Sciences. Available at: http://nces.ed.gov/surveys/nls72/ (accessed May 2, 2011).

———. (2007). *The Education Longitudinal Study of 2002* (ELS02), Restricted Use Second Follow-up Data Files, Data File Documentation, and Electronic Codebook System. Washington: U.S. Department of Education, Institute of Education Sciences. Available at: http://nces.ed.gov/surveys/els2002/ (accessed May 2, 2011).

Oreopoulos, Philip. 2003. "The Long-Run Consequences of Growing Up in a Poor Neighborhood." *Quarterly Journal of Economics* 118(4): 1533–75.

Solon, Gary, Marianne Page, and Greg Duncan. 2000. "Correlations Between Neighboring Children in Their Socioeconomic Status as Adults." *Review of Economics and Statistics* 82(3): 383–92.

Speakman, Robert, and Finis Welch. 2006. "Using Wages to Infer School Quality." In *Handbook of the Economics of Education*. Vol. 2, edited by Eric Hanushek and Finis Welch. Amsterdam: Elsevier B.B.

Chapter 17

Year-by-Year and Cumulative Impacts of Attending a High-Mobility Elementary School on Children's Mathematics Achievement in Chicago, 1995 to 2005

Stephen W. Raudenbush, Marshall Jean, and Emily Art

High rates of residential and school mobility are a pervasive aspect of life among the inner-city poor in contemporary America. Urban families living in poverty frequently move, usually over short distances. Moving across school-catchment boundaries often triggers a change of school. In this chapter we ask whether attending a school characterized by high levels of student mobility depresses learning in the general student population. In particular, we ask whether and to what extent influxes of new students during the school year reduce students' mathematics achievement during the elementary years. We ask whether these effects cumulate with time, whether they vary as a function of student background, and whether exposure to high mobility is an important factor in understanding racial-ethnic inequality in learning.

The first set of analyses is based on a cohort of 23,344 students from ages 8 to 10 attending 445 elementary schools from 1997 to 2000 and focuses on schoolwide effects. The second set of analyses considers 313,310 children who attended 515 Chicago public schools while 8 to 10 years of age during the years 1995 to 2005 and focuses on within-school differences in grade-level in-migration rates. We find that African American students and students at high-poverty schools are at the greatest risk of attending schools characterized by high within-year in-migration. We find small but reliably negative effects of school-level and grade-level in-migration year by year; the school-level effects are larger than the within-school effects by grade. These effects cumulate with time. The negative effects are equally important for "stable students" and mobile students. The grade-level effects are most pronounced for African American students and particularly for those with low initial achievement. We conclude that high student mobility exacts a small but real cost on the general student population in Chicago and contributes modestly to racial inequality in mathematics achievement.

By the time they had reached third grade, almost half of the U.S. children entering kindergarten in 1998 had changed schools at least once. Among the developed nations, residential mobility is unusually high in the United States and often leads to school mobility; such mobility is particularly high among disadvantaged urban families (de la Torre and Gwynne 2009; Kerbow

1996; Hanushek, Kain, and Rivkin 2004). Children from ethnic-minority families are especially likely to change schools (Burkham, Lee, and Dwyer 2009). David Kerbow (1996) reported that only 38 percent of Chicago elementary students attended the same school through their elementary years. Although residential mobility is the most important cause of school mobility, children change schools not only because their residence changes, but also to seek better schools, because their schools close, or, in rare cases, because of expulsion.

HOW IN-MIGRATION AFFECTS SCHOOLS

In this chapter we ask whether attending a "high-mobility school" undermines student achievement in mathematics during grades K–8. In particular, we ask whether schools subjected to a large influx of new students during the school year are less effective than they would have been without such within-year in-migration. There are several reasons to suspect that within-year in-migration harms teaching and learning.

Instructional Disruption

It may be that when large numbers of students enter a school during the year, it is difficult for teachers to sustain effective instruction (Lash and Kirkpatrick 1990; Kerbow 1996). How a teacher manages instruction when there is an influx of new students may especially undermine the learning of the highest achievers, the lowest achievers, or the mobile students themselves.

It may be hard to sustain a reasonable pace of mathematics instruction when many new students appear in a classroom during the academic year. The new students may require substantial review in order to catch up with the class or substantial orientation to the expectations and procedures of class work. As a result, nonmobile as well as mobile students might suffer diminished learning opportunities when attending high-mobility schools. Slowing the pace of instruction might especially reduce the learning opportunities of the most able students. If so, we would expect the highest achievers to suffer the largest negative impacts of high levels of in-migration.

A teacher confronted with a large number of new students faces a dilemma. On the one hand, the teacher might take pains to effectively integrate the new students into classroom life. Although helpful to the new students, such a choice might reduce the time the teacher has to provide special help to nonmobile students, with particularly negative consequences for those who are furthest behind and therefore need the most help. In this case, high levels of in-migration would produce negative effects on low achievers.

On the other hand, a decision to continue to focus on the nonmobile students while allowing the new students to "sink or swim" would presumably reduce the learning opportunities of those mobile students. In this case, high levels of within-school migration would be most negative for the mobile students themselves. Our data do not provide information on how teachers manage these instructional dilemmas. However, we ask whether high levels of in-migration disproportionately affect high achievers, low achievers, or the mobile students themselves.

Disrupted Social Networks

An influx of new students may disrupt pro-academic social networks. Dana L. Haynie, Scott J. South, and Sunita Bose (2006) and South and Haynie (2004) found that schools with high mobility rates were more likely than other schools to be characterized by antisocial peer networks, leading to high dropout rates. Rebecca C. Fauth, Tama Leventhal, and Jeanne Brooks-Gunn (2005) found that highly mobile students were more likely than others to be victimized by violence. David Wood et al. (1993) noted high levels of behavior problems in schools with high mobility.

Challenges to School Organization

A large influx of new students during the year would presumably tax the administrative capacity of a school and its leadership. Indeed, Anthony S. Bryk and colleagues (2009) cite high rates of student mobility within inner-city schools as a formidable barrier to school improvement. In an era of high accountability, the work of the school principal has increasingly turned from managerial tasks to instructional leadership. High levels of in-migration, however, confront the school leaders with the extra burden of meeting new parents, enrolling their children, and placing them in classes. Preoccupation with these tasks may decrease emphasis on schoolwide instructional leadership. Moreover, if high mobility undermines pro-academic peer networks, the extra administrative burden would be even more pronounced.

SCHOOL-LEVEL VERSUS GRADE-LEVEL MOBILITY RATES

For all of the reasons cited, we expect that high levels of in-migration during the year will undermine a school's instructional effectiveness and thereby reduce the rate of student learning. Such effects might be limited to the classrooms in which the new students are placed; or these effects might, in addition, spill over and affect the entire school. If in-migration affects student learning solely by impairing classroom instruction, the negative effects of such in-migration might be restricted to those classes in which the new students are placed. However, the negative effects might be schoolwide: negative peer relations in one class might spill over into the hallways, the lunchroom, and the playground. Alternatively, negative social relations in those locations might influence life in the classroom. Moreover, if in-migration reduces the effectiveness of a principal's instructional leadership, the effects could be felt in every classroom. It is therefore useful to separate the classroom-specific effects of in-migration from the schoolwide effects, as we hypothesize that both kinds will be negative.

Unfortunately, we do not have access to data on the level of in-migration at the classroom level. However, we do have measures of in-migration at the grade level and at the school level for all of Chicago's public elementary schools from 1995 to 2005, and we have annual test scores from students during those years. Our analytic strategy has two focuses. The first is on the school-level impact of in-migration. For simplicity, we henceforth label school-level in-migration "school-level mobility." The effect of school-level mobility presumably reflects the combined effect of classroom instructional disruption, social-network disruption, and the extra administrative burden.

Our second analytical focus is on isolating the impact of in-migration at the grade level after removing the school-level effect. Again, to simplify the language, we refer to in-migration at the grade level as "grade-level mobility." We reason that high grade-level mobility reflects the impact of in-migration on classroom processes.

RELATIONSHIP TO PAST RESEARCH ON STUDENT MOBILITY

Many researchers have studied the effects of changing schools on the students who move. We refer to this kind of study as one of the impacts of "student-level mobility." This work is related but fundamentally different from our focus on how high rates of school-level and grade-level mobility affect the learning of all students, including those who don't move.

Work on student-level mobility generally suggests that changing schools is statistically associated with low achievement (see the review by Reynolds, Chen, and Hebers 2009). There are several possible explanations for this association. First, it may be that frequent school changes disrupt instructional continuity, undermining sustained opportunities to learn. It also may be that school changes undermine children's capacity to become integrated in social networks, and the resulting isolation or alienation may undermine school engagement and motivation to learn. However, the negative association between student-level mobility and achievement may not be causal. After all, we know that those who move frequently are disadvantaged in other ways that predict low achievement, and we suspect that the frequent residential moves that often trigger school moves may themselves undermine learning. Moreover, changing schools may be a response to a student's difficulties rather than a cause. Isolating the causal effect of student-level mobility is also difficult because the disruptive effect of changing schools may be offset if the move is to a better school or amplified if it is to a worse school.

It is not surprising, then, that evidence regarding the effects of student-level mobility on student learning is mixed. Kerbow (1996) found that the initial negative effects associated with changing schools faded within two years so long as students did not experience a second move during that time. Indeed, a key claim in Arthur J. Reynolds, Chin-Chih Chen, and Janette E. Hebers's meta-analysis (2009) is that frequent moves are especially harmful. Other careful studies find that once student demographic background and prior achievement are controlled, associations between student mobility and test scores diminish to nonsignificance (Alexander, Entwisle, and Dauber 1996; Hanushek, Kain, and Rivkin 2004; see Rumberger's 2003 review).

It is quite plausible, however, that if policies were enacted to stabilize school membership or to ameliorate its effects, school leaders and teachers who could then count on a stable population could become more effective. For example, children moving across school-catchment areas could be allowed or encouraged to stay in the school they had attended, and school districts might enact common curricula so that school changes are not associated with drastic changes in curricular content. Influxes of new students during the year would then plausibly be less common and less disruptive when they do occur, not only for the mobile students, but for their classmates. Moreover, it may be that school improvement reduces student mobility and its effects. There is some evidence that increased school quality reduces the number of school changes young children experience and that part of the positive effect of attending high-quality schools is attributable to their reduced mobility rates (Reynolds, Chen, and Hebers 2009).

YEAR-BY-YEAR AND CUMULATIVE EFFECTS OF SCHOOL-LEVEL AND GRADE-LEVEL MOBILITY

Although many researchers have studied student-level mobility, studies of the impact of high rates of school-level mobility on the general student population are remarkably rare. Indeed, Eric A. Hanushek, John F. Kain, and Steven G. Rivkin's (2004) article is singularly notable in taking pains to identify the causal effects of school-level and grade-level mobility. Analyzing data from Texas, they found that attending schools characterized by high levels of within-year in-migration statistically significantly reduced the test scores of students attending those schools. Although the effects in any one year were small, the authors reasoned that, on the basis of their model, the cumulative effects of multiple years of exposure would be substantial. However, they did not assess the magnitude of these cumulative effects empirically.

Our chapter builds on their work by estimating the annual and cumulative effects of school-level and grade-level mobility in an urban setting with a high concentration of low-income, minority students. Our aims are similar to those of Hanushek, Kain, and Rivkin (2004), but we want to explicitly study the cumulative effects that their model predicts. This goal requires a somewhat different methodological strategy from theirs, although we also apply approaches similar to theirs.

IMPLICATIONS FOR UNDERSTANDING ETHNIC INEQUALITY

If high levels of school mobility thus defined suppress student achievement, many students in Chicago will have been affected. Rates of school mobility have been quite high there, though they have decreased slowly with time. In 1995, the school-mobility rate was, on average, 11.4 percent, but declined to 7.1 percent in 2007. For African American students, the rates have been higher and have declined less, from 12.5 percent in 1995 to 9.5 percent in 2007 (de la Torre and Gwynne 2009). Substantial numbers of children, particularly African American children, attend schools in which as many as 18 percent of the students enrolled at the end of the school year joined the school during the year. If high levels of school-level or grade-level mobility undermine student learning, such effects would exacerbate racial inequality in learning, given that black students are substantially more likely than others to attend schools characterized by high mobility rates. This tendency to increase racial inequality would be even more pronounced if the impacts of school-level and grade-level mobility were especially pronounced for black students. We therefore consider the implications of school- and grade-level mobility for understanding racial inequality in outcomes.

METHODOLOGICAL STRATEGY

We adopt several methods, each based on different assumptions, to estimate the impact of school-level and grade-level mobility. In each case, we estimate annual and cumulative effects, and we investigate whether the effects vary by prior achievement, ethnicity, and prior mobility status. In addition, in each case, we consider the implications of our results for understanding racial inequality in achievement. We focus on mathematics achievement during grades 3 through 5. We concentrate on mathematics as an outcome because it is well known that, by the time they reach elementary school, children learn math almost entirely in school rather than at home (compare with Bryk and Raudenbush 1988). Therefore, if school-level mobility disrupts instruction, it should reduce learning in mathematics.

School-Level Mobility: Year-by-Year Effects

The first set of analyses focuses on the impact of school-level mobility on math achievement. Our key methodological challenge arises because children who attend schools with high mobility rates likely differ in many ways from children who attend schools with more stable student populations. Therefore, we might expect these children to display different learning rates even if school-level mobility had no effect. To cope with this problem, we have obtained considerable data on the prior achievement, social background, and prior exposure to mobility of 23,334 children who began third grade in 1998.

To estimate the annual effect of school-level mobility, we first develop a statistical model that uses this prior data to predict the degree of school-level mobility to which each child will have been exposed in 1998. We then subclassify children into fifty-three strata such that, within strata, all children have nearly identical predicted levels of exposure to school-level mobility. Yet within those strata, we find that the actual levels of school mobility vary across children. Given the similar backgrounds of the children within these strata, we regard the association between the actual level of school-level mobility and math achievement within these fifty-three strata as representing the causal effect of exposure to high school-level mobility during 1998. We repeat this approach in 1999 and 2000, each year using prior data to predict exposure to school-level mobility the next year, then assessing the association between actual school-level mobility and achievement during that next year. Following Paul R. Rosenbaum and Donald B. Rubin (1983), we call this method "propensity-score stratification," because we have stratified children on their predicted propensity to attend a school with a given rate of school-level mobility.

School-Level Mobility: Cumulative Effects

To estimate the cumulative effects of school-level mobility, we combine the data from the same 23,344 students across the three years 1998, 1999, and 2000. We then use these data to study the growth in mathematics achievement during these three years, regarding a student's achievement each year as depending on age and on that student's cumulative exposure to school-level mobility. Although we could have used propensity-score stratification to remove bias, as in the case of the yearly effects, we did not. Propensity-score stratification is a reasonable approach when one has obtained substantial data that can be used to predict exposure to an intervention before that intervention has occurred. When the aim is to estimate cumulative effects, this approach is problematic because the outcomes of one year's experience in a high- or low-mobility school might influence the decision to stay in that school or move. Statisticians call this the problem of "time-varying confounding": an outcome of last year's experience becomes a confounding variable in assessing the impact of next year's experience. Although measured time-varying confounders pose no problem when the aim is to estimate year-by-year effects, they pose a major challenge when one uses a growth model to estimate cumulative effects.

To cope with this problem, we adopt the method of "inverse probability of treatment weighting" developed by James Robins, Miguel Ángel Hernán, and Babette Brumback (2000). We modify the simple growth model by weighting each child's contribution to the data each year inversely proportional to the probability that that child will receive the "dose" of school-level mobility actually received. This insures that children whose unfolding characteristics strongly predict the dosage they actually receive will be down-weighted; such children are effectively "overrepresented" in the sample of children who received that dose. This approach effectively eliminates selection bias in school-level mobility based on observable stable and time-varying student characteristics that predict selection.

Grade-Level Mobility: Year-by-Year Effects

The second set of analyses focuses on variation in grade-level mobility rates within a school. Such grade-level variation should more closely reflect the classroom-level influences of mobility as distinct from the schoolwide effects. To estimate these effects, we again use the method of propensity-score stratification, just as described in the case of school-level mobility. Recall that propensity-score stratification removes bias associated with measured prior characteristics of students that predict exposure to mobility. However, this method cannot control for unobserved characteristics of students. Indeed, a crucial assumption underlying propensity-score stratification is that unobserved confounding variables are irrelevant when the observed confounding variables are controlled. This assumption may be reasonable when the set of observed student characteristics is rich, but one never knows whether unobserved confounders might still be relevant.

However, when focusing on grade-level mobility, there is an alternative analytic strategy that provides estimates of year-by-year causal effects under different assumptions. We therefore adopt this additional approach—comparing children who attended the same school at the same age but in different years. This approach is based on the assumption that children who attend the same school at the same age are similar in characteristics that we cannot observe as well as in characteristics that we can observe. A key criticism of such an approach is that school composition can change with time; for example, as a neighborhood "gentrifies" or declines, its student composition may gradually become more or less advantaged. To cope with this problem, we remove year-specific schoolwide mean differences in achievement. This approach is similar to that used by Hanushek, Kane, and Rivkin, who described it as using school-by-year and school-by-grade fixed effects. It has the advantage of removing not only school-specific year effects but also school-specific differences in average growth rates.

Grade-Level Mobility: Cumulative Effects

We studied the cumulative effects of grade-level mobility using the same methods as described in the case of school-level mobility.

Specification Checks

To check the robustness of our results, we compared results across identification strategies that use different assumptions, examined sensitivity to covariate specification, and reestimated our models with a nonparametric control for prior achievement.

Comparing the Propensity Stratification and Fixed-Effects Specification   Each strategy for assessing causal effects is based on assumptions that cannot be checked empirically. Therefore, no strategy is foolproof. However, if strategies relying on quite different assumptions produce convergent evidence, the credibility of the causal inferences is enhanced. When we study the impact of school-level mobility, we cannot compare propensity stratification to the strategy that removes school-specific year and age effects: removal of year-specific, schoolwide mean differences in achievement would eliminate any possible effects of year-to-year differences in schoolwide mobility. However, it is possible to use both approaches to study grade-level mobility effects. We did so, and we found that the two approaches produced similar results. This suggests that findings based on propensity-score stratification are not likely attributable to assumptions specific to that methodology, and this fact lends some credence to the schoolwide mobility results based on propensity stratification.

Introducing Time-Varying Predictors in the Fixed-Effects Specification   The fixed-effects strategy uses within-school, within-grade deviations of grade-level mobility to remove within-school, within-grade differences in mean achievement—after removing school-specific year and age effects. Might there be a time-varying factor that would confound this effect? To test this hypothesis, we introduced measures of time-varying child characteristics, including the presence of residential moves and measures of the social status of the block group in which the student resides, into the fixed-effects model. Doing so had no discernable consequence on our estimates of the association between grade-level mobility and mean achievement.

Other Strategies for Reducing Bias and Checking Results   We used the Iowa Test of Basic Skills as an outcome. Researchers at the Consortium for Chicago School Research have used item response theory to create a scale that was equated across years and thus designed to reveal growth. We found that initially lower-achieving students displayed, on average, substantially larger rates of growth on this metric than did initially high-achieving students. We therefore stratified students into ten deciles of prior achievement and estimated the impacts of mobility within strata, controlling for stratum-specific effects of age. Our estimates of the average effects of school-level and grade-level mobility were not sensitive to this control; however, we found this stratification useful in uncovering the variable impact of school-level and grade-level mobility on children of varied academic background and ethnicity. The online appendix describes all of our analytic strategies in detail (http:www.russellsage.org/duncan_murnane_online_appendix.pdf).

RESULTS

We begin by describing school-level mobility rates in 515 Chicago elementary schools from 1995 to 2005. We consider the demographic background and prior achievement of students attending those schools, then assess the student and school characteristics that predict exposure to high mobility rates. These descriptive findings create a context for interpreting our estimates of the impact of school- and grade-level mobility.

School-Level Mobility in Chicago

Our first causal variable of interest is the school-level mobility rate, that is, a school's rate of in-migration during the academic year, defined as

$$\text{school mobility} = \text{rate of within-year in-migration}$$

(17.1)
$$= \frac{n_j \ new}{n_j \ in \ May}$$

where $n_j \ new$ is the number of students who joined the school after the beginning of the school year and $n_j \ in \ May$ is the school's enrollment in May of that year. The grade-level mobility rate is computed identically, after replacing n_j by the number of students in a given grade within a given school. The online appendix provides mean school-level mobility rates from 1995 to 2000 for the ages of children in our study.

Table 17.1 describes the study sample of 313,310 students attending Chicago schools in grades 3 through 5 from 1995 to 2000. First, note that school-level mobility has a mean of about 0.10 and a standard deviation of about 0.05. Given the slightly positively skewed distribution of this variable, it is plausible to find students attending schools in which as many as 20 percent of the students enrolled at the end of the school year had migrated in during the year. Given that the average enrollment of the elementary schools in our sample is just under 800 students, this means that as many as 160 new students might plausibly migrate into a school during the year, or about 5 per classroom.

Second, the table shows important ethnic differences in exposure to schools with high mobility rates: for African American students, the average rate during the entire period is about 11 percent, as compared with less than 7 percent for European American students; for Hispanic American students, the average rate is between these two extremes. For African American students in Chicago throughout all grades, the rates have been higher and have declined much more slowly with time than for other students (de la Torre and Gwynne 2009).

The table reveals the comparatively difficult circumstances experienced by African American children in Chicago. We see that the achievement levels of blacks and Hispanics are lower than those of whites and Asians; blacks experience slightly smaller annual gains than whites, whose gains are slightly smaller than those of Hispanics. As mentioned, blacks experience the highest levels of school- and grade-level mobility, with Hispanics in between. Moreover, blacks are much more likely than whites or Asians to live in neighborhoods characterized by high levels of disadvantage, as indicated by percentage of the population in poverty, percentage of unemployed adults, per-

TABLE 17.1   *Analytic Sample, 1995 to 2005*

Variable	African American (N = 175,132) M (SD)	European American (N = 31,281) M (SD)	Asian American (N = 9,105) M (SD)	Hispanic American (N = 97,140) M (SD)	Overall (N = 313,310[a]) M (SD)
Math achievement age eight	−1.364 (1.09)	−0.4363 (1.20)	−0.0274 (1.12)	−1.029 (1.04)	−1.128 (1.14)
Math achievement age nine	−0.7496 (1.03)	0.1965 (1.14)	0.6351 (1.02)	−0.3436 (0.971)	−0.4872 (1.08)
Math achievement age ten	−0.1810 (1.03)	0.7908 (1.15)	1.270 (1.04)	0.2888 (0.980)	0.0920 (1.092)
School-level mobility	0.1082 (0.049)	0.0676 (0.039)	0.0688 (0.042)	0.0817 (0.040)	0.0950 (0.048)
Grade-level mobility	0.0996 (0.057)	0.0635 (0.046)	0.0640 (0.046)	0.0757 (0.047)	0.0877 (0.055)
Neighborhood concentrated disadvantage	1.630 (0.534)	0.7693 (0.286)	0.8376 (0.266)	1.012 (0.293)	1.335 (0.568)

Source: Authors' compilation of data provided by the Consortium on Chicago School Research (de la Torre and Gwynne 2009).

[a]Overall statistics include 652 students coded as Native American.

centage of families receiving welfare, and percentage of single-parent families. The mean level of disadvantage for Hispanics is about midway between that of blacks and that of whites. Taken together, these facts suggest that blacks, who compose 56 percent of the student population, are multiply disadvantaged, living in the most challenged neighborhoods and being exposed to the highest levels of school mobility. A key question for this study is to understand the role that exposure to school- and grade-level mobility plays in generating racial inequality in achievement.

Table 17.2 describes the data from the cohort (those in third grade in 1998) we have selected for intensive analysis using propensity stratification and inverse probability of treatment weighting. This table shows the same trends as table 17.1 but elaborates a bit by adding information on school composition. It shows that blacks have the highest level of school mean disadvantage (the school aggregate of child-specific neighborhood disadvantage) and the highest levels of poverty concentration, as indicated by the percentage of children eligible for free lunch. Moreover, blacks attend remarkably segregated schools: on average, black children attend schools that are 2.6 percent white and 89.6 percent black.

Correlates of School-Level Mobility

School and neighborhood characteristics that predict high school-level mobility also predict low levels of achievement, as indicated in table 17.3. It may then be that exposure to high levels of school mobility helps explain the association between neighborhood and school disadvantage and low academic achievement.

Effects of School-Level Mobility: Year-by-Year

To implement the propensity-stratification approach for 1998, we formulated a model to predict the school-level mobility from twenty-seven explanatory variables.[1] We classified students

TABLE 17.2   *Analytic Sample for 1998 Cohort*

	African American (N = 16,350) M (SD)	European American (N = 2,731) M (SD)	Asian American (N = 709) M (SD)	Hispanic American (N = 5,033) M (SD)
Math achievement age eight, 1998	−2.22 (0.96)	−1.59 (1.05)	−1.20 (1.05)	−2.10 (0.91)
Math achievement age nine, 1999	−1.59 (1.06)	−0.77 (1.67)	−0.32 (1.12)	−1.34 (0.97)
Math achievement age ten, 2000	−0.89 (1.11)	−0.03 (1.14)	0.49 (1.05)	−0.52 (1.01)
School-level mobility, 1998	0.114 (0.046)	0.072 (0.039)	0.072 (0.043)	0.089 (0.038)
School-level mobility, 1999	0.111 (0.047)	0.073 (0.040)	0.074 (0.041)	0.093 (0.044)
School-level mobility, 2000	0.109 (0.046)	0.074 (0.041)	0.074 (0.044)	0.093 (0.041)
Neighborhood disadvantage, 1998	1.64 (0.052)	0.79 (0.29)	0.84 (0.26)	1.02 (0.30)
School mean of neighborhood disadvantage, 1998	1.62 (0.044)	0.87 (0.22)	0.92 (0.22)	1.04 (0.23)
School percentage black	89.6 (23.0)	16.1 (18.4)	18.0 (17.5)	13.1 (18.5)
School percentage white	2.6 (8.5)	38.5 (21.8)	22.5 (17.0)	15.2 (16.7)
Percentage Hispanic	6.9 (16.9)	37.4 (25.3)	30.9 (19.8)	68.1 (25.7)
School percentage eligible for free or reduced lunch	89.5 (13.3)	65.3 (23.8)	72.7 (20.9)	86.6 (14.2)
School percentage limited English proficiency	3.6 (9.4)	21.6 (15.6)	26.8 (14.5)	32.8 (16.0)
School mean math achievement, 1998	−2.69 (0.46)	−2.26 (0.59)	−2.32 (0.66)	−2.59 (0.47)

Source: Authors' compilation of data provided by the Consortium on Chicago School Research (de la Torre and Gwynne 2009).

into fifty-three strata such that, within each stratum, students shared virtually the same predicted school mobility. We then estimated the average association between a student's actual school-level mobility and math achievement within levels of these strata, controlling also for the continuous-propensity score and, to increase precision, controlling for prior math achievement. The results, summarized in table 17.4, were reasonably consistent across years. For each year, we see small, negative, statistically significant effects. In 1998, the estimated coefficient is −0.573 ($t = −2.02$). To interpret this effect, imagine that a "low-mobility" school with an enrollment of 800 received 40 new students (1 or 2 per classroom) This compares with a "high-mobility" school of the same size that received 120 new students during the year (4 or 5 per class). These two schools represent

TABLE 17.3   *Neighborhood and School Correlates of Exposure to School-Level Mobility*

	Correlation with School-Level Mobility	Correlation with Mean Math Achievement
Neighborhood disadvantage, 1998	0.25	−0.49
School mean of neighborhood disadvantage, 1998	0.29	−0.57
School percentage black	0.26	−0.44
School percentage eligible for free or reduced lunch	0.48	−0.69

Source: Authors' calculations based on data presented in table 17.1, provided by the Consortium on Chicago School Research (de la Torre and Gwynne 2009).

TABLE 17.4   *Estimated Average Effects of School-Level Mobility, 1998 to 2000*

Year	Age of Child	Coefficient Estimate	T-Ratio	Fraction of a Year's Growth
1998	Eight years old	−0.572	−2.02	0.089
1999	Nine years old	−0.529	−2.22	0.083
2000	Ten years old	−0.729	−3.06	0.113

Source: Authors' calculations of data presented in table 17.2, provided by the Consortium on Chicago School Research (de la Torre and Gwynne 2009).

a contrast between −1.0 and 1.0 standard-deviation units on the school-level mobility scale. We would expect the high-mobility school's annual average mathematics learning rate to be 8.9 percent lower than the average learning rate in the low-mobility school.[2] This difference represents a little less than one month's growth in math learning. The corresponding numbers are similar in 1999 (coefficient of −0.529, $t = -2.22$) and a bit higher in 2000 (coefficient of −0.721, $t = -3.06$).

Effects of School-Level Mobility: Cumulative Results

A key aim of this chapter is to investigate whether year-by-year effects of school-level mobility cumulate with time. If so, even small annual effects may become quite consequential. To estimate these cumulative effects, we used inverse probability of treatment weighting, as described earlier. For each year, we used the results of our propensity-score models to predict the school-mobility level for the next year. We weighted each participant's data for that year inversely proportional to the probability density of exposure to the observed level of school mobility. Using a cross-classified random-effects model (repeated measures crossed by students and schools) with weighting as developed by Guanglei Hong and Stephen W. Raudenbush (2008), we estimated a growth model in which math achievement depends on student age and exposure to school-level mobility.

Our estimate of the cumulative effect is, on average, −0.721 per year ($t = -2.71$), about the same size as the annual effects. This result is important because it suggests that annual and cumulative effects of school-level mobility are similar in magnitude to the year-specific effects. Given that attending a high-mobility school reduces annual growth by almost one month, as described previously, the implication is that a student attending such a high-mobility school for three consecutive years would fall almost three months behind a similar student who had attended a low-mobility school for three consecutive years.

Interaction Effects

We found no evidence that the impact of school-level mobility is different for children who themselves move during the study year than it is for students who stay in their school during the study year. In each year, the impact estimates for the nonmovers were negative and similar in magnitude to the overall estimate. We also found no evidence that the impact of school-level mobility varied by student ethnicity. We did find evidence each year that the impact of school-level mobility depends on students' prior achievement. However, given the overall small size of the effect and the fact that these results are based on data from a single cohort, these interaction effects were not estimated precisely. We therefore defer discussion of interactions with prior ability until we discuss grade-level effects, when the sample size increases to more than 300,000 and the estimated interaction effects are very precise.

FIGURE 17.1   *Estimated Effect of Grade-Level Mobility for African American Students as a Function of Initial Mathematics Achievement; Low Achievers Experience the Largest Negative Effects, Though Effects for the Highest Achievers Are Also Negative*

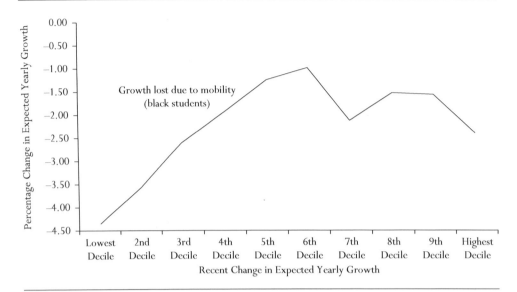

Source: Authors' calculations based on data from the Consortium of Chicago School Research (de la Torre and Gwynne 2009).

Effects of Grade-Level Mobility

Our main analytic strategy for estimating effects of grade-level mobility used fixed effects of 10 years and 3 ages for each of 515 schools in addition to 10 fixed effects of student prior ability and 20 ability-by-age fixed effects. We estimated effects within each ability decile for blacks, whites, and Hispanics, and we estimated the average of these effects.

Average Year-by-Year Effects   We estimated the average effect of grade-level mobility to be small but highly statistically significant (coefficient $= -0.0087$, $t = -9.31$). If this effect is causal, we would predict that a student attending a high-mobility class (four to five new students during the year) would experience a reduction of 1.7 percent of a year's growth in mathematics test scores as compared with the growth rate expected in a low-mobility classroom (one to two new students during the year). When we estimated grade-level effects using the propensity-score method, we found slightly larger effects.[3]

Interaction Effects   We found no significant effects of grade-level mobility for whites (coefficient $= -0.001$, $t = -0.32$) or for Hispanics (coefficient $= -0.003$, $t = -0.80$). However, the effects for black students were, on average, significantly negative (coefficient $= -0.010$, $t = -3.45$). Moreover, these effects varied significantly and substantially by students' prior math ability, as displayed in figure 17.1. The estimated impact of grade-level mobility is largest for the students displaying the lowest initial achievement. There is also a suggestion that the highest achieving students suffer negative effects, a result that was also apparent in the school-level analysis. We emphasize that none of the effects in figure 17.1 is large: for the lowest achieving students, the impact of high versus low grade-level mobility (defined as a contrast of two standard deviations) is a 4 percent reduction in annual growth according to our model estimates.

Cumulative Effects of Grade-Level Mobility   As in the case of school-level mobility, we used inverse probability of treatment weighting to estimate the cumulative effects of grade-level mobility. Again, the evidence suggests that the annual effects do cumulate (coefficient $= -0.666$, $t = -7.07$). These estimated effects were significantly larger than those generated by the fixed-effects analysis, but very similar in magnitude to the year-by-year and cumulative school-level effects. There are several possible explanations for the discrepancy. First, recall that the fixed-effects analysis removes any possible effect of mobility that operates schoolwide. The cumulative-effects analysis does not do so. Second, the cumulative effects may be larger than the year-by-year effects. Third, the two methods may have different biases.[4] Based on our assumptions, we estimate that the grade-level cumulative effects are -0.666 per year, as compared with the estimated school-level effects of -0.721 per year discussed earlier.

DISCUSSION

About 10 percent of the students attending a typical Chicago public school in the spring of 1998 had moved into that school during the current year, but that number varied substantially from school to school. Some schools experienced little mobility, whereas in others almost 20 percent of the students had joined during the year. Thus, it would not have been unusual to locate elementary schools in which 160 of the students present in the spring of 1998 had entered the school during the year, equivalent to 5 to 7 students per classroom. Research suggests that such in-migration during the year makes it hard for teachers to sustain coherent instruction at a reasonably fast pace and with adequate attention to struggling students. Moreover, past research suggests that a large influx of new students during the year can undermine the social networks that enable teachers and students to support sustained school-related efforts. And it seems likely that large influxes of new students absorb substantial administrative attention and undermine the instructional leadership a principal might provide to the whole school.

The impact of a large influx of new students might be felt mainly within classrooms, when teachers are forced to make difficult decisions: Time focused on the newcomers might slow instruction, hurting the high achievers, or it might absorb the teachers' attention to the detriment of the lowest achievers who need the most help. Yet failing to attend to the newcomers would undermine their learning. On the basis of this reasoning, we wondered whether high levels of in-migration would disproportionately affect high achievers, low achievers, or mobile students.

The impact of mobility might be felt schoolwide—even in classrooms that did not receive many new students. This could occur if high school-level mobility disrupts social networks, leading to behavior problems outside the classroom, or if high school-level mobility prevents school leaders from focusing on academic leadership. For these reasons, we decided to study schoolwide effects of mobility as well as grade-specific effects that would primarily reflect classroom processes.

We are also interested in the implications of high school-level mobility for racial inequality in achievement. We found that African American students are exposed to significantly higher levels of school mobility than are other students. If school-level mobility reduces student learning, then such mobility would contribute to racial inequality in achievement. This would be especially true if the impact of mobility on African American students is particularly acute.

We think our findings shed some light on these questions. Let us briefly summarize these findings and then consider their implications for policy.

School-Level Mobility

We found statistically significantly negative effects of schoolwide mobility for children ages eight to ten years old. The effects are small but not negligible. Consider a child attending a low-mobility school in which about forty new students would enter the school (one or two per classroom). Such a school would be about 1 standard deviation below the Chicago average. Our model suggests that such a student would gain about 9 percent more during that year than if the child's school had a high mobility rate, that is, a school in which 120 new children enter the school each year (4 to 5 per classroom). Such a high-mobility school would be 1 standard deviation above the Chicago average. This effect is equivalent to a standardized regression coefficient of about −0.026 and is remarkably similar to the estimate provided by Hanushek, Kain, and Rivkin (2004), based on their analysis of statewide data from Texas. If such an effect accumulated with time, as those authors speculated, it could become substantial. We tested that speculation and found evidence that the effects do, in fact, cumulate. Attending a high-mobility school for three consecutive years would leave a student three months behind where that student would be if he or she had attended a low-mobility school. We found some evidence that low and high achievers were especially vulnerable to the impact of school-level mobility. The estimated impacts for stable students were similar to those for the sample as a whole, though our data did not provide a precise estimate of the effect of schoolwide mobility on the mobile students. We did not find strong evidence that the effects were different for students of different ethnic backgrounds.

Grade-Level Effects

Our grade-level analysis removed between-school differences and focused on differences between cohorts within a school at the same grade level who experienced different levels of mobility. Although eliminating schoolwide effects from consideration, this approach focused more sharply on grade-level effects, which presumably largely reflect classroom processes. Our estimates of these effects were considerably smaller than the schoolwide estimates, though the average effect was highly statistically significant and negative. This analysis was very powerful statistically, as it was based on more than 300,000 students attending 515 elementary schools between 1995 and 2005. Perhaps the most consequential finding from this analysis is that the impact of grade-level mobility was restricted to African American students and was most pronounced for the lowest achieving among them. For these most vulnerable students, the impact was about half of the schoolwide impact described earlier. The estimates of impact of grade-level mobility on non–African American students were, on average, very close to zero. We also found that the average impact of grade-level mobility cumulated over a child's school career.

Implications for Understanding Racial Inequality

As mentioned, black children experienced significantly higher levels of school-level mobility than did white children. On average during the period from 1995 to 2005, this difference was 4.06 percent. Given our estimate of the average effect of school-level mobility of −0.61, we speculate that school-level mobility accounts for $(-0.61) \times (4.06) = 0.025$ points in math achievement per year. If such an effect were to accumulate over three years (between grades three and five in our study), it would account for 7.6 percent of the black-white achievement-test score gap of 0.972 points observed in this study at the end of grade five. Grade-level mobility would by itself explain less than 2 percent of the achievement gap.

We conclude that the impact of school-level mobility on mathematics learning is reliably negative and is relevant to understanding racial inequality in learning. However, our results urge caution against overemphasizing the importance of mobility. Most social scientists would regard the effect as small. However, one can realistically assess the magnitude of the effect in relation to the cost of actions we might recommend for reducing mobility or its effects.

Implications for Policy

Crafting policy options to reduce school mobility, which is especially salient for African American children, is a complex problem. Reducing housing instability would seem an especially expensive way to reduce school mobility, though such an option may have many other important benefits. Encouraging families who move short distances to keep their children in the same school would be much cheaper, though we don't know how effective such a strategy might be. Improving school quality would likely encourage parents to avoid changing schools, though the cost associated with this improvement is a question of seminal importance and a complex one.

Finally, policies to ameliorate the impact of school mobility are worth considering. Increasing curricular and instructional conformity across schools would require strong district leadership and would seem to run counter to the current trend of encouraging schools to experiment with novel governance and instruction. However, coordinating instruction might have other benefits, such as enabling districts to provide more effective professional development and making accountability more coherent. In sum, the problem of crafting policies to reduce mobility or ameliorate its effects is complex, because policy options vary not only in cost but also in terms of their broader impact on the quality of schooling. Our findings suggest that these policy issues are worth pursuing in light of the real if modest impact of mobility.

These results also encourage future research. An obvious option would be to design an experimental intervention to reduce school mobility or ameliorate its effects. A well-designed experiment is, in principle, effective in reducing uncertainty about the causal effect of mobility, and such an experiment might be particularly useful for policy. However, the small size of the effects we see implies that very large sample sizes would be needed to clarify experimentally the size of these effects for subgroups of students and at different base levels of mobility, and such a large-sample experiment would be very expensive.

It is sensible to extend this research to the secondary level. Hypothesized negative effects of school-level mobility on social networks may prove more important at the secondary than at the elementary level, and effects on antisocial behavior may be manifest at that level. This research will give a clearer picture of the cumulative effects of school-level mobility during the public-school careers of urban students, with potentially important implications for policy.

The research reported here was supported by a grant from the MacArthur Foundation entitled "Identifying Mobility Pathways and Effects of Mobility on Peer Social Networks and Academic Achievement in Chicago Elementary Schools" and by a contract from the Brookings Institution as part of its Project on Social Inequality and Educational Disadvantage. We wish to thank Marisa de la Torre, Julia Gwynne, and John Easton of the Consortium for Chicago School Research for sharing their knowledge about school mobility in Chicago and for developing excellent indicators of school mobility. Mario Small and Micere Keels have been instrumental in conceptualizing the MacArthur-funded project.

NOTES

Online appendix available at: http://www.russellsage.org/duncan_murnane_online_appendix.pdf.

1. These included prior student math achievement, prior student reading achievement, school means of prior achievement, prior school-level mobility, concentrated disadvantage of the block group of the student's residence, school mean of neighborhood concentrated disadvantage, "social status" of the block group (a composite of percentage professional and percentage with a college education on the block group), school mean of social status, school percentage low income, school ethnic composition, school percentage of students with limited English proficiency, school size, prior class size, student gender, age, having repeated a grade, and having changed schools in the last year; prior school-level mobility status, prior grade-level mobility status; and achievement in reading and math during the two years prior.

2. The standard deviation of school-level mobility is a little less than 0.05, and the average growth rate between grades 3 and 5 is about 0.606 points per year. Thus, a contrast of 2 standard deviations is approximately $(2 \times 0.05 \times 9 - 0.57)/0.606 = 0.089$, or 8.9 percent of a year's average achievement growth.

3. We would expect the estimates based on propensity-score stratification to be a bit larger than those based on the fixed effects even in the absence of any bias. Recall that the fixed-effects method eliminates the schoolwide effects and focuses on within-school differences associated with grade-level mobility. The propensity-score approach does not remove these schoolwide differences.

4. The fixed-effects analysis removes the influences of unobserved confounding that are time invariant within schools but does not remove the effect of time-varying confounding. The weighted analysis removes the effects of observable confounding that are time invariant and time varying.

REFERENCES

Alexander, Karl L., Doris Roberts Entwisle, and Susan L. Dauber. 1996. "Children in Motion: School Transfers and Elementary School Performance." *Journal of Educational Research* 90(1): 3–12.

Bryk, Anthony S., and Stephen W. Raudenbush. 1988. "Toward a More Appropriate Conceptualization of Research on School Effects: A Three-level Hierarchical Linear Model." *American Journal of Education* 97(1): 65–108.

Bryk, Anthony S., Penny B. Sebring, Elaine Allensworth, Stuart Lupescu, and John Easton. 2009. *Organizing Schools for Improvement: Lessons from Chicago.* Chicago: University of Chicago Press.

Burkham, David T., Valerie E. Lee, and Julie Dwyer. 2009. "School Mobility in the Early Elementary Grades: Frequency and Impact from Nationally Representative Data." Paper prepared for the National Academy of Sciences Committee on the Impact and Change in the Lives of Young Children, Schools, and Neighborhoods. Presented at a workshop on the Impact of Mobility and Change on the Lives of Young Children, Schools, and Neighborhoods, Washington, D.C. (June 29 to 30). Available at: http://www.fcd-us.org/sites/default/files/ReynoldsSchoolMobilityAndEducational Success.pdf (accessed March 20, 2011).

de la Torre, Marisa, and Julia Gwynne. 2009. *Changing Schools: A Look at Student Mobility Trends in Chicago Public Schools Since 1995.* Chicago: Consortium on Chicago School Research.

Fauth, Rebecca C., Tama Leventhal, and Jeanne Brooks-Gunn. 2005. "Early Impacts of Moving from Poor to Middle-Class Neighborhoods on Low-Income Youth." *Journal of Applied Developmental Psychology* 26(4): 415–39.

Hanushek, Eric A., John F. Kain, and Steven G. Rivkin. 2004. "Disruption Versus Tiebout Improvement: The Costs and Benefits of Changing Schools." *Journal of Public Economics* 88(9–10): 1721–46.

Haynie, Dana L., Scott J. South, and Sunita Bose. 2006. "The Company You Keep: Adolescent Mobility and Peer Behavior." *Sociological Inquiry* 76(3): 397–426.

Hong, Guanglei, and Stephen W. Raudenbush. 2008. "Causal Inference for Time-Varying Instructional Treatments." *Journal of Educational and Behavioral Statistics* 33(3): 333–62.

Kerbow, David. 1996. "Patterns of Urban Student Mobility and Local School Reform." *Journal of Education for Students Placed at Risk* 1(2): 147–69.

Lash, Andrew A., and Sandra L. Kirkpatrick. 1990. "A Classroom Perspective on Student Mobility." *Elementary School Journal* 91(2): 177–92.

Reynolds, Arthur J., Chin-Chih Chen, and Janette E. Hebers. 2009. "School Mobility and Educational Success: A Research Synthesis and Evidence on Prevention." Paper prepared for the National Research Council's Board on Children, Youth, and Families. Presented at a Workshop on the Impact and Change in the Lives of Young Children, Schools, and Neighborhoods. Washington, D.C. (June 29 to 30).

Robins, James M., Miguel A. Hernán, and Babette Brumback. 2000. "Marginal Structural Models and Causal Inference in Epidemiology." *Epidemiology* 11(5): 550–60.

Rosenbaum, Paul R., and Donald B. Rubin. 1983. "The Central Role of the Propensity Score in Observational Studies for Causal Effects." *Biometrika* 70(1): 41–55.

Rumberger, Russell W. 2003. "The Causes and Consequences of Student Mobility." *Journal of Negro Education* 72(1): 6–21.

South, Scott J., and Dana L. Haynie. 2004. "Friendship Networks of Adolescents." *Social Forces* 83(1): 315–50.

Wood, David, Neal Halfon, Debra Scarlatta, Paul Newacheck, and Sharon Nessim. 1993. "Impact of Family Relocation on Children's Growth, Development, School Function, and Behavior." *Journal of the American Medical Association* 270(11): 1334–38.

Chapter 18

The Effect of School Neighborhoods on Teachers' Career Decisions

Don Boyd, Hamp Lankford, Susanna Loeb,
Matthew Ronfeldt, and Jim Wyckoff

Recent research has confirmed a widely held belief that teachers matter for students' educational outcomes. Students consistently learn more during the course of a school year with some teachers than they do with other teachers. Yet not all students have access to teachers of the same quality. Schools with low salaries and poor working conditions, particularly poor support from school leadership, face a weaker supply of teachers, on average. A substantial body of research also shows that schools with large populations of poor, nonwhite, and low-achieving students, on average, have more difficulty attracting and retaining teachers. This difficulty in recruiting teachers to schools with high concentrations of low-income students likely reduces the educational opportunities of students in areas of concentrated poverty. As income segregation grows (see chapter 16 in this volume), the impact on students of inequalities in the teacher workforce likely also grows.

The neighborhoods in which schools are located may also affect the supply of teachers, but little research has assessed the extent to which differences in neighborhoods either affect teacher recruitment and retention or explain the observed relationship between school characteristics and teachers' career choices. This chapter uses newly compiled data on the neighborhoods of all schools in New York City, linked to a unique data set on teachers' applications to transfer, to assess the effects of neighborhoods on teachers' career decisions.

To make this assessment, the study uses indicators of the fifty-nine community districts in New York City as well as additional information on the characteristics of neighborhoods surrounding each school. The study distinguishes neighborhoods by community districts because these districts are responsible for reviewing and monitoring quality-of-life issues for New York City neighborhoods and because the community districts were designed to align with historical neighborhood boundaries. The study also includes measures of the characteristics of the neighborhoods surrounding each school such as median family income, population density, racial composition, percentage of households that are married with children, percentage of vacant lots, whether the neighborhood experiences a lot of violent crime, the distance to a subway station, and retail amenities such as grocery stores, restaurants, movie theaters, parks, libraries, bookstores, drugstores, hardware stores, and clothing stores. The study examines both the probability that a teacher will seek to transfer *to* a given school and the probability that a teacher will seek to transfer *away from* a given school as a function of that school's neighborhood.

The analyses show that neighborhoods affect teachers' choices. First, neighborhoods add substantial predictive power to models that include relatively rich measures of school characteristics. Second, neighborhood characteristics predict teachers' choices. The effects of neighborhood characteristics differ between urban areas with relatively low and high population densities. Not surprisingly, neighborhood characteristics are more important to teachers in high-density areas. In lower-density areas, it is likely easier for teachers to travel, and so the immediate surroundings of the school are less important. In applying to schools, teachers tend to favor neighborhoods with higher median family income and less violent crime. In higher-density areas, teachers also favor neighborhoods with greater local amenities, particularly for practical (grocery stores, hardware stores, drugstores) and leisure (bars, fitness centers, coffee shops, movie theaters) purposes. When teachers apply for new jobs, they are also less likely to try to leave schools in neighborhoods with high median family income, and in high-population-density areas, they are less likely to try to leave schools near local amenities.

Overall, this study finds that although neighborhood characteristics matter somewhat to teachers when they choose where to work, their influence is modest relative to teachers' preferences to teach in schools serving relatively low proportions of African American students and low-achieving students. The effects of neighborhoods may compound the effects of school characteristics in that schools in low-income neighborhoods tend to lose teachers more rapidly than schools in higher-income neighborhoods and have fewer applicants for teaching positions. It is likely more difficult for schools in these neighborhoods to create strong, stable teaching staffs. Whether the effects operate through schools, neighborhoods, or a combination of both, to the extent that students with fewer supports for education are increasingly concentrated in a subset of schools (see chapter 16 in this volume) and are more dependent on schools for their educational opportunities (see chapter 9 in this volume), the lower supply of teachers to these schools as well as the higher teacher turnover rates can have increasingly detrimental effects on achievement and attainment.

Public schools are the most extensive public intervention in the lives of children and youth, and teachers and peers are the most immediate factors influencing school experiences for students. Thus, understanding differences in teacher quality across schools can give insight into the equity and effectiveness of public interventions. Teachers affect students' educational achievement, and differences in effectiveness across teachers can be substantial (Rockoff 2004; Rivkin, Hanushek, and Kain 2005). There is also clear evidence that the characteristics of teachers vary across schools, with poor students, black students, and low-achieving students consistently in classrooms with teachers who are less experienced and less academically able, as measured by their own test performance (Lankford, Loeb, and Wyckoff 2002; Clotfelter, Ladd, and Vigdor 2005). However, qualifications and quality are not the same. There is far less evidence on the distribution of teacher quality across schools, largely because it is difficult to compare teacher quality across different contexts. Even so, researchers can observe the career choices of teachers and use this information to better understand the distribution of quality teachers across schools. To the extent that teachers' choices of whether to teach in a particular school signal differences in the supply of teachers, they also reflect the potential for schools to select and retain effective teachers and provide high-quality educational opportunities for students.

Teacher attrition is not substantially greater than attrition in other occupations (Harris and Adams 2007); however, some schools have substantially more difficulty retaining teachers than do other schools. As an example, 27 percent of first-year teachers in New York City's lower-performing schools do not return the following year, compared to 15 percent in the quartile of schools having the relatively highest student achievement (Boyd et al. 2005).[1] Nearly 44 percent of elementary teachers and 55 percent of middle-school teachers in the lowest-performing schools in the city left within two years (Boyd et al. 2011).

Teacher attrition is not always bad. Recent research shows that more effective teachers, on average, stay in teaching and remain in their school more than do less effective teachers (Boyd, Grossman, et al. forthcoming; Boyd, Lankford et al. forthcoming; Goldhaber, Gross, and Player 2007; Hanushek et al. 2005). However, the differential attrition of more and less effective teachers appears to be similar across school types, and average attrition differences across schools are largely the result of differences in the appeal of teaching in those schools (Boyd, Lankford, et al. forthcoming). Teachers are more likely to leave schools with high proportions of low-income, black, and low-achieving students, as well as schools with less supportive leadership and lower salaries (Ingersoll and Smith 2003; Hanushek, Kain, and Rivkin 2004; Boyd et al. 2005). This greater attrition disadvantages schools because of the cost of recruiting and hiring, the greater instability of instructional programs, and the greater probability of hiring first-year teachers who have been shown to be less effective, on average (see, for example, Rockoff 2004). In addition, it likely signals a less desirable pool of teachers interested in filling vacancies.

Not only are schools with concentrations of low-income, non-white, and low-achieving schools disadvantaged in the teacher labor market, the effect of this disadvantage is likely to be more pronounced for these students because of fewer resources in the home to support their education (Kaushal, Magnuson, and Waldfogel, chapter 9 in this volume; Phillips, chapter 10 in this volume). While higher-income families can buffer their children from the effects of poorer educational opportunities at schools, lower-income families, on average, have less ability to do so. In addition, lower-income students tend to enter school with greater needs, as reflected by lower scores on measures of school readiness (Duncan and Magnuson, chapter 3 in this volume). Without effective teachers, these students are likely to continue to trail their higher-income peers.

While it is clear that school characteristics affect teachers' career choices, no research that we know of has identified the effects of neighborhood characteristics on teachers' decisions. There is, however, substantial research on the relationship between neighborhood characteristics and student outcomes. The evidence is mixed. Lisa Sanbonmatsu et al. (2006) analyze a sample of more than five thousand students from the Moving to Opportunity (MTO) program in Boston, Baltimore, Chicago, Los Angeles, and New York whose families were randomly assigned to vouchers for housing in higher-income communities. They find no effect of voucher receipt on student test scores four to seven years after random assignment, even though the characteristics of neighborhoods were strongly affected by the treatment. The findings of this aggregate study are in keeping with some earlier work that also found little effect of neighborhood change on students' later achievement (Leventhal and Brooks-Gunn 2004; Jacob 2004), and they are also in keeping with some careful correlational studies of neighborhood effects (such as Solon, Page, and Duncan 2000). However, other smaller experimental studies such as Chicago's Gautreaux program (Rosenbaum 1995) and the initial analyses of the Baltimore MTO program (Ludwig, Ladd, and Duncan 2001) do show positive effects of neighborhood transitions. Substantial research also demonstrates correlations between neighborhood characteristics and child and youth outcomes (for example, Chase-Lansdale and Gordon 1996). However, it is difficult to separate potentially omitted family characteristics that lead families to locate in a given neighborhood from the effect of the neighborhood itself.

Omitted variables bias is a concern in correlational studies of the effects of neighborhoods on student outcomes, and it is a concern in assessing the effects of neighborhoods on teachers as well. In particular, if we see higher attrition of teachers in one neighborhood than in another, this difference could be driven by neighborhood characteristics, but it could also be driven by differences in school characteristics across neighborhoods or by differences in teacher characteristics across neighborhoods that we are not measuring. In the analyses that follow, we adjust for school and teacher characteristics that could differ across neighborhoods using an unusually rich data set on New York City schools; however, there is still some concern that neighborhood characteristics could be reflecting unobserved characteristics of schools and teachers.

In addition to the potential bias caused by omitted variables, estimates of the effects of neighborhood characteristics are complicated by the potential variation in effects across contexts. A neighborhood characteristic such as ample public transportation may have a different effect in an area where there is easy access by car and easy parking than it would in an area without this access. In this study, we use data from one large urban school district, so there is more uniformity in location than there would be in a state or national study; we do not, for example, need to worry about differential effects in urban and rural areas. Nonetheless, there is variation in density within New York City. In some of the city's outer areas, teachers drive to work, therefore amenities such as parking may be salient and the distance to a coffee shop or subway station less salient; in the most densely populated areas, driving to work is not an option and local amenities and public transportation may be particularly important. To address these differences in location, we look separately at the effects of neighborhood characteristics in high- and low-population-density locations.

The analysis of teacher career decisions also presents challenges of its own. Most studies of teachers' choices examine whether teachers are more likely to quit or to transfer to other schools when they work in one type of school relative to when they work in another type of school. Yet transferring across schools is a two-sided choice; the teacher has to be willing to transfer, and the school has to be willing to accept the teacher. Transfers reflect both teacher and school preferences. In this chapter, we are able to isolate teacher preferences by using data on applications to transfer, instead of on the actual transfer (Boyd, Lankford, et al. forthcoming). We detail these data next.

DATA

Our work is the result of the analysis of multiple sets of data, including that from the New York City Department of Education and the New York State Department of Education, the 2000 United States Census, and WalkScore.com.

Transfer Request System Data

The primary data for this chapter come from the New York City Department of Education Transfer Request System. The data include the applications for open positions for the 2006 to 2007 and 2007 to 2008 academic years. Each application identifies the teacher as well as characteristics of the open positions such as the school and the subject area. These data also indicate which applicants were hired for a given position.[2]

These data are relatively newly available and are the results of policy changes in New York City. In 2005, the Department of Education and its teachers union decided to reform prior hiring policies to move away from a system that was based on seniority and gave teachers and principals little input in hiring decisions to a more free-market approach. Previously, teachers applied for and received transfers through the central human-resources or district offices, "a behind the scenes process that many teachers and schools found inscrutable" (Daly et al. 2008, 14). Teachers who were displaced from their jobs for any number of reasons, such as school closure or changing enrollment, were assigned to new placements by human-resources staff, often without teacher or principal input. The new policy requires that all teachers seeking transfer—both voluntary and involuntary—enter an open applications system in which hiring decisions are made mutually by both teacher and principal. Senior teachers can no longer claim the positions of novice teachers because of their seniority, a practice that previously had tied the hands of principals in the hiring process. To achieve these objectives, the district instituted a more centralized hiring system, including an online infrastructure for searching job postings and applying to them directly. The open-market system allows for transfers during a window that begins the last week in April and closes the first week in August. Transfers that occur outside of this period are not subject to the open-market process. The data for this study come from the first two years that the new applications system was in place. Across that time, about half of all transfers occurred through the open-market system and about half outside of it. Each year, approximately 8 percent of all active teachers submitted at least one application through the Transfer Request System. Of those who applied across two years, 42 percent transferred. We use information on which teachers applied to transfer and to which schools they applied.[3]

Other School and District Data

To these data, we have linked an array of additional data on teachers and schools in the New York City School District. Data on teacher characteristics include demographic information (race, gender, age), information on professional preparation pathway, years of experience, scores on the general-knowledge certification exam, and whether teachers attended a competitive undergraduate college. Data on schools include school level (elementary school, middle school, high school, or other grade combination), student race or ethnicity, student eligibility for free or reduced-price lunch, student English-learner status, when the school was established, the experience of teachers in the school, school enrollment, crime rates, and a host of other variables.[4]

Neighborhood Data

To assess the effects of neighborhoods, we use indicators of the fifty-nine community districts in New York City as well as additional information on the characteristics of neighborhoods surrounding each school. The community districts, shown in figure 18.1, were established in 1975 in order to help city agencies administer public services. They review and monitor quality-of-life issues for New York City neighborhoods. We choose community districts as categories of neighborhoods because of this administrative role and because the community districts were designed to align with historical neighborhood boundaries. As shown in figure 18.2, each community district is composed of multiple neighborhoods. For example, Community District 1 in the Bronx includes the neighborhoods of Mott Haven, Port Morris, and Melrose, while District 2 includes Longwood and Hunts Point.

We also collected data on the characteristics of the neighborhood surrounding each school. Because schools can be located on the boundaries of community districts and historic neighborhoods, we choose to use measures of characteristics based on geographic distance. We start with administrative data on the latitude and longitude of each school in New York City. We then link the schools to all Census tracts within one mile of the school, as measured by distance

FIGURE 18.1   *New York City Community Districts*

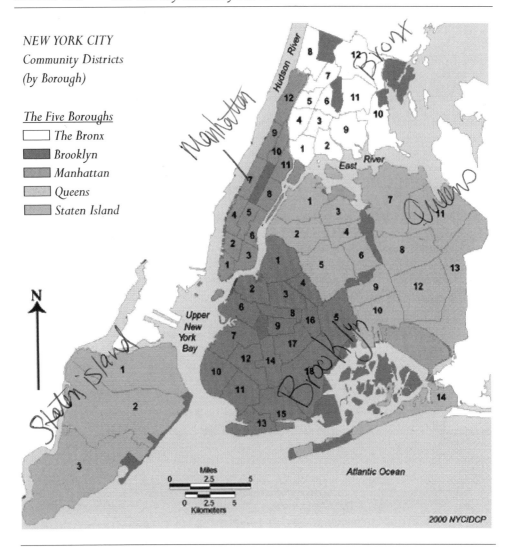

Source: New York City Department of City Planning (2008).

to the tract centroid, until the square area of the aggregated tracts is 0.64 square miles. We use this area, which is equivalent to 0.8 by 0.8 miles, because it is a reasonable walking distance for teachers in New York City. We then aggregated the values of each neighborhood's characteristics across all such nearby tracts and computed relevant variables from these aggregated tracts.

The Census data include multiple measures of the local community, but the data do not have information on the retail amenities surrounding schools. Amenities such as shopping opportunities may matter to teachers because they provide entertainment and ease of accomplishing household chores, even though teachers spend most of their day within school build-

FIGURE 18.2   *Neighborhoods Within Community Districts*

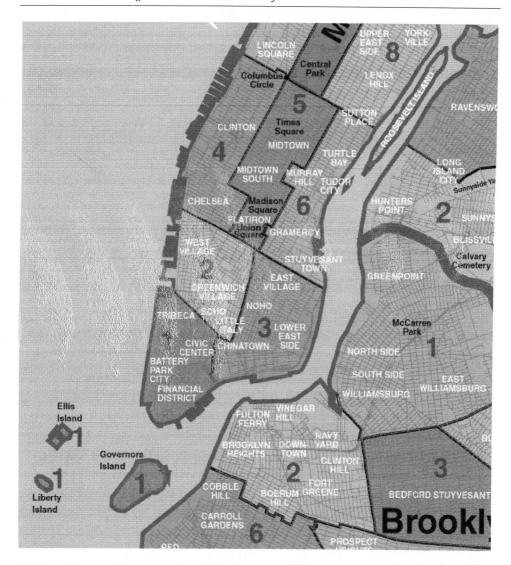

Source: New York City Department of City Planning (2011).

ings. In order to get this information, we use the Walk Score website (www.walkscore.com). For each address, the website provides data on up to eight grocery stores, restaurants, coffee shops, bars, movie theaters, other schools, parks, libraries, bookstores, fitness facilities, drugstores, hardware stores, clothing stores, and music stores within any given distance of the school. We use a half-mile to designate distance, and because of the high correlation across amenities, we created an aggregate measure of local amenities using factor analysis. We also collect information on the distance to the closest amenity in each group and use this measure for robustness checks.

TABLE 18.1   *Descriptive Statistics on Active Teachers*

| | Full Sample | | By Population Density | |
	Observations	Overall	Low Population Density	High Population Density
Proportion black	75,364	0.19	0.18	0.20
Proportion Hispanic	75,364	0.13	0.09	0.16
Proportion other, nonwhite	75,364	0.06	0.05	0.07
Proportion white	75,364	0.62	0.68	0.57
Proportion female	77,751	0.76	0.76	0.75
Age	77,755	41.27	41.79	40.76
Proportion college-recommending	71,748	0.43	0.48	0.39
Proportion teaching fellows	71,748	0.12	0.09	0.14
Proportion Teach for America	71,748	0.02	0.01	0.03
Proportion temporary license	71,748	0.22	0.20	0.23
Proportion "other" path	71,748	0.21	0.21	0.22
LAST score	53,023	248.00	246.77	249.12
Years of experience	77,755	7.51	7.97	7.06
Proportion competitive college	58,991	0.33	0.31	0.36

Source: Authors' calculations based on data from New York City Department of Education (2006–2008), not publicly available.

Descriptive Statistics

Table 18.1 provides the descriptive statistics for the teachers in the sample. We see that there are more than 75,000 teachers. Nineteen percent of the teachers are black, 13 percent are Hispanic, and 62 percent are white. Most teachers (76 percent) are female, and they average forty-one years of age. Less than half the teachers entered New York City schools through the traditional college-recommended route (43 percent), while another 14 percent came through the two most common early-entry or alternative routes, the New York City Teaching Fellows and Teach for America. Although 22 percent of teachers initially entered teaching with a temporary license, as of 2003 they all must have completed a recognized teacher preparation pathway and so now have a valid certification.

About 33 percent of active teachers graduated from colleges rated in the top two out of four tiers of competitiveness according to Barron's ratings. As part of their New York City certification requirements, the teachers had to take the Liberal Arts and Sciences Test (LAST), intended to measure "knowledge and skills in the liberal arts and sciences, in teaching theory and practice, and in the content area of the certificate title" (New York State Teacher Certification Examinations 2009). The exam includes a multiple-choice section covering scientific, mathematical, and technological processes; historical and social-scientific awareness; artistic expression and humanities; communication and research skills; and written analysis and expression. There is also a component requiring teachers to prepare a written response to an assigned topic. Teachers had an average score on the LAST exam of 248 (s.d. = 30), where 220 is required to pass for certification. Active teachers had an average of about seven and a half years of teaching experience. More than one-third of teachers (36 percent) had three or fewer years of experience; less than one-third (32 percent) had more than ten years of experience.

Table 18.1 also includes similar descriptive statistics for areas of the city with high and low population density, as this distinction proves important in the analyses. We define high-density areas as those with greater than fifty thousand people per square mile and low-density areas as those

TABLE 18.2   *Descriptive Statistics on Schools*

	Full Sample		By Population Density	
	Observations	Overall	Low Population Density	High Population Density
Proportion elementary schools	1,363	0.54	0.61	0.48
Proportion middle schools	1,363	0.20	0.17	0.22
Proportion high schools	1,363	0.26	0.22	0.30
Percentage black	1,357	36.25	36.98	35.62
Percentage Hispanic	1,357	40.11	31.36	47.75
Percentage Asian	1,357	10.89	13.65	8.48
Percentage English language learners (ELLs)	1,295	13.24	9.98	16.24
Percentage female	1,357	49.82	49.42	50.18
Percentage qualifying for free or reduced-price lunch	1,301	69.58	63.16	75.46
Percentage level 1 (lowest) math achievement	901	14.51	12.78	16.38
Enrollment	1,357	745.65	827.78	674.05
Attendance rate	1,301	90.38	90.87	89.93
Percentage of faculty with five-plus years' experience	1,347	47.44	51.56	43.82
Suspension and enrollment	1,347	0.05	0.04	0.06
Proportion high violent crime (top quartile)	1,236	0.25	0.22	0.28

Source: Authors' calculations based on data from New York City Department of Education (2006–2008), not publicly available.

♡ Sam

with less than fifty thousand people per square mile. This categorization splits the sample of teachers approximately in half. On average, teachers in high-population-density areas of the city are more likely to be Hispanic and to have entered teaching through alternative pathways. They are also slightly less experienced, on average, and were more likely to attend a competitive college.

Table 18.2 provides similar descriptive statistics for the schools in New York City. Just more than half of all schools are elementary, with another 20 percent middle schools and 26 percent high schools. The average enrollment in these schools is 746 students, with approximately 70 percent of students qualifying for a free or reduced-price lunch. The attendance rate averages 90 percent, and the racial distribution of students is 40 percent Hispanic, 36 percent black, 13 percent white, and 11 percent Asian. On average, there is a somewhat greater representation of elementary schools in the low-population-density areas. In addition, the enrollments are slightly higher; the percentage of students eligible for subsidized lunch, lower; the percentage of Hispanic students, lower; and the percentage of low-achieving students, somewhat lower.

Table 18.3 provides information on neighborhoods. The median family income of neighborhoods averages $43,500 and is somewhat higher in low-population-density areas than in high-population-density areas. Eighteen percent of households are married couples with children; this is lower in high-density areas. Almost 6 percent of housing units are vacant, and 61 percent of the population is living in the same house that they lived in five years before. On average, there are almost fifty amenities within a half-mile of a school, but schools in low-density areas have substantially fewer local amenities.

While we measure multiple neighborhood characteristics, if these characteristics are highly correlated then we might not be able to distinguish among them in the multivariate analyses. Online appendix table 18.A1a gives the correlation coefficients for the neighborhood variables (online

TABLE 18.3   *Descriptive Statistics on Neighborhoods*

| School Neighborhood Features | Full Sample | | By Population Density | |
	Observation	Overall	Low Population Density	High Population Density
Median family income ($10,000)	1,320	4.35	4.64	4.07
Population density (10,000)	1,320	5.41	3.10	7.75
Percentage of population who are nonwhite	1,320	61.18	57.28	65.13
Percentage of households married couple with kids under eighteen	1,320	17.83	20.38	15.23
Percentage of housing units vacant	1,320	5.88	5.58	6.18
Percentage of population living in same house five years ago	1,320	61.40	62.97	59.80
Percentage of population age twenty-five with B.A.	1,320	9.38	8.73	10.04
Distance from school to nearest subway (miles)	1,320	0.56	0.86	0.26
High violent-crime rate (top quartile)	1,424	0.24	0.18	0.30
General amenities factor—centered	1,346	0.00	−0.56	0.52
Sum of amenities within 0.5 miles	1,347	49.16	35.00	62.49

Source: Authors' calculations based on data from U.S. Bureau of the Census (2000) and WalkScore (2011).

appendix available at: http://www.russellsage.org/duncan_murnane_online_appendix.pdf). The strongest correlation in the table is between median family income and the percentage of the adult population with greater than a bachelor's degree (0.89). It will be difficult to separate the effects of these two neighborhood characteristics. Median family income also varies strongly with the percentage of white residents (0.68). The other strong correlation is between the amenities factor and population density (0.66). Because of the relatively high correlations among measures, we use the neighborhood variables both together as a group and individually in the multivariate analyses. When entered individually, a given variable likely measures an aggregate characteristic of the neighborhood and not the specific characteristic included in the model.

Online appendix table 18.A1b provides the correlations between school and neighborhood characteristics. Independent variation at each level is necessary in order to distinguish the effects of neighborhoods from the effects of schools. The table shows relatively high correlations between school and neighborhood race—0.61 between the percentage of black students and the percentage of nonwhite residents—and between student poverty and neighborhood median family income—0.61 between the percentage of students eligible for a lunch subsidy and neighborhood median family income. However, even in these areas there is meaningful independent variation, and all other correlations are low.

METHODS

We assess the effects of neighborhoods on teacher choices using three approaches. First, we model the number of applicants a school receives for each position using ordinary least-squares regression. We use these models to estimate the importance of neighborhoods using the community-district indicator variables. Second, we use logit models to estimate the relationship between neighborhood characteristics and a teacher's decision of whether or not to apply for transfer to another school. Finally, we use conditional logit models to estimate where a teacher applies, given that he or she applies to schools within the transfer system. In this way, we can examine the kinds of neighborhoods to which teachers are trying to transfer. This section describes each of these approaches.

Applications per Vacancy

Equation 18.1 describes the first set of analyses in which the log of applications per vacancy is modeled as a function of school and neighborhood characteristics as well as community-district indicator variables. We use the log transformation of the applications measure because of the skewed distribution (see online appendix figure 18.A1a).

$$(18.1) \qquad \ln A_{sy} = \beta_0 + S_{sy}\beta_1 + N_{sy}\beta_2 + C_s + \tau_y + \varepsilon_{sy}$$

The log of applications, A, for school s in year y is a function of that school's characteristics, S, the neighborhood characteristics specific to the school, N, as well as indicator variables for the community district, C, and the year. We compare results from the full model to results of specifications that do not include the neighborhood measures in order to assess the importance of including neighborhood measures.

Whether a Teacher Applies to Transfer

Although the first set of analyses benefit from simplicity, they are unable to adjust for the characteristics of teachers, which may differ across neighborhoods and schools. A more thorough analysis uses teacher-level data. In this set of analyses, we model active teachers' choices of whether to apply.[5] We model the likelihood of applying for transfer as a function of teacher characteristics, school characteristics, and neighborhood characteristics as given by equation 18.2:

$$(18.2) \qquad P_{tsy}\left(\text{teacher } t \text{ applying}\right) = \frac{e^f}{1+e^f},$$

where $f = \alpha_0 + T_{tsy}\alpha_1 + S_{sy}\alpha_2 + N_{sy}\alpha_3 + \sigma_y + \omega_{sy}$. The probability that teacher t in school s in year y applies to transfer is a function of that teacher's characteristics, T, the characteristics of the school from which he or she is applying, S, the neighborhood characteristics of the school from which he or she is applying, N, an indicator variable for the year, s, and a random error, w.

Where a Teacher Applies to Transfer

Finally, to model preferences of where to apply, we use a logit model for applying to a given school. We limit the sample to elementary schools so that we do not need to distinguish teaching fields. In this model, each teacher has a separate observation for each school to which he or she could apply. The standard errors are then clustered by school to adjust for the multiple teachers with the option to apply to each school. Equation 18.3 summarizes this approach:

$$(18.3) \qquad P_{tly}\left(\text{teacher applying to school } l\right) = \frac{e^g}{1+e^g},$$

where $g = \gamma_0 + T_{ty}\gamma_1 + S_{ly}\gamma_2 + N_{ly}\gamma_3 + \rho_y + \varphi_{tly}$. In equation 18.3, the probability that teacher t applies to school l in year y is a function of the teacher's characteristics, T, the characteristics of the school to which he or she might apply, S, the characteristics of the neighborhood of the school

TABLE 18.4   *Modeling Log (Applicants per Vacancy) as a Function of School Characteristics, at the School Level*

Variables	Model 1	Model 2	Model 3	Model 4
Proportion middle schools	−0.480***	−0.454***	−0.471***	−0.472***
Proportion high schools	−0.021	0.093	0.069	0.078
Proportion "other," nonelementary schools	−0.925*	−0.787*	−0.663~	−0.695~
Enrollment (per 1,000)	−0.011*	−0.014**	−0.014**	−0.016**
Percentage qualifying for free or reduced-price lunch	−0.004*	0.001	0.001	0.002
Attendance rate	0.010	0.011	0.010	0.009
Percentage black	−0.006**	−0.006*	−0.008**	−0.004
Percentage Hispanic	−0.004~	−0.003	−0.006*	−0.002
Percentage Asian	0.004~	−0.001	0.000	0.000
Percentage ELL	−0.001	−0.003	−0.002	−0.003
Percentage female	0.002	−0.002	−0.000	−0.002
Percentage of faculty with five-plus years' experience	0.000	−0.000	0.001	0.001
Suspensions/enrollment	0.291	0.081	0.132	0.012
High-violent-crime school (top quartile)	−0.100	−0.134~	−0.102	−0.120~
Observations	1015	1013	980	980
R-squared	0.188	0.285	0.217	0.295
District indicators		x		x
Neighborhood controls			x	x

Source: Authors' calculations based on data from the New York City Department of Education (2006–2008), not publicly available.

Note: x indicates the item in the left column was included in the regression.

***$p < 0.001$, **$p < 0.01$, *$p < 0.05$, ~$p < 0.1$

to which he or she might apply, N, an indicator variable for the year, ρ, and a random error term, φ.

Additional Models

As just discussed, because of the potential differential role of neighborhood characteristics in areas with different population densities, we run the analyses that estimate the effects of neighborhood characteristics (equations 18.2 and 18.3) separately for teachers in high- and low-population-density schools. In addition, we assess the differential effects of neighborhoods on teachers with different characteristics using both interaction and separate equations.

RESULTS

Let us now turn to the results of our analyses.

Applicants per Vacancy

Table 18.4 gives the results of the first set of analyses modeling the log of applicants per vacancy. Because of space, table 18.4 includes only the estimates for the school characteristics. Models 1 to 4 include all schools. The first column gives the coefficients for when only the school characteristics are included in the model. The second column adds in fifty-eight indicator variables for the fifty-nine community school districts. The third column does not include these indicator variables but does include the neighborhood characteristics. The final column has both the indicators and the characteristics. Looking first at the R-square, we see that neighborhood measures explain a substantial proportion of the variation in applications. The school characteristics alone account for 18.8 percent of the variation. The addition of the neighborhood characteristics in model 3 increases this explained variation to 21.7 percent. The community district indicators further increase this explained variation to 29.5 percent.

Now consider the coefficients on the school characteristic variables. Middle schools, in particular, receive fewer applicants per position. They are relatively evenly spread across neighborhoods, so neighborhood characteristics do not explain the relationship between middle schools and applications. The inclusion of neighborhood characteristics does little to change the estimates on the school-level measures. Similarly, the relationship between school enrollment and applicants per vacancy is not meaningfully affected by neighborhood controls. On average, larger schools receive fewer applicants per position than do smaller schools.

Neighbor characteristics that are included in these models explain only a small amount of the relationship between student characteristics and teachers choices. The characteristics of schools most clearly tied to teacher retention in other analyses using administrative data on schools are the percentage of students eligible for subsidized lunch (a measure of poverty) and the percentage of black students.[6]

Table 18.4 shows that once neighborhood characteristics are included in the model, the percentage of poor students is no longer negatively associated with applications per transfer. This student measure has also tended to be the weakest of these measures for predicting teachers' career trajectories in earlier analyses. The inclusion of neighborhood characteristics does less to reduce the negative relationship between the percentage of black students and the number of applicants per position. The coefficients lose significance in some models, but the point estimates are only partially reduced. For example, the coefficient on percentage of black students falls from −0.006 to −0.004 in the full model. Across models, schools in the top quartile of violent crime receive fewer applicants per vacancy, though the effect is only borderline significant.[7]

Overall, we find evidence that neighborhoods affect teachers' decisions but that they do not explain the relationships between school characteristics and teacher application decision. We now move on to model the relationship between neighborhood characteristics and teachers' choices more carefully.

Whether a Teacher Applies for Transfer

Table 18.5 summarizes the results from models predicting the likelihood that a teacher applies to transfer as a function of neighborhood characteristics surrounding his or her current school.[8] All models include controls for both teacher and school characteristics. Estimates in the section on the left are from multivariate models. In univariate models, on the right, each neighborhood characteristic is entered separately so that the coefficient represents a separate estimation, with the exception of linear and squared terms for the same measure being included together. Within each section, the first column displays estimates from the full sample, the second column from the sample of teachers working in schools in low-population-density neighborhoods, and the third column from the sample of teachers in high-population-density neighborhoods.

Table 18.5 shows across all models that teachers are less likely to seek to transfer if they currently teach in a neighborhood with higher median family income. An increase in family income of $10,000 reduces the odds of applying by approximately 8 percent. As shown in online appendix table 18.A2a, without teacher controls, teachers in neighborhoods with a higher proportion of nonwhite residents are more likely to seek transfer and those in neighborhoods with a higher

TABLE 18.5   *The Odds Ratios That a Teacher Applies for Transfer as a Function of the Neighborhood Characteristics Surrounding His or Her Current School*

	Multivariate Models			Univariate Models		
	Full Sample	Low Density	High Density	Full Sample	Low Density	High Density
Median family income/$10,000	0.917**	0.948	0.891*	0.963**	0.945*	0.977
Population density/10,000	1.050	1.093	1.232~	1.051	1.076	1.122
Population density squared	0.998	0.996	0.989	0.997	0.999	0.994
Percentage nonwhite	0.999	0.997	0.999	1.003	1.001	1.002
Percentage households married with kids	0.994	0.989	0.998	0.995	0.987~	0.999
Percentage lots vacant	1.010	1.011	1.014	1.003	1.005	1.000
Percentage same house for five years	1.004	1.001	1.009	1.006	1.004	1.011
Percentage education B.A. or more	1.016~	0.998	1.034*	0.994	0.993	0.997
Subway distance	1.143	1.270	0.942	1.065	1.114	1.054
Subway distance squared	0.972	0.953	0.878	0.976	0.968	0.779
High violent crime	0.975	0.992	1.004	1.055	1.065	1.010
Amenity factor	0.918	0.995	0.753**	0.975	1.019	0.858~
Amenity factor squared	0.985	0.999	1.081	0.982	0.994	1.073
Observations	76300	39535	36765			
χ^2	1117.685	641.2161	615.4564			

Source: Authors' calculations based on data from U.S. Bureau of the Census (2000) and WalkScore (2011) and the data in table 18.1.
Note: All models include controls for teacher and school characteristics. For univariate models, each neighborhood characteristic is estimated separately. Standard errors clustered by current school. Complete results presented in online appendix tables 18.A2a to 18.A2c.
***$p < 0.001$, **$p < 0.01$, *$p < 0.05$, ~$p < 0.1$

proportion of households with families are less likely to seek transfer. However, these relationships do not hold up to the inclusion of any of the controls.

As discussed, neighborhood characteristics could have different effects in different types of neighborhoods. Because of this, we rerun the models for low- and high-density areas separately. The multivariate models in table 18.5 show that, although teachers working in neighborhoods with higher median family income are less likely to seek transfer in general, the effects are strongest in neighborhoods with high population densities.[9] In these areas, teachers are also less likely to apply to transfer if the amenities in the area are greater. Later, we explore whether certain kinds of amenities are more highly associated with transfer requests.

Where a Teacher Applies for Transfer

Factors affecting whether a teacher applies to transfer may differ from factors that affect where he or she applies for transfer. Table 18.6 presents the likelihood a teacher applies to transfer to a school as a function of that school's surrounding neighborhood characteristics. Models reflect the same approach taken for the estimates presented in table 18.5. Online appendix tables 18.A3a to 18.A3c display alternative model specifications as well as standard errors. Beginning with the full sample results, teachers are more likely to apply to transfer to schools in neighborhoods with higher median family income. An increase in median income of $10,000 increases the odds of applying to a given school by approximately 8 percent. Teachers are also more likely to apply to

TABLE 18.6   *The Odds Ratios That a Teacher Applies for Transfer to a School as a Function of the Neighborhood Characteristics Around That School*

	Multivariate Models			Univariate Models		
	Full Sample	Low Density	High Density	Full Sample	Low Density	High Density
Median family income/ $10,000	1.069*	1.116*	0.978	1.081***	1.111***	1.059*
Population density/10,000	0.984	0.978	1.343***	0.943	0.969	1.354***
Population density squared	1.002	0.993	0.986***	1.005*	0.980	0.986***
Percentage nonwhite	0.998	1.002	0.993	0.993**	0.995	0.991**
Percentage households married with kids	1.000	1.001	1.000	0.997	1.015*	0.978**
Percentage lots vacant	1.000	1.020	0.995	1.007	1.010	1.000
Percentage same house for five years	0.988~	0.989	0.993	0.983***	0.988~	0.975**
Percentage education B.A. or more	0.995	1.001	1.010	1.015***	1.009	1.024***
Subway distance	1.234	0.995	5.779*	1.042	1.123	3.103
Subway distance squared	0.981	1.023	0.312	1.010	1.003	0.479
High violent crime	0.971	0.691*	1.192	0.821*	0.614***	0.9685
Amenity factor	1.029	0.816~	0.996	1.066*	0.886	1.1678*
Amenity factor squared	1.021	0.916*	1.188*	1.047*	0.976	1.142*
Observations	1540257	852171	756066			
χ^2	22307.050~	889.3649	1984.586***			

Source: Authors' calculations based on data from U.S. Bureau of the Census (2000) and WalkScore (2011) and the data in table 18.1.

Note: Only elementary-level, nonspecialist teachers are included in these analyses. All models include controls for teacher and school characteristics. For univariate models, each neighborhood characteristic is estimated separately. Standard errors clustered by school to which teachers applied. Complete results are presented in appendix tables 18.A3a to 18.A3c.

***$p < 0.001$, **$p < 0.01$, *$p < 0.05$, ~$p < 0.1$

schools in neighborhoods with a higher proportion of white residents. A 10 percent increase in white residents increases the probability of applying by approximately 6 percent. Although the local violent crime rate did not affect a teacher's propensity to apply for transfer, it is related to where a teacher applies.[10] Teachers are substantially less likely to apply to schools in neighborhoods in the top quartile of violent crime. In addition, they are more likely to apply to schools in neighborhoods with many amenities; however, this relationship does not hold up to the inclusion of other neighborhood characteristics.

Comparing results between low- and high-population-density neighborhoods, we see that median family income appears more salient for schools in low-density neighborhoods, while amenities are far more important in high-density areas. In fact, the relationship between amenities and applications is negative for low-density areas, perhaps indicating other disadvantages such as greater difficulty parking in close proximity to retail amenities. Violent crime is also more predictive of applications in low-density areas than in high-density areas.

Differential Relationships for Different Teachers

These results show the average relationship for all teachers, but there is likely variation across teachers in their preferences for neighborhood characteristics. Surprisingly, we find only small differences in the relationship between neighborhood characteristics and application behavior by teacher race/ethnicity, gender, and age (online appendix tables 18.A4a and 18.A5a give these results).[11]

For the teachers in schools in low-density areas, we found slight evidence that they were less likely to apply from schools in higher-median-income neighborhoods (coefficients of 0.94–0.97). In separate estimates by teacher characteristics, we find a stronger relationship for white teachers (0.91) than for black or Hispanic teachers (1.05 and 0.95, respectively) and a stronger relationship for female teachers (0.92) than for male teachers (1.01), but the estimates are not statistically different from zero. For teachers in schools in high-population-density areas, we find that on average, teachers are less likely to apply to transfer if they currently work in neighborhoods with higher median income or stronger amenities. When we estimate the models separately by teacher characteristics, we find that across the board, teachers are less likely to apply to transfer from schools in higher-median-income neighborhoods. Amenities also predict fewer applications to transfer away, though the effect appears stronger for women than for men.

The models of applications to schools in low-density areas show that teachers are more likely to apply to schools in neighborhoods with higher median income and less violent crime, while in high-density areas, they are more likely to apply to neighborhoods with more amenities. For schools in low-density neighborhoods, the positive relationship with median family income is relatively consistent across teacher groups. The relationship between violent crime and applying is negative for most teacher groups, but less strong for black teachers and for older teachers. For schools in high-density areas, the nonlinear relationship with population density holds up across teacher types, while the relationship with amenities is stronger for white teachers and for female teachers.

Effects of Different Kinds of Amenities

As we have described, in high-density areas, teachers are less likely to request transfers from and more likely to request transfers to neighborhoods with greater amenities. We wondered, however, whether some kinds of amenities are more highly associated with transferring than other kinds. By rotating the general amenity factor loadings, we create four orthogonal measures of amenities: leisure, practical, residential, and community. The "leisure" factor signals areas with nearby bars, fitness centers, movie theaters, and coffee shops. Neighborhoods characterized as having "practical" amenities have a higher concentration of grocery, hardware, clothing, and drugstores. The "residential" factor signals areas with few amenities of any kind. Finally, the "community" factor represents neighborhoods with many parks, schools, and libraries.

Table 18.7 reports estimates for whether (on left) and where (on right) teachers apply for transfer as a function of the different amenity factors. In the overall sample, including both high- and low-population-density areas, teachers are less likely to apply for transfer from and more likely to apply for transfer to "community" neighborhoods—those with many parks, schools, and libraries. Consistent with prior analyses, the relationships between amenities and requests for transfer are stronger in higher-population-density areas. More specifically, teachers in high-density neighborhoods are significantly less likely to request transfer from neighborhoods that have many practical amenities and are significantly more likely to apply for transfer to schools that have more amenities for leisure nearby.

DISCUSSION

To our knowledge, this is the first study to estimate the effects of neighborhood characteristics on teachers' career decisions. We find that neighborhoods do play a role in teachers' choices. First, neighborhoods add substantial predictive power to models that include rela-

TABLE 18.7   *Modeling Whether and Where a Teacher Applies to Transfer as a Function of Different Kinds of Amenities (Odds Ratios Presented)*

	Whether Teacher Applies for Transfer			Where Teacher Applies for Transfer		
Kinds of Amenities	Overall	Low Density	High Density	Overall	Low Density	High Density
Leisure	0.940	0.954	0.889~	1.046	0.921	1.154*
	(0.040)	(0.050)	(0.063)	(0.050)	(0.068)	(0.072)
Practical	0.947	1.023	0.784**	0.962	0.992	0.886~
	(0.038)	(0.045)	(0.068)	(0.046)	(0.057)	(0.059)
Residential	1.008	0.997	1.072	1.013	1.001	0.965
	(0.028)	(0.026)	(0.089)	(0.039)	(0.046)	(0.090)
Community	0.930*	0.947	0.911~	1.090*	0.988	1.076
	(0.029)	(0.040)	(0.045)	(0.041)	(0.062)	(0.053)
Neighborhood controls	x	x	x	x	x	x
School controls	x	x	x	x	x	x
Teacher controls	x	x	x	x	x	x

Source: Authors' calculations based on data from U.S. Bureau of the Census (2000) and WalkScore (2011) and the data in table 18.1.

Note: x indicates item in left column was included in the regression.

***$p < 0.001$, **$p < 0.01$, *$p < 0.05$, ~$p < 0.1$

tively rich measures of school characteristics. Second, neighborhood characteristics predict teachers' choices.

The effects of neighborhood characteristics differ between urban areas with relatively low and high population density. Not surprisingly, neighborhood characteristics are more important to teachers in high-density areas. In lower-density areas, it is likely easier for teachers to travel, and thus, the immediate surroundings of the school are less important. In applying to schools, teachers tend to favor neighborhoods with higher median family income and less violent crime. In higher-density areas, teachers also favor neighborhoods with greater local amenities, particularly for practical (grocery, hardware, drugstores) and leisure (bars, fitness centers, coffee shops, movie theaters) purposes.

There are two important caveats to these findings. First, it may be that our estimates of the importance of neighborhood characteristics are biased by important omitted variables. If a school characteristic that we do not include in the model is correlated with neighborhood characteristics in the model, then these neighborhood characteristics may simply proxy for school characteristics. The potential omitted variables bias seems more concerning in regards to neighborhood median family income than amenities, since the correlation between median income and measured school characteristics is much stronger than is the correlation between amenities and these school characteristics. Nonetheless, bias remains a concern in this study's analyses, which are all correlational.

A second caveat is that though neighborhood characteristics are potentially salient, they explain little of the relationship between the student characteristics of schools and teachers' career choices. Teachers demonstrate preferences for schools with lower proportions of black students and low-achieving students. Including neighborhood indicator variables and neighborhood characteristics in the models does little to change these relationships. Nonetheless, whether teachers respond to neighborhoods or to the more immediate school environment, they are systematically leaving schools serving students who are likely to have the least supports for education at home. These labor-market dynamics likely disadvantage these students further.

NOTES

Online appendix available at: http://www.russellsage.org/duncan_murnane_online_appendix.pdf.

1. An expanded version of this chapter is available at www.teacherpolicyresearch.org/portals/1/pdfs/Explaining_ the_short_careers_of_high_achieving_teachers_AER_final.pdf (accessed March 20, 2011).

2. We know if a teacher was hired but do not know who else may have received a job offer for the same position. In terms of estimating school preferences for teachers, we would prefer to know all teachers who received job offers in the first place.

3. Boyd, Lankford, et al. (forthcoming) provide more detail on the transfer-system data.

4. Boyd et al. (2005) provide more detail on the sources of these data.

5. By "active" teacher we mean teachers that are in the human-resources database as paid regular teachers at the beginning of the school year who are working at 70 percent of full-time or more. Teachers who had taken leave, had quit, or were of unknown status were dropped from our sample. This reduced our sample down to more than 70,000 teachers each academic year. For instance, although teachers who quit or were on leave make up some of the teachers who entered the Transfer Request System, there were relatively few. It did not make sense to include these teachers because we were interested in accounting for the effects of teachers' current school workplace on their applying and transferring behaviors. Since these teachers were not currently in schools, such models could not apply.

6. We also ran models that included the percentage of lowest-performing students in schools. Schools with more lowest-achieving students received fewer applicants per vacancy, on average. The effect was moderately significant in model 1 and was statistically significant in models with district indicators (models 2 and 4). Because we only have test-score data on grades 4 through 8, the inclusion of this measure greatly reduces the sample. We do not present these results here, but they are available upon request from the authors.

7. In a related study, Boyd et al. (forthcoming) used a composite measure for school crime that included violent crime in addition to other forms of crime. Schools with higher crime on this general measure received significantly fewer applicants per vacancy. We used violent crime here to match our neighborhood measures for crime that focus on violent crime.

8. Online appendix tables 18.A2a to 18.A2c present results from the full models with alternative specifications and standard errors. Because the sample changes across different model specifications, we also reran all models using a constant sample. The results were similar and are available on request from the authors.

9. Online appendix table 18.A2b presents some evidence that teachers in low-population-density areas, more than teachers in high-density areas, are less likely to apply for transfer when working in neighborhoods with higher proportions of families with kids.

10. We tried examining whether teachers' choices about whether and where to apply for transfer were associated differentially with different neighborhood crime measures, such as property crime, rape, murder, and assault. However, the propensities of the different forms of crime were so highly correlated that we could not distinguish their separate effects.

11. We also looked separately at less experienced (five or fewer years) and high-value-added (above the mean) teachers. The relationships between neighborhood characteristics and decisions about whether and where to apply were not statistically different for novice and high-value-added teachers than for other teachers. We do not present the results here, but they are available upon request from the authors.

REFERENCES

Boyd, Donald, Pamela Grossman, Marsha Ing, Hamilton Lankford, Susanna Loeb, and James Wyckoff. 2011. "The Influence of School Administrators on Teacher Retention Decisions." *American Education Research Journal* 48(2): 303–33.

————. Forthcoming. "Who Leaves? Teacher Attrition and Student Achievement." *Economics of Education Review.*

Boyd, Donald, Hamilton Lankford, Susanna Loeb, Mathew Ronfeldt, and James Wyckoff. Forthcoming. "Separating Supply and Demand: Using Applications-to-Transfer to Uncover Preferences of Teachers and Schools." *Journal of Policy Analysis and Management.*

Boyd, Donald, Hamilton Lankford, Susanna Loeb, and James Wyckoff. 2005. "Explaining the Short Careers of High-Achieving Teachers in Schools with Low-Performing Students." *American Economic Review Proceedings* 95(2): 166–71.

Chase-Lansdale, L. P., and R. A. Gordon. 1996. "Economic Hardship and the Development of Five- and Six-Year-Olds: Neighborhood and Regional Perspectives." *Child Development* 67(6): 3338–67.

Clotfelter, C. T., H. F. Ladd, and Jacob Vigdor. 2005. "Who Teaches Whom? Race and the Distribution of Novice Teachers." *Economics of Education Review* 24(4): 377–92.

Daly, T., D. Keeling, R. Grainger, and A. Grundies. 2008. "Mutual Benefits: New York City's Shift to Mutual Consent in Teacher Hiring." The New Teacher Project policy brief. Available at: http://www.tntp.org/files/Mutual Benefits.pdf (accessed March 20, 2011).

Goldhaber, D., P. Gross, and D. Player. 2007. "Are Public Schools Really Losing Their 'Best'? Assessing the Career Transitions of Teachers and Their Implications for the Quality of the Teacher Workforce." Working paper 12. Washington, D.C.: Urban Institute, National Center for Analysis of Longitudinal Data in Education Research.

Hanushek, Eric, J. Kain, and S. Rivkin. 2004. "Why Public Schools Lose Teachers." *Journal of Human Resources* 39(2): 326–54.

Hanushek, Eric, J. Kain, D. O'Brien, and S. Rivkin. 2005. "The Market for Teacher Quality." NBER Working Paper No. 11154. Cambridge, Mass.: National Bureau of Economic Research.

Harris, D., and S. Adams. 2007. "Understanding the Level and Causes of Teacher Turnover: A Comparison with Other Professions." *Economics of Education Review* 26(3): 325–37.

Ingersoll, R., and T. Smith. 2003. "What Are the Effects of Mentoring and Induction on Beginning Teacher Turnover?" *American Educational Research Journal* 41(3): 681–714.

Jacob, B. A. 2004. "Public Housing, Housing Vouchers, and Student Achievement: Evidence from Public Housing Demolitions in Chicago." *American Economic Review* 94(1): 233–58.

Lankford, Hamilton, Susanna Loeb, and James Wyckoff. 2002. "Teacher Sorting and the Plight of Urban Schools: A Descriptive Analysis." *Education Evaluation and Policy Analysis* 24(1): 37–62.

Leventhal, T., and Jeanne Brooks-Gunn. 2004. "A Randomized Study of Neighborhood Effects on Low-Income Children's Educational Outcomes." *Developmental Psychology* 40(4): 488–507.

Ludwig, J., Helen F. Ladd, and Greg J. Duncan. 2001. "Urban Poverty and Educational Outcomes." Brookings-Wharton Papers on Urban Affairs. Washington, D.C.: Brookings Institution Press.

New York City Department of City Planning. 2008. *New York City Community Data Portal: The Five Boroughs* [map]. Available at: http://www.nyc.gov/html/dcp/html/neigh_info/nhmap.shtml (accessed May 4, 2011).

———. 2011. *New York: A City of Neighborhoods* [map]. Available at: http://www.nyc.gov/html/dcp/html/neighbor/neighe.shtml (accessed May 4, 2011).

New York State Teacher Certification Examinations. 2009. "Liberal Arts and Sciences Test, Preparation Guide." Available at: www.nystce.nesinc.com/NY_viewSG_opener.asp (see "Tests for Teacher Certification" link; accessed March 20, 2011).

Rivkin, S., Eric Hanushek, and J. Kain. 2005. "Teachers, Schools, and Academic Achievement." *Econometrica* 73(2): 417–58.

Rockoff, J. 2004. "The Impact of Individual Teachers on Student Achievement: Evidence from Panel Data." *American Economic Review Proceedings* 94(2): 247–52.

Rosenbaum, J. E. 1995. "Changing Geography of Opportunity by Expanding Residential Choice: Lessons from the Gautreaux Program." *Housing Policy Debate* 6(1): 231–69.

Sanbonmatsu, Lisa, J. R. Kling, Greg J. Duncan, and Jeanne Brooks-Gunn. 2006. "Neighborhoods and Academic Achievement: Results from the Moving to Opportunity Experiment." *Journal of Human Resources* 41(4): 649–91.

Solon, G., M. E. Page, and Greg J. Duncan. 2000. "Correlations Between Neighboring Children in Their Subsequent Educational Attainment." *Review of Economics and Statistics* 82(3): 383–92.

U.S. Bureau of the Census. 2000. *2000 Decennial Census* [various data]. Available at: http://www.census.gov/main/www/cen2000.html (accessed May 6, 2011).

WalkScore. 2011. Available at: http://www.walkscore.com (accessed May 6, 2011).

Chapter 19

Crime and the Production of Safe Schools

David S. Kirk and Robert J. Sampson

Violence in and around U.S. schools is a major barrier to the physical and emotional well-being of students and ultimately to their prospects of educational attainment. A fundamental challenge to schools is therefore to produce a safe environment that fosters learning instead of fear and anxiety about crime. A common policy response is "zero tolerance" of delinquent students; one infraction may lead to suspension, expulsion, and even incarceration. The assumption behind such measures is that allowing problem students to remain in school produces an environment in which little academic learning takes place. But the practice of excluding or arresting students who have engaged in criminal conduct may have the undesirable consequence of reducing the educational attainment and life chances of these same students. A criminal label and dropping out of school may thus be linked; taken together, these life-course snares portend an especially bleak future. It follows that schools must balance the conflicting goals of providing support for troubled youth and fostering a school climate in which academic learning can prosper.

To shed light on these issues, we investigate how criminal behavior among the student body of public schools hinders the ability of the school to provide a productive, safe learning environment, and whether a criminal record limits the future educational prospects of troubled youth. The study design combines individual-level data from the Project on Human Development in Chicago Neighborhoods (a three-wave longitudinal cohort study of more than six thousand randomly sampled children, adolescents, and young adults), the Chicago Police Department, the Illinois State Police, and the Chicago Public Schools with neighborhood- and school-level data from the U.S. census, the Teacher and Student Surveys of the Chicago Public Schools, and a community survey of almost 9,000 residents of the city of Chicago. This unique assemblage of data brings together information on the organization and functioning of neighborhoods, families, and schools with data on individual-level characteristics and behaviors over time.

Our analyses reveal that schools with a high rate of arrested students tend to be located in areas of Chicago that produce high arrest rates in general, but the overall relationship is quite modest. This finding means that crime-ridden neighborhoods do not always contain schools overrun with students who have had contact with the criminal justice system. Within schools, we find that crime can be a major obstruction to the learning process. Schools with large numbers of criminal youths tend to be poorly functioning learning environments, characterized by fear and a lack of commitment among teachers. The criminality among students may be as much a consequence of deficient learning environments as its cause, implying that the expulsion of problem students may do little to remedy the core educational deficiencies of a school or to stem educational inequality in urban America. In fact, it may make things worse. Our analyses demonstrate that a criminal-arrest record has negative consequences for educational attainment: most students with an arrest record subsequently drop out of high school (73 percent) compared with half of those who have not been arrested, controlling for confounding factors common to both groups. We conclude with a discussion of alternatives to zero-tolerance policies and other tools of exclusion designed to enhance school safety and learning. We find promise in educational reforms designed to foster trust and a sense of community among teachers, principals, parents, and students.

Exposure to crime and violence is unfortunately common in the lives of many American students. More than 5 percent of public and private high school students skip school at least once a month because they feel unsafe at school or on their journeys to or from school. More than one-third of students are involved in at least one physical fight a year (Centers for Disease Control and Prevention [CDC] 2008). Eighteen percent of students report carrying a weapon of some sort (gun, knife, or club) at least one day out of thirty; 5 percent report carrying a gun (CDC 2008).

In Chicago, the site of our investigation, the figures are even more staggering. Forty percent of high school students in Chicago are involved in a fight at least once per year, and 12 percent of students skip school one or more times each month because of fear for their safety. Research on Chicago adolescents reveals that exposure to firearm violence in the community doubles the likelihood that an adolescent will perpetrate violence (Bingenheimer, Brennan, and Earls 2005). The implications of exposure to violence extend well beyond crime, moreover, including influences on outcomes as diverse as posttraumatic stress disorder, anxiety, and depression (Fitzpatrick and Boldizar 1993; Margolin and Gordis 2000). The mental-health consequences of exposure to violence may in turn impair cognitive development and hinder educational attainment (Grogger 1997; Margolin and Gordis 2000; Harding 2009).

Thus, there is growing evidence that violence in and around primary and secondary schools is a major barrier to physical, emotional, and educational well-being. Since crime and violence cluster in select urban neighborhoods, particularly those marked by concentrated poverty (see, for example, Shaw and McKay 1942; Morenoff, Sampson, and Raudenbush 2001), educational inequality is in part a byproduct of the uneven distribution of crime and violence across geographic space. The challenge to already overburdened schools is therefore to provide a safe environment that fosters learning instead of fear and anxiety.

The good news is that national trends reported by the National Center for Education Statistics reveal that school crime and victimization have declined at least since the early 1990s (Robers et al. 2010). For instance, the number of nonfatal violent crimes against students at school declined from forty-eight per one thousand students in 1992 to twenty-four in 2008. The bad news is that declines have been unevenly distributed; private and suburban schools appear to have benefited more from these declines than have public and urban schools. The percentage of middle and high school students victimized in school during a six-month period declined nearly 60 percent in private schools between 1995 and 2005, compared to 55 percent in public schools. The gap is substantially more drastic between urban and suburban schools. Victimizations at school declined by nearly 60 percent in suburban schools during this time, yet by only 43 percent in urban schools. Students' fear of being attacked at school declined between

1995 and 2005 in both urban and suburban schools, but it fell substantially more in suburban schools. Thus, despite aggregate declines in school crime and fear, inequality by race and social class in educational experiences has likely increased because declines have been relatively more concentrated in suburban and private schools.

One response to the problem of school crime and violence during the past two decades has been the increased use of punitive measures against delinquent students, including suspension, expulsion, and even incarceration. The practice of "zero tolerance" has become widespread in school districts in the United States, yet it remains unclear whether "get tough" policies and practices for problem students have resulted in safer learning environments (American Psychological Association 2008). Moreover, there may be unintended negative repercussions from the use of suspension and expulsion as a tool for promoting school safety, or from segregating problem students into specialized programs. Ultimately, these practices may lead to educational failure, thereby ensuring that the problems of a troubled adolescent translate into reduced employment prospects and a higher likelihood of adult criminality. Much like the case for adult punishment (Western 2006), the collateral consequences of policies and practices designed to promote school safety need to be weighed against the potential benefits.

This chapter takes seriously the complex social consequences for education of juvenile crime and arrest. On the one hand, allowing problem students to remain in school may create an environment in which little academic learning takes place. On the other hand, the practice of excluding students who have engaged in criminal conduct may reduce their educational attainments and life chances. Schools must balance the conflicting goals of providing support for troubled youths and creating environments in which all students' academic learning can prosper. To shed light on these issues we draw on an extensive array of data from the Project on Human Development in Chicago Neighborhoods and the Chicago Public Schools to study how criminal behavior among public-school students hinders the ability of the school to provide a productive, safe learning environment, and the extent to which a criminal record limits the educational prospects of troubled youths.

Our data reveal that a criminal-arrest record has negative consequences for educational attainment, virtually ensuring that students drop out of high school. We also find that graduation rates are drastically lower in schools populated with large numbers of criminally inclined students, and that characteristics conducive to educational attainment, such as a safe school environment and committed teachers, tend to be absent from schools with high arrest rates. Yet our findings also suggest that criminality among students may be a consequence of deficient learning environments as well as a cause. Thus, expelling problem students as a policy solution may do little to remedy the core educational deficiencies of a school or to stem educational inequality in urban America.

DISCIPLINE IN THE CHICAGO PUBLIC SCHOOLS

School systems have in place a number of policies and practices designed to provide a safe and effective learning environment for students, yet many such policies and practices may ultimately lead to the exclusion of problem students from the normal schooling process. In the Chicago Public School (CPS) system, student behavior is regulated by the Student Code of Conduct (Chicago Public Schools [CPS] 2009b), which applies to the actions of all students while they are on school property or attending school-sponsored events. Students may also be disciplined for certain inappropriate behaviors occurring off-campus, namely, Group 5 or Group 6 acts of misconduct, if the behavior disrupts the orderly educational process. Group 5 and Group 6 acts involve serious criminal behavior, including lethal violence. Students who commit Group 5 or

Group 6 acts of misconduct may be expelled from school and assigned to Alternative Safe Schools (CPS 2009b).[1]

The goal of the CPS Safe Schools program is to give students who have been expelled the opportunity to earn credits toward a high school diploma while expelled. In addition to support services and small class sizes, CPS Safe Schools provide a special curriculum focused on core academic subjects and social skills. Although CPS reports that 77 percent of Safe Schools students ultimately complete the specialized program and return to their regular school (CPS 2009a), to the extent that expulsion or assignment to alternative programs either stigmatizes students or weakens their social bonds to school, dropping out of school may still be the end result of this process (see, for example, Hirschi 1969). The research evidence buttresses this point. For instance, although some students may benefit from the dedicated attention and specialized support found in alternative programs, the most common transition from participation in alternative programs is not to high school graduation, but rather to school dropout (Kelly 1993). In addition, Russ Skiba and Reece Peterson (1999) report that zero-tolerance policies and corresponding sanctions, such as school suspension and expulsion, are consistent predictors of school dropout. Ethnographic research (Bowditch 1993) shows that school officials actively use practices of exclusion and suspension as a way to push troublemakers and students deemed unlikely to succeed out of school. Thus, schools have in place institutional mechanisms designed to produce a safe learning environment, whose collateral consequences often include the exclusion of problem or arrested students.

In the empirical analyses that follow, we contrast the enormous challenge that urban schools face in fostering a safe learning environment with the challenge of providing an education and prosocial development to those students most at risk of crime and educational failure.

DATA AND STRATEGY

This study uses a research design that combines individual-level data from the Project on Human Development in Chicago Neighborhoods Longitudinal Cohort Study (PHDCN-LCS), the Chicago Police Department, the Illinois State Police, and CPS with neighborhood- and school-level data from the U.S. Census, the Teacher and Student Surveys of the Chicago Public Schools, and the PHDCN Community Survey. This unique assemblage of data brings together information on the organization and functioning of neighborhoods, families, and schools with data on individual-level characteristics and behaviors.

As part of the PHDCN-LCS, seven cohorts of child or adolescent subjects and their primary caregivers were interviewed up to three times between 1995 and 2002. The focus of our analysis is on the twelve-year-old and fifteen-year-old cohorts; these youths were approximately eighteen and twenty-one years old by the end of the data collection, in 2002. The LCS data contain a wealth of information on youth and family characteristics, including IQ, primary- and secondary-school enrollment, college enrollment, school and residential mobility, grade retention, family structure and supervisory processes, peer characteristics, and criminal offending (see tables 19.1 and 19.2 for a list of youth, family, and peer characteristics drawn from the PHDCN-LCS data). Importantly, these cohort data also contain indicators of youths' neighborhood of residence and school of attendance, allowing us to combine the cohort data with other data repositories containing information about the characteristics and functioning of Chicago neighborhoods and schools.

Neighborhood data were gathered from the 1990 U.S. Census and the 1995 PHDCN Community Survey of Chicago residents. School demographic data come from the CPS Office of Research, Evaluation, and Accountability. In addition, we use school data from the 1997

Teacher and Student Surveys of the Chicago Public Schools, conducted by the Consortium on Chicago School Research (CCSR). These surveys include information on the social organization of schools, human resources in the school, instructional quality, relations among school actors, and student behavior (Bilcer 1997).

Using key identifiers, such as Social Security number, name, and birth date, we linked CPS student enrollment and attendance records from 1990 to 2005 with the PHDCN-LCS data. Our individual-level measure of school dropout is drawn from these CPS student records. These data indicate precisely when the dropout was registered by the CPS system, allowing us to determine temporal ordering with criminal-arrest events. From the CPS student records, we have determined under what circumstances a student exited the CPS system: if students completed high school, if they transferred to a non-CPS school, if they were "lost" by the CPS system (in other words, former students who could not be located by CPS), or if they dropped out of CPS without transferring to a different school district. To develop our dropout measure, we include students designated as dropouts by CPS as well as those students who obtained a GED and students who could not be located by CPS.[2] Note that, by law, students cannot drop out of the CPS system prior to age sixteen, and they cannot be dropped from school by CPS (for example, for excessive truancy) before this age.[3]

Finally, we linked official arrest records from 1995 through 2001 from the Illinois State Police and the Chicago Police Department with the PHDCN-LCS data. We use these arrest records to investigate whether a criminal record hinders an individual's educational attainment. The arrest data contain information on all arrests of youths who are in the sample that occurred throughout the State of Illinois during the specified time period. Arrest is a binary variable indicating whether the student had been arrested at any point after enrolling in grade nine and prior to graduating or dropping out.[4] Thirteen percent of the sample was arrested during high school prior to graduating or dropping out. Our analytic sample consists of 659 respondents from the twelve-year-old and fifteen-year-old LCS cohorts who were enrolled in the Chicago public schools during ninth grade and who then either completed their schooling in a Chicago public school or dropped out of the system. We exclude from our analytic sample students who transferred to a non-CPS school.

Our analytic strategy is designed to accomplish four goals. First, we ground our study in a descriptive summary of the extent of arrest in and around Chicago public schools. Good descriptive data are surprisingly rare in this area. Second, we examine the challenges of cultivating a learning environment in schools characterized by high levels of criminality. We describe characteristics and conditions in three types of high schools: those with minimal arrest prevalence, with moderate arrest, and with substantial proportions of students arrested. This school-level analysis, which is based on data from the Teacher and Student Surveys of the Chicago Public Schools, addresses whether criminal behavior among the student body hinders the ability of a school to provide a productive, safe learning environment. Third, we provide an individual-level description of the characteristics of arrested and nonarrested youths. If arrest is implicated in dropping out of high school at a later point, as we hypothesize, it is imperative to examine the individual, familial, peer, neighborhood, and school conditions that put adolescents on the path to crime and educational failure before attempting to ascertain causal relationships.

Having examined the multiple sources of juvenile arrest, our fourth goal involves analytic questions more causal in nature. We use statistical modeling techniques most suitable to the observational data we have to estimate the effect of arrest on dropout for individuals otherwise equivalent in terms of their frequency of criminal offending (disaggregated by violent, property, and drug offenses) as well as individual, family, peer, neighborhood, and school characteristics. With this analytic design, we compare the likelihood of dropping out for each arrested subject with the three most similar nonarrested subjects (that is, we statistically match each arrested

FIGURE 19.1   *The Distribution of Arrests in Chicago Neighborhoods and Chicago Public Schools*

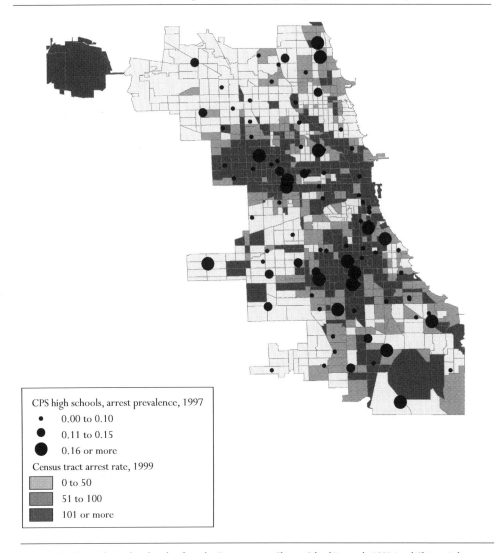

Source: Authors' compilation, based on data from the Consortium on Chicago School Research (1997a) and Chicago Police Department (2008).

individual with up to three nonarrested subjects and assess whether those arrested are any more likely to later drop out of school). If there are differences, we may cautiously conclude that arrest significantly impairs an adolescent's prospects of completing high school.

SCHOOL AND NEIGHBORHOOD PATTERNS

To understand the repercussions of crime and arrest for the educational trajectories of Chicago students, we begin by charting the geographic distribution of arrest in Chicago in figure 19.1. The shaded census tracts in the map display the 1999 arrest rate per one thousand tract residents as reported by the Chicago Police Department. The graduated circles denote high school locations, with the size of the circle reflecting the proportion of students in the school who self-reported being arrested sometime during the school year (from the beginning of the school year in the fall of 1997 through the point of survey administration the following February).[5] Student arrests include incidents that occurred at school and anywhere else.

The dark tract shading reveals that arrests tend to concentrate in the central-west section and on the south side of Chicago. Schools with high proportions of arrested students also tend to be located in these geographic areas, yet not all schools on the central-west and south sides of Chicago have high proportions of arrestees enrolled. Community areas on the west side such as Austin, North Lawndale, Humboldt Park, and West and East Garfield Park have several public schools with low proportions of arrestees.[6] Similarly, communities in the Bronzeville area on the south side with high arrest rates, such as Grand Boulevard and Washington Park, have some schools with proportionally few arrestees. Overall, the correlation between the proportion of students arrested in a school and the arrest rate in the tract surrounding the school is only 0.15. The modest association between these two measures suggests that crime-ridden neighborhoods do not always contain schools overrun with students who have had contact with the criminal justice system.[7] This is not surprising, in that school catchment boundaries do not necessarily overlap with residential boundaries. With respect to our interest in the effect of arrest on school dropout, figure 19.1 suggests that the repercussion of arrest for educational attainment is an issue than spans numerous neighborhoods across the city.

School Characteristics by Prevalence of Arrest

To explore the repercussions of student arrest for educational attainment, we display in figure 19.2 the association between arrest prevalence in a school (the proportion of students arrested during the school year) and high school graduation rates. The points on the scatterplot represent high schools.[8] The linear fit in the figure reveals that there is a strong negative correlation (-0.51, $p < 0.001$) between graduation rates and arrest. In schools with the highest arrest rates, only half of entering freshmen will graduate four years later. Prior research yields similar conclusions. For instance, Grogger (1997) finds a significant, negative association between school violence and high school graduation; serious levels of school violence lower the likelihood of graduation by nearly six percentage points.

What are the factors underlying the negative relationship between arrest and graduation? In figures 19.3 and 19.4, we describe the variation in characteristics among schools with low, moderate, and high proportions of criminalized students. In general, the findings reveal substantial differences across school types in demographic, structural, and social-organizational characteristics. Figure 19.3 shows that schools with high percentages of arrested students have greater percentages of students who qualify for free or reduced-price lunch (that is, students who are low income) and more African American students relative to low- and moderate-arrest schools. Low-arrest schools tend to have more Latino and white students and more students with limited English proficiency.

Figure 19.4 compares school structural and social-organizational characteristics across low-, moderate-, and high-arrest schools. In this figure, values on all school characteristics have been converted to z-scores to facilitate the presentation of results.[9] Results reveal considerable differences across schools in student enrollment and the number of teachers, but not average teacher tenure. High-arrest schools tend to have substantially more disciplinary problems than low- and moderate-arrest schools, and students perceive high-arrest schools to be less safe. There are few differences across schools in student engagement yet significant differences in

FIGURE 19.2   *Association Between Chicago Public Schools High School Graduation Rates and*
Prevalence of Arrest, 1997

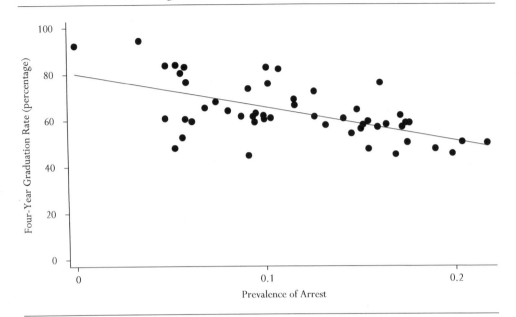

Source: Authors' compilation, based on data from Chicago Public Schools (1998) and Consortium on Chicago School Research (1997a).

FIGURE 19.3   *Demographic Characteristics of Chicago Public Schools High Schools,*
by Prevalence of Arrest

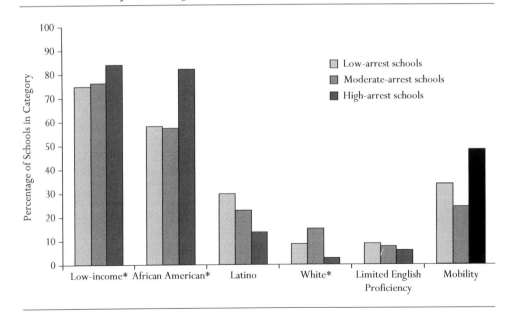

Source: Authors' compilation based on data from Consortium on Chicago School Research (1997a).
*Differences between schools are statistically significant.

FIGURE 19.4   *Structural and Social Organizational Characteristics of Chicago Public Schools High Schools, by Prevalence of Arrest*

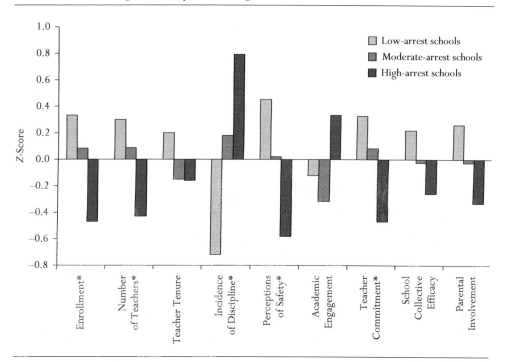

Source: Authors' compilation based on data from Consortium on Chicago School Research (1997a, 1997b).
*Differences between schools are statistically significant.

teacher commitment. Parental involvement and school collective efficacy, defined like neighborhood collective efficacy (Sampson, Raudenbush, and Earls 1997) as the activation of social ties among teachers in order to control student behavior (Kirk 2009), are lower in high-arrest schools than in low-arrest schools, although the differences across schools are not statistically significant.

Findings presented in figures 19.3 and 19.4 reveal that not only the demographic characteristics of schools but also their social organization and the schooling process more generally vary by arrest levels. Schooling characteristics conducive to educational attainment, such as a safe environment and committed teachers, are notably absent from schools with high arrest rates. Yet we must take care not to conclude a causative relationship from these correlations. The fact that schools with high proportions of arrested students have characteristics of poor academic environments does not necessarily mean that an abundance of criminal youth—or a high incidence of neighborhood crime—produced such school conditions. The relationship between school or neighborhood crime and school climate may be explained by some other factor.

To explore the association between crime and school characteristics in greater detail, in figure 19.5 we present correlations between the prevalence of arrest among students and school safety as well as correlations between the neighborhood violent-crime rate and school safety. School safety is a measure from the Student Surveys of the Chicago Public Schools describing students' sense of safety within and immediately surrounding their school (see Bilcer 1997). The

FIGURE 19.5   *Correlation Between Prevalence of Student Arrest and School Safety, and Neighborhood Violence and School Safety*

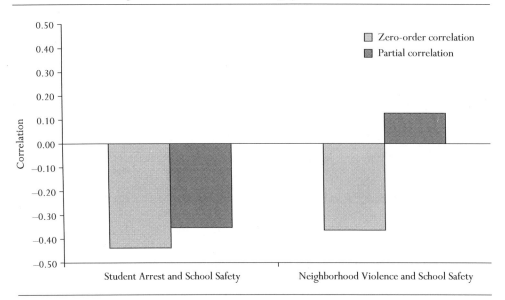

Source: Authors' compilation based on data from Consortium on Chicago School Research (1997a, 1997b); Project on Human Development in Chicago Neighborhoods (1995a, 1995b); and Chicago Police Department (1998).
Note: All associations are significantly different from zero (*p* < 0.01) except for the partial correlation between neighborhood violence and school safety.

light gray columns in the figure represent the zero-order correlations between safety and either school arrest or neighborhood violence, respectively. The dark gray columns represent the partial associations between safety and school arrest or neighborhood violence, after controlling for relevant characteristics of schools that are predictive of safety. These characteristics include school racial and ethnic composition, the socioeconomic status of students, school enrollment, teacher commitment, student-teacher trust, school collective efficacy, and neighborhood collective efficacy.

The far left column in figure 19.5 reveals a strong, significant zero-order correlation between school arrest prevalence and school safety ($r = -0.44$). After partialing out the influence of several other correlates of school safety, we still find a significant correlation between school arrest and safety, although the magnitude has declined slightly, to -0.35. Although we cannot rule out the possibility that school arrest and safety are spuriously related, these results do suggest that the prevalence of arrest has an influence on student perceptions of school safety. With neighborhood violence, however, we find that the correlation with school safety diminishes substantially and even reverses direction (from -0.36 to 0.13) once controlling for relevant correlates of safety. This result indicates either that neighborhood violence is indirectly related to school safety or that these two measures are each explained by a common third factor, such as neighborhood collective efficacy.

To further disentangle whether crime and arrest impair school functioning, we consider whether the direction of the relationship may be reversed (or reciprocal). Criminal behavior among the student body may be a *consequence* of a dearth of committed teachers, instead of a factor that *causes* teachers to become uncommitted to their school. The direction of the rela-

FIGURE 19.6   *Correlation Between Prevalence of Student Arrest and Teacher Commitment*

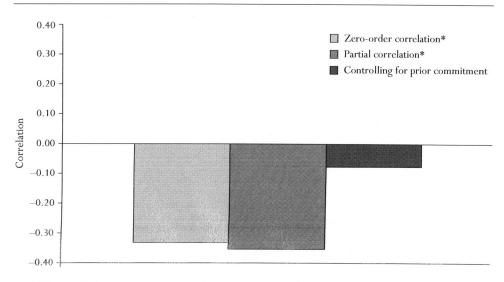

Source: Authors' compilation based on data from Consortium on Chicago School Research (1997a, 1997b).
*Correlation between teacher commitment and arrest is significantly different from zero.

tionship between the prevalence of arrest and characteristics of school organization and climate has substantial bearing on the policy levers that could be employed to promote educational attainment. If criminally disposed students disrupt learning environments, then expelling or banishing them to specialized programs should allow schools to be more effective, at least with educating the noncriminal students. If, however, ineffective schools prompt criminal behavior in the first place, then "get tough" school policies may have limited utility. Instead of only punishing individuals, education reform would need to be focused more on improving school quality.

To attempt to sort out this crucial question of directionality, we present in figure 19.6 a series of correlations between teacher commitment and the prevalence of school arrest. Teacher commitment is a measure describing the extent to which teachers are loyal to the school and look forward to work each day. The left column in figure 19.6 reveals a strong, significant correlation between school arrest prevalence and teacher commitment ($r = -0.33$), an association that becomes slightly stronger ($r = -0.35$) when controlling for correlates of teacher commitment (such as school racial and ethnic composition, the socioeconomic status of students, school enrollment, and teacher influence). With the column on the far right, we account for prior levels of teacher commitment, as measured in 1994. Our findings indicate that controlling for the lagged measure of commitment renders the association between teacher commitment and school arrest nonsignificant, with a partial correlation of -0.08. Thus, a lack of teacher commitment is not necessarily the product of large numbers of criminally inclined students; instead, criminality among the student body may be rooted in the fact that students attend schools with uncommitted teachers. Perhaps more reasonably, our findings may be interpreted as evidence of a reciprocal relationship between teacher commitment and arrest. Low levels of teacher commitment lead to higher rates of arrest, which then feeds back to further undermine teacher commitment.

The results to this point have underscored the unfortunate dilemma that urban schools face on a daily basis. Schools with large numbers of criminal youths tend to be poorly functioning learning environments, and yet it is imperative that schools do what is necessary to provide a safe learning environment for students. Our results suggest that policies such as zero tolerance, designed to expel or segregate problem youths, may enhance perceptions of school safety, but they will not necessarily remedy the core deficiencies of a poor learning environment such as a lack of committed teachers. Arrest is a natural extension of zero tolerance and may produce unintended negative consequences. We therefore investigate the following question: Does a criminal record limit the educational attainment of arrested students?

Individual-Level Arrest Results

Schools have in place institutional mechanisms to foster a safe learning environment, yet the collateral consequences of such practices may ultimately be educational failure among those students in trouble with the law. Of course, criminal arrest is the result of a cumulative process characterized by family disruption, exposure to deleterious neighborhood conditions, associations with delinquent peers, and school disengagement (Kirk 2008). It follows that before examining the link between arrest and educational attainment, we must compare the characteristics of youths with an arrest record with those youths who have not been arrested.

Table 19.1 presents a comparison of individual and demographic characteristics between arrested and nonarrested members of the PHDCN sample. This table reveals that arrestees are more likely to be male and African American than nonarrestees, and less likely to be Mexican or white. It is important to note that youths of different racial and ethnic groups often reside in substantially different neighborhood and family contexts, such that the difference in contexts explains differences in criminal outcomes between groups (Kirk 2008). Black youths, in particular, face multiple layers of disadvantage, such that even the worst neighborhood contexts in which whites reside, in terms of disadvantage and family disruption, are still better than the average black neighborhood (Sampson 1987, 353–54).

In terms of cognitive and schooling characteristics, little difference exists between arrestees' and nonarrestees' IQ and in student mobility. However, arrested youths are more likely to have failed a grade and to have been enrolled in remedial or special education. Arrested youths also tend to have less self-control and persistence, and they are more commonly sensation seeking. With respect to problem behavior, those arrested tend to be less anxious and depressed and are more likely to use marijuana, although these differences are only marginally significant. Not surprisingly, arrested adolescents are significantly more likely to engage in violent offenses, property crime, and drug distribution than those who have not been arrested. Thus committing a criminal offense is a crucial determinant of arrest; nevertheless, prior research reveals that family, peer, neighborhood, and school factors also predict both arrest and criminal offending (see, for example, Kirk 2008, 2009).

Table 19.2 displays summary statistics for family and peer covariates by group. There are significant differences between groups' immigrant generational status as well as in the proportion of students with married parents. Surprisingly, there is little difference between groups' family socioeconomic status, supervision, and support. Parents of arrested youths tend to be more controlling, and arrested adolescents are more likely to have mothers with substance-abuse problems and to have experienced parent-child conflict. In terms of peer influence and characteristics, we see that arrestees are significantly and substantially more likely to associate with deviant peers, a finding consistent with a long line of criminological research and one that validates the data.

TABLE 19.1   *Descriptive Characteristics of Arrested and Nonarrested Youths, 1995*

	Means		
			T-Statistic
Youth Characteristics	Arrested	Nonarrested	of Difference
Male	0.71	0.41	5.26***
Race-ethnicity			
African American	0.72	0.40	5.58***
Mexican	0.18	0.32	−2.74**
Puerto Rican or other Latino	0.08	0.13	−1.34
White	0.01	0.11	−2.80**
Other race-ethnicity	0.01	0.03	−1.13
Cohort 12 (versus 15)	0.54	0.51	0.62
Age (Wave 1)	13.52	13.63	−0.61
IQ	96.59	99.39	−1.68
Student mobility	2.79	2.60	1.25
Truancy	0.02	0.03	−0.13
Ever retained in grade	0.27	0.14	3.34***
Ever special education	0.50	0.26	4.84***
Temperament			
Lack of control	2.74	2.42	2.87**
Lack of persistence	2.66	2.39	2.66**
Decision time	3.13	2.97	1.63
Sensation seeking	2.94	2.73	2.26*
Activity	3.70	3.59	1.09
Emotionality	2.88	2.69	1.54
Sociability	3.71	3.68	0.33
Shyness	2.41	2.48	−0.66
Problem behavior			
Withdrawal	3.56	3.68	−0.43
Somatic problems	3.89	4.08	−0.52
Anxiety or depression	4.87	5.92	−1.87
Aggression	9.79	8.94	1.17
Internalization	12.08	13.28	−1.24
Externalization	14.04	12.46	1.62
Violent offending	0.70	0.12	5.28***
Property offending	0.23	0.07	2.28*
Drug distribution	0.21	−0.06	3.72***
Marijuana use	1.30	1.14	1.81

Source: Authors' compilation based on data from Project on Human Development in Chicago Neighborhoods (1995b); Illinois State Police (2003); and Chicago Police Department (2003).
Note: Sample from wave 1 of the PHDCN-LCS.
*p < 0.05; **p < 0.01; ***p < 0.001

Table 19.3 illustrates differences between groups in terms of neighborhood of residence and school attended. There are significant differences in the racial-ethnic composition of groups' neighborhoods and schools, and arrested subjects tend to reside in neighborhoods characterized by substantially more poverty, disorder, and violent crime and substantially less immigration than do the nonarrested. As expected, collective efficacy is weaker in neighborhoods where arrested youths tend to live. Arguably, then, there is a crucial ecological dimension to criminal behavior and arrest. In addition, to the extent that arrest hinders educational attainment, our results suggest that being arrested is one key pathway through which family processes and neighborhood and school conditions affect adolescents' life chances.

TABLE 19.2   *Family and Peer Characteristics of Arrested and Nonarrested Youths, 1995*

Characteristics	Means		T-Statistic of Difference
	Arrested	Nonarrested	
Family characteristics			
Immigrant generation			
First	0.07	0.13	−1.66
Second	0.15	0.30	−2.81**
Third or higher	0.78	0.57	3.72***
Family socioeconomic status	−0.02	−0.10	0.53
Married parents	0.31	0.48	−2.96**
Length of residence	5.45	5.60	−0.28
Extended family in household	0.28	0.20	1.77
Num. of children in household	3.73	3.41	1.54
Family supervision	−0.07	−0.09	0.19
Family control	60.19	58.30	1.97*
Family conflict	49.51	47.76	1.50
Family religiosity	61.82	60.82	1.25
Family support	−0.11	−0.04	−0.62
Paternal criminal record	0.11	0.11	−0.19
Paternal substance use	0.19	0.14	1.14
Maternal substance use	0.13	0.03	4.00***
Maternal depression	0.15	0.17	−0.33
Parent-child conflict	0.25	−0.08	3.78***
Home environment			
Access to reading	−0.26	−0.08	−0.88
Developmental stimulation	−0.02	−0.07	0.39
Parental warmth	−0.16	−0.09	−0.35
Hostility	0.18	0.52	−0.64
Parental verbal ability	0.07	−0.01	0.40
Family outings	0.02	−0.14	1.78
Home interior	−0.14	−0.19	0.24
Home exterior	−0.19	−0.10	−0.61
Peer characteristics			
Friend support	0.02	0.04	−0.29
Peer attachment	−0.10	0.03	−1.57
Peer school attachment	0.13	0.04	1.79
Peer pressure	0.21	0.08	0.96
Deviance of peers	0.46	0.04	4.63***

Source: Authors' compilation based on data from Project on Human Development in Chicago Neighborhoods (1995b); Illinois State Police (2003); and Chicago Police Department (2003).
Note: Sample from wave 1 of PHDCN-LCS.
*p < 0.05; **p < 0.01; ***p < 0.001

Estimating the Effect of Juvenile Arrest on School Dropout

There are considerable differences in graduation rates by arrest status—26 percent for arrestees versus 64 percent for nonarrestees—and these are not the only points of divergence. Arrested and nonarrested students, on average, differ on numerous individual, family, peer, neighborhood, and school characteristics.[10] Prior research using the PHDCN respondents reveals that in addition to criminal offending, the likelihood of arrest is strongly related to parental marital status,

TABLE 19.3   *Neighborhood and School Characteristics of Arrested and Nonarrested Youths, 1995*

	Means		*T*-Statistic of Difference
	Arrested	Nonarrested	
Neighborhood			
Percentage African American	54.89	36.80	3.99***
Percentage Latino	25.66	32.08	−1.89
Concentrated poverty	0.35	−0.06	4.87***
Concentrated affluence	−0.33	−0.28	−0.72
Immigrant concentration	0.12	0.38	−2.08*
Residential stability	−0.08	0.02	−0.88
Neighborhood organizations	−0.28	−0.43	2.29*
Neighborhood youth services	−1.65	−1.81	1.87
Legal cynicism	2.54	2.52	1.63
Neighborhood disorder	1.95	1.87	2.48*
Tolerance of deviance	4.21	4.24	−1.76
Collective efficacy	3.81	3.88	−2.63**
Resident victimization	0.44	0.42	0.58
LN (1995 violent crime rate)	9.29	8.94	5.26***
School			
Percentage African American	65.72	48.20	4.22***
Percentage Latino	25.42	36.03	−2.99**
Enrollment	1,462.64	1,879.60	−4.51***
Poverty	79.54	76.74	1.57
School mobility	59.29	31.04	2.74**
Percentage with English proficiency	9.55	12.27	−1.82

Source: Authors' compilation based on data from Project on Human Development in Chicago Neighborhoods (1995a, 1995b); Illinois State Police (2003); Chicago Police Department (2003); Chicago Public Schools (1998); and U.S. Bureau of the Census (1990).
Note: Sample from wave 1 of PHDCN-LCS.
*$p < 0.05$; **$p < 0.01$; ***$p < 0.001$

family structure, socioeconomic status, neighborhood racial-ethnic composition, and concentrated poverty (Kirk 2008). Research reveals that these family and neighborhood factors are also strong predictors of numerous other types of problem behavior, including dropping out of school (see, for example, Cairns, Cairns, and Neckerman 1989; Ekstrom et al. 1986; Rumberger 1983). Therefore, it is important to determine if any apparent relationship between school dropout and arrest is due to the fact that both outcomes have a similar set of antecedents.

Kirk and Sampson (2010) isolate the effect of arrest on high school dropout by comparing arrested and nonarrested sample members who are otherwise similar to each other in all of the characteristics displayed in tables 19.1, 19.2, and 19.3. This is accomplished through propensity-score matching (Rosenbaum 2002, chapter 10), where the intent is to approximate an experimental design in which "treated" youths (those arrested) are equivalent to a control group (the nonarrested). The propensity score is defined as the probability that a particular youth is arrested, given all that we observe about the youth and his or her family, peers, neighborhood, and school. We specifically used all of the covariates displayed in tables 19.1, 19.2, and 19.3 to predict the propensity of arrest, including the frequency of self-reported criminal offending as measured in the first wave of the PHDCN-LCS survey.[11] Therefore, treated and control-group youths are statistically equivalent not only in personal, school, and neighborhood factors but in the frequency with which they engage in the following crimes: violent offending (carried a hidden weapon, assault, assault with a weapon, use of force, gang fighting), property offending (purposely damaged or destroyed property, entered or broke into a building to steal something, theft from a store, theft from a household member, theft from a car, knowingly bought or sold stolen goods), drug distribution (sold marijuana, cocaine, crack, or heroin), and drug use (marijuana use in the last thirty days).

Numerous factors beyond the control or background of an individual influence whether a given criminal act will culminate in an arrest. Two key determinants include whether the crime is made known to the police and police discretion as to whether to arrest. Yet most crimes are not reported to the police, and the police arrest proportionally few of the known suspects of a crime. For instance, Donald J. Black and Albert J. Reiss (1970) find that only 15 percent of police contacts with juveniles resulted in an official arrest, suggesting considerable discretion on the part of police. In fact, most criminal incidents do not end in arrest. Thus, unlike many other behaviors under the control of an individual (selection), the arrest decision, which we conceptualize analytically as the "treatment," is made by the police on the basis of a host of external and often idiosyncratic reasons in addition to the criminal behavior and other characteristics of the individual that we measure.

For this reason juvenile arrest has a random component, making it likely that two individuals in the PHDCN sample who were otherwise equivalent in terms of criminal offending and other pretreatment covariates could end up with different officially defined fates because one of them got arrested after committing a crime whereas the other one did not. Indeed, much attention in the criminological and juvenile justice literature has focused on the seemingly random and thus "inequitable" nature of juvenile-arrest outcomes. Efforts to standardize arrest encounters and limit police discretion have, with few exceptions (for example, domestic violence), met with little success. As a result, there are strong substantive and empirical reasons to expect that there is overlap in the likelihood of arrest between the treatment (arrested) and control (nonarrested) groups, which we exploit empirically through matching in order to estimate the effect of juvenile arrest on school dropout.

After matching propensity scores of arrestees and nonarrestees we find that not a single statistically significant difference remains between these groups on any of the eighty covariates from tables 19.1 through 19.3 that were used to estimate the propensity score. Having achieved balance between groups through propensity-score matching, we are able to proceed with our comparison of dropout across groups. As depicted in figure 19.7, our propensity-based results reveal that the probability of dropping out of school is 0.22 greater for arrested adolescents than for very similar adolescents who were not arrested. This difference is large and statistically significant. On average, arrested youths have a 0.73 probability of subsequently dropping out of public school. In contrast, youths who avoid the snare of arrest have a probability of dropping out equal to 0.51.[12] The data thus reveal that the likelihood of completing high school is tragically low overall for students in the Chicago public school system. Yet for those youths who commit crimes and get caught, the repercussions of sanctioning via the criminal justice system drastically limit their already dismal chances of graduating from high school.

As described in the theoretical framework section, there are several potential mechanisms that explain why, exactly, arrest leads to school dropout. The stigma of arrest may weaken a student's bond to school, and schools may react to arrest by initiating a variety of exclusionary practices designed to expel problem students or separate them from the general school population. Here we explore one particular mechanism: arrest may lead to dropping out because time spent moving through the juvenile justice system increases school absences, making it more difficult to successfully complete high school.[13]

FIGURE 19.7   *Probability of Dropping Out of Chicago Public Schools Following Arrest,
Individually Matched Arrested and Nonarrested Youths*

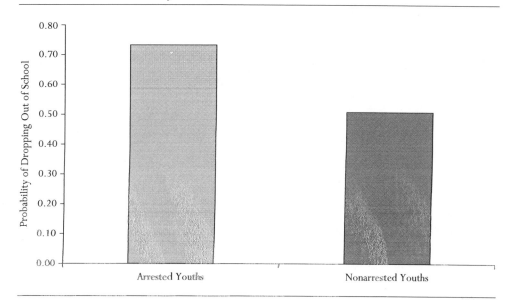

Source: Authors' compilation based on data from Project on Human Development in Chicago Neighborhoods (1995a, 1995b);
Illinois State Police (2003); Chicago Police Department (2003); and Chicago Public Schools (1998, 2006).
Note: Differences in dropout between groups are statistically significant.

Figure 19.8 compares arrestees' and nonarrestees' average frequency of absences at the
start of ninth grade and during the last semester of enrollment. We find that absences
increased substantially from the first semester of ninth grade through the last semester of
enrollment for both groups. Nonarrested youths averaged nine absences during the first
semester of ninth grade, which nearly doubled (seventeen absences) by their final semester.
Those arrested averaged fourteen absences at the start of ninth grade, which increased to
twenty-five by their last semester. Roughly 80 percent of students in both groups had more
absences in their last semester of school than in their first. Since the percentage increase in
absences over time is similar for arrested and nonarrested students, we tentatively conclude
that juvenile arrest does not adversely affect the frequency with which high school students
attend class.[14] Attendance at school plummets over time regardless of whether a student is
arrested. Sorting out the other potential mechanisms underlying the observed effect of arrest—
besides changes in attendance—is an important area of future research that we are exploring,
but it is beyond the scope of this chapter.

CONCLUSION

Our findings reveal that crime is a major snare for both schools and their students. The key
dilemma is that the quality and organization of schooling is strongly related to the criminality of
students, but at the same time one of the major policies to deal with criminality—arrest—
appears to have a substantively large and unintended negative effect on educational attainment.
Consider, for example, that graduation rates are low in schools that have large numbers of criminally inclined students (figure 19.2), and that schooling characteristics conducive to educational

FIGURE 19.8   *Changes in Groups' School Absences, Ninth Grade to the Last Semester of Enrollment*

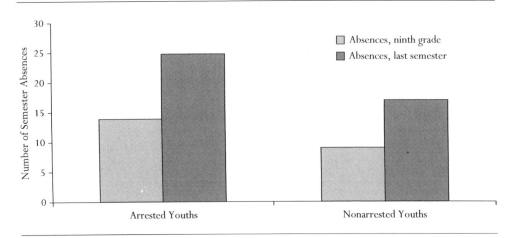

Source: Authors' compilation based on data from Project on Human Development in Chicago Neighborhoods (1995b); Illinois State Police (2003); Chicago Police Department (2003); and Chicago Public Schools (2006).
Note: The increases in the average number of absences from ninth grade to the last semester of enrollment between arrested and nonarrested youths are not statistically different.

attainment, such as safety, tend to be absent from schools with high arrest rates (figure 19.4). Still unanswered is the question: What is the most advantageous solution to the issue of school safety? Our findings suggest that misbehavior among students may be as much a consequence of school organizational characteristics (for example, lack of teacher commitment) as a cause (figure 19.6). It follows, then, that expelling problem students may do little to reverse the core educational deficiencies of a school. Among otherwise similar adolescents, 73 percent of those arrested later dropped out of high school compared with 51 percent of those not arrested, a substantial difference of 22 percent (figure 19.7).

Although there is no easy solution, we end here with some observations and recommendations for fostering school safety and, ultimately, educational attainment. As our findings demonstrate, a variety of social contexts influence educational attainment and youths' development. Schools are just one key context, with families and neighborhoods also of vital importance. Certainly the interdependency of school, family, and neighborhood influences bears upon the shape of human lives. For instance, Kirk (2009) finds that certain school characteristics accentuate the effect of neighborhood conditions on student misbehavior. In particular, he finds that a lack of neighborhood collective efficacy and a lack of school-based social controls combine to exert a substantial increase in the likelihood of student arrest.

Our concluding point, then, is that it is not sufficient to merely exhort or adjure schools to resolve the issue of school safety. A multicontext approach to fostering learning and acceptable social behavior is required. In contrast to strategies targeting the symptoms of educational failure and student misbehavior, we find promise in strategies designed to address the root causes. Fostering trust and a sense of community among teachers, principals, parents, and students should enhance the capacity of a school to provide a safe, productive learning environment (Bryk and Schneider 2002; Bryk, Lee, and Holland 1993; Coleman 1987; Kirk 2009). The solution to educational inequality and the related problem of crime is thus not to be found primarily in the criminal justice system, but is embedded in social contexts.

NOTES

Online appendix available at: http://www.russellsage.org/duncan_murnane_online_appendix.pdf.

1. All students in violation of the CPS Code of Student Conduct are afforded due process in disciplinary cases. Inappropriate behaviors are categorized into six groups, by increasing severity. Students engaging in Group 5 acts of misconduct are subject to up to ten days of suspension as well as expulsion. Those committing Group 6 acts are subject to ten days of suspension and expulsion for a minimum of one year. At expulsion hearings, both the CPS chief executive officer and the suspected student are provided the opportunity to present evidence. At the conclusion of the hearing, the hearing officer issues an opinion to the Chief Executive Officer with a disciplinary recommendation. Placement in alternative safe schools may be recommended for the period of expulsion. The chief executive officer then makes the final approval of the course of disciplinary action (Chicago Public Schools 2009b).

2. Gary Orfield and colleagues (2004) highlight a number of individual-level issues with the computation and reporting of statistics on dropping out of high school, which lead to widely varying estimates of dropout rates even from the same data sources. One issue is whether to consider "lost" students as dropouts or as students who relocated to another school district. For the purposes of this study, we adhere to practices established by CPS and CCSR, and we treat "lost" students as dropouts.

3. This policy changed on January 1, 2005. Now students must be seventeen years of age to drop out of the CPS system. However, all analyses are based on observation years prior to the policy change, when age sixteen was the cutoff for eligibility to drop out.

4. With information on the date of arrest, we are specifically able to determine whether the arrest occurred prior to the arrestee's dropout. Several longitudinal self-report studies of the effect of criminal justice sanctions on dropout have been unable to fully establish temporal ordering because arrest and dropout responses were given during the same survey wave with no indication of precedence (Bernburg and Krohn 2003; Hjalmarsson 2008; Sweeten 2006). One advantage of using school and police records in this study is thus the ability to establish the precise timing of life events.

5. Geographic addresses of arrests from the Chicago Police Department are available only from 1999 onward; however, self-report survey measures of arrest are not available for the 1999 Student Surveys of the Chicago Public Schools. We therefore must use different years of data in these analyses (1997 for student arrest prevalence and 1999 for the neighborhood arrest rate).

6. Community areas are aggregations of census tracts, averaging about 38,000 residents.

7. Similarly, we find modest correlations between the prevalence of school arrest and the neighborhood's rate of violent crime.

8. CPS computes a four-year graduation rate as the total number of students graduating from a school in June of the academic year divided by the number of students who entered the ninth grade in the fall four years earlier.

9. To compute a z-score for a given value, the mean value across the sample for a given variable is subtracted from the value for a specific observation, and this difference is then divided by the sample standard deviation. Converting to z-scores allows us to present results using a standard metric.

10. The difference between groups is known as imbalance. Imbalance is a problem if there are differences across groups in confounding factors—characteristics of youths that are related to the likelihood of both arrest and school dropout. If groups are imbalanced, a comparison of the prevalence of school dropout between arrestees and nonarrestees will not produce a valid estimate of the effect of arrest on educational attainment. To resolve any issues of imbalance, we adjust for differences between groups through propensity matching, described later in this chapter.

11. We estimated the propensity of arrest for each student using a logit model with arrest at any point during high school as the binary outcome variable. We dealt with the problem of missing data by implementing the multiple imputation by chained equation (MICE) algorithm to create five imputed data sets, and we calculated a propensity score of arrest for each observation in each of the imputed data sets (see Kirk and Sampson 2010 for further details). We then averaged the propensity scores for each respondent across the five imputed data sets. Following estimation of the propensity score, we matched each "treated" subject (arrested) with up to three control subjects (nonarrested) with very similar propensity scores (within a threshold of 0.03), with the objective of producing treatment and control groups that are indistinguishable except for the receipt of treatment after conditioning on propensity scores.

12. Of the 85 youths in the sample who had been arrested, we were able to match 79 to at least one and up to three otherwise similar nonarrested youths. Our matching procedure allowed for matches to be made with replacement—that is, each control observation could be used as a match for more than one treated observation.

In total, 117 control observations were used in the matching procedure. There were six arrestees in the sample whose propensity to be arrested for a crime was not similar to that of any of the nonarrested youths and therefore they not be statistically matched to any of the nonarrested youths. These six youths all had a predicted probability of being arrested of at least 0.70, and some were considerably greater. The 0.22 difference in school dropout reported in the text refers to the comparison between matched youth and excludes the six unmatched arrestees from the analysis. See Kirk and Sampson (2010) for a more extensive examination of the effect of arrest on educational attainment, including a sensitivity analysis that investigates the robustness of results to hidden biases from unobserved data.

13.   We thank Larry Katz for making this suggestion.

14.   The changes in the average number of absences from ninth grade to the last semester of enrollment between arrestees and nonarrested students are not statistically different.

REFERENCES

American Psychological Association (Zero Tolerance Task Force). 2008. "Are Zero Tolerance Policies Effective in the Schools? An Evidentiary Review and Recommendations." *American Psychologist* 63(9): 852–62.

Bernburg, Jon Gunnar, and Marvin D. Krohn. 2003. "Labeling, Life Chances, and Adult Crime: The Direct and Indirect Effects of Official Intervention in Adolescence on Crime in Early Adulthood." *Criminology* 41(4): 1287–1318.

Bilcer, Diane King. 1997. *User's Manual, Version 1: A Survey of Students and Teachers in the Chicago Public Schools.* Report. Chicago: Consortium on Chicago School Research.

Bingenheimer, Jeffrey B., Robert T. Brennan, and Felton J. Earls. 2005. "Firearm Violence and Serious Violent Behavior." *Science* 308(5726): 1323–26.

Black, Donald J., and Albert J. Reiss, Jr. 1970. "Police Control of Juveniles." *American Sociological Review* 35(1): 63–77.

Bowditch, Christine. 1993. "Getting Rid of Troublemakers: High School Disciplinary Procedures and the Production of Dropouts." *Social Problems* 40(4): 493–509.

Bryk, Anthony S., Valerie E. Lee, and Peter B. Holland. 1993. *Catholic Schools and the Common Good.* Cambridge, Mass.: Harvard University Press.

Bryk, Anthony S., and Barbara Schneider. 2002. *Trust in Schools: A Core Resource for Improvement.* New York: Russell Sage Foundation.

Cairns, Robert B., Beverley D. Cairns, and Holly J. Neckerman. 1989. "Early School Dropout: Configurations and Determinants." *Child Development* 60(6): 1437–52.

Centers for Disease Control and Prevention. 2008. "Youth Risk Behavior Surveillance—United States, 2007." *Morbidity and Mortality Weekly Report* 57 (No. SS-4). Surveillance Summaries, June 6. Atlanta: Centers for Disease Control and Prevention. Available at: http://www.cdc.gov/mmwr/preview/mmwrhtml/ss5704a1.htm (accessed on November 18, 2009).

Chicago Police Department. 1998. *Reported Crime Data, 1997.* Chicago: Chicago Police Department [producer and distributor].

————. 2003. *Arrest Data, 1995–2001.* Chicago: Chicago Police Department [producer]. Chicago: Chapin Hall at the University of Chicago [distributor].

————. 2008. *Citywide Arrest Data, 1999.* Chicago: Chicago Police Department [producer and distributor].

Chicago Public Schools. 1998. *School & Citywide Reports, 1997.* Chicago: Chicago Public Schools Office of Research, Evaluation, and Accountability [producer and distributor].

————. 2006. *Student-level Enrollment and Attendance Data, 1990–2005.* Chicago: Chicago Public Schools [producer]. Chicago: Chapin Hall at the University of Chicago [distributor].

————. 2009a. "Alternative Safe Schools." Information available at: www.cps.edu/Programs/Pathways_to_success/Alternative_education_and_transition/Pages/AlternativeSafeSchools.aspx (accessed March 21, 2011).

————. 2009b. "Student Code of Conduct for the Chicago Public School Students for the 2009–2010 School Year." In *Chicago Public Schools: Policy Manual.* Available at: http://policy.cps.k12.il.us (accessed November 18, 2009).

Coleman, James S. 1987. "Families and Schools." *Educational Researcher* 16(6): 32–38.

Consortium on Chicago School Research. 1997a. *Student Survey of the Chicago Public Schools, 1997.* Chicago: Consortium on Chicago School Research [producer and distributor].

————. 1997b. *Teacher Survey of the Chicago Public Schools, 1997.* Chicago: Consortium on Chicago School Research [producer and distributor].

Ekstrom, Ruth E., Margaret E. Goertz, Judith M. Pollack, and Donald A. Rock. 1986. "Who Drops Out of School and Why: Findings from a National Study." *Teachers College Record* 87(3): 356–73.

Fitzpatrick, Kevin M., and Janet P. Boldizar. 1993. "The Prevalence and Consequences of Exposure to Violence Among African-American Youth." *Journal of the American Academy of Adolescent Psychiatry* 32(2): 424–30.

Grogger, Jeffrey. 1997. "Local Violence and Educational Attainment." *Journal of Human Resources* 32(4): 659–82.

Harding, David J. 2009. "Collateral Consequences of Violence in Disadvantaged Neighborhoods." *Social Forces* 88(2): 757–82.

Hirschi, Travis. 1969. *Causes of Delinquency*. Berkeley: University of California Press.

Hjalmarsson, Randi. 2008. "Criminal Justice Involvement and High School Completion." *Journal of Urban Economics* 63(2): 613–30.

Illinois State Police. 2003. *Arrest Data, 1995–2001*. Chicago: Illinois Criminal Justice Information Authority [producer]. Chicago: Chapin Hall at the University of Chicago [distributor].

Kelly, Deirdre R. 1993. *Last Chance High: How Girls and Boys Drop In and Out of Alternative Schools*. New Haven, Conn.: Yale University Press.

Kirk, David S. 2008. "The Neighborhood Context of Racial and Ethnic Disparities in Arrest." *Demography* 45(1): 55–77.

———. 2009. "Unraveling the Contextual Effects on Student Suspension and Juvenile Arrest: An Examination of School, Neighborhood, and Family Controls." *Criminology* 47(2): 479–520.

Kirk, David S., and Robert J. Sampson. 2010. "Collateral Damage in the Transition to Adulthood: The Case of Juvenile Arrest and Later Educational Attainment." Working paper. Austin: University of Texas at Austin, Department of Sociology.

Margolin, Gayla, and Elana B. Gordis. 2000. "The Effects of Family and Community Violence on Children." *Annual Review of Psychology* 51: 445–79.

Morenoff, Jeffrey D., Robert J. Sampson, and Stephen W. Raudenbush. 2001. "Neighborhood Inequality, Collective Efficacy, and the Spatial Dynamics of Homicide." *Criminology* 39(3): 517–60.

Orfield, Gary, Daniel Losen, Johanna Wald, and Christopher B. Swanson. 2004. *Losing Our Future: How Minority Youth Are Being Left Behind by the Graduation Rate Crisis*. Cambridge, Mass.: Harvard University, Civil Rights Project.

Project on Human Development in Chicago Neighborhoods. 1995a. *Project on Human Development in Chicago Neighborhoods: Community Survey, 1995*. Boston: Harvard Medical School [producer and distributor].

———. 1995b. *Project on Human Development in Chicago Neighborhoods: Longitudinal Cohort Study*. Boston: Harvard Medical School [producer and distributor].

Robers, Simone, Jijun Zhang, Jennifer Truman, and Thomas D. Snyder. 2010. *Indicators of School Crime and Safety: 2010*. Washington, D.C.: National Center for Education Statistics, and Bureau of Justice Statistics.

Rosenbaum, Paul R. 2002. *Observational Studies*. New York: Springer.

Rumberger, Russell W. 1983. "Dropping Out of High School: The Influence of Race, Sex, and Family Background." *American Educational Research Journal* 20(2): 199–220.

Sampson, Robert J. 1987. "Urban Black Violence: The Effect of Male Joblessness and Family Disruption." *American Journal of Sociology* 93(2): 348–82.

Sampson, Robert J., Stephen W. Raudenbush, and Felton Earls. 1997. "Neighborhoods and Violent Crime: A Multilevel Study of Collective Efficacy." *Science* 277(5328): 918–24.

Shaw, Clifford R., and Henry D. McKay. 1942. *Juvenile Delinquency and Urban Areas*. Chicago: University of Chicago Press.

Skiba, Russ, and Reece Peterson. 1999. "The Dark Side of Zero Tolerance: Can Punishment Lead to Safe Schools?" *Phi Delta Kappan* 80(5): 372–82.

Sweeten, Gary. 2006. "Who Will Graduate? Disruption of High School Education by Arrest and Court Involvement." *Justice Quarterly* 23(4): 462–80.

U.S. Bureau of the Census. 1990. *Census of Population and Housing, 1990*. Washington: U.S. Department of Commerce, Bureau of the Census [producer and distributor].

Western, Bruce. 2006. *Punishment and Inequality in America*. New York: Russell Sage Foundation.

Chapter 20

Immigrants and Inequality in Public Schools

Amy Ellen Schwartz and Leanna Stiefel

In the study described in this chapter, we conduct a descriptive analysis exploring the context of immigration in the United States and, importantly, the relationship between academic performance and immigrant share in schools. Given the significant socio-economic inequality in the United States and the emphasis on improving educational outcomes for all students, understanding the impact that immigrants have on schools is critical, particularly for urban school districts, which disproportionately educate diverse immigrant and native-born student populations. We begin by analyzing national data detailing the large variation in the immigrant population over time and across the United States. We then focus on the New York City (NYC) experience and probe the differences in immigrant exposure to racial and ethnic subgroups in schools. We conclude with an analysis of the complex relationship between immigrant share in schools and grades and immigrant and native-born student performance.

First, we find that today's immigrants are different from immigrants of the past. Notably, there have been significant changes in the composition of the foreign-born population resulting from the passage of the Immigration and Nationality Act of 1965. Broadly, we see that today's immigrants are more likely to be Asian, Hispanic, poor, and limited English-proficient (LEP) than immigrants from previous decades. The foreign-born are not evenly distributed across the nation, which is reflected in the significant variation in immigrant populations between and within states, cities, and, significantly, school districts.

Second, the variation within the immigrant population means that although there are significant differences between foreign- and native-born students, there are also differences among immigrant students. Although large numbers of immigrants are poor or come from homes where no English is spoken, many come from families who are quite well off and speak only English. Thus, we need to be specific about the outcomes for the actual immigrants we study.

Although there is reason to be concerned about immigrant segregation, particularly into poorly performing and low-resourced schools, we find that immigrant isolation is lower than racial isolation. Further, consistent with previous research on resource allocation, we find that the NYC school district is no less generous in providing resources to immigrants than otherwise similar native-born students. There are stark differences in the types of schools attended by students of different races, however. Further, there is evidence that some foreign-born groups are more isolated than others, which appears to be due at least partially to ethnic clustering. In sum, the differences in exposure mean that immigrants with different socioeconomic characteristics are exposed to different native-born peers and vice versa, suggesting sorting and the possibility of differing impacts.

Turning to the implications for performance, we find that although immigrants, on average, outperform their native-born peers, there is variation within the immigrant population. Given the differences in exposure and in student performance, we hypothesize that there may be different associations between immigrant share and student performance. Estimates from a baseline ordinary least-squares regression show that schools with larger shares of immigrants have better performance. When we explore this relationship by native-born race group, however, we find that this overarching association masks heterogeneity within the native-born population. Specifically, we find that blacks and Hispanics have higher performance in schools with larger shares of immigrants, but the opposite is true for whites and Asians. Further, when we parse the variation to look specifically within schools and within grades, we find no positive relationship between immigrant share and achievement.

There are many questions that remain unanswered—specifically, exploring the causal relationships and identifying the mechanisms operating within schools. Undertaking this research may help more fruitfully illuminate this complicated relationship. In addition, it may provide policy makers and education administrators with the information needed to better address the needs of the diverse student populations in urban areas—a critical piece in mitigating disparities in educational outcomes arising from socioeconomic inequality.

The change in the size, distribution, and composition of the U.S. immigrant population during the past decades and the emphasis on improving academic performance and lessening disparities in achievement has led to a growing body of new research analyzing how newcomer students perform in U.S. schools. Notably, research has explored disparities within the immigrant student community by comparing differences in regions of origin, generational differences (first versus second), differences in language proficiency, or differences in the influence of coethnic communities (see Biavaschi, Stiefel, and Schwartz 2009; Glick and White 2003; Kao and Tienda 1995; Rumbaut and Portes 2001; Zhou and Bankston 1998). Although fewer studies have examined differences in performance between immigrants and their native-born peers, the existing research suggests that similar individual, family, and school characteristics that affect native-born performance also drive immigrant achievement. Very little work in the United States has explored the impact of the share of immigrant students (in a student's grade or school) on the achievement of native-born students in schools and grades, however, which is a notable omission in our understanding of whether and how the sorting of students into different schools perpetuates disadvantage. This chapter begins to fill that gap.

Much of the previous work examining the effect of immigrants on the native-born focuses on labor markets. Although this work generally has found that an increase in a community's immigrant population has a negative effect on the wages of low-skilled, native-born workers, evidence on the size of this impact is mixed. Some authors, such as Rachel M. Friedberg and Jennifer Hunt (1995) and David Card (2001), find that immigration has a small negative effect on employment rates and wages of low-skilled native-born workers. More recent work by George J. Borjas (2003), however, finds a larger negative impact on the wages of low-skilled native-born workers, particularly those without high school diplomas. At the same time, Gianmarco Ottaviano and Giovanni Peri (2005) argue that the small negative impact of immigration on low-skilled native-born wages and employment is outweighed by increased demand for higher-level workers and improved physical capital.

Although interest has been increasing recently, researchers have devoted less attention to the effect of immigrants in schools on the academic performance of fellow immigrant and native-born classmates. Peter Jensen and Astrid Wurtz Rasmussen (2008) conclude that a higher concentration of immigrants in Danish schools has a negative impact on the reading scores of immigrant and native students, although controlling for sorting in different neighborhoods yields a more modest negative impact on native Danes and no effect on immigrants. Similarly, Kalena E. Cortes (2006) finds that after controlling for nonrandom selection into immigrant enclave schools, there is no effect of attending an enclave school on reading or math test performance or assimilation profiles. Using data from Israel, Eric D. Gould, Victor Lavy, and M. Daniele Paserman (2008) show negative short- and long-term effects of high immigrant concentrations on the native-born, but the impact on fellow immigrant students is less clear. Jane Friesen and Brian Krauth (2008) find that the effect varies by immigrant group and attribute this variation to differences in human capital and cultural norms across immigrant groups. They do not explore the impact of immigrant concentration on the native-born. Thus, whether—and how—immigrants shape the performance of the native-born is not well understood.

At the same time, improving education in the United States and closing disparities among demographic groups require understanding how immigration affects the composition of schools and the achievement of native-born students. Schools are key institutions in promoting intergenerational mobility, and understanding whether and how immigrants affect them is important to correcting educational disparities and social inequality. In this chapter we begin to fill this gap in the literature, exploring the relationship between the presence of immigrants and the performance of native-born school and grade mates. Before turning to empirical work, it is worthwhile to consider the mechanisms through which immigrant presence might matter to native-born students.

First, variations in the proportions of immigrants might affect the level or kinds of resources allocated to schools. In addition to between-school differences, there might be impacts resulting from how resources are distributed within schools, if, for example, resources are channeled to educate immigrants in special language classes or acculturation programs.

Second, immigrants might affect academic performance through their interactions as peers. As is well known, obtaining clean estimates of peer effects is difficult, but there is some evidence that peers matter in important ways and that students are affected by the academic performance and socioeconomic status of their schoolmates.[1] If immigrants are particularly motivated students with high academic aspirations who receive encouragement from their families and communities, these traits could boost peer performance. Alternatively, if immigrants have poor academic skills or limited family and community resources and support, they may be "low-quality" peers. Thus, the impact of immigrants may depend on their own characteristics (limited English proficient [LEP], poverty, family background, ties to their ethnic community), and the extent to which they interact with other students. To the extent that immigrants with different socioeconomic characteristics are unevenly concentrated in different neighborhoods and schools, there likely will be different impacts on student performance.

In this chapter we explore whether and how changes in the size and composition of the foreign-born population during the past half-century shape the relationship between academic performance and the proportion of immigrants in schools. We begin with a broad perspective, drawing on previous literature and national data to examine trends in immigration, the variation between states and cities, and the changes in the composition of schools and student performance. Because understanding how immigrants affect schools is particularly important for urban districts, which disproportionately attract large immigrant communities and face the challenge of educating diverse student populations with limited resources, we then focus on the New York City (NYC) experience to gain insight into the relationship between the characteristics and concentration of immigrants and resource distribution and native-born performance.

As the largest and perhaps most diverse K–12 public school system in the country, NYC provides an excellent setting to study immigrants and inequality in public schools. NYC has a higher proportion of foreign-born people than the rest of the United States: 28.3 percent of the population and 9 percent of school-age children, which is considerably more than the 12.6 percent of the nation's population and 5 percent of its school-age children.[2] Only Miami and Los Angeles have larger percentages of foreign-born populations.

In addition, NYC's immigrant students are incredibly varied. Of the nearly 17 percent of NYC's public elementary- and middle-school students who were born outside the United States, there is substantial racial-ethnic, socioeconomic, and cultural diversity. NYC's foreign-born students hail from more than 200 countries and speak more than 160 languages.[3]

We are able to explore this broad variation using rich administrative data from the NYC Department of Education. In this chapter we use data on all third- through eighth-grade students in NYC public schools between 1997 and 2002.[4] The data include detailed demographic and academic information for each student, including birthplace, race, gender, English-language ability, language spoken at home, poverty, resource-room (or part-time special education) participation, and standardized test scores. We define a student as foreign-born if his or her birthplace is not in the United States.

The remainder of the chapter proceeds as follows: We begin by exploring how the context of U.S. immigration varies with time and between and within cities. In the next section, we explore the distribution of immigrant students across recipient schools in NYC and, particularly, the possibility that they are disproportionately located in poorly resourced or low-performing schools. We then look at the performance of immigrant students in U.S. schools and compare differences between the foreign- and native-born on raw performance measures, measures adjusted for selected student characteristics, and measures by region of origin. Finally, we look at the relationship between performance and representation of foreign-born students in NYC schools. We conclude with explanations and suggestions for future research that might fruitfully illuminate this complicated relationship.

TWENTY-FIRST-CENTURY IMMIGRANTS IN THE UNITED STATES

Although the size of the foreign-born population in the United States is larger than ever, immigrants today represent a smaller percentage of the total population than they did a century ago, because much of the twentieth century saw the proportion of foreign-born decline significantly (see figure 20.1). The share of foreign-born in the total U.S. population peaked in 1910, at 14.7 percent and then fell to 4.7 percent by 1970; it rose above 10 percent only after 2000. An important explanation of these trends is the change in U.S. immigration policy. The Immigration Act of 1924 formally established a national-origins quota system that excluded immigrants from Asia and limited the number of immigrants of other nationalities.[5] Forty years later, the Immigration and Nationality Act of 1965 repealed the quota system, which resulted in increases in the number and proportion of foreign-born among the overall population.

Composition of the New Immigrant Population

At the same time, the composition of this new immigrant population significantly changed. Today's immigrants are less likely to be European and are more likely to be South American or Asian than immigrants of the twentieth century.[6] In the early twentieth century more than 85 percent of the

FIGURE 20.1   *Trends in U.S. Immigration, 1850 to 2000*

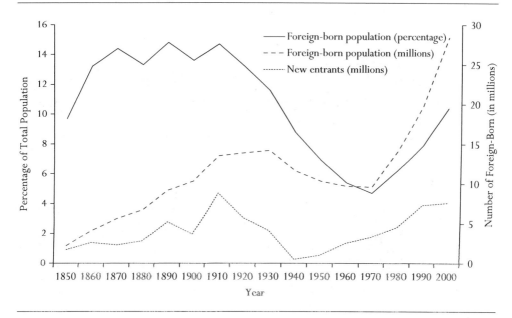

Source: Authors' adaptation of Schmidley (2001, figures 1.1 and 1.2).

foreign-born emigrated from Europe; one century later, a majority (51 percent) hailed from Latin America. Interestingly, in 2000, one-quarter of the overall foreign-born population was Mexican, representing the largest share any country has held since the Germans dominated in 1890 with 30 percent (see figure 20.2).[7]

An important point is that today's immigrants are also more likely than their predecessors to be poor. As reported by Steven Raphael and Eugene Smolensky (2009), the proportion of immigrants in poverty increased from roughly 15 percent to 18 percent between 1970 and 2005, although no such increase occurred for the native-born. The rise largely reflects increases in the shares of immigrants from high-poverty countries—there was little change in the poverty rates within groups of immigrants from particular countries.[8] As a result, on average, the overall immigrant population is poorer than the native-born. Recent poverty rates for the foreign-born are roughly six percentage points above rates for the native-born (see figure 20.3).

Unsurprisingly, immigrant students nationally are quite diverse. Descriptive statistics for immigrant children up to age seventeen show significant variation in their racial background, language ability, and economic status, as well as that of their native-born peers. (See online appendix table 20.A3, available at http://www.russellsage.org/duncan_murnane_online_appendix.pdf.) Many immigrants are still learning English, but many others speak English well. In fact, nearly 16 percent speak only English. Further, many native-born students speak a language other than English at home (13 percent are bilingual), and nearly 4 percent of native-born students qualify for English-language services in school. In addition, both immigrant and native-born students are racially and economically diverse. For example, though more than half of foreign-born students are Hispanic, there are sizable Asian (21 percent), white (18 percent), and African American populations (8 percent). Although the racial distribution is different among the native-born—a much larger white population in particular (60 percent)—nearly 20 percent of the native-born are

FIGURE 20.2   *Immigrants' Region of Origin, 1960 to 2000*

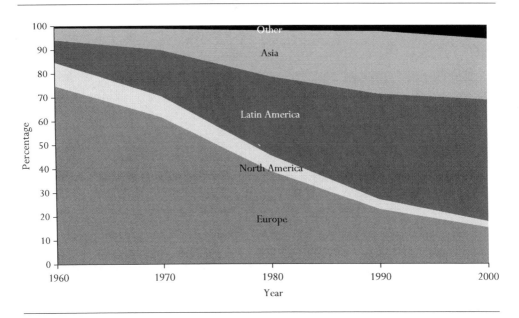

Source: Authors' adaptation of Schmidley (2001, figure 2.2).

FIGURE 20.3   *Poverty Rates, by Region of Origin, 1995, 2000, and 2005*

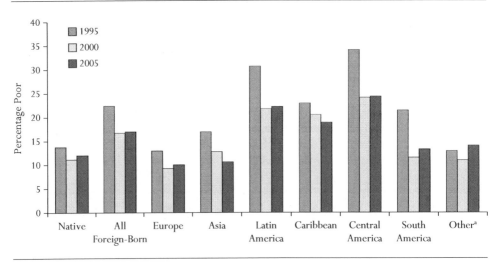

Source: Authors' compilation, based on U.S. Bureau of the Census (1995, 2000, 2005).
[a]Includes immigrants from Africa, Oceania, and North America.

Hispanic and more than 15 percent are black. In addition, although larger shares of immigrant children live in poverty (58 percent are below twice the poverty line), many native-born children also come from low-income families (38 percent are below twice the poverty line) or families with low education levels (11 percent have parents who did not graduate high school).

Variation in Size of Immigrant Communities Between and Within States and Cities

Although some states experience little immigration, others have large immigrant communities. In particular, the populations of six states—California, New York, Florida, Texas, New Jersey, and Illinois—include more than one million foreign-born residents. Combined, these represent more than 70 percent of the foreign-born population, considerably more than the 40 percent of the total U.S. population residing in these states (Schmidley 2001).

The same demographic diversity seen at the national level is evident in the six largest immigrant-recipient states (see online appendix table 20.A4). In these states, relative to their native-born peers, the foreign-born are more likely to be LEP, poor, or come from families with lower levels of education. There are, however, significant differences in the composition of immigrants across states. For example, in California and Texas, more than 60 percent of immigrant children up to seventeen years old are Hispanic and 40 percent are LEP. In contrast, in New Jersey and New York, less than 40 percent are Hispanic and, as in Florida, less than 30 percent are LEP.

Notice, however, that there is also significant diversity in the composition of native-born students across states. For example, Hispanic native-born children range from less than 18 percent in New Jersey to 47 percent in California. These same children are almost 9 percent LEP in California but less than 5 percent in New Jersey. At the same time, immigrants disproportionately settle in large urban areas. As noted by Jennifer E. Glick and Michael J. White (2009), more than half of the foreign-born in the United States live in the ten largest U.S. cities. Further, Schmidley (2001) estimates that nearly 95 percent of the foreign-born live in large metropolitan areas. That said, there is wide variation in the characteristics of immigrant communities across metropolitan areas. As shown in figure 20.4, Miami and Houston schools educate immigrants who are almost entirely from the Americas; foreign-born students in the Los Angeles schools are also largely from the Americas, but more than one in five are Asian. In contrast, NYC and Chicago schools have greater diversity—including significant populations from many continents—and more closely mirror the national composition.

The NYC data allow us greater insight into the differences between native-born and foreign-born students in 2000. As shown in table 20.1, foreign-born students are four times as likely to be LEP, twice as likely to speak a language other than English at home, and slightly more likely to be poor than their native-born peers. As might be expected, race and ethnicity matter here: LEP students are particularly concentrated among the Hispanic foreign-born (44.4 percent) and native-born (12.5 percent) and, to some extent, among the Asian foreign-born (13.4 percent) as well. Blacks and whites, regardless of nativity, have low levels of participation in LEP programs.[9] This is further reflected in the large percentages of Hispanic and Asian students who do not speak English at home (more than 70 percent for all racial-ethnic subgroups). In addition, we see that poverty is concentrated among the black and Hispanic populations, both native- and foreign-born; at least 85 percent are poor.

To summarize, the dramatic shift in the composition of the foreign-born in the United States in terms of country of origin, poverty, and race during the last fifty years has led to considerable heterogeneity in immigrant- and native-student populations. Although some immigrants are LEP

FIGURE 20.4   *Immigrant Concentrations, Nationally and for Five Large School Districts, 2006 Estimates*

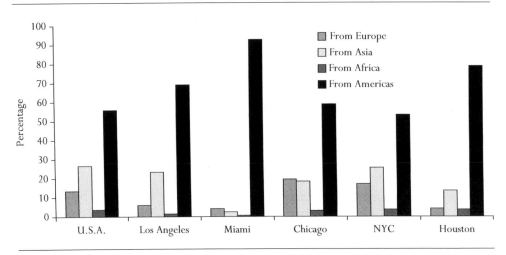

Source: Authors' compilation, based on U.S. Bureau of the Census (2006, school-district-level estimates).

TABLE 20.1   *NYC Third-Through Eighth-Grade Student Characteristics, by Race and Nativity, 2000 (Percentages)*

	Overall		White		Black		Hispanic		Asian	
	NB	FB	NB	FB	NB	FB	NB	FB	NB	FB
Female	50.8	49.6	49.1	48.5	51.8	51.6	51.0	50.1	48.4	47.8
Poor	76.4	80.7	34.7	55.9	84.5	85.8	87.9	92.9	62.5	74.6
Resource room	6.6	3.3	7.2	3.1	6.2	3.7	7.7	3.6	3.0	2.6
LEP	5.3	21.6	0.6	5.5	0.8	4.2	12.5	44.4	2.7	13.4
English not spoken at home	37.7	72.1	16.4	92.1	5.2	14.0	73.2	94.9	70.0	75.4
Observations	343,821	63,852	54,873	10,766	132,087	13,988	127,838	23,829	29,023	15,269

Source: Authors' calculations using data from the year 2000 from New York City Department of Education (1997–2002).
Note: NB denotes native-born and FB denotes foreign-born.

or poor, others are quite wealthy and benefit from well-educated families. There are significant populations of immigrants of every racial and ethnic group, matching the similar variation in the native-born population, and implying that the impact of immigrants on schools is likely to be varied and dependent on the students' educational needs and characteristics. Further, if immigrants of different backgrounds and needs are unevenly distributed across schools, their impact on native-born students is likely to vary across schools. Moreover, to the extent that the characteristics of native-born and immigrant students are related, perhaps because poor immigrants are more likely to enroll in schools with poor native-born students, the impact on native-born populations may well be uneven. Obtaining a more comprehensive understanding of how social and economic inequalities contribute to challenges in K–12 education thus requires a more detailed examination of the roles immigrants play, accounting for their varied socioeconomic backgrounds.

THE PLACEMENT AND TREATMENT OF IMMIGRANTS
IN U.S. PUBLIC SCHOOLS

There is considerable evidence of segregation along racial and socioeconomic lines, but less is known about current segregation of immigrants between neighborhoods and schools. That said, the long history of school segregation and immigrant enclaves in the United States suggests that immigrants are unevenly distributed across schools within cities. Even more, our previous research suggests that some groups may be concentrated in poorly resourced, low-performing schools.[10]

To set the stage, we examine data from the Neighborhood Change Database to examine the concentration of immigrants in the population of school-attendance zones used by NYC (the practice in much of the United States) to assign elementary and middle school students to schools.[11] Although some students attend school "out of zone," the composition of the residents of the school zone significantly shapes the composition of the student body as well as community support for the school.

The average NYC school zone has a mix of races and backgrounds, but there is substantial variation in the level of concentration of representation of the foreign-born, as well as other racial-ethnic groups, income classes, and so on (see online appendix table 20.A6). Although the average school zone is 31 percent white, 30 percent black, 29 percent Hispanic, and 9 percent Asian, some zones are racially quite homogeneous, with more than 90 percent of residents belonging to a single racial-ethnic group (white, black, or Hispanic).

At the same time, there is broad variation in the representation of immigrants (see online appendix figure 20.A1). Most NYC school zones have significant shares of immigrants, and in some of them immigrants are a majority. Although the average zone is roughly one-third immigrant, some are almost entirely native-born (roughly 95 percent), and, at the other extreme, some zones are almost three-quarters foreign-born. Thus, there is a concentration of immigrants in some school zones.

Differences in neighborhoods' immigrant concentrations alone are unlikely to result in unequal distributions of resources across schools. There is little in school-resource-allocation formulas that explicitly links resources to the characteristics of the overall population of a zone. According to the NYC school-district policies, school resources are distributed according to formulas that allocate resources on the basis of student and school characteristics. Differences in students drive some of the differences in school resources: a variety of federal and state programs direct additional resources toward schools serving students who are poor (Title I), have special education needs (English as a second language), and so on. Much previous research documents the relationship between resources and school populations: schools with higher percentages of poor students and minority students are often found to have more money and higher numbers of teachers per student than otherwise similar schools (see Rubenstein et al. 2007). Their teachers, however, are more likely to be inexperienced and to receive lower salaries (see, for example, Clotfelter, Ladd, and Vigdor 2006; Iatarola and Stiefel 2003; Lankford, Loeb, and Wyckoff 2002; Rubenstein et al. 2007).

Taken together, then, the racial and economic diversity of NYC public schools and the differences in school resources create conditions under which the impact of immigration can be quite different for students of different racial or economic backgrounds. Thus, we examine whether—and in what way—school resources, characteristics, and peers differ among students of different races and nativity.

To begin, we note that research on the relationship between immigrants and resource allocation is particularly limited, but existing research provides no evidence that schools are less generous in providing resources to immigrants relative to otherwise similar native-born students. Although Amy Ellen Schwartz and Alec Ian Gershberg (2001) find that immigrant children, on average, attend schools with fewer resources, this relationship disappears when the composition of the school's students is controlled (see Schwartz and Stiefel 2004). School resources differ because of differences in educational needs (LEP, special education, and so on) but not because of nativity in and of itself.

We reexamine this finding using NYC Department of Education administrative data for 2000 and note that the differences in school resources experienced by foreign-born and native-born students are not large (see online appendix table 20.A7a). On average, foreign-born students attend larger schools than native-born (1,151 students versus 1,012, respectively), but differences in other variables are modest. But we find that there are large disparities in the characteristics of the teachers of students of different races. Whites and Asians, both native- and foreign-born, attend schools with more qualified and educated teachers than their black and Hispanic peers. The nativity differences between the schools experienced by the foreign-born and the native-born of the same race are no larger than two percentage points, whereas differences in schools attended by different races are wide. In the end, disparities in teaching resources seem to fall along racial, not nativity, lines.

Of course, school resources are not limited to purchased inputs; peers also matter. To examine the relevance of peers, we look at the exposure of students of particular nativity-race groups to students of other sociodemographic groups (see online appendix table 20.A7b). We see a gap of approximately seven percentage points between native- and foreign-born children's exposure to foreign-born students in schools overall, which may reflect the residential concentration of immigrants in particular school zones. The gap in exposure to foreign-born students is largest among whites: the average foreign-born white student attends schools where more than a quarter of the students are foreign-born, whereas an average native-born white student attends schools that are only 13.5 percent foreign-born. Interestingly, as is the case with purchased resources, the differences between nativity within race are much smaller than those among races. For example, exposure to students of the same race group (racial isolation) is significant: although the average school is roughly 16 percent white, 33 percent black, 33 percent Hispanic, and slightly more than 10 percent Asian, we find that blacks, Hispanics, and native-born whites all attend schools where more than 50 percent of the students are of their own race.[12] Further, there are differences in exposure to poverty: both native- and foreign-born blacks and Hispanics attend schools where a significantly larger proportion of the student body is poor.

Taken together, these statistics show that students of different races in NYC attend schools that are very different, which points to the challenges that schools face in addressing social inequality and facilitating equality of opportunity. On average, whites and Asians (whether immigrant or native) go to schools that are racially isolated and have higher-quality teachers. Hispanics and blacks are less likely to attend school with whites and Asians and are significantly more likely to go to schools suffering from high levels of poverty. This not only highlights the level of segregation and inequality that remains in the public school system, but also suggests that subgroups of students face challenges that other subgroups may not encounter.

Although immigrants do not appear to be segregated from the native-born, we do see different exposure to subgroups of immigrant peers, which is of particular relevance for this analysis. Overall, the average foreign- and native-born student is exposed to similar immigrant schoolmates, with calculated exposure indices differing by around 2 percent; the exceptions are the exposure to foreign-born blacks (28 percent versus 22 percent) and Asians (19 percent versus 24 percent; see online appendix table 20.A7c). Looking at different race groups, however, again reveals notable differences. For example, the average student in each race group, whether native- or foreign-born, goes to school where the majority of the immigrant population is of the same race. Further, both black and Hispanic native- and foreign-born students attend school where more than 85 percent of the immigrant population is poor. There are also differences in the exposure to foreign-born students with limited English proficiency: whites, regardless of nativity, attend schools where less than 10 percent of the foreign-born are LEP. Native-born Hispanics, however, attend schools where 30 percent of the foreign-born are not English proficient—and the share is higher for the average foreign-born Hispanic (nearly 36 percent). This implies that the distribution of immigrants among schools may contribute to preexisting socioeconomic differences between schools, as they appear to attend schools with native-born students of similar social and economic backgrounds.

Finally, race plays an important role in exposure to immigrants from different regions (see table 20.2), which, as we highlight later in this chapter, has significant implications for the background characteristics and raw performance of their immigrant peers. An average white student is more likely to go to school with students from the former U.S.S.R. (note that foreign-born whites attend schools where nearly 40 percent of their foreign-born schoolmates are from the former U.S.S.R.), whereas an average black student goes to school where more than 50 percent of the foreign-born population are from the Dominican Republic or the Caribbean, and an average Hispanic student goes to school where more than one-fifth of the foreign-born population is from Mexico and another 40 to 50 percent are from the Dominican Republic or another Caribbean island. Thus, if country of origin signals differences in academic preparation or educational disadvantage, then these differences may translate into important differences in the peers that black, Hispanic, white, and Asian students have in NYC public schools.

In summary, although these exposure indices provide troubling evidence of stark disparities in school resources, composition, and peers, they provide no explanations as to why such variations occur. The differences in resources and student-body composition may have important implications for understanding the relationship between performance and immigrant share. White, native-born students attending schools where the immigrant population is majority white, Asian, proficient in English, and from high-income families are exposed to immigrants in ways that are significantly different from native-born Hispanic students who do not speak English at home and go to a school with immigrants who are majority black, Hispanic, LEP, and poor. We turn next to the implications for student performance.

IMMIGRANT PERFORMANCE IN U.S. PUBLIC SCHOOLS

Although a large body of research examines varied achievement by race and ethnicity, fewer quantitative studies explore differences in performance between native- and foreign-born students.[13] There are several reasons that nativity might matter.[14] First, immigrant students may differ in family and home circumstances (such as income, education, family composition, or parental marital status), which may influence their academic achievement.[15] Second, depending on their age at immigration, foreign-born students enter U.S. schools with a different educational background than their native-born peers. These backgrounds may hinder performance if immigrants come from countries with less rigorous education systems and have low levels of English proficiency or may enhance performance if they come from countries with well-developed education systems and there is selective migration. Third, there may be cultural differences in the emphasis, support, and encouragement an immigrant student's family and community place on education that may cause immigrant children to succeed academically (Waters 1999). Finally, there may be differences in the experiences that foreign- and native-born students have in school—either between schools (differences in resources or composition) or within schools or classrooms (such as ability grouping or special language classes).

Importantly, these potential explanations imply that there is no one immigrant experience and that a variety of factors may influence immigrant performance in U.S. schools. As a result, it is not

TABLE 20.2   Exposure Index:ᵃ Origin of Foreign-Born Schoolmates, New York City Public Schools, by Race and Nativity, 2000 (Percentages)

Region of Birth	Overall		White		Black		Hispanic		Asian	
	Native-Born	Foreign-Born	Native-Born	Foreign-Born	Native-Born	Foreign-Born	Native-Born	Foreign-Born	Native-Born	Foreign-Born
Former U.S.S.R.	7.0	10.3	20.0	37.8	3.3	2.9	3.8	2.7	13.2	9.7
Other Eastern Europe	3.7	3.5	9.4	8.7	1.3	1.0	3.5	2.5	4.3	3.6
Western Europe	3.6	2.6	6.8	4.1	3.4	2.8	2.5	1.7	3.7	2.8
China	4.8	6.5	8.5	7.7	1.7	1.1	3.8	3.2	16.6	15.8
East Asia	4.4	4.2	9.2	4.6	2.6	2.4	3.1	2.9	8.8	7.4
South Asia	6.0	7.7	8.7	9.1	3.6	2.9	5.8	5.9	12.4	13.9
West Asia or North Africa	2.3	2.2	5.3	4.4	1.3	1.0	1.7	1.4	3.4	3.0
Sub-Saharan Africa	3.9	2.4	2.2	1.3	5.5	4.4	3.3	2.3	1.7	1.4
Dominican Republic	21.3	20.2	5.2	4.3	18.1	11.1	34.8	40.3	7.2	8.5
Other Caribbean	19.9	17.1	6.7	4.9	36.7	50.1	10.9	8.5	8.1	8.9
Non-Spanish South America	6.1	6.4	2.5	1.7	8.9	11.0	4.8	4.5	5.8	8.3
Mexico, Central and South America	16.2	16.5	15.2	11.2	12.1	8.6	21.3	23.6	14.5	16.3
Observations	343,584	63,852	54,866	10,766	131,924	13,988	127,774	23,829	29,020	15,269

Source: Authors' calculations using data from the year 2000 from New York City Department of Education (1997–2002).
ᵃThe exposure indices report the share of a school's population belonging to a certain group for an average student of particular nativity and race.

FIGURE 20.5   *Raw Scores, NYC Third- Through Eighth-Graders, 2000*

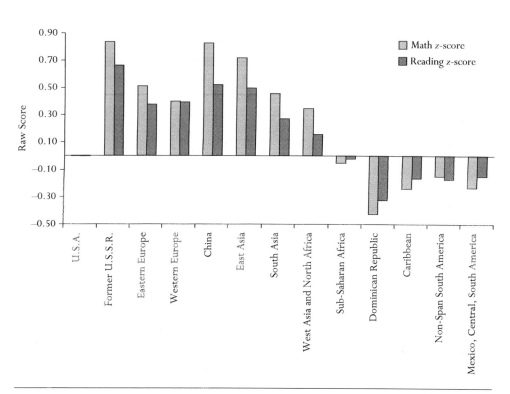

Source: Authors' calculations, based on data from the year 2000 from NYC Department of Education (1997–2002).
Note: See online appendix table 20.A8 for sample sizes among test takers from each subgroup. Raw test scores for students from the United States are slightly negative but essentially zero.

surprising that studies rarely present data for raw performance on aggregate native- and foreign-born scores, and those that do (or at least reference raw test scores) tend to report different findings. For example, using data on NYC immigrants, Schwartz and Stiefel (2006) find that immigrants have higher raw scores than their native-born peers on standardized math and reading tests. In contrast, using two cohorts of students from the 1980 High School and Beyond Survey and the 1988 National Education Longitudinal Study, Glick and White (2009) find that immigrant students have lower raw test scores than their peers who have been in the United States longer.

To begin, we examine the performance of NYC students by country of origin. As shown in figure 20.5, we find sizable differences in raw test scores by region for NYC students in grades 3 through 8 in 2000, with some immigrants performing better than the native-born and others performing worse. Immigrants from China and East Asia have particularly high scores, as do children from the former Soviet Union, whereas immigrants from Latin America have lower scores, and children from the Dominican Republic perform particularly poorly.

Fully controlling for background characteristics yields findings that are more consistent across the literature. Holding constant a host of student and family background and socioeconomic characteristics, research consistently finds that immigrants outperform otherwise similar native-born peers.[16] Simply put, the variation in performance among the foreign-born seems to be driven by factors similar to those driving the variation in performance among the native-born.[17] Specifically, immigrants who are white, Asian, and English-proficient and who come from higher-income and better-educated families have higher achievement levels, on average, than others.[18]

It is notable that the variation in performance among immigrants seen in figure 20.5 persists even after controlling for student, parent, school, and neighborhood characteristics (see Chiswick and Deb Burman 2004; Glick and White 2003; Kao 1999; Perreira, Harris, and Lee 2006; Rumbaut and Portes 2001; Portes and MacLeod 1996). In previous work, although we still found evidence of interregional differences among the foreign-born using an education production function, the estimated disparities between the foreign- and native-born favored immigrant students, regardless of region (Schwartz and Stiefel 2006).[19]

THE RELATIONSHIP BETWEEN IMMIGRANT CONCENTRATIONS AND THE PERFORMANCE OF NATIVE STUDENTS

To explore the relationship between performance and the concentration of immigrants in a school, we estimate a series of regression models linking a student's performance and the size and characteristics of immigrants in his or her school or grade.[20] The most parsimonious model is as follows:

$$(20.1) \qquad TEST_{it} = \alpha + \beta \ PERCENTFB_{it} + \varepsilon_{it},$$

where $TEST_{it}$ captures the performance of student (i) in year (t) on standardized math (reading) tests, $PERCENTFB$ measures the percentage of students in student i's school in year t who are immigrants, ε_{it} is a statistical-error term with usual properties, and β captures the average difference in student i's test score that is associated with a 1 percentage point increase in the share of immigrant students in his or her school in year t. As described earlier, we use data on students in grades 3 through 8 in NYC public schools to calculate the percentage of immigrant students in a school (grade) for each year (1997 to 2002).

The relationship estimated in this model reflects the variation both between and within schools. To disentangle the "between-schools" from the "within-schools" components, we next introduce school fixed effects to the model. In this way, the fixed effects capture the time-invariant differences between schools, and the association captured by β is only identified by variation within schools over time. Finally, we replace the school fixed effects with grade-school effects, which probe the variation within grades over time. Thus, we attempt to parse this relationship into the pieces that are due to variation within and between grades and schools.

Following the discussion earlier, we explore the relationship first for all students, then separately for the native- and foreign-born, and then, finally, by race group. In the end, we hope to shed light on whether the observed relationships reflect associations that are consistent for all groups or specific to the subgroup.

Is Performance Lower in Schools with More Immigrants?

We measure performance using both math and reading scores, measured as z-scores.[21] The results indicate that both math and reading performance are higher in schools with more immigrants overall, and for both the foreign-born and native-born populations separately (see table 20.3). Although the point estimates differ, the associations are both positive.

The strength of this association differs for subgroups. Blacks and Hispanics have slightly higher performance in schools with larger immigrant populations, but whites and Asians do not.[22] Although the performance of whites and Asians decreases with higher immigrant shares,

TABLE 20.3   Math and Reading Performance, by School's Percentage Immigrant, by Nativity and Race, 1997 to 2002

	All (1)	Foreign-Born (2)	Native-Born (3)	Native-Born			
				Black (4)	Hispanic (5)	Asian (6)	White (7)
Math							
School's percentage immigrant	0.0043***	0.0058***	0.0036***	0.0005***	0.0016***	−0.0035***	−0.0057***
Standard error	(0.0001)	(0.0002)	(0.0001)	(0.0001)	(0.0001)	(0.0002)	(0.0002)
Observations	2,241,280	357,899	1,883,381	724,282	695,543	157,324	306,231
R-squared	0.002	0.005	0.001	0.001	0.000	0.002	0.004
Reading							
School's percentage immigrant	0.0018***	0.0030***	0.0009***	0.0010***	0.0006***	−0.0055***	−0.0067***
Standard error	(0.0001)	(0.0002)	(0.0001)	(0.0001)	(0.0001)	(0.0002)	(0.0002)
Observations	2,113,801	303,144	1,810,657	704,351	655,774	152,536	297,995
R-squared	0.000	0.001	0.000	0.000	0.000	0.005	0.005

Source: Authors' calculations using data from New York City Department of Education (1997–2002).
Note: All models include year dummies. Robust standard errors in parentheses.
***$p < 0.01$.

their higher initial levels of performance (z-scores above 0.6 for both compared to z-scores below −0.2 for Hispanics and blacks) mean that each group remains above the performance levels of Hispanics and blacks (see online appendix figure 20.A2). Further, at approximately 14.5 percent (the average exposure to foreign-born students among the native-born), white and Asian performance is still quite high.

Parsing the Variation: Digging Deeper

The parsimonious specification means that we estimated the relationship identified both by variation between schools and by variation within schools. Thus, the associations reflect persistent differences between schools—the fact that some are "immigrant destination" schools with high immigrant representation—as well as the variation over time within schools whose share of immigrant students waxes or wanes. To disentangle these effects, we reestimate the model including school fixed effects. For brevity, we show only models for math performance.[23]

We find that higher shares of immigrants are consistently associated with lower performance in math—overall, for both the foreign- and native-born, and, within the native-born, for blacks, Hispanics, and whites (see table 20.4). Although there is little variation in the magnitudes of these relationships, ranging from −0.0029 to −0.0076, only for the native-born Asians is there no significant relationship. Thus, there is no evidence of a positive association between immigrants and academic performance.

Next, we parse the association more finely by substituting grade-school effects for school effects, controlling for differences between grades within a school (for example, differences in the rigor of the curriculum both between grades at the same school and in the same grade at different schools).[24] To do so, we measure the proportion of immigrant students at the grade level and then estimate the association between performance on standardized tests and the percentage of immigrants in a student's grade in a given school in a given year.

These relationships are less clear than the school results (see the second panel of table 20.4), but again, no evidence of a positive association is found. An increase in the proportion of immigrants in a particular grade at a particular school is associated with slightly lower performance overall (−0.0011). There is a negative association between the percentage of immigrant students in a grade and immigrants' math scores (−0.0048). The association between performance and all the native-born subgroups is insignificant.

DISCUSSION

What do these results mean? Students in schools with more immigrants have higher performance. That said, our fixed-effects regressions show that this positive association largely reflects variation between schools, some of which have more immigrants and some, less, suggesting that the distribution of immigrants among schools may be driving the results. Looking just at the variation within schools, we find a negative relationship. Variation within grades suggests, again, a small negative or insignificant relationship between performance and immigrant share. Importantly, however, these are descriptive findings and do not identify underlying causal mechanisms, which may have to do with peer groups, within-school effects, or mobility more broadly.

The different exposures of subgroups of native-born children to different subgroups of immigrants mean that the peer-group effects of immigrants may be substantially heterogeneous. As always, disentangling the causal impact of peers is challenging because peer groups are endogenous. If peer groups were randomly assigned, then we might estimate the impact by including an appropriate set of variables that would capture the characteristics of the peer group

TABLE 20.4   *Math Performance, by School's or Grade's Percentage Immigrant, by Nativity and Race, 1997 to 2002*

	All (1)	Foreign-Born (2)	Native-Born (3)	Native-Born			
				Black (4)	Hispanic (5)	Asian (6)	White (7)
School fixed effects							
School's percentage immigrant	-0.0046***	-0.0076***	-0.0035***	-0.0035*	-0.0029**	-0.0000	-0.0036***
Standard error	(0.0011)	(0.0016)	(0.0011)	(0.0019)	(0.0013)	(0.0018)	(0.0017)
Number of fixed effects	1,090	1,086	1,090	1,087	1,089	1,046	1,034
R-squared	0.195	0.223	0.194	0.106	0.093	0.175	0.147
Grade school fixed effects							
Grade's percentage immigrant	-0.0011**	-0.0048***	-0.0003	-0.0006	-0.0001	0.0011	-0.0002
Standard error	(0.0006)	(0.0009)	(0.0005)	(0.0009)	(0.0006)	(0.0011)	(0.0009)
Number of fixed effects	3,732	3,671	3,731	3,705	3,709	3,345	3,234
R-squared	0.202	0.233	0.202	0.117	0.103	0.191	0.157
Observations	2,241,280	357,899	1,883,381	724,282	695,543	157,324	306,231

Source: Authors' calculations using data from New York City Department of Education (1997–2002).

Note: All models include year dummies. Test scores measured as z-scores. A grade school fixed effect allows each grade in every school to have a unique intercept. This means that the intercept for third-graders in school A will be different from the intercept for fourth-graders in school A and for third-graders in school B. Robust standard errors, adjusted for within-school clusters, in parentheses.

***$p < 0.01$, **$p < 0.05$, *$p < 0.1$

in a model. Unfortunately, peer groups are rarely randomly determined and instead, as is well known, typically reflect important socioeconomic processes that would bias regression results (Manski 1993).

To be concrete, immigrants may disproportionately reside in schools serving neighborhoods with low rents, and these neighborhoods may also be home to low-performing, low-income native-born students. In this case, a naïve interpretation of estimated regression coefficients might suggest that immigrants harm the performance of native-born students, even though the underlying causal mechanism is quite different. One way of dealing with this endogenous sorting is to use instrumental variables. Although locating an appropriate instrument is challenging, exploring the use of the ethnic concentration in a larger geographic area (citywide or at a school) as an instrument for localized ethnic concentration may be a good place to start (see Andersson, Burgess, and Lane 2009; Jensen and Wurtz Rasmussen 2008).

Causality may be better understood by focusing inside the school. We would benefit from knowledge on how immigrants are distributed by grade level and whether that distribution matters. How are the foreign-born distributed among classrooms at the grade level: are they evenly distributed or segregated, and how does that distribution affect the quality of teachers who are teaching foreign- and native-born students? In addition, do concentrations of foreign-born students from different parts of the world have different effects, and why? If they do, is it because these students enter the school system predominantly at different grade levels or with different levels of English-language proficiency, or for some other reason? Finally, it may be that within-school resources are distributed in favor of immigrant students; perhaps schools have acculturation programs that benefit incoming immigrants but take time away from instruction or activities that would otherwise benefit the native-born.

Perhaps most important, however, is exploring and understanding student mobility and isolating the effects of immigration from the effects of mobility. Student mobility is widespread in the United States and is particularly prevalent in large, urban school districts (see, for example, Ingersoll, Scamman, and Eckerling 1989; Kerbow 1996). Data from the 2000 Census show that 15 to 18 percent of school-age children moved in the previous year.[25] Further, there is significant variation in the types of moves and types of movers. Moves can be promotional, as when a student moves from a K–5 to a 6–8 school; strategic, as when a student leaves a poorly performing school for a higher-quality educational environment; intradistrict nonresidential, as when a student remains at the same residence but changes schools; interdistrict, when a student changes both residence and school district; or international, when a student comes from abroad when entering a new school. The exact type of move may lead to different conclusions regarding its effects, yet there is little nuance in the way current research typically approaches nativity and mobility. Ultimately this leads to mixed results and conflated estimates in studies exploring and quantifying the relationship between mobility broadly (both national and international) and achievement.

In this chapter we do not attempt to disentangle immigration from mobility and do not disentangle the stock of foreign-born students from the flow of newcomers, which may be critical to our findings.[26] In previous work on NYC public school students, we found evidence that mobility, rather than immigration per se, plays a larger role in shaping student performance. Specifically, we found that newcomer immigrants arriving in high school outperform their stable high school classmates, regardless of nativity; notably, they also outperform newcomer migrants, who do very poorly (Stiefel, Schwartz, and Conger 2010). This finding might lead one to ask whether the negative impact of increased concentrations of immigrants in schools is really about the fact that the students are foreign-born or that they were mobile. It would be interesting to see whether the same relationship exists between performance and all "newcomer" students—

those moving from a different school in NYC, those moving from a different district, and those moving from a different country.

CONCLUSIONS

Immigration to the United States has changed dramatically during the past half-century, but what has not changed is that the foreign-born population remains very diverse. It is a well-known and oft-cited fact that urban schools face a number of challenges in educating a diverse population of students, and have limited resources to do so. Understanding whether and in what ways increases in the share of foreign-born students affect academic outcomes is important in recommending actionable and effective policy.

The positive results we see initially show that among native-born blacks and Hispanics, performance is higher in schools with more immigrants, which may be telling us something about where the foreign-born move. However, when we look within schools we do not find this pattern. In fact, nothing we see suggests that more immigrants are associated with higher performance. We observe negative and zero associations only.

That said, many important questions need to be answered and a concerted effort needs to be made to isolate the causal relationships between immigrant share and achievement. Uncovering the true effect that immigrants have on achievement will require a nuanced approach—looking at newcomer immigrants separately, examining the role of mobility, exploring how resources are allocated within schools, and focusing attention within schools. Unexpected results, such as those presented in this chapter, present opportunities to further understand the ways in which school composition affects student outcomes. Gaining greater insight into the mechanisms underlying our findings is an important step in understanding whether and how concentrations of social and economic inequality perpetuate, persist, and prevent educational institutions from facilitating intergenerational mobility. We look forward to seeing the results of such work.

We thank Elizabeth Debraggio for her excellent research assistance and Richard Murnane, Rebecca Blank, Richard Freeman, Greg Duncan, and Dylan Conger for helpful comments on an earlier draft.

NOTES

Online appendix available at: http://www.russellsage.org/duncan_murnane_online_appendix.pdf.

1. For example, Caroline Hoxby (2000) finds that students are affected by the achievement levels of their peers, and Russell Rumberger and Gregory Palardy (2005) find that net of other background factors, the average socioeconomic level of students' schools has as much impact on their achievement growth as their own socioeconomic status.

2. American Community Survey 2007 1-Year Estimates, MSA level. See online appendix table 20.A1 for more detail, available at http://www.russellsage.org/duncan_murnane_online_appendix.pdf.

3. A large fraction of K–12 students in NYC attend private schools, which may account for the higher proportion of immigrant children among students in NYC public elementary and middle schools (if, for example, parents of native-born children better understand the private school system or are wealthier than foreign-born parents). According to the American Community Survey 3-Year Estimates, roughly 22 percent of NYC's K–8 students attend private school, as do 19 percent of ninth- to twelfth-graders. These figures are larger than those for most other major cities. See online appendix table 20.A2.

4. We include students who appear in at least two years of data and who have at least one standardized-test score (in reading and/or math). Our final sample size includes 665,408 unique students (a total of 2,265,062 student observations during the six-year period).

5. See U.S. Department of State (n.d.).

6. This dramatic shift in origin occurred after 1960 (see figure 20.2). Since that year, the European share declined by nearly sixty percentage points, while the shares from Latin America and Asia increased by forty and twenty percentage points, respectively.

7. See A. Dianne Schmidley (2001).

8. See figure 5.1 in Raphael and Smolensky (2009).

9. Probing the language question further, of the more than 400,000 third- to eighth-grade students in NYC in 2000, 15.7 percent were foreign-born, of whom only 21.5 percent were LEP. Put differently, roughly 56 percent of students receiving LEP services were native-born. Although the foreign-born are more likely to be LEP, the two characteristics are not perfectly correlated (see appendix table 20.A5). The most likely explanation of why native-born students are LEP is that they are children or grandchildren of one or more immigrants. In 2000, 11.5 million children lived in a household with a foreign-born householder; of these children, 77.7 percent were native-born (Schmidley 2001). In a 2009 brief on Children of Immigrants, the Urban Institute noted that as of 2007, more than one in five children in the United States have at least one immigrant parent (Fortuny et al. 2009).

10. In previous work, we (with coauthors Ingrid Ellen and Katherine O'Regan [2002]) examined segregation of immigrants and the consequences for resources and peers. See also Schwartz and Stiefel (2004).

11. The Neighborhood Change Database, developed by the Urban Institute and GeoLytics, Inc. (Tatian 2003), compiles tract-level social, demographic, economic, and housing data from the U.S. Census. A school-zone aggregate-level data set was constructed by the authors and Ingrid Ellen using tract-level statistics, reallocated and reweighted to reflect the representation of each tract in the zone.

12. The average foreign-born white student attends schools where 43 percent of his or her peers are white.

13. A significant body of research focuses on demographic differentials in student achievement. These studies often draw on education production function models to explain differences in academic performance between students and schools (see Hanushek 1986; Todd and Wolpin 2003). Studies using this model consistently highlight the importance of family characteristics to student achievement (for example, Phillips, Crouse, and Ralph 1998; Todd and Wolpin 2007). In particular, many of these studies seek to explain achievement differences between racial or ethnic groups (for example, Phillips, Crouse, and Ralph 1998; Todd and Wolpin 2007; Fryer and Levitt 2004, 2006). Using data from the Texas Schools Project, Steven G. Rivkin, Eric A. Hanushek, and John F. Kain (2005) conclude that teacher quality has a strong influence on student achievement, yet achievement is not related to traditional measures of teacher quality such as experience and education. Also using Texas Schools Project data, Hanushek, Kain, and Rivkin (2009) found that segregation, student mobility (2004), and special education (2002) also matter to student outcomes.

14. This draws on our prior research on nativity. See Schwartz and Stiefel (2006) for further detail.

15. Grace Kao (1999) and Glick and White (2003) control for these kinds of factors in their analyses.

16. See online appendix table 20.A9 for a list of studies exploring differences in immigrant and native-born performance.

17. See Kao and Marta Tienda (1995); Michael Glick and Jennifer White (2003); Charles Hirschman (2001); Krista M. Perreira, Kathleen Mullan Harris, and Dohoon Lee (2006); Suet-Ling Pong and Lingxin Hao (2007); and Schwartz and Stiefel (2006), who find differences in the composition (income, race, parents' education) of high- and low-performing foreign-born students.

18. Research finds no evidence of convergence with time; that is, the immigrant advantage does not fade as the children mature. Kao (1999), Kao and Tienda (1995), Glick and White (2003), and Constanza Biavaschi, Stiefel, and Schwartz (2009) all find that first-generation immigrants outperform the native-born; the results for the second generation are mixed.

19. The only exception was students from Guyana, who, relative to their native-born peers, had lower reading performance on both raw test scores and after controlling for a range of sociodemographic characteristics.

20. For the purpose of our analyses, we define the percentage in a school as the share of students in grades three through eight. Similar results are obtained for estimates using the share in K–8.

21. z-scores are test scores that have been normalized to have a mean of 0 and a standard deviation of 1. Results obtained using only a single cross-section of data for 2000 are similar and are presented in online appendix table 20.A10.

22. Note, however, that this relationship, though alarming, may not be substantively important. A typical native-born white student attended school with approximately 13.5 percent foreign-born students. For such a student, the

effect of the concentration of foreign-born, ceteris paribus, is lower performance of 0.04 standard deviations (−0.003 × 13.5), which is a small effect. As a benchmark, the raw-test-score difference between white and black students in NYC is around 0.7 standard deviations, and the regression-adjusted gap is around 0.1 standard deviations.

23. Results for models estimating the relationship between reading performance and immigrant share are presented in the online appendix table 20.A11.

24. More technically, a grade-school fixed effect allows each grade in every school to have a unique intercept. This means that the intercept for third-graders in school A will be different from the intercept for fourth-graders in school A and for third-graders in school B.

25. See Schachter (2001).

26. Although defining immigrants based on birth country alone has the advantage of being clear and consistent, it groups all students born abroad together, including those immigrating as infants and those immigrating as ten-year-olds. Clearly, there are important differences between these students that are worth exploring.

REFERENCES

Andersson, Fredrik, Simon Burgess, and Julia Lane. 2009. "Do as the Neighbors Do: The Impact of Social Networks on Immigrant Employment." IZA Discussion Paper No. 4423. Bonn: Institute for the Study of Labor.

Biavaschi, Constanza, Leanna Stiefel, and Amy Ellen Schwartz. 2009. "Testing the Convergence Hypothesis in Immigrant Academic Achievement: A Longitudinal Analysis." Unpublished paper, prepared for the Annual Conference of the American Education Finance Association. Nashville, Tennessee (March).

Borjas, George J. 2003. "The Labor Demand Curve Is Downward Sloping: Reexamining the Impact of Immigration on the Labor Market." *Quarterly Journal of Economics* 118(4): 1335–74.

Card, David. 2001. "Immigrant Inflows, Native Outflows, and the Local Labor Market Impacts of Higher Immigration." *Journal of Labor Economics* 19(1): 22–64.

Chiswick, Barry R., and Noyna Deb Burman. 2004. "Educational Attainment: Analysis by Immigrant Generation." *Economics of Education Review* 23(4): 361–76.

Clotfelter, Charles T., Helen F. Ladd, and Jacob L. Vigdor. 2006. "Teacher-Student Matching and the Assessment of Teacher Effectiveness." *Journal of Human Resources* 41(4): 778–820.

Cortes, Kalena E. 2006. "The Effects of Age at Arrival and Enclave Schools on the Academic Performance of Immigrant Children." *Economics of Education Review* 25(2): 121–32.

Ellen, Ingrid G., Katherine O'Regan, Amy Ellen Schwartz, and Leanna Stiefel. 2002. "Immigrant Children and New York City Schools: Segregation and Its Consequences." Brookings-Wharton Papers on Urban Affairs. Washington, D.C.: Brookings Institution.

Fortuny, Karina, Randy Capps, Margaret Simms, and Ajay Chaudry. 2009. "Children of Immigrants: National and State Characteristics." Report. Brief 9. Washington, D.C.: Urban Institute.

Friedberg, Rachel M., and Jennifer Hunt. 1995. "The Impact of Immigrants on Host Country Wages, Employment and Growth." *Journal of Economic Perspectives* 9(2): 23–44.

Friesen, Jane, and Brian Krauth. 2008. "Enclaves, Peer Effects, and Student Learning Outcomes in British Columbia." Working paper series, no. 80-08. Burnaby, B.C.: Simon Fraser University, Metropolis Centre. Available at: http://mbc.metropolis.net/assets/uploads/files/wp/2008/WP08-08.pdf (accessed March 21, 2011).

Fryer, Jr., Roland G., and Steven D. Levitt. 2004. "Understanding the Black-White Test Score Gap in the First Two Years of School." *Review of Economics and Statistics* 86(2): 447–64.

———. 2006. "The Black-White Test Score Gap Through Third Grade." *American Law and Economics Review* 8(2): 249–81.

Glick, Jennifer E., and Michael J. White. 2003. "The Academic Trajectories of Immigrant Youths: Analysis Within and Across Cohorts." *Demography* 40(4): 759–83.

———. 2009. *Achieving Anew: How New Immigrants Do in American Schools, Jobs, and Neighborhoods.* New York: Russell Sage Foundation.

Gould, Eric D., Victor Lavy, and M. Daniele Paserman. 2008. "Does Immigration Affect the Long-Term Educational Outcomes of Natives? Quasi-Experimental Evidence." IZA Discussion Paper No. 1883. Bonn: Institute for the Study of Labor.

Hanushek, Eric A. 1986. "The Economics of School Production and Efficiency in Public Schools." *Journal of Economic Literature* 24(3): 1141–77.

Hanushek, Eric A., John F. Kain, and Steven G. Rivkin. 2002. "Inferring Program Effects for Special Populations: Does Special Education Raise Achievement for Students with Disabilities?" *Review of Economics and Statistics* 84(4): 584–99.

———. 2004. "Disruption Versus Tiebout Improvement: The Costs and Benefits of Switching Schools." *Journal of Public Economics* 88(9–10): 1721–46.

———. 2009. "New Evidence About *Brown v. Board of Education:* The Complex Effects of School Racial Composition on Achievement." *Journal of Labor Economics* 27(3): 349–83.

Hirschman, Charles. 2001. "The Educational Enrollment of Immigrant Youth: A Test of the Segmented-Assimilation Hypothesis." *Demography* 39(3): 317–36.

Hoxby, Caroline. 2000. "Peer Effects in the Classroom: Learning from Gender and Race Variation." NBER working paper W7867. Cambridge, Mass.: National Bureau of Education Research.

Iatarola, Patrice, and Leanna Stiefel. 2003. "Intra-District Equity of Public Education Resources and Performance." *Economics of Education Review* 22(1): 69–78.

Ingersoll, Gary, James Scamman, and Wayne Eckerling. 1989. "Geographic Mobility and Student Achievement in an Urban Setting." *Educational Evaluation and Policy Analysis* 11(2): 143–49.

Jensen, Peter, and Astrid Wurtz Rasmussen. 2008. "Immigrant and Native Children's Cognitive Outcomes and the Effect of Ethnic Concentration in Danish Schools." Study paper 20. Odense: University Press of Southern Denmark.

Kao, Grace. 1999. "Psychological Well-Being and Educational Achievement Among Immigrant Youth." In *Children of Immigrants: Health, Adjustment, and Public Assistance,* edited by Donald J. Hernandez. Washington, D.C.: National Academy Press.

Kao, Grace, and Marta Tienda. 1995. "Optimism and Achievement: The Educational Performance of Immigrant Youth." *Social Science Quarterly* 76(1): 1–19.

Kerbow, David. 1996. "Patterns of Urban Student Mobility and Local School Reform." *Journal of Education of Students Placed at Risk* 1(2): 147–69.

Lankford, Hamilton, Susanna Loeb, and James Wyckoff. 2002. "Teacher Sorting and the Plight of Urban Schools: A Descriptive Analysis." *Educational Evaluation and Policy Analysis* 24(1): 37–62.

Manski, Charles. 1993. "Identification of Endogenous Social Effects: The Reflection Problem." *Review of Economic Studies* 60(3): 531–42.

New York City Department of Education (1997–2002). Student-Level Administrative Data [dataset not publicly available]. New York: Department of Education.

Ottaviano, Gianmarco I. P., and Giovanni Peri. 2005. "Rethinking the Gains from Immigration: Theory and Evidence from the U.S." NBER working paper 11672. Cambridge, Mass.: National Bureau of Education Research.

Perreira, Krista M., Kathleen Mullan Harris, and Dohoon Lee. 2006. "Making It in America: High School Completion by Immigrant and Native Youth." *Demography* 43(3): 511–36.

Phillips, Meredith, James Crouse, and John Ralph. 1998. "Does the Black-White Test Score Gap Widen After Children Enter School?" In *The Black-White Test Score Gap,* edited by Christopher Jencks and Meredith Phillips. Washington, D.C.: Brookings Institution Press.

Pong, Suet-Ling, and Lingxin Hao. 2007. "Neighborhood and School Factors in the School Performance of Immigrants' Children." *International Migration Review* 41(1): 206–341.

Portes, Alejandro, and Dag MacLeod. 1996. "Educational Progress of Children of Immigrants: The Roles of Class, Ethnicity and School Context." *Sociology of Education* 69(4): 255–75.

Raphael, Steven, and Eugene Smolensky. 2009. "Immigration and Poverty in the United States." In *Changing Poverty, Changing Policies,* edited by Maria Cancian and Sheldon Danziger. New York: Russell Sage Foundation.

Rivkin, Steven G., Eric A. Hanushek, and John F. Kain. 2005. "Teachers, Schools, and Academic Achievement." *Econometrica* 73(2): 417–58.

Rubenstein, Ross, Amy Ellen Schwartz, Leanna Stiefel, and Hella Bel Hadj Amor. 2007. "From Districts to Schools: The Distribution of Resources Across Schools in Big City School Districts." *Economics of Education Review* 26(5): 532–45.

Rumbaut, Ruben, and Alejandro Portes. 2001. *Legacies: The Story of the Immigrant Second Generation.* Berkeley: University of California Press.

Rumberger, Russell, and Gregory Palardy. 2005. "Does Segregation Still Matter? The Impact of Student Composition on Academic Achievement in High School." *Teachers College Record* 107(9): 1999–2045.

Schachter, Jason. 2001. "Geographical Mobility: March 1999 to March 2000." *Current Population Reports,* Series P20-538. Washington: U.S. Government Printing Office for U.S. Bureau of the Census. Available at: www.census.gov/prod/2001pubs/p20-538.pdf (accessed March 21, 2011).

Schmidley, A. Dianne. 2001. "Profile of the Foreign-Born Population in the United States: 2000." *Current Population Reports,* Series P23-206. Washington: U.S. Government Printing Office for U.S. Bureau of the Census.

Schwartz, Amy Ellen, and Alec Ian Gershberg. 2001. "Immigrants and Education: Evidence from New York City." Research report. In *Proceedings from the Annual Meeting of the National Tax Association.* Santa Fe (November 9–11). Washington, D.C.: National Tax Association.

Schwartz, Amy Ellen, and Leanna Stiefel. 2004. "Immigrants and the Distribution of Resources Within an Urban School District." *Educational Evaluation and Policy Analysis* 26(4): 303–28.

———. 2006. "Is There a Nativity Gap? The Achievement of New York City Elementary and Middle School Immigrant Students." *Education Finance and Policy* 1(1): 17–49.

Stiefel, Leanna, Amy Ellen Schwartz, and Dylan Conger. 2010. "Age of Entry and the High School Performance of Immigrant Youth." *Journal of Urban Economics* 67(3): 303–14.

Tatian, Peter. 2003. "Neighborhood Change Database (NCDB)." Washington, D.C.: Urban Institute. Available at: http://www2.urban.org/nnip/cua/ncdb/NCDB_LF_DataUsersGuide.pdf (accessed March 21, 2011).

Todd, Petra, and Kenneth Wolpin. 2003. "On the Specification and Estimation of the Production Function for Cognitive Achievement." *Economic Journal* 113(485): 3–33.

———. 2007. "The Production of Cognitive Achievement in Children: Home, School, and Racial Test Score Gaps." *Journal of Human Capital* 1(1): 91–136.

Urban Institute. 2009. "Children of Immigrants Data Tool." Available at: http://datatool.urban.org (accessed March 21, 2011).

U.S. Bureau of the Census. 1995. "Foreign-Born Population of the United States: Current Population Survey—March 1995 Detailed Tables, Tables 1.11 and 3.11." Available at: www.census.gov/population/www/socdemo/foreign/for95dtabs.html (accessed April 21, 2011).

———. 2000. "Foreign-Born Population of the United States: Current Population Survey—March 2000 Detailed Tables, Tables 1.11, 3.11, and 4.11." Available at: www.census.gov/population/www/socdemo/foreign/p20-534.html (accessed April 26, 2011).

———. 2005. "Foreign-Born Population of the United States: Current Population Survey—March 2005 Detailed Tables, Tables 1.11, 3.11, and 4.11." Available at: www.census.gov/population/www/socdemo/foreign/cps2005.html (accessed April 26, 2011).

———. 2006. "American Community Survey (ACS)." Available at: http://www.factfinder.census.gov/servlet/CTGeoSearchByListServlet?ds_name=ACS_2006_EST_G00_&_lang=en&_ts=321886595415 (accessed March 21, 2011).

U.S. Department of State. n.d. "Milestones: 1921–1936: The Immigration Act of 1924 (The Johnson Reed Act)." Available at: http://history.state.gov/milestones/1921-1936/ImmigrationAct (accessed March 22, 2011).

Waters, Mary C. 1999. *Black Identities: West Indian Immigrant Dreams and American Realities.* New York: Russell Sage Foundation and Harvard University Press.

Zhou, Min, and Carl L. Bankston, III. 1998. *Growing Up American: How Vietnamese Children Adapt to Life in the United States.* New York: Russell Sage Foundation.

Chapter 21

School Desegregation and the Black-White Test Score Gap

Jacob L. Vigdor

Racial segregation in American public schools has persisted over the past twenty-five years in spite of a contemporaneous trend toward residential integration. This discrepancy reflects a tendency for school districts to reduce their efforts to integrate schools, a trend that seems likely to continue in the wake of recent judicial decisions. This chapter considers the prospective impact of this trend on racial inequality in educational outcomes.

Many theories propose mechanisms linking school segregation to racial disparities in academic performance and behavior. Many of these mechanisms suggest that segregation disadvantages black students relative to whites, but some mechanisms suggest the opposite. On the one hand, segregation may harm black students relative to whites because it introduces disparities in educational aspirations and expectations, because it leads to differences in the quality of school inputs—most important, teachers—or because it alters the peer composition of students' classrooms in detrimental ways. On the other hand, separation may permit beneficial specialization in terms of both curriculum and personnel. Integration accomplished through busing may not fairly apportion the costs of extra travel time, and integration at the school level may be offset by segregation at the classroom level. Finally, integration may promote the development of an oppositional culture.

Estimating a causal relationship between school segregation and educational outcomes is difficult because segregation may result from both residential sorting and potentially endogenous school district policies. Randomized experiments assigning entire metropolitan areas to either integrated or segregated schools are infeasible. The best available causal evidence, represented by Jonathan Guryan (2004) and Byron F. Lutz (2005), examines the impact of court-mandated shifts of school integration policy and finds that segregation increases black dropout rates. Additional studies, predicated on the notion that classroom assignments within a school are in some cases close to random, have found modest relationships between segregation and test score gaps among younger children. Although these studies represent the state of the art on this subject, each is subject to a standard set of validity concerns.

After briefly reviewing the literature (treated more thoroughly in Vigdor and Ludwig 2008), this chapter introduces new descriptive evidence based on the experience of Charlotte-Mecklenburg schools, which ceased busing under court order in 2002. Evidence from the elementary and middle school grades shows no obvious detrimental impact on the performance of black students compared to that of whites in the same district or to that of black students in a comparable district that continued busing over the same time period.

FIGURE 21.1   *State-Level Correlation Between Segregation in School Districts and the Black-White Gap in Fourth-Grade National Assessment of Educational Progress Math Test Scores, 2003*

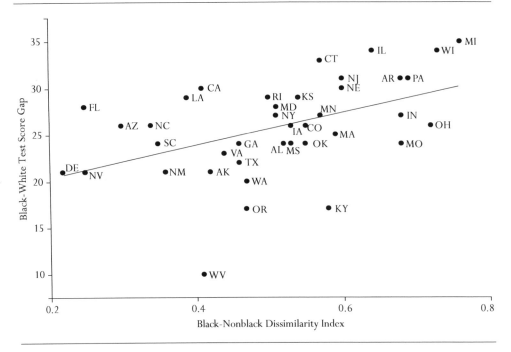

Source: Vigdor and Ludwig (2008).
$r = 0.47$
$p < 0.01$

If nothing else, this evidence indicates that any adverse impact of segregation on the test score gap can potentially be offset by policy initiatives such as those undertaken by Charlotte-Mecklenburg during this time period—including a controlled school choice plan, salary differentials to make jobs in disadvantaged schools more attractive, and restrictions on teacher mobility across schools. These countervailing policies, which are generally more amenable to evaluation with rigorous research design, deserve more attention as potential tools to improve black students' achievement.

The prospects for achieving racial balance in American public schools dimmed considerably over the first decade of the twenty-first century. A series of adverse court rulings, culminating in the Supreme Court's 2007 decision opposing busing plans in Louisville and Seattle, introduced significant obstacles to race-aware school assignment policies.[1] Some districts have attempted to preserve busing by considering factors other than race in school assignment, but these efforts entail political risk.[2]

Does the end of busing necessarily imply a widening of the black-white test score gap? Basic cross-sectional evidence, such as the plot of state-level test score gaps and segregation levels in figure 21.1, is consistent with this view. Time-series evidence, which shows contemporaneous inflections in the test score gap and segregation levels in the mid-1980s, is consistent with it as well. This basic evidence can be assailed on a number of fronts, however; internally valid estimates of the relationship between these two factors are in fact hard to come by.

In this chapter I outline the theoretical basis of arguments for and against this proposition, build on multiple recent surveys of the empirical evidence, and provide new empirical evidence based on the experience of Charlotte-Mecklenburg public schools, which under court order ended their race-aware busing policy after the 2001–2002 school year. A complete reading of the evidence indicates an adverse impact of school segregation on the test score gap; however, this effect is likely to be slight and could potentially be offset by the simultaneous adoption of countervailing policies. In Charlotte-Mecklenburg, the retreat from busing has not been accompanied by a wholesale decline in the academic performance of black students. In fact, these students have improved their performance relative to black students in Wake County, the North Carolina district that continued busing by socioeconomic status over this time period.

Ultimately, the empirical difficulties in assessing whether school integration has a beneficial impact argue against making busing the centerpiece of a strategy promoting equality in educational outcomes. The case of Charlotte-Mecklenburg illustrates that the effects of resegregation, to the extent they exist, are moderate enough to be offset by modest compensatory policies. These policies themselves generally are amenable to causal identification using experimental or quasi-experimental methods. Given the general consensus that the academic performance of disadvantaged groups has not reached an acceptable level, pursuit of these policies would seem a worthy goal regardless of future trends in school segregation levels.

THEORIES LINKING SCHOOL SEGREGATION TO THE TEST SCORE GAP

Some social scientific theories that posit a link between school segregation and the black-white test score gap imply a causal link; others suggest a noncausal correlation. For purposes of forecasting the impact of future changes in school segregation, only the first type matter. Among theories supporting a causal link, some models predict a positive effect of segregation on the test score gap, while others predict a negative impact. These theories are not mutually exclusive, and each one may hold some truth. The question of which theories are most important, then, is ultimately empirical in nature.

Proposed Causal Mechanisms

A causal mechanism linking segregation to the test score gap, by definition, implies that a change in segregation patterns, holding all other determinants of student performance constant, would raise or lower the performance of black students relative to white students. There are several hypothesized reasons to think that an increase in segregation would widen the test score gap; there are also reasons to think that an increase in segregation would narrow the gap.

Mechanisms Indicating that Segregation Widens the Test Score Gap   The Supreme Court's 1954 decision in *Brown v. Board of Education* held that "[s]eparate educational facilities are inherently unequal."[3] The inherent inequality, according to the unanimous opinion, stemmed from the underlying justification for de jure segregation: the presumed inferiority of one race relative to another. This presumption of inferiority was in turn hypothesized to negatively impact motivation to learn, which in turn would worsen academic achievement.

It is unclear whether such an argument would hold equally in a world of de facto, rather than de jure, segregation. Modern school segregation reflects underlying differences in residential location, not any presumed difference in different racial groups' intellectual capacity. Students may, however, realize that differences in residential location are themselves a function of disparities in income and wealth, as well as real or perceived discrimination in housing markets. Given the remarkable persistence of neighborhood racial characteristics over time, residential settings for many children reflect actions taken in the era before the Fair Housing Act. If children make inferences regarding their future prospects on the basis of what they observe in their school and neighborhood, then school segregation may have a negative effect on the aspirations of low-income minority children quite similar to the effect hypothesized by the Supreme Court in 1954.

A related, though not identical, mechanism stems from the role of a student's peers and teachers in developing his or her educational aspirations and expectations. Students may benefit from the presence in their peer group of positive role models, who exemplify the potential returns on effort in the classroom. These role models may be harder to come by in a segregated school environment. In the face of uncertainty about each student's true academic potential, teachers may engage in a form of statistical discrimination, making inferences about a student's intelligence on the basis of skin color or other easily observed characteristics. Such inferences may be more common in a segregated school environment, particularly when teachers lack experience with that type of environment in their personal history.

Peers and teachers play roles that go beyond setting expectations or aspirations. Teachers have a direct, significant impact on the achievement of students in their own classroom.[4] Were schools perfectly integrated, students of any race would have an equal likelihood of being taught by a high-quality teacher. When schools are segregated, the possibility exists that the highest-quality teachers will gravitate away from schools that offer some combination of lower salaries and poorer working conditions. In fact, considerable evidence shows that teachers—particularly those with strong credentials—are more likely to take jobs in schools serving more advantaged students (Clotfelter, Ladd, and Vigdor 2005a; Hanushek, Kain, and Rivkin 2004).[5]

A policy that equalized teacher quality across segregated schools would not affect potential mechanisms operating through peers. One such mechanism, the use of schoolmates as role models for academic expectations and aspirations, has already been discussed. Even if all students share the same high aspirations, though, exposure to a disproportionate number of disadvantaged peers may be detrimental for a number of reasons, largely stemming from family background factors that result in lower levels of school readiness at the point of entry into the public system, as well as elevated rates of residential mobility, antisocial behavior, and attention problems (see chapters 3 and 17 in this volume). Disadvantaged peers may also be at higher risk for specific disruptive life events, such as domestic violence, that filter into both their own and peers' school behavior and academic performance (see chapter 4 in this volume; Carrell and Hoekstra 2010).

Even in the elementary grades, when most schoolwork is intended to reflect individual rather than group effort, students may learn through informal interaction with classmates. Exposure to disadvantaged classmates may reduce these opportunities for direct peer-to-peer learning. Multiple social scientific models suggest that exposure to disruptive peers reduces learning opportunities through other mechanisms as well. Classroom disruption may directly reduce the amount of time a teacher dedicates to instruction (Lazear 2001; Carrell and Hoekstra 2010). Contagion models of social interaction imply that high-risk students may alter their behavior when exposed to fellow high-risk students, leading to reductions in the students' own learning and potentially that of other students as well (Glaeser, Sacerdote, and Scheinkman 1996; Kinsler 2009).

Mechanisms Indicating that Segregation Narrows the Test Score Gap[6]   Many of the mechanisms enumerated previously refer to classroom dynamics. The integration of public schools promotes equality of classroom-level factors across races so long as each classroom is itself integrated. This is not necessarily the case, however. Classroom-level segregation is fairly common within secondary schools. Even though students generally attend more integrated schools as they age because secondary schools serve larger geographic areas, the classrooms in these schools often become more segregated (Clotfelter, Ladd, and Vigdor 2005b). A policy of busing students to achieve integration might accomplish little if the effects of that policy were undone by sorting patterns within schools.[7]

One reason why schools separate students is to deliver specialized curricula. "Tracking" policies that segment students by ability offer the promise of delivering more challenging material to students who are ready for it, while building up basic skills among students who have yet to master them. This sort of segmentation could benefit students throughout the ability spectrum; indeed, one of the few studies to evaluate tracking policies using a randomized design has shown improvements for students regardless of track assignment (Duflo, Dupas, and Kremer 2009). Tracking has been criticized, however, for invoking many of the same mechanisms hypothesized to link segregation with wider test score gaps.

Tracking is not the only potential source of specialization. Several empirical studies have documented that students tend to perform better when their race conforms to that of their classroom teacher (Dee 2004, 2005). This pattern may itself reflect mechanisms described previously: same-race teachers may serve as positive role models, or they may carry different sets of expectations or aspirations for the children they teach. For example, empirical evidence has shown that white teachers discriminate against nonwhite students in subjective assessments (Ehrenberg, Goldhaber, and Brewer 1995; Taylor 1979; see Ferguson 1998 and Irvine 1988 for summaries of other studies). A mismatch between teacher and race might also cause stereotype threat (Steele 1997; Steele and Aronson 1995). Regardless of the mechanism underlying the effect, full integration of public school classrooms would necessitate abandoning any advantage associated with matching students and teachers by race.

As noted previously, it is hypothesized that integration could influence classroom dynamics by introducing lower-performing students to higher-performing peers. This exposure of ability levels to each other might inspire lower-performing students to exert greater effort in their schoolwork. It might also, however, serve to discourage lower-performing students if they interpret the performance gap as impassable and beyond their control. Along similar lines, students who belong to an observable race- or class-based group with low average achievement may demonstrate loyalty to the group by restraining their own academic efforts. This "acting white" or "oppositional culture" mechanism would presumably be more salient in a classroom that featured substantial diversity (Ogbu 1992).

Given the existence of residential segregation, school integration can be achieved only by assigning some children to relatively distant schools. Indeed, one great barrier to complete school integration is the substantial physical distance between segregated neighborhoods in many metropolitan areas—primarily those in the northeastern and midwestern regions of the country (Cutler, Glaeser, and Vigdor 1999). Attending a school distant from one's home could be detrimental for several reasons. Time spent in transit may crowd out more productive activities. Distance may impede parental involvement in a child's education. Children from different neighborhoods who attend the same school may face difficulties in socially integrating; for instance, those who live close to a school most likely enjoy advantages in terms of arranging transport to shared after-school activities. Given these advantages of attending school close to home, a school integration policy that forces children of one racial group to more frequently attend schools at some distance from their homes might easily place those children at a disadvantage.

Other Potential Distinguishing Features of Causal Mechanisms   Proposed causal mechanisms linking segregation and the test score gap may vary along dimensions other than valence. In some cases, the hypothesized differences between otherwise identical children attending segregated and integrated schools may widen as the duration of exposure to the school environment increases. For example, the disadvantage associated with having a more disruptive peer group may compound as exposure to the peer group increases. It is unclear whether every mechanism features such a dose response. Individual expectations and aspirations may be established relatively early in life and exhibit low responsiveness to subsequent environmental conditions.

The possibility that causal mechanisms apply only during "critical periods" of a child's development applies to other examples as well. Mechanisms associated with peer interaction may be activated in later childhood and adolescence, as the student's focus reorients from the family to same-age peers. Some educational research has shown that sensitivity to school-based environmental characteristics such as class size is heightened in early childhood. In that case, the impact of exposure to a lower-quality teacher might be larger in the early elementary years than in the secondary years.

These mechanisms might also exhibit interaction and nonlinearity. Exposure to a low-quality teacher for one or two isolated years might have only a negligible long-range impact on a student's development. At the same time, prolonged exposure for several consecutive years might have a very large long-run impact. Certain mechanisms might apply only to certain subsets of the population. For example, the "acting white" phenomenon is typically ascribed to higher-achieving black students.

Noncausal Mechanisms

The existence of a correlation between the degree of school segregation in a state and the black-white test score gap in that state is impossible to dispute. The association has a fairly obvious noncausal explanation, however. The process of assigning students to schools is governed largely by the decisions of each student's own family, and characteristics of the chosen alternative are quite likely to be correlated with characteristics of the family itself.

The traditional method of assigning students to schools, at least in the United States, is based on residential location. When schools are allocated by residential sorting, prices and zoning laws can create stratification by income across schools, even when all families place an equally high value on school quality. Families may, of course, differentially value school quality, in which case we would expect the lowest-quality schools to serve families with some combination of low incomes and low valuations of school quality. Family income and valuation of school quality may in turn correlate with other factors that influence student achievement, including early-life experience, exposure to books in the household, or time spent with a parent while young.

To at least some extent, the link between family income and school quality has been weakened by school-choice initiatives, including the use of magnet schools, charter schools, private school voucher programs, and related policies (see chapter 23 in this volume for a review of evidence on major charter school initiatives). In some cases, the existence of other means of entering a favored school means that families no longer need to compete for scarce housing in a favored school's zone. School-choice programs do not, however, promise to offset the effect of differential valuation of school quality. Given the complexities of choosing a nondefault public

FIGURE 21.2   *Conceptual Framework Showing Hypothesized Factors Linking School Segregation and Outcome Disparities*

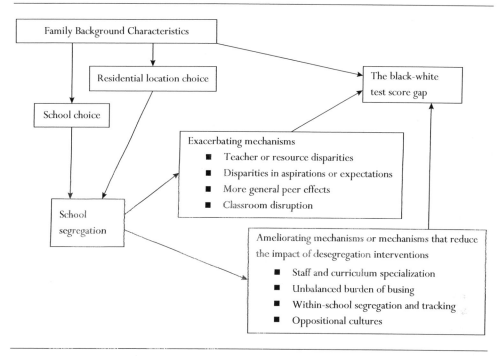

Source: Authors' figure.

school option, families that value school quality highly are more likely to fill available slots at more desired schools.

The hypothesized factors linking causal and noncausal school segregation and outcome disparities are summarized in figure 21.2. The complex nature of the assignment of students to school environments, coupled with the equally complex web of possible causal mechanisms linking environments to outcomes, makes the task of accurately measuring purported effects incredibly difficult.

REVIEWING THE EXISTING EVIDENCE

Jacob L. Vigdor and Jens O. Ludwig (2008) provide a thorough review of the empirical literature related to the link between segregation and the test score gap. For this reason, the following review of existing evidence will be brief, providing only a basic sense of the literature.[8]

The traditional scientific means of isolating the causal impact of an explanatory factor is to conduct a controlled experiment, in which identical or nearly identical sets of research subjects are assigned to either a "treatment" or "control" condition. In the case of school segregation, the ideal experiment would randomly assign entire metropolitan regions to operate either segregated or integrated schools. It is unlikely that anything resembling the ideal experiment has ever been implemented or that it will be in the future.

In the absence of a feasible experimental strategy, two basic nonexperimental methods have been used to support inferences regarding the impact of school segregation on test score gaps and other outcome disparities. The first strategy focuses on discrete changes in the degree of segregation in a district, usually brought about by a court order. The second associates variation in classroom environments within a school with variation in student outcomes, under the hypothesis that the confounding selection processes associated with school choice do not operate within schools, only between them.[9]

Event studies promise to identify the causal impact of school segregation by, for example, comparing the educational outcomes of the last cohorts to attend school under a segregated regime to those of the first cohorts to attend under an integrated regime. Underlying family background characteristics presumably do not vary all that much between one age cohort and another, so long as the temporal distance between cohorts is not great. Event studies are best suited to evaluate policy changes with instantaneous effects and little if any dose response. The suitability of the method for studying the impact of school segregation can easily be questioned.[10]

Within-school studies have the potential to capture some of the hypothesized mechanisms related to classroom dynamics, provided that the degree of variation in classroom characteristics within a school comes close to matching variation between schools. This provision may be problematic in certain settings. Classrooms within an elementary school might vary between 45 and 55 percent black, for example, whereas elementary schools themselves might vary between 10 and 90 percent black. Extrapolating from the within-school results would be appropriate only if the proposed mechanisms operate linearly.

Not all the proposed mechanisms are expected to operate within schools. Teacher quality might vary substantially according to the racial composition of a school. It is not necessarily the case that teacher quality varies so systematically across classrooms. In some cases, particularly in elementary schools, the degree of variation in student characteristics is small enough to be consistent with a random assignment algorithm. If schools randomly assigned students to classrooms and randomly assigned teachers to those classrooms, we would not expect to find any evidence of a teacher sorting mechanism at all. This hypothetical situation may in fact be a close approximation of reality.

Finally, any within-school analysis must make use of a data source that identifies which classroom each student attends. By contrast, the event-study methodology can make use of retrospective data collected in adulthood. In sum, there is no perfect method of distinguishing correlation from causality. The world may never see a definitive estimate of the causal impact of segregation on racial test score gaps. Instead, researchers and policymakers must content themselves with interpreting the limited available evidence—a task to which we now turn.

Quasi-Experimental Event Studies

Court orders mandating the desegregation of public school districts, or in more recent years orders reversing these earlier decisions, provide the most promising opportunities to examine the short-run impacts of segregation on educational outcomes.

Most desegregation orders in the United States were issued in a relatively short time span between the late 1960s and the mid-1970s.[11] Jonathan Guryan's (2004) study of the impact of court orders links data on the timing of these orders with 1970 and 1980 U.S. Census data. The census data contain information on school enrollment; Guryan used this variable to compute the proportion of fifteen- to seventeen-year-olds not enrolled in school. His results indicate that the black dropout rate, thus computed, declined between 1970 and 1980 in districts that received a court order for desegregation during the 1970s. Results indicate that black dropout rates in these districts declined by as many as four percentage points, from a base rate of 14 percent—a sizable decline.

Although Guryan's study presents some of the best evidence available on this topic, important caveats are worth mentioning. Census data in many cases do not permit identification of a respondent's school district; geographic identification is in most cases limited to the county level. More important, the comparison of cohorts separated by an average of ten years of age introduces the possibility of confounding trends. Guryan's analysis checks for some of these confounding patterns, including selective migration into the desegregating districts, and finds the results to be generally robust. Other possible concerns, including changes in the school and local public finance environment resulting from "white flight," are more difficult to fully discount.

Byron F. Lutz (2005) adopted an empirical strategy similar to Guryan's to study the impact of court decisions ending busing plans during the 1990s. Using census data from 1990 and 2000, he finds an increase in black dropout rates in school districts that stopped busing. The effect is concentrated among students in non-Southern districts. Since the research design mirrors Guryan's, it is subject to comparable concerns about potential confounding factors operating over the decade-long period. Like Guryan, Lutz pays some attention to the question of whether migration might skew the results.

Overall, then, the event-study literature provides evidence of a longer-run impact of desegregation orders on test scores. This evidence is subject to certain caveats, but authors have generally been diligent about testing for the most obvious confounding relationships. The analysis presented in this chapter will examine relatively short-run impacts of a desegregation plan, using more high-frequency data.

Within-School Analyses

The selection bias problems associated with basic cross-section analyses linking school environment to individual outcomes can be solved, at least to some extent, by analyzing only variation in the school environment experienced by students attending the same school. As noted, however, this restriction excludes much of the potentially important variation in environmental conditions.[12]

Bearing this caveat in mind, the within-school literature has produced varying estimates of the impact of classroom racial composition on the black-white test score gap. Both Eric Hanushek, John F. Kain, and Steven Rivkin (2009) and Caroline Hoxby (2000) use administrative data on public school students in Texas to demonstrate that black students who belong to more integrated school cohorts tend to perform better than their counterparts in less integrated cohorts. Vigdor and Thomas S. Nechyba (2007), by contrast, find no such relationship when comparing students assigned to different classrooms in the same North Carolina elementary school. Even focusing on the Texas evidence, however, the implied magnitudes of the effects of segregation are small. In any case, it is difficult to conclude much from this evidence, given the acknowledged exclusion of potentially important causal mechanisms.

A CASE STUDY: RESEGREGATION
IN CHARLOTTE-MECKLENBURG

Following the Supreme Court's 1971 decision in *Swann v. Charlotte-Mecklenburg Board of Education* (402 U.S. 1), the Charlotte-Mecklenburg school system pursued a policy of busing students to achieve racial balance among public schools. In the late 1990s, the district faced a new set of legal challenges, this time from parents who argued that the district's practice of maintaining racial preferences for enrollment in certain schools was unconstitutional. The U.S. Fourth Circuit Court of Appeals ruled in favor of these challengers in 2000, and the Supreme Court

FIGURE 21.3   *Exposure-Based Segregation Index in the Charlotte-Mecklenburg Schools, 1992 to 2008*

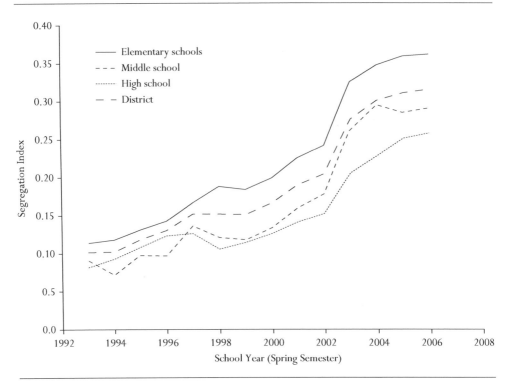

Source: Authors' calculations based on North Carolina School Activity Reports (North Carolina Department of Public Instruction, various years-a).

declined to rehear the case soon afterward. As a consequence, the Charlotte-Mecklenburg system abandoned its busing policy following the 2001–2002 school year.

Figure 21.3 plots the degree of segregation in the Charlotte-Mecklenburg system, using an index measure commonly used in the literature. The index is zero when the nonwhite share in the school attended by the "typical" white student equals the overall nonwhite proportion in the district—complete integration. The index is 1 when whites and nonwhites never attend the same schools. A discrete jump in segregation is observed between 2001–2002 and 2002–2003 in the district overall as well as when the data are stratified by school level (elementary, middle, high).[13]

Beyond the obvious impact of the policy change in 2002, several noteworthy points are made visible by the figure. The degree of school segregation rose gradually for several years prior to the policy change and continued to rise slightly in the years immediately after. The 2002 increase is substantial, though, even in comparison to this trend. The degree of school segregation increased as much between the spring and fall semesters of 2002 as it had in the six previous years.

A second important point is that even after 2002, the degree of segregation in Charlotte-Mecklenburg schools does not come close to the level that would be witnessed in a regime of de jure segregation. For the district as a whole, the degree of segregation is approximately one-third of the distance between the extremes of perfect integration and complete separation by race. In a district that is roughly two-thirds nonwhite, the typical white student attends a school that is about 45 percent nonwhite.

FIGURE 21.4   *Percentile of Black Median in White Distribution, Math Scores*

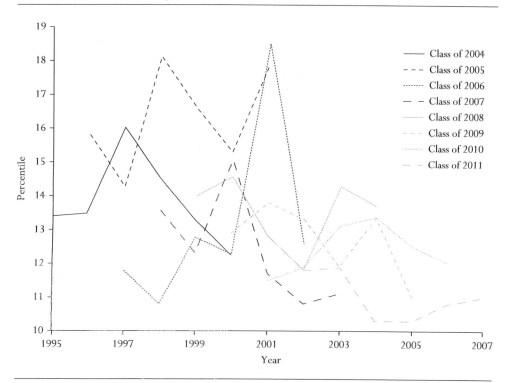

Source: Authors' calculations based on North Carolina End-of-Grade test score database (North Carolina Department of Public Instruction, various years-b).

The 2002 policy change in Charlotte-Mecklenburg has already been associated with a significant re-sorting of teachers, as documented by C. Kirabo Jackson (2009). It remains to be seen, however, whether this effect on teacher sorting translates into a net effect on the black-white test score gap.

Has the Test Score Gap Widened in Charlotte-Mecklenburg?

The abandonment of the busing policy in Charlotte-Mecklenburg was accompanied by expressions of concern regarding the potential impacts on the district's racial test score gap. It is reasonable to ask, then, whether a significant change in the black-white test score gap accompanied the jump in school segregation around 2002.[14]

Figures 21.4 and 21.5 display information on the black-white test score gap in Charlotte-Mecklenburg for students belonging to eight age cohorts, the high school classes of 2004 through 2011. The figures use test score data spanning third grade to eighth grade for each cohort. The test score gap is measured by evaluating the performance of the median black student against the distribution of white test scores. Lower numbers on this scale indicate a wider test score gap. This measure is preferable to simpler measures such as the mean difference in test scores because it is immune to concerns about the scale of test scores, such as ceiling and floor effects. The percentile measure is invariant to any monotonic transformation of the underlying test scores.[15]

FIGURE 21.5   *Percentile of Black Median in White Distribution, Reading Scores*

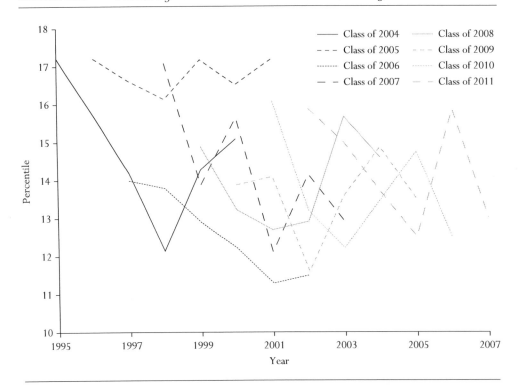

Source: Authors' calculations based on North Carolina End-of-Grade test score database (North Carolina Department of Public Instruction, various years-b).

At first glance, the data in figure 21.4 appear to show a pattern consistent with wider math test score gaps after 2002. The cohorts that completed eighth grade no later than 2002, depicted with darker lines, range widely across the graph, with the black median falling anywhere from the 11th to the 18th percentile in the white distribution for the same grade in the same year. The unweighted average across cohorts and years, focusing only on these early cohorts, is 14.4; that is, for the average cohort in the average year, the black median falls around the 14th percentile of the white distribution.

By contrast, the data points collected after the end of busing in 2002 are much more tightly arranged around a lower average value. For all cohorts and years, the black median never reaches higher than the 14th percentile of the white distribution. The unweighted average is 12.

This pattern becomes more difficult to interpret when we consider the pre-2002 performance of cohorts observed after 2002. Even before the cessation of busing in Charlotte-Mecklenburg, these later cohorts exhibited a wider test score gap than their predecessors. Tracing the lighter colored trend lines back before 2002, we discover that even in the busing era, the black median exceeded the 14th white percentile only twice; the unweighted average of all data points is 12.8. The end of busing in Charlotte-Mecklenburg thus came at a time when successive cohorts of students were already exhibiting growing black-white test score gaps. This pattern could in fact be the result of the gradual increase in segregation observed in the years prior to 2002, or it could reflect any number of extraneous factors.

FIGURE 21.6   *Gap-Based Segregation Index, Charlotte-Mecklenburg and Wake County Schools,*
1992–1993 to 2005–2006

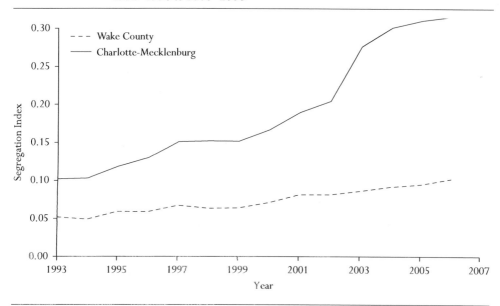

Source: Authors' calculations based on North Carolina School Activity Reports (North Carolina Department of Public
Instruction, various years-a).

Figure 21.5 shows the position of the black median in the white distribution of reading test
scores, by cohort and year. Here, little if any pattern can be discerned. The black median fluctu-
ates between approximately the 11th and 17th percentiles of the white test score distribution.
Interestingly, the pre-2002 cohorts appear quite different from one another: the graduating class
of 2005 has a persistently narrow gap, whereas the class of 2006 has a larger gap that widens over
time. This apparent trend is not continued in later cohorts.

In summary, if we ask a fairly straightforward question, whether the cessation of busing was
accompanied by an increase in the black-white test score gap, the straightforward answer is no,
or perhaps "at most a small increase, in math only." This straightforward question is fundamentally less interesting, however, than the question of whether the cessation of busing *caused* a widening of the black-white test score gap. Although the evidence presented so far suggests an answer
of no, it is limited because no counterfactual has been identified. A before-after comparison is
inherently a weaker test of causal influence than a design that incorporates a contemporaneous
counterfactual.

A Possible Counterfactual: Wake County Schools

As noted in the introductory section of this chapter, although Charlotte-Mecklenburg schools
underwent a rise in segregation following a court order to discontinue busing for racial balance,
schools in the Wake County School District, the state's second-largest district, maintained some
degree of integration, in part by changing the rationale for busing from racial balance to socioeconomic and academic achievement balance.[16] Figure 21.6 illustrates the sharp contrast in segregation trends in the two districts. Charlotte-Mecklenburg schools are more segregated at all

TABLE 21.1   *Trends in the Black Population, 2000 to 2005–2007*

	Mecklenburg County	Wake County
Growth in population	26%	30%
Change in poverty rate	+4%	+5%
Change in high school dropout rate among adults	−5%	−5%
Change in median household income (2007 dollars)	−$5,875	−$7,780
Change in proportion of single-parent families	+5%	+4%

Source: Authors' calculations based on data from Census 2000 (U.S. Bureau of the Census 2003), and the American Community Survey (U.S. Bureau of the Census 2010).

points from the beginning of observation in 1993 until 2006, and the segregation index shows at least some upward trend in both districts. The rise in segregation is much steeper in Charlotte-Mecklenburg, however. If the goal of a counterfactual is to illustrate what would have happened in Charlotte-Mecklenburg in the absence of a sharp rise in segregation, Wake County looks like a promising candidate.

The ideal counterfactual would be a district identical to Charlotte-Mecklenburg in every way save the trend in segregation. Table 21.1 examines a series of demographic and socioeconomic trends in the two counties. To do so it compares figures from the 2000 census to later estimates based on the American Community Survey of 2005 to 2007. Comparisons are restricted to the black population.

In both counties the black population rose substantially over the period in question; the metropolitan regions of North Carolina were among the fastest growing in the nation. At the same time, however, the economic fortunes of black residents in the two counties show evidence of a roughly comparable decline. In both counties the poverty rate and the proportion of black families headed by a single parent both increased. Initially, then, trends other than school segregation appear fairly similar in the two counties.

Our analysis of educational trends in the two counties will focus on the absolute performance of black students rather than the achievement gap per se. The achievement gap widens whenever the performance of white students improves more rapidly than the performance of black students. Were one county to achieve a reduction in the achievement gap solely because the performance of white students declined dramatically while black students' performance remained stagnant, it would be difficult to label the reduction a success. The more relevant question, then, is whether the black students in the district undergoing resegregation (Charlotte-Mecklenburg) over- or underperformed the black students in the counterfactual district (Wake County).

Figure 21.7 shows the math test score performance of two cohorts of black students from third through eighth grade. The high school graduating class of 2006 consists of students who completed eighth grade in 2002, immediately prior to the end of busing in Charlotte-Mecklenburg. The high school class of 2012 entered eighth grade in 2003 and are thus observed entirely in the period after resegregation, though these students began their education prior to the end of busing in Charlotte-Mecklenburg.[17] The information in the figure supports a crude difference-in-differences estimation of whether black students in Charlotte-Mecklenburg lost ground relative to their counterparts in Wake County after the cessation of busing. The graph effectively displays six difference-in-differences estimates, two of which might be considered falsification tests, since both the early and late cohort are observed before resegregation. In figure 21.7, dark lines represent the cohorts before the policy change; lighter lines show the cohorts after the change.

FIGURE 21.7   *Average Math Test Scores, Normalized Relative to the Statewide Distribution of White Test Scores, for Black Students in Charlotte-Mecklenburg and Wake County, High School Classes of 2006 and 2012*

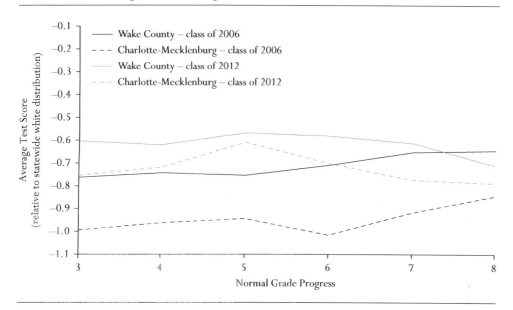

Source: Authors' calculations based on North Carolina End-of-Grade test score database (North Carolina Department of Public Instruction, various years-b).

In both districts, the black students in the later cohort improved their performance relative to the statewide mean for white students. The improvement is most pronounced in the early grades; by eighth grade there is little or no difference across cohorts in Charlotte-Mecklenburg, and the later cohort actually appears slightly worse off in Wake County. In both cohorts, black students in Wake County consistently outperform those in Charlotte-Mecklenburg.

Perhaps surprisingly, Charlotte-Mecklenburg's performance does not show strong signs of weakening in the post-resegregation cohort. Black students in the high school class of 2012 in Charlotte-Mecklenburg come very close to eliminating the deficit relative to Wake County in the fifth grade, having spent the previous three years in "resegregated" elementary schools. From this apex, however, the gap between Charlotte-Mecklenburg and Wake County widens slightly, as students in both counties exhibit a decline in relative performance that lasts through eighth grade.

The critical question in evaluating this evidence is how much of the improvement of Charlotte-Mecklenburg's later cohort can be attributed to factors other than resegregation. The third grade data point suggests that this cohort's performance might have been substantially better than its predecessors even before the end of busing in Charlotte-Mecklenburg. From this baseline, the narrowing trend in the elementary schools followed by a widening trend thereafter suggests that the cessation of busing had net positive effects in the early grades, followed by net negative effects thereafter. Some logical consistency supports this interpretation. The benefits of neighborhood schooling, to the extent they exist, should be most pronounced in the elementary years, when schools tend to be small and serve compact geographic areas. Many of the negative

FIGURE 21.8   *Average Reading Test Scores, Normalized Relative to the Statewide Distribution of White Test Scores, for Black Students in Charlotte-Mecklenburg and Wake County, High School Classes of 2006 and 2012*

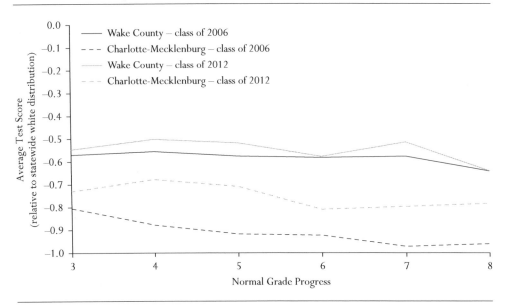

Source: Authors' calculations based on North Carolina End-of-Grade test score database (North Carolina Department of Public Instruction, various years-b).
Note: A value of zero would indicate that a group's mean is equivalent to the statewide mean for whites.

peer dynamics hypothesized to accompany segregation most likely arise in the secondary school years. Importantly, the quasi-experimental event studies summarized here associate segregation with lower rates of high school completion and not any outcome observed earlier in childhood.

Figure 21.8 repeats the analysis for reading test scores. In Wake County there is virtually no difference between the early and late cohorts. In Charlotte-Mecklenburg, by contrast, the late cohort outperforms the early cohort fairly consistently from third through eighth grade. If we accept the possibility that the performance of the class of 2012 in third grade largely reflects experiences accrued prior to the cessation of busing, the evidence appears to indicate that this policy change had little if any impact on reading performance.

Why Don't We See Anything Happening in Charlotte-Mecklenburg?

There are two possible reasons for the general lack of compelling evidence in the figures. First, we may be failing to observe an effect because we are looking in the wrong place. The true effects of school segregation might be most pronounced among high school students; this would be consistent with evidence linking court orders to changes in dropout rates, summarized previously. Evidence from randomized lotteries suggests that the effects of school quality are more pronounced for adolescent behavioral outcomes, including criminal activity and college attendance, relative to traditional test score measures (Cullen and Jacob 2009; Cullen, Jacob, and Levitt 2006; Deming 2009; Deming et al. 2010) than for younger students. The benefits of attending integrated schools might operate through social networks and opportunities rather than traditional academic channels (Linn and Welner 2007). Alternatively, the "critical period" for school segregation effects might be in early childhood. The cohort entering kindergarten in 2002–2003 has not been the subject of analysis here, largely because test score records for this cohort are as yet incomplete. Given the lag between school entry and the onset of standardized testing in third grade, it may be impossible to accurately measure this type of effect.

The second possible explanation for the lack of any observed effect is that there may in fact be no net effect. The positive and negative hypothesized mechanisms linking school segregation to the test score gap may in practice cancel each other out. Alternatively, the onset of resegregation in Charlotte-Mecklenburg may be confounded with other policy interventions that themselves had impacts strong enough to negate any effect of segregation per se.

Several policy interventions could have blunted the impact of resegregation in Charlotte-Mecklenburg. Beginning in 2002, Charlotte-Mecklenburg operated a "controlled choice" system, assigning students to zones and offering them a relatively unrestricted choice of schools within that zone. The system was scrapped shortly thereafter, but the district continues to operate a number of partial and full magnet programs in the urbanized portion of the district. The establishment of choice may have invoked any of several theorized mechanisms linking school competition to improved student outcomes.

Charlotte-Mecklenburg also operates programs to make disadvantaged schools more attractive workplaces for teachers or to limit teachers' ability to transfer from disadvantaged to advantaged schools. The "Equity Plus" program funnels extra resources, including teacher pay differentials, into schools with a high proportion of disadvantaged students. The system also has followed a policy of closing teacher vacancies in certain schools to job candidates who would transfer from another school in the system. Although such a policy could make the district a less attractive work environment overall, in the short term the impact might be to lower teacher turnover rates in disadvantaged schools. Empirical evidence on teacher re-sorting in Charlotte-Mecklenburg suggests that these policies did not completely close the gap in perceived workplace attractiveness for teachers (Jackson 2009); however, the magnitude of re-sorting might have been larger in the absence of these policies.

CONCLUSION: PROSPECTS FOR A RESEGREGATING WORLD

All available evidence indicates that the era of busing is drawing to a close. The Supreme Court provided a very unambiguous statement to this effect in its 2007 rulings. The voters of Wake County, North Carolina, have brought to a close the nation's most prominent example of involuntary busing for socioeconomic balance. Setting aside those districts that maintain a commitment to socioeconomic diversity in the context of a comprehensive school choice plan (as in Cambridge, Massachusetts; Berkeley, California; and San Francisco), the three districts that have continued involuntary busing for socioeconomic diversity have a combined enrollment about one-fourth that of Wake County (Kahlenberg 2007).[18]

Several factors promise to mitigate any negative impact of resegregation on the black-white test score gap. American cities are more racially integrated now than they were forty years ago, when court orders first mandated busing for racial balance (Glaeser and Vigdor 2003).[19] The neighborhood school of 2010 is in most cases a more integrated place than it would have been in 1970 or earlier. Importantly, no court ever mandated that students be bused across district lines. The city-suburban racial divides particularly prominent in the Northeast and Midwest were never truly breached by involuntary busing, so the end of busing carries little importance for them.

Beyond this background trend, arguments for mitigated effects of resegregation flow directly from the hypothesized mechanisms described previously. The costs of busing plans have in many cases been divided unequally among the races. Inner-city neighborhoods are frequently assigned to suburban schools, but the recruitment of suburban children for inner-city schools invokes more voluntary measures such as the establishment of magnet programs. Segregation may enable certain beneficial mechanisms such as matching students to teachers of their own race or tailoring curriculum more narrowly to students. For every argument that interaction within a diverse group of peers benefits students, a counterargument suggests that peer dynamics might operate in a different manner.

These statements should not in any way be read as a segregationist manifesto. The effects of de facto school segregation on the life trajectories of disadvantaged youth are at best poorly understood, and there is sufficient evidence of a negative impact in at least some circumstances for us to consider compensatory strategies appropriate in the event that a school district abandons efforts to balance schools.

Given widespread public concern that the academic performance of disadvantaged racial and socioeconomic groups is too low, the case for pursuing and evaluating compensatory strategies is strong. Regardless of whether resegregation will widen, narrow, or have little effect on achievement gaps, no argument suggests that it will eliminate them. For those who value greater equity in educational outcomes, the focus must now shift from strategies of relocation to strategies of differential investment. This shift is not all for the worst. As this chapter has made clear, the prospects for learning definitively whether school desegregation improved the academic performance of disadvantaged students are quite dim. Compensatory policies can be implemented using strategies more amenable to causal evaluation. Society will be able to learn more rapidly whether efforts to promote equity are bearing fruit.

NOTES

Online appendix available at: http://www.russellsage.org/duncan_murnane_online_appendix.pdf.

1. The Seattle and Louisville cases were *Parents Involved in Community Schools v. Seattle School District No. 1 et al.* and *Meredith v. Jefferson County Board of Education,* respectively.

2. See Richard D. Kahlenberg (2007) for a review of these efforts. The most prominent example, in North Carolina's Wake County, inspired a political backlash that culminated in the 2009 election of a slate of school board candidates committed to dismantling the busing policy.

3. 347 U.S. 483 (1954), page 495.

4. Since the mid-1990s, studies using large administrative data sets have attempted to measure teachers' "value added," or the gain in academic achievement that a student can expect from being assigned to one particular teacher rather than another. A recent review of this literature cites estimates that students achieve as much as an extra year's worth of learning when assigned to a high- rather than low-quality teacher (Hanushek and Rivkin 2006).

5. In theory this effect could be offset by countervailing measures that make jobs in disadvantaged schools more attractive to teachers. In practice, research has found that modest salary differentials could influence teachers' labor-market decisions; however, evidence also indicates that the most qualified teachers are less sensitive to salary differences (Clotfelter, Ladd, and Vigdor 2010).

6. To argue that certain mechanisms associated with school segregation might narrow the test score gap is not the same as arguing that the total effect of segregation is negative. Rather, any such mechanisms serve to offset the mechanisms just discussed—those that lead to a positive relationship between segregation and the test score gap. The degree of offset may be partial, in which case segregation widens the gap on net; complete; or more than complete. Bear in mind that the actual validity of any of these mechanisms, as well as the net relationship between school segregation and the test score gap, can only be resolved empirically and not through rhetorical argument.

7. Even in elementary schools, where self-contained classrooms tend to balance fairly evenly by race and other indicators, specialized pull-out programs may have the impact of reducing contact between races or socioeconomic groups.

8. There have been several noteworthy studies using basic cross-sectional analysis to infer the impact of segregation on black-white educational differentials. David Cutler and Edward Glaeser (1997) found evidence of wider racial disparities in more segregated metropolitan areas; the possibility that these disparities are a function of selective migration rather than a true treatment effect is supported by Elizabeth Oltmans Ananat (2007). David Card and Jesse Rothstein (2007) similarly document a correlation between segregation and gaps in SAT scores at the metropolitan-area level; this study is also subject to concerns about selective migration.

9. A third, more basic, strategy involves examining the correlation between school segregation and educational outcome disparities, possibly controlling for a range of family background characteristics. This strategy will not be discussed in great detail here, as the primary drawback—the possibility of selection on unobservables—is fairly obvious.

10. Event studies may also face external validity limitations to the extent that events themselves occur nonrandomly. For example, families may bring suit to force a policy change only in jurisdictions where judges are predisposed to the policy change in the first place. These jurisdictions might not be representative of the population as a whole.

11. Although the mandate to integrate public schools dates to the Supreme Court's 1954 decision in *Brown v. Board of Education,* there was little scope for enforcement. State and local authorities had little interest in enforcing the law, and the federal government's options for enforcement were limited. Elizabeth Cascio et al. (2010) provide evidence that financial incentives embedded in Title I of the Elementary and Secondary Education Act of 1965 prodded many school districts to act.

12. It is also possible that selection bias occurs within a school, as students with differing unobservable characteristics sort into different classroom environments. There is at least some evidence, though, that this within-school sorting imparts relatively little selection bias, at least in the generally untracked primary school setting (Clotfelter, Ladd, and Vigdor 2006).

13. Note that the index used in figure 21.3 is different from the index used in figure 21.1. Figure 21.1 uses a dissimilarity index, which measures the degree to which students of different races attend different schools. Figure 21.3 uses an exposure index, which focuses on the degree to which students share schools with students of different races. The two indexes are highly correlated.

14. Note that any attempt to make inferences on the basis of trends in Charlotte-Mecklenburg is subject to the same caveats associated with the event studies discussed earlier. This research design is well suited to capture causal mechanisms that operate instantaneously. It is less well suited for evaluating causal mechanisms with a significant dose response. Given the lack of test score data for students in the early primary years or the high school years, it is also not well suited to capture effects that are confined to critical periods within those years.

15. These percentile-to-percentile comparisons can be conducted at various other points in the distribution; for example, the 90th percentile in the black distribution can be placed in the white distribution, or the median in the white distribution can be placed in the black distribution. Some evidence indicates that lower-percentile blacks rise in the white distribution as they age, while higher-percentile blacks decline (Clotfelter, Ladd, and Vigdor 2009). This pattern is consistent with a mechanism whereby teachers focus effort on struggling students, who are more likely to share a classroom with high-performing blacks than high-performing whites.

16. In some sense, this switch of rationale makes Wake County an imperfect counterfactual, as the ideal comparison would be between Charlotte-Mecklenburg and a district that maintained a steady busing policy. As figure 21.6 illustrates, the switch to socioeconomic balancing in Wake County did not have a substantial effect on racial segregation. There may be an additional concern, however, that the switch in rationale for busing altered Wake County's focus on narrowing achievement gaps. Ultimately, there are numerous reasons for considering Wake County an imperfect counterfactual, including differences in industrial composition, growth and socioeconomic patterns in the nonblack population, and so forth. The perfect counterfactual does not exist. This basic analysis thus suffers from the same core problems that plague other attempts to infer the causal impact of school segregation.

17. As North Carolina's standardized tests utilize a developmental scale, it is possible to include retained students in this longitudinal sample, under the presumption that their score postretention is interpretable on the scale used in the grade to which they would have otherwise progressed.

18. The three districts in question are Brandywine, Delaware; La Crosse, Wisconsin; and McKinney Independent School District, Texas.

19. It should be noted, however, that economic segregation, by several measures, increased over much of this period (Jargowsky 1996; Watson 2009). Thus the prototypical "neighborhood school" of 2010 would simultaneously be more racially integrated and less economically integrated than the neighborhood school of 1970. Increased economic segregation could have an impact on racial achievement gaps to the extent that the effects of exposure to students—or neighbors—of different income levels vary by race.

REFERENCES

Ananat, Elizabeth Oltmans. 2007. "The Wrong Side(s) of the Tracks: The Causal Effect of Racial Segregation on Urban Poverty and Inequality." NBER Working Paper No. 13343. Cambridge, Mass.: National Bureau of Economic Research.

Card, David, and Jesse Rothstein. 2007. "Racial Segregation and the Black-White Test Score Gap." *Journal of Public Economics* 91 (11–12): 2158–84.

Carrell, Scott E., and Mark L. Hoekstra. 2010. "Externalities in the Classroom: How Children Exposed to Domestic Violence Affect Everyone's Kids." *American Economic Journal: Applied Economics* 2(1): 211–28.

Cascio, Elizabeth, Nora Gordon, Ethan Lewis, and Sarah Reber. 2010. "Paying for Progress: Conditional Grants and the Desegregation of Southern Schools." *Quarterly Journal of Economics* 125(1): 445–82.

Clotfelter, Charles T., Helen F. Ladd, and Jacob L. Vigdor. 2005a. "Who Teaches Whom? Race and the Distribution of Novice Teachers." *Economics of Education Review* 24(4): 377–92.

———. 2005b. "Classroom-Level Segregation and Resegregation in North Carolina." In *School Resegregation: Must the South Turn Back?,* edited by John Charles Boger and Gary Orfield. Chapel Hill: University of North Carolina Press.

———. 2006. "Teacher-Student Matching and the Assessment of Teacher Effectiveness." *Journal of Human Resources* 41(4): 778–820.

———. 2009. "The Academic Achievement Gap in Grades 3 Through 8." *Review of Economics and Statistics* 91(2): 398–419.

———. 2010. "Teacher Labor Markets, Segregation, and Salary-Based Policies to Combat Inequality Across Schools." Unpublished paper. Duke University.

Cullen, Julie B., and Brian A. Jacob. 2009. "Is Gaining Access to Selective Elementary Schools Gaining Ground? Evidence from Randomized Lotteries." In *The Problems of Disadvantaged Youth: An Economic Perspective,* edited by Jonathan Gruber. Chicago: University of Chicago Press.

Cullen, Julie B., Brian A. Jacob, and Steven D. Levitt. 2006. "The Effect of School Choice on Participants: Evidence from Randomized Lotteries." *Econometrica* 74(5): 1191–1230.

Cutler, David, and Edward Glaeser. 1997. "Are Ghettoes Good or Bad?" *Quarterly Journal of Economics* 112(3): 827–72.

Cutler, David M., Edward L. Glaeser, and Jacob L. Vigdor. 1999. "The Rise and Decline of the American Ghetto." *Journal of Political Economy* 107(3): 455–506.

Dee, Thomas S. 2004. "Teachers, Race, and Student Achievement in a Randomized Experiment." *The Review of Economics and Statistics* 86(1): 195–210.

———. 2005. "A Teacher Like Me: Does Race, Ethnicity, or Gender Matter?" *American Economic Review* 95(2): 158–165.

Deming, David. 2009. "Better Schools, Less Crime?" Unpublished paper. Harvard University.

Deming, David, Justine Hastings, Thomas Kane, and Douglas Staiger. 2010. "School Choice and College Attendance: Evidence from Randomized Lotteries." Unpublished paper. Harvard University.

Duflo, Esther, Pascaline Dupas, and Michael Kremer. 2009. "Peer Effects, Teacher Incentives, and the Impact of Tracking: Evidence from a Randomized Evaluation in Kenya." Unpublished paper. Massachusetts Institute of Technology.

Ehrenberg, Ronald G., Daniel D. Goldhaber, and Dominic J. Brewer. 1995. "Do Teachers' Race, Gender, and Ethnicity Matter? Evidence from NELS88." NBER Working Paper No. 4669. Cambridge, Mass.: National Bureau of Economic Research.

Ferguson, Ronald F. 1998. "Teacher Perceptions and Expectations and the Black-White Test Score Gap." In *The Black-White Test Score Gap,* edited by Christopher Jencks and Meredith Phillips. Washington, D.C.: Brookings Institution Press.

Glaeser, Edward, Bruce Sacerdote, and Jose Scheinkman. 1996. "Crime and Social Interactions." *Quarterly Journal of Economics* 111(2): 507–48.

Glaeser, Edward, and Jacob L. Vigdor. 2003. "Racial Segregation: Promising News." In *Redefining Urban and Suburban America: Evidence from Census 2000,* edited by Bruce Katz and Robert Lang. Vol. 1. Washington, D.C.: Brookings Institution Press.

Guryan, Jonathan. 2004. "Desegregation and Black Dropout Rates." *American Economic Review* 94(4): 919–43.

Hanushek, Eric, John F. Kain, and Steven Rivkin. 2004. "Why Public Schools Lose Teachers." *Journal of Human Resources* 39(2): 326–54.

———. 2009. "New Evidence About *Brown v. Board of Education*: The Complex Effects of School Racial Composition on Achievement." *Journal of Labor Economics* 27(3): 349–83.

Hanushek, Eric, and Steven Rivkin. 2006. "Teacher Quality." In *Handbook of the Economics of Education,* edited by Eric A. Hanushek and Finis Welch. Vol. 2. Amsterdam: Elsevier North Holland.

Hoxby, Caroline M. 2000. "Peer Effects in the Classroom: Learning from Gender and Race Variation." NBER Working Paper No. 7867. Cambridge, Mass.: National Bureau of Economic Research.

Irvine, Jacqueline J. 1988. "An Analysis of the Problem of Disappearing Black Educators." *Elementary School Journal* 88(5): 503–13.

Jackson, C. Kirabo. 2009. "Student Demographics, Teacher Sorting, and Teacher Quality: Evidence from the End of School Desegregation." *Journal of Labor Economics* 27(2): 213–56.

Jargowsky, Paul. 1996. "Take the Money and Run: Economic Segregation in U.S. Metropolitan Areas." *American Sociological Review* 61(6): 984–98.

Kahlenberg, Richard D. 2007. "Rescuing *Brown v. Board of Education*: Profiles of Twelve School Districts Pursuing Socioeconomic School Integration." New York: Century Foundation.

Kinsler, Joshua. 2009. "School Policy and Student Outcomes in Equilibrium: Determining the Price of Delinquency." Unpublished paper. University of Rochester.

Lazear, Edward. 2001. "Educational Production." *Quarterly Journal of Economics* 116(3): 777–803.

Linn, Robert L., and Kevin G. Welner. 2007. *Race-Conscious Policies for Assigning Students to Schools: Social Science Research and the Supreme Court Cases.* Washington, D.C.: National Academy of Education.

Lutz, Byron F. 2005. "Post *Brown v. the Board of Education*: The Effects of the End of Court-Ordered Desegregation." Finance and Economics Discussion Series 2005-64. Washington, D.C.: Board of Governors of the Federal Reserve System (U.S.).

North Carolina Department of Public Instruction. Various years-a. *School Activity Reports.* Electronic resource available through the North Carolina Education Research Data Center, Duke University.

———. Various years-b. *End of Grade Test Score Files.* Electronic resource available through the North Carolina Education Research Data Center, Duke University.

Ogbu, John U. 1992. "Understanding Cultural Diversity and Learning." *Educational Researcher* 8(8): 5–14.

Steele, Claude M. 1997. "A Threat in the Air: How Stereotypes Shape the Intellectual Identities and Performance of Women and African Americans." *American Psychologist* 52(6): 613–29.

Steele, Claude M., and Joshua Aronson. 1995. "Stereotype Threat and the Intellectual Test Performance of African-Americans." *Journal of Personality and Social Psychology* 69(5): 797–811.

Taylor, Marylee C. 1979. "Race, Sex, and the Expression of Self-Fulfilling Prophecies in a Laboratory Teaching Situation." *Journal of Personality and Social Psychology* 37(6): 897–912.

U.S. Bureau of the Census. 2003. *Census 2000 Summary File 3, Census of Population and Housing.* Electronic resource. Washington: U.S. Bureau of the Census.

———. 2010. *American Community Survey (ACS): Three-year Public Use Microdata Sample (PUMS), 2005–2007.* Electronic resource.

Vigdor, Jacob L., and Jens O. Ludwig. 2008. "Segregation and the Test Score Gap." In *Steady Gains and Stalled Progress: Inequality and the Black-White Test Score Gap,* edited by Katherine Magnuson and Jane Waldfogel. New York: Russell Sage Foundation.

Vigdor, Jacob L., and Thomas S. Nechyba. 2007. "Peer Effects in North Carolina Public Schools." In *Schools and the Equal Opportunity Problem,* edited by Paul E. Peterson and Ludger Woessmann. Cambridge, Mass.: MIT Press.

Watson, Tara. 2009. "Inequality and the Measurement of Residential Segregation by Income." *Review of Income and Wealth* 55(3): 820–44.

Chapter 22

The Challenges of Finding Causal Links Between Family Educational Practices and Schooling Outcomes

Frank F. Furstenberg

Several key mechanisms in the family are thought to affect children's educational success: parental expectations, involvement, social connections and knowledge of the school system, and investment of resources. Over the past several decades, there have been numerous attempts to design and evaluate programs aimed at enhancing the success of children in school by altering one or another of these mechanisms. The problem with such an approach is that it assumes that key features of family socialization are readily amenable to modification one by one. I contend that, on the contrary, children are affected by a multitude of overlapping and simultaneous processes that are themselves influenced and reinforced by their immediate surroundings: their social and kin networks, neighborhoods, and schools.

Social class, ethnicity, and even geography shape the contexts in which the family is embedded. The family has its boundaries, but the outside world penetrates them in a variety of ways to affect the culture and practice of families regarding education. Just as a seed needs soil, sunlight, and water to thrive, and a deficit of any of these conditions will result in a failure to thrive regardless of the quality of the others, so, too, children fail to thrive without a combination of complementary conditions. It is therefore naïve to expect to alter families' approaches to their children's school practices by isolating one particular element of family life without acknowledging how families operate as social systems.

This perspective draws on a large literature in developmental psychology stretching back to Kurt Lewin (1935) and Urie Bronfenbrenner's (1979) theoretical approach to the study of human development, and in sociology to the contributions of symbolic interactionists and life-course theorists (Cairns, Elder, and Costello 2001; Mead 1934; Thomas and Volkart 1951). The chapter juxtaposes the central findings from two research streams: nonexperimental research, which has largely focused on description from observational and survey research, and experimental interventions designed to test whether parents can be taught more effective practices. The match between the descriptive studies showing the powerful influence of the family and the experimental studies designed to apply the lessons of that literature is modest at best. The discussion in later sections of the chapter explains why programs designed to alter family practices to improve children's educational prospects generally have achieved only modest, if not minimal, impacts.

The chapter concludes with an exercise in theory and imagination to envision studies and experiments that might engage the family more fully. This is not to say that what we currently know is an insufficient basis to devise some cost-effective programs for children at risk of failing in school. Still, it is useful to think more boldly about more powerful interventions for helping families realize their nearly universal aspirations of seeing their children reach their potential in school.

Long before social scientists began to explore how parents influence their children's success in later life, theologians, philosophers, historians, and ordinary citizens offered aphorisms and observations instructing parents (Hulbert 2003). Not until the past century, with the emergence of the disciplines of anthropology, economics, psychology, and sociology and the mandate of universal education, did researchers begin to measure these practices and examine their impact on success in school. A voluminous and diverse èmpirical literature on the family's role in preparing children for school and sustaining educational commitment has appeared in the last several decades.

This chapter reviews a select portion of that literature from the critical perspective of a sociologist, with an eye to distilling what has been learned about how families, and parents in particular, contribute (in a causal sense) to success in school. My focus is on the United States, although I refer to research in other nations where appropriate. The emphasis on examining the causal pathways is quite deliberate because my ultimate aim is to identify promising policies and programs that have some likelihood of helping families promote educational success.

For a host of reasons discussed later, this task is a not simple one. The field has developed increasingly sophisticated methods for discerning causal impacts, and there is a substantial body of evidence gained from interventions involving parents and families that have employed random assignment designs (hereafter referred to as "experimental methods"). However, the approach to understanding and measuring how—not just how much—families influence children's success in school remains fairly primitive. Social science's methods for modeling how complex systems work have not yet faithfully simulated what happens within families. Parenting behaviors have not always been well measured or faithfully applied in experiments designed to measure causality. Even when they have, it is not always evident how these behaviors are perceived and responded to by children, who are presumed to be affected by parenting interventions. Providing an accurate picture of how children acquire "school smarts" and how their competence in school is sustained and supported by practices and processes within the family remains a formidable challenge.

This effort calls for thinking about how systems such as the family work in practice. Much of the research has relied on quantitative study that treats family processes as "variables" or vectors of potential causal influence. These variables might, for example, include altering styles of parenting, increasing family-school communication, or attempting to raise educational expectations. Although standard practice in quantitative social science, this variable-centered approach leaves something to be desired in understanding how processes in family systems actually affect children's attitudes and behaviors. It runs the risk of falsely specifying family influences that purportedly are amenable to change by singling out particular features of a more multifarious package of related practices. For example, promoting family involvement in schools may or may not enhance student commitment or skill development, even if that involvement has been shown to be related to school success in nonexperimental research. I will amplify this argument later in the chapter.

Viewing parents and their children as part of an interacting system requires that we think of causality in less mechanical terms than is our custom. The family does not operate like a game of billiards, where parents hold the cue and children are the balls to be placed in the far pocket. A more useful analogy is to imagine families as physicists view a system of elementary particles: mutually reacting, often in paradoxical ways, to the presence of one another. Our approach to modeling causality in ongoing systems requires a different way of thinking about how and under what conditions influence occurs. Likewise, researchers and policymakers must take care not to assume that affecting a child at a particular developmental period or at a singular point in time establishes a permanent trajectory for educational success.

In the past ten years or so, developmental social science with a policy focus has targeted the early years of childhood, when the influence of parents and families is formative and pervasive (Duncan, Huston, and Weisner 2007; Heckman and Lochner 2000). The premise that early interventions aimed at influencing children in the preschool years are more effective than reme-dial efforts in later childhood has been backed up by both theory and research, some of which will be cited later in this chapter and the accompanying online appendix (see, for example, Nelson et al. 2007). No doubt, getting off to a good start is essential to school success in the pri-mary years, and doing well in the early years is essential to later performance.

However, sustaining school success demands continuous support, supervision, and involve-ment by parents and educators beyond the primary years. Managing school choice, when pos-sible, is often a critical ingredient in success during middle and high school. Further, monitoring school activities, selecting curriculum, supervising peers, and a number of other practices that well-educated parents routinely provide are associated with educational attainment in later life. Moreover, family support, particularly in the form of resources for higher education, undoubt-edly plays a role in college entrance and completion. Accordingly, I adopt a life-course perspec-tive and consider the different family processes in play during childhood, adolescence, and early adulthood (Elder 1974). A life-course perspective sensitizes us to changing contexts, transitions, and turning points, as well as potential interventions for students and their families during ado-lescent and postadolescent years.

THE EMBEDDED FAMILY: A BRIEF REVIEW OF NONEXPERIMENTAL RESEARCH

Before examining the ongoing experimental efforts to influence children's success in school, it is worth taking a cursory look at the nonexperimental research. (A more extended review is available in the online appendix.) Doing so can help illustrate how the many different processes within the family operate concurrently to produce variation in children's school success.

Prior research points to several different mechanisms within families that could account for the sharp differences in school readiness and success across social strata. These mechanisms include parenting practices as they relate to language acquisition and literacy, peer choices, and educational ambitions (Hart and Risley 1995; Hess and Holloway 1984; Lareau 2008). A long tradition of studies, beginning with the seminal work of Diana Baumrind (1967), Eleanor E. Maccoby and J. A. Martin (1983), and Robert D. Hess and Susan D. Holloway (1984), finds that parents' habits of managing emotion, anger, and disobedience may shape children's ability to function outside the home, particularly in school. Likewise, according to Reginald Clark (1983), a constellation of val-ues, habits, and practices give children "school survival skills" to beat the odds. Specifically, fami-lies that instill high educational values take a set of discrete actions to reinforce their expectations. These actions include engendering a culture of literacy in the home, closely monitoring their chil-dren's schoolwork, providing feedback and responding to their children's educational activities, creating rituals and routines to establish good habits, advocating for their children, and finding resources in the community (Clark 1983).

These mechanisms also include parents' social and cultural capital (Clark 1983; Coleman 1988) and broader influences such as family structure (McLanahan and Sandefur 1994) and neighborhood access (Brooks-Gunn, Duncan, and Aber 1997). When families are embedded in a community of like-minded parents, they are more likely to succeed in promoting their own values (Coleman 1988).

Family resources are strongly linked to educational outcomes as well. Greater resources allow families to select more protective and positive environments, while lack of resources generally leaves the families to fend for themselves in otherwise uncongenial environments. Income begets better schools and neighborhoods. Low-income parents are constantly preoccupied with emergencies and stresses that consume time and energy, upset family routines, and increase flux in household composition, moves, and school changes (Furstenberg et al. 1999).

Genetics, too, come into play. Genetic predispositions interact with parenting practices—any parent with more than one child can testify to this! (See, for example, Dunn, Plomin, and Daniels 1986.) Judith Rich Harris (1998), among others, has argued that ignoring genetic factors as well as the ongoing power of peers has led researchers to overstate the influence of parents in the socialization process. Her views are controversial and perhaps overstated, but she does make an important point. American social beliefs assign an unusually powerful role to parents in shaping their children's destinies, yet a host of factors, including genetics and peer influences and most of all schooling opportunities, affects their success. Notably, Harris argues almost exactly the opposite of James S. Coleman and his colleagues (1966) in their earlier study of the modest impact of schools compared with the powerful impact—or so he presumed—of families on children's education attainment.

In all likelihood these many mechanisms overlap, mutually reinforcing each other and playing out over time because they are all linked to the family's social position (see, for example, Entwisle, Alexander, and Olson 1997). This is not to say that social position "determines" what families do, but the recurrent and consistent patterns of family beliefs and practices mean that these behavioral patterns will create sharply divergent patterns of school success by socioeconomic status. Significant variations occur in capacity building at very early ages, creating a daunting problem for schools as they attempt to compensate for learning differences in the family. Indeed, many preschool programs are explicitly designed to offset the gap in learning advantages imparted by well-educated parents.

In examining the causal impacts in the next section, it is important not to lose sight of the possibility that families are creating very different learning environments for their children, differences that flow from their own social position. The repertoire of skills they bring as parents to educate their children, the assets they can command to introduce their children to attractive school settings and like-minded playmates and peers, and their capacity to take action when they discern learning problems all contribute to the distinctions that play out over children's school lives.

EXPERIMENTS TO STRENGTHEN THE FAMILY'S INFLUENCE ON SCHOOL READINESS AND SUCCESS

Policymakers and social scientists over many decades have attempted to put into practice some of the discoveries from the nonexperimental literature. Reaching as far back as the early antipoverty, community-based programs of the late 1960s, a long progression of interventions has aimed at altering features of family life and practice in attempts to enhance children's school readiness and performance. Many of these programs include explicit attempts to involve parents and augment their role as educators. These include home visiting, parent education, and outreach efforts to spur parent interaction in the home and involvement in the schools.

By now there is a robust tradition of using random assignment experiments to test the efficacy of many of these interventions (Mbwana, Terzian, and Moore 2009). Therefore, as I look broadly at this research, I ask, what have we learned about the success of interventions designed to strengthen the family's capacity to foster positive school outcomes? Because this review focuses on the "causal impact" of family practices, I restrict it to studies employing random-assignment designs, omitting a large literature, mostly by economists, that has employed quasi-experimental techniques for estimating causality (Slavin and Madden 2001).

Several Caveats Worth Bearing in Mind

It is important to acknowledge several limitations of this literature. First, the research concerns itself largely with the most disadvantaged portion of the population. Therefore, much of what we have learned comes from comparing low-income families that have received a treatment or intervention with those that have not. Within this low-income subset, researchers generally compare volunteers or recruits who are randomly assigned to program or control groups. This means that we cannot easily generalize beyond relatively "motivated" populations of low-income families. Sometimes, as in the case of preschool programs, it is possible to reach very deep into the population of the "truly disadvantaged." Other programs may do less well in reaching the least well-off and least organized families. In any event, little of what we have learned could be safely generalized to families of modest to moderate means.

A second limitation is that although most of the programs are fairly comprehensive and long-lasting by standards of most interventions, few are designed to be both intensive and long-lasting. There are some exceptions, such as the Harlem Children's Zone (Dobbie and Fryer 2009; see also chapter 23 in this volume), but I am not familiar with evaluated programs that work intensely with parents or whole families over long spans of their children's lives. Even if successful, this type of program model may be difficult to implement on a large scale because of cost. Yet, as I will argue later in the chapter, most short-term programs aimed at creating lasting influences do not fulfill their promise. At least to date, I know of none that have similar impacts to, let us say, the premier preschool interventions.

Third, although there are some important exceptions (for example, Cowan and Cowan 2002; Schultz, Cowan, and Cowan 2006), few experimental programs aimed at changing family practices to better promote children's educational success work with more than one parent, much less whole families. The difficulty of launching and sustaining services for couples or for couples and children is monumental. There are some encouraging efforts in this direction, but the vast majority of experimental programs attempt to change, improve, or augment one or another of the mechanisms by which families appear to influence their children's prospects in school. In short, few adopt a holistic approach to changing families as might be advocated by clinicians who adopt a "family systems" approach (Haley 1971; Minuchin et al. 1967).

A literature on changing families with behavioral problems is growing out of the work of clinical researchers such as G. R. Patterson (1976), Kenneth Dodge and Gregory S. Pettit (2003), and many others whose work is based on a family systems model. Many interventions have been subjected to random assignment evaluations (Shadish et al. 1993; Stanton and Shadish 1997). It is an open question whether this work might be generally extended to improving school performance or ultimate educational attainment among a nonclinical population. For example, parents may be more committed to interventions aimed at reducing problem behaviors in school than to those aimed at improving children's academic performance. Clearly, children with serious behavioral problems often have problems in school, but a review of this work falls outside the purview of this chapter.

Finally, and a source of frustration to any reviewer of the experimental literature, most studies suffer from serious limitations in measurement that make it difficult to discern how interventions play out within the family. Namely, the vast majority of experimental studies do not adequately assess how the intervention affects family processes. They also frequently do not measure child impacts directly. Rarely do we find examples of experiments aimed at changing family practices that contain good measures of both family processes and resulting school outcomes.

Nonetheless, there is much to be learned from existing experiments, and I summarize some of the prominent meta-analyses and meta-summaries of policies and programs aimed at affecting family features believed to be causally linked to child achievement.

Home Visitor Programs

The home visitor program, often referred to as nurse-family partnerships, is among the most widely adopted and evaluated programs involving a family intervention in very early childhood. This program is considered a model for educating, monitoring, and supporting parents after birth (Olds, Sadler, and Kitzman 2007). One review estimates that this program, in one form or another, reaches nearly a half-million families with newborns every year (Daro and McCurdy 2007). The program is a continuing effort to educate, monitor, and assist parents (recent mothers), usually with an intensive schedule of visits, sometimes extending up to three years. A nurse or health educator reaches parents in the home and instructs families on best practices in early infant care and development, including nutrition and health, parenting skills (involving such things as infant stimulation), and management practices for getting help and services. The program has been widely evaluated (Gomby 2005).

Relatively recently, several teams of researchers carried out a meta-analysis of the evaluations (Barnett 1995; Gomby, Culross, and Behrman 1999; Sweet and Appelbaum 2004). The assessments (or interpretations of them) do not always concur, but almost all show some positive effects on certain parent and child outcomes. The most consistent of the results points to reductions of child maltreatment and visits to emergency rooms. It is less clear whether such programs affect school readiness either directly or indirectly. Although there is some evidence that home visitor programs can improve behavioral adjustment in the transition to school, the results are typically smaller for the better-designed random evaluations.

The long-term impacts on school readiness are inconsistent, but the evidence suggests there could be very modest effects on children's social adjustment and cognitive skills. In short, the program, when faithfully implemented, is successful at bending the twig, but only slightly.

Early Parent Involvement and School-Readiness Programs

When we turn more broadly to education programs for parents aimed at enhancing their ability to provide a stimulating home environment, the results are less consistent and less encouraging (Mbwana, Terzian, and Moore 2009). A randomized experiment of Even Start, a federally supported family literacy program providing early childhood education, produced few measurable impacts (Brooks-Gunn 2003; St. Pierre, Ricciuti, and Rimdzius 2005). In a review of some 200 parenting-support programs, including experimental and nonexperimental evidence, Barbara Dillon Goodson (2005) reports no effects to modest effects (the strongest were about one-quarter of a standard deviation on the outcome variable). She concludes: "Debate continues about the effectiveness of parent support interventions on outcomes for children. Program evaluations have shown the difficulty of producing sustained and comprehensive changes in parents. The subsequent link between changes in parents and positive consequences for their children's development has been even harder to prove" (4).

In another recent review of pre-K–3, including efforts to change family behavior, Arthur Reynolds, Katherine Magnuson, and Suh-Ruu Ou (2006) concluded that programs are more effective when they extend services for a longer period of time and include an "intensive family support component." Yet, as they note, few of the existing studies of such comprehensive programs are able "to parse out the unique effects of parental involvement."

Jane Waldfogel (2006), in a recent assessment of the international literature on early education and parenting programs, concluded that although the nonexperimental evidence suggests that parenting matters, the effectiveness of parenting programs in enhancing parental skills, much less affecting children's school achievement, is far weaker (see also Magnuson and Duncan 2004; Magnuson and Votruba-Drzal 2008).

A similar review in Britain by Charles Desforges (2003) reached identical conclusions. Desforges concluded that the nonexperimental literature shows that the "spontaneous" influence of parents is even greater than the quality of the schools. However, policy and program interventions to alter parental involvement have been extensive but "so technically weak that it is impossible on the basis of publicly available evidence to describe the scale of the impact on pupils' achievement" (5). Desforges goes on to conclude that the programs can raise "nonspontaneous" parental involvement, but it is unclear that such increases make a difference for student achievement.

On the basis of several independent reviews of the experimental and quasi-experimental literature, we still do not know whether programs designed to improve parents' skills in preparing their children for school can be successful. My own conclusion is that such efforts might at best have a small, positive effect when combined with early school education and programs aimed at easing the transition to primary school. The effects of increasing family involvement appear to be greater when they are integrated with early school education (Love et al. 2005).

Programs to Increase Parental Resources

The strong link between resource deprivation and school readiness and later school success has led many developmental and educational policy researchers to consider programs to provide income or material resources to low-income families as a means of improving their adjustment to school (Dearing, McCartney, and Taylor 2001; Reynolds et al. 2001). There are numerous reasons to believe that resource-starved parents have a harder time preparing their children for school. Poor parents are continually stressed, move more frequently, and find it harder to obtain high-quality child care, among other reasons (Yeung, Linver, and Brooks-Gunn 2002). Much of the experimental evidence seems to support the importance of resources, particularly in preschool and during the transition to primary school.

Greg Duncan, Katherine A. Magnuson, Pamela Morris, and their colleagues have done extensive reviews of this literature (Morris, Duncan, and Rodrigues 2007; Duncan and Magnuson 2005; Kalil and Deleire 2004; see also Huston et al. 2005b; Morris and Gennetian 2003). Some of the important interventions have tried to improve child outcomes by increasing parental education and employment; others have examined the impact of programs that increase income directly through income transfers or the Earned Income Tax Credit. As I noted earlier, few studies have used experimental methods to examine how increases in income or resources to the family change how parents function, much less the impact of changed parental behaviors on child outcomes.

Morris, Duncan, and Christopher Rodrigues (2007), drawing on data from random-assignment experiments, developed a set of instruments to identify causal effects of added income. They report "selective effects of income on school achievement," particularly in families with young children. These impacts disappear for children in middle childhood, however. In another study focusing on the impact of New Hope, a program aimed at increasing income, Aletha C. Huston et al. (2005a) found significant impacts in school achievement, motivation, and social behavior, particularly for males. They suggested that the added income allowed parents to make better use of organized child care and after-school activities. Magnuson and Elizabeth Votruba-Drzal's (2008, 22) recent review of nonexperimental and experimental studies of the effects of poverty on child development concluded that it was "difficult to isolate the causal effects of income from that of other related disadvantages and family characteristics." These authors note that impacts on educational attainment may amount to as much as one-third of a standard deviation.

Again, the studies conflict to some degree, but generally suggest a modest to moderate impact of interventions to enhance resources in low-income families. The problem is attempting to isolate the specific causal effects of bolstering resources, in part because most studies do not trace these effects through changes in family processes. The results similar to other intervention programs indicate effects are greater on families with young children, and particularly young boys.

Stepping back from these three separate literatures on interventions among families with preschool and primary school children, we can draw the reasonable (though hardly ironclad) conclusion that programs aimed at affecting developmental processes through direct intervention with parents or by increasing parental resources have modest causal impacts on children's school performance. These programs might have larger impacts if combined with early education programs. Their impact on boys may be greater than on girls. How much these effects persist into the middle school or high school years is an open question, but there is little support from the experimental and quasi-experimental studies to suggest that any interventions with parents or, more broadly, the family have a strong and lasting effect on children's school performance beyond the primary grades.

FAMILY INTERVENTIONS IN MIDDLE CHILDHOOD

For both theoretical and practical reasons, interventions aimed at increasing parental involvement decline after preschool and the transition to primary school in large measure because parents tend to withdraw from schools and schools lack either the will or the capacity to engage parents in middle school and beyond. Nonetheless, this decline is a gradual one, and there is a large and growing literature on efforts to support parents and provide guidance, monitoring, and outreach during the middle childhood years. In part stimulated by the efforts of the MacArthur Foundation Network on Middle Childhood and the work of leading developmental psychologists, researchers have begun to devote more effort to designing programs to keep parents involved, particularly as children make the transition from primary to middle school (Cooper et al. 2005; Huston and Ripke 2006).

The nonexperimental studies offer strong evidence that children do better in school when their parents communicate with them, show interest in their school, offer assistance, monitor their children's participation in school, and, most important, when they set clear expectations about school (see Fan and Chen 2001; Magnuson, Duncan, and Kalil 2006). The experimental evidence examining program interventions is less extensive, and unfortunately, the results of the two main meta-analyses are not in accord. William H. Jeynes (2005) examined forty-one studies of school programs involving urban students, only some of which involved random-assignment evaluations. He found a strong impact of parental involvement on student achievement (on average, about three-quarters of a standard deviation). Moreover, the quality of the evaluation and the specific nature of the intervention were not generally linked to the effect sizes, although homework supervision seemed unrelated to student outcomes. The results were not specific to population subgroups.

Jeynes's assessment stands in contrast to a meta-analysis by Doreen J. Mattingly and colleagues (2002, 549), also summarizing forty-one studies. They found "little empirical support for the widespread claim that parental involvement programs are an effective means of improving student achievement or changing parent, teacher or student behavior." Compared with Jeynes's assessment, Mattingly and her collaborators concluded that most of the studies they reviewed did not meet rigorous design criteria. Although it is possible to explain away the differences between these two papers by the differences in the studies included and the attention to research design, I am inclined to put more weight on the paper by Mattingly et al. (2002) because of its careful attention to the quality of the evaluation. They concluded that efforts to enhance parental involvement possibly might be effective; so far, studies using rigorous designs have not demonstrated a causal effect (see also White, Taylor, and Moss 1992).

In still another study focusing on the impact of family resources in middle childhood, Morris, Duncan, and Elizabeth Clark-Kauffman (2005) reviewed the longer-term effects of welfare policies designed to improve employment and income among families in poverty. On the basis of seven random-assignment experiments, they concluded that the policies had positive effects on children's transition into middle childhood but slight negative effects on children's transition into adolescence (see also Epps and Huston 2007; Huston and Ripke 2006). These results also mirror the results of a large-scale federal program, Moving to Opportunity (MTO). The MTO program relocated families from high-poverty neighborhoods to communities with lower rates of poverty, on average. Younger children in these families generally fared better than older children entering a new school in their early adolescent years.

Finally, it is worth taking note of another line of research aimed at improving parental and family functioning as a means to reduce children's problem behaviors in the middle years. Building on a long line of experimental studies by clinical researchers whose work was cited in an earlier part of this chapter, concerted efforts have been devoted to strengthening positive parenting practices in order to reduce child misbehavior in home and at school. A particularly intriguing set of studies by Marc S. Schulz, Philip Cowan, and Carolyn Cowan (2006) indicate that couple and father interventions may help to reduce problem behaviors. Clearly, family-oriented interventions have had some success in easing problem behaviors; however, it is less certain whether this family-oriented therapeutic and educational approach translates into better school performance (Hughes and Gottlieb 2004).

All in all, the studies in middle childhood reveal a more mixed pattern of success in promoting family involvement, changing parental practices, and thereby improving child outcomes. I am inclined to concur with Desforges and Alberto Abouchaar (2003, 70), who say, "The available evidence . . . would seem to suggest that levels of involvement can be raised. The jury is still out on whether this makes a difference to pupil achievement."

FAMILY INTERVENTIONS IN ADOLESCENCE
AND EARLY ADULTHOOD

The experimental research on family interventions during adolescence and early adulthood is very thin. Most social scientists and policymakers believe it is difficult to alter family practices at this stage, the family exerts less direct influence on adolescents and young adults, and regular involvement by parents in school activities drops off (Booth and Dunn 1996). In part, schools tend to put parents at a distance, and parents, particularly those with low education, may feel intimidated by teachers and the curriculum (Eccles and Harold 1993). At the same time, there is mounting evidence that the major school transitions (into high school and into postsecondary education) need parental guidance and support (Patrikakou 2004). For example, school choice and curriculum selection have important consequences for educational attainment. Similarly, nonexperimental studies show that parental encouragement and economic support have powerful consequences for whether young adults attend college and obtain a postsecondary degree (Hobcraft 2004; Teachman 1987).

It might be possible to examine the experimental literature cited above to explore whether effects persist in the high school years, but it is important to examine parents' actions regarding high school and beyond to determine whether they have consequences for their children's educational performance. There is a growing literature on parental involvement in choice of high school; however, few of the studies involved random-assignment experiments or quasi-experimental designs that manipulated parental characteristics (Falbo, Lein, and Amador 2001). This could potentially be a promising area for experimentation.

Dropout-prevention programs similarly command a great deal of attention in the educational literature. A subset of these programs is aimed at increasing parental monitoring and control. Again, however, I was unable to locate experiments that permit one to assess the components that include enhancing parental support or helping parents to coordinate their efforts with schools. There is, however, encouraging experimental evidence on the efficacy of some school-based interventions, most notably a program run by the National Guard called ChalleNGe (Bloom 2010).

Although we know that parents contribute heavily to supporting their children in college or technical school, there are no experiments aimed at increasing parental resources (Schoeni and Ross 2005). Virtually all of the literature looks at the role of educational support for students directly, even though family income is taken into account in most programs (Brock 2010). We really do not know whether increased support provided to parents would result in increased rates of matriculation in postsecondary education or college completion. Very little research has been carried out on whether student performance in high school or beyond can be affected by increasing parental information, support, and resources, even though the nonexperimental studies suggest that parents continue to have relevance for school success and educational attainment.

EXPLAINING THE GAP BETWEEN NONEXPERIMENTAL AND EXPERIMENTAL RESEARCH

Nonexperimental studies uniformly show pervasive and powerful effects of parental socialization and management on school success and educational attainment in later life. However, results of family interventions involving random-assignment experiments have been mixed at best. This does not necessarily indicate that the nonexperimental research has exaggerated the importance of the family's influence (Harris 1999). However, the experimental studies show that it is difficult to translate what we think we know about how the family shapes children's school readiness into programs that improve performance in primary and middle school, much less increase children's success in secondary and postsecondary education.

Because families are small social systems, passing on cultural values and beliefs, rituals, and routines, it is difficult to imagine any interventions that could even begin to narrow substantially the disparity that exists by the time children enter primary school. And this disparity between affluent and disadvantaged children continues to widen during the early and middle years of school (Alexander and Entwisle 1996; Entwisle, Alexander, and Olson 1997). By adolescence the inequalities have become, it might be said, overdetermined by a set of conditions that are increasingly difficult to compensate for: exposure to extracurricular activities, summer camp, and associations with peers, coaches, and mentors, to mention but a few of the sources that contribute to the advantages of children from well-off families.

Because of the high degree of redundancy and interdependence in values, parental practices, and resources (or the lack of them), most interventions are simply not up to the task of modifying family characteristics linked to the development and persistence of school skills. The family system and the social ecology in which families are embedded are highly self-reinforcing and difficult to modify by simply changing one feature or another (even when interventions are successfully implemented). The result is that interventions designed to increase parental involvement, raise educational expectations, extend resources, inform parental decisionmaking, or provide guidance and support as children move through the education system are not powerful enough to make much of a difference in children's school outcomes when weighed against the accumulated history of family inputs.

Families, much like larger organized systems, are sensitive to influences and incentives devised by policy and programs, but it is frequently the case that policies or programs cannot offset, overcome, or compensate for huge preexisting differences created by social position and long-standing differences in family culture and practices.

It is instructive to think about huge shocks to the family system that conceivably should alter children's education trajectories, such as the death of a parent or divorce. Important as they are, research indicates that even significant shocks to the family generally have only moderate impacts on children's school success or its extent (Amato and Booth 1997; Furstenberg and Kiernan 2001; Sigle-Rushton and McLanahan 2004). Why then should we expect that most programs aimed at reorienting parents' beliefs and behaviors would produce large and lasting impacts?

Added to these impediments is the problem of resources, which in the nonexperimental studies is strongly linked to educational outcomes of children. Income provides for better schools and neighborhoods. As noted earlier, low-income parents are preoccupied by emergencies and stresses that detract from stable family and school routines. Higher income allows parents to purchase favorable peer environments; low income constrains parents' ability to manage peers and other adult influences.

Families, of course, consist of more than parents and a child. They include siblings and often extended kin living nearby who take an active part in child care and child rearing. Siblings constitute a special form of peer influence that, as noted earlier, may reinforce or undermine parents' actions. Similarly, regular involvement by extended kin may support parents' actions or divert the influence of parents. We know relatively little about the impact of these influences on school readiness or long-term achievement. However, it is not unreasonable to assume that siblings and extended family reinforce the ability of better-off families to promote educational success, while having just the opposite impact in disadvantaged families.

The notion that families are interacting systems, dependent on support from the surrounding contexts of school and community, makes the task of intervention far more challenging than most policymakers generally perceive. Changing one feature of the system rarely produces the ripple effect on children that is often imagined. How, then, can we get inside families to make more radical change? I turn to that question now.

RETHINKING FAMILY INTERVENTIONS TO PROMOTE EDUCATIONAL SUCCESS

Available evidence suggests that the influence of families, parents in particular, on their children's school success is very difficult to modify, particularly in the long term, by programmatic interventions aimed at changing parental socialization practices. This is not to say efforts such as these are not worthwhile or even cost-effective; rather, for a number of reasons discussed in this chapter, programmatic interventions are bound to have relatively small impacts and go only a small way in mitigating the huge family differences created and sustained by the uneven opportunities provided children in different social strata. Reginald Clark (1983) demonstrated years ago that individual families can overcome the educational handicaps imposed by cultural and social milieus if they are very motivated and highly directed. However, most parents lack the repertoire of skills that the odds-defying families possess. It is unrealistic to build a policy to reduce educational inequalities by mobilizing parents to adopt and mimic the techniques of the most motivated and capable families.

The main line of attack instead must involve better schools equipped with more skilled teachers that provide a more extensive program of education with longer days and summer months. (See, for example, the preliminary effects of the Harlem Children's Zone as discussed in Dobbie and Fryer 2009; also see chapters 23 and 24 in this volume.) The less affluent—especially low-income—families need access to better schools, better-trained teachers, and more instruction time to compensate for skills not acquired in the home. Most parents will welcome such efforts, particularly if day-care and summer-care programs offer more in the way of school preparation, tutoring, and support. Direct efforts to increase parental involvement with schools, teachers, and educational information can be a useful component in preschool education, as it often is in many high-quality programs, but as a stand-alone program, it will probably have a limited effect on school success, much less long-term educational attainment.

There are other potentially promising alternatives in reducing educational inequality that have not yet been carefully assessed or evaluated. It would be highly desirable, for example, to examine the long-term impacts on children of efforts to increase parental education and income. Many parents return to school after having children. In my own Baltimore study, which followed teenage mothers after their first child was born, a very high fraction of women returned to school in their twenties and thirties. It appears that the children of these mothers did better in school than the counterparts whose mothers did not go back to school (Weiss and Furstenberg 1997). Given the widespread availability of adult education, it is possible that increasing parents' educational attainment could have a very positive benefit for their children's school success. However, the findings of this small study are only suggestive and should be examined in experimental settings. It might be possible to pool data from MDRC and other research organizations that routinely evaluate educational and income programs with an eye toward examining their long-term impacts on children.

A second strategy for getting greater traction with existing programs is to build longer-lasting structures of opportunity for children by linking preschool programs (with parent involvement) to enhanced educational programs in the schools as is being attempted in the Harlem Children's Zone. The idea of building more continuous enrichment efforts is not a new one, but it has not been a prominent approach in changing children's educational trajectories. More typically, children complete preschool programs only to enter poor schools with limited curriculums whose effect is often to retard the child's progress. These schools extinguish whatever gains the child achieved in preschool. We know that quality preschool education produces gains for children, but we also know that most of these gains will be erased later on. Building quality educational tracks that resemble the schooling offered to more affluent children is absolutely necessary if there is to be any hope of improving disadvantaged children's long-term educational prospects.

A third strategy involves immersing parents and children together in intensive programs. Some communities offering high-quality summer programs or camps for disadvantaged and moderately disadvantaged children have applied this approach already, though not many have made it part of a deliberate attempt to engage, if not immerse, the family in building school skills and management strategies aimed at promoting educational success. An annual summer camp could offer classes to both parents and children simultaneously along with recreational and skill-building opportunities.

Such programs, of course, face formidable challenges because parents are frequently unable to miss work, but it is possible to negotiate with employers to permit a week or two weeks in which parents and their children would be exposed to a range of enjoyable and educational activities. The idea is to immerse parents in an environment with like-minded families aimed at providing information and imparting skills. A program of this sort might be designed to maintain contact with parents during the year, offering counseling and assistance when problems in schooling arise and building what amounts to a community of supportive families. This type of program might target preschool children, but it would be appropriate for families with older children as well. Indeed, it might be desirable to direct this sort of programmatic intervention at families whose children are making transitions in the school system: to primary, middle, and high school.

A fourth strategy involves enhancing communication between schools and parents by making better use of the Internet and email (Hill and Chao 2009). School districts are gradually adopting these communication tools. Of course, the digital divide continues to exist, but it has narrowed over time. School districts might be able to mount programs to make the Internet available to all families (with supplementary grants from government or private funding sources). This strategy permits teachers to communicate with parents on a more regular basis, but it might require training teachers to make better use of the Internet to keep parents informed and more involved in what is happening in the classroom, to provide information on community resources such as tutoring or after-school programs, and to explain policies and practices in the school. This kind of intervention might be particularly useful as children move into middle school and high school, where parent involvement generally drops off. Such programs may only help the more motivated and capable parents, but they nonetheless offer a low-cost way of enhancing communication and family involvement.

Limited financial resources affect the capacity of low- and moderate-income families to implement their educational goals, apart from the disadvantages they face owing in part to insufficient cultural and social capital. Although research demonstrates that resource constraints are particularly consequential during early childhood, resources also play a part in constraining children's chances of making it through high school and beyond. In particular, adolescents and young adults from low-income households confront a number of income-related barriers to college. The children of poor and near-poor families are less likely to enter college, taking account of other factors that influence education, and they are less likely to complete a degree. Poorer families may also be less knowledgeable about financial assistance for higher education; they may be less willing and able to borrow funds to aid their offspring. In experimental studies on community college achievement, MDRC found that financial aid for low-income students increased course completion. In other words, providing direct monetary assistance to students may be one of the most effective ways of converting early school success into educational attainment. This strategy reminds us that supporting families' ambitions for their children ultimately requires greater aid for higher education, no matter how diligent policymakers may be about helping children get off to a good start in school.

A stream of recent research by economists has been devoted to finding out whether cash transfers conditional on performance of parents and children can be a useful approach to keeping children in school. Most work on this strategy has been carried out in developing nations, especially Latin America. The results are encouraging, but only a little of this work has examined the long-term impact on educational attainment (Ponce and Bedi 2010). New York City is currently evaluating a program designed for families with young children in collaboration with

MDRC. It is too early to tell just how useful this approach will turn out to be, but it deserves consideration as a potentially effective tool for aiding low-income parents.

Some have argued that directing resources to lower-income families either through tax policies such as the Earned Income Tax Credit or through child care, preschool programs, health care, after-school tax rebates, summer education programs, or tuition assistance would do more to help reduce educational inequality than interventions aimed at changing family practices. However, we need not pose the macro-level policies and the micro-level policies as strict alternatives. Instead, they can be seen as complementary approaches to reducing educational inequality.

Without policies directed toward reducing family instability, it will be difficult to make significant headway in raising the school achievement of poor children. This review shows that parents can also benefit from information and knowledge as well as assistance in dealing with intermittent crises that inevitably occur in all families, and more frequently in poorer families. It seems likely that for such interventions to be successful, they must be present throughout children's lives, not just during the preschool and primary school years. Building on earlier programs and paying particular attention to transitional points in school are potentially propitious approaches to assisting parents with limited cultural and social capital.

CONCLUSION

Policymakers appear to believe that intimately involving parents with low education and income in preparing children for school and helping them to succeed is a potent way to reduce educational inequality (see Mbwana, Terzian, and Moore 2009). Although this idea has some plausibility and merit, both theory about how family systems operate and evidence from experimental studies suggest we may be overestimating our capacity to alter family practices in ways that will reduce the achievement gap between advantaged and disadvantaged children.

It seems unlikely that children's mobility will be changed dramatically by micro-level programs aimed at helping families. Such efforts by themselves, especially in their current restricted form, will not do much to change the inequality gap. Macro-level programs that address income inequality and permit less-advantaged families greater access to higher-quality day care, preschool, summer learning opportunities, and ultimately better schools offer more promise of later success in the educational system. If such macro-level policies are in place, the micro-level interventions that help parents make better educational decisions for their children may likely have an even greater payoff than they currently do.

Ultimately, we may learn more about the role of both macro- and micro-level policies by cross-national comparisons that focus on how to mitigate the pervasive effects of social class on educational success. Studies of how and how much redistribution policies, educational policies, and programs aimed at increasing educational involvement enhance the level of intergenerational educational mobility would provide insight on what works in other nations to reduce educational inequality.

Finally, there may be other indirect strategies about which we have only limited evidence from nonexperimental studies that could lessen the burdens on disadvantaged parents, such as helping them to increase their own educational standing, control unintended childbearing, improve their health, or reduce involuntary housing moves (many of which require children to switch schools) that ultimately affect their children's chances of educational attainment.

American policymakers and the public at large strongly believe that the route to educational success runs largely through the family. Nonexperimental studies support this conviction. Yet the evidence from experimental studies aimed at changing family practices suggests that our ability to alter family processes to reduce educational inequality is largely inefficient. Although the nonexperimental studies may exaggerate the impact of families, results from the experiments probably underestimate the effect, largely because intervention programs have had little traction in altering family practices in a meaningful way.

I wish to thank Katherine Magnuson, Dick Murnane, Greg Duncan, Ruth Neild, and Barbara Ray, as well as participants in the November 2009 conference sponsored by the Russell Sage Foundation, "Rethinking the Role of Neighborhoods and Families on Schools and School Outcomes for American Children," for their helpful comments.

Online appendix available at: http://www.russellsage.org/duncan_murnane_online_appendix.pdf.

REFERENCES

Alexander, Karl L., and Doris R. Entwisle. 1996. "Schools and Children at Risk." In *Family-School Links: How Do They Affect Educational Outcomes?*, edited by Alan Booth and Judith F. Dunn. Mahwah, N.J.: Lawrence Erlbaum.

Amato, Paul, and Alan Booth. 1997. *A Generation at Risk: Growing Up in an Era of Family Upheaval.* Cambridge, Mass.: Harvard University Press.

Barnett, W. Steven. 1995. "Long-Term Effects of Early Childhood Programs on Cognitive and School Outcomes." *Future of Children* 5(3): 25–50.

Baumrind, Diana. 1967. "Child Care Practices Anteceding Three Patterns of the Preschool Behavior." *Genetic Psychology Monographs* 75(1): 43–88.

Bloom, Daniel. 2010. "Programs and Policies to Assist High School Dropouts in the Transition to Adulthood." *The Future of Children* 20(1): 89–108.

Booth, Alan, and Judith F. Dunn, eds. 1996. *Family-School Links: How Do They Affect Educational Outcomes?* Mahwah, N.J.: Lawrence Erlbaum.

Brock, Thomas. 2010. "Young Adults and Higher Education: Barriers and Breakthroughs to Success." *The Future of Children* 20(1): 109–32.

Bronfenbrenner, Uri. 1979. *The Ecology of Human Development: Experiments by Nature and Design.* Cambridge, Mass.: Harvard University Press.

Brooks-Gunn, Jeanne. 2003. "Do You Believe in Magic? What We Can Expect from Early Childhood Intervention Programs." *Social Policy Report* 17(1): 3–15.

Brooks-Gunn, Jeanne, Greg Duncan, and Lawrence Aber, eds. 1997. *Neighborhood Poverty I: Context and Consequences for Children.* New York: Russell Sage Foundation.

Cairns Robert B., Glen Elder, and E. Jane Costello. 2001. *Developmental Science.* Cambridge: University of Cambridge.

Clark, Reginald. 1983. *Family Life and School Achievement: Why Poor Black Children Succeed or Fail.* Chicago: University of Chicago Press.

Coleman, James. 1988. "Social Capital in the Creation of Human Capital." *American Journal of Sociology* 94: S95–S120.

Coleman, James S., Ernest Q. Campbell, Carol J. Hobson, James McPartland, Alexander M. Mood, Frederic D. Weinfeld, and Robert L. York. 1966. *Equality of Educational Opportunity.* Washington, D.C.: U.S. Government Printing Office.

Cooper, Catherine R., Cynthia T. Garcia Coll, W. Todd Bartko, Helen Davis, and Celina Chatman, eds. 2005. *Developmental Pathways Through Middle Childhood: Rethinking Contexts and Diversity as Resources.* Mahwah, N.J.: Lawrence Erlbaum.

Cowan, Philip A., and Carolyn P. Cowan. 2002. "What an Intervention Design Reveals About How Parents Affect Their Children's Academic Achievement and Behavior Problems." In *Parenting and the Child's World: Influences on Intellectual, Academic, and Social-Emotional Development,* edited by John. G. Borkowski, Sharon L. Ramey, and Marie Bristol-Powers. Mahwah, N.J.: Lawrence Erlbaum.

Daro, Deborah D., and Karen McCurdy. 2007. "Interventions to Prevent Child Maltreatment." In *Handbook of Injury and Violence Prevention,* edited by Lynda S. Doll, Sandra E. Bonzo, David A. Sleet, and James A. Mercy. Secaucus, N.J.: Springer.

Dearing, Eric, Kathleen McCartney, and Beck A. Taylor. 2001. "Change in Family Income-to-Needs Matters More for Children with Less." *Child Development* 72(6): 1779–93.

Desforges, Charles, with Alberto Abouchaar. 2003. "The Impact of Parental Involvement, Parental Support and Family Education on Pupil Achievements and Adjustment: A Literature Review." Research Report RR433. London: Queen's Printer. Available at: http://www.bgfl.org/bgfl/custom/files_uploaded/uploaded_resources/18617/Desforges.pdf (accessed March 22, 2011).

Dobbie, Will, and Roland G. Fryer, Jr. 2009. "Are High Quality Schools Enough to Close the Achievement Gap? Evidence from a Social Experiment in Harlem." NBER Working Paper No. 15473. Cambridge, Mass.: National Bureau of Economic Research.

Dodge, Kenneth A., and Gregory S. Pettit. 2003. "A Biopsychosocial Model of the Development of Chronic Conduct Problems in Adolescence." *Developmental Psychology* 39(2): 189–90.

Duncan, Greg J., Aletha C. Huston, and Thomas S. Weisner. 2007. *Higher Ground: New Hope for the Working Poor and Their Children.* New York: Russell Sage Foundation.

Duncan, Greg J., and Katherine A. Magnuson. 2005. "Can Family Socioeconomic Resources Account for Racial and Ethnic Test Score Gaps?" *The Future of Children* 15(1): 35–52.

Dunn, Judy, Robert Plomin, and Denise Daniels. 1986. "Consistency and Change in Mothers' Behavior Toward Young Siblings." *Child Development* 57(2): 348–56.

Eccles, Jacquelynne, and Rena D. Harold. 1993. "Parent-School Involvement During the Early Adolescent Years." *Teachers College Record* 94(3): 568–87.

Elder, Glen H., Jr. 1974. *Children of the Great Depression.* Chicago: University of Chicago Press.

Entwisle, Doris R., Karl L. Alexander and Linda S. Olson. 1997. *Children, Schools, and Inequality.* Boulder, Colo.: Westview Press.

Epps, Sylvia R., and Aletha C. Huston. 2007. "Effects of a Poverty Intervention Policy Demonstration on Parenting and Child Behavior: A Test of the Direction of Effects." *Social Science Quarterly* 88(2): 344–65.

Falbo, Toni, Laura Lein, and Nicole A. Amador. 2001. "Parental Involvement During the Transition to High School." *Journal of Adolescent Research* 16(5): 511–29.

Fan, Xitao, and Michael Chen. 2001. "Parental Involvement and Students' Academic Achievement: A Meta-Analysis." *Educational Psychology Review* 13(1): 1–22.

Furstenberg, Frank F., Thomas D. Cook, Jacquelynne Eccles, Glen H. Elder, Jr., and Arnold Sameroff. 1999. *Managing to Make It: Urban Families and Adolescent Success.* Chicago: University of Chicago Press.

Furstenberg, Frank F., and Kathleen Kiernan. 2001. "Delayed Parental Divorce: How Much Do Children Benefit?" *Journal of Marriage and the Family* 63(2): 446–57.

Gomby, Deanna S. 2005. "Home Visitation in 2005: Outcomes for Children and Parents." Invest in Kids Working Paper 7. Washington, D.C.: Committee for Economic Development.

Gomby, Deanna S., Patti L. Culross, and Richard E. Behrman. 1999. "Home Visiting: Recent Program Evaluations: Analysis and Recommendations. *The Future of Children* 9(1): 4–26.

Goodson, Barbara Dillon. 2005. "Parent Support Programs and Outcomes for Children." In *Encyclopedia on Early Childhood Development,* edited by Richard E. Tremblay, Ronald G. Barr, and Ray deV. Peters. Cambridge, Mass: Abt Associates. Available at: http://www.child-encyclopedia.com/documents/GoodsonANGxp.pdf (accessed March 22, 2011).

Haley, Jay. 1971. *Changing Families: A Family Therapy Reader.* New York: Grune and Stratton.

Harris, Judith Rich. 1998. *The Nurture Assumption: Why Children Turn Out the Way They Do.* New York: Free Press.

Harris, Marian S. 1999. "Comparing Mothers of Children in Kinship Foster Care: Reunification vs. Remaining in Care." In *Kinship Care: Improving Practice Through Research,* edited by James P. Gleeson and Creasie Finney Hairston. Washington, D.C.: Child Welfare League of America.

Hart, Betty, and Todd R. Risley. 1995. *Meaningful Differences in the Everyday Experiences of Young American Children.* Baltimore: Paul H. Brookes.

Heckman, James J., and Lance Lochner. 2000. "Rethinking Education and Training Policy: Understanding the Sources of Skill Formation in a Modern Economy." In *Securing the Future: Investing in Children from Birth to College,* edited by Sheldon Danziger and Jane Waldfogel. New York: Russell Sage Foundation.

Hess, Robert D., and Susan D. Holloway. 1984. "Family and School as Educational Institutions." In *Review of Child Development Research,* edited by Ross Parke. Chicago: University of Chicago Press.

Hill, Nancy E., and Ruth K. Chao, eds. 2009. *Families, Schools, and the Adolescent: Connecting Research, Policy, and Practice.* New York: Teachers College Press.

Hobcraft, John N. 2004. "Parental, Childhood and Early Adult Legacies in the Emergence of Adult Social Exclusion: Evidence on What Matters from a British Cohort." In *Human Development Across Lives and Generations: The Potential for Change,* edited by P. Lindsay Chase-Lansdale, Kathleen E. Kiernan, and Ruth J. Friedman. New York: Cambridge University Press.

Hughes, Jean R., and Laurie N. Gottlieb. 2004. "The Effects of the Webster-Stratton Parenting Program on Maltreating Families: Fostering Strengths." *Child Abuse and Neglect* 28(10): 1081–97.

Hulbert, Ann. 2003. *Raising America: Experts, Parents, and a Century of Advice About Children.* New York: Knopf.

Huston, Aletha C., Greg J. Duncan, Vonnie McLoyd, D. A. Crosby, Marika R. Ripke, T. S. Weisner, and C. A. Eldred. 2005a. "Impacts on Children of a Policy to Promote Employment and Reduce Poverty for Low-Income: New Hope after Five Years." *Developmental Psychology* 41: 902–18.

Huston, Aletha, and Marika N. Ripke. 2006. *Developmental Contexts in Middle Childhood.* New York: Cambridge University Press.

Huston, Aletha C., Rashmita S. Mistry, J. Bos, E. Lowe, and M. S. Shim. 2005b. "Well-Being of Low-Income Adults in a Period of Historical Changes in Welfare and Employment Policies." In *Historical Influences on Lives and Aging,* edited by K. W. Schaie and Glen H. Elder, Jr. New York: Springer.

Jeynes, William H. 2005. "A Meta-Analysis of the Relation of Parental Involvement to Urban Elementary School Student Academic Achievement." *Urban Education* 40(3): 237–69.

Kalil, Ariel, and Thomas C. DeLeire, eds. 2004. *Family Investments in Children's Potential: Resources and Parenting Behaviors That Promote Success.* Mahwah, N.J.: Lawrence Erlbaum.

Lareau, Annette. 2008. *Unequal Childhoods: Class, Race, and Family Life.* Berkeley: University of California Press.

Lewin, Kurt. 1935. *A Dynamic Theory of Personality.* New York: McGraw-Hill.

Lowe, John, Ellen Eliason Kisker, Christine Ross, Jill Constantine, Kimberly Boller, Rachel Chazan-Cohen, Christy Brady-Smith, Allison Sidle Fuligni, Helen Raikes, Jeanne Brooks-Gunn, Louisa Banks Tarullo, Peter Z. Schochet, Diane Paulsell, and Cheri Vogel. 2005. "The Effectiveness of Early Head Start for 3-Year Old Children and Their Parents: Lessons for Policy and Programs." *Developmental Psychology* 41(6): 885–901.

Maccoby, Eleanor E., and J. A. Martin. 1983. "Socialization in the Context of the Family: Parent-Child Interaction." In *Handbook of Child Psychology,* edited by Paul H. Mussen and E. Mavis Hetherington. New York: Wiley.

Magnuson, Katherine, and Greg Duncan. 2004. "Parent- vs. Child-Based Intervention Strategies for Promoting Children's Well-Being." In *Family Investments in Children: Resources and Behaviors that Promote Success,* edited by Ariel Kalil and Thomas De Leire. Mahwah, N.J.: Lawrence Erlbaum.

Magnuson, Katherine, Greg J. Duncan, and Ariel Kalil. 2006. "The Contribution of Middle Childhood Contexts to Adolescent Achievement and Behavior." In *Developmental Contexts in Middle Childhood,* edited by Aletha Huston and Marika N. Ripke. New York: Cambridge University Press.

Magnuson, Katherine, and Elizabeth Votruba-Drzal. 2008. "Enduring Influences of Childhood Poverty." In *Changing Poverty,* edited by Maria Cancian and Sheldon Danziger. New York: Russell Sage Foundation.

Mattingly, Doreen J., Radmila Prislin, Thomas L. McKenzie, James L. Rodriquez, and Brenda Kayzar. 2002. "Evaluating Evaluations: The Case of Parent Involvement Programs." *Review of Educational Research* 72(4): 549–76.

Mbwana, Kassim, Mary Terzian, and Kristin A. Moore. 2009. "What Works for Parent Involvement Programs for Children: Lessons from Experimental Evaluations of Social Interventions." *Child Trends Fact Sheet.* Publication 2009–47. Washington, D.C.: Child Trends.

McLanahan, Sara, and Gary Sandefur. 1994. *Growing Up with a Single Parent: What Hurts, What Helps.* Cambridge, Mass.: Harvard University Press.

Mead, George H. 1934. *Mind, Self, and Society.* Chicago: University of Chicago Press.

Minuchin, Salvador, Montalvo Braulio, Bernard G. Guerney, Jr., Bernice Rosman, and Florence Schumer. 1967. *Families of the Slums: An Exploration of Their Structure and Treatment.* New York: Basic Books.

Morris, Pamela, Greg J. Duncan, and Elizabeth Clark-Kauffman. 2005. "Child Well-Being in an Era of Welfare Reform: The Sensitivity of Transitions in Development to Policy Change." *Developmental Psychology* 41(6): 919–32.

Morris, Pamela, Greg J. Duncan, and Christopher Rodrigues. 2007. "Does Money Really Matter? Estimating Impacts of Family Income on Young Children's Achievement with Data from Random-Assignment Experiments." Next Generation Working Paper 27. New York: MDRC.

Morris, Pamela, and Lisa A. Gennetian. 2003. "Identifying the Effects of Income on Children's Development: Using Experimental Data." *Journal of Marriage and the Family* 65(3): 716–29.

Nelson, Charles A., Charles H. Zeanah, Nathan A. Fox, Peter J. Marshall, Anna T. Smyke, and Donald Guthrie. 2007. "Cognitive Recovery in Socially Deprived Young Children: The Bucharest Early Intervention Project." *Science* 318(5858): 1937–40.

Olds, David, Lois Sadler, and Harriet Kitzman. 2007. "Programs for Parents of Infants and Toddlers: Recent Evidence from a Randomized Trial." *Journal of Child Psychology and Psychiatry* 48(3–4): 355–91.

Patrikakou, Eva. 2004. "Adolescence: Are Parents Relevant to Students' High School Achievement and Post-Secondary Attainment?" The Harvard Family Research Project. Family Involvement Network of Educators: Research Digests. Cambridge, Mass.: Harvard School of Education. Available at: http://www.hfrp.org/publications-resources/browse-our-publications/adolescence-are-parents-relevant-to-students-high-school-achievement-and-post-secondary-attainment (accessed March 22, 2011).

Patterson, Gerald R. 1976. *Living with Children: New Methods for Parents and Teachers.* Champaign, Ill.: Research Press.

Ponce, Juan, and Arjun S. Bedi. 2010. "The Impact of a Cash Transfer Program on Cognitive Achievement: The *Bono de Desarrollo Humano* of Ecuador." *Economics of Education Review* 29(1): 116–25.

Reynolds, Arthur J., Katherine A. Magnuson, and Suh-Ruu Ou. 2006. "P–3 Education Programs and Practices That Work in Children's First Decade." Working Paper. New York: Foundation of Child Development.

Reynolds, Arthur J., Judy A. Temple, Dylan L. Robertson, and Emily A. Mann. 2001. "Long-Term Effects of an Early Childhood Intervention on Educational Achievement and Juvenile Arrest: A 15-Year Follow-Up of Low-Income Children in Public Schools." *Journal of the American Medical Association* 285(18): 2339–46.

Schoeni, Robert F., and Karen E. Ross. 2005. "Material Assistance from Families During the Transition to Adulthood." In *On the Frontier of Adulthood: Theory, Research, and Public Policy,* edited by Richard A. Settersten, Jr., Frank F. Furstenberg, and Ruben G. Rumbaut. Chicago: University of Chicago Press.

Schulz, Marc S., Philip Cowan, and Carolyn Cowan. 2006. "Promoting Healthy Beginnings: A Randomized Controlled Trial of a Preventive Intervention to Preserve Marital Quality During the Transition to Parenthood." *Journal of Clinical and Consulting Psychology* 74(1): 20–31.

Shadish, William R., L. M. Montgomery, P. Wilson, M. R. Wilson, I. Bright, and T. Okwumabua. 1993. "Effects of Family and Marital Psychotherapies: A Meta-Analysis." *Journal of Consulting and Clinical Psychology* 61(6): 992–1002.

Sigle-Rushton, Wendy, and Sara McLanahan. 2004. "Father Absence and Child Well-Being: A Critical Review." In *The Future of the Family,* edited by Daniel P. Moynihan, Timothy M. Smeeding, and Lee Rainwater. New York: Russell Sage Foundation.

Slavin, Robert A., and Nancy A. Madden. 2001. *Success for All: Research and Reform in Elementary Education.* New York: Routledge.

Stanton, M. Duncan, and William R. Shadish. 1997. "Outcome, Attrition, and Family-Couples Treatment for Drug Abuse: A Meta-Analysis and Review of the Controlled, Comparative Studies." *Psychological Bulletin* 122(2): 170–91.

St. Pierre, Robert G., Anne E. Ricciuti, and Tracy A. Rimdzius. 2005. "Effects of a Family Literacy Program on Low-Literate Children and Their Parents: Findings from an Evaluation of the Even Start Family Literacy Program." *Developmental Psychology* 41(6): 953–70.

Sweet, Monica A., and Mark I. Appelbaum. 2004. "Is Home Visiting an Effective Strategy? A Meta-Analytic Review of Home Visiting Programs for Families with Young Children." *Child Development* 75(5): 1435–56.

Teachman, Jay. 1987. "Family Background, Educational Resources and Educational Attainment." *American Sociological Review* 52(4): 548–57.

Thomas, William I., and Edmund H. Volkart. 1951. "Social Behavior and Personality." In *Contributions of W.I. Thomas to Theory and Social Research,* edited by Edmund H. Volkart. New York: Social Science Research Council.

Waldfogel, Jane. 2006. *What Children Need.* Cambridge, Mass.: Harvard University Press.

Weiss, Christopher, and Frank F. Furstenberg. 1997. "Schooling Together: Mutual Influences on Educational Success of Teenage Mothers and their Children." Paper presented at the biennial meetings of the Society for Research on Adolescence, Washington, D.C. (April 3–6).

White, Karl R., Matthew J. Taylor, and Vanessa D. Moss. 1992. "Does Research Support Claims About the Benefits of Involving Parents in Early Intervention Programs?" *Review of Educational Research* 62(1): 92–125.

Yeung, W. Jean, Niriam R. Linver, and Jeanne Brooks-Gunn. 2002. "How Money Matters for Young Children's Development: Parental Investment and Family Processes." *Child Development* 73(6): 1861–79.

Chapter 23

It May Not Take a Village: Increasing Achievement Among the Poor

Vilsa E. Curto, Roland G. Fryer Jr., and Meghan L. Howard

One of the triumphs of recent research on the causes of racial inequality has been the discovery that many of the disparities that exist in wages, incarceration rates, and health outcomes can be explained by racial disparities in educational achievement. Minority children are woefully unprepared to compete in the labor market: the average black seventeen-year-old reads at the proficiency level of the average white thirteen-year-old, and minority children consistently score lower than their white counterparts on national assessments in every subject and at every grade level. However, the correlation between educational achievement and life outcomes offers hope. Important progress toward achieving racial inequality may be made if we close the racial achievement gap.

In this chapter we survey targeted social interventions aimed at increasing the academic achievement of minority students. We restrict our attention to evaluations that use a credible experimental or quasi-experimental design. These interventions can be categorized conceptually as community investments, school investments, or some combination of the two. Furthermore, one can loosely characterize the intensity of each investment as low, medium, or high. Equipped with this framework, we provide an overview of these interventions and their effectiveness at raising student achievement.

The programs we review cover a broad spectrum of community-based and school-based interventions, including charter schools, housing vouchers for low-income families to move to low-poverty neighborhoods, cash transfers to encourage parents to engage in behaviors that support education, a boarding school for disadvantaged youths, and a social experiment in Harlem that couples rigorous charter schools with deep-dive community investments. We conclude that the most promising results come from a set of gap-closing, high-quality charter schools that have certain core institutional elements in common. These schools employ a "No Excuses" model that usually involves aggressive human-capital strategies; extended school days or school years; a high level of commitment from students, parents, and faculty; and the use of data-driven instruction. In addition, the evaluation of the Harlem Children's Zone allows us to conclude that a high-quality school coupled with community-based interventions does not produce better results than a high-quality school alone, offering further evidence that school investments offer higher social returns than community-based interventions.

Admittedly, there are aspects of the No Excuses model that raise concerns about the feasibility of its widespread implementation in public schools. For instance, an aggressive human-capital strategy that involves firing many teachers could be problematic if executed on a large scale. Furthermore, charter school students and their parents may compose a particularly motivated and unrepresentative sector of the population, and charter school practices may not be as effective in the traditional public school system.

Nevertheless, the most promising avenue for future research will be rigorous empirical investigation and experimentation to pinpoint the charter school practices that would translate most effectively into improved student outcomes if they were introduced into the traditional public school system. Evaluating these strategies and implementing only those that drive student achievement, though difficult, holds enormous promise as a step toward achieving racial equality.

One of the most important developments in the study of racial inequality in the past quarter-century has been the quantification of the importance of premarket skills in explaining differences in economic and social outcomes between minorities and nonminorities (Neal and Johnson 1996; O'Neill 1990). Using the National Longitudinal Survey of Youth 1979 (NLSY79), a nationally representative sample of 12,686 individuals age fourteen to twenty-two in 1979, Derek A. Neal and William R. Johnson (1996) show that educational achievement among fifteen- to eighteen-year-olds explains all of the black-white wage gap between young women and 70 percent of the gap between men. Important critiques such as racial bias in the achievement measure (Darity and Mason 1998; Jencks 1998), labor-market dropouts, or the possibility that forward-looking minorities underinvest in human capital because they anticipate discrimination in the market cannot explain the stark results.[1] Roland Fryer (forthcoming) shows that the key insight from Neal and Johnson (1996) is robust to including the most recent wage data (in which individuals are fifteen years older than in the original analysis) and extends far beyond income. Accounting for educational achievement reduces disparities in employment by 53 percent, incarceration by 79 percent, and health outcomes by 88 percent (defined by the Physical Component Score of the twelve-item Short Form Health Survey).

In developing countries, eradicating poverty requires a large and diverse set of strategies: battling disease, fighting corruption, building schools, providing clean water, and so on (Schultz and Strauss 2008). In the United States, important progress toward racial equality can be made by ensuring that African American and white children obtain the same skills.

The problem is that despite decades of interventions, we do not know how to close the racial achievement gap. Early-childhood interventions such as Perry Preschool, Head Start, the Nurse-Family Partnership, and the Milwaukee Project boost kindergarten readiness, but the effects on cognitive ability often fade after children enter school (Currie and Thomas 1995; Puma et al. 2010). School district–based strategies such as smaller schools and classrooms (Jepsen and Rivkin 2002; Krueger 1999); mandatory summer school (Jacob and Lefgren 2004); merit pay for principals, teachers, and students (Fryer 2010; Podgursky and Springer 2007); after-school programs (Lauer et al. 2006); budget, curricula, and assessment reorganization (Borman et al. 2003); ending social promotion (Jacob and Lefgren 2009); and policies to lower the barrier to teaching via alternative paths to accreditation (Decker, Mayer, and Glazerman 2004; Kane, Rockoff, and Staiger 2008) have not substantially reduced the gap in even the most reform-minded districts. In an analysis of policies to foster the development of human capital in poor children, Brian Jacob and Jens Ludwig (2008) estimate that targeted investment in early-childhood education, smaller class sizes, and bonuses for teachers in hard-to-staff schools all pass a cost-benefit analysis, but cannot close the achievement gap by themselves.

FIGURE 23.1 *Conceptual School Quality and Environmental Quality Matrix*

		Low	Medium	High
School Quality	Low	Status quo	Moving to Opportunity	------
	Medium	Typical charter school	------	------
	High	No Excuses charter school	Harlem Children's Zone and SEED charter school	------ *

Environment

Source: Authors' figure.
*A Better Chance scholarship program provides low-income minority students with high-quality schools and high-quality environments, but there is no credible evaluation of its impacts. See note 14.

The lack of progress in closing the racial achievement gap has led some to assert that we need more supportive communities and neighborhoods; stronger, more intact families and engaged parents; or less income inequality to eliminate racial disparities in achievement (Brooks-Gunn and Markman 2005; Duncan and Magnuson 2005; Rothstein 2004). Others have interpreted the lack of progress as prima facie evidence that genetics or other cultural dysfunctions are holding blacks back and argue that these problems cannot be solved by government interventions (Ferguson 2001; Herrnstein and Murray 1994; Jensen 1973; Rushton 1995). A third group argues that the presence of labor unions makes true reform impossible (Hoxby 1996; Thernstrom and Thernstrom 2004), dismissing the current school-based interventions as being tantamount to "fiddling while Rome burns." Understanding how and where to invest our resources—communities, schools, families, and so on—is a subject of intense debate and vicious disagreement. The answer is of first-order importance for the direction of public policy designed to eliminate racial inequality.

In this chapter we describe recent social experiments and evaluations of investments in schools, communities, and family engagement strategies and use these data to argue that it may not take a village to increase the educational achievement of the poorest minority children. We envision a three-by-three conceptual matrix: school quality categorized as low, medium, and high, and environment quality categorized similarly (figure 23.1 is an illustration).

As an anchor, we assume that the typical low-income minority student is now in a low-quality school and is being reared in a low-quality environment. We do not want to quibble over words here, so consider this a normalization. On the opposite end, there are several features that seem common among high-quality schools, including challenging coursework (college preparatory at the secondary level); orderly, respectful, and safe environments; and high expectations for student success. These and other characteristics are necessary elements of what Thernstrom and Thernstrom (2004) call the No Excuses model that many charter schools have adopted. We realize that the placement of particular interventions into a category in our conceptual matrix will, to some extent, be ad hoc. We do our best to adhere to a clear and principled assignment mechanism, although we recognize that all such mechanisms will cause some amount of concern for the reader.

With these important caveats in mind, we use recent evaluations of charter schools across the United States to show that providing high-quality schools to children who live in low-quality environments can significantly increase their achievement. Yet, changing environments by moving individuals to different neighborhoods or placing them in boarding schools to create a more nurturing and stimulating substitute home environment does not significantly alter achievement.[2] Taken together, the evidence to date suggests it may not take a village to increase the achievement of the poorest minority students, just a high-quality school.[3]

STATUS QUO FOR LOW-INCOME MINORITY CHILDREN

The racial achievement gap is a persistent fact of life in the United States. Although there are no cognitive differences between black and white infants, cognitive differences can be observed as early as two years of age (Fryer and Levitt forthcoming), and these differences can thereafter be observed at every grade level in every subject (Campbell, Hombo, and Mazzeo 2000; Neal 2005). The typical black seventeen-year-old reads at the proficiency level of the typical white thirteen-year-old (Campbell, Hombo, and Mazzeo 2000). On the SAT, black college-goers score, on average, more than one standard deviation below white college-goers (Card and Rothstein 2004).

The differences are even more dramatic in large urban areas. On the National Assessment of Educational Progress (NAEP), only 14 percent of black fourth-graders in large cities are at least proficient in mathematics, compared with 55 percent of white fourth-graders; for reading, these figures are 14 and 47 percent, respectively. In eighth grade, 10 percent of black students in large cities are proficient in math, compared with 47 percent of white students; the figures for reading are 11 and 41 percent, respectively.

Even these numbers cannot fully describe the lack of achievement of black students in some urban areas. In Detroit, for example, 4 percent of black fourth-graders are proficient in math; by eighth grade, 3 percent are proficient. Similarly, 5 percent of black fourth- and eighth-graders in Cleveland are proficient in math. In Milwaukee, 6 percent of black fourth-graders and 3 percent of black eighth-graders are proficient in math. Of the eighteen districts in the NAEP Trial Urban District Assessment (TUDA) sample, at least half of the black students in fourteen of these districts score at the "below basic" level on eighth grade math.

High-poverty urban public schools can often be characterized by certain recurring qualities. A MetLife study (2001) of principals, teachers, and students reports that teachers and principals in heavily minority or low-income schools have lower expectations for their students and report lower teaching quality than teachers and principals in schools with lower poverty rates or lower concentrations of minority students. Students in low-income schools report that the curriculum and courses are not challenging. Teachers and principals from low-income schools also report lower quality of instruction and lower quality of the physical school environment than teachers in more affluent schools.

The community and home environments of black children also offer a stark picture of racial inequality. According to the 2008 American Community Survey, 67 percent of black women between the ages of fifteen and fifty who gave birth in a twelve-month period were unmarried, compared with only 26 percent of white women. One-third of black children live below the poverty level; for whites, 11 percent do. Twenty percent of black households received food stamps in 2008, compared with 6 percent of white households.[4] At the end of the 1990s, one-third more black men were under the jurisdiction of the corrections system than were enrolled in colleges or universities (Ziedenberg and Schiraldi 2002).

With these facts in mind, we label the status quo for low-income minority children as low-quality schools and a low-quality environment. In what follows, we describe interventions in terms of how they change either the social environment in which students live or the schools that students attend.

CHARTER SCHOOLS

One of the most promising education reforms in the past fifty years has been the creation of char-ter schools. Charter schools are publicly funded but privately run schools that are playing an increasingly significant role in the field of public school reform, especially in large urban areas. Minnesota passed the first charter school law in 1991; today, thirty-nine states and the District of Columbia have laws to authorize charter schools. The laws vary significantly from state to state. Some states cap the number of charter schools, some do not; some states require charter school teachers to remain covered by collective bargaining agreements, others do not.[5] As of the 2009–2010 school year, more than 1.6 million students were attending 4,638 charter schools across the country. Most charter schools are located in cities and serve a student popu-lation that is disproportionately black.[6] At their current rate of growth, it will take charter schools forty years to educate every student. Owing to their relative freedom, charter schools use an array of intervention strategies, which include parental pledges of involvement and aggressive human capital strategies that tie teacher retention to value-added measures. There has been a recent flurry of work on the efficacy of charter schools, which we describe next.

National Sample of Charter Schools

Philip Gleason et al. (2010) conducted a national study of thirty-six charter middle schools in fifteen states. By limiting the set of analyzed schools to include only those that were oversub-scribed and that used a lottery to determine student enrollment, the authors are able to credi-bly estimate the causal relationship of attendance at these schools on student achievement. They find that, on average, the charter schools studied are no more or less successful at improving student achievement than traditional public schools. Taken on its own this average, however, masks the sizable variance in the effect size of different schools. The effects on students' read-ing scores after two years were estimated to be greater than zero in eleven sites and less than zero in seventeen sites, and the estimates were significant for only four sites. For math, the effects were greater than zero in ten sites and less than zero in eighteen sites, and the estimates were significant for ten sites. The authors also find that charter middle schools in large urban areas have significant positive impacts on math achievement, while charter middle schools in other settings have negative effects in this domain.

It is important to note that there are some significant demographic differences between the charter schools included in this study and charter schools in general. In the charter schools included in the study, students were less likely to be eligible for free or reduced-price lunch (44 versus 62 percent), were less likely to be minority students (47 versus 62 percent), and were less likely to have scored below proficiency on the state assessment before entering the charter lottery. Because this chapter focuses on interventions aimed at improving the educational or environmental experiences of low-income minority students, the relevance of these results must be interpreted carefully. Next, we explore analyses of charter schools that more specifically serve this target population.

New York City

Caroline Hoxby and Sonali Murarka (2009) use matched charter school and New York City public schools data from forty-two of New York City's forty-seven charter schools that were operating during the 2005–2006 school year to analyze the impact of charter schools on student performance.[7] They first examine the comparability of students who entered charter school lotteries and students from similar public schools in New York City who did not enter charter school lotteries. They then compare winners and losers of the lotteries for spots in charter schools. Comparing charter school applicants and nonapplicants using weighted averages of the traditional public schools from which the charter schools draw applicants, Hoxby and Murarka find that charter school applicants and their comparison group are quite similar in terms of gender ratios and the percentage that are non-Hispanic white, Asian, or "other" race. The charter applicants group, however, is significantly more black (64 percent versus 50 percent) and less Hispanic (32 percent versus 45 percent) than the comparison group.[8] They also conclude that charter school applicants are more likely to be eligible for free or reduced-price lunch than those in the comparison group, are equally likely to be special education students, and are less likely to be English Language Learners (ELL).

The forty-two charter schools that Hoxby and Murarka (2009) examine differ substantially in their methodology, inputs, and ultimate results. The authors sort the styles of charter schools in New York City into five groups: those with a child-centered, progressive educational philosophy; general or traditional educational program; rigorous academic focus; schools that target a specific population of students; and those that focus on a specific aspect of the curriculum. The schools that are considered to have a rigorous academic focus are likely to be of high quality, but only twelve of the schools (serving 25 percent of charter students in the study) can be classified as fitting this model (Hoxby and Murarka 2009). Some New York City charter schools have been closed owing to poor performance, so we also know that some of the charter schools are likely of low quality. Because of the wide variance in charter school quality in this study, we believe that, on average, New York City charter schools are of medium quality. The environments in which these students are reared can be considered low-quality, so an analysis of this intervention allows us to examine the impact of medium-quality schools and a low-quality environment.

By New York law, oversubscribed charter schools must assign admission via random lottery. When comparing lottery winners to lottery losers, Hoxby and Murarka (2009) find no significant differences between the groups in terms of the observable characteristics described above. Between lottery winners who attend and lottery winners who do not attend, those who attend are slightly more likely to be female and slightly less likely to be special education or ELL students. Using only those lotteries that were balanced, Hoxby and Murarka find that charter schools in New York City increase student achievement in grades three through eight by 0.09 standard deviations in math and 0.04 standard deviations in reading for each year that a student spends in the school.[9] Thus, providing students with average-quality schools while maintaining their low-quality social environment produces modest results.

Boston

Atila Abdulkadiroglu and his colleagues (2009) compare charter school attendance with traditional public school or pilot school attendance in Boston.[10] Restricting their analysis to only oversubscribed charter schools that were operating when data were collected and that had available lottery data, the authors are able to include five charter middle schools and four charter high schools in their analysis. Comparing the charter school population with the overall population of Boston public schools, the authors find that Boston charter schools with available lottery data have a higher percentage of black students (59 percent versus 47 percent in middle schools; 68 percent versus 51 percent in high schools) and a smaller percentage of Hispanic students (19 percent versus 37 percent in middle schools; 23 percent versus 36 percent in high schools) than traditional public schools, a finding similar to that of Hoxby and Murarka (2009) in New York City. Charter students are less likely to be eligible for free or reduced-price lunch or to be English Language Learners than students in traditional public schools. Incoming middle and high school charter students also have substantially higher previous year's test scores in math and English language arts than their public school peers. They conclude, however, that those who enroll in charter schools are similar to the overall charter lottery group on these characteristics.[11]

Although it seems clear that Boston charter schools attract a stronger student group than the average Boston public school, it is difficult to determine whether the Boston charter schools examined in this study are themselves medium- or high-quality schools. To answer this question, we examine the individual schools included in the study. All five of the included middle schools are considered by themselves and others to be No Excuses charter schools. Of the four high schools, one is explicitly a No Excuses school, while two others have features that lead many to consider them to fit into that model.[12] For these reasons, we consider this study to be an analysis of the impact of mainly high-quality schools on above-average students in low-quality environments.

Abdulkadiroglu et al. (2009) find that charter middle school students outperform charter school applicants who attend traditional public schools by 0.149 standard deviations per year in English language arts and 0.405 standard deviations per year in math. Charter high school students' English language arts scores are 0.187 standard deviations higher per year and their math scores are 0.274 standard deviations higher per year.[13]

Lynn, Massachusetts

The Knowledge is Power Program (KIPP) is the nation's largest charter school network. In 2009–2010, there were eighty-two KIPP schools in nineteen states and the District of Columbia serving more than 21,000 students. KIPP was founded as a middle school curriculum model, in Houston, Texas, in 1994, by two Teach for America alumni. The KIPP Foundation has since expanded to preschool, elementary, and high school instruction, although KIPP still serves students mostly in grades five through eight. KIPP schools are characterized by high expectations (both academically and behaviorally), more time-on-task (longer school day and school year than in traditional public schools), selective teacher hiring, and a high-commitment requirement for students, parents, and faculty—the features that distinguish a school as a No Excuses adherent.

KIPP Academy Lynn, in Lynn, Massachusetts, north of Boston, was founded in 2004, and in 2007–2008 served 326 students in grades five through eight. The school serves a student body that is about half Hispanic and 22 percent black. Eighty-three percent of the student body is eligible for free or reduced-price lunch, and 17 percent of the school's students are classified as having special needs.[14]

Like other KIPP schools and the majority of the Boston charter schools examined by Abdulkadiroglu et al. (2009), KIPP Lynn is a No Excuses charter school, suggesting that this, too, falls into the matrix category of high-quality school and low-quality environment. The important distinction between KIPP Lynn and the Boston charter schools is that, as demonstrated by Joshua D. Angrist et al. (2010), KIPP Lynn students are quite representative of the general population

FIGURE 23.2   *Student Achievement in KIPP Lynn*

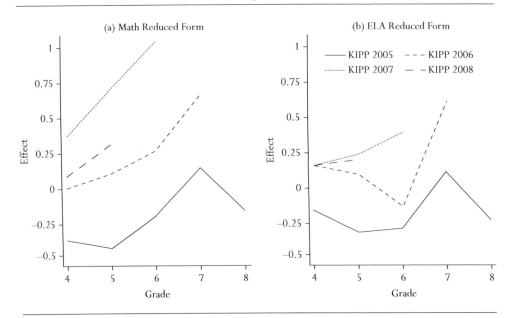

Source: Angrist et al. (2010), with permission.

from which they are drawn, whereas the Boston charter school analysis informs us about the impact of this combination (high-quality school, low-quality environment) on above-average students. Therefore, the analysis of KIPP Lynn allows us to draw stronger conclusions about the impact of high-quality schools on typical students from a low-quality environment.

Because of state regulations, KIPP Lynn must fill its incoming class using a lottery if more students apply than there are spots available. This random assignment of students into—and out of—the program allows for reliable evaluation of program effects. Angrist et al. (2010) use lottery data from KIPP Lynn and student data from the Massachusetts Student Information Management System (SIMS) to compare the performance of KIPP Lynn lottery winners with the performance of those who entered the lottery but did not win a spot in the school.[15] Using test scores from the Massachusetts Comprehensive Assessment System (MCAS) and a two-stage least squares analysis strategy, with the random lottery assignment serving as an instrument for time spent at KIPP Lynn, Angrist and colleagues find that KIPP Lynn significantly improves student performance. Students improve by 0.35 standard deviations in math and 0.1 to 0.15 standard deviations in English language arts for each year at KIPP Lynn.

Figure 23.2 plots estimates of the impact of being offered admission into KIPP Lynn on math (panel A) and reading (panel B) achievement from Angrist et al. (2010). In particular, the figure plots the coefficients from a regression of achievement-test scores on the lottery-offer dummy interacted with dummies for achievement-test grade times application year, including basic and demographic controls. In math, the effect of KIPP is quite large and relatively linear over time for all cohorts except the 2005 cohort in their eighth grade year. Reading achievement follows a similar, though more muted, pattern.

Angrist et al. (2010) also examine the effects of attending KIPP Lynn for various subgroups of students. A major criticism of charter schools is that although schools like KIPP Lynn serve

largely poor and minority communities, these schools often have lower percentages of special education or English Language Learners than traditional public schools serving the same community
and that the gains made by students in these schools are made by students at the upper end of the
ability distribution among poor and minority students. Angrist and colleagues find that the opposite is true at KIPP Lynn: gains in English language arts are actually driven by the English Language
Learner group, which also experiences stronger gains in math than non-ELL students. Special
education students have similar results. Furthermore, Angrist et al. find that students whose baseline scores are 0.5 standard deviations below the mean have achievement gains that are 0.05 to
0.08 standard deviations higher than students whose baseline achievement is at the mean.

SOCIAL ENVIRONMENT INTERVENTIONS

There have been many efforts to vary the social environment of poor minority children with the
goal of increasing academic achievement. James E. Rosenbaum (1995) documents the impact
of the Gautreaux housing program on the outcomes of low-income families in Chicago.[16] The
Gautreaux program granted housing vouchers to more than five thousand families, quasi-randomly
assigning the families to move either to middle-income, predominantly white suburbs or to low-
income, predominantly black, urban neighborhoods. Rosenbaum finds that students from families that moved to suburban neighborhoods were more likely to attend college and, if not
attending college, to be employed full-time than children whose families were relocated to low-
income urban neighborhoods. Using data from the 1989 NBER Boston Youth Survey, Anne Case
and Lawrence Katz (1991) find that measured family background traits are highly correlated
with the socioeconomic outcomes of disadvantaged youth. They also conclude that neighborhood effects in the form of peer influences have a strong impact on youth outcomes: youths who
live in neighborhoods with high rates of crime, drug use, and idleness are more likely to have
similar outcomes.

The most comprehensive effort to quantify the importance of neighborhood effects was the
Moving to Opportunity (MTO) experiment. Operating under the same general model as the
Gautreaux program, MTO provided housing vouchers to low-income families in a randomized
manner. One group of families received housing vouchers that were eligible for use in low-
poverty neighborhoods ("restricted vouchers"), one group received regular Section 8 housing
vouchers that had no neighborhood restrictions, and one group received no housing vouchers
but was still eligible for public housing. The program operated between 1994 and 1997 in
Boston, Baltimore, Chicago, Los Angeles, and New York and included 4,248 families. Forty-
seven percent of the restricted voucher families and 59 percent of the Section 8 voucher families used their vouchers to move to a new apartment (Sanbonmatsu et al. 2006).

MTO succeeded in changing the neighborhood environments of the children from families
that were offered restricted vouchers. These families lived in neighborhoods with lower poverty
rates and lower unemployment rates, and they reported feeling safer in their neighborhoods,
among other neighborhood improvements (Kling, Liebman, and Katz 2007; Sanbonmatsu et al.
2006). The program's effects on improving school quality for the children who moved were
much smaller than neighborhood effects, however. Schools attended by treatment students had
only marginally better state exam scores than schools attended by control students (19th percentile versus 15th percentile) and a slightly lower percentage of students eligible for free lunch,
and there was no difference in the average student-teacher ratio at these schools (Sanbonmatsu
et al. 2006). Because the school quality was largely unchanged for these children, we consider the schools they attended to be of low quality. The neighborhoods they moved to, however, were a significant improvement over the status quo on measurable characteristics; thus

we consider the environments to be of medium quality. Therefore, MTO allows us to examine the impact of low-quality schools and medium-quality neighborhoods on student achievement.[17]

Sanbonmatsu et al. (2006) find that MTO had insignificant effects on student achievement in reading and math, grade retention, student engagement in school, and enrollment in either gifted or remedial education courses. Jeffrey R. Kling, Jeffrey B. Liebman, and Lawrence F. Katz (2007) find that living in an area with lower poverty rates leads to large decreases in mental health issues (−1.84 [0.50] standard deviations) and risky behavior (−0.94 [0.39] standard deviations) for female youths. However, they find an increase in physical health problems (1.07 [0.49] standard deviations) and risky behavior (1.46 [0.54] standard deviations) for male youths. Kling, Ludwig, and Katz (2005) find a similar female-male differential in arrest rates: females in MTO had fewer lifetime violent crime arrests, lifetime property crime arrests, and total lifetime arrests than control-group females, while MTO male youths experienced an increase in lifetime property crime arrests compared to control-group males and had higher scores on the self-report behavior problems index. On the basis of this evidence, we conclude that changing a student's neighborhood from low to medium quality while keeping school quality constant does not increase achievement.

PARENTAL AND HOME ENVIRONMENT INTERVENTIONS

Many argue that to improve children's educational outcomes, one must improve the family and social environments in which the children are reared. A myriad of programs have attempted to change a student's family environment in ways that are believed to improve educational outcomes. Opportunity NYC is a conditional cash transfer program that offers cash incentives to families living in high-poverty communities in New York in return for specific education, health care, and employment target behaviors. For instance, families are given $25 per parent-teacher conference they attend, $50 for obtaining a library card, and $600 for each Regents exam that their high school children pass. Cynthia Miller, James Riccio, and Jared Smith (2009) find that after one year in this program, there are no effects on elementary or middle school students and that there are small effects for high school students on attendance, number of credits attempted (but not number of credits completed), and percentage of students taking and passing at least one Regents exam. However, these effects are largely driven by the particular subgroup of ninth-graders considered academically prepared for high school.

Overall, research on the impact of parent intervention programs on student achievement has been weak. In chapter 22 in this volume, Frank Furstenberg reviews the existing literature, both experimental and nonexperimental, on parental and family intervention programs at different stages in a child's development. He concludes that policymakers likely overestimate the impact of "micro-level" intervention programs designed to change parental or family habits along a specific dimension.

COUPLING COMMUNITY AND SCHOOL INVESTMENTS

In what follows, we examine interventions that combine a community-based approach with substantial school investments.

The SEED School

SEED (School for Educational Evolution and Development) schools, America's only urban public boarding schools, provide a rich laboratory to help understand the social environment versus schools debate. Located in Washington, D.C., and Baltimore, the two SEED schools serve students in grades six through twelve. They combine a curriculum model that shares some characteristics with many of the successful charter schools with a residential boarding program. Students live on campus five days a week, returning home only for weekends.

Academic Program The academic component of the SEED model is composed of a middle school program and a high school program. The middle school curriculum is focused on basic skills with the goal of allowing all students to enter the high school program performing at or above grade level. The benchmark standards that middle school students must master before promotion to high school are referred to as the "gate." Students who need more time to master grade-level skills can take a "growth year" during middle school. The middle school curriculum uses a readers and writers workshop model for language arts instruction and is designed such that all students will have taken algebra before entering high school.

The high school curriculum is a college-preparatory program for all students. To graduate, students must complete four years each of English and mathematics (through Algebra II); three years each of social studies, science, and a foreign language; one and a half years of physical education and health; one year of arts; a half-year each of U.S. government and politics, District of Columbia history, and technology; and five and a half years' worth of elective courses. In addition to course requirements, students must also take the SAT or ACT college admissions test, apply to at least five colleges or universities, and complete sixty hours of community service to graduate. The school offers advanced-placement courses in English literature, English language, U.S. history, government, and biology.

Both the D.C. and Maryland SEED schools have an extended school day at the middle and high school levels, from 8 A.M. until 4 P.M., and provide students with extensive after-school tutoring as needed. Instruction within the schools relies heavily on data. SEED uses internal interim assessments and has data days every quarter for the staff (both academic and boarding) to review student data. There is a strong emphasis on college preparation from the time the students enter the school, which begins more informally in middle school and is a formal part of the curriculum in high school. The SEED model espouses year-round education; although the SEED schools are only open for a traditional school year, they strive to place all of their students in educational programs during the summer months.

Residential Program From Sunday evening through Friday afternoon, students live on campus in double bedrooms in same-sex dorms. Within the dormitories students are organized into houses of twelve to fourteen students. The houses are all named for a college or university and the house members have study hall and meal times together, as well as other activities such as book clubs, field trips, and community service. The school offers a wide range of athletic and other extracurricular activities to students after school hours, as well as a program known as HALLS (Habits for Achieving Life-Long Success) that teaches students study skills, time management, and interpersonal communication, among other valuable life skills. Students can complete homework in their dorm rooms or in one of the common study spaces available throughout the dormitory. Each dorm room has a computer as do the common areas, and the residential staff is available during homework times to answer any questions. The residential staff is separate from the school faculty, although the two groups interact often to discuss student progress.

Despite students' living away from their families for the majority of the week, SEED emphasizes parental involvement to whatever level possible. Through events such as community dinners, SEED attempts to draw parents into the school community; parents can also serve as tutors during study hall, assist during extracurricular activities, and participate in book clubs.

We argue that SEED provides its students with a medium-quality environment. Although the schools offer students a very structured, safe, and nurturing environment that is somewhat removed from the risks and distractions they would normally face in their status quo low-quality environments, the schools are still located in Washington and Baltimore. The D.C. SEED School is located in one of the most impoverished wards in the city, an area marked by public housing and other signs of urban blight. In addition, SEED sends its students home to low-quality environments every weekend.

We also argue that SEED is a high-quality school, similar to other No Excuses charter schools. SEED provides a rigorous college preparatory curriculum and incorporates many of the elements common to No Excuses schools, such as extended instructional time and the use of data to drive student instruction. Thus, SEED allows us to examine the effect on student achievement of the interaction of high-quality schools and a medium-quality environment.

Vilsa Curto and Roland Fryer (2011) estimate the impact of being offered admission into SEED schools on reading and math achievement. For the 2007 and 2008 cohorts of lottery applicants to the SEED School in Washington, the impact of being offered admission into SEED is 0.188 (0.087) standard deviations in reading and 0.218 (0.081) in math. If one instruments for years of enrollment in SEED with lottery assignment, the standard approach in the charter school evaluation literature (Abdulkadiroglu et al. 2009; Angrist et al. 2010; Dobbie and Fryer 2009), the impact of attending SEED schools on achievement is 0.198 (0.093) standard deviations in reading and 0.230 (0.084) in math, per year.[18] These effects are large and comparable in magnitude to those reported for high-performing charter schools such as the Harlem Children's Zone (Dobbie and Fryer 2009) and KIPP (Angrist et al. 2010), but they come at a far steeper price—the cost to educate a student at SEED is approximately $39,000 per year. An important qualification regarding the success of SEED is that the positive effects are entirely driven by the performance of girls. That is, the impact of attending SEED for boys is statistically zero (−0.138 [0.145] in reading and 0.037 [0.156] in math), and for girls is 0.382 (0.155) in reading and 0.265 (0.142) in math. The overall evidence from the SEED School in Washington suggests that changing a student's social environment and putting the student in high-quality schools has positive results, though these are mainly driven by female students.

Harlem Children's Zone

The Harlem Children's Zone (HCZ) began in 1970 as an amalgam of after-school programs, truancy-prevention services, and antiviolence training for teenagers in New York City schools. It offers an extremely rare chance to estimate the impact on student achievement of being exposed to No Excuses charter schools and significant community investments. The actual "zone" is an area of ninety-seven blocks bounded by 116th and 143rd Streets, 8th Avenue on the west, and Madison Avenue on the east.

HCZ offers a number of programs, which we have categorized into "community" investments and "school" investments. Community programs are available to anyone living near HCZ, and serve 8,058 youths and 5,291 adults. School programs are available only to the approximately 1,300 students who attend the HCZ public charter schools.

Community Investments   HCZ has more than twenty programs in its ninety-seven blocks designed to help and empower individuals. These investments include early childhood programs such as Head Start; public elementary, middle, and high school programs such as karate, dance, and after-school tutoring; a college success office; family, community, and health programs; foster-care prevention services (whose purpose is to stabilize and strengthen families to avoid placement of children in foster care); and so on. The vision of Geoffrey Canada, CEO of the Harlem Children's Zone, is to "create a tipping point" in the neighborhood so that children are surrounded by an enriching environment of college-oriented peers and supportive adults. This is consistent with the vision articulated by scholars and policymakers who argue that communities, not schools, are responsible for the achievement gap. For a more detailed analysis of HCZ community programs, see Dobbie and Fryer (2009).

School Investments   The HCZ Promise Academy public charter schools began in fall 2004 with the opening of the HCZ Promise Academy elementary and middle schools, followed in fall 2005 by the opening of the HCZ Promise Academy 2 Elementary School.[19] The HCZ Promise Academy will enroll a new kindergarten and sixth-grade cohort each year until it is a full K–12 school, and HCZ Promise Academy 2 will enroll a new kindergarten cohort each year until it is a full K–12 school.[20]

The HCZ Promise Academies have an extended school day and year, with coordinated after-school tutoring and additional classes on Saturdays for children who need remediation in mathematics and English language arts. Our rough estimate is that HCZ Promise Academy students who are behind grade level are in school for twice as many hours as a traditional public school student in New York City. Students who are at or above grade level still attend the equivalent of about 50 percent more school in a calendar year. Some would argue that these extended hours necessarily constitute an environmental intervention, given that for these hours, the school acts as a substitute for the home or neighborhood environment. Although we do not debate the existence of this substitution effect, we nonetheless consider this extended time model to be a school intervention. During the extended time, students are receiving traditional instruction, as opposed to participating in more piecemeal or community-based extracurricular activities. Furthermore, extended time is an intervention that schools can implement on their own; many No Excuses charter schools require more in-school hours from students than traditional public schools. In this and other ways, we consider school interventions to be those policies within the control of schools, rather than the set of policies common to all high-achieving schools, as we imagine the second list would be rather short.

Both schools emphasize the recruitment and retention of high-quality teachers and use a value-added measure based on students' test scores to create incentives and evaluate current teachers. The schools have had high turnover as they search for the most effective teachers: 48 percent of HCZ Promise Academy previous year's teachers did not return for the 2005–2006 school year, 32 percent of them left before 2006–2007, and 14 percent left before 2007–2008. Each teacher has an annual meeting with Canada to discuss his or her performance and is supported by myriad behind-the-scenes efforts to make sure his or her time is spent primarily on teaching and not on administrative tasks.

Another key element of HCZ's instructional model is the reliance on data-driven instruction at the HCZ Promise Academy. The schools administer formative assessments to all students at regular intervals. The results of these assessments are analyzed to determine which skills each student has not yet mastered, and teachers create plans to correct these weaknesses. The remediation plans often include after-school tutoring or Saturday school time devoted to improving these skills in a way that is coordinated with and integrated into the regular school curriculum.

The schools provide free medical, dental, and mental health services (students are screened upon entry and receive regular checkups through a partnership with the Children's Health Fund); student incentives for achievement (such as money or trips to France); high-quality and nutritious cafeteria meals; support for parents in the form of food baskets, meals, bus fare, and so forth; and less tangible benefits such as the support of a committed staff. The schools also

FIGURE 23.3   *Student Achievement in HCZ (Math)*

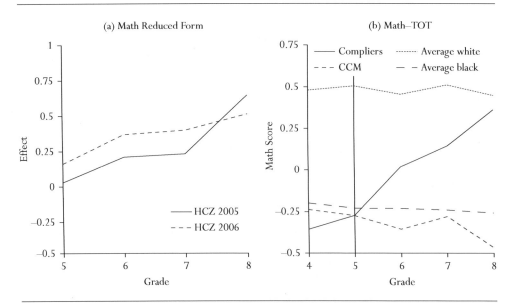

Source: Authors' adaptation of Dobbie and Fryer (2009).

make a concerted effort to change the culture of achievement, surrounding students with reminders of the importance of hard work in achieving success. These types of school investments are consistent with those recommended by experts who argue that high-quality schools are enough to close the achievement gap.

Will Dobbie and Roland Fryer (2009) use two separate statistical strategies to estimate the causal impact of HCZ charter schools on student achievement. First, they exploit the fact that HCZ charter schools are required to select students by lottery when the number of applicants exceeds the number of available slots for admission. In this scenario, the treatment group is composed of students who are lottery winners and the control group consists of students who are lottery losers. The second identification strategy explored in Dobbie and Fryer (2009) uses the interaction between a student's home address and his or her cohort year as an instrumental variable. This approach takes advantage of two important features of the HCZ charter schools: (1) anyone is eligible to enroll in HCZ's schools, but only students living inside the zone are actively recruited by HCZ staff; and (2) there are cohorts of children who are ineligible owing to their age at the time of the schools' openings.

Both statistical approaches lead to the same basic story. Harlem Children's Zone is effective at increasing the achievement of the poorest minority children, closing the gap between poor minority students and the average white student in New York City public schools in math and English language arts in elementary school and math in middle school.

Figure 23.3 provides a visual representation of the basic results from HCZ Promise Academy middle school, reported in Dobbie and Fryer (2009). Panel a of figure 23.3 plots yearly, raw, mean state math test scores from fourth to eighth grade for four subgroups: lottery winners, lottery losers, white students in New York City public schools, and black students in New York City public schools. The difference between the lottery winners and losers represents the impact of being offered admission to HCZ Promise Academy.

FIGURE 23.4   *Student Achievement in HCZ (ELA)*

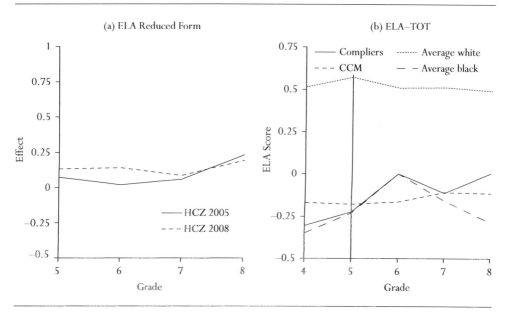

Source: Authors' adaptation of Dobbie and Fryer (2009).

In fourth and fifth grade, before entering middle school, math test scores for lottery win-ners, losers, and the typical black student in New York City are virtually identical, and roughly 0.75 standard deviations behind the typical white student.[21] Lottery winners have a modest increase in sixth grade, followed by a more substantial increase in seventh grade and even larger gains by eighth grade.

The effect of attending the HCZ Promise Academy Middle School on math scores is depicted in panel b of figure 23.3. These results follow a similar pattern, showing remarkable convergence between children in the middle school and the average white student in New York City. After three years of being enrolled, HCZ Promise Academy students have nearly closed the achievement gap in math. They are behind their white counterparts by 0.121 standard devia-tions (p-value = 0.113). If one adjusts for gender and free lunch, the typical eighth grader enrolled in the HCZ middle school outscores the typical white eighth grader in New York City public schools by 0.087 standard deviations, although the difference is not statistically signifi-cant (p-value = 0.238).

Figure 23.4 plots yearly state English language arts test scores from fourth to eighth grade. Treatment and control designations are identical to those in panel a of figure 23.3. In fourth and fifth grade, before they enter the middle school, ELA scores for lottery winners, losers, and the typical black student in New York City are not statistically different, and are roughly 0.65 stan-dard deviations behind those of the typical white student.[22] Lottery winners and losers have very similar English language arts scores from fourth through seventh grade. In eighth grade, HCZ Promise Academy students diverge from the control group. These results are statistically mean-ingful, but much less so than the math results. The estimate of the effect of attending HCZ Promise Academy on English language arts scores, depicted in panel b of figure 23.4, follows an identical pattern with marginally larger differences between enrolled middle school students and the control group. Adjusting for gender and free lunch pushes the results in the expected direction.[23]

BETTER NEIGHBORHOODS, ENGAGED PARENTS, MORE EFFECTIVE SCHOOLS, OR ALL OF THE ABOVE?

The ideal data to distinguish whether we should invest in neighborhoods or schools would come from an experiment in which we randomly distributed a common population into high-quality schools, high-quality schools coupled with a better social environment, and a better social environment without high-quality schools. We do not have these data, but we know the impact of high-quality schools from Abdulkadiroglu et al. (2009) and Angrist et al. (2010). We also have a good sense of the impact of changing the social environment from MTO and SEED. Taken together, these examples provide good, but clearly not gold standard, evidence that high-quality schools are enough to significantly improve the academic achievement of the poorest minority students.

Four additional pieces of evidence, taken together, suggest that it does not take a village to close the racial achievement gap—just a great school. First, Dobbie and Fryer (2009) find no correlation between participation in community programs in HCZ and academic achievement. Second, Dobbie and Fryer (2009) report that children who live inside the zone garnered the same benefit from the schools as those who live outside the zone, suggesting that proximity to the community programs is unimportant. Third, siblings of HCZ students who are in regular public schools, but likely have better-than-average access and information about HCZ community programs, have marginally lower absences but their achievement is unchanged (Dobbie and Fryer 2009). Fourth, Curto and Fryer (2011) show that students admitted to SEED schools (No Excuses charter schools with a five-day-a-week boarding program) have similar increases in achievement as similar students admitted to No Excuses schools that do not contain a boarding option. This, coupled with the results from MTO, suggests that the marginal benefit on achievement of taking students out of their home environment is small. Again, we still need to run the ideal experiment and our conceptual matrix is admittedly ad hoc, but the only fair reading of the available data is that schools are a stronger driver of student achievement than is environment.

CONCLUSION: FOUR CAVEATS TO THE SUCCESS OF NO EXCUSES CHARTER SCHOOLS

There is a tremendous amount of enthusiasm surrounding the success of charter schools and their ability to educate even the poorest minority students. In July 2009, the federal government announced "Race to the Top," a two-phase grant program in which states apply for a share of $4.35 billion to improve public schools. The program is designed to give states incentives to advance education reform in specific areas. Charter schools have been leading the way in many of the targeted reform areas, such as data-driven instruction and performance pay for teachers. U.S. Secretary of Education Arne Duncan declared that states that sought to limit the growth of charter schools would "jeopardize" their Race to the Top applications. Another federal government grant program, the Public Charter Schools Program, explicitly targets the expansion of charter school coverage, awarding grants to state educational agencies to support the planning, development, and initial implementation of charter schools.

The private sector is also investing in the success of charter schools. The Charter School Growth Fund is a social venture investment fund that is backed by more than $100 million and supports charter school operators who can demonstrate evidence of improving the educational achievement of underserved students. These are just a few of the many programs and initiatives that reflect a growing consensus that charter schools are the way forward to close the racial achievement gap and improve educational achievement for all children.

However, what if charter schools are not the panacea that people increasingly believe them to be?

We conclude with four potentially important caveats to the recent success of charter schools that are worth considering carefully and for which, to date, there are no solid data to lead the way. First, can charter school strategies educate every child? Many charter schools have strict entry requirements or a tedious application process. KIPP makes parents sign a pledge that holds them responsible for their children's attendance (including on Saturdays and during the summer), for their children's adherence to the school dress code, and for their children's behavior, among other commitments. Achievement First has a similar parent contract requirement. The 2007–2008 application for the SEED school in Washington, D.C., was twelve pages long, including a student essay portion. The Maryland SEED application process currently requires parents to request an application, which is mailed to them and which they must then complete and return.

All three of these networks—KIPP, Achievement First, and SEED—have a strong college focus from the time students enter, which could serve to attract only more motivated students and families. The average charter student who enters a charter school is more academically prepared than the typical public school student with similar demographics. Lottery estimates are only valid for making inferences about the (potentially self-selected) set of people who signed up for a lottery. Estimates based on these individuals do not necessarily generalize to the larger public. Discussing the effectiveness of randomized control trials in development economics, Angus Deaton (2009) argues that randomization is not enough to measure the impact of policy interventions because what randomized control trials truly allow one to assess is the local average treatment effects of the program, rather than the impact of the program across all treatment recipients or the impact that the program would have on the population as a whole. We do not have a good sense of how effective charter strategies might be in an average public school with parents who might refuse to sign a pledge, might be unwilling to fill out a twelve-page application, and so on.

Furthermore, many charter school critics argue that even if charter schools originally admit a random sample of the community, there is a significant difference in attrition rates between charter and traditional public schools (for example, Buckley and Schneider 2009; Frankenberg, Siegel-Hawley, and Wang 2010). Although there is a large variance in attrition rates in charter schools, those such as the KIPP schools in the San Francisco Bay Area garnered much attention when they lost over half of their 2003 cohort between fifth and eighth grades (Woodworth et al. 2008). Martha Abele MacIver and Elizabeth Farley-Ripple (2007) find that the students who left KIPP schools had lower test scores than those who stayed, suggesting that there is some degree of differential attrition in charter schools.

This latter critique is not likely an issue because the estimates of the impact of being offered admission into a charter school include all students who won the lottery whether or not they attended the school. Per usual, these estimates are smaller than the estimates of the impact of actually attending a charter school, but taking the former estimates at face value would likely generate the same level of enthusiasm. The concern in Deaton (2009), however, is still potentially very important.

Second, many charter schools have aggressive human-capital strategies: many charter schools hire only experienced teachers with a proven record of increasing student achievement, require longer hours from their teaching staff, and dismiss those teachers who are not producing the required student gains. We have little idea what the equilibrium in the teacher market would look like if all schools were to implement these strategies. In the first year, Harlem Children's Zone fired 48.6 percent of its teachers. No Excuses charter schools routinely require their teachers to work sixty-plus hours per week with only a two-week break over the summer (Carter 2000). At KIPP, teachers are expected to be available twenty-four hours a day by phone to students. Teacher attrition in charter schools is 20 to 25 percent overall, but close to 40 percent for new teachers (Miron and Applegate 2007). Many have argued that this strategy might not be sustainable, as it might lead to teacher burnout among even experienced, talented, reform-minded teachers (Hubbard and Kulkarni 2009). Samuel Casey Carter (2000) describes effective charter principals as having to "scour the country" for suitable teachers, which further suggests that the teacher recruiting model of successful charter schools might not be scalable. It is unclear whether the supply can keep pace with demand in this environment. On the other hand, as charter management organizations such as KIPP and HCZ grow to encompass an entire K–12 model, the heroic effort by teachers to ensure that students are achieving at grade level may take substantially less effort, since students will be less likely to fall as far behind in the first place.

A third question is whether the increases in achievement test scores will translate into college graduation and other desirable life outcomes. Although we know that educational achievement is correlated with positive life outcomes, we have not yet determined the causal impact of education on these outcomes. Early anecdotal evidence suggests that some charter schools are struggling to get their students through college, despite their early emphasis on college completion and high achievement-test scores. From the first graduating class (2004) at the SEED School in Washington, only two students completed college within four years; only seven students—or 33 percent—completed college within six years. One of the goals of KIPP NYC is for 75 percent of their eighth-grade alumni to complete college within six years of high school graduation, but currently only 50 percent of eighth-grade alumni are on this track.

A final question, which encompasses some of the concerns just discussed, is whether charter school practices can be boiled down into a form that can be used in traditional public schools. KIPP seems to be highly successful at building new schools, but it is too early to tell whether their early successes are being replicated. Many of the charter management organizations that manage networks of charter schools provide some evidence that it is possible. Yet it is unclear whether there are enough people like Dave Levin, Mike Feinberg, Geoffrey Canada, and the other dynamic leaders who manage these organizations to meet this demand.

Assuming that we do not have this ample supply, there are two options: allow market forces to ensure that only gap-closing schools can thrive or figure out what makes charter schools work and try to replicate those strategies in traditional public schools. For this reason, and because of the caveats discussed, it will be a difficult task. If it is successful, however, there is a chance to transform the state of poverty and racial inequality in the United States.

NOTES

Online appendix available at: http://www.russellsage.org/duncan_murnane_online_appendix.pdf.

1. Kevin Lang and Michael Manove (2008) show that including years of schooling in the Neal and Johnson (1996) specification causes the gap to increase—arguing that when one controls for performance on the Armed Forces Qualification Test (AFQT), blacks have higher educational attainment than whites and that the labor market discriminates against blacks by not financially rewarding them for their greater education.

2. It is imperative to note that no interventions that have moved students from low- to high-quality environments, such as the A Better Chance program, have been credibly evaluated.

3. Although Brighouse and Schouten (chapter 24, this volume) argue that separating influences that are internal to school from those that are external to school creates a false dichotomy that is harmful to the policy debate around

improving educational outcomes for disadvantaged students, we argue that this distinction is real and significant and frame our categorization of the various interventions we examine to reflect these differences.

4. These statistics can all be accessed through the American FactFinder on the U.S. Census Bureau website and refer to the 2008 American Community Survey 1-Year Estimates.

5. A state-by-state description of charter laws as of 2010 can be found at the Center for Education Reform website, http://www.charterschoolresearch.com (accessed March 23, 2011). This site also ranks the relative "strength" of states' charter school laws.

6. These and other important charter school statistics about schools and students can be found at the National Alliance for Public Charter Schools website, http://www.publiccharters.org/dashboard/home (accessed March 23, 2011).

7. Two schools that were excluded did not have any students in test-taking grades, so their omission has no impact on the analysis of achievement outcomes. One school was in the process of closing during the 2005–2006 school year and the authors could not obtain lottery information from this school. The New York Center for Autism Charter School was excluded because of obvious comparability issues. The United Federation of Teachers Elementary Charter School declined to participate in the study.

8. It should be noted that the comparison group is not representative of the overall population of NYC public schools, which enroll a much larger percentage of both white and Asian students than can be found in the charter applicant or comparison groups.

9. The specification that produced these results was a treatment-on-treated analysis with gender, race-ethnicity, free and reduced-price lunch status, special education status, ELL status, and previous year's test score controls, as well as grade, school, and lottery fixed effects and robust standard errors clustered at the school level.

10. Pilot schools occupy a theoretical middle ground in the Boston schools landscape, with more autonomy than traditional public schools but less than that enjoyed by charter schools. For this discussion, we focus on the charter school results. See Abdulkadiroglu et al. (2009) for results on the effectiveness of pilot schools.

11. This is not true of fourth grade ELA and math test scores for incoming middle school students. The test scores of those who enter the charter school lotteries are higher than those of students who ultimately enroll in charter schools.

12. The fourth high school, Health Careers Academy (HCA), is a Horace Mann Charter, which means that it shares some important characteristics with pilot schools, such as a unionized teacher pool. Abdulkadiroglu et al. (2009) conduct separate analyses, one including HCA as a charter school and one including HCA as a pilot school. See Abdulkadiroglu et al. (2009) for more on these distinct specifications.

13. These are treatment-on-treated analysis results that include demographic controls.

14. These figures are taken from the KIPP Report Card 2008, which can be accessed on the KIPP website at http://www.kipp.org/about-kipp/results/annual-report-card (accessed June 30, 2011).

15. Because of differential rates of matching, Angrist et al. (2010) use only data from those students who entered the KIPP Lynn lottery who were initially in Lynn public schools. The authors posit that students who were enrolled in private schools who entered and lost the lottery remained in private school and thus did not have data in SIMS.

16. The program was the response by the Chicago Housing Authority to the Supreme Court decision in *Hill v. Gautreaux* (1976), which declared that the Chicago Housing Authority needed to provide more dispersed housing to public housing residents who were at the time living in high-poverty public housing projects.

17. A Better Chance (ABC) was founded in 1963 to give low-income minority students with above-average achievement the opportunity to live and attend school in more affluent environments. Originally, many of the students attended independent schools, many of which were elite boarding schools. Today, some students attend independent schools, while others live in ABC houses and attend private or public schools in suburban communities. This program theoretically allows us to examine the impact of high-quality schools and a high-quality environment on the academic achievement of low-income students. George Perry and Nancy Kopperman (1973) evaluate this program and find positive effects on college attendance and on the selectivity of the colleges attended by ABC alumni. However, these findings must be taken with a grain of salt for two reasons. First, the evaluation is nearly forty years old, and it is difficult to say whether the findings would be the same today. Second, there is an issue of selection bias in the sample. Perry and Kopperman attempted to match ABC scholarship recipients to nonrecipients based on a set of observed characteristics. The program selection was not random, however, so it is possible

that those selected for the program differed in some important way from those not selected for the program. In addition, because of ABC's mission to specifically serve high-performing disadvantaged youth, the program cannot tell us anything about the impact of high-quality schools and a high-quality environment on average low-income minority youth.

18. Reported estimates include controls for baseline test scores and demographic characteristics. For the 2007 and 2008 D.C. cohorts, Curto and Fryer (2011) are able to match 94 percent of the students who signed up for the charter school lottery with test scores from either the District of Columbia Comprehensive Assessment System (DCCAS) or the Maryland School Assessment (MSA). Their analysis is based on results from the SEED School of Washington, D.C., which has been in operation since 1998. The SEED School of Maryland has only been open since 2008. The first year of operation is usually difficult; estimates of effect sizes from the first year may not be representative of the typical effect sizes one would expect (Zimmer et al. 2009).

19. Promise Academy 2 held kindergarten and first-grade lotteries in its first year, enrolling forty students in each grade. After its first year of operation, Promise Academy 2 relocated, and in the process lost a number of students. To simplify our analysis and abstract from the issues created by this relocation, we focus our analysis on Promise Academy.

20. In the fall of 2007, Promise Academy did not enroll a new sixth-grade cohort, and expelled the entire existing eighth-grade cohort (the 2004 lottery cohort). HCZ was unhappy with the performance of the middle school to this point, and the decision was made to focus on the existing sixth- and seventh-grade cohorts in reforming the school. Test data, made public months after the decision was taken, showed that the 2004 cohort did quite well (Tough 2008). In 2008, the lottery was moved back to fifth grade (Tough 2008).

21. This is similar in magnitude to the math racial achievement gap in nationally representative samples (0.882 in Fryer and Levitt 2006, and 0.763 in Campbell et al. 2000), and samples with an urban focus (Fryer forthcoming).

22. This is smaller than the reading racial achievement gap in some nationally representative samples (0.771 in Fryer and Levitt 2006, and 0.960 in Campbell et al. 2000), but similar to gaps in data with an urban focus (Fryer forthcoming).

23. Interventions in education often have larger impacts on math scores than on reading or ELA scores (see, for example, Decker, Mayer, and Glazerman 2004; Jacob 2005; Rockoff 2004). This may be because it is relatively easier to teach math skills, or because reading skills are more likely to be learned outside of school. Another explanation is that language and vocabulary skills may develop early in life, making it difficult to impact reading scores in adolescence (Hart and Risley 1995; Nelson 2000). For a detailed explanation of the brain development that occurs early in life that can impact a child's language skills, see chapter 2 of this volume.

REFERENCES

Abdulkadiroglu, Atila, Joshua Angrist, Susan Dynarski, Thomas J. Kane, and Parag Pathak. 2009. "Accountability and Flexibility in Public Schools: Evidence from Boston's Charters and Pilots." NBER Working Paper No. 15549. Cambridge, Mass.: National Bureau of Economic Research.

Angrist, Joshua D., Susan M. Dynarski, Thomas J. Kane, Parag A. Pathak, and Christopher R. Walters. 2010. "Who Benefits from KIPP?" NBER Working Paper No. 15740. Cambridge, Mass.: National Bureau of Economic Research.

Borman, Geoffrey D., Gina M. Hewes, Laura T. Overman, and Shelley Brown. 2003. "Comprehensive School Reform and Achievement: A Meta-Analysis." *Review of Educational Research* 73(2): 125–230.

Brooks-Gunn, Jeanne, and Lisa B. Markman. 2005. "The Contribution of Parenting to Ethnic and Racial Gaps in School Readiness." *The Future of Children* 15(1): 139–68.

Buckley, Jack, and Mark Schneider. 2009. *Charter Schools: Hope or Hype?* Princeton: Princeton University Press.

Campbell, Jay R., Catherine M. Hombo, and John Mazzeo. 2000. "NAEP 1999 Trends in Academic Progress: Three Decades of Student Performance." National Center for Education Statistics Reports, no. 2000-469. Washington: U.S. Government Printing Office.

Card, David, and Jesse Rothstein. 2004. "Racial Segregation and the Black-White Test Score Gap." Unpublished paper. Princeton University.

Carter, Samuel Casey. 2000. *No Excuses: Seven Principals of Low-Income Schools Who Set the Standard for High Achievement.* Washington, D.C.: Heritage Foundation.

Case, Anne, and Lawrence F. Katz. 1991. "The Company You Keep: The Effects of Family and Neighborhood on Disadvantaged Youth." NBER Working Paper No. W3705. Cambridge, Mass.: National Bureau of Economic Research.

Currie, Janet, and Duncan Thomas. 1995. "Does Head Start Make a Difference?" *American Economic Review* 85(3): 341–64.

Curto, Vilsa, and Roland Fryer. 2011. "Estimating the Returns to Urban Boarding Schools: Evidence from SEED." NBER Working Paper No. 16746. Cambridge, Mass.: National Bureau of Economic Research.

Darity, William A., and Patrick L. Mason. 1998. "Evidence on Discrimination in Employment: Codes of Color, Codes of Gender." *Journal of Economic Perspectives* 12(2): 63–90.

Deaton, Angus. 2009. "Instruments of Development: Randomization in the Tropics, and the Search for the Elusive Keys to Economic Development." NBER Working Paper No. 14690. Cambridge, Mass.: National Bureau of Economic Research.

Decker, Paul T., Daniel P. Mayer, and Steven Glazerman. 2004. "The Effects of Teach for America on Students: Findings from a National Evaluation." Discussion paper 1285-04. Madison: University of Wisconsin, Institute for Research on Poverty.

Dobbie, Will, and Roland Fryer. 2009. "Are High Quality Schools Enough to Close the Achievement Gap? Evidence from a Social Experiment in Harlem." NBER Working Paper No. 15473. Cambridge, Mass.: National Bureau of Economic Research.

Duncan, Greg J., and Katherine A. Magnuson. 2005. "Can Family Socioeconomic Resources Account for Racial and Ethnic Test Score Gaps?" *The Future of Children* 15(1): 35–54.

Ferguson, Ronald. 2001. "Test Score Trends Along Racial Lines, 1971 to 1996: Popular Culture and Community Academic Standards." In *America Becoming: Racial Trends and Their Consequences,* edited by Neil J. Smelser, William Julius Wilson, and Faith Mitchell. Vol. 1. Washington, D.C.: National Academies Press.

Frankenberg, Erica, Genevieve Siegel-Hawley, and Jia Wang. 2010. "Choice Without Equity: Charter School Segregation and the Need for Civil Rights Standards." Los Angeles: UCLA, The Civil Rights Project/Proyecto Derechos Civiles.

Fryer, Roland. 2010. "Financial Incentives and Student Achievement: Evidence from Randomized Trials." Working paper 15898. Cambridge, Mass.: National Bureau of Economic Research.

———. Forthcoming. "Racial Inequality in the 21st Century: The Declining Significance of Discrimination." In *Handbook of Labor Economics, Volume 4,* edited by Orley Ashenfelter and David Card. Amsterdam and New York: North Holland.

Fryer, Roland, and Steven Levitt. 2006. "The Black-White Test Score Gap Through Third Grade." *American Law and Economics Review* 8(2): 249–281.

———. Forthcoming. "Testing for Racial Differences in the Mental Ability of Young Children." *American Economic Review.*

Gleason, Philip, Melissa Clark, Christina Clark Tuttle, and Emily Dwoyer. 2010. *The Evaluation of Charter School Impacts: Final Report.* NCEE 2010-4030. Washington, D.C.: U.S. Department of Education.

Hart, Betty, and Todd R. Risley. 1995. *Meaningful Differences in the Everyday Experience of Young American Children.* Baltimore: Brookes.

Herrnstein, Richard J., and Charles Murray. 1994. *The Bell Curve: Intelligence and Class Structure in American Life.* New York: Free Press.

Hoxby, Caroline Minter. 1996. "How Teachers' Unions Affect Education Production." *Quarterly Journal of Economics* 111(3): 671–718.

Hoxby, Caroline M., and Sonali Murarka. 2009. "Charter Schools in New York City: Who Enrolls and How They Affect Their Students' Achievement." NBER Working Paper No. 14582. Cambridge, Mass.: National Bureau of Economic Research.

Hubbard, Lee, and Rucheeta Kulkarni. 2009. "Charter Schools: Learning from the Past, Planning for the Future." *Journal of Educational Change* 10(2): 173–89.

Jacob, Brian A. 2005. "Accountability, Incentives and Behavior: Evidence from School Reform in Chicago." *Journal of Public Economics* 89(5–6): 761–96.

Jacob, Brian A., and Lars Lefgren. 2004. "Remedial Education and Student Achievement: A Regression Discontinuity Analysis." *Review of Economics and Statistics* 86(1): 226–44.

———. 2009. "The Effect of Grade Retention on High School Completion." *American Economic Journal* 1(3): 33–58.

Jacob, Brian, and Jens Ludwig. 2008. "Improving Educational Outcomes for Poor Children." Working paper 14550. Cambridge, Mass.: National Bureau of Economic Research.

Jencks, Christopher. 1998. "Racial Bias in Testing." In *The Black-White Test Score Gap,* edited by Christopher Jencks and Meredith Phillips. Washington, D.C.: Brookings Institution Press.

Jensen, Arthur A. 1973. *Educability and Group Differences.* New York: Free Press.

Jepsen, Christopher, and Steven Rivkin. 2002. *Class Size Reduction, Teacher Quality, and Academic Achievement in California Public Elementary Schools.* San Francisco: Public Policy Institute of California.

Kane, Thomas J., Jonah E. Rockoff, and Douglas O. Staiger. 2008. "What Does Certification Tell Us About Teacher Effectiveness? Evidence from New York City." NBER Working Paper No. 12155. Cambridge, Mass.: National Bureau of Economic Research.

Kling, Jeffrey R., Jeffrey B. Liebman, and Lawrence F. Katz. 2007. "Experimental Analysis of Neighborhood Effects." *Econometrica* 75(1): 83–119.

Kling, Jeffrey R., Jens Ludwig, and Lawrence F. Katz. 2005. "Neighborhood Effects on Crime for Female and Male Youth: Evidence from a Randomized Housing Voucher Experiment." *Quarterly Journal of Economics* 120(1): 87–130.

Krueger, Alan B. 1999. "Experimental Estimates of Education Production Functions." *Quarterly Journal of Economics* 114(2): 497–532.

Lang, Kevin, and Michael Manove. 2008. "Education and Labor-Market Discrimination." NBER Working Paper No. 12257. Cambridge, Mass.: National Bureau of Economic Research.

Lauer, Patricia A., Motoko Akiba, Stephanie B. Wilkerson, Helen S. Apthorp, David Snow, and Mya L. Martin-Glenn. 2006. "Out-of-School-Time Programs: A Meta-Analysis of Effects for At-Risk Students." *Review of Educational Research* 76(2): 275–313.

MacIver, Martha Abele, and Elizabeth Farley-Ripple. 2007. "The Baltimore KIPP Ujima Village Academy, 2002–2006: A Longitudinal Analysis of Student Outcomes." Baltimore: Johns Hopkins University, Center for Social Organization of Schools.

MetLife Insurance, Inc. 2001. *The MetLife Survey of the American Teacher 2001: Key Elements of Quality Schools.* Rochester, N.Y.: Harris Interactive, Inc.

Miller, Cynthia, James Riccio, and Jared Smith. 2009. "A Preliminary Look at Early Educational Results of the Opportunity NYC—Family Rewards Program (A Research Note for Funders)." New York: MDRC.

Miron, Gary, and Brooks Applegate. 2007. "Teacher Attrition in Charter Schools." East Lansing: Great Lakes Center for Education Research and Practice.

Neal, Derek. 2005. "Why Has Black-White Skill Convergence Stopped?" NBER Working Paper No. 11090. Cambridge, Mass.: National Bureau of Economic Research.

Neal, Derek A., and William R. Johnson. 1996. "The Role of Premarket Factors in Black-White Wage Differences." *Journal of Political Economy* 104(5): 869–95.

Nelson, Charles A. 2000. " The Neurobiological Bases of Early Intervention." In *Handbook of Early Childhood Intervention,* edited by Jack P. Shonkoff and Samuel J, Meisels. New York: Cambridge University Press.

O'Neill, June. 1990. "The Role of Human Capital in Earnings Differences Between Black and White Men." *Journal of Economic Perspectives* 4(4): 25–45.

Perry, George, and Nancy Kopperman. 1973. "A Better Chance: Evaluation of Student Attitudes and Academic Performance, 1964–1972." Boston: A Better Chance, Inc.

Podgursky, Michael J., and Matthew G. Springer. 2007. "Teacher Performance Pay: A Review." *Journal of Policy Analysis and Management* 26(4): 909–49.

Puma, Michael, Stephen Bell, Ronna Cook, and Camilla Heid. 2010. "Head Start Impact Study: Final Report." Washington, D.C.: Administration for Children and Families.

Rockoff, Jonah E. 2004. "The Impact of Individual Teachers on Student Achievement: Evidence from Panel Data." *American Economic Review* 94(2): 247–252.

Rosenbaum, James E. 1995. "Changing the Geography of Opportunity by Expanding Residential Choice: Lessons from the Gautreaux Program." *Housing Policy Debate* 6(1): 231–269.

Rothstein, Richard. 2004. *Class and Schools: Using Social, Economic, and Educational Reform to Close the Achievement Gap.* Washington, D.C.: Economic Policy Institute.

Rushton, J. Philippe. 1995. "Thirty Years of Research on Race Differences in Cognitive Ability." *Psychology, Public Policy, and Law* 113(2): 235–94.

Sanbonmatsu, Lisa, Jeffrey R. Kling, Greg J. Duncan, and Jeanne Brooks-Gunn. 2006. "Neighborhoods and Academic Achievement: Results from the Moving to Opportunity Experiment." *Journal of Human Resources* 41(4): 649–91.

Schultz, T. Paul, and John Strauss, eds. 2008. *Handbook of Development Economics*. Vol. 4. Amsterdam and New York: North-Holland.

Thernstrom, Abigail, and Stephan Thernstrom. 2004. *No Excuses: Closing the Racial Gap in Learning*. New York: Simon & Schuster.

Tough, Paul. 2008. *Whatever It Takes: Geoffrey Canada's Quest to Change Harlem and America*. New York: Mariner Books.

Woodworth, Katrina R., Jane L. David, Roneeta Guha, Haiwen Wang, and Alejandra Lopez-Torkos. 2008. "San Francisco Bay Area KIPP Schools: A Study of Early Implementation and Achievement. Final Report." Menlo Park, Calif.: SRI International.

Ziedenberg, Jason, and Vincent Schiraldi. 2002. "Cellblocks or Classrooms? The Funding of Higher Education and Corrections and Its Impact on African American Men." Unpublished paper. Washington, D.C.: Justice Policy Institute.

Zimmer, Ron, Brian Gill, Kevin Booker, Stephane Lavertu, Tim R. Sass, and John Witte. 2009. *Charter Schools in Eight States: Effects on Achievement, Attainment, Integration, and Competition*. Santa Monica, Calif.: RAND Corporation.

Chapter 24

Understanding the Context for Existing Reform and Research Proposals

Harry Brighouse and Gina Schouten

It is commonplace to categorize reforms intended to ameliorate educational disadvantage as either "external" or "internal" to the school. The usefulness of this distinction is limited in the case of policy interventions. Many interventions do fit neatly into one category, but some fit into both and others into neither category. Furthermore, advocates of reform do not fit the strict dichotomy: some advocate an exclusive internal-to-school agenda, others a mixed strategy of internal and external to school. None, however, advocates an exclusively external-to-school agenda. More important, policymakers—whose contexts, funds, and feasible sets vary—must seek the combination of interventions that has the best chance of success, and they should be open to considering items in each category, both categories, or neither one.

The division into two categories may have strengthened support for a reform agenda that includes promoting "high-commitment" schools—charter schools serving poor neighborhoods—by having longer school days, stringent disciplinary norms, and rigorous "basics" academic curriculums. Some advocates of these schools have attacked efforts to promote an external-to-school agenda as making "excuses" for failing schools. Several large funders of reform, as well as both the previous and the current presidential administrations, display enthusiasm for this model. We argue that the evidence concerning those schools in many contexts does not warrant making them the core of an agenda to tackle educational disadvantage.

Richard Rothstein's chief contention in *Class and Schools: Using Social, Economic, and Educational Reform to Close the Black-White Achievement Gap* (2004) is that policymakers concerned with educational disadvantage have focused too narrowly on internal-to-school reform strategies, whereas the preponderance of the evidence shows that the causes of educational disadvantage lie outside of schools. He advocates more political attention to external-to-school factors.

Both of Rothstein's central claims are plausible. The U.S. Department of Education's *Strategic Plan for Fiscal Years 2007–12* (2007) mentions few factors outside the control of schools as causes of educational disadvantage, and its strategic focus is relentlessly school-based. The three leading nonprofit funders of educational reform—the Bill and Melinda Gates Foundation, the Broad Foundation, and the Walton Family Foundation—have focused almost entirely on schools and school-governance structures, or on school-focused advocacy groups, such as the Education Trust and the Education Sector. As the largest nongovernmental funder of education reform, the Gates Foundation focused its first phase of operations on reforming the structure of high schools, and its current phase is focused on reforming school curriculums and identifying high-quality instructors. However, the evidence is compelling that factors over which schools have little or no control—such as the health states of children, the employment status and income of their parents, and the concentrations of disadvantage within their neighborhoods— have a substantial impact on educational disadvantage.

Although Rothstein insists that "many of the curricular and school organizational reforms promoted by education critics have merit, and should be intensified" (2004, 9), he argues that policymakers should pay much more attention than they do to external-to-school factors. Some leading advocates of internal-to-school reform strategies have criticized him for this, the worry being that paying attention to the factors over which schools have no control gives schools an excuse for the poor performance of their students and thereby reduces their incentive and will to improve.

In this chapter we argue that although placing factors implicated in the production of educational disadvantage into a dichotomous taxonomy of internal-to-schools and external-to-schools categories provides a nice heuristic and captures a considerable part of the conceptual and empirical space concerning the *causes* of disadvantage, is misleading, especially for policymakers and practitioners. Some important factors do not fit neatly into either category, and others seem to fit well into both. Policy advocates, too, do not divide neatly into corresponding categories: the advocacy space is occupied by proponents of exclusively internal-to-schools strategies and advocates of mixed external and internal strategies, but no one proposes exclusively external strategies. And because many policy and practical interventions influence what happens both within and outside the school, the dichotomy does not help policymakers answer their central question: "Which among the feasible policies in my circumstances will ameliorate educational disadvantage most cost-effectively?" In any given circumstances, the most cost-effective package of feasible policies may include items from both categories and items that do not fit neatly into either. So policymakers must consider, and need relevant evidence concerning, many discrete items on a large menu that does not respect the dichotomy.

We start with a discussion of the meaning and causes of educational disadvantage and then consider how knowledge about causation relates to how we should think about policy agendas. We subsequently sketch versions of the external-to-schools and internal-to-schools reform agendas, and explain why we think that dichotomous taxonomy is misleading. We focus on the specific case of what we call "high-commitment" schools, a central item on the internal-to-schools policy agenda, and we challenge the conviction that such schools have a central role to play in large-scale efforts to ameliorate educational disadvantage. Finally, we examine the policy dilemmas that would arise if high-commitment schools *were* given such a role.

WHAT IS EDUCATIONAL DISADVANTAGE AND WHAT CAUSES IT?

The current project concerns the connections between social inequality and educational disadvantage. As Sean Reardon (chapter 5 in this volume) observes, we have a wealth of analysis of the (declining) correlations between race and educational achievement; his contribution is an analysis of the (larger and growing) correlation between household income and educational achievement. Much of the evidence concerning what actually causes educational disadvantage is at best suggestive. Educational disadvantage refers to the way that some children are put at a disadvantage relative to others in their ability to negotiate the adult world by how they interact with whatever educational institutions are available to them. But not only do we not have precise measures of the skills and traits that educational institutions can produce and that influence how well people succeed over their life course; we do not even know precisely what those skills and traits are. The standard measures are as follows:

- Attainment—the number of years a child attends school

- Graduation—whether a child graduates from high school

- Achievement—how well he or she performs on tests of narrowly defined achievement, usually reading and mathematics

A fair amount is known about which factors influence variation in attainment, graduation, and achievement, and we have reason to think that factors influencing poor performance on these measures cause educational disadvantage. But even if precise weights could be assigned to these factors, attainment, graduation, and achievement are sufficiently distant from the traits and skills that make for successful negotiation of the economy and civic and social life that we could not conclude a great deal about the relative weight of the factors causing overall educational disadvantage.

Given this definition, an exclusive focus on the "achievement gap" can be misleading. In contemporary usage, "achievement gap" has come to mean a gap among two or more groups in the percentage that reaches a proficiency cutoff score on a test. But even if two groups are identical in the proportions that achieve proficiency, one group may be disadvantaged if, say, only 10 percent of its members achieve significantly above proficiency, whereas 80 percent of the other group achieves significantly above proficiency. Because "proficiency" is an arbitrarily set cutoff, the gap varies depending on where the cutoff is set (Rothstein 2004, 15–16). Finally, scores on math and reading tests, which tell us something about the level of reading and math competence of the students, are only part of the story of how schools influence students' life-course outcomes.

Eliminating educational disadvantage ("closing the achievement gap") would mean that valuable educational outcomes no longer correlate with social class, race, or ethnicity. Though some philosophers argue that this is part of educational justice (see, for example, Brighouse and Swift 2008; Koski and Reich 2008), it seems not to be a central goal of public policy. Even advocates of closing the achievement gap seem centrally concerned not with eliminating all educational disadvantage, but with raising the floor: muting the worst educational disadvantage. Accordingly, we shall talk of *ameliorating* or *reducing,* rather than *eliminating,* educational disadvantage.

Educational advantage and disadvantage are realized in the interaction between educational institutions and students. How successful that interaction is depends on what both parties bring to it—how well equipped the student is to take up what the institution offers, and how well designed the institution is to offer opportunities that the student can take up. What the student brings to the interaction is influenced by her experiences outside the school and whatever unchangeable traits she was born with; the socially designated purpose of the school is to create educationally productive interactions. So the standard taxonomy of causes of educational disadvantage distinguishes factors that are external to schools (those that operate on the student outside the purview of the school) from those that are internal to schools (even though those, too, are obviously influenced by external factors such as government policy, the economic environment, and social attitudes about teaching). Here, then, is a non-exhaustive list of factors, broken down by the standard taxonomy.

External to Schools

Factors to educational disadvantage that are external to schools include variations in how well families prepare children to interact with school, in family income and wealth, effectiveness of public health measures, access to health care and, hence, health states, levels of parental stress and parental health, types of parental employment, family structure, levels of neighborhood crime, quality of policing in the neighborhood, concentrations of disadvantage or advantage in the neighborhood, quality of physical environment (especially as it affects health), frequency of moving homes, and the peer group within the neighborhood.

Internal to Schools

Factors to educational disadvantage that are internal to schools include variations in spending within and among schools, teacher quality, principal quality, curriculum and instruction, disciplinary regime, peer group within the school, and the physical environment of the school, especially as relating to health.[1]

CAUSES AND POLICIES

One natural thought is that policies for ameliorating educational disadvantage should directly tackle the fundamental causes of educational disadvantage where they are found: according to Rothstein, largely outside of schools. Some of Rothstein's critics, such as Stephan and Abigail Thernstrom, worry that Rothstein's analysis will make teachers and school leaders, who have very little ability to tackle the causes on which Rothstein focuses, complacent about those things they can influence, genuine problems within schools: Stephan Thernstrom (2005) refers to Rothstein as the "excuser in chief" for his emphasis on the external factors that prepare students unequally for school (see also chapter 25 in this volume). Whatever the merit of this worry, there is no reason to think that fundamental causes must be addressed. If a city is built on a floodplain, policymakers do not attempt to change either of the fundamental causes of its proneness to flooding, tidal patterns and location; instead, they try to manipulate where the flooding will occur by engineering protections for the most socially valued and vulnerable sites. They cannot alter tidal patterns, and relocating the city is too costly. The same holds for purely social phenomena: we may not know how to alter some causes, and it may be unduly expensive to alter others. So even though most fundamental causes of educational disadvantage may indeed lie outside the school, the only known or knowable, or cost-effective, or feasible levers to ameliorate the disadvantage may lie within the school.[2]

External-to-Schools Reforms

Rothstein is the most prominent advocate of an external-to-schools agenda, and the agenda of the Broader, Bolder Approach to Education (BBA) coalition reflects his book's arguments. Neither he nor the BBA denies that internal-to-school reforms can be effective; rather, they argue against exclusive focus on schools, contending that a panoply of external-to-school reforms are more likely to be effective than many internal-to-school measures. The "Main BBA Statement" says:

Education policy in this nation has typically been crafted around the expectation that schools alone can offset the full impact of low socioeconomic status on learning. Schools can—and have—ameliorated some of the impact of social and economic disadvantage on achievement. Improving our schools, therefore, continues to be a vitally important strategy for promoting upward mobility and for working toward equal opportunity and overall educational excellence.

Evidence demonstrates, however, that achievement gaps based on socioeconomic status are present before children even begin formal schooling. Despite the impressive academic gains registered by some schools serving disadvantaged students, there is no evidence that school improvement strategies by *themselves* can close these gaps in a substantial, consistent, and sustainable manner.

Nevertheless, there is solid evidence that policies aimed directly at education-related social and economic disadvantages can improve school performance and student achievement. The persistent failure of policymakers to act on that evidence—in tandem with a school-improvement agenda—is a major reason why the association between social and economic disadvantage and low student achievement remains so strong. (BBA 2010)

Figure 24.1 displays the causal model Rothstein endorses: he sees the background institutions rather than schools as the key causes of educational disadvantage. The policy agenda is informed, though not determined, by this view. It is useful to distinguish two main strands of his agenda:

Background Institutions. These include such measures as reducing income inequality by, for example, increasing the minimum wage, using collective bargaining, expanding the earned-income tax credit, and establishing a commitment to full employment as a central part of economic policy; stabilizing low-income housing by mechanisms that make it easier for low-income renters to stay in their homes; integrating housing by socioeconomic class through inclusionary zoning ordinances; and improving public health measures affecting disadvantaged neighborhoods and health-care access for low-income families.[3]

Support to Schools. These include such measures as school integration by socioeconomic status; establishing school-community clinics that would serve both parents and children; improving prenatal and postnatal care through visiting nurse programs and improved health-care access; expanding high-quality early childhood education for low-income and minority children that emphasizes social skills as well as literacy, mirroring middle-class early childhood experiences; establishing stable and high-quality after-school and summer programs.

Internal-to-Schools Reforms

The assumption that schools currently operate below the production-possibility frontier—that given the level of resources they currently deploy, they could, with some reorganization, produce better results—is plausible. Researchers find that resources are used less effectively than they might be for a range of reasons, including poor management, a deficient school culture, teachers' inadequacies in pedagogical knowledge or skill, and deficient discipline (see, for example, Fullan 2007; Elmore 2004; Payne 2008). At least some of these problems could in principle be corrected without radical personnel changes or budget increases. Different agendas locate the inefficiencies in different places. One approach locates the central inefficiency in the structure and culture of the teaching profession, which prevents managers from learning what the

FIGURE 24.1   *Rothstein Causal Model*

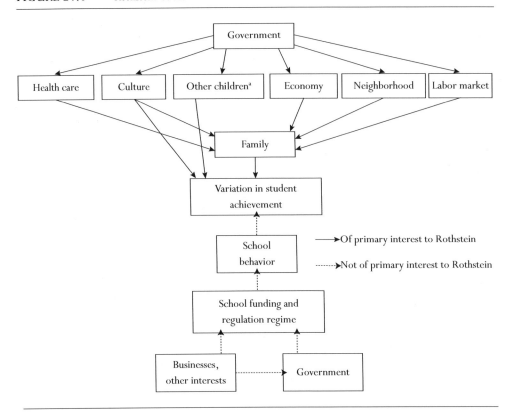

Source: Authors' figure based on Rothstein (2004).
[a] Rothstein does not consider "other children" to be an in-school factor, because schools have limited control over student characteristics.

effective instructional practices are and teachers from implementing them. (For examples of this approach, see Elmore 2004; Wagner 2010; McLaughlin and Talbert 2001.) An alternative approach locates the problem in schools' failure to appropriately accommodate the cultural expectations and norms of children from demographic groups that exhibit lower achievement (see, for example, Apple 2006; Ladson-Billings 1994). (For a state-of-the-art account and analysis of current school improvement strategies, see chapter 25 in this volume.)

How could improving schools ameliorate educational disadvantage? The hunch is that disadvantaged children generally attend schools that are less efficient than average, and that within heterogeneous schools, efficiency gains from school improvement can be turned disproportionately to benefit lower achievers. There is no reason to believe this will happen as a matter of course: one review of U.K.-based studies from the 1980s and early 1990s indicates that school improvement in that context tended to widen achievement gaps because the gains flowed disproportionately to those who were already the higher achievers (Mortimer and Whitty 1997). On a societywide basis, if efforts were equally distributed among schools, it is easy to imagine that, other things being equal, school-improvement efforts would be more likely to take root and succeed in schools with relatively advantaged populations than in schools with relatively disadvantaged populations.

Abigail Thernstrom and Stephan Thernstrom (2003) propose a variant of the internal-to-schools reform agenda specifically designed to address disadvantage. Because elements of their agenda have been influential and are shared by large funders and by the George W. Bush and Barack Obama administrations, we think it is worth outlining in some detail. The Thernstroms start from surveys of schools that "beat the odds" by producing achievement among disadvantaged students similar to what we can expect from more advantaged children.[4] The Thernstroms argue that these successes are evidence that schools can narrow the gap, and they propose that we replicate what these schools do in order to narrow the gap on a larger scale. The agenda includes recommendations for policymakers concerning regulation, but we shall concentrate on their template for the "No Excuses" school.[5]

Lengthened School Day and Year   Success requires that African American and Latino students spend a good deal more time at school than is standard and that most of this additional time be devoted to instruction.[6] Moreover, children are expected to continue studying outside the school gates.[7]

Basics Curriculum   The curriculum emphasizes basics. Fact-based emphasis on the core subjects, traditional-style drilling, and insistence on mastery of basics are preferable to "progressive, fuzzy new-age" teaching methods (Thernstrom and Thernstrom 2003, 62–63).

Discipline   Successful schools must make it clear to their students what constitutes misbehavior and that it will not be tolerated, and ensure that consequences for misbehavior are administered consistently and reliably. A well-publicized system of rewards and penalties is strictly enforced. Knowledge Is Power Program (KIPP) schools, for example, set out expectations in contracts, signed by teachers, parents, and students.[8] Expectations include "coming to school on time, attending every class, listening with their full attention, burning the midnight oil" (Thernstrom and Thernstrom 2003, 7).

Emphasis on Teaching and Learning   The schools have excellent teachers, meeting the criteria set forth by principals, which include subject knowledge, ability to inspire, and dedication. If teachers can manage their classrooms effectively, fewer are needed, and more money can be spent elsewhere.[9] Principals control budgets and management with entrepreneurial discretion and autonomy, but are primarily instructional leaders who "coach teachers, helping them plan lessons to reach all children, and so forth"; and teachers have ample collaboration time in which they "meet, they watch each other, they discuss strategies, and see themselves as a team dedicated to finding the best way to reach their students—a collective responsibility" (Thernstrom and Thernstrom 2003, 53).

Ethos of Disconnection from Home Culture   The schools maintain an ethos that makes limited concessions to the home culture of the students, since "too heavy a dose of African-American history and literature arguably reinforces the isolation" (Thernstrom and Thernstrom 2003, 77). The school sends the optimistic message about America that hard work opens doors (74–75) and teaches students to "think of themselves as unique, free to choose their identity" (78). Students see themselves as members of a team; their school is their second home (71), and students take responsibility for the appearance of both the school and themselves; clothes, for example, are not a means of self-expression. If the expectations of the school conflict with their culture, students must "leave their culture at the door" (Thernstrom and Thernstrom 2003, 69).

Many of these elements are common to other school reform agendas. The distinctive feature is the combination of two key components: an emphasis on academic basics in the instructional regime and a disciplinary regime that is highly regimented and seems to prepare the students for the corporate culture they are liable to experience in the semiskilled jobs largely in the service economy for which many of them are bound.

PROBLEMS WITH THE "INTERNAL-EXTERNAL" DICHOTOMY

What is wrong with the dichotomous taxonomy of "internal" and "external" reforms? The first problem is obvious from a careful glance at the two sketched agendas. One prominent item—increasing the length of the school day and school year—appears on both. In the most obvious sense it seems school-based. But it is also a neighborhood-changing reform, because when children spend more time in school, several features of the neighborhood change. Their parents are less limited in the hours they can engage in the labor force: they can spend more hours working, more flexibly. The period between the end of the school day and the arrival home of working parents is the time when teenagers are most at risk of involvement with drugs, crime, and early sexual experiences: reducing that period reduces their risks (Waldfogel 2006, 167). It also reduces the risks to neighborhood residents of becoming victims of juvenile crime (Jacob and Lefgren 2003). Consider the limiting case of the lengthened school day: boarding school. Curto, Fryer, and Howard (this volume, chapter 23) describe SEED schools—public college-preparatory boarding schools in Washington, D.C., and Baltimore for students grades six through twelve—as offering a "very safe and structured nurturing environment that is somewhat removed from the risks and distractions [students] would normally face in their status quo low-quality environments" (14). But they also change those very environments—both the families and the neighborhoods—by removing the children from them Sunday evening till Friday afternoon every week of the school year.

Thernstrom and Thernstrom (2003) regard the lengthened school day and school year as part of a larger package of internal-to-school reforms because these are part of what the successful schools they take their cue from do. Rothstein simply makes it one item on a menu: he is inspired by the work on the summer learning gap, which indicates that the achievement gap between members of different socioeconomic classes and racial groups remains constant while children are in school, but grows during the summer. The inference is that something happens when children are not in school that increases the gap, so reducing that time will diminish the gap. Rothstein does insist that summer programs for poor children should replicate the kinds of experiences middle-class children are having (2004, 143–44). But even this does not amount to requiring a change in the character of what happens within schools during the school year. And if the findings about the summer learning gap are correct, simply doing more of what happens in the school year should ameliorate disadvantage. So, quite independently of the effects such programs are likely to have on neighborhoods, categorizing them as "internal" seems forced.

After-school tutoring programs also fit both categories. Some are conducted on the school grounds, some outside, some by school employees, some by other service providers; some are coordinated with the school curriculum and instructional practices, others not. They affect the neighborhood and the family by keeping children out of the home and off the street; but if they affect the school and its operations, it is by doing the same things as well as by supplementing students' learning.

Now consider a second problematic case: items that do not naturally fit either category. Many of Rothstein's proposals have this character. Consider school-community clinics. Rothstein (2004, 37–38) observes that many disadvantaged children enter kindergarten with undiagnosed (and hence untreated) visual and hearing impairments:

> Children with vision problems have difficulty reading and seeing what teachers write on the board. Trying to read their eyes may wander or have difficulty tracking print or focusing. . . . Poor children have severe vision impairment at twice the normal rate. . . . Lower-class children are more likely to suffer from vision problems because of their less adequate prenatal development. . . . [V]isual deficits also arise because poor children are more likely to watch more television, activity that does not train the eye to develop hand-eye coordination and depth perception.

These conditions are diagnosed prior to school in more advantaged children because their parents teach them to read and therefore are more likely to discover an impairment if there is one. Vision problems sometimes underlie unruly behavior, which is punished, leading to further alienation. Poor children also suffer much higher rates of hearing problems, poor dental health, lead exposure, exposure to smoke, fetal alcohol syndrome, low birth weight, poor nutrition, and asthma, all of which affect their interactions with school. As a partial corrective, Rothstein (2004, 138–39), proposes

> . . . establishment in lower-class neighborhoods of school clinics that serve children through their high school years and their parents as well. To narrow the achievement gap, a school-community clinic should include services that middle-class families take for granted and that ensure children can thrive in school . . . includ[ing] obstetric and gynecological services . . . pediatric services . . . dentists and hygienists . . . optometrists and vision therapists . . . social workers to refer families to other services, community health educators and psychologists or therapists to assist families and children who are experiencing excessive stress and other emotional differences.

Notice that establishing school-community clinics does not deal with the fundamental causes of poor vision and other health issues outside the school: low-income children inhabit conditions that tend to promote worse health, and that their parents have less access to health care. It simply treats the symptom so that the child can function better in school. And it seems odd to call it an external-to-school reform, because the proposal is to place it inside the school. But nor is it natural to call the establishment of a school-community clinic an internal-to-school reform. It does affect what happens in the school and may require a change in the job description of the principal (who now becomes a manager of a health-care facility), but it does not influence the way that the school conducts its core mission—curriculum and instruction.

Consider two other kinds of programs often mentioned in holistic approaches to ameliorating educational disadvantage: nurse visiting programs and parent education schemes. Susan Neuman (2009, 86; see also chapter 22 in this volume) describes the Nurse-Family Partnership:

> Helping women improve the outcomes of pregnancy, child health and development, and maternal life course, the program uses a "person-process-context" model that draws heavily upon research in self-efficacy, attachment, and human ecology. . . . Home visits [by nurses] are considered essential in developing these close, therapeutic alliances with mothers and other family members. As [one visiting nurse] reports, "We're on their own turf—it breaks down barriers."

The Nurse-Family Partnership looks like an external-to-schools intervention. But now consider the Baby College and the early-childhood programs in the Harlem Children's Zone (HCZ), which the Obama administration promises to replicate across twenty cities. Like the Nurse-Family Partnership, Baby College attempts to teach young parents and parents-to-be how to raise their children more effectively, using Saturday classes to teach what are widely regarded as "middle-class parenting techniques" such as, when discipline is needed, using time-outs rather than hitting a child, and reasoning with children rather than commanding them. The subsequent stages of the HCZ early-childhood program, which starts with children at age three, prepare children for entry to the charter elementary schools run by the HCZ. The HCZ's early-childhood programs look like an extension of school—in the way that the lengthened school day is an extension of school—but its aims are similar to those of the Nurse-Family Partnership and are informed by similar analyses of the problems. And, again, neither attempts to change the underlying background conditions that give rise to educational disadvantage: the cultural assumptions of the communities the parents inhabit, the disadvantages they endure and the stress they are under, the health-affecting physical conditions in their homes. Instead they intervene at an intermediate stage, attempting to block the transmission of the disadvantage. From the perspective of the policymaker, whether one or the other is external to school or internal to school is neither here nor there.

The dichotomy does not, furthermore, really describe the political advocacy map. Whereas the Gates Foundation, Thernstrom and Thernstrom (2003), and the U.S. Department of Education (2007) all focus exclusively or almost exclusively on changing what schools do and make little or no mention of the external factors causing the educational disadvantage, neither Rothstein (2004) nor the Broader, Bolder Coalition (2010) advocates exclusively "external" measures. We quoted Rothstein earlier to the effect that many school-based reforms were valuable; the first on the Broader, Bolder Coalition's list of four priorities is to "continue to pursue school improvement efforts." The focus on external measures is meant to correct, not replace, an unduly narrow focus on schools.

Before moving on, we want to alert readers to an issue we shall discuss at length later. Although we accept that the inside-outside dichotomy quite naturally captures most of the causal factors of educational disadvantage, there is one exception. Peer effects on learning are widely thought to be significant and are usually counted as school-based factors from the point of view of the researcher looking at causes. But from the policy point of view, this seems wrongheaded. In a nonchoice system of allocating children to schools, schools have little or no control over who the schoolmates of a particular child are, so one would not want to design a policy that punished or rewarded schools for peer effects. In a choice-based system of allocation, it is true that oversubscribed schools can influence who attends (either by skewing the applicant pool or by actively selecting children with particular characteristics); but this is at the expense of other schools. Internal-to-school reforms cannot change the fact that there is pool of children who are likely to affect others negatively and that these children will have to be in some school or another.

ASSESSING FEASIBILITY AND PROBABILITY IN CONTEXT

Rothstein's aim is not to deflect decisionmakers from attending to school improvement. Rather, he alerts them to other features of the social environment over which they may have more leverage than schools have, and suggests changes that may be more promising in ameliorating educational disadvantage. Decisionmakers have limited resources and, depending on their situation, face different feasibility constraints. Even though changes in instructional practices would not be expensive and would be effective in ameliorating disadvantage, a particular principal may not be able to implement them because she may be unable to activate the staff turnover necessary to make the change, or because her district leadership may block the necessary resource reallocations. She may, though, be able to access county funds to establish regular health visits or private grants to supply prescription eyeglasses. Another principal may have changes in instructional practices forced on her by a district leadership and be in a position to influence those changes positively. The Thernstroms (2003) rely heavily on choice and charter schools to produce the changes they desire; officials in districts where introducing such measures is unfeasible must look for other ameliorative measures. In other words, whether internal or external factors are more significant in the production of disadvantage is not what the decisionmaker needs to know; she needs to be alert to the wide range of measures, each of which may have some ameliorative promise, and be able to judge which are feasible and which package of those is most likely to work in her circumstances. The optimal feasible package may include items from both categories, and items that fit neither.

HIGH-COMMITMENT SCHOOLS

The Thernstroms' model is inspired by a small group of what we label "high-commitment" schools identified by the Heritage Foundation and Education Trust as high-performing. We label these "high-commitment" schools because they exhibit features such as parental contracts, long school days and long school years, and demanding long hours from teachers, including substantial after-school hours interacting with parents. Most are middle or elementary-through-middle schools, and almost all are small charter schools serving low-income communities, admission to which is controlled by choice. Many belong to the Knowledge Is Power Program (KIPP) franchise founded by David Levin and Michael Feinberg in Houston in 1994 (described in detail in Mathews 2009). These schools are not only the model for the Thernstroms but also for the instructional style of the Promise Academies in the Harlem Children's Zone, which the Obama administration has promised to replicate in other cities and which appear to have influenced the Obama administration's insistence on states' removing barriers to the expansion of charter schools for the Race to the Top competition and for the plans to reauthorize the Elementary and Secondary Education Act. The KIPP schools, the schools on the Heritage Foundation and Education Trust's lists, and the advocates for KIPP appear to have had considerable influence in establishing the internal-external dichotomy in the policy arena—which we reject—by influencing advocates and policymakers to believe that internal-to-school reform efforts alone can ameliorate, or perhaps even eliminate, educational disadvantage. So a separate discussion of their status is essential to a comprehensive presentation of our case.

The available evidence does not establish that these "high-performance" schools have profound effects on educational disadvantage. We do not mean to criticize the schools, still less to urge that they be excluded from the menu of options for tackling disadvantage. Rather, we urge caution in seeing them as the central element of a national strategy. Why should we be cautious about making them the basis of a large-scale improvement strategy? First, it is not clear how many "high-performance" schools systematically improve achievement. Rothstein reports his examination of the Education Trust's 1,320 schools, at least half of whose students were both poor and minorities, and whose test scores in math and reading were in the top third of their states: "Only a third of the high-flying schools had high scores in *both* reading and math. Only a 10th were high in reading and math in *more than one grade*. Only 3% were high in reading and math in at least two grades for *two years running*. Less than half of one percent of these high poverty and high minority schools were truly high flying, scoring well consistently" (Rothstein 2004, 76; emphasis added). Doug Harris's (2007, 384) further analysis with a sample of 18,365 schools finds that when "high-performing" is defined to include consistency over time, fully 93 percent of schools identified as high performing for a year drop out of the category.[10] He finds that on the more demanding definition, "the likelihood that a low-poverty-low-minority school is high-performing is *89 times* greater than for a high-poverty-high-minority school" (385; emphasis added).

Second, as Rothstein (2004, 71–83) argues at length, the Thernstroms' model schools have special characteristics that cannot necessarily be replicated at scale. Most practice some form of selection. A few schools cherry-pick promising students (Rothstein 2004, 72). Many, however, because they are schools of choice, probably unintentionally exclude many of the students most likely to perform very badly and to consume high levels of disciplinary attention. For example, KIPP schools require parents to opt in and sign a contract and then enforce the contract by expelling students who display major behavioral problems thus concentrating the most difficult students in other schools. Some schools rely heavily on a limited supply of young teachers who have not yet started their own families (the KIPP schools appear to do this; see Mathews 2009) and have found exceptional principals. The Thernstroms ignore the possible magnetic effect of excellent principals on good teachers who may concentrate in particular schools, producing remarkable results at a cost to other schools; nor do they discuss the need to increase the supply of high-quality teachers and principals. Yet a large-scale strategy must deal with all these issues.

Will Dobbie and Roland Fryer (2009) find remarkable test score gains for children in the Promise Academies in the Harlem Children's Zone, which is taken by some commentators as evidence that such schools contain the key to eliminating disadvantage. David Brooks ("The Harlem Miracle," *New York Times,* May 8, 2009, A31) described the schools as follows:

> The typical student entered the charter middle school, Promise Academy, in sixth grade and scored in the 39th percentile among New York City students in math. By the eighth grade, the typical student in the school was in the 74th percentile. The typical student entered the school scoring in the 39th percentile in English Language Arts (verbal ability). By eighth grade, the typical student was in the 53rd percentile. Forgive some academic jargon, but the most common education reform ideas—reducing class size, raising teacher pay, enrolling kids in Head Start—produce gains of about 0.1 or 0.2 or 0.3 standard deviations. If you study policy, those are the sorts of improvements you live with every day. Promise Academy produced gains of 1.3 and 1.4 standard deviations. That's off the charts. In math, Promise Academy eliminated the achievement gap between its black students and the city average for white students. Let me repeat that. It eliminated the black-white achievement gap.

The problems here are twofold. First, test scores are only one indicator of educational disadvantage, possibly not the most important. To know the contribution to ameliorating disadvantage, we need to know whether these gains persist through high school and whether they influence dropout rates, involvement in crime, and other outcomes. Second, it is clear from Paul Tough's (2009) laudatory description of the Harlem Children's Zone that in the period Dobbie and Fryer studied, raising test scores became an obsessive focus for Geoffrey Canada, CEO of the Harlem Children's Zone. He removed the school principal for maintaining a more balanced curriculum and threatened her successor with replacement by the KIPP team if test score gains were not considerable. Variation in test scores may well tell us a good deal about the relative preparation and skill levels of different students, but it is not clear whether big improvements in test scores are a useful measure for the elimination of educational disadvantage (Booher-Jennings 2005; Deming et al. 2010; Jennings and Beveridge 2009).

What can children attending these schools really expect? The schools are said to raise substantial numbers of students above proficiency in state-mandated tests—yet such successes fall short of college readiness. The culture and disciplinary regime that the Thernstroms advocate is not harsh by any standards, but it emphasizes deference to authority, hard work, and abnegation of self in the school setting; this emphasis may reminding readers of Samuel Bowles and Herbert Gintis's (1976) arguments that education's function is not to teach knowledge and skills, but to form the personality of future workers so as to fit them for the employment they can expect. This is not what advantaged parents seek or provide for their children (Lareau 2003).

Suppose that what the instructional and disciplinary regimes of these schools in fact prepare students well for is semiskilled service jobs. Whether a strategy producing this result is justified depends on what the feasible alternatives are. If an alternative strategy for preparing the same students to be college-ready is feasible, and jobs requiring college readiness are available, that justifies adoption of the alternative. If, by contrast, the feasible alternatives do not prepare students to take and hold on to even semiskilled service jobs, the strategy is more defensible, despite the nonideal state to which the students are consigned. A different possibility, of course, is that the schools are designed to prepare students well for jobs that are disappearing (or have already disappeared)—skilled manufacturing jobs in urban areas. If so, there's a case against what the schools are doing, though one that would be mitigated if preparation for those nonexistent jobs had collateral effects enabling students to perform in actually existing jobs well.[11]

Our final observation raises, but does not resolve, a serious policy dilemma. The high-commitment schools use two mechanisms for selecting students. Parents must choose the school, in an environment in which the necessity of making choice is not the default condition. And parents have to sign a contract with the school making a commitment to ensure that the student abides by its norms and rules, and must maintain that agreement. This is not cherry-picking the strongest students: students attending these schools are disadvantaged relative to the general population. But careful analyses of these schools emphasize that the effects can only be shown for the kind of student who actually attends, and nothing is known about their likely effects for other kinds of students (Dobbie and Fryer 2009, 4). Students whose parents do not enter the lottery—student who are liable to be among the very most disconnected and disadvantaged—are concentrated in regular schools. The more concentrated the presence of high-commitment schools in a region, the higher will be the concentration of extreme disadvantage in the regular schools in that region.

There is evidence, furthermore, of peer effects on student learning: that learning in a classroom with harder-working, higher-achieving, and less disruptive peers increases a student's own learning; the converse is that less-hardworking, lower-achieving, and more disruptive peers harms a student's own learning (Ding and Lehrer 2007; MacCoun et al. 2008; Hoxby 2000; Vigdor and Nechyba 2004; but see chapter 5 in this volume, by Sean Reardon, for a skeptical view). If so, then some if not all of the amelioration of educational disadvantage that high-commitment schools generate may be gained at the cost of increasing the educational disadvantage of those students who concentrate in the regular nonchoice schools.

Those who analyze such schools must be alert to this possibility. One necessary piece of information for evaluating a strategy involving the schools is how large the negative effect on the outcomes that really matter is on *other* children, whether these relevant outcomes are seen to be academic achievement or later life-course outcomes. Suppose these effects are small, whereas the benefits of attending No Excuses schools are considerable; if that is so, the negative effects on other children do not support a case against the strategy. Suppose, by contrast, that the negative effects on other children are considerable; this would constitute a reason to object to the agenda. On the other hand, the benefits to attending children might be so large that these effects might justify the agenda despite the downsides to other children. (By analogy, some regard affirmative action as justified even if it benefits more advantaged members of racial minorities at some cost to less advantaged members.) The dilemma for policymakers—whether to adopt policies that benefit some but harm others among the disadvantaged—requires a nuanced understanding of how to properly distribute the benefits and burdens among subgroups of the educationally disadvantaged, as well as detailed information about what the effects of putative policies on all of those subgroups actually are.

CONCLUSION

The evidence concerning the success of high-commitment schools does not warrant the conclusion that internal-to-schools reform is the best, or even a central, strategy for ameliorating educational disadvantage. Depending on their context and the level at which they make decisions, policymakers have a wide array of options—some internal to schools, others external to schools, and others that don't naturally fit either category. The policymaker must judge, among the feasible items on a large menu including internal and external strategies, which combination has the highest probability of paying off in her context.

We want to reiterate a word of caution we sounded earlier. We have defined educational disadvantage as referring to the way that children are put at a disadvantage relative to others in their ability to negotiate the adult world by the way they interact with whatever educational institutions are available to them. Any given policymaker has limited space for action and is unlikely to make a huge impact on educational disadvantage. Good evidence about what might work in her circumstances will be sparse, because the variable she is trying to influence is not something as readily measurable as test scores or graduation rates or attainment. Studies demonstrating changes in those variables, even if they can identify the mechanisms responsible, do not, in themselves, demonstrate reductions in educational disadvantage. So policymakers have to make difficult judgments. Categorizing interventions dichotomously as "internal" and "external" does not make those judgments easier or better.

We are especially grateful to Richard Murnane and Greg Duncan for comments on earlier drafts; to many other participants in the project, especially Susanna Loeb; to our commentator, Richard Nelson; and to Richard Rothstein for valuable discussions.

NOTES

Online appendix available at: http://www.russellsage.org/duncan_murnane_online_appendix.pdf.

1. Our goal in this chapter is to criticize the internal-external taxonomy's value for policymakers. Beyond this weakness, however, the taxonomy does not work perfectly even for merely itemizing causes. Consider Sean Reardon's documentation (chapter 5 in this volume) of the increasing educational returns to living in a higher-income household. The income distribution fits well within the external category. But the mechanisms that he suggests might be at work don't fit in either one: parent-school interactions, for example, are shaped by factors outside and inside the school, and have consequences beyond as well as within the school (Lareau 1989).

2. Frank Furstenberg suggests this (see chapter 22 in this volume).

3. Note that programs designed specifically to alter the internal life of the family of the kind surveyed, largely negatively, by Furstenberg (chapter 22 in this volume) feature in this very broad category.

4. Their "starting point" in seeking these schools was the Heritage Foundation list of twenty-one high-performing, high-poverty schools. Most, but not all, are charter schools (the notable exception is Hobart Elementary in Los Angeles, where Rafe Esquith teaches).

5. Note that not all elements of the agenda fit well with one another or with the causal assumptions at play.

6. "Almost all the schools we describe added hours to the day and days to the year," and "almost the entire day is devoted to learning core subjects . . . every minute is regarded as precious" (Thernstrom and Thernstrom 2003, 46, 54).

7. "At good schools, the day is organized for nonstop learning, and the children generally go home with hefty home-work assignments" (Thernstrom and Thernstrom 2003, 55).
8. Several of the model schools belong to the KIPP franchise. For a detailed, and strongly partisan, account of the development of this franchise, see Jay Mathews (2009). For a more measured discussion, see Paul Tough (2008).
9. According to Thernstrom and Thernstrom (2003): "Great teaching is central to this success. . . . In part, the right people were hired; in part, talent is nurtured; and in part, the teachers are freed up to teach. The administrative headaches are gone. The lunch duty is gone. The paperwork is gone. Teachers are in the school a very long day, but we build in a minimum of two and a quarter hours of lesson planning time'" (50). Teachers receive "more professional training, mentoring, and collegial advice" (51).
10. Similarly, a team of researchers examining "beating the odds" schools in California found that "365 elementary schools were beating the odds during 2002 and 307 schools were beating the odds during 2003; however, only 61 elementary schools were beating the odds every year over the 2002–05 time period" (Pérez et al. 2007).
11. This is not the place to defend a full account of the considerations we should be attentive to when making an "all things considered" judgment of policy alternatives (see Brighouse 2009 for a sketch of an account). But we do want to mention a relevant consideration here that might count in favor of the high-commitment school; what the school environment contributes to the quality of the youth's childhood. If a youth's home life is lacking in order, it might be very beneficial for his or her everyday experiences to be in a highly ordered school setting with clear rules and boundaries. We suspect that the children with the most disorderly home lives do not attend No Excuses schools because their parents are unlikely to engage in the choice process, but this consideration might count in favor of making the schools they do attend more like No Excuses schools.

REFERENCES

Apple, Michael. 2006. *Educating the "Right" Way: Markets, Standards, God, and Inequality*. New York: Taylor & Francis.

Broader, Bolder Coalition (BBA). 2010. "A Broader, Bolder Approach to Education: Main BBA Statement." Available at: http://www.boldapproach.org/statement.html (accessed June 9, 2010).

Booher-Jennings, Jennifer. 2005. "Below the Bubble: 'Educational Triage' and the Texas Accountability System." *American Educational Research Journal* 42(2): 231–68.

Bowles, Samuel, and Herbert Gintis. 1976. *Schooling in Capitalist America: Educational Reform and Contradictions of Economic Life*. New York: Basic Books.

Brighouse, Harry. 2009. "Moral and Political Aspects of Education." In *Oxford Handbook to Philosophy of Education*, edited by Harvey Seigel. Oxford: Oxford University Press.

Brighouse, Harry, and Adam Swift. 2008. "Putting Educational Equality in Its Place." *Education Finance and Policy* 3(4): 444–66.

Deming, David, Justine Hastings, Thomas Kane, and Douglas Staiger. 2010. "School Choice and College Attendance: Evidence from Randomized Lotteries." Unpublished manuscript. Authors' collection.

Ding, Weili, and Steven F. Lehrer. 2007. "Do Peers Affect Student Achievement in China's Secondary Schools?" *Review of Economics and Statistics* 89(2): 300–312.

Dobbie, Will, and Roland G. Fryer, Jr. 2009. "Are High-Quality Schools Enough to Close the Achievement Gap?: Evidence from a Bold Social Experiment in Harlem." NBER Working Paper No. 15473. Cambridge, Mass.: National Bureau of Education Research. Available at: http://www.economics.harvard.edu/faculty/fryer/files/HCZ_Nov2009_NBERwkgpaper.pdf (accessed April 12, 2010).

Elmore, Richard. 2004. *School Reform from the Inside Out: Policy, Practice, and Performance*. Cambridge, Mass: Harvard Educational Press.

Fullan, Michael. 2007. *The New Meaning of Educational Change*. New York: Teachers College Press.

Harris, Douglas N. 2007. "High Flying Schools, Student Disadvantage and the Logic of NCLB." *American Journal of Education* 113(3): 367–94.

Hoxby, Caroline. 2000. "Peer Effects in the Classroom: Learning from Gender and Race Variation." NBER Working Paper No. 7867. Cambridge, Mass.: National Bureau of Education Research.

Koski, William S., and Rob Reich. 2008. "When 'Adequate' Isn't: The Retreat from Equality in Educational Law and Policy and Why It Matters." *Emory Law Journal* 56(3): 545–88.

Jacob, Brian A., and Lars Lefgren. 2003. "Are Idle Hands the Devil's Workshop? Incapacitation, Concentration, and Juvenile Crime." *American Economic Review* 93(5): 1560–77.

Jennings, Jennifer L., and Andrew A. Beveridge. 2009. "How Does Test Exemption Affect Schools' and Students' Academic Performance?" *Educational Evaluation and Policy Analysis* 31(2): 153–75.

Ladson-Billings, Gloria. 1994. *The Dreamkeepers: Successful Teachers of African American Children.* San Francisco: Jossey-Bass.

Lareau, A. 1989. *Home Advantage: Social Class and Parental Intervention in Elementary Education.* London: Falmer Press.

———. 2003. *Unequal Childhoods: Class, Race, and Family Life.* Berkeley: University of California Press.

MacCoun, Robert, Philip J. Cook, Clara Muschkin, and Jacob L. Vigdor. 2008. "Distinguishing Spurious and Real Peer Effects: Evidence from Artificial Societies, Small-Group Experiments, and Real Schoolyards." *Review of Law & Economics* 4(3). Available at: http://www.bepress.com/rle/vol4/iss3/art2 (accessed July 14, 2010).

Mathews, Jay. 2009. *Work Hard. Be Nice: How Two Inspired Teachers Created the Most Promising Schools in America.* Chapel Hill, N.C.: Algonquin.

McLaughlin, Milbrey W., and Joan E. Talbert. 2001. *Professional Communities and the Work of High School Teaching.* Chicago: University of Chicago Press.

Mortimer, Peter, and Geoff Whitty. 1997. *Can School Improvement Overcome the Effects of Disadvantage?* London: Institute of Education.

Neuman, Susan B. 2009. *Changing the Odds for Children at Risk: Seven Essential Principles of Educational Programs that Break the Cycle of Poverty.* Westport, Conn.: Praeger.

Payne, Charles. 2008. *So Much Reform, So Little Change: The Persistence of Failure in Urban Schools.* Cambridge, Mass.: Harvard Educational Press.

Pérez, María, Priyanka Anand, Cecilia Speroni, Tom Parrish, Phil Esra, Miguel Socías, and Paul Gubbins. 2007. *Successful California Schools in the Context of Educational Adequacy.* Stanford, Calif.: American Institutes for Research. Available at: http://irepp.stanford.edu/documents/GDF/STUDIES/17-AIR-Successful-Schools/17-Successful-California-Schools(3-07).pdf (accessed June 16, 2010).

Rothstein, Richard. 2004. *Class and Schools: Using Social, Economic, and Educational Reform to Close the Black-White Achievement Gap.* Washington, D.C.: Economic Policy Institute.

Thernstrom, Abigail, and Stephan Thernstrom. 2003. *No Excuses: Closing the Racial Gap in Learning.* New York: Simon & Schuster.

Thernstrom, Stephan. 2005. "Must Schools Fail? An Exchange." *New York Review of Books* 52(3) (February 24). Available at: http://www.nybooks.com/articles/17764 (accessed November 21, 2009).

Tough, Paul. 2009. *Whatever It Takes: Geoffrey Canada's Quest to Change Harlem and America.* New York: Houghton Mifflin Harcourt.

U.S. Department of Education. 2007. *Strategic Plan for Fiscal Years 2007–12.* Washington, D.C.: U.S. Government Printing Office.

Vigdor, Jacob, and Thomas Nechyba. 2004. "Peer Effects in North Carolina Schools." Unpublished manuscript. Available at: http://www.hks.harvard.edu/pepg/PDF/events/Munich/PEPG-04-20Nechyba.pdf (accessed on June 17, 2010).

Wagner, Tony. 2010. *The Global Achievement Gap: Why Even Our Best Schools Don't Teach the New Survival Skills Our Children Need—and What We Can Do About It.* New York: Basic Books.

Waldfogel, Jane. 2006. *What Children Need.* Cambridge, Mass.: Harvard University Press.

Chapter 25

Intervening to Improve the Educational Outcomes of Students in Poverty: Lessons from Recent Work in High-Poverty Schools

Brian Rowan

In this chapter I describe what America's high-poverty schools are doing to improve the educational outcomes of students in poverty. A major question asked here is whether these efforts have been targeted mainly at improving students' academic learning or whether they also have been aimed at improving students' socioemotional learning. The question is important because research has shown that students' academic and socioemotional learning are correlated and jointly affect students' success in school.

This correlation is especially relevant for poor children. It is well known that children in poverty enter kindergarten with lower academic-achievement scores than more advantaged children. As early as when they first begin school, poor children are less attentive to schoolwork and more likely to engage in behaviors that get them into trouble in school settings. Research suggests that if these conditions are not dealt with, poor students' subsequent trajectories through schooling are negatively affected, since early patterns of low academic achievement, low engagement, and misbehavior exacerbate the risk of academic failure, including dropping out of school (see, for example, chapters 3 and 4 in this volume).

Thus, the key question considered in this chapter is whether school-improvement efforts in high-poverty settings should focus solely on improving students' academic learning or whether they also should aim to improve students' broader socioemotional learning.

Problems of academic and socioemotional learning loom large in schools where high percentages of students live in poverty. In this country the percentage of high-poverty schools (defined as schools with more than 75 percent of students eligible for free or reduced-price lunches) has increased during the past decade, climbing from 12 percent of schools a decade ago to 17 percent of schools in 2011. As of 2011, about 20 percent of all elementary-age children attend high-poverty schools, and about 6 percent of high school students attend such schools (Aud et al. 2010). These schools are disproportionately located in central cities but also can be found in rural and urban fringe areas, and they typically enroll high percentages of minority (primarily African American and Latino) youths. Indeed, 34 percent of all children attending high-poverty schools are black, 46 percent are Hispanic, and 25 percent have limited English proficiency.

Perhaps the most obvious problem in high-poverty schools is lagging academic achievement. In high-poverty elementary schools, about 55 percent of all students perform below grade level on standardized tests, and this hardly improves as they move to the middle grades. As a result, by the time students enter ninth grade in high-poverty high schools, around 80 percent are over-age for their grade or have reading and math skills that are below the seventh-grade level (Aud et al. 2010). Moreover, 20 to 40 percent of students entering high-poverty high schools fail so many classes in ninth grade that they have to repeat that grade, and 40 to 60 percent ultimately drop out. For these reasons, high-poverty elementary and secondary schools disproportionately face sanctions under today's education accountability regimes, and high-poverty high schools are often labeled "dropout factories."

High-poverty schools face more than academic problems, however. Students in these schools are also less engaged in school life generally. In high-poverty elementary schools, for example, student absenteeism is higher than in other schools, and teachers report more disciplinary problems. These issues persist in high-poverty middle and high schools. At this level of schooling, student absenteeism continues to be higher than in other schools, and students in high-poverty secondary schools do less homework, are less likely to participate in sports or extracurricular activities, and spend more time watching TV during out-of-school time. Sadly, it is not just students who seem disengaged from schooling in high-poverty schools. Teacher absenteeism is higher, and parents are less likely to talk with their children about schoolwork, participate as school volunteers, or attend school events (Lippman et al. 1996).

Problems from the surrounding environment also spill into high-poverty schools. Crime rates are higher in high-poverty secondary schools (peaking in the middle grades and declining thereafter), and as a result, both students and teachers are more likely to feel unsafe (Aud et al. 2010). In high-poverty schools, more students engage in risky behaviors such as substance use and sexual activity, and more have mental-health problems. Despite this, high-poverty schools have about the same ratios of student support personnel (nurses, psychologists, social workers, counselors) per pupil as do schools serving less disadvantaged populations.

Finally, there is a good deal of instability in high-poverty schools. Because of precarious economic circumstances and substandard living conditions, poor students experience higher rates of school transfer. In high-poverty elementary schools, for example, it is not uncommon for only half the students who enter a school at kindergarten to remain through sixth grade (Beatty 2010). Rates of teacher mobility are also high in high-poverty schools, with 15 percent of teachers leaving each year. About a third of the teacher mobility in high-poverty schools is the result of school staffing actions, another third is due to teacher dissatisfaction, and the remainder occurs for personal reasons.

Given these multifaceted problems, I look at three issues in this chapter. First, I briefly review research on current trends in school improvement in high-poverty schools. Second, I discuss a number of "exemplary" school-improvement programs that have been shown in prior research to have positive effects on student outcomes, separately reviewing programs for elementary and secondary schools and examining the extent to which the reviewed programs seek to improve academic learning, socioemotional learning, or both. In the final section of the chapter, I summarize this discussion and draw some conclusions about the state of school improvement in the United States.

TRENDS IN SCHOOL IMPROVEMENT

I begin with a description of what school improvement looks like on the "shop floor" of the U.S. school system. For more than two decades, virtually all state accountability systems in this country have required local schools to engage in a regular process of improvement planning and to file annual school-improvement plans with state education offices. Recent research by Heinrich Mintrop (2004) shows that local planning efforts proceed as follows: First, local school-improvement teams look at data from state accountability systems and use these data to set measurable schoolwide goals for student achievement, attendance, office referrals, suspensions, and so on. As a next step, school-improvement teams theorize about the root causes of any gaps between present performance on these indicators and the school's goals. Here, Mintrop has found that educators in high-poverty schools typically identify external factors (such as scarce resources, student mobility, and the socioeconomic status of students) as responsible for such gaps rather than internal causes (such as limitations in teachers' skills and knowledge, leadership weaknesses, or organizational-structural issues).

Finally, school-improvement teams enumerate the actions to be taken to achieve performance goals. Here, Mintrop has found that school-improvement plans typically identify about fifty discrete school-improvement activities each year, involving organizational and governance changes, changes in relationships to parents and communities, and changes in instruction. On closer inspection, it turns out that most of these activities focus on improving the achievement scores of specific subgroups of students, with the most common activities involving the provision of instructionally relevant professional development to teachers. Thus, most school improvement in U.S. schools is internally focused and does not emphasize the kinds of "external" reforms discussed by Harry Brighouse and Gina Schouten (chapter 24 in this volume).

Although this internal focus leads schools to emphasize academic achievement in their improvement plans, research suggests that schools also focus on issues of socioemotional learning and that in doing so, schools attend to factors external to the academic core of schooling. For example, a recent study found that 63 percent of schools in the United States provide team and family meetings for students with behavioral problems, and 20 percent offer mental-health services on-site. However, most of these services are short-term interventions, such as brief assessments, behavior-management consultations, crisis-intervention services, and referrals to special education or other specialized services. Beyond this, 59 percent of schools report the use of curriculum programs for students with behavioral problems. Only 15 percent of schools engage in schoolwide screening for behavioral and emotional problems (Foster et al. 2005).

An issue that has surfaced in research is the lack of coherence in many school-improvement efforts. As we have seen, school-improvement plans call for educators to undertake many activities, focused on numerous student subgroups, with multiple academic and nonacademic targets of change. They also require teachers and administrators to participate in many separate professional-development workshops, in which educators learn about numerous (but sometimes unconnected) "best practices." Too often, research suggests, teachers and administrators attend these workshops on their own and implement these practices without much organized support in the schools and classrooms where they work (Garet et al. 1996). Research suggests that this leads to a "Christmas tree" pattern of innovation in schools, where the school-improvement agenda becomes cluttered with loosely coupled and potentially contradictory initiatives (Bryk et al. 1998).

To counteract this Christmas-tree approach, many school districts have begun to take deliberate steps to promote what Fred Newmann and colleagues (2001) call "instructional program coherence." To promote instructional coherence, districts either have become directly involved in school-based instructional improvement efforts or have contracted with externally developed school-reform providers. In either case, school-based improvement efforts share a common framework for promoting instructional change. First, district leaders or external providers focus on improving a particular area of the curriculum—say, reading or math. They then develop a specific vision of how changes in that area of the curriculum should proceed. This involves developing a clear definition of the academic learning goals to be achieved by students, the instructional materials and practices to be used, any changes to instructional grouping arrangements that are required, and any assessments that will be used to monitor student learning. In a final step, districts or external providers organize supports for implementation. In both district-led and externally supported instructional improvement efforts, this involves delegating clear authority for the direction of school-improvement efforts to particular people at school sites, ensuring the support of school principals for change efforts, and moving coaches or other support staff directly into schools to support implementation of the plan. In all cases, there is close and ongoing monitoring of instructional improvement efforts.

Accumulating research suggests that many districts and external providers are succeeding with this approach (Rowan et al. 2009; Sykes, O'Day, and Ford 2009). By contrast, research suggests that schools are less successful in their efforts to improve students' socioemotional learning. In part, this is because the field of education has yet to develop a sound understanding of how to implement broader "prevention" programming in schools (Greenberg 2004; Payne 2009). In a recent study of prevention programming in schools, for example, Allison Payne (2009, 152) found that most schools offered short-term prevention programs on an irregular basis. She also found that only half of these programs were built around specific content or practices shown to be effective in the research literature. However, she did manage to identify characteristics of programs, schools, and communities that positively influenced program implementation, and here, the parallels to studies of instructional improvement are striking. For example, programs that provide clear and explicit materials to teachers, clear guidelines for implementation, and intensive implementation support by trainers and principals are put into practice with greater fidelity. Finally, at least some evidence suggests that prevention programs are better implemented when they are treated as an integral part of normal school operations (Greenberg 2004).

This last point, however, has proved to be a major stumbling block in getting "nonacademic" improvement programs implemented inside schools. Mark Greenberg (2004) discussed various strategies that can be used to facilitate implementation of programs. One strategy has been to integrate socioemotional or other prevention programming directly into regular classroom activities through curriculum modules that can be established quickly, an approach that is sometimes also coupled with a tiered intervention approach that identifies students with more severe emotional or behavioral problems for additional out-of-class intervention. An alternative strategy has been to change the school environment more broadly—for example, by working to improve the school and classroom climate through a combination of class meetings, peer leadership, family involvement, and whole-school, community-building activities or by making structural changes, such as establishing smaller units within schools to increase trust and support among students, teachers, counselors, and others. Finally, an even broader approach seeks to reach beyond the school through integration of school, family, or community programs. Current research on school improvement includes studies on each of these approaches.

EXEMPLARY SCHOOL-BASED INTERVENTION PROGRAMS

There have been numerous reviews of school-improvement research during the past ten years. In general, research on district-led reform efforts has been conducted using case-study methods, and it has been difficult to establish clear effects of such efforts on student outcomes. In the best studies, however, increases in student achievement resulting from district-led efforts appear to be temporary, in part because of constantly changing leadership and an unstable policy environment in America's largest school systems (see Sykes, O'Day, and Ford 2009, especially figure 59.1). For these reasons, this chapter contains a review of research on school-improvement programs developed by external providers, typically not-for-profit organizations that provide schools with intervention services such as design assistance, professional development programming, and curricular materials. The research base here consists of many field experiments and quasi-experiments, which renders it easier for researchers to make causal claims about program effectiveness, although these studies often ignore the question of how intervention programs are sustained over time.

My review of these programs is broken into two sections, one on elementary school programs and the other on secondary school programs. I begin each of these sections by looking at what are known as comprehensive school reform (CSR) programs—a set of school-improvement programs that emerged out of the New American Schools initiative in order to stimulate coherent, whole-school designs for instructional improvement. Geoffrey Borman and colleagues (2003) conducted an extensive review of research on twenty-nine of the most widely implemented of these CSR programs, and that meta-analysis found that, on average, these diverse programs had only a small effect on students' academic achievement (Cohen's $d_{s.d.} = 0.12$ in comparison group studies). However, there was a great deal of program-to-program variability in effect sizes in this meta-analysis, with Cohen's $d_{s.d.}$ ranging from -0.13 to $+0.92$ in comparison group studies, depending on the program being evaluated.

In light of this variability, I focus here only on a few of the most effective CSR programs, chosen to illustrate theoretically important variations in program design.[1] In describing these programs, I ask what each program does to improve instruction and whether that program also is geared to improving students' socioemotional learning. As we shall see, the successful elementary school programs that I discuss tend to focus on academic goals and do so by intervening directly in classrooms. By contrast, the secondary school programs that I discuss tend to have a broader focus on socioemotional and academic learning and work on reorganizing schools as wholes rather than focusing on classroom instruction. In general, the programs I discuss have what Brighouse and Schouten would identify as an "internal" focus (see chapter 24 in this volume).

Elementary School Programs

Two academically oriented and highly effective CSR programs for elementary schools are Success for All and America's Choice. Of the two, Success for All is by far the larger (now operating in more than 1,200 schools) and the most frequently evaluated (more than forty-six quasi-experimental comparisons and one large, randomized field trial). In evaluation studies, Success for All typically has positive but small effects on students' reading achievement, the curricular domain in which it works to make instructional improvements. In general, within a range of reading outcomes for elementary-aged children, the average effect size on reading achievement is about $d_{s.d.} = 0.20$, with effects somewhat larger on early reading skills such as decoding and somewhat lower on reading comprehension (Borman et al. 2007).

America's Choice, formerly operated by the National Center for Education and the Economy, has not been as widely implemented as Success for All and has not been as frequently evaluated (about seventeen quasi-experimental studies). This program works to improve both reading and mathematics instruction in elementary schools and has moderate support for effectiveness, with an average effect size on achievement of about $d_{s.d.} = 0.19$. In the most careful evaluation done on this program (May and Supovitz 2006), its effects were found to be larger in later grades than earlier grades, and larger in mathematics than reading. For example, program effects in grades one through three were $d_{s.d.} = 0.16$ for reading and $d_{s.d.} = 0.28$ for math; in grades four through 8, the effect sizes were $d_{s.d.} = 0.36$ for reading and $d_{s.d.} = 0.39$ for math.

Both programs bring about major changes in the "academic infrastructure" of schools, although they take different approaches. Success for All, which attempts only to change reading practices, institutes a ninety-minute reading period in schools, and because all certified teachers in a school teach reading, it lowers reading-class sizes to eighteen to twenty students per teacher. In kindergarten and first grade the program uses its own instructional materials, but in later grades, schools choose from commercially available texts. At all grade levels students are administered curriculum-aligned, formative assessments, which are used every nine weeks to place students in different grades into groups of pupils with the same reading level. In every class period, teachers are strongly encouraged to follow lesson scripts calling for high levels of fast-paced, direct instruction in all domains of reading instruction. Success for All lessons employ a variety of instructional strategies such as use of explicit teaching of content and cooperative groups, and students engage in various reading-comprehension activities such as answering brief oral questions, answering multiple-choice or fill-in-the-blank comprehension questions, writing brief answers to comprehension questions, and discussing the text with peers. Students whose achievement lags behind that of their peers also receive one-on-one tutoring outside of class, with priority given to students in the earlier grades. At each school, a locally employed program facilitator and the principal work to assure that teachers are faithfully implementing this program; monitoring for program fidelity is a high priority for Success for All (Rowan and Miller 2007).

The America's Choice program also works to change the academic infrastructure of elementary schools. In reading, it recommends use of the Open Court reading series, a textbook series found to have positive effects on reading achievement, and schools are asked to set aside a two-hour block for teaching an integrated program of reading and writing that Richard Correnti and Brian Rowan (2007) called a "literature-based" reading program. Unlike Success for All, there are no lesson scripts, nor are students from different grades and classes regrouped. Rather, teachers form skill groups within classes. Extensive job-embedded professional development helps teachers learn to enact program-recommended lesson routines, and teachers are taught how to use students' work as a means of frequent formative assessment. This professional development is supplemented by coaching, with coaches working inside classrooms to facilitate program implementation. Like Success for All, the model is typically well implemented, although there is a bit more site-to-site variation in implementation than there is in Success for All (Rowan and Correnti 2009).

Both Success for All and America's Choice are good models of how to achieve instructional program coherence, but neither model pursues a broad reform agenda. Instead, the focus is on classroom instruction and the improvement of students' academic learning. Interestingly, this contrasts sharply with another high-profile CSR, program developed by James Comer and known as the School Development Program. The SDP does not focus on instruction per se, but rather aims to improve student development along six broad pathways: physical, cognitive, psychological, language, social, and ethical. To achieve these broad goals, the SDP works on improving the larger environment of schools (rather than a school's instructional core) through an organizational-development intervention that establishes three teams at each School Development Program school: a school planning and management team, a student and staff support team, and a parent team. Thomas Cook, Robert F. Murphy, and H. David Hunt (2000) have discussed the theory guiding this intervention. The idea is that School Development Program's organizational-development process is guided by three core principles: cooperation (rather than fault finding), problem solving, and decisionmaking by consensus. School Development Program developers assume that if each team uses these principles to organize its work, interpersonal relationships among students, teachers, and staff will improve; students will become more engaged in their schoolwork; and students will become more oriented to conventional behavior. In theory, this will lead to improvements in student achievement.

Is this approach effective, especially in comparison to approaches that work more directly on instructional improvement? The research on this point is weak, but evidence from four studies suggests that School Development Program implementation has only small effects on school climate and very little effect on student achievement. In particular, in a well-designed study of ten School Development Program schools (plus controls) conducted by Cook, Murphy, and Hunt (2000), students in SDP schools showed some gains in socioemotional learning (such as endorsement of positive norms for behavior and control of anger), and student perceptions of school climate improved in School Development Program schools compared to those at control sites. However, SDP students gained only about three percentage points more on achievement tests over the interval from grades five to eight than did students in the no-treatment control schools.

There are a number of reasons that the School Development Program might not fully achieve its aims. Cook, Murphy, and Hunt (2000) report that there is a great deal of school-to-school variability in School Development Program implementation, and, in addition, they show that the program's approach to intervention support is generally weak. But another reason the School Development Program might have only weak effects on students' achievement is that its guiding theory is wrong. Put differently, it could be that intervening to improve the larger school environment and thus students' socioemotional learning does *not*, in fact, produce improved academic achievement.

Positive Action is another school-based intervention that, like the School Development Program, is designed to improve students' socioemotional learning (see the What Works Clearinghouse at the website of the U.S. Department of Education's Institute of Education Sciences, www.ies.ed.gov/ncee/wwc; accessed April 25, 2010). This program is built around a sequenced curriculum for socioemotional learning developed for use in grades K–12. In contrast to the School Development Program, Positive Action sells curriculum kits that contain an instructor's manual with scripted fifteen-minute lessons, along with student activity booklets, journals, and other hands-on materials. Thus, it differs from the School Development Program approach in that its approach to intervention is narrowly targeted and well specified and works directly inside classrooms. It also provides schools with a variety of training options to support implementation.

Data from two randomized field trials reported in the What Works Clearinghouse show strong effects on reading and mathematics achievement in one study but statistically insignificant results in another (the average effect on reading and math achievement was listed as plus fourteen percentile points in all the studies). These and other studies further suggest that the Positive Action program reduces student absenteeism, retention in grade, disciplinary referrals, and violent behavior. So this program holds out at least the promise that a simple addition to classroom programming might actually represent a major way of making instructionally focused CSR programs more comprehensive.[2]

A final approach to elementary school reform that is worthy of attention seeks to enhance students' academic and socioemotional learning by working outside regular school hours. This includes summer school programming designed to allocate additional academic learning time to lower-achieving students. A meta-analysis by Harris Cooper and colleagues (2000) found that the average effect of summer school programs on student achievement was $d_{s.d.} = 0.19$. Another approach would add after-school programming to the mix of intervention strategies, although here, results have been more variable. For example, a recent review of thirty-five out-of-school program evaluations found positive effects on average for the academically oriented programs under study, although these effects varied between grades: $d_{s.d.} = 0.22$ for lower-elementary students, $d_{s.d.} = 0.09$ for middle-grades students, and $d_{s.d.} = 0.25$ for secondary-school students (Lauer et al. 2006). There also was large program-to-program variation in these effect sizes, so program design issues seem especially important to the effectiveness of after-school programs.

Secondary School Programs

Approaches to secondary school reform differ in important ways from those pursued in elementary schools. In elementary schools, successful school-improvement efforts have tended to focus squarely on instructional improvement, but at the secondary level, internally oriented improvement efforts have focused more broadly on "school restructuring," on attempts to change the overall environments of secondary schools rather than to intervene intensively inside classrooms.

There are a number of reasons for these differences between elementary and secondary programs.[3] One is the difference in the way the curriculum is organized at the two levels of schooling. Elementary schools are built around a core curriculum in basic skills that is common for all students and spiraled across grades to give children repeated coverage of common strands of work. Moreover, teachers in elementary schools typically are subject-matter generalists who teach this common core in its entirety. To do so, these teachers work with small groups of thirty or so students for six hours a day for an entire year. In addition, elementary schools are smaller than secondary schools. All of this means that elementary school teachers know each other and their and other teachers' students well, so the school environment is quite personalized. In addition, teachers in a given elementary school share many commonalities: they teach the same curriculum, to the same students, who come mostly from the same neighborhood(s). These circumstances naturally tend to produce more collegiality and cooperation among elementary school teachers and administrators than among secondary school staff, and these conditions facilitate cooperative, schoolwide improvement efforts at the elementary level.

At the same time, elementary school teachers lack power in the educational system, partly because elementary teaching historically has been women's work and partly because the elementary grades are where accountability systems are most highly developed as a result of a legacy of achievement testing at these grades. For these reasons, it has been much more logical, and easier, for authorities and change agents to target instructional improvements at the elementary level. Elementary schools produce measurable achievement, the teachers are accustomed to working collegially, and they lack power within the system.

The situation is quite different in secondary schools. In contrast to elementary schools, high schools are typically larger in size, and the curriculum is organized differently. More subjects are taught, and these are broken into discrete and sequenced courses, each with its own distinctive content. Teachers are organized as subject-matter specialists, and they teach hundreds of students every semester, spending only about fifty minutes a day with each class. In this environment, a teacher's main reference group is often his or her academic department and academic discipline. Because of school size and academic specialization, teachers at the secondary level are much less subject to direct administrative control over their teaching work. They also are under much less individual pressure to produce achievement outcomes on standardized tests, relying more on grades and passing rates as salient measures of learning. In this larger and more differentiated environment, the social climate is also much less personalized than in elementary schools. But all of this occurs at a time when students are still learning the limits of their independence. As a result, problems of order have always been a major threat to the smooth running of secondary schools—and for good reason.

In this environment, secondary school reform has usually proceeded as follows. First, policy-makers have worked to reform secondary schools largely by ratcheting up graduation require-ments, which are easily defined within the highly institutionalized structure of credit hours and course titles. However, the instructional substance of courses typically has been left to the dis-cretion of teachers, who are, after all, subject-matter specialists. When direct efforts at improv-ing classroom instruction do occur in the typical American high school, they tend to be organized around collegial interactions among departmental faculty or through larger networks of subject-area specialists, not by administrative authorities (Little and McLaughlin 1993). Instead of work-ing on a schoolwide basis to change instruction, reformers have tended instead to attack the problem of social order in secondary schools—attempting to stop the gradual disengagement of many students from schooling and to stem disciplinary problems. They have done this through "school restructuring"—breaking larger schools into smaller and more personalized units by organizing schools-within-a-school or developing other teaming arrangements designed to make the high school environment more personalized. In point of fact, this is a good place to begin schoolwide reform in high schools, since the problem of order is shared by all teachers, whereas issues of instructional reform differ from subject to subject.

However, the high school programs I focus on in this chapter take a deeper and more instructionally focused approach to school reform than is typical. To illustrate how this process works, I have chosen two programs: the Talent Development High School and First Things First. Both programs began primarily as school "restructuring" efforts, but they have since expanded their intervention designs to work more intensively on changing instructional practices in class-rooms. Moreover—and this is important—both Talent Development High School and First Things First are designed to operate under the "normal" constraints of urban secondary school-ing. That is, these programs are deliberately deployed in regular-enrollment, high-poverty high schools and operate under existing labor contracts and district budgets. They are therefore not what might be called "high-commitment" interventions, like the KIPP schools or the Promise Academies in the Harlem Children's Zone, both of which are schools of choice, require parental and student commitment, and extend school hours radically—although both Talent Develop-ment High School and First Things First could, in principle, be operated in high-commitment settings, and both share design elements in common with these high-commitment models. In choosing to focus on Talent Development High School and First Things First, I am making a deliberate choice to examine what has been done in the name of "whole-school" reform under what might be called "normal" operating conditions. (See chapter 23 in this volume for a discus-sion of research on "high-commitment" reforms.)[4]

Both Talent Development High School and First Things First originated in the 1990s. The Talent Development program began in 1994 as a cooperative project between Johns Hopkins University and a single high school in Baltimore. Since then it has expanded, and as of 2011 oper-ates in about forty high schools nationwide. Only a handful of systematic evaluations of Talent Development High School have been conducted, and these have tended to report on educational outcomes for ninth-grade students—the early focus of the program's efforts. The results of one of these evaluations (reported by the Comprehensive School Reform Quality Center) found "moderate" program effects on ninth-grade students' reading achievement ($d_{s.d.} = 0.30$) and mathematics achievement ($d_{s.d.} = 0.25$). Another study of five Talent Development High School schools, conducted by James Kemple and Caroline Herlihy (2004), however, reported sub-stantial impacts on ninth-grade students' core-course completion and promotion rates; the proportion of students completing core courses in Talent Development schools rose from about 43 percent prior to treatment to 56 percent after treatment, and the schools experienced a six-percentage-point increase in rates of promotion to tenth grade.

The other model of high school reform, First Things First, is operated by the nonprofit Institute for Research and Reform in Education. It was introduced into high schools in Kansas City, Kansas, in 1996 and has since expanded to middle schools in a handful of other school systems. The Kansas City effort has been the subject of two evaluations discussed by the Comprehensive School Reform Quality Center, one of which was conducted by Janet Quint and colleagues (2005) after the program had been in operation for three years in four Kansas City high schools. The results of this evaluation showed large reductions in the percentage of tenth- and eleventh-grade students failing the state mathematics and reading examinations (minus twenty-one percentage points in reading, minus eighteen percentage points in mathematics), a 6 percent increase over baseline in attendance rates, and a 15.7 percent increase in graduation rates over baseline.

The Talent Development High School Program

One way to characterize Talent Development High School (TDHS) is as a school restructuring program, because at the ninth grade the program creates self-contained schools-within-a-school, known as ninth-grade academies. Each academy has about 100 students and an interdisciplinary team of 4 teachers, a design that is intended to create a more personalized learning environment for students at the beginning of high school. At later grades, students then enter career academies—self-contained, theme-based groups of 250 to 350 students who are chosen on the basis of their interests. Talent Development High School also reshapes the high school schedule, reducing it from the usual six-period day to a four-period day, with classes of 80 to 90 minutes. One goal of this rescheduling is to provide teachers with additional time to teach in-depth using a variety of instructional strategies. But another goal is to allow students to complete a year-long course in one semester, thus accelerating the academic progress of students who enter high school below grade level or who fail a course during a school year.

Talent Development High School makes other efforts to enhance low-achieving students' academic success. All freshmen take a first-semester seminar course designed to improve study skills, goal setting, and peer relations. In addition, "double-dose" academic courses are offered in the first semester of each year to help students performing below grade level prepare for grade-appropriate coursework in the second semester. In ninth grade students take Strategic Reading and Transition to Advanced Math; in tenth grade, Reading and Writing in Your Career and Geometry Foundations; in eleventh grade, College Prep Reading and Writing and Algebra II Foundations. Talent Development High School also offers failing students after-hours credit-recovery programs, an alternative program called Twilight School, and other summer and weekend activities for academic assistance.

To support program implementation, schools are encouraged to join the National Network of Partnership Schools, which helps schools form Action Teams for Partnership consisting of parents, teachers, administrators, and community members. These teams plan activities and strategies that focus on school goals and improvement plans. Like the elementary school programs discussed earlier, Talent Development High School also provides professional development and technical assistance to guide and monitor implementation of both the organizational and curricular components of the model. TDHS schools also hire an organizational facilitator and curriculum coaches, who are part of the school team. These facilitators receive additional training from the program and are supported by instructional facilitators from program offices, who perform implementation checks and troubleshooting via phone, email, and school visits, when possible.

The First Things First Program

Like Talent Development High School, the First Things First program involves a substantial restructuring of high schools. First Things First also forms theme-based schools-within-a-school, called small learning communities. Each small learning community is staffed by a team of teachers, and is composed of about 350 students from each grade level. A major goal of First Things First is to avoid remediation, but students who are substantially behind academically are placed temporarily in a transitional community or go to a school's "opportunity center." The expectation is that students will spend only a year in this center, which features reduced class sizes. In the opportunity center, students take only academic courses, and have no electives. Like Talent Development High School, First Things First schools use block scheduling, with eighty- to ninety-minute periods, and attempts are made to reduce class size for reading and mathematics classes. Unlike Talent Development High School, First Things First is only beginning to develop a specific curriculum package; currently, the model relies on teacher planning groups to improve instruction. In this model, teachers are given a minimum of three hours of planning time each week. In addition, First Things First has developed a family-advocate system in which each staff member in a given small learning community serves as an advocate for fifteen to seventeen students and their families. This arrangement lasts the entire time a student is in the school. Family advocates meet regularly with their students, communicate at least monthly with every family through phone calls, e-mails, or notes home, meet with every student's family twice yearly, and otherwise work with other SLC staff to support each student.

Throughout the years, First Things First has evolved an ever more specified design and more intensive approach to implementation support. In the current model, a program coordinator is located at the district office, a school-improvement coordinator is located at each school, and a small learning community coordinator works with each team. First Things First also provides ongoing and sequenced professional development for these and other school staff. In this effort, teachers are explicitly taught various processes of instructional improvement and how to use group-planning time well. Further, First Things First coordinators closely monitor program implementation by observing each classroom twice annually and entering data into a software program called Measuring What Matters, which collates this and other information from student records to monitor student outcomes. These data are then fed back to school and small learning community planning groups for the purposes of continuous improvement.

DISCUSSION

One thing that is striking about the CSR programs described here is the extent to which they work intensively at improving instructional quality in high-poverty schools. At both the elementary and secondary levels, schools are reorganized through innovative schedules and grouping arrangements, new materials are purchased, innovative assessments are designed to track student learning, schoolwide staff-development programs are mounted to help teachers learn to use program-developed instructional strategies, coaches are brought to schools to work directly with teachers to improve classroom practices, and more. Data suggest that well-structured efforts along these lines succeed in changing instructional practices, at least at the elementary grades, where there are good data on this point. Indeed, studies that have carefully tracked implementation fidelity after elementary-school teachers become involved in well-designed instructional interventions typically find that 70 to 80 percent of teachers implement program-approved practices (Garet et al. 2008; Rowan and Correnti 2009).

As we have seen, at the elementary level, all of this can have positive effects on students' achievement, with effects sizes for effective programs typically reported to be on the order of 0.20 to 0.30. At the secondary level, CSR programs designed for high-poverty high schools have had a tougher time making instructional changes, largely because high schools are more complex organizationally and tougher to change. Yet even here, my review suggests that two of the most well developed programs, Talent Development High School and First Things First, can reduce student failure rates and increase students' progress toward high school graduation.

A problem, however, is that none of the successful efforts described in this chapter has fully succeeded in reducing the gaps in educational outcomes that exist between poor and nonpoor students. At the elementary level, the average student in Success for All and America's Choice schools continues to perform below grade level in reading, despite the demonstrable effectiveness of these program schools in comparison to similar high-poverty schools that do not participate in the intervention programs (see, for example, Rowan et al. 2009). One reason this occurs is that educationists have yet to design truly powerful instructional interventions. But another is that high rates of teacher and student mobility militate against students receiving "full" and well-implemented doses of these interventions. More speculatively, a final reason these programs might achieve limited success is that instructionally focused interventions pay insufficient attention to the socioemotional-learning needs of elementary school students, although it remains an open question whether the coupling of academic interventions with socioemotional interventions will be sufficient to markedly improve poor students' performance much beyond the current state of the art.

Similar comments can be made about secondary school improvement programs. As my review showed, the Talent Development High School program had statistically significant positive effects on ninth-graders' completion of core courses and increased rates of promotion to tenth grade, but in the high schools under study where the program was deployed, 45 percent of students still did not complete core courses on time, and there was only a six-percentage-point increase in promotion rates. Similarly, despite the fact that the First Things First program had statistically significant effects on students' state high school assessment scores and produced increases in attendance and graduation, 56 percent of students in First Things First high schools were still failing tenth-grade state assessments in mathematics, and 31 percent were failing the eleventh-grade state assessment in reading. Moreover, 30 percent of students were not graduating from high school. Therefore, although the two high school programs reviewed here made a significant impact on the high schools where they worked, much research and development remains to be done to improve program effectiveness.

How, then, are educators in high-poverty schools to solve the immediate problem of school improvement? One implication of the discussion presented here is to intervene early and continuously in poor students' academic preparation for schooling. This would entail expanding access to and improving the quality of preschool programming, continuing to reform instruction in the elementary grades to better prepare students for secondary school, and continuing to improve secondary schooling by developing more powerful instructional interventions. But it remains to be seen whether such academic interventions alone can enable poor students to catch up to nonpoor students in achievement outcomes, graduation rates, and postsecondary enrollment.

This suggests that high-poverty schools also need to mount academically oriented after-school and summer programs in order to increase the academic learning time of students whose achievement lags behind peers. Here, however, school systems face budgetary constraints, students must be motivated to attend, and if costs are passed on to parents, low-income families will need some form of tuition assistance. To my knowledge, these practical problems have not been worked out, except through various "high-commitment" schools of choice, such as the KIPP schools and Promise Academies.

Beyond these well-developed approaches to intervention, the time also might be ripe for schools to explore intervention programs aimed at enhancing students' socioemotional learning. The idea here is that such programs would improve students' abilities to benefit from high-quality instruction and teach students to avoid the kinds of behavioral problems associated with school failure. Throughout this chapter, I describe some existing approaches to this problem, but I also note how the field of prevention research has yet to come up with sound approaches to integrating such programming into schools. Therefore, any pursuit of this strategy for improving the academic outcomes of students in poverty would seem to require additional development efforts.

Finally, as other chapters in this volume suggest, there is a pressing need to connect debates about education reform to discussions of social policy more generally. If poverty places students at risk of educational failure through the mechanisms described in this book, would not intervening in poverty directly contribute to educational improvement?

NOTES

Online appendix available at: http://www.russellsage.org/duncan_murnane_online_appendix.pdf.

1. My choices are based on work by the Best Evidence Encyclopedia (www.bestevidence.org), a free website created by the Johns Hopkins University School of Education's Center for Data-Driven Reform in Education.

2. At this point, however, it is worth noting that the most widely researched curriculum for socioemotional learning, the Fast Track program, has not fared well in randomized field trials. Fast Track starts with a universal socioemotional-learning curriculum and then adds indicated treatment for students with behavior problems, including parent-training groups, home visits, child social-skills training, one-on-one tutoring in reading, and children's friendship-enhancing groups. In an extensive body of research, Fast Track has had surprisingly small effects on student outcomes and therefore was not judged as cost-effective by a panel of practitioners (Foster and Jones 2007). This has led some researchers to suggest that an alternative approach should be taken to providing indicated treatment to students. This would involve training existing student-personnel professionals in schools to provide students with evidence-based mental-health services. As John R. Weiss, Amanda Jensen-Doss, and Kristin M. Hawley (2006) discuss, many evidence-based therapies now exist for common childhood emotional and behavioral problems, but practitioners in the field seldom implement existing treatment protocols faithfully. This is an area that school-based prevention research could fruitfully turn to in order to improve indicated treatment plans.

3. The discussion here and in the next paragraph is based on the research of Robert J. Miller and Brian Rowan (2003, 2006).

4. Note, also, that I do not focus here on the New York City "small schools of choice" program that was recently evaluated by MDRC (Bloom, Thompson, and Unterman 2010)—MDRC's evaluation report was issued at about the time this volume went to press. However, the outcomes of that program are discussed in the introductory chapter of this volume, by Richard Murnane and Greg Duncan, and tend to reinforce the general argument made in this chapter. For example, the New York City schools evaluated by MDRC have many of the characteristics of the high schools working with the school-reform programs I discuss in this chapter: they are small; built around designs that emphasize academic rigor, personalization, and community partnerships; and have access to many outside resources. In MDRC's evaluation study, Bloom and colleagues compared academic-achievement outcomes for students who were and were not admitted to these schools via a lottery. The effects reported in that study are very similar to the program effects discussed here for the Talent Development High Schools and First Things First models. Thus, this new study adds confidence to the review of research on the TDHS and FTF models provided here.

REFERENCES

Aud, Susan, William Hussar, Michael Planty, Thomas Snyder, Kevin Bianco, Mary Ann Fox, Laure Frohlich Jana Kemp, and Lauren Drake. 2010. *The Condition of Education 2010*. NCES 2010028. Washington: U.S. Department of Education, National Center for Education Statistics (May).

Beatty, Alexandra. 2010. *Student Mobility: Exploring the Impact of Frequent Moves on Achievement: Summary of a Workshop*. Washington, D.C.: National Academies Press.

Bloom, Howard S., Saskia Levy Thompson, and Rebecca Unterman. 2010. *Transforming the High School Experience: How New York City's Small Schools Are Boosting Student Achievement and Graduation Rates.* New York: MDRC.

Borman, Geoffrey D., Gina M. Hewes, Laura T. Overman, and Shelly Brown. 2003. "Comprehensive School Reform and Achievement: A Meta-Analysis." *Review of Educational Research* 73(2): 125–230.

Borman, Geoffrey D., Robert E. Slavin, Alan C. K. Cheung, Anne M. Chamberlain, Nancy A. Madden, and Bette Chambers. 2007. "Final Reading Outcomes of the National Randomized Field Trial of Success for All." *American Educational Research Journal* 44(3): 701–31.

Bryk, Anthony S., Penny B. Sebring, David Kerbow, Sharon Rollow, and John Q. Easton. 1998. *Charting Chicago School Reform: Democratic Localism as a Lever for Change.* Boulder, Colo.: Westview Press.

Cook, Thomas D., Robert F. Murphy, and H. David Hunt. 2000. "Comer's School Development Program in Chicago: A Theory-Based Evaluation." *American Educational Research Journal* 37(2): 535–97.

Cooper, Harris, Kelly Charlton, Jeff C. Valentine, Laura Muhlenbruck, and Geoffrey D. Borman. 2000. "Making the Most of Summer School: A Meta-Analytic and Narrative Review." *Monographs of the Society for Research in Child Development* 65(1): 1–127.

Correnti, Richard, and Brian Rowan. 2007. "Opening Up the Black Box: Literacy Instruction in Schools Participating in Three Comprehensive School Reform Programs." *American Educational Research Journal* 44(2): 298–33.

Foster, E. Michael, and Damon Jones. 2007. "Issues in the Economic Evaluation of Prevention Programs." *Applied Developmental Science* 7(2): 76–86.

Foster, Susan, Mary Rollefson, Teresa Doksum, Denise Noonan, Gail Robinson, and Judith Teich. 2005. *School Mental Health Services in the United States, 2002–2003.* DHHS Pub. No. (SMA) 05-4068. Rockville, Md.: Center for Mental Health Services, Substance Abuse and Mental Health Services Administration.

Garet, Michael S., Stephanie Cronin, Marian Eaton, Ana Kurki, Meredith Ludwig, Wehmah Jones, Kazuaki Uekawa, Audrey Falk, Howard S. Bloom, Fred Doolittle, Pei Zhu, Laura Sztejnberg, and Marsha Silverberg. 2008. *The Impact of Two Professional Development Interventions on Early Reading Instruction and Achievement.* NCEE 2008–4030. Washington: U.S. Department of Education, Institute for Education Sciences.

Garet, Michael S., Andrew C. Porter, Laura Desimone, Beatrice F. Barman, and Kwan Suk Yoon. 1996. "What Makes Professional Development Effective: Results from a National Sample of Teachers." *American Educational Research Journal* 38(4): 915–45.

Greenberg, Mark T. 2004. "Current and Future Challenges in School-Based Prevention: The Researcher Perspective." *Prevention Science* 5(1): 5–13.

Kemple, James J., and Caroline Herlihy. 2004. *The Talent Development High School Model: Context, Components, and Initial Impacts on Ninth-Grade Students' Engagement and Performance.* New York: Manpower Development Research Corporation.

Lauer, Patricia A., Motoko Akiba, Stephanie B. Wilkerson, Helen S. Apthorp, David Snow, and Mya L. Martin-Glenn. 2006. "Out-of-School-Time Programs: A Meta-Analysis of Effects for At-Risk Students." *Review of Educational Research* 76(2): 275–313.

Lippman, Laura, Shelley Burns, Edith McArthur, Robert Burton, Thomas M. Smith, and Phil Kaufman. 1996. *Urban Schools: The Challenge of Location and Poverty.* NCES 96-184. Washington: U.S. Department of Education, National Center for Education Statistics (June).

Little, Judith W., and Milbrey W. McLaughlin. 1993. *Teachers' Work: Individuals, Colleagues, and Contexts.* New York: Teachers College Press.

May, Henry A., and Jon A. Supovitz. 2006. "Capturing the Cumulative Effects of School Reform: An 11-Year Study of the Impacts of America's Choice on Student Achievement." *Educational Evaluation and Policy Analysis* 28(3): 231–57.

Miller, Robert J., and Brian Rowan. 2003. "Source and Consequences of Organic Management in Elementary and Secondary Schools." In *Studies in Leading and Organizing Schools,* edited by Wayne K. Hoy and Cecil Miskel. Greenwich, Conn.: Information Age Press.

———. 2006. "Effects of Organic Management on Student Achievement." *American Educational Research Journal* 43(2): 219–53.

Mintrop, Heinrich. 2004. *Schools on Probation: How Accountability Works (and Doesn't).* New York: Teachers College Press.

Newmann, Fred M., BetsAnn Smith, Elaine Allen Worth, and Anthony S. Bryk. 2001. "Instructional Program Coherence: What It Is and Why It Should Guide School Improvement Policy." *Educational Evaluation and Policy Analysis* 23(4): 297–321.

Payne, Allison A. 2009. "Do Predictors of the Implementation Quality of School-Based Prevention Programs Differ by Program Type?" *Prevention Science* 10(2): 151–67.

Quint, Janet, Howard S. Bloom, Alison Rebecca Black, and Ladler Stephens with Theresa M. Cakey. 2005. *The Challenge of Scaling Up Educational Reform: Findings and Lessons from Findings and Lessons from First Things First*. New York: Manpower Development Research Corporation.

Rowan, Brian, and Richard Correnti. 2009. "Interventions to Improve Instruction: How Implementation Strategies Affect Instructional Change." In *Studies in School Improvement: A Volume in Theory and Research in Educational Administration*, edited by Wayne W. K. Hoy and Michael DiPaola. Greenwich, Conn.: Information Age.

Rowan, Brian, Richard Correnti, Robert J. Miller, and Eric Camburn. 2009. "School Improvident by Design: Lessons from a Study of Comprehensive School Reform Designs." In *Handbook of Education Policy Research*, edited by David N. Plank, Gary Sykes, and Barbara L. Schneider. New York: Routledge.

Rowan, Brian, and Robert J. Miller. 2007. "Organizational Strategies for Promoting Instructional Change: Implementation Dynamics in Schools Working with Comprehensive School Reform Providers." *American Educational Research Journal*, 44(2): 252–97.

Sykes, Gary, Jennifer O'Day, and Timothy G. Ford. 2009. "The District Role in School Improvement." In *Handbook of Education Policy Research,* edited by David N. Plank, Gary Sykes, and Barbara L. Schneider. New York: Routledge.

Weiss, John R., Amanda Jensen-Doss, and Kristin M. Hawley. 2006. "Evidence-Based Youth Psychotherapies Versus Usual Clinical Care: A Meta-Analysis of Direct Comparisons." *American Psychologist* 61(7): 671–89.

INDEX

Boldface numbers refer to figures and tables.